Americans Living Abroad
What You Should Know
While You are There

Gladson I. Nwanna, Ph.D., Editor

Frontline Publishers
Baltimore, Maryland

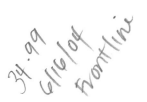

Copyright © 2004 by Gladson I. Nwanna

Library of Congress Cataloging-in-Publication Data

Americans living abroad : what you should know while you are there /
Gladson I. Nwanna, editor.
    p. cm.
Includes bibliographical references and index.
  ISBN 1-890605-11-5 (alk. paper)
  1. Americans--Foreign countries--Handbooks, manuals, etc. I. Nwanna,
Gladson I.
E184.2 .A45 2004
910'.2'0208913--dc22

                2003021473

ISBN, paperback ed 1-890605-11-5
ISBN, PDF ed :   1-890605-28-X
ISBN, LIT ed :   1-890605-29-8

Cover Design by David E. Ricardo

Printed in the United States of America

Visit Frontline Publishers Website at **http://www.frontlinepublishers.com**

Acknowledgement

I would like to thank Mrs. Phyllis Desbordes for her assistance with editing parts of this book and for all of her valuable suggestions.

A special thanks and credit goes to various departments and agencies of the government and other private agencies whose research and publications have been reproduced in this book

Preface

Each year thousands of Americans travel overseas to take up temporary or permanent residency, and each year a large number of them experience one type of trouble or another with a range of consequences including jail time, deportation, abduction, victims of terrorism, illness, hospitalization, loss of citizenship and even death.

Americans who travel abroad to take up residency can find their stay to be safe, enriching and exciting with careful and adequate planning and preparation. On the other hand, they could find their stay to be wasteful, expensive, boring an embarrassing nightmare and even deadly if they are not adequately informed.

Many prospective foreign residents or returning U.S. residents, find the process rather time-consuming and expensive, are unaware of available resources and find available information confusing.

A good number, on the other hand, do not have access to relevant and reliable information and resources in a timely manner to maximize their energy and knowledge. This book addresses most of these issues and should be of help to those Americans living abroad or planning to take up residence abroad.

It is the primary motive of the author to compile a book that is informative and comprehensive in form and at the same time reliable and authoritative as a source. This book provides a one stop source for the little publicized information and resources for Americans living abroad. Furthermore, it provides answers and sources of references for frequently asked questions, issues, and concerns faced by Americans who reside abroad.

This book has several unique features that distinguishes it from other books available to travelers. Information contained in this book.

- reflects the post September 11, 2001, travel and world-wide events and concerns

- should be useful to Americans living abroad or who plan to live abroad for an extended time period or for a short time period

- should be useful to American students studying abroad

- addresses issues of safety relating to terrorism, abduction, kidnapping etc.

- addresses matters that should be of concern to concern returning residents

In addition, the Appendix section of the book is filled with valuable addresses and telephone numbers of institutions, agencies, and other information not readily accessible to American residents abroad.

Finally, I must note an additional and unique feature of this book - its wide appeal. Most of the information should be useful and beneficial to every American citizen living abroad.

It is my hope that readers who reside abroad or are planning to reside abroad who consult this book will find the information useful, particularly in ensuring that their stay overseas will be safe, enjoyable and incident-free, and that their return trip to the U.S. will be a happy and successful one and without disappointments.

It is also my expectation that the information contained in this book will make a difference, particularly in ensuring a safe, enjoyable, rewarding and hitch-free trip for the thousands of Americans who reside or plan to reside abroad. We, at WTI hope that your expectations will be met and when they are, we will appreciate hearing from you. Should we fall short in meeting your expectations or in addressing adequately your overseas travel concerns, we would like to hear from you, so that an effort can be made to improve future editions. Suggestions and letters should be mailed to Public Relations Department, Frontline Publishers, P.O. Box 32674, Baltimore, Maryland 21282-2674.

Editor's Note:

[1]   Perhaps little is known about the numerous publications and services for Americans traveling or living abroad made available by the United States Government through its various agencies such as the U.S. Department of State. A great deal of information is also available from several non-governmental agencies and organizations. Unfortunately, many overseas travelers are not aware of these resources. In this book, an effort has been made to fill in that gap by reproducing most of those publications with adequate references to other useful services and resources available to overseas travelers. Similarly, expert advice and answers to questions of interest to travelers is available in the media, but is often limited to those who subscribe to travel newsletters and magazines. This book provides these sources by incorporating the advice of experts in the field. To all these sources, I must say THANKS for facilitating the process of preparing this book.

[2]   The author, editor and publisher have made a determined effort to reproduce all the borrowed materials verbatim and in their entirety. For the most part, this objective was accomplished. In a few instances, it was necessary to make minor alterations in order to facilitate reading and to ensure consistency and uniformity. This is particularly the case with pagination, cross referencing and with the use of chapter, section and text in the place of brochure, publication, bulletin, pamphlet and leaflet as used in the original documents. I must point out an important but deliberate feature of this book that could easily become obvious to a meticulous reader; that is, a seeming repetition of titles,

topics, ideas, paragraphs and sections. This is a deliberate action due in part to my determination to represent borrowed materials in their original forms and structure. It is also due to my desire and resolve to ensure that important tips and advice are not missed by those travelers or readers who, under the pressures of daily life, may not have the time to read the entire book and might only concentrate on a few select chapters. Furthermore, where repetition appears to be the case, it underscores my own belief in the importance of the information being conveyed.

[3]   We live in changing times, which include changing political, social, cultural and economic climates both at home and abroad that, may impact on international travels. Most of the information contained in this book will remain valid perhaps through the ages, but some is bound to change. I have anticipated that to be the case; hence, I have provided you with relevant references, including addresses (mailing & web), phone numbers, and e-mail addresses of government and non-government agencies and organizations that will keep you up-to-date. See Chapter 25.

Similarly, I caution readers that some information contained in this book, including those related to prices of publications cited here and addresses and phone numbers of various organizations cited throughout the book are subject to change and may already have been changed by their respective sources by the time you consult this book. Lastly, for a book of this size, even with all the carefulness and diligence on the part of the publisher, errors and omissions both typographical and in content are bound to occur and I have acknowledged that. I urge you to inform us whenever you find such errors and omissions, so that we may correct them in the next edition. Whereas, at the time this book went to press, every effort was made to ensure that all of the prices and references are accurate. I must, however, make the following explicit disclaimer:

DISCLAIMER

The author and Frontline Publishers shall have neither liability nor responsibility to any person or entity with respect to any loss or damage caused, or alleged to have been caused, directly or indirectly, by information contained in this book. Nor will they be held responsible for the experiences of readers while they are traveling or while they are living abroad. The information contained in this book is meant to serve only as a general guide and to assist you in your travel plans and not as the only source or the ultimate source of information for Americans living abroad or plan living abroad. This information is neither all inclusive, exhaustive nor cast in bronze. Similarly, we warn that neither the author nor the publisher recommends or attests to the legal status, reliability and quality of services and products provided by any of the agencies, organizations, and business firms mentioned in this book. Independent verification and assessment are strongly recommended, including checking out other information sources such as your local government's Consumer Affairs Office, and the Better Business Bureau. If you do not wish to be bound by the above, you are advised not to purchase this book.

TABLE OF CONTENTS

CHAPTER 3: PERSONAL SECURITY 29

CHAPTER 4: SECURITY GUIDELINES FOR AMERICAN FAMILIES LIVING ABROAD 4

xi

CHAPTER 14: INTERNATIONAL ADOPTIONS *133*

CHAPTER 15: KNOW BEFORE YOU GO: US CUSTOMS HINTS FOR RETURNING RESIDENTS 151

CHAPTER 16: MOVING HOUSEHOLD GOODS TO THE UNITED STATES: A GUIDE TO CUSTOMS

REGULATIONS 169

CHAPTER 17: BRINGING PETS, WILDLIFE INTO THE U.S. *183*

CHAPTER 18: TIPS ON BRINGING FOOD, PLANT, AND ANIMAL PRODUCTS INTO THE U.S. *189*

CHAPTER 19: BUYING A CAR OVERSEAS? BEWARE *195*

CHAPTER 20: IMPORTING A CAR/PLEASURE BOAT *199*

CHAPTER 24: : MORE INFORMATION AND ADVICE FROM THE U.S. STATE DEPARTMENT, CUSTOMS,

TRANSPORTATION, AGRICULTURE, SOCIAL SECURITY... 241

CHAPTER 25: REFERENCES AND RESOURCES FOR OVERSEAS TRAVELERS & RESIDENTS 293

APPENDIXES

INDEX

Chapter 1

Tips for Americans Residing Abroad

[The information in this chapter is reprinted verbatim from a bulletin issued by the U.S. State Department, Bureau of Consular Affairs. It is intended to serve as advice to Americans traveling abroad.]

FOREWORD

The Department of State's Bureau of Consular Affairs has prepared information contained in this chapter for Americans considering residence abroad as well as for the more than three million U.S. citizens who are currently residing in a foreign country. The Bureau's goal is to provide assistance to and protect the welfare of American citizens who live abroad.

Before taking up a foreign residence, there are many details that you will need to consider. This chapter will acquaint you with the wide range of services provided to American citizens by U.S. embassies and consulates worldwide. We are committed to providing prompt, courteous, and effective assistance.

BEFORE YOU GO

LEARN ABOUT THE HOST COUNTRY

Read as much as possible about the country where you plan to reside. Learning about a nation's culture, customs, people, and history will make your stay more meaningful. Libraries, bookstores and tourist bureaus are good resources for this information. Keep abreast as well of the international news for the latest political developments in the country where you will live. Although English is spoken in many countries, learning the language of the nation in which you plan to reside will make the transition to your new environment easier.

One of the best ways to learn about living in a foreign country is to get advice from U.S. citizens already residing there. Countries with large numbers of U.S. expatriates often have a U.S. Chamber of Commerce, a bicultural organization, or clubs for Americans that could give you information on living in that country. In countries with fewer U.S. residents, you may be able to meet fellow expatriates through a local international club. The Consular Section of the U.S. embassy or consulate may be able to assist you in finding these organizations.

Background Notes

The Department of State publishes *Background Notes* on countries around the world. These are brief, factual pamphlets with information on each country's people, culture, geography, history, government, economy, and political conditions. They are available for about 170 countries worldwide and often include a reading list, travel notes, and maps. To purchase copies, contact the Superintendent of Documents, U.S. Government Printing Office, Washington, D.C. 20402 or call (202) 512-1800. Select issues are also available on the Department of States home page on the Internet at http://www.state.gov.

Consular Information Program

The U.S. Department of State issues fact sheets on every country in the world called Consular Information Sheets. The sheets contain information on crime and security conditions, areas of instability and other details relevant to travel in a particular country.

The Department of State also issues Travel Warnings and Public Announcements. Travel Warnings are issued when the State Department recommends deferral of travel by Americans to a country because of civil unrest, dangerous conditions, terrorist activity and/or because the U.S. has no diplomatic relations with the country and cannot assist an American in distress. Public Announcements are issued as a means to disseminate information quickly about terrorist threats and other relatively short-term and/or transnational condition which would pose significant risks to American travelers.

How to Access Consular Information Sheets, Travel Warnings and Public Announcements

Consular Information Sheets, Travel Warnings and Public Announcements may be heard any time by

1

dialing the Office of Overseas Citizens Services at (202) 647-5225 from a touchtone phone. The recording is updated, as new information becomes available. They are also available at any of the 13 regional passport agencies, and U.S. embassies and consulates abroad, or, by sending a self-addressed, stamped envelope and indicating the desired country to the Office of Overseas Citizens Services, Bureau of Consular Affairs, Room 4811, U.S. Department of State, Washington, D.C. 20520-4818.

By Fax

From your fax machine, dial (202) 647-3000, using the handset as you would a regular telephone. The system prompts you on how to proceed.

By Internet

Information about travel and consular services is now available on the Internet's World Wide Web. The address is http://travel.state.gov. Visitors to the web site will find Travel Warnings, Public Announcements and Consular Information Sheets, passport and visa information, travel publications, background on international adoption and international child abduction services, international legal assistance, and the Consular Affairs mission statement. There is also a link to the State Department's main site on the Internet's World Wide Web that provides users with current foreign affairs information. The address is http://www.state.gov.

Tips for Travelers Series [All current issues of TIPS FOR TRAVELERS are reproduced elsewhere in this book. Check the Table of Contents for location**]**

REQUIRED DOCUMENTS

U.S. Passports

[The information on PASSPORTS originally slotted for this section is provided in detail in **Chapter 23**]

Visas

All governments require foreigners to have an appropriate visa to reside in their country. This endorsement or stamp placed in your passport by a foreign government permits you to enter that country for a specified purpose. If you are planning to reside in a country for an indefinite period of time, most countries will require you to

seek residence status. See the section on Citizenship to learn what effect this may have on your U.S. citizenship.

Applying for a Visa

In most instances you must obtain the necessary visa before you leave the United States. Apply for your visa directly from the embassy or nearest consulate of the country in which you plan to reside. A listing of foreign embassies and consulates in the U.S. should be available at your local library or by ordering the publication Foreign Consular Offices in the United States from the U.S. Government Printing Office. You can write or call them at Superintendent of Documents, U.S. Government Printing Office, Washington, D.C. 20402; telephone (212) 512-1800 to check pricing and stock information.

Work Permits

A work permit is usually required and is a separate document from your visa or residency permit. It is necessary if you plan on working in a foreign country. It may be obtained either before you leave the U.S. or after you arrive in the foreign country, depending on the laws of the particular country. It is usually applied for at the same time as the residency permit or visa. (Note: The Department of State cannot help you obtain visas or work permits.)

HEALTH MATTERS

Health Insurance

The Social Security Medicare Program does not cover hospital or medical services outside the United States. The Department of Veterans Affairs will only pay for hospital and medical service outside the United States if you are a veteran with a service-related disability.

When considering medical insurance, first find out how citizens of the country where you will reside pay their medical bills and if the same coverage is available to resident foreigners. Some countries have government-sponsored health insurance that may also provide coverage to foreign residents, while others have a dual system with national health supplemented by private insurance. In countries where many American expatriates reside, such as Mexico, you may find that local private international health insurance companies will offer coverage to U.S. citizen residents. Once you arrive, check with organized groups in the American community to learn about these companies.

Wherever possible, try to get the best medical insurance available. If good coverage is not available where you will live, you may have to rely on a U.S. medical insurance company. Before taking up residence abroad, learn which U.S. medical services or health insurance plans provide coverage for Americans living overseas. Check with the insurance company on whether the coverage offered abroad includes both routine and emergency medical treatment, hospitalization, and medical evacuation should it be necessary. Once you obtain health insurance, remember to carry your policy's identity card and to keep a supply of insurance claim forms handy. The U.S. government cannot pay for hospital or medical services for Americans overseas and cannot pay to evacuate you for treatment in the United States.

There are a number of emergency medical assistance companies operating internationally who offer urgent medical treatment for their member travelers. Although the service is designed primarily for tourists who encounter a medical or personal emergency while on vacation, some companies offer yearly memberships which may be available to Americans residing overseas. Contact a travel agent to learn more about these emergency assistance companies.

Medication

For your protection, leave all medicines in their original, labeled containers. If you require medication containing habit-forming drugs or narcotics, carry a copy of the doctor's prescription attesting to that fact. These precautions will make customs processing easier and also will ensure you do not violate the laws of the country in which you live. If you have allergies, reactions to certain medicines, or other unique medical problems, consider wearing a medical alert bracelet or carrying a similar warning at all times.

Immunizations

Under the International Health Regulations adopted by the World Health Organization, some countries require International Certificates of Vaccination against yellow fever from international travelers. A few countries still require a certificate of cholera immunization as well. A helpful guide to immunizations and preventive measures for international travel is the booklet, Health Information for International Travel. It is available for $14 from the Superintendent of Documents,

U.S. Government Printing Office, Washington, D.C. 20402. Specific information may also be obtained from local and state health departments, physicians, or travel clinics that advise international travelers. You may also reach the Centers for Disease Control & Prevention on (404) 332-4559 or via their Internet address at http://www.cdc.gov for immunization recommendations.

AIDS /HIV Testing

Many countries require long-term foreign residents and students to submit proof that they are free of the HIV virus. Some of the countries that require this proof may accept certified test results from the United States. Consult the embassy of the country you will be residing in on whether an AIDS/HIV test is required and if test results from the United States are accepted. If not, check on the type of test to be performed and if it is permissible to supply your own disposable needle. If you are overseas, consult the nearest U.S. embassy or consulate for information and advice, keeping in mind that you are in a foreign country and are subject to its laws and requirements.

Glazed Ceramic Purchases

Be careful when purchasing ceramic tableware and clay pottery while overseas. The U.S. Food and Drug Administration has determined that there are dangerous levels of lead found in the glazes of some ceramic dinnerware and pottery sold abroad. Because there is no way of knowing whether a particular item is safe, the Food and Drug Administration recommends that you use such wares for decorative purposes only.

PRACTICAL MATTERS

Federal Benefits

If you are receiving monthly benefits from a Federal or state agency (Social Security, Department of Veterans Affairs, Office of Personnel Management, etc.), contact the appropriate agency prior to your departure from the United States to advise them of your residence abroad and to inquire about the procedures for having your benefits checks sent overseas.

Driver's License

Many countries do not recognize a U.S. driver's license. Some, however, will accept an international driver's permit, but it would be a good idea to qualify for an in-country driver's license as soon as possible. International driver's

3

permits are not always valid in every country for the length of your stay. It is usually only a matter of courtesy that the holder of the permit is allowed to drive with it for any length of time.

International driver's licenses are usually only valid if presented in conjunction with a valid U.S. or local license. To renew a license contact, the Department of Motor Vehicles in your home state. It is illegal to drive without a valid license and insurance in many countries. You should check with the embassy of the country where you plan to reside, to find out more about driver's license requirements.

Customs Hints
The pamphlet *Know Before You Go* contains information about U.S. Customs regulations and procedures. Single copies are available from any U.S. Customs office abroad or by writing to U.S. Customs, P.O. Box 7407, Washington, D.C. 20044.

Taking A Pet Overseas
If you decide to bring your pet with you overseas, check specific requirements with the country's embassy. Many countries have strict health, quarantine, agriculture, wildlife, and customs requirements and prohibitions. (Note: There are U.S. government regulations forbidding evacuation or emergency assistance to pets during a crisis abroad)

LIVING OVERSEAS

HELP FROM THE U.S. GOVERNMENT

Assistance From American Consuls
U.S. consular officers are located in over 260 foreign service posts abroad. They are available to advise and help you, especially if you are in any kind of serious trouble. In addition, consular agents in approximately 46 foreign cities without U.S. embassies or consulates provide a limited range of emergency and other consular services.

Consular officers are responsive to the needs of Americans traveling or residing abroad. However, the majority of their time is devoted to assisting Americans who are in serious legal, medical, or financial difficulties. They can provide the names of local doctors, dentists, medical specialists, and attorneys, and give you information about any dangerous or unusual situations. Consular officers also perform non-emergency services, including

information on absentee voting, selective service registration, and acquisition and loss of U.S. citizenship. They can arrange for the transfer of Social Security and other U.S. government benefits to beneficiaries residing abroad, provide U.S. tax forms, and notarize documents. They may also provide information on how to obtain foreign public documents.

Because of the limited number of consular officers and the growing number of U.S. tourists and residents abroad, consuls cannot provide tourism or commercial services. For example, consuls cannot perform the work of travel agencies, lawyers, information bureaus, banks, or the police. They cannot find you jobs, get residence or driving permits, act as interpreters, search for missing luggage, or settle commercial disputes.

Registration at U.S. Embassies or Consulates
As soon as you arrive at your permanent residence abroad, you should register in person or by telephone with the nearest U.S. embassy or consulate. Registration will make your presence and whereabouts known in case it is necessary to contact you in an emergency. In accordance with the Privacy Act, information on your welfare or whereabouts may not be released to inquirers without your expressed written authorization. If you register in person, you should bring your U.S. passport with you. Your passport data will be recorded at the embassy or consulate, thereby making it easier for you to apply for a replacement passport should it be lost or stolen.

Missing Persons
When a U.S. citizen abroad loses contact with friends or relatives in the United States, the U.S. consul is often requested to give information about that individual's welfare and whereabouts. Similar requests often come from American private and official welfare organizations attempting, for example, to track down an errant parent who failed to make child support payments. The U.S. consul tries to comply with such requests after determining carefully the reasons for the inquiry. If the consul has the address of the U.S. citizen about whom the inquiry is being made, the consul will inform the American of the inquirer's interest in getting in touch with them and pass on any urgent messages. Consistent with the Privacy Act, the consul then reports back to the inquirer the results of their search efforts. Except in emergency situations, the consul will not release any details about a U.S. citizen's welfare and whereabouts

4

without the citizens expressed consent.

Helpful Information for Americans Arrested Abroad

When living abroad, you are subject to local--i.e. foreign--laws. If you experience difficulties with the local authorities, remember American officials are limited by foreign laws, U.S. regulations, and geography as to what they can do to assist you. The U.S. government cannot fund your legal fees or other related expenses.

Should you find yourself in a dispute that may lead to police or legal action, consult the nearest U.S. consular officer. Although consular officers cannot get you out of jail, serve as your attorneys or give legal advice, they can provide lists of local attorneys and help you find legal representation. However, neither the Department of State nor U.S. embassies or consulates can assume any responsibility for the caliber, competence, or professional integrity of these attorneys.

If you are arrested, immediately ask to speak to the consular officer at the nearest U.S. embassy or consulate. Under international agreements and practice, you have a right to get in touch with the U.S. consul. If you are turned down, keep asking--politely, but persistently.

Consular officers will do whatever they can to protect your legitimate interests and ensure that you are not discriminated against under local law. Upon learning of your arrest, a U.S. consular officer will visit you, provide a list of local attorneys and, if requested, contact family and friends. In cases of arrest, consuls can help transfer money, food, and clothing from your family and friends to you. They also try to get relief if you are held under inhumane or unhealthy conditions or treated less equitably than others in the same situation.

Drug Arrests

Despite repeated warnings, drug arrests and convictions of American citizens are still a problem. If you are caught with any type of narcotics overseas, you are subject to local--not U.S. laws. Penalties for possession or trafficking are often the same. If you are arrested, you will find the following:

-- Few countries provide a jury trial.
-- Most countries do not accept bail.
-- Pre-trial detention, often in solitary confinement,

may last many months.
-- Prisons may lack even minimal comforts--bed, toilet, washbasin.
-- Diets are often inadequate and require supplements from relatives and friends.
-- Officials may not speak English.
-- Physical abuse, confiscation of personal property, degrading or inhumane treatment, and extortion are possible.

If you are convicted, you may face one of the following sentences:
-- Two to ten years in most countries.
-- A minimum of six years' hard labor and a stiff fine.
-- The death sentence in some countries.

Learn what the local laws are and obey them.

Marriage Abroad

Consular officers abroad cannot perform a marriage for you. Marriages abroad are generally performed by local civil or religious officials. Once your marriage is performed overseas, U.S. consular officers can advise you on how your foreign marriage document can be authenticated. A marriage which is valid under the laws of the country where the marriage was performed is generally recognized by most states in the United States. If you are married abroad and need confirmation that your marriage will be recognized in the United States, consult the Attorney General of your state of residence in the United States.

Marriages abroad are subject to the residency requirements of the country where the marriage is performed. There is almost always a lengthy waiting period. Some countries require that the civil documents which are presented to the marriage registrar abroad be translated and authenticated by a foreign consular official in the United States. This process can be time consuming and expensive. Unlike in the United States, civil law countries require proof of legal capacity to enter into a marriage contract. If it is necessary to obtain this proof overseas, you can execute an affidavit of eligibility to marry at a U.S. embassy or consulate for a small fee (currently $10). There are also individual requirements, which vary from country to country, i.e. parental consent and blood tests. Before going abroad, check with the embassy or tourist information bureau of the country where you plan to marry to learn of any specific requirements. In addition, the Office of Overseas Citizens Services, Room 4811, Department of State, Washington, D.C. 20520 has some general information on marriage in a number of countries overseas. If you are already abroad, consult with the nearest U.S. embassy or consulate.

Divorce Abroad

The validity of divorces obtained overseas will vary according to the requirements of an individual's state of residence. Consult the authorities of your state of residence in the United States for these requirements.

Birth Abroad of a U.S. Citizen

Most children born abroad to a U.S. citizen parent or parents acquire U.S. citizenship at birth. As soon as possible after the birth, the U.S. citizen parent should contact the nearest American embassy or consulate. When it is determined that the child has acquired U.S. citizenship, a consular officer prepares a Consular Report of Birth Abroad of a Citizen of the United States of America (Form FS-240). This document is recognized by U.S. law as proof of acquisition of U.S. citizenship and is acceptable evidence of citizenship for obtaining a passport, entering school, and most other purposes.

Death of a U.S. Citizen Abroad

When a U.S. citizen dies abroad, the nearest U.S. embassy or consulate should be notified as soon as possible. Upon notification, the consular officer, in accordance with local laws, may do the following:
-- Require proof of the decedent's citizenship (for example, U.S. passport, birth certificate, or naturalization certificate).
-- Report the death to the next of kin or legal representative.
-- Obtain instructions and funds from the family to make arrangements for local burial or return of the body to the United States.
-- Obtain the local death certificate and prepare a Report of Death of an American Citizen Abroad (Form OF-180) to forward to the next of kin or legal representative. (This document may be used in U.S. courts to settle estate matters.)
-- Serve as provisional conservator of a deceased Americans estate and arrange for disposition of those effects.

Because the costs for local burial or transporting a deceased body back to the United States can be quite expensive, you may wish to obtain insurance to cover this cost. Otherwise, your relative or next of kin must bear these expenses. The U.S. Government cannot pay to have your body buried overseas or returned to the United States.

Federal Benefits Services Abroad

Federal agency monthly benefits checks are generally sent from the Department of the Treasury to the U.S. embassies or consulates in the countries where the beneficiaries are residing. When you move overseas, report your change of residence to the nearest U.S. embassy or consulate. The usual procedure is for the embassy or consulate to then forward the check through the local mail system to you. It may be possible to make arrangements to have your check deposited directly into a bank account located in the United States or in the country where you reside. Check with the benefits paying agency or the nearest U.S. embassy or consulate for further information.

If your check does not arrive or you have other questions about your benefits, contact a consular officer at the nearest U.S. embassy or consulate. If the consular officer cannot answer your inquiry, he or she will contact the appropriate paying agency, such as the Social Security Administration, and make inquiries on your behalf. If you move, notify the nearest U.S. embassy or consulate at least 60 days before the move. This will enable the Federal agency to update its records so your checks are sent to the correct address.

Assistance In Voting in U.S. Elections

Americans who reside abroad are usually eligible to vote by absentee ballot in all Federal elections and may also be eligible to vote in many state and local U.S. elections. Eligibility depends upon the laws and regulations of your state of residence in the United States. To vote absentee, you must meet state voter registration requirements and apply for the ballot as early as possible from the state of your last domicile. Should your state ballot not arrive in sufficient time, you may be eligible to use a Federal write-in ballot known as a F.W.A.B. You should consult the nearest U.S. embassy or consulate for additional information.

Selective Service Registration

Section I-202 of the Presidential Proclamation of July 2, 1980, reinstituting registration under the Military Selective Service Act, states:

Citizens of the United States who are to be registered and who are not in the United States on any of the days set aside for their registration, shall present themselves at a U.S. embassy or consulate for registration before a diplomatic or consular officer of the United States or before a registrar duly appointed by a diplomatic or consular officer of the United States. Check with the nearest U.S. embassy or consulate if you need to comply.

FAMILY MATTERS

Adopting A Child Overseas

If you plan to adopt a child overseas, you should be aware that the U.S. Government considers foreign adoptions to be a private legal matter within the judicial sovereignty of the nation where the child is residing. U.S. authorities have no right to intervene on behalf of American citizens in the courts in the country where the adoption takes place. However, there are a number of ways that U.S. embassies and consulates can assist prospective parents.

The U.S. embassy or consulate can provide you with information on the adoption process in the country where you reside. Consular officers can make inquiries on your behalf regarding the status of your case in the foreign court and will assist in clarifying documentary requirements if necessary. Embassies and consulates will also ensure that as an American you are not being discriminated against by foreign courts and will provide you with information on the visa application process for your adopted child.

Because children in foreign adoptions are considered to be nationals of the country of origin, prospective parents must comply with local laws. One way to achieve this is by dealing only with a reputable international adoption agency experienced in handling adoptions in the country where you are living. In the case of a private adoption, you should hire a local attorney with expertise in adoptions. Because of the potential for fraud in international adoptions, you need to be aware of the pitfalls. The U.S. embassy or consulate can offer you advice on what problems you might encounter.

Foreign children adopted overseas by U.S. citizens can gain U.S. citizenship if the adoptive parents apply for the child's naturalization after they return to the United States. In most cases, the adoptive parents would merely apply for a Certificate of Citizenship from the Immigration and Naturalization Service (INS) after the adoption. However, until they return to the United States,

the adopted child remains a national of their country of origin. Before returning to the United States with your adopted child, you will need to petition the INS for your child's immigrant visa. For further information on adoption procedures, obtain INS Form M-249 entitled, *The Immigration of Adopted and Prospective Adoptive Children*. You can also contact the Department of State, Overseas Citizens Services Office of Children's Issues, telephone (202) 736-7000 to learn more about foreign adoption procedures and to order the booklet *International Adoptions*. This booklet is also available on the Internet at http://travel.state.gov and contains useful information for U.S. citizens who plan to adopt a foreign child.

International Child Custody Disputes

For parents involved in a child custody dispute, there are limits on the assistance that U.S. authorities can provide. In cases where an American child is abducted overseas by a parent, the U.S. Governments role is confined to helping the remaining parent locate the child, monitoring the child's welfare, and providing general information about child custody laws and procedures in the country where the abduction took place. Consular officers overseas can issue a U.S. passport to a child involved in a custody dispute if the child appears in person at the U.S. embassy or consulate and there is no court order issued by the foreign court of that country which bars the child's departure from the country.

U.S. consuls cannot take custody of a child, force the child's return to the United States, or attempt to influence child custody proceedings in foreign courts. If the parents cannot work out an amicable settlement of a child custody dispute, the only recourse is usually court action in the country where the child is residing. A custody decree originating in the United States is not automatically recognized overseas. On the contrary, foreign courts will decide custody in accordance with the laws of that country. If you are involved in a custody dispute, you will need to obtain a foreign attorney to represent you in court. You can obtain a list of such attorneys from the U.S. embassy or consulate in the country where your child has been taken.

Parents who are involved in a custody battle overseas should find out whether the country you are in is a party to the Hague Convention on the Civil Aspects of International Child Abduction.

Under the Hague Convention, a child who has been wrongfully removed may be returned to his or her place of habitual residence. For further information on the Hague Convention contact the Office of Children's Issues in Overseas Citizens Services. That office also has copies of the booklet International Parental Child Abduction which contains helpful information on what U.S. citizen parents can do to prevent their child from becoming a victim of parental child abduction. If you are overseas and would like information on this subject, contact the nearest U.S. embassy or consulate for guidance.

PRECAUTIONS

Safeguarding Your Passport
Your passport is a valuable document which should be carefully safeguarded. When living overseas, the Department of State recommends that you keep your passport at home in a safe, secure place. Although a passport kept at an available storage facility outside the home might offer maximum security, keep in mind that an emergency requiring immediate travel may make it difficult or impossible to obtain your passport before departure. In such a case, it may not be possible to obtain a replacement or temporary passport in time to make the intended travel.

Loss or Theft of a U.S. Passport
If your passport is lost or stolen abroad, report the loss immediately to the nearest foreign service post and to local police authorities. If you can provide the consular officer with the information in the old passport, it will facilitate issuance of a new passport. Therefore, you should photocopy the data page of your passport and keep it in a separate place for easy retrieval.

Passport Fraud
Multiple and fraudulent U.S. passports are used in many types of criminal activity, including illegal entry into the United States. In processing lost passport cases, the Department of State must take special precautions that may delay the issuance of a new passport. If you suspect a U.S. passport is being used fraudulently, do not hesitate to contact the nearest passport agency in the United States or American embassy or consulate overseas.

CITIZENSHIP AND NATIONALITY

U.S. Citizenship and Residence Abroad
U.S. citizens who take up residence abroad or who are contemplating doing so frequently ask whether this will have any effect on their citizenship. Residence abroad, in and of itself, has no effect on U.S. citizenship and there is no requirement of U.S. law that a person who is a naturalized U.S. citizen must return to the United States periodically to preserve his or her U.S. citizenship. Contact the nearest U.S. embassy or consulate if you have any questions about nationality.

Acquisition and Loss of Citizenship
U.S. citizenship may be acquired by birth in the United States or by birth abroad to a U.S. citizen parent or parents. However, there are certain residency or physical presence requirements that U.S. citizens may need to fulfill before the child's birth in order to transmit citizenship to their child born overseas. A child born abroad in wedlock to one citizen parent and one alien parent acquires U.S. citizenship only if the citizen parent was physically present in the United States for 5 years prior to the child's birth, at least 2 years of which were after the age of 14. Living abroad in military service or U.S. Government employment, or as an unmarried dependent in the household of someone so employed, can be considered as presence in the United States. A child born out of wedlock to a U.S. citizen mother acquires U.S. citizenship if the mother was physically present in the United States for 1 continuous year prior to the child's birth. A child born out of wedlock to a U.S. citizen father must establish a legal relationship to the father before age 18 or be legitimated before reaching age 21, depending on the date of birth, if he/she is to acquire U.S. citizenship through the father. For further information on these legal requirements, consult the nearest U.S. embassy or consulate. Citizenship may also be acquired subsequent to birth through the process of naturalization. (For more information, contact the Immigration and Naturalization Service at 1-800-755-0777.)

Loss of citizenship can occur only as the result of a citizen voluntarily performing an act of expatriation as set forth in the Immigration and Nationality Act with the intent to relinquish citizenship. Such acts most frequently performed include the following:

• Naturalization in a foreign state;
• Taking an oath or making an affirmation of allegiance to a foreign state;
• Service in the armed forces of a foreign state;
• Employment with a foreign government; or
• Taking a formal oath of renunciation of

allegiance before a U.S. consular or diplomatic officer.

If you have any question about any aspect of loss of nationality, contact the nearest U.S. embassy or consulate or the Office of Overseas Citizens Services, Bureau of Consular Affairs, Room 4811, Department of State, Washington, D.C. 20520.

Dual Nationality

A foreign country might claim you as a citizen of that country if:

- You were born there.
- Your parent or parents are or were citizens of that country.
- You are a naturalized U.S. citizen but are still considered a citizen under that country's laws.

If you fall into any of the above categories, consult the embassy of the country where you are planning to reside or are presently living. While recognizing the existence of dual nationality, the U.S. Government does not encourage it as a matter of policy because of the problems it may cause. Claims of other countries upon dual-national U.S. citizens often place them in situations where their obligations to one country are in conflict with U.S. law. Dual nationality may hamper efforts by the U.S. Government to provide diplomatic and consular protection to individuals overseas. When a U.S. citizen is in the other country of their dual nationality, that country has a predominant claim on the person. If you have any question about dual nationality, contact the nearest U.S. embassy or consulate or the Office of Overseas Citizens Services at the address in the previous section.

FINANCIAL AND BUSINESS MATTERS

U.S. Taxes

U.S. citizens must report their worldwide income on their Federal income tax returns. Living or earning income outside the United States does not relieve a U.S. citizen of responsibility for filing tax returns. However, U.S. citizens living and/or working abroad may be entitled to various deductions, exclusions, and credits under U.S. tax laws, as well as under international tax treaties and conventions between the United States and a number of foreign countries. Consult the Internal Revenue Service (IRS) for further information.

For information on taxes and locations of IRS offices overseas, contact any office of the IRS or write to the Forms Distribution Center, Post Office Box 25866, Richmond, Virginia 23289. That office also has copies of Publication 54, Tax Guide for U.S. Citizens and Resident Aliens Abroad; Publication 901, U.S. Tax Treaties; Publication 514, Foreign Tax Credit for Individuals and Publication 520, Scholarships and Fellowships. The IRS has also put together a package of forms and instructions (Publication 776) for U.S. citizens living abroad. The package is also available through to the Forms Distribution Center. During the filing period, you can usually obtain the necessary Federal income tax forms from the nearest U.S. embassy or consulate.

If you have access to a personal computer and a modem, you can get forms and publications electronically from the IRS. The forms and publications are available through IRIS, the Internal Revenue Information Services on FedWorld, a government bulletin board. On the Internet, you can telnet to fedworld.gov. or for file transfer protocol services, connect to ftp.fedworld.gov. If you are using the Internet's World Wide Web, connect to http://www.ustreas.gov.

Foreign Country Taxes

If you earn any income while you are overseas, you may be required to pay tax on that income. You should check the rules and regulations with that country's embassy or consulate before you leave the United States, or consult the nearest U.S. embassy or consulate abroad.

Bank Accounts

Some countries will permit you to maintain a local bank account denominated in dollars or in another foreign currency of your choice. This may be a good idea if the U.S. dollar is strong and the local currency in the country you reside in is weak. If that country does not permit you to maintain U.S. dollar bank accounts, another idea would be to keep your dollars in a bank in the United States. That way you could convert them to the local currency as you need them rather than all at once. This would protect you in the event that the country you are living in devalues its currency.

Wills

To avoid the risk of running afoul of foreign laws, if you own property or other assets both in the United States and overseas, consider the idea of having two wills drawn up. One should be prepared according to the legal system of your adopted country, and the other according to the legal system of the U.S. Each will should mention the other.

Having two wills should ensure that your foreign property is disposed of in accordance with your wishes in the event of your death.

Property Investment
A major decision that you will have to face when you live abroad is whether or not to purchase a home or property. Because prices in many foreign countries may seem like a bargain compared to the United States, there may be some merit to investing in real estate. However, you will need to keep several things in mind. First, check to see whether the country where you plan to invest permits foreigners to own property. Many foreign countries do not permit foreigners without immigrant status to buy real estate. Also, there may be restrictions on areas in which you may buy property and on the total number of foreigners who may purchase property in any one year.

One way for a foreigner to purchase real estate overseas may be to set up a bank trust and then lease the property. For your protection, you should first consult with a local real estate agent and then hire a reputable attorney. Check with the U.S. embassy or consulate in the country where you plan to purchase property to obtain a list of lawyers. A good lawyer will provide you with information about having your real estate contract notarized, registered, and if necessary, translated. Your attorney should also be able to advise you on protection against unscrupulous land deals.

Before you make a real estate purchase, learn the customs and laws of the foreign government with regard to real estate. In the event of a dispute, you will have to abide by local and not U.S. laws. A good rule to follow is that before you invest in any real estate take the same precautions which you normally would take before you make a sizeable investment in the United States.

RETURNING TO THE U.S.

U.S. Immigration and Customs
If you leave the U.S. for purposes of traveling, working, or studying abroad, and return to resume U.S. residence, you are considered a returning U.S. resident by the U.S. Customs Service.

When you go through immigration and customs at the port of entry, have your passport ready. Where possible, pack separately the articles you have acquired abroad to make inspection easy. Have your receipts handy in case you need to support your customs declaration. If you took other documents with you, such as an International Certification of Vaccination, a medical certificate, or a customs certificate of registration for foreign-made personal articles, have them ready also. If you are returning to the U.S. by car from either Mexico or Canada, a certificate of vehicle registration should be available.

Articles acquired abroad and brought back with you are subject to duty and internal revenue tax. As a returning U.S. resident, you are allowed to bring back $400 ($600, if you are returning directly from a Caribbean Basin Economy Recovery Act country) worth of merchandise duty free. However, you must have been outside the United States for at least 48 hours, and you must not have used this exemption within the preceding 30-day period. The next $1,000 worth of items you bring back with you for personal use or gifts are dutiable at a flat 10% rate. (Your duty free exemption may include 100 cigars, 200 cigarettes, and 1 liter of wine, beer or liquor.)

Restrictions on Products Entering the U. S.
Fresh fruit, meat, vegetables, plants in soil, and many other agricultural products are prohibited from entering the United States because they may carry foreign insects and diseases that could damage U.S. crops, forests, gardens, and livestock. Other items may also be restricted, so be sure to obtain details of regulations before departing for your trip back to the U.S. These restrictions also apply to mailed products. Prohibited items confiscated and destroyed at U.S. international postal facilities have almost doubled in recent years. For more information and to request the pamphlet, *Travelers Tips on Prohibited Agricultural Products* contact the agricultural affairs office at the nearest U.S. embassy or consulate, or write to the Animal and Plant Health Inspection Service, U.S. Department of Agriculture, 4700 River Road, Unit 51, Riverdale, MD 20737.

Importing A Car
If you plan to bring a car back with you, before purchasing it, make sure it conforms to U.S. emission standards established by the Environmental Protection Agency. If your vehicle does not conform to standards, it may be banned from entering the country. For further information, obtain the pamphlet, *Buying a Car Overseas?*

10

Beware! from the U.S. Environmental Protection Agency, Public Information Center, Mail Code 3406, 401 M Street, S.W., Washington, D.C. 20460.

Wildlife and Wildlife Products

While you were overseas, if you purchased any articles made from endangered animals and plants or any live wild animals to bring back as pets, you need to be aware that U.S. laws and international treaties make it a crime to bring many wildlife souvenirs into the United States. Some prohibited items include those made from sea turtle shell, most reptile skins, crocodile leather, ivory, furs from endangered cat species, and those from coral reefs. Do not buy wildlife souvenirs if you are unsure of being able to bring them legally into the United States. The penalties you risk are severe and your purchases could be confiscated. To learn more about endangered wildlife and guidelines governing restrictions on imports into the United States, you can obtain the pamphlet, *Buyer Beware!* For a free copy, contact the Publications Unit, U.S. Fish and Wildlife Service, Department of the Interior, Washington, D.C. 20240. Additional information on the import of wildlife and wildlife products can be obtained through TRAFFIC (U.S.A.), World Wildlife Fund--U.S., 1250 24th Street, N.W., Washington, D.C. 20037.

OTHER IMPORTANT PUBLICATIONS

(several of these publications have been reprinted elsewhere in this book. Check the Table of Contents]

U.S. Embassies and Consulates

Key Officers of Foreign Service Posts: Guide for Business Representatives has names of key officers and addresses for U.S. embassies, consulates, and missions abroad.

Your Trip Abroad

Your Trip Abroad contains helpful tips on obtaining a passport, things to consider in preparing for your overseas trip, other resources for travel and customs information. To obtain a copy, contact the GPO for price and availability.

Tips for Older Americans

Travel Tips for Older Americans provides general information on passports, visas, health, currency, and other travel tidbits for elderly U.S. citizens planning to travel overseas. Copies are available from the Internet at http://travel.state.gov or Consular Affairs automated fax at (202) 647-3000.

A Safe Trip Abroad

A Safe Trip Abroad contains helpful precautions to minimize the chance of becoming a victim of terrorism and also provides other safety tips for Americans traveling overseas. To obtain a copy, contact the GPO for price and availability.

Crisis Abroad

Crisis Abroad--What the State Department Does summarizes the work by the State Department during a crisis and its efforts to obtain reliable information from local authorities abroad for concerned relatives and friends of Americans located in the disaster area. Copies are free by sending a stamped, self-addressed business-size envelope (SASE) to CA/P, Room 6831, Department of State, Washington, D.C. 20520-4818.

Overseas Citizens Services

The booklet Office of Overseas Citizens Services contains information about the assistance that the office provides in four major categories: deaths, arrests, welfare/whereabouts inquiries, and financial-medical emergencies. The booklet is free by sending a SASE to CA/P at the address above

General Advice For Americans Resident Overseas

January 24, 2003

Among the highest priorities of the Department of State and our missions abroad is the safety and security of locally-resident Americans overseas. In the past year, the Department has intervened to assist in the evacuation of Americans from half a dozen countries throughout the world as a result of serious political or economic unrest, natural disasters, and terrorist attacks. Hundreds of expatriate Americans each year are forced by personal emergencies (e.g. death or illness in the family) to return to the U.S. on short notice. Evacuations, especially under crisis conditions, are inevitably very disruptive and distressing for those involved.

The State Department routinely provides standard advice to its employees on prudent steps to take to ensure they would be prepared in the event of such an evacuation. This and other advice on crisis preparedness is available on the Department's Web site at http://travel.state.gov, and we are summarizing the principal points below. The

Department commends these elementary steps to you for your careful consideration.

- Assemble all vital documents such as passports, birth and marriage records, vaccination, insurance and bank records in one readily accessible location;
- Check to be sure your passport and any necessary visas are valid and that you are registered at the Embassy/Consulate with your current address and phone number. If you need to obtain a new passport or to update your registration, please do so at the Embassy as soon as possible (fill in the times and days).
- Visa processing can take several weeks. Immediate family members should keep their U.S. visas current and apply for visas with as much time in advance of planned travel as possible.
- Make or update as necessary a complete inventory of your household effects, in duplicate.
- Maintain an adequate supply of food, water, and necessary medications in your home. Make sure your car is in good working order. Keep the gas tank full and check oil, coolant, tires, and battery.

We do not want American citizens to become unduly alarmed. These are precautionary measures only. Given the potential for acts of violence, terrorism, or anti-American demonstrations, we believe it is important for all citizens to maintain readiness for all possibilities in case of an emergency. We will promptly inform you of any significant developments and advise you accordingly.

The Department of State encourages all American citizens residing abroad to register their presence and obtain up-to-date information on security conditions at the nearest American Embassy or Consulate.

Chapter 2

Security Awareness Overseas

[The information in this chapter is reprinted verbatim from a bulletin issued by the U.S. State Department, Bureau of Diplomatic Security. It is intended to serve as advice to Americans traveling abroad.]

Introduction

Personal security abroad is a major concern of individuals and companies. Information in this chapter, and infact the entire book should make a strong contribution to the security and well-being of American citizens who live and work abroad.

This chapter is intended as a guideline for business persons in the private sector who travel or reside abroad.

A rapidly changing political world has not lessened the attention one should pay to personal security when overseas. Natural disasters will continue, as will acts of terrorism. Indeed, one might expect increased incidents of civil unrest, some directed against Americans, as political situations remain unresolved. The guidelines, which follow, are suggested to assist American companies and their personnel abroad in planning to meet their individual needs and circumstances. Individuals should ensure, however, that any approach chosen is best suited to their individual situation.

Take the time to think through your upcoming travel and to use this chapter to plan for emergencies and other special contingencies. Hopefully, you will never be required to act upon your plan, but if an emergency does develop, the time spent planning may ensure your safety and that of your family.

Introduction

We gain a great sense of security and self confidence knowing we are prepared for potential crises. This chapter provides assistance in preparing us to face those emergencies we may encounter while living or traveling overseas. Many potential overseas crises may be eased or averted by taking the time to read and study the information that follows.

Cultural misunderstandings and inadequate local support services often make crises abroad more intense than similar situations in the United States. Overseas, we must assume greater responsibility for our own safety.

Information and suggestions in this chapter have been collected from several government and private sources. Personal experiences of those who have been through particular crises abroad have added substantially to the store of ideas and advice. The experience of each-whether hostage, crime victim, evacuee, or other-is distinct. Yet there are common threads that provide guidelines on how to handle crises successfully. We hope, in this chapter, to pass those guidelines on to you.

Although we have attempted to organize tips and information according to whether your stay will be temporary or permanent, most apply to either situation.

Preparing To Travel

Have Your Affairs in Order
Many hostages have expressed regret that their affairs were not left in better order for their families. An evacuation, illness, or death can often place a family in a similar situation. Three actions, taken before you depart, will alleviate this potential problem:

Discuss and plan with your family what should be done in the case of any emergency separation. All adult family members should be aware of these plans.

Supply family and close friends with the emergency notification numbers found on this page. They serve both to notify you while you are overseas in the event of an illness or death in your family in the United States and to provide your family in the U.S. with information about you in case of a crisis abroad.

See that all important papers are up-to-date. List papers and leave originals with a family member or attorney in the United States. Carry only copies to your overseas assignment. Safe deposit boxes and bank accounts are very useful but may be sealed on the death of an owner. Therefore, make sure your representative has joint right of access.

Important Papers

Your collection of important papers might include:
  Will
  Birth and marriage certificates
  Guardianship or adoption papers for children
  Power of attorney for spouse or relative
  Naturalization papers
  Deeds, mortgages, stocks and bonds, car titles
  Insurance papers-car, home, life, personal effects, ... medical
  Tax records
  Proof of termination of previous marriage(s)
  Child support/alimony agreements Proof of membership in any organization or union that entitles the estate to any benefits

Useful Information

An Information List might include:
  Bank account numbers and addresses
  Passport numbers
  Duplicate passport pictures in case passport needs to be replaced due to loss
  U.S. and local driver's license numbers
  Insurance policy numbers and names of carriers
  Social Security numbers
  Credit card numbers
  Travelers check numbers and issuing bank
  Medical and dental information, distinguishing marks and scars, and medicine and eyeglass prescriptions
  Assets and debts
  Names and addresses of business and professional contacts
  Updated inventory of household and personal possessions with pictures/videos
  Employment records for each family member; resumes, references,

commendations
Personal address list
Fingerprints, current photos/videos, voice recording, known handwriting samples of family members

Emergency Notification

While abroad, you may need to be notified of an emergency involving someone in the United States. And during a political, social, or natural crisis abroad, your family in the United States will be anxious to get news of you.

The appropriate telephone numbers below should be given to your family for such purposes.
  U.S. Embassy/consulate
  ...... (Day)
  ...... (Night)
  U.S. Corporate HQ
  ...... (Day)
  ...... (Night)
  Corporate Security
  Local Legal Counsel
  Local Police
  Airline(s)
  Red Cross
  Department of State
  Host Country Embassy, Washington, D.C.
  Local Company Office
  Residence
  International Operator
  Relatives

Before initiating calls, the caller in the United States should have the following information available:
  Your name, company, and current location
  Name and relationship of family member
  In case of death-Date of death
  In case of illness-Name, address, and telephone number of attending physician or hospital

Miscellaneous Tips

The corporate traveler should also consider the following, which will assist and possibly protect him/her during the actual journey:
  Obtain International Driving Permit.
  Prepare a wallet card identifying your blood type, known allergies, required medications, insurance company, and name of person to contact in case of emergency.
  Remove from wallet all credit cards and other items not necessary for trip.
  Remove unessential papers, such as reserve,

military, or humorous cards, e.g., "Honorary Sheriff."

Put a plain cover on your passport (covers available in stationery stores);

Use hard, lockable luggage.

Be sure luggage tags contain your name, phone number, and full street address; that information is concealed from casual observation; and that company logos are not displayed on luggage.

Inform family member or friend of specific travel plans. Give your office a complete itinerary. Be sure to notify the local company manager of your travel plans.

Obtain the name(s) and address(es) of your local office(s).

Obtain small amount of local currency if possible.

Be aware of airline safety records when booking vacation trips while overseas; do not include company name in reservation.

When possible, mail personal papers to yourself at the local overseas office.

Stay informed! Check for any travel advisories pertinent to countries you plan to visit. Call the Department of State's Citizens Emergency Center (see Chapter 10), or your company's Corporate Security Department.

In Transit

Most of the following suggestions apply to any travel; several are specifically directed at surviving a terrorist situation. It is recognized that the level of risk varies from country to country and time to time, so that you may need to choose among the suggested options or modify the concepts to meet your needs.

If you plan to stay in one country any length of time while traveling, especially in a country that is in a period of civil unrest, register with the embassy or consulate and provide a copy of your itinerary. Registration makes it easier to contact you in case of an emergency and to evacuate you if necessary.

On the Plane

Carry-on luggage should contain a supply of any regularly taken prescription medicines (in original containers labeled with the pharmacy name and prescribing physician), an extra pair of eyeglasses, passport, and carefully chosen personal documents (copies only!).

Dress inconspicuously to blend into the international environment.

Consider wearing no jewelry.

On foreign carriers, avoid speaking English as much as possible. Do not discuss business or travel plans with fellow passengers, crew, or even traveling companions. Select a window seat in the coach section. This position is less accessible by hijackers inflicting indiscriminate violence.

Memorize your passport number so you do not have to reveal your passport when filling out landing cards.

At an Overseas Airport

Maintain a low profile, and avoid public areas as much as possible. Check in quickly and do not delay in the main terminal area. Do not discuss travel plans indiscriminately.

Stay away from unattended baggage. Verify baggage claim checks before and after flight. Always maintain custody of your carry-on bag.

Survey surroundings, noting exits and safe areas.

If an incident occurs, survival may depend on your ability to remain calm and alert. During a terrorist attack or rescue operation, you do not want to be confused with the terrorists and shot. Avoid sudden moves; hide behind something and drop to floor.

Car Rentals

Ideally, choose a conservative model car with locking trunk, hood, and gas cap; power brakes and steering; seat belts; quick accelerating engine; heavy duty bumpers; smooth interior locks. In a hot climate, choose air conditioning. Keep the gas tank at least half full.

Before getting into the car, examine it for strange objects or wires inside, around, or underneath it. If found, do not touch; clear the area and call police.

When driving, lock the doors, keep windows rolled up, avoid being boxed in by other cars. Vary routes. Check for suspicious individuals before getting out of the car.

Lock the car when unattended. Never let anyone place a package inside or enter the car unless you are present.

Public Transportation

Stay on your guard against pickpockets and petty thieves while in a bus/train terminal or at a taxi stop. Avoid carrying a wallet in your hip or easily accessible coat pocket. Carry a purse/handbag that you may firmly grip or secure to your body. Beware of people jostling you at busy stations.

Take only licensed taxis. Generally those found in front of terminals and the better hotels are the safest. You may pay a bit more, but the companies are reputable and normally the drivers have been screened. Be sure the photo on displayed license is of the driver. Have the address of your destination written out in local language and carry it with you. Get a map and learn the route to your destination; note if taxi driver takes you a different or longer way.

Try not to travel alone in a taxi, and never get out in deserted areas. If the door doesn't lock, sit near the middle of the seat so you will thwart thieves who might open the door to grab a purse, briefcase, or wallet.

On subways, choose a middle car but never an empty car. On buses, sit in an aisle seat near the driver. Stand back from the curb while waiting for a bus.

Avoid arriving anywhere at night and using dim or vacant entrances to stations or terminals. Utilize only busy, well-lit stations.

Take as little luggage as possible; ideally, no more than you can comfortably carry.

In-Transit Accommodations

Accommodations in many countries differ considerably from those found in North America and Western Europe. Safety features required in U.S. hotels, such as sprinkler systems, fire stairwells, and emergency lighting, often are either lacking or inoperable. The following measures will enable you to better plan for unforeseen contingencies in hotels.

Hotel Crime

Stay alert in your hotel. Put the "do not disturb" sign on your door to give the impression that the room is occupied. Call the maid when you are ready for the room to be cleaned. Consider leaving the light or TV on when you are out of the room.

Carry the room key with you instead of leaving it at front desk. Do not use your name when answering the phone. Do not accept packages or open the door to workmen without verification from the front desk.

When walking, remain on wide, well-lit streets. Know where you are going when you leave the hotel if on a tour, enlist a reputable guide. Generally, the hotel will recommend or procure one. Do not take shortcuts through alleys or off the beaten path. If alone, be back in the hotel by dark. Never resist armed robbery; it could lead to violence. Always carry some cash to appease muggers who may resort to violence at finding no reward for their efforts.

Civil Unrest

In some areas of the world, civil unrest or violence directed against Americans and other foreigners is common. Travelers should be alert to indicators of civil unrest and take the following precautions in the event of such situations:

If in your hotel, stay there. Contact the U.S. Embassy, consulate or other friendly embassy. Hire someone to take a note to them if phones are out of order.

Contact your local office representative.

Do not watch activity from your window, and try to sleep in an inside room which provides greater protection from gunfire, rocks, grenades, etc.

If you are caught outside in the middle of a riot or unrest, do not take sides or attempt to gather information. Play the tourist who just wants to get home to his/her family.

Hotel Fires

Many hotels abroad are not as fire-resistant as those in the United States. Interior materials are often extremely flammable. Escape routes may not be posted in hallways and exits may be few or sealed. Fire fighting equipment and water supplies may be limited. There may be no fast method for

alerting a fire department. Sprinkler systems and smoke detectors may be nonexistent.

You must aggressively take responsibility for the safety of yourself and your family. Think "contingency plan" and discuss it with your dependents. Begin planning your escape from a fire as soon as you check in to a hotel. When a fire occurs, you can then act without panic and without wasting time.

Stay in the most modern hotel; consider a U.S. chain. Request a lower floor, ideally the second or third. Selecting a room no higher than the second floor enables you to jump to safety. Although most fire departments can reach above the second floor, they may not get to you in time or position a fire truck on your side of the building.

Locate exits and stairways as soon as you check in; be sure the doors open. Count the number of doors between your room and exit or stairway. In a smoke-filled hallway, you could have to "feel" your way to an exit. Form a mental map of your escape route.

If the hotel has a fire alarm system, find the nearest alarm. Be sure you know how to use it. You may have to activate it in the dark or in dense smoke.

Ensure that your room windows open and that you know how the latches work. Look out the window and mentally rehearse your escape through it. Make note of any ledges or decks that will aid escape.

Check the smoke detector by pushing the test button. If it does not work, have it fixed or move to another room. Better yet, carry your own portable smoke detector (with the battery removed while traveling). Place it in your room by the hall door near the ceiling.

Keep the room key and a flashlight on the bedside table so that you may locate the key quickly if you have to leave your room.

If a Fire Starts

If you awake to find smoke in your room, grab your key and crawl to the door on your hands and knees. Don't stand-smoke and deadly gases rise while the fresher air will be near the floor.

Before you open the door, feel it with the palm of your hand. If the door or knob is hot, the fire may be right outside. Open the door slowly. Be ready to slam it shut if the fire is close by. If your exit path is clear, crawl into the hallway. Be sure to close the door behind you to keep smoke out in case you have to return to your room. Take your

key, as most hotel doors lock automatically. Stay close to the wall to avoid being trampled.

Do not use elevators during a fire. They may malfunction, or if they have heat-activated call buttons, they may take you directly to the fire floor.

As you make your way to the fire exit, stay on the same side as the exit door. Count the doors to the exit.

When you reach the exit, walk down the stairs to the first floor. Hold onto the handrail for guidance and protection from being knocked down by other occupants.

If you encounter heavy smoke in the stairwell, don't try to run through it. You may not make it. Instead, turn around and walk up to the roof fire exit. Prop the door open to ventilate the stairwell and to keep from being locked out. Find the windward side of the roof, sit down, and wait for fire fighters to find you.

If all exits are blocked or if there is heavy smoke in the hallway, you'll be better off staying in your room. If there is smoke in your room, open a window and turn on the bathroom vent. Don't break the window unless it can't be opened. You might want to close the window later to keep smoke out, and broken glass could injure you or people below.

If your phone works, call the desk to tell someone where you are, or call the fire department to report your location in the building. Hang a bed sheet out the window as a signal.

Fill the bathtub with water to use for fire fighting. Bail water onto your door or any hot walls with an ice bucket or waste basket. Stuff wet towels into cracks under and around doors where smoke can enter. Tie a wet towel over your mouth and nose to help filter out smoke. If there is fire outside your window, take down the drapes and move everything combustible away from the window.

If you are above the second floor, you probably will be better off fighting the fire in your room than jumping. A jump from above the third floor may result in severe injury or death.

Remember that panic and a fire's byproducts, such as super-heated gases and smoke, present a greater danger than the fire itself. If you know your plan of escape in advance, you will be less likely to panic and more likely to survive.

Terrorism

Although for most of us it is not a probability, terrorism is a fact. The likelihood of terrorist incidents varies according to country or area of the world, generally depending on the

stability of the local government and the degree of frustration felt by indigenous groups or individuals.

Although the number of incidents worldwide has increased at the rate of 10 percent per year, less than a quarter of these have been directed against American businesses or their employees. Most acts of terrorism are directed against citizens of the country where they occur.

When an act of terrorism does occur, it often has dire consequences: murder, hostage taking, property destruction. Much has been learned about the mentality of terrorists, their methods of operation, and the behavior patterns of both victims and perpetrators.

Alert individuals, prepared for possible terrorist acts, can minimize the likelihood that these acts will be successfully carried out against them. While there is no absolute protection against terrorism, there are a number of reasonable precautions that can provide some degree of individual protection.

U.S. Policy

U.S. policy is firmly committed to resisting terrorist blackmail.

The U.S. Government will not pay ransom for the release of hostages. It will not support the freeing of prisoners from incarceration in response to terrorist demands. The U.S. Government will not negotiate with terrorists on the substance of their demands, but it does not rule out contact and dialogue with hostage takers if this will promote the safe release of hostages.

In terrorist incidents abroad affecting Americans, our government looks to the host government to provide for the safety of U.S. citizens in accordance with international agreements.

The U.S. Government is prepared to offer terrorist

experts, specialized assistance, military equipment, and personnel should the foreign government decide such assistance could be useful.

Terrorist Demands

U.S. Government policy is to make no concessions to terrorist demands. However, such a decision on the part of private individuals or companies is a personal one and in some special circumstances may be made by the family or company of the victim. Whatever the decision, it should conform to local law.

Terrorist Surveillance

Terrorists may shadow an intended victim at length and with infinite patience before an actual abduction or assassination is attempted. Initial surveillance efforts may be clumsy and could be spotted by an alert target. In most cases, more than one individual is a likely candidate for the terrorist act. Usually the choice is based on the probability of success. In one documented instance, both an American and another country's representative were under surveillance. Though the American was the first choice of the terrorists, their surveillance showed that it would be more difficult to kidnap him. Consequently, the other individual was abducted and spent a long period in captivity.

Precise risks of surveillance and popular local tactics can be explained by your company's security representative. However, you must also learn to cultivate a "sixth sense" about your surroundings.

Know what is normal in your neighborhood and along your commute routes, especially at choke points. If you know what is ordinary, you will notice anything extraordinary-people who are in the wrong place or dressed inappropriately, or cars parked in strange locations.

Be particularly observant whenever you leave your home or office. Look up and down the street for suspicious vehicles, motorcycles, mopeds, etc. Note people near your home who appear to be repair personnel, utility crew teams, even peddlers. Ask yourself if they appear genuine.

Become familiar with vehicle makes and models; learn to memorize license numbers. Determine if a pattern is developing with specific vehicles. See if cars suddenly pull out of parking places or side streets when you pass. Cars with extra mirrors or large mirrors are suspicious.

Be aware of the types of surveillance: stationary (at residence, along route, at work); following (on foot, by car); monitoring (of telephone, mail); searching (of luggage, personal effects, even trash); and eavesdropping (electronic and personal). An elaborate system involving several people and cars might be used.

Make their job tougher by not being predictable. Eat at different times and places. Stagger professional and social activities; don't play tennis "every Wednesday at three," for example.

Know the choke points on your routes and be aware of other vehicles, vans, or motorcycles as you enter those bottleneck areas. Search out safe havens that you can pull into along the route.

Drive with windows rolled up to within 2 inches of the top and lock all doors. Report any suspicious activity promptly to law enforcement.

Avoid using unlicensed cabs or cabs that appear out of nowhere. Do not permit taxi drivers to deviate from desired route.

Be circumspect with members of the press, as terrorists often pose as journalists. Do not submit to interviews or allow photographs to be made in or of your home.

Always speak guardedly and caution children to do the same. Never discuss travel or business plans within hearing of servants. Surveillants consider children and servants to be a prime source of information. Always assume that your telephone is tapped.

In elevators, watch for anyone who waits for you to select your floor, then pushes a button for the one just above or below yours.

If you become aware of surveillance, don't let those watching you know you are onto them. And certainly never confront them. Immediately notify your appropriate company representative. Memorize emergency numbers, and carry change for phone calls.

Hijackings

The experience of others will be helpful to you if you are the victim of a hijacking. Blend in with the other airline passengers. Avoid eye contact with your captors. Remember there may be other hijackers covertly mixed among the regular passengers.

Although captors may appear calm, they cannot be trusted to behave reasonably or rationally at all times. Stay alert, but do not challenge them physically or verbally. Comply with their instructions.

If interrogated, keep answers short and limited to nonpolitical topics. Carry a family photo; at some point you may be able to appeal to captors' family feelings.

Minimize the importance of your job. Give innocuous reasons for traveling. Never admit to any accusations.

Armed Assault on the Ground

Hostages taken by ground assault are in a situation similar to hijacking except that it occurs within buildings. Business offices, banks, embassies, and trains have been targets. The same advice for dealing with hijackers applies to ground assaults. Should shooting occur, seek cover or lie flat on the floor.

Kidnappings

Kidnapping is a terrifying experience, but you possess more personal resources than you may be aware of to cope with the situation. Remember, you are only of value to them alive, and they want to keep you that way.

The common hostage responses of fear, denial, and withdrawal are all experienced in varying degrees. You may be blindfolded, drugged, handled roughly, or even stuffed in the trunk of a car. If drugs are administered, don't resist. Their purpose will be to sedate you and make you more manageable; these same drugs may actually help you to get control of your emotions, which should be your immediate goal. If conscious, follow your captors' instructions.

Captivity

A hostage-taking situation is at its worst at the onset. The terrorists are nervous and unsure, easily irritated, often irrational. It is a psychologically traumatic moment for the hostage. Violence may be used even if the hostage remains passive, but resistance could result in death.

If taken hostage, your best defense is passive cooperation. You may be terrified, but try to regain your composure as soon as possible and to organize your thoughts. Being able to behave rationally increases your chances for survival. The more time that passes, the better your chances of being released alive.

Behavior Suggestions

Each captivity is different, but some behavior suggestions apply to most:

Try to establish some kind of rapport with your captors. Family is a universal subject. Avoid political dialogues, but listen attentively to their point of view. If you know their language, listen and observe; and if addressed, use it.

Plan on a lengthy stay, and determine to keep track of the passage of time. Captors may attempt to confuse your sense of time by taking your watch, keeping you in a windowless cell, or serving meals at odd hours. However, you can approximate time by noting, for example, changes in temperatures between night and day; the frequency and intensity of outside noises-traffic, whistles, birds; and by observing the alertness of guards.

Maintain your dignity and self respect at all times.

Manage your time by setting up schedules for simple tasks, exercises, daydreaming, housekeeping.

Build relations with fellow captives and with the terrorists. If hostages are held apart, devise ways to communicate with one another. Where hostages are moved back and forth, to bathrooms for example, messages can be written and left. However, do not jeopardize your safety or the safety or treatment of others if attempting to communicate with fellow captives seems too risky.

Maintain your physical and mental health; it is critical to exercise body and mind. Eat food provided without complaint; keep up your strength. Request medical treatment or special medicines if required.

Establish exercise and relaxation programs. Exercise produces a healthy tiredness and gives you a sense of accomplishment. If space is confined, do isometrics. Relaxation reduces stress. Techniques include meditation, prayer, daydreaming.

Keep your mind active; read anything available. Write, even if you are not allowed to retain your writings. If materials are not available, mentally compose poetry or fiction, try to recall Scripture, design a house, even "play tennis" (as one hostage did).

Take note of the characteristics of your captors and surroundings: their habits, speech, contacts; exterior noises (typical of city or country); and other distinctive sounds. This information could prove very valuable later.

If selected for early release, consider it an opportunity to help remaining hostages. Details you have observed on the terrorists and the general situation can assist authorities with a rescue.

You can expect to be accused of working for the government's intelligence service, to be interrogated extensively, and to lose weight. You may be put in isolation; your captives may try to disorient you. It is important that you mentally maintain control.

Avoidance of Capture or Escape

Efforts to avoid capture or to attempt escape have in most cases been futile. The decision, however, is a personal one, although it could affect fellow hostages by placing them in jeopardy. Several other considerations should be weighed.

To have any chance of success, you should be in excellent physical condition and mentally prepared to react before the terrorists have consolidated their position. This, also, is the riskiest psychological time. You would need to have a plan in mind, and possibly have been trained in special driving tactics or other survival skills.

If you are held in a country in which you would stand out because of race or other physical characteristics, if you know nothing of the language or your location, or if you are held in a country where anti-American or anti-Western attitudes prevail, you should consider the consequences of your escape before attempting it.

20

If you conclude that an escape attempt is worthwhile, take terrorists by surprise and you may make it. If their organization has a poor track record of hostage safety, it may be worth the risk.

Rescue

The termination of any terrorist incident is extremely tense. If an assault force attempts a rescue, it is imperative that you remain calm and out of the way. Make no sudden moves or take any action by which you could be mistaken for a terrorist and risk being injured or killed.

Even in a voluntary release or surrender by the terrorists, tensions are charged and tempers volatile. Very precise instructions will be given to the hostages, either by the captors or the police. Follow instructions precisely. You may be asked to exit with hands in the air, and you may be searched by the rescue team. You may experience rough treatment until you are identified and the situation has stabilized.

Finally, it's worth keeping in mind three facts about terrorism:

> The overwhelming majority of victims have been abducted from their vehicles on the way to or from work.

> A large number of people taken hostage ignored the most basic security precautions.

> Terrorist tactics are not static. As precautions prove effective, they change their methods. There is a brief "window of vulnerability" while we learn to counter their new styles.

Additional Precautions

Do not settle into a routine. Vary times and routes to and from work or social engagements.

Remember, there is safety in numbers. Avoid going out alone. When traveling long distances by automobile, go in a convoy. Avoid back country roads and dangerous areas of the city.

A privately owned car generally offers the best security. Avoid luxury or ostentatious cars. Keep your automobile in good repair and the gas tank at least half full. Driving in the center lane of a multiple lane highway makes it difficult for the car to be forced off the road.

Overseas Crisis Planning

Culture Shock

Culture shock is the physiological and psychological stress experienced when a traveler is suddenly deprived of old, familiar cues-language, customs, etc. Both the seasoned traveler and the first-timer, whether in transit or taking up residence, are susceptible. The sensation may be severe or mild, last months or only hours, strike in a remote village or in a modern European city, in one country, but not another-or not at all.

Culture shock is most prevalent in the second or third month after arrival when the novelty of the new country fades. Symptoms typically disappear by the fourth to sixth month, when the family has settled in and a sense of equilibrium is restored.

Traveler disorientation is a form of culture shock. You may encounter so many strange sounds, sights, and smells upon arrival in a country new to you that you may be more vulnerable to accidents or crime. You may experience this disorientation on a fast-paced business trip to several different cultures.

You can combat traveler disorientation by gathering, in advance, information of a practical nature-knowing the routine at the airport, which taxis are recommended, knowing the exchange rate, etc. Pay particular attention to any host nation cultural behavior which may affect your security or safety.

As with any type of stress, culture shock may manifest itself both physically and emotionally. If you should experience it at a time when you need to be alert to security concerns, your awareness could be impaired. But if you understand it, you can successfully deal with it.

Symptoms

In children, you may notice a drop in school work and disruptive or regressive behavior. Teens may rebel with drugs or sex.

Symptoms to watch for in adults and children include:
> Sleepiness, apathy, depression
> Compulsive eating or drinking
> Exaggerated homesickness
> Decline in efficiency
> Negative stereotyping of nationals
> Recurrent minor illnesses

Successful Handling

The trauma of culture shock is most successfully dealt with if you:

Realize that operating in a new setting with strange sights, sounds, smells, and possibly a new language, is a different experience for each person in the family.

Communicate with each other; have patience and understanding; be sensitive to each others' feelings and difficulties.

Exercise! Lack of proper rest, diet, and exercise aggravate culture shock stress symptoms. Establish a daily exercise schedule quickly.

Use the support system of experienced associates at first. Begin to participate in the life of the new country to whatever extent possible. There are many possibilities for family or individual activities within the American and international communities and in the new country. Sightsee, join a tennis club, enroll at the university, join a church, go to a concert, volunteer with the Red Cross, join Rotary.

We never build up an absolute immunity to culture shock. Yet that same sensitivity to change also means that we have the capacity to be enriched by the new experience travel brings us. Remember, each positive effort at stepping into the local culture usually opens yet another door of opportunity and diminishes the effects of culture shock.

If severe culture shock symptoms persist past six months, seek professional help.

Helping Children Adjust

Before the Move

Set the stage with children before the transfer process begins. Discuss the contents of this chapter with them and share what you have learned about the new country. Keep discussions informal. Bring up selected subjects during routine activities-dinner or a weekend hike. Be careful not to be apologetic about any restrictions that living overseas may place on them.

Talk to them about:

- Cultural restrictions: Teens need to understand any dress or behavior restrictions ahead of time. Help children accept the local mores rather than resent them. Make your guidelines clear.

- Health precautions: It may be the first time children have not been able to drink tap water or eat the local fruits, vegetables, and meats. They may require shots or pills to prevent the onset of local diseases.

- Stress factors: Discuss with them the stress placed on a family by such a move and how they can relieve it. Many children instinctively reduce stress through play with others or a pet or by spending hours on the phone with friends. Still, they may express anger at relocation and anxiety about what the future holds. Flashbacks and nightmares are not uncommon in these situations.

Relocation Crisis

Children are creatures of habit. Settling them into a daily routine helps them adjust more successfully to any situation-whether it's a normal move, an evacuation, a separation, or a catastrophic disaster that has affected the whole community.

Give them information on the crisis appropriate to their age level. Listen to them. Talk to them. Let them express their anxieties. Acknowledge their feelings.

Encourage them to be physically active. Little ones can play games, teenagers can help with community needs related to the crisis, such as organizing activities for younger children or cleaning up earthquake damage. Vigorous exercise and sports are good for everyone during periods of high stress.

Make opportunities for them to be with peers. The older the child the more important this is, but most need to interact with children their own age. Insist they attend school, as this is the center of life with peers.

Let them feel that they have complete parental support. In times of crisis, children regress to earlier developmental stages. Young children can become almost infantile, forget toilet training, cling to parents. School-age children may refuse to go to school, be disruptive. Even teens, who have begun to break away from parents, may need reassurance that they are still securely within the family circle.

Stress During Crisis

A crisis is best handled collectively. Parents, teachers, family, and friends can play a part in helping any child handle a crisis. Adults should support each other in guiding children through the crisis; there is no need to feel you're in this alone. Play groups or support groups may be formed.

Parents and teachers are models. If they handle a crisis calmly, children will be less anxious.

Children "borrow" strengths from adults around them. Help them put labels on their reactions; encourage them to verbalize feelings. Play is a natural form of communication for children; it will discharge bottled-up feelings. If allowed to work through their fears, most children will emerge strengthened from a crisis.

Children need to see you express your feelings of fear and grief, too. By example, parents and other adults can show children how these feelings are handled. It's important that they see not only the expression of grief and sadness, but that they understand that the feeling will pass.

Some parents attempt to protect children by not allowing discussion about a crisis. The healthy route is to let them discuss it until they can get some psychological distance from it. Verbal repetition is a natural cathartic process.

Give them information-real details in language appropriate to their ages. Children are more painfully aware of what's going on than adults realize. And, if it's not discussed, what they do know, or think they know, can become unpleasantly distorted in their minds.

If a child requires medical attention, someone from the immediate family should stay with him or her. See that the procedures that are to be done are explained to the child.

Security for Children

Rules for Children

Children must be taught:

    To keep a parent in sight in public places and to go to a store clerk if lost and in need of help.
    Not to go anywhere with anyone without a parent's permission.

...... A password known only to family and close friends.
Not to accept packages or letters from people you don't now.
To know at least key phrases in the local language.
To let someone know their location and plans.

Rules for Parents

Parents need to:

    Teach your child never to get into a car or go into a house without your permission. Don't leave your child alone in a public place, even for a moment.

    Teach your child your home address and telephone number. Children should know how to use public phones. Keep a list of emergency numbers by your phone and make children aware of them.

    Train children not to give personal information over the phone, even though the caller purports to be a friend. "Personal information" includes whether family members are away, travel plans, where parents work, or recreation and school routines.

    Explain the importance of never divulging any information in front of strangers.

    Caution children to always keep doors locked, and never to unlock a door to a stranger without adult approval.

    Listen when your child tells you he or she does not want to be with someone; there may be a reason. Have the child present when you interview a servant who will be caring for him or her; observe their reactions.

Child-Watch Checklist

Post an information list by each phone. Your sitter should be familiar with every item.

    Family name
    Address
    Phone number
    Fire
    Police
    Medical
    Poison
    Neighbor's name

Neighbor's address
Neighbor's phone
Nearest fire call box
Miscellaneous information of importance

Checklist for Babysitters

Ensure all doors and windows are locked and that doors are not opened to anyone.

Do not give out any information over the telephone. Simply state that Mr./Mrs. X cannot come to the phone right now. Take a message.

Never leave the children alone, even for a minute.

Know the dangers to children of matches, gasoline, stoves, deep water, poisons, falls.

Know the locations of all exits (stairs, doors, windows, fire escapes) and phones in case of emergency.

List the names and ages of children.

Evacuation

Many evacuations have taken place in past years for reasons of political instability, acts of terrorism, and natural disasters. In a number of cases, people have gone back to their new home after a short time; in others they have not returned at all. Notification times can range from a couple of hours to several weeks.

No two evacuations are the same. But there are common threads that run through all; knowing them can make an evacuation easier. What we have learned, both as a government and from individuals who have been evacuated, is distilled here for you.

Preparation

Be prepared. Assume an evacuation could occur at any point and have everything in place to execute it. It is better to be ready and not need it, than to need it and be unprepared.

Determine the "who and where" with your family. Who should be contacted and where your family would go in case of an extended evacuation. This is especially important for single parents; employees could be required to stay in the new country while children must leave. Parents should make arrangements for emergency child care

before leaving the United States.

Establish a line of credit to cover emergencies. Obtain individual credit cards for you and your spouse. Open two checking accounts; use one as an active account, and keep the other in reserve. If possible, arrange for your paycheck to be deposited in a U.S. bank. Keep only a small account in a local bank for currency exchange or local purchases.

Know the emergency evacuation plan of the school. If there is none, be an active parent organizer and ensure that one is instituted. Join or start a safety network of parents.

Keep a small bag packed with essentials-clothing changes, snack food (dry, nonperishable), bottled water, medications. Small means small; anything over 10 pounds is not small.

In your residence, group important papers together along with checkbooks, U.S. credit cards, some traveler's checks, a small amount of cash, and U.S. driver's licenses. Maintain a basic emergency supply of food, water, gasoline, and first-aid supplies.

Meet your neighbors. Learn the location of the nearest hospital, police station, and friendly embassy or consulate.

Remember pets; have inoculations current and arrange for a suitable home in case they must be left behind.

If Evacuated

In the event an evacuation order is given, it is crucial for parents to discuss with children what is going to happen. Even if there is very little time before a departure, talk with them about the parent who will be staying. Reassure them; explain what will take place in the evacuation. They also need to know that the same rules and routines that structured their lives during normal times will continue.

Establish a daily routine with the children as soon as possible after evacuation and relocation. Be sure to incorporate family rituals-bedtime stories, family meals, church, pancakes on Saturday morning, whatever! Accentuate any advantages of the alternate location museums, amusement park, proximity to grandma and grandpa.

Minimize separation from the remaining parent as much as possible. Try not to use day care for a while. The child's fear of abandonment will be intense for a time.

Residential Fire Safety
Although fire does not sound as dramatic as terrorism, in fact it kills far more people each year than does terrorist activity overseas. In many countries fire regulations do not exist, fire fighting equipment is antiquated, water sources are inadequate, and buildings are constructed with minimum standards.

Each year thousands of people die in home fires, half of them killed in their sleep by the toxic gases and smoke. Many who do survive spend months in hospitals and suffer lifelong physical and emotional scars. Children are often killed because they panic and try to hide from fire under beds and in closets.

Most of this devastation can be prevented. In only a few years, the use of smoke detectors in the United States has cut in half the number of annual fire fatalities. Fire prevention education is gradually making the odds even better.

Take these basic steps to protect your family from fire, whether you are in the United States or overseas:
> Use smoke detectors in your home.
> Prepare a fire escape plan with your family.
> Conduct a fire drill at least once every six months.

Smoke Detectors
If fire occurs in your home, you may never awaken; smoke and toxic gases kill quietly and quickly. Yet you can be saved by the same smoke that can kill you-if it activates a smoke detector.

A smoke detector sounds a warning before you can even smell the smoke or see any flames. Smoke detectors should be installed, on each floor of the residence. If you have only one, place it on the ceiling outside the sleeping area.

Smoke detectors must be tested once a month and whenever you return from vacation. Never paint them. Once a year they should be vacuumed to remove any dust or cobwebs inside that would interfere with their functioning. Be sure everyone in the family recognizes the sound of the alert; test it with all members in the bedrooms with doors closed to be sure that they can hear it.

Fire Escape Plan
Since fire and smoke travel quickly, you have, at most, only minutes to escape. It is imperative that each member of the family knows what to do, automatically.

A fire escape plan is your best bet. With your family, draw a floor plan of your house marking all possible exits. Since fire could block any exit, always have an alternative way to escape. Know in advance where to go. Double check exits to be sure they open and that children can handle doors or windows by themselves.

Show all windows, doors, and outdoor features. Note escape aids such as a tree or balcony; check to ensure that they would work. Locate the nearest fire alarm box or the neighbor's house. Teach your children how to report a fire.

Designate a meeting place outside the house. You must know immediately who may be trapped inside.

Tape a copy of the floor plan by the telephone. Advise household employees and babysitters

Fire Drills
Practice your plan! Regular fire drills assure that everyone knows what to do. Change the imaginary situation from drill to drill. Decide where the "fire" is and what exits are blocked. When small children learn what to do by rote, they will be less likely to panic in real life situations.

Pets cannot be considered. The dangers of a fire are overwhelming, and the primary consideration is saving human lives. Often pets will escape before you do, anyway.

Fire Extinguishers
Every home should have at least one fire extinguisher and one smoke detector. Be sure that the extinguisher works and that you know how to operate it.

Portable fire extinguishers can be effective on a small, confined fire, such as a cooking fire. But if a fire is large and spreading, using an extinguisher may be unsafe; you risk the dangers of inhaling toxic smoke and having your escape route cut off.

Use a fire extinguisher only after you:

25

Are sure everyone else is out of the building.
Have called the fire department.
Are certain you can approach the fire safely.

Use of Window Escapes

Before using a window escape, be sure that the door to the room is closed; otherwise, a draft from the open window could draw smoke and fire into the room.

Use an escape ladder or balcony if possible. If there is none, don't jump, wait for rescue as long as you can. Open a window a few inches at the top and bottom while you wait; gases will go out through the top and fresher air will enter through the bottom.

Children must know that it is all right to break a window. Discuss how to do it, using a baseball bat or a chair. Stand aside to avoid flying glass shards. Place a rug or blanket over the sill before crawling out.

Lower small children from the window. Don't leave first and expect them to follow. If they panic and refuse to jump, you will be unable to get them.

A Summary of Fire Safety Reminders

After a smoke detector warns you of a fire, you have only a few moments to escape.

Even concrete buildings are not fireproof. Virtually all the contents of your home or office will burn very quickly and produce toxic gases that can overpower you.

Sleep with bedroom doors closed. A closed door can hamper the spread of a fire, and the chances of a fire starting in a bedroom are remote.

To escape, keep low and crawl on hands and knees. A safety zone of cleaner air exists nearer the floor.

Once out, no one should be permitted to re-enter a burning house for any reason. Hold on to children who may impulsively run back inside. Children panic in fire and tend to attempt hiding as a means of escape. Train them to react correctly. As you escape, try to close every door behind you. It may slow the fire's progress.

Feel every door before you open it. If it is hot, don't open it. If it is cool, brace yourself against the door and open it slowly, checking for fire. A fire that has died down due to lack of oxygen could flare up once the door is open. If that happens, close the door immediately. Never waste time getting dressed or grabbing valuables.

If clothes catch fire, drop to the ground and roll to extinguish flames, or smother the fire with a blanket or rug. Never run. Teach children to stop, drop, and roll.

The Final Word

Fires are preventable. The major causes of home fires are:

Carelessness with cigarettes. Never smoke in bed; poisonous gases from a smoldering mattress can kill long before there are flames. After a party, look under cushions for smoldering cigarettes.

Faulty electrical wiring. Many homes in lesser developed countries are wired insufficiently to handle the simultaneous use of many electrical appliances. Don't overload circuits. Limit appliances plugged into the same extension cord. Major appliances should have their own heavy-duty circuit. Know where the fuse box is and instruct older children and household employees on how to shut off power in case of an electrical fire. Household current and plugs/sockets in many countries are different than in the United States. Transformers may be required to adapt U.S. appliances to the local current. Be sure your appliance, transformer, and the local current are compatible before using.

Faulty lighting equipment. Check electrical cords for cracks, broken plugs, poor connections. Use correct size bulbs in lamps, and be sure shades are not too close to bulbs.

Carelessness with cooking and heating appliances. Don't leave food cooking unattended. Have heating system and fireplaces inspected professionally once a year.

Children playing with matches. Teach children fire safety; keep matches and combustibles out of their reach.

Community Participation in Security

Safety in Numbers

26

As you consider the issues of safety and security, remember you are not alone. Overseas, you have the support and guidance of your company, the U.S. Embassy, colleagues, and their families. The best security results from information and support flowing between these entities.

Remember, you also have a responsibility to them. Do your part to contribute to the safety and security of the community.

What You Can Do

Keep abreast of current events, not only in the country, but internationally. Know what's going on in the country and in the world that could affect that country. Watch TV news programs, read newspapers, attend embassy security briefings periodically. It is your responsibility to keep current.

Locate yourself in relation to emergency services and places of refuge. Assist newcomers to do the same.

Other Useful Steps

Assemble a list of telephone numbers.
Maintain a set of local maps.
Meet neighbors and friendly people in your neighborhood.
Locate fire department and police stations.
Pinpoint nearest hospitals and clinics.
Know how to reach friendly diplomatic missions.
Know how to get accurate information.
Don't repeat rumors.
Establish an I.D. system for children.
Establish and participate in a neighborhood warden plan and a buddy system.
Prepare and keep current a telephone notification system.
Identify an alternative notification system in the event telephone service is lost.
Be a good listener. Be sensitive to special needs in your community. Single parents and employed couples may need help arranging security for their children. People who are ill, pregnant, or have new babies may have limited mobility. Elderly, dependent parents are a growing concern. Those who are isolated may need help in getting information. You can refer those with needs to the appropriate person.
......

Resources (See Chapter 25)
Conclusion

Although this chapter contains many tips for successful travel and residence abroad, it is by no means all inclusive. Additional information is available from a variety of sources, ranging from travel brochures, magazines, and books, to conversations with persons who have lived or traveled to your assigned country.

You can never know too much about what you're getting into. Prior organization and preparation will significantly reduce your anxieties, lessen the shock of adjustment, and enable you to settle in with relative ease to a safe and enjoyable experience abroad

27

Chapter 3

Personal Security

[The information in this chapter is reprinted verbatim from a bulletin issued by the U.S. State Department, Bureau of Diplomatic Security. It is intended to serve as advice to Americans traveling abroad

Introduction

For Americans living overseas, the most serious obstacle to personal safety is an attitude of complacency or fatalism. "It can't happen to me" and "if it's going to happen, it's going to happen" is dangerous thinking. Recent political events throughout the world have changed-but not necessarily diminished the threats you face. Today, the most prevalent threat you face overseas is crime. A criminal attack against you or your family can take place at any post, as can a fire or other disaster. However, you can influence what happens to you by assuming more responsibility for your own security.

The information presented in this chapter is general. Not all the information applies to all posts. Ask for post-specific information from your Regional Security Officer (RSO) or Post Security Officer (PSO).

Residential Security

Residential security is a critical component of any personal security program. The following guidelines should be used in reviewing your residential security.

All entrances, including service doors and gates, should have quality locks- preferably deadbolt. Check your: Front Door, Rear Door, Garage Door(s), Service Door(s), Patio Door, Sliding Glass, Door Gate, Swimming Pool Gate, Guest House Door(s)

- Don't leave keys "hidden" outside the home. Leave an extra key with a trusted neighbor or colleague.
- Keep doors locked even when you or family members are at home.
- Have window locks installed on all windows. Use them.
- Lock louvered windows-especially on the ground floor.
- Have locks installed on your fuse boxes and external power sources.
- If you have window grilles and bars, review fire safety. Don't block bedroom windows with permanent grilles if the windows may be used for emergency exits.
- If you have burglar or intrusion alarms, check and use them.
- Keep at least one fire extinguisher on each floor, and be sure to keep one in the kitchen. Show family members and household help how to use them.

Periodically check smoke detectors and replace batteries when necessary.

- Keep flashlights in several areas in the house. Check the batteries often, especially if you have children in your home. (They love to play with flashlights!)
- A family dog can be a deterrent to criminals. But remember, even the best watchdog can be controlled by food or poison. Do not install separate "doggy doors" or entrances. They also can admit small intruders.
- Choose a location that offers the most security. The less remote, the safer your home will be, particularly in a neighborhood close to police and fire protection.
- Know your neighbors. Develop a rapport with them and offer to keep an eye on each other's homes, especially during trips.
- If you observe any unusual activity, report it immediately to your RSO.
- Establish safe family living patterns. If you understand the importance of your contribution to the family's overall security, the entire household will be safer.
- While at home, you and your family should rehearse safety drills and be aware of procedures to escape danger and get help.
- Educate family members and domestic help in the proper way to answer the
- Vary daily routines; avoid predictable

- Know where all family members are at all
- Use these same guidelines while on leave telephone at home. patterns. times. or in travel status.

Establishing a Safehaven
Follow three basic steps in setting up a safehaven in your home:
- Designate an internal room;
- Install a two-way communications system or telephone; and
- Furnish the safehaven with an emergency kit.

It is highly unlikely you would spend more than a few hours in a safehaven; however, the supplies listed below are suggested for your maximum safety. Your security officer can tell you more about how to select and secure your safehaven.

The following is a checklist of possible safehaven supplies.
Fire extinguisher
Fresh water
5-day supply of food
Candles, matches, flashlight
Extra batteries
Bedding
Toilet facilities
Sterno stove, fuel
Shortwave or other radio
Medical/first aid kit
Other items for your comfort and leisure-a change of clothing, books, games

Home Security While You Are Away
- Notify your RSO or PSO of your departure and return dates but don't otherwise publicize your travel or vacation plans. Leave contact numbers with appropriate mission personnel.
- Arrange to have a friend or colleague pick up your newspapers, mail, or other deliveries daily.
- Secure your home. Close and lock all windows and doors. Don't forget to lock garage or gate doors.
- Consider purchasing timers to turn on outside and inside lights automatically at various times throughout the night.
- Check outside lighting and replace older light bulbs. You don't want a light burning out while you are away.
- Ask a friend or colleague to check your residence periodically, ensuring your furnace or air conditioning is functioning and that timers and lights are working.
- The decision to set the automated alarm system may vary from region to region.

Power outages and brownouts may trip alarm systems. Check with your security officer for advice on setting alarm systems when you are away for long periods of time.
- Unplug all unnecessary appliances such as televisions, stereos, and personal computers.
- Mow your lawn just before leaving; make arrangements to have someone mow it again if you will be gone for an extended period of time. Also arrange for watering, if that is likely to be needed.
- In the winter, make arrangements to have someone shovel walkways if it snows. At a minimum, have a neighbor walk from the street to your door several times.
- If possible, ask a neighbor to park a car in your driveway (if you are taking yours).
- If you use a telephone answering machine, turn off the ringer on the telephone. If you don't have an answering machine, unplug or turn off ringers on all telephones.
- Lock all jewelry, important papers, currency, and other valuable portables in a safe place such as a safe deposit box or home safe.
- Ensure all personal and home insurance policies are up-to-date and that your coverage is adequate.

Personal Security while Traveling.

- Notify your RSO or PSO of your departure and return dates, but don't otherwise publicize your travel or vacation plans.
- Leave contact numbers with appropriate mission personnel.
  Check plane, train, and bus times before you travel.
- Sit near other people or near aisles or doors. Learn the location of emergency alarms and exits.
- Stay awake and alert when using public transportation.
- Consider purchasing special clothing or accessories to hide your passport, money, or credit cards. Keep the majority of your funds in travelers checks and hidden; carry some in your wallet or handbag. Use a money clip. If you are robbed, you may lose the money in the clip but will retain important credit cards and documents.
- Keep valuables out of sight and luggage close at hand. If carrying a handbag, keep it in front of you, closed, with the fastening toward your body. Keep a wallet in your front pants pocket. . Let go if your bag is snatched.
- Do some research on the area you are visiting
- Talk to your security officer or consular colleagues regarding travel advisories or warnings.

- When traveling, dress casually; dress down where appropriate. Be aware of local customs.
- Don't wear excess jewelry. Reduce wallet and purse contents, particularly cards denoting affiliations, memberships, accounts, etc.
- At airports, proceed through security checks and go to the boarding area as quickly as possible. These areas are usually the most secure in the airport.
- In any crowded situation, be aware of any crowding or jostling, even if it appears innocent. This is often a ploy by pickpockets to distract you.
- Be very careful any time you use a telephone calling card. Fraudulent uses of these cards are on the rise. Look for people observing your card or your fingers as you dial your code. Avoid being heard giving the number to local telephone operators.

Personal Security in Hotels
- Do not discuss your business or travel plans in public areas where they may be overheard. Discuss your travel plans and movements during your stay with as few people as possible.
- Selecting a hotel room on the third to fifth floor generally will keep you out of reach of criminal activity from the street but still within reach of most fire truck ladders.
- Do not entertain strangers in your hotel room.
- Be alert to overly friendly locals who may have criminal intentions. They may offer to take you to a "special" restaurant. Their ruse may be to offer drugged refreshments.
- Never leave valuables in your hotel room exposed or unattended, even in a locked suitcase.
- Place valuables-money, jewelry, airplane tickets, credit cards, passport-in a hotel safe deposit box or room safe.
- Familiarize yourself with escape routes in case of fire or other catastrophe.
- Use the door chain or bolt lock whenever you are in your room.
- Use the door viewer (peephole) before opening the door to visitors.
- Do not discuss your room number while standing in the lobby or leave your room key on restaurant or bar tables. . Keep your room neat so you will notice disturbed or missing items quickly.

Fire Safety at Home
Statistics about fire are frightening. In America, about 30,000 people are injured and nearly 4,800 die from fire each year. This rate is lower than in most other countries. Differences in fire codes, building and electrical standards, and even fire

fighting capabilities can increase your threat from fire if you live overseas. Three vital facts you should know about fire:

- It isn't usually fire that kills, it is the products of combustion-smoke, toxic gases, or superheated air.
- Fire travels at lightning speed-up to 19 feet per second. . The critical hours for a house fire are 11 PM to 6 AM when most people are asleep. This means you need to detect fire early, and you must move quickly when you do. You and your family can avoid becoming a statistic if you:
- Install smoke detectors in your home.
- Create and practice a fire escape plan.
- Take fire preventive measures such as those listed on the next page.

Smoke Detectors. A smoke detector can mean the difference between life and death. They are inexpensive and are battery operated; they are not at the mercy of sporadic electrical service. You should have one on every level of your home, particularly in the hallway outside bedrooms. Test your detectors regularly, and replace the batteries as needed-usually twice a year.

Exit Drills
You and your family should create a fire exit plan together. Learn how to escape the house from every room. Locate two exits from each bedroom. Designate a meeting place outside the house. Most importantly-especially if you have children- PRACTICE YOUR PLAN!

Preventive Measures
Carelessness with cigarettes is the most frequent cause of house fires. Never smoke in bed! Open flames and the resulting sparks are dangerous
- Don't place barbecue grills or other open flames on the balcony or near the house. Check for: faulty electrical wiring; overloaded circuits; faulty equipment, including cooking and heating appliances; leaking propane tanks; overloaded or frayed extension cords; dirty chimneys and vents; and flammable liquids.

- Keep a fire extinguisher in the house, preferably one on every level but particularly in the kitchen. Teach older children and household help how to use the extinguisher.

Security Do's for Children
- Teach children never to admit strangers into the home.

31

•Teach children local emergency phone numbers, the mission number, and how to use the two-way radio. Make sure younger children know their name, address, and phone number.

•Caution teenagers about "blind dates" or meeting anyone they do not know.

• Teach younger members of your family not to open mail or packages.

• Teach young children how to answer the telephone so that they do not give out personal information, such as home address, absence of adults, etc.

•Teach children how to say no to strangers.

• Teach children how to exit the house in case of emergency.

Letter and Parcel Bombs

Letter and parcel bombs generally are "victim activated" meaning that a victim or intended target must activate the device by opening it. They do not normally contain timing devices. Bombs can range from the size of a cigarette package to a large parcel. Letter and package bombs have been disguised as letters, books, candy, and figurines. Delivery methods have included mail systems, personal delivery, or placement at the recipient's site. A letter or parcel bomb might have some of the following indicators:

• Suspicious origin-especially if the postmark or name of sender is unusual, unknown, or no further address is given.

• Excessive or inadequate postage.

• Off-balance or lopsided letter or package.

• Unusual weight for the size of the letter or package. Letters also may be unusually thick.

• Stiffness or springiness of contents. (When checking, do not bend excessively.)

• Protruding wires or components; unusual grease or oil stains on the envelope.

•Strange smell, particularly almond or other suspicious odors.

•Handwriting of sender is not familiar or indicates a foreign style not normally received by recipient.

• Common words or names are misspelled.

• Rub on or block lettering.

•Restrictive markings such as "confidential" or "personal" or an honorific title appended to the name of the addressee.

• Small hole in the envelope or package wrapping that could be a provision for an arming/safety wire.

•Rattling inside the envelope or package- possibly loose components of a device.

•Visual distractions (i.e., currency, pornography). If you identify a letter or package as suspicious,

don't let anyone near it. Notify your RSO or PSO immediately, and leave the letter or package in an open area, such as a courtyard, where it is easily accessible to bomb squad personnel.

• Never submerge it in water.

Carjacking

• When in your car, always keep the doors locked. Any time you drive through areas containing stoplights, stop signs, or anything that significantly reduces vehicular speed, keep your windows up.

• Leave ample maneuvering space between your vehicle and the one in front of you. If you are approached by suspicious persons while you are stopped, do not roll down windows; drive away quickly.

• If you are being followed or harassed by another driver, try to find the nearest police station, hotel, or other public facility. Once you find a place of safety, don't worry about using a legal parking space. Park as close as you can, and get inside fast.

• If another driver tries to force you to pull over or to cut you off, keep driving and try to get away. Try to note the license plate number of the car and a description of the car and driver. If this effort places you in danger, don't do it. The information is not as important as your safety.

• If you are being followed, never lead the person back to your home or stop and get out. Drive to the nearest police station, public facility, or U.S. mission. (You could verify surveillance by going completely around an arbitrarily chosen block.) Always report these incidents to the RSO or PSO.

• If you are traveling alone and a car "bumps" into you, don't stop to exchange accident information. Go to the nearest service station or other public place to call the police. (Check with your RSO or PSO to see if this advice is appropriate for your post.)

•Never, ever pick up hitchhikers!

• When you park, look for a spot that offers good lighting and is close to a location where there are a lot of people. Lock valuables in the trunk, and lock all doors.

• Extra precautions are necessary when shopping. If you take packages out to lock them in your trunk, then plan to return to the stores to do more shopping, it may be a good idea to move your car to another section of the parking lot or street. The criminal knows that you will be coming back and can wait to ambush you. By moving your car, you give the impression you're leaving. If you think you are being followed, do not go back to your car. Return to the safety of the occupied shopping area or office building and contact the authorities.

• If you have car trouble on the road, raise your hood. If you have a radio antenna, place a handkerchief or other flag there. When people stop to help, don't get out of the car unless you know them or it's the police. Ask the "good samaritan" to stop at the nearest service station and report your problem.

• If you are in a parking lot or parked on the street and have trouble, be wary of personal assistance from strangers. Go to the nearest telephone and call a repair service or friend for assistance. If you feel threatened by the presence of nearby strangers, lock yourself in your car and blow the horn to attract attention of others. By using these basic safety tips and your own common sense, you can help protect yourself. You should:

Surveillance

The purpose of surveillance is to identify a potential target based on the security precautions that individual takes, and the most suitable time, location, and method of attack. Surveillance may last for days or weeks. Naturally, the surveillance of a person who has set routines and who takes few precautions will take less time. Detecting surveillance requires a fairly constant state of alertness and, therefore, must become a habit. A good sense of what is normal and what is unusual in your surroundings could be more important than any other type of security precaution you may take. Above all, do not hesitate to report any unusual event. There are three forms of surveillance: foot, vehicular, and stationary. People who have well-established routines permit surveillants to use methods that are much more difficult to detect.

If, for example, you leave the office at the same time each day and travel by the most direct route to your home or if you live in a remote area with few or no alternate routes to your home, surveillants have no need to follow you all the way to your residence.

• Vary your routes and times of travel.

• Be familiar with your route and have alternate routes.

•Check regularly for surveillance.

Stationary surveillance is most commonly used by terrorist organizations. Most attacks take place near the victim's residence, because that part of the route is least easily varied. People are generally most vulnerable in the morning when departing for work because these times are more predictable than evening arrivals. Many surveillance teams use vans with windows in the sides or back that permit observation from the interior of the van. Often the van will have the name of a business or utility company to provide some pretext for being in the area.

Where it is not possible to watch the residence unobserved, surveillants must come up with a plausible reason for being in the area. Women and children are often used to give an appearance of innocence. Try to check the street in front of your home from a window before you go out each day. If you suspect that you are being followed, drive to the nearest police station, fire station, or the U.S. mission. Note the license numbers, color and make of the vehicle, and any information printed on its sides that may be useful in tracing the vehicle or its occupants. Don't wait to verify surveillance before you report it. Be alert to people disguised as public utility crews, road workers, vendors, etc., who might station themselves near your home or office.

Whenever possible, leave your car in a secured parking area. Be especially alert in underground parking areas. Always check your vehicle inside and out before entering it. If you notice anything unusual, do not enter the vehicle. Household staff and family members should be reminded to look for suspicious activities around your residence; for example, surveillance, attempts to gain access to your residence by fraudulent means, and telephone calls or other inquiries requesting personal information. Tell your household staff and family members to note descriptions and license numbers of suspicious vehicles. Advise them to be alert for details. Household staff can be one of the most effective defensive mechanisms in your home- use them to your advantage. While there are no guarantees that these precautions, even if diligently adhered to, will protect you from terrorist violence, they can reduce your vulnerability and, therefore, your chances of becoming a victim.

Sexual Assault Prevention

• Be alert. Don't assume that you are always safe. Think about your safety everywhere. Your best protection is avoiding dangerous situations.

• Trust your instincts. If you feel uncomfortable in any situation, leave.

• Always walk, drive, and park your car in well-lit areas.

33

• Walk confidently at a steady pace on the side of the street facing traffic.

• Walk close to the curb. Avoid doorways, bushes, and alleys.

• Wear clothes and shoes that allow freedom of movement.

• Walk to your car with keys in your hand.

• If you have car trouble, raise the hood and stay inside your car. If a stranger wants to help, have him or her call for help. Don't leave your car.

• Keep your car doors locked and never pick up hitchhikers.

• Make sure all windows and doors in your home are locked, especially if you are home alone.

• Never give the impression that you are home alone if strangers telephone or come to the door.

• If a stranger asks to use your phone, have him wait outside while you make the call.

• If you come home and find a door or window open or signs of forced entry, don't go in. Go to the nearest phone and call Post 1 or the local law enforcement authorities.

Crisis Awareness and Preparedness

Crisis Awareness

Keeping Informed About A Crisis: When a crisis occurs abroad involving large numbers of U.S. citizens, such as a natural disaster, transportation accident, civil or political unrest or a terrorist incident, the Department of State and the U.S. Embassy abroad utilize a variety of means of communicating with the American public, including the Internet.

Monitoring the Consular Updates on the Internet: Monitor the Department of State, Bureau of Consular Affairs home page and the home page for the U.S. Embassy in the foreign country for up-to-date information about the crisis.

Communicating With Families of U.S. Citizens Involved in a Crisis: Families in the United States whose U.S. citizen relatives abroad are directly affected by the crisis can also communicate with the Department of State through our Office of American Citizens Services and Crisis Management at (202) 647-5225. If a 24-hour task force or working group is established in the Department of State Operations Center to manage the crisis, you will be directed to the Task Force at (202) 647-0900.

Letting Your Family Know You Are Okay: If a crisis occurs in a country you are visiting, contact your family in the United States to reassure them regarding your safety.

If You Are in a Foreign Country Involved in a Crisis:

• Contact the U.S. Embassy or Consulate if you need help.

• Be sure to register with the U.S. Embassy or Consulate by phone, fax or in person.

• Monitor the U.S. Embassy and State Department home pages.

• Monitor Voice of America and BBC broadcasts for announcements.

Crisis Preparedness

The following information may be helpful to you in preparing for a crisis abroad. While some of the material was designed by other U.S. Government agencies for a crisis occuring in the United States, the guidance about preparedness may be useful to Americans making plans for similar emergencies abroad. Visit the Department of State web site for information on preparedness.

Chapter 4

Security Guidelines For American Families Living Abroad

[The information in this chapter is adapted from a bulletin issued by The Overseas Security Advisory Council (OSAC). It is intended to serve as advice to Americans living abroad]

The guidelines outlined in this chapter are designed to facilitate personal security and protection of property. They will help protect American families living and working abroad from the threat of terrorism.

They focus on self-help techniques, as well as on assistance available through the U.S. Government. They can help save the lives of you and your loved ones.

Like personal safety, personal security cannot be totally delegated to others. Reading this chapter closely, implementing its recommendations in full will go a long way in achieving personal security and protection of property.

Effective security precautions require a continuous and conscious awareness of your environment. This is especially true when living in a foreign country where it will be necessary to adapt to new cultures, customs, and laws which, in most instances, are very different than those to which Americans are accustomed in the United States.

Security precautions not only lessen your vulnerability to criminal and terrorist acts, but greatly facilitate the assistance the U. S. Government can render, where possible, to all Americans and their families living abroad.

The Council recognizes that many American organizations, especially the larger ones, employ numerous foreign nationals at locations abroad. It would be presumptuous of the Council to suggest security guidelines from an American perspective to these foreign nationals in their native land. For this reason, these security guidelines are primarily for American citizens living abroad.

Section I. Introduction

This chapter is a compilation of diverse security measures for consideration by American private sector employees and their families living and working outside the United States. Obviously, the implementation of security precautions described herein should be consistent with the level of risk currently existing in the foreign country of residence.

Diverse political climates, local laws and customs, and a wide range of other variables make it impossible to apply standard security precautions worldwide.

Levels of risk can change very rapidly, sometimes overnight, triggered by internal or external incidents or circumstances. It is advisable, therefore, to monitor continually the political climate and other factors which may impact the level of risk. Remember that establishing a family residence abroad requires much more security planning than a short-term visit to a foreign country for business or pleasure.

It is essential that security precautions be kept under constant review so that they may be adapted to respond effectively to any changes in the level of risk. An inflexible security posture would be indicative of a disregard for the climate of risk and will almost certainly result in a lack of preparedness.

Section II. Preliminary Residential Security Planning

Need for Planning

Begin to develop a tentative Residential Security Plan for yourself and all members of your family before leaving the U.S. This is essential in providing you the guidelines for selecting your future home and determining where your children will go to school, the type of car you will buy, the kind of clothing you will wear (and not wear) and the information required to live securely in your forthcoming overseas location.

Your Residential Security Plan should progress from a tentative to an active plan. The latter, however, is not to be considered final because you should keep it under continuing review and update it regularly as circumstances dictate.

Primary Concept — Low Profile

A single concept, more than any other, should permeate all planning activities, namely keep a low profile. In other words, do not draw attention to yourself as an American by driving a big American car, having American publications delivered to residential mail box or doorsteps, or having displays at your residence which will identify you as an American. Common sense and a knowledge of local cultures and mores must guide you to what extent you should blend into local environs. Appearing to "go native" may subject you to ridicule and be counter-productive in keeping a low profile.

Keeping a low profile also entails staying away from civil disturbances, protesters and mobs, and not visiting or, if possible, traversing high-risk areas.

Information Required, and Where to Get It

· To keep a low profile and to know what pitfalls must be avoided, you need to inform yourself about your new location if you are to live safely there. Much professional help is available for the family moving overseas. Major multinational corporations have large international departments and corporate security departments which may serve as valuable resources for Residential Security Planning. Libraries have an abundance of current reference materials on working and living abroad.

Obtain a current issue of U.S. Department of State Publication #7877 entitled: Key Officers of Foreign Service Posts   A   Guide   for Business Representatives

This small, paperback volume can be obtained for $3.75 a copy from the Superintendent of Documents, U.S. Government Printing Office, Washington, D.C. 20402 (Telephone: 202-783-3238). This publication lists all key U.S. State Department Officials, including the Regional Security Officer (RSO), mailing addresses, phone numbers and telex numbers for all U.S. Embassies and Consulates.

Obtain a current political profile of the country to which you will be moving to aid you in assessing the level of risk. Corporate Security Directors of large multinational companies can identify a number of commercial organizations which publish political profiles of most countries as well as periodic updates.

You and your family should study the culture and customs of the country. Use library sources and reference works. Two excellent publications relating to the prospective country of residence are available for sale by the Superintendent of Documents, U.S. Government Printing Office, Washington, D.C. 20402.

1. *Background Notes*, published by the U.S. Department of State, Bureau of Public Affairs (Publication Number 7757 - One for each country).

2. **Foreign Area Studies**, The American University has published a detailed volume on each of 108 foreign countries for the Department of the Army. Request the volume by country name in the Country Studies/Area Handbook Program.

Schools

If you have school-age children, information about schooling will no doubt also be of major concern to you. Therefore, in addition to "in-house" guidance from your organization and from those who have been or are assigned to the country to which you are going, you may obtain information and advice from the Office of Overseas Schools (A/OS), Department of State about schooling abroad.

A/OS has six Regional Education Officers, each assigned to a specific geographic area, and it publishes a one-page "Fact Sheet" on each overseas American-sponsored school it assists —

during the 1992-93 school year it assisted 183 schools in 113 countries. The schools assisted are independent, non-profit, non-denomination schools established on a cooperative basis by U.S. citizens residing in foreign communities.

These are considered essentially American schools.

A/OS also publishes detailed "Summary School Information Forms" (SSI) on over 700 overseas schools — preschools, elementary and high schools, and boarding schools — including information on course offerings, special programs, programs for children with special needs, extracurricular activities, graduation requirements, etc. A/OS can be reached by phoning: (703) 875-7800; by faxing: (703) 875-7979. The mailing address is: Office of Overseas Schools, Room 245, SA-29, Department of State, Washington, D.C. 20522-2902. O/AS office hours are 8:15 am to 5:00 pm, Monday through Friday.

Section III. Assessing the Level of Risk at Overseas Location

Two factors must be taken into consideration when evaluating the seriousness of the personal risk to you and your family when contemplating a move abroad:

A risk assessment of the location to which you will be moving.

The profile of the company for which you work. Highly visible defense contractors may not be welcome in some parts of the world.

The threat assessment designators below were formulated by the Department of State Threat Analysis Division in the Diplomatic Security Service. The assessments are reevaluated by the Department of State quarterly with new levels being assigned when and where appropriate.

This assessment information is available to the business community through the Regional Security Officer (RSO) at the U.S. Embassy. The level assigned to a particular country is the result of the political/terrorist/criminal environment in that country.

High - The threat is serious and forced entries and assaults on residents are common or an active terrorist threat exists.

Medium - The threat is moderate with forced entries and some assaults on residents occurring, or the area has potential for terrorist activity.

Low - The threat is minimal and forced entry of residences and assault of occupants is not common. There is no known terrorist threat.

Section IV. Location of the Residence

Finding a Safe Neighborhood

The first step in the residence selection process should be choosing a safe neighborhood. The local police, the RSO or Post Security Officer (PSO) at the nearest U.S. diplomatic post, i.e. Embassy or Consulate, other American residents, and other sources, will facilitate this process.

Street Conditions

During the neighborhood selection process, particular attention should be paid to the condition of the streets, e.g., paved or unpaved, maintenance condition, wide or narrow, one-way or two-way traffic (two-way is preferred). Parked and/or double-parked vehicles could impede access to, or egress from, the residence. Density of pedestrian traffic could create security hazards. Dense vehicular and/or pedestrian traffic facilitates retention of anonymity of criminals and surveillants.

Note the overall security precautions that are taken in the neighborhood, such as barred windows, security fences, extensive lighting, large dogs, and security guards. Such visible precautions may indicate a high level of security awareness or a high crime area. Ensure you properly interpret reasons for same by checking the crime levels with RSO or local police.

Susceptibility to Clandestine Approach

You should examine the quality of lighting at night time to determine whether it is sufficient to illuminate the entrance to homes in the area. At the very least it should suffice to deter someone from lurking undetected in adjacent areas. Also, you should assure that there are no trees or shrubbery on the grounds which provide cover for a clandestine approach and concealment, or that you may remove them if you move in.

Access Routes

Statistics of kidnappings and assassinations have shown that the vast majority occur close to the residence when the victim is leaving or returning home. Therefore, it is essential that access routes to and from the residence provide sufficient alternatives which do not lock you into predictable patterns. Specifically, it is essential that dead-end streets or narrow one-way streets be avoided. If possible, your residence also should afford more than one point of entrance/exit.

Parking

Underground parking, unless tightly controlled, should be avoided particularly in high threat areas and in multi-story buildings. Ideally, a garage that can be locked is the most suitable means of securing vehicles at single family dwellings. Carports and driveways within fenced or guarded areas will also normally suffice. Parking the car on the street should be avoided.

Nearby Friends

You may want to consider residences located near friends or co-workers. This could enable you to car pool, especially during periods of high stress and to have them share with you any observations of suspicious activities in the neighborhood.

Section V. Selection of Residence

Apartment vs Single Dwelling

Given a choice between apartment or single dwelling living, an apartment offers greater protection against criminal intrusion. An apartment, especially one above the second floor, presents a more difficult target, provides the tenant some degree of anonymity, provides the benefit of close neighbors, and is almost always easier and less expensive to modify with security hardware. In the event of an emergency and loss of communications, neighbors can often be relied upon to come to another tenant's assistance. At

the very least, they can notify the authorities.

Apartment Pros and Cons

Apartments on the first or second floors should be avoided because of their immediate and easy accessibility from the street level or from trees, tops of large vehicles, or porch roofs. Foreign objects can easily be introduced to first and second floor apartments from the outside area accessible to the public.

Although an apartment above the second or third floor is preferred, do not select apartments on floors above the fire fighting and rescue capabilities of the local fire department. Even the most sophisticated fire and rescue equipment has limitations. In most countries it would be well not to live above the seventh floor.

It is important that access to the lobby of the apartment building be tightly controlled by a doorman or an electronic system such as card key readers or CCTV.

Surveillance of a particular target is sometimes more difficult in an apartment building because of multiple tenants.

Single Dwelling Pros and Cons

The private or single dwelling allows the occupant greater opportunity to establish more rigid access control to the property. However, since single dwelling residences are seldom designed or built with security as a major consideration, it is usually more difficult to achieve good security.

Safe Haven Suitability

In certain areas where an active terrorist threat exists or there is a serious crime threat with forced entries and assaults on residents being common, it may be prudent to consider the need for a safe haven in any residence that may be selected, i.e. a place in a residence which can serve as an area where occupants may take refuge for short periods of time until help arrives.

If it is determined that there is a need for a safe haven, this factor should be included in the selection of a residence. Then the type, layout and construction of a residence should be assessed to decide whether it lends itself to constructing such an area.

A basic requirement for a safe haven is that it be furnished with a substantial door equipped with a door viewer or with a grill gate. The door or gate should be equipped with a strong deadbolt lock. (NOTE: A "substantial" door is made of material which is strong enough to prevent someone from breaking through by kicking, throwing body weight against it, or striking it with a heavy item such as a rock or hammer. A door below this standard may suffice if it is used with a good quality grill gate.)

The safe haven area also should be equipped with reliable communications and accessible windows/openings should be secured against forced entry. Furthermore, a desirable feature would be to have the area afford a secondary means of escape. This could be an opening from which to reach the ground safely (not from a high upper floor) or to reach an unobservable intermediate location in the building such as a rear stairwell. (Secondary escape routes from areas with grilled windows/openings would, of course, have to be in accordance with fire and safety regulations.)

Even if all elements of a safe haven can not be achieved, a strong secure area in which to take refuge for a brief period may still be attainable. Of course, in an apartment without accessible openings/windows or balconies, the "safe haven" may be the whole residence, starting with the entrance door.

Long-Term Lease Availability

A factor to consider in the selection of a residence is the availability of a long-term lease. Obtaining such a lease may be particularly desirable if sizeable expenditures are required on security hardware and security-related modifications, as well as on other residence-related expenditures.

Section VI. After Moving In

Passport Registration

Take your passport to the U.S. Embassy or Consulate and register as soon as possible following arrival in a foreign country.

All countries abroad where Americans are permitted to conduct business have a U.S. Embassy or American Interests Sector of a friendly embassy in the capital city of that country. In other major population centers there is often times a U.S. Consulate.

Registration greatly facilitates emergency evacuation from the country of residence, if it becomes necessary.

Neighborhood Familiarization

When you have finally moved into your new residence, make an immediate effort to familiarize yourself with your new surroundings. Walk around the neighborhood and drive around the area to get a good idea of where you are located. Note the layout of the streets. Make a mental note of one way streets. Drive around at night. Streets and buildings look much different in the dark with artificial light.

Get acquainted with at least one neighbor as quickly as possible. You may need a neighbor in an emergency or for a temporary "safe haven" in the event of a burglary or other type of incident.

Learn the location of the nearest hospital and police station. Drive the route to the hospital in daylight and at night. Go directly to the Emergency Room entrance so no time is lost if you really have to use the facility. Check on traffic conditions during rush hours and at other times. Determine how long it will take you to reach the Emergency Room at various times during day and at night.

U.S. Government Advice on Security Concerns

American Embassies and Consulates will upon request, advise any American citizen or business representative on possible terrorist threats in foreign countries. The Regional Security Officer (RSO) or Post Security Officer (PSO) is the point of contact in embassies or consulates who can provide advice and guidance relative to your security concerns. However, it must be noted that the RSO/PSO must limit his assistance to the private sector to security services of an advisory nature. The RSO or other designated officer at a diplomatic or consular post can provide the following information:

The nature, if any, of the general terrorist threat in a particular country.

Whether private American citizens or companies have been the target of terrorist threats or attacks in the recent past.

Specific areas in cities or countryside that are considered dangerous for foreigners.

Recommended host government contacts, including police officials; local employment requirements for private security services.

Methods and agencies available for security and background checks on local employees.

Local laws and regulations concerning ownership, possession, and registration of weapons.

Local government laws, regulations, and policies on paying ransom or making concessions to terrorists.

U. S. Government Assistance to Terrorist Victims

In the case of a terrorist action against an American citizen or company, the Embassy or Consulate can:

• Facilitate communication with the home office and the family of the victim if normal channels are not adequate.

• Help establish useful liaison with local authorities.

• Provide information and suggest possible alternatives open to the family or company of the victim. The U.S. Government, however, cannot decide whether or not to accede to terrorist demands. Such a decision can be made only by the family or company of the victim, but it should be in consonance with local law. The official U.S. Government policy, as publicly stated, is not to make any concessions to terrorist demands and, while such policy is not necessarily binding on the private sector, the private sector is well advised to

review its proposed action in time of crisis with the Embassy or Consulate.

(In regard to the comment in the foregoing paragraph that your decision should be in consonance with local law, keep in mind that, unlike some U.S. Government employees who enjoy diplomatic immunity while living and working in the host country, U.S. private sector employees and their families are subject to all laws of the host country. It is well to remember that the constitutional safeguards enjoyed by all Americans in the U.S. do not apply to the actions of foreign governments.)

Emergency Preparations

Once an emergency strikes it is too late to obtain needed equipment or to make necessary preparations, including the following:

Obtain emergency fire and safety equipment as soon as possible, including but not limited to fire extinguishers, first-aid kits, blankets, matches and candles, flashlights and battery operated radios with spare batteries. Consider storing a seven day supply of canned food, juices, water and staples for all members of the family. Supplies should be stored for emergency use and inspected on a regular basis.

Family members and domestic employees should be trained and tested on the use of each item of emergency equipment.

Know beforehand where you will turn for help. Familiarize yourself with the identities of nearby neighbors, their servants, and their vehicles. This will facilitate the identification of a stranger or an unauthorized individual in the area.

Investigate the possibility of participating in an alert-calling list in event of emergencies. If such a list does not exist, create one.

Be cognizant of host country fire regulations and telephone numbers. Determine if the emergency number has someone on the other end who can understand you if you do not speak the local language. Arrange alternate emergency numbers which can forward your call in the local language if necessary.

40

It is highly recommended that an "Employee and Family Profile" form be filled out for each family and updated at least once a year. Keep one copy at home and one at the office with supervisor or person responsible for security. Include current photos of each family member. (see Part I).

Section VII. Perimeter Security

General Parameters

Generally, there are two lines of defense for a residence, the outer and the inner perimeter. The outer ordinarily is a property line in the case of a single residence, or the outer lobby door in an apartment or high-rise condominium. A third, or remote outer perimeter, may exist if your home or apartment is situated in a private compound or club environment.

Outer Perimeter

Any perimeter barrier, even if it is only a symbolic hedge, serves as a deterrent. An intruder must commit an overt act in crossing the barrier and run the risk of being seen. Therefore, it is recommended that, where possible, a single family dwelling overseas have a perimeter barrier.

The type of barrier employed should be carefully considered as each has its advantages and disadvantages. Different type barriers include:

Hedges and Natural Growth Material

This type of barrier is useful in marking the property line. However, unless they are thick and covered with thorns or pointed leaves, they can easily be breached.

Picket and Chain Link Fences

Advantages include view of outside area by resident, while not providing a hiding place for a potential intruder. Residual benefit is restraint for watchdog.

Solid or Block Fences/Walls

Although a solid wall limits the occupant's observation out of the compound and could provide concealment for an intruder, it is usually the most secure perimeter barrier.

The perimeter barrier is no stronger than the gate. A solid wooden gate is appropriate for a hedge or picket fence, a chain link gate is appropriate for a hedge, a picket fence or a chain link fence, and a solid wooden or metal gate is appropriate for a solid fence or wall. The gate should be well anchored to the fence or wall, swing outward with hinges on the inside, and be provided with a high security lock. Keys to locks should be stored in a secure but accessible location in the residence.

Shrubbery around a single detached dwelling should be trimmed in such a way that it does not provide a hiding place.

Consider installation of a contingency or emergency exit through the rear of the property, to be utilized only in high risk situations.

Inner Perimeter — Grills and Shatter Resistant Film

All building exterior openings over 96 square inches in size on the ground floor or accessible from trees, vehicle tops or porches should be grilled. Bars of solid steel, flat or round stock, spaced five to seven inches apart, with horizontal braces 10-12 inches apart to provide adequate rigidity, and securely imbedded on all sides to a depth of at least three inches into the adjacent wall or frame, should be installed. Use clip anchors or bend the end of the bars when grouting them into the wall. Otherwise, where possible, the bars should extend through the wall and be secured on the interior.

Shatter resistant film, a high quality clear plastic sheeting glued to windows, is recommended and should be applied to windows and doors before the grills are installed. Decorative grills should be so designed that the protection afforded is equal to the conventional type grills. Wherever possible, grillwork should be installed on the interior of the opening.

At least one grill in each section of the sleeping quarters should be hinged and equipped with an emergency release to permit emergency exit in the event of fire. Houses with a single corridor access to all sleeping quarters should have an iron grill

41

gate to control the bedrooms at night time. This grill gate would constitute an inner perimeter protection for the sleeping quarters. Where grillwork is required, a complete early warning fire detection and alarm system must be installed.

Inner Perimeter — Locks and Key Control
Locks
These are described in several ways and the various descriptions tend to confuse the layman. For example, they are described by their use (primary or auxiliary), by their locking mechanism (pin tumbler, wafer disc, lever, magnetic, cipher, etc.), by the type of cylinder (single or double), or by the type of mounting (key-in-the-knob, mortised, rim, etc.).

All primary residential entry doors should be equipped with both a primary and auxiliary lock. Additionally, each entry door should have a 190 degree optical viewer or equivalent.

Primary locks are the main lock on a door and are identified by the fact they have handles. These locks are usually key-in-the-knob or mortised type locks with the locking hardware located in a cavity in the door. Unless they have a latch or bolt that extends into the door jamb 5/8 inch to one inch, they do not provide sufficient protection.

Auxiliary locks usually are deadbolts which are mortise or rim/surface mounted, located on the inner door and door frame surface, and do not have handles. This type lock does not have to be keyed and may be nothing more than a sliding deadbolt. The exception to this rule is where there is a window or side light within 40 inches of the lock.

Change all exterior locks, including garage door and mail box lock (if in an apartment) prior to moving into new residence abroad, in either a new or used home. It is possible to change only the lock cylinder or to repin the cylinder on good quality locks without changing the complete locking device.

Exterior doors with or near glass panels should be equipped with dead bolts which are key operated on both interior and exterior. It is advisable to place an extra key for this type lock in a concealed area in the immediate proximity to the inside lock in case of emergencies. All residents should be aware of its location. Never leave the key in the inside lock for personal convenience.

Lock all fuse boxes and electrical panels located on the exterior of the residence.

Electronic garage door openers have advantages and disadvantages and, therefore, should be installed with discretion. A security advantage, in addition to the convenience, is that it is not necessary to leave the security of your locked car to enter and lock your garage behind you. The disadvantage is that such devices can often be compromised by a variety of inexpensive transmitters. If installed, insure maximum protection is installed on door between garage and interior of house. Discuss with competent locksmith.

Have a qualified locksmith install effective locking devices on sliding glass doors which are highly vulnerable. Avoid using louvered or jalousie windows which are a very easy mark for even the most inexperienced burglar.

Maintaining Perimeter Security

Maintain strict key control on all exterior locks. Never hide an exterior door key outside the house. Sophisticated burglars know all the hiding places.

Install an intercom between primary entrance and the inside foyer or protected area. In apartments and homes the intercom should be backed up with a peep hole in solid core door with an angle of visibility of 190 degrees.

Remove all name identification from your gate and doors. Avoid displays which identify you as an American.

Burglars/terrorists are always on the alert for an easy way to enter a residence. Doors, windows, and garages should be closed and locked at all times when the residents are away from home, no matter how short the time. If there is any doubt about accountability of keys to a home, have the lock cylinders replaced or re-pinned. Keys should be controlled and only given to mature family members or trusted friends. When domestic employees are given a key, it should only be to the primary lock of one entry door. They should never be given keys to both the primary and auxiliary locks. This ensures that the occupants can always secure the residence in the evenings or when the domestic staff is absent. Insure that access to the residence is not permitted through domestic employee's quarters.

Any padlocks used for residential security should always be stored in the locked position. Sophisticated burglars sometimes will replace a padlock with a similar one to which they alone have the key.

Section VIII. Intrusion Alarms and Security Lighting

Objective

Intrusion or alerting devices are any means by which a resident and/or the local police/security force are made aware of the attempted or forcible entry of a residence. This includes alarm systems, guards, dogs, noisemakers, and communications systems.

Alarm Systems

Basically, alarm systems perform two functions: they detect an intruder, and they report the intrusion. However, for the purpose of residential security use overseas, an alarm system in a residence should be considered as a deterrent device. In areas abroad where forced entry of a residence is commonplace, or where an active terrorist threat is present, the use of a good residential alarm system is highly recommended.

Minimum desired alarm system features are:

Capable of operating on the local electrical current and have a rechargeable battery backup.

Relatively easy to install and trouble-shoot. Many local electricians may not be capable of installing or repairing a complex alarm system.

Equipped with a time delay feature to allow the occupant to arm or disarm the system without activating the alarm.

Capable of being wired with a fixed or mobile panic switch, a device which permits manual activation of the alarm system. Panic switches should be installed in the safe haven, in the living portion of the residence and outside as well for use by residential guards.

Security Lighting

Security lighting should be an integral part of the intrusion system.

Lighting - Most intruders will go to great lengths to escape visual detection. Therefore, they will normally strike at a residence that appears vacant or is dark.

Outdoor lighting can be a major deterrent against criminal intrusion. Properly used, it can discourage criminal activity and aid observation.

The important elements of protective outdoor lighting are coverage and evenness of light. It is possible that in some residential settings existing street lighting, along with one or two porch lights, will furnish sufficient lighting. However, it may be necessary to install additional lighting in order to achieve the degree of security desired. If outdoor lighting is to be used as a protective measure, all accesses to vulnerable areas of the property and house should be lighted.

Lighting should be placed in such a manner that it covers the walls of the residence and the ground area adjacent to the perimeter walls. Also, it should illuminate shrubbery and eliminate building blind spots.

If security lighting is deemed advisable in your location, it should consist of two independent systems. Cosmetic or low level tamper-resistant fixtures installed in the eaves or overhangs for continuous perimeter illumination, and emergency floodlights tied to the alarm system so that they will turn on automatically when the alarm is activated. A manual switch should be installed in the living quarters of the single family residence, so that they may be turned on independent of the alarm system.

It is a good idea to connect the cosmetic lighting to a photo electric cell which automatically turns them on at dusk and off at dawn. They should be connected to a dimmer, so that the light level can

43

be adjusted to the extent that it would discourage an attack on the house by burglars but at the same time would not be offensive to the neighbors.

Insure that all lighting systems are installed in compliance with local codes.

Consider installation of diesel powered auxiliary generator which turns on automatically when electric power fails. Turn on at least once each quarter to insure it's in good working order.

"Mushroom" lights which are installed along the foundation of the house and cast a light up the side of the structure are easily compromised and should be avoided.

Section IX.   Extended Absences From the Residence

Extended absences present the burglar with his easiest opportunity to target a residence. There are many indicators to a burglar that a residence is unoccupied. For example, discussing the planned absence in the office or in the neighborhood, forgetting to cancel deliveries, leaving the home unlighted and the blinds or drapes drawn, and closing the shutters.

While residents are away, automatic timers or photoelectric switches should turn on inside lights, a radio, or even an air-conditioner to create the illusion that someone is home.

Invite a reliable neighbor to park a car in your driveway at times during your absence, especially at night.

Ask close friends or neighbors to look after the home and turn on and off different lights, put out trash as usual, etc.

In many foreign locations it is advisable to have trusted domestic employees remain in the residence during extended absences.

If you live in a single-family house or if the servants are on vacation, you could hire a guard but do not give him access to enter the house. He should only patrol the garden area which encircles the house.

Hook up of a telephone answering device serves to defeat the telephone call that is made by the terrorist/criminal to determine if someone is home.

Section X.   Domestic Hires Screening and Responsibilities

Domestic employees can either be a valuable asset to residential security or a decided liability. The chances of obtaining the services of a reliable servant can be improved by hiring one employed and recommended by a friend, acquaintance or neighbor.

Prospective applicants should be required to produce references and should be interviewed thoroughly.

It is wise to personally check with references to confirm their existence and obtain information concerning the reliability, honesty, attitudes and work habits of prospective applicants.

In some countries, the authorities will conduct background investigations upon request.

In some foreign countries, it is an accepted practice to request full personal data from applicants for employment. This data should be copied from either a National Government I.D. card or a passport.

Do not accept the person's word as to their name and date of birth without an authentic government document to back up their claim.

Obtain the following information:

● Government Identity Card or passport, etc., for number, date of birth, nationality, full names, valid date, place of registry.

● Letters of reference: Be sure you know who wrote it and what it says. (Usually written in local language.)

● Obtain the address of the former employer and the company he represented.

● Good domestic employees are generally referred by your predecessor, although this is not always the case.

This entire procedure should only require a few days if you utilize good contacts with competent police recommended by the embassy, consulate or your predecessor. If you are unable to establish good contacts, contract the job out to reliable investigative consultants.

Caution

Do not permit domestics of untested integrity and reliability in your home. If you must engage a cook or house servant before investigation is completed, do not entrust keys or an unoccupied house to the employee in question.

When you have hired a servant, record his/her complete name, date and place of birth, identity card number, telephone number, and address as well as the names of spouse, parent or close relative.

Domestic help should be briefed on security practices. It is critical that they be rehearsed and rebriefed from time to time to refresh their memory and to update previous instructions. Domestic staff should be briefed on visitor control, how to report suspicious or unusual activity, proper telephone answering procedures, and admittance of maintenance men to the residence. They should also be made aware of emergency telephone numbers. They should be able to reach the man or woman of the house by phone to report critical situations at the residence.

Domestic employees should be trained to answer the door rather than members of the household. They should not be allowed to admit visitors without specific approval. When visitors, repair or services personnel are expected, domestic employees should be informed of their probable time of arrival and identification and should not unlock or open the door until they have been properly identified.

Domestic employees should never give a caller the impression that no one is home, nor should they tell when the occupants are expected. They should be directed to reply that occupants are "Unable to come to the phone right now but will return the call, if the caller will leave his name and telephone number."

Domestic employees should not be allowed to overhear family plans and official business. Sensitive and confidential letters such as those dealing with business strategies, hiring or firing practices, employee disciplinary matters and other matters which are closely guarded at the office, should be equally guarded at home. Travel itineraries, purchasing negotiations and bids, labor negotiation strategies, pricing and marketing information, to name but a few, are other examples of official business which should not be shared with domestics in any form, written or oral, and documents relating to same should not be left unsecured about the residence.

Terrorists or burglars do not always break in; sometimes people let them in. Family members should be wary of salesmen, or unexpected visits from repairmen or utility company representatives, even if they are in uniform. Ask to see their credentials or call their office to verify their bonafides. If a stranger asks to use the telephone, do not let him in. Make the call for him. Do not hesitate to be suspicious if the situation warrants it. An intercom system can be used to determine a stranger's business before he is allowed access to the residence.

Frequently brief all domestic hires, such as maids, cooks, gardeners, handymen and chauffeurs, on security precautions. Be very specific in making clear what you expect of them. It is advisable to select one member of the domestic staff and make him/her responsible for the actions of others.

Instruct the domestic help to report to the man or woman of the house the presence of strangers in the neighborhood. Virtually all kidnappings and terrorist assaults have indicated that the perpetrators had an intimate knowledge of the victims' habits developed through surveillance prior to attack.

Do not allow domestic help to invite anyone into your home without prior approval.

As a final word of caution, do not, in front of domestic employees, make comments which could be construed as being disrespectful of local customs or people. Even when they make critical remarks about themselves or their government do not join in. Remember that we would probably consider criticism of the U.S. by a foreigner even

45

if justified as an indication of anti-Americanism, especially if made repeatedly. And remember further, the security of you and your family may depend on these employees and their fellow nationals.

Section XI. Family and Company Cars

Selection of Make and Model

Purchase or lease a car that blends in well with local passenger car environment. Remember, keep a low profile!

Safety and Security Precautions:

● Consider installation of burglar alarm on car consistent with risk level.

● Make sure gas cap, spare tire, and engine compartment are lockable in the interest of good safety and security.

● Always have the fuel tank at least half full.

● Keep vehicle(s) locked at all times.

● Never park your vehicle on the street for long periods of time.

● Keep your vehicle(s) housed in a garage.

● Make sure that you have both right and left side rear view mirrors.

● Visibility around your vehicle is critical.

● Do not leave registration papers in your car.

● If legal to do so, have your car license plate registered to a Post Office Box rather than to your home or office. List the P.O. Box to your office.

● Keep extra water and oil in the trunk.

● Keep emergency equipment in the trunk — flashlight, flares, fire extinguisher, first aid kit, etc.

·● Do not use stickers or personalized license plates.

● If possible, install a communication device, such as a two-way radio or telephone in your car.

Section XII. Auto Travel

Travel Precautions

Potential victims of kidnapping and assault are probably most vulnerable when entering or leaving their home or office.

● Never enter a car without checking the rear seat to insure that it is empty.

● Do not develop predictable patterns during the business day or during free time. For example, do not leave home or the office at the same time and by the same route every day. Do not have a standard tee-off time for golf, tennis, hand ball, etc.

● If possible, exchange company cars, swap with co-workers occasionally.

● Know the location of police, hospital, military, and government buildings. Ascertain when they are open and which are 24-hour operations. These areas can provide a safe haven along normal transportation routes.

● Even the slightest disruption in travel patterns may disrupt a surveillance team sufficiently for them to tip their hand or abandon their efforts.
● Avoid trips to remote areas, particularly after dark. If it is essential to go into such an area, travel in a group or convoy and advise trusted personnel of your itinerary.

● Select well traveled streets as much as possible.

● Keep vehicles well maintained at all times, including a useable spare tire. Install additional rear-view mirrors so passengers may see what is behind.

● If chauffeur driven, consider riding up front next to the driver sometimes, in keeping with the low profile concept.

● Chauffeurs and high-risk personnel should be trained in offensive and evasive driving techniques.

46

● When driving, keep doors and windows locked.

● Be constantly alert to road conditions and surroundings, to include possible surveillance by car, motorcycle, or bicycle. All passengers should be vigilant. If a surveillance or some other danger is detected, drive to the closest safe haven, such as police station, hospital emergency room, fire station, etc., lock your car and go inside. Advise authorities as appropriate.

● When traveling, pre-plan your route and one alternate.

● Be prepared for local environmental conditions (snow, rain, etc.).

● Never pick up hitchhikers.

● Whenever possible, drive to the center of the road, especially in rural settings, to avoid being forced off the road.

● Remain a safe distance behind the vehicle ahead to allow space for avoidance maneuvers, if necessary.

● Check side and rear view mirrors routinely.

● Carry 3 x 5 cards with important assistance phrases printed on them to assist with language problems. Always carry appropriate coin denomination for public phones. Practice use of public telephones.

● Report as appropriate all suspicious activity to the company security contact, embassy or consulate, or local police as soon as possible.

● Consider keeping a small hand-held cassette recorder in the glove box at all times, descriptions of suspicious persons, activities, license plate numbers, etc., can be dictated while driving. It's impossible to make notes while driving or in stressful situations.

● Never leave identifying material or valuables in the vehicle.

Surveillance

If surveillance is suspected, consider the following actions:

● Divert from originally intended destination, make a few turns to see if the surveillant still persists.

● Immediately determine any identifying data that you can observe. (For example: make, color of car, license number, number and description of occupants.)

● Remember, do not panic if surveillance is confirmed. Surveillance teams are normally neither trained nor have the mission to assault the potential target.

Parking Precautions

● Always lock the vehicle, no matter where it is located.

● Do not leave the car in the care of a valet parking service such as hotel, restaurant or club.

● Require chauffeurs to stay with the car.

● Avoid leaving the vehicle parked on the street overnight.

● Never exit vehicle without checking the area for suspicious individuals. If in doubt, drive away.

Section XIII. Telephones

One can never be sure of the true identity of a person on the other end of a telephone line. For this reason, it behooves all of us to exercise the following telephone security precautions:

● Do not answer the telephone by stating the name of the family.

● If a caller inquires, "To whom am I speaking?", respond with a question like, "Who are you calling?"

● Do not give the residence telephone number in response to wrong-number telephone calls. If the caller asks, "What number did I reach?" respond with another question like, "What number are you calling?"

● Report repetitive wrong-number telephone calls

47

to the telephone company, the person in charge of security at your company, if there is such a person, and to the police as appropriate.

• Be suspicious of any caller alleging to represent the telephone company and advising that the telephone service may be interrupted.

• Be skeptical of telephone calls from strangers advising that a family member has been injured or has won a prize, or making any other assertion that is followed by a request for the family member to leave the home immediately. Verify the telephone call by looking up the number of the caller in the directory, check it against the one given by the caller, and then call the number to verify the information given.

• Children should be advised not to converse with strangers on the telephone for any reason. When an adult is not present, a child will occasionally answer the phone. Children should be instructed to tell callers in such circumstances that the adult being called is not available to come to the phone, rather than reveal that the adult is absent from the home.

• When practical, home telephone numbers should be unlisted and unpublished.

• Do not list home phone numbers in company directories unless circulation is highly restricted.

• Family members and domestic help should not divulge personal information or travel plans over the telephone to anyone without specific authority to do so.

• Avoid party lines.

• Consider use of answering devices for ALL incoming calls in order to be selective in which calls you choose to answer.

• Report ALL suspicious activity to your security contact at the company or the local police.

• Locate the nearest public telephone to your home and inform the family and household members of its location for their use in an emergency. Also, locate the nearest non-public telephone to your home to which you have access, perhaps a friendly neighbor's phone, for the same reason.

• All family members should carry the phone number of one or more trusted neighbors who have a clear view of your home, either front or rear. A pseudo-extortionist may call you at your office and claim that family member(s) are being held at gunpoint at your home and, unless a sum of money is paid to a third party or placed at a designated location, they will be harmed. A telephone call to a neighbor who has a clear view of your home may, by simply looking out the window, determine that your family is in no jeopardy at all and thereby determine with reasonable certainty that the call is a hoax. If a strange vehicle is parked in the driveway, the police should be notified as appropriate.

• Emergency telephone numbers of police, fire, medical and ambulance service should be available for quick reference at each telephone in the home. Check accuracy of list every six months or so.

• You and your family members, should practice the use of public telephones.

• If available, maintain two portable two-way radios - one in your own home and one in a neighbor's home - in the event wire communications are severed. Telephone service in many foreign countries is highly unreliable.

• In certain emergencies, it may become necessary on short notice to locate and account for all members of the family. Make it a habit to know generally where family members will be every day. Make a list of phone numbers of all places frequently visited by family members such as neighbors, friends homes, clubs, beauty salons, barbers, favorite restaurants, schools, etc. All family members should carry a copy of the list and a copy kept at home for domestics and one at the office. Update regularly.

Section XIV. Mail

Businessmen should discourage the delivery of mail to their private residence. Either rent a Post Office Box registered to your office or have your personal mail delivered to your office.

Family members and domestic help should accept no mail parcels or other unexpected deliveries unless they are sure of the source.

Do not open the door to accept strange deliveries. Packages should be left by the door. Wait a considerable time before opening the door to retrieve the package.

If deliveryman requires a signature, have him slide receipt under the door.

Continuously remind yourself and others in the household to be suspicious of all incoming mail and parcels and to remain alert for the following danger signs:

Appearance

● Is it from a strange place?

● Is there an excessive amount of postage?
● Are there stains on the item?

● Are wires or strings protruding or attached to the item in an unusual location?

● Is the item marked conspicuously with the receiver's name: i.e., Personal for Mr. Smith, Confidential for Mr. Smith?

● Is the spelling on the item correct?

● Does the letter or package contain an inner letter or package addressed to a particular individual or tied with a string, tape, wire, rubber band, or any compression item?

● Do the return address and the postmark differ?

Odor

● Do the items smell peculiar? Many explosives used by terrorists smell like shoe polish or almonds.

Weight

● Is the item unusually heavy or light?

● Is the item uneven in balance or lopsided?

Caution

If parcel is at all suspicious, STOP further

handling, place item against exterior corner of room. DO NOT IMMERSE ITEM IN WATER. This may make paper soggy and cause spring-loaded device to detonate. Open windows and evacuate the immediate area. Call appropriate authorities.

Section XV. Banking and Charge Accounts

Checking accounts, charge accounts and loan applications create audit trails which divulge more about you and your family than you may wish to be known. Purchasing habits can reveal much about the value of household goods and personal valuables that are kept in your residence and which might become attractive to potential thieves. It may be prudent to utilize major U.S. credit cards as opposed to writing checks on local banks, in order to reduce the audit trail your financial transactions can leave.

When requested to write a phone number on checks or credit card slips, use the office number and have family members do the same.

DO NOT imprint your home address or phone number on personalized checks.

Section XVI. Trash Removal

Trash containers have been proven to be excellent sources of intelligence for curiosity seekers and terrorists.   Therefore, do not place material in them which can be exploited to the detriment of yourself or a member of your family. To preclude this possibility, incinerate, disintegrate or shred trash consisting of private papers, letters, correspondence including drafts of outgoing correspondence, bills, invoices, cancelled checks as well as any papers with your signature or facsimile thereof, or any other type of materials which might result in
embarrassment to or compromise the security of any other member of your household. As a rule of thumb, all paper products, used carbons and discs or tapes, exclusive of wrapping paper and publications not annotated by a member of your household should be destroyed as indicated above.

Trash receptacles should be stored inside the residence or outside in a secure shed, to preclude easy access by the curiosity seeker or the placement of dangerous objects.

Section XVII. Quality of Law Enforcement Protection

Police Capability

Assessment of police protection available to a given area is necessary. Determine if the police have sufficient officers and means of transportation and communication to respond to residential crimes in a timely manner. Every effort should be expended to establish quick, dependable communication links to the local security or police force to insure their effective response in an emergency. You should be aware of the attitude of the government, police and the populace towards other nationals, particularly Americans. A strong anti-American attitude may be cause for diminished police responsiveness.

Private Guard Service

Where police capability is in doubt, the use of a private guard service should be considered. However, the use of guards is costly and the quality of guards vary significantly from area to area. Most guards are poorly trained and ineffective. However, if the guard can at least alert the resident to an attack on the residence by tripping a "panic" switch, sounding a horn, or blowing a whistle, he has done his job.

All guards should be subjected to a security check. As much as possible should be known about the employed guards, particularly where and how effectively he has worked previously. At a minimum, guards should be physically capable of performing their shift duties during the normal work day. They should be provided with the following: written guard orders (both in English and native language), a uniform, a communication or alerting device, e.g., air horn, whistle, alarm panic switch, two-way radio, etc., a flashlight, and a defensive weapon such as a club or a chemical deterrent (mace). In rare instances where the threat warrants and local laws and customs allow, a side arm should be considered provided the guard is fully trained in its use.

Section XVIII. Firearms in Foreign Countries

Firearms restrictions and/or requirements differ from country to country. Persons assigned overseas should contact the local police authority to ascertain the law of the land concerning private ownership of weapons.

If authorized by the host country, weapons must be maintained and used n accordance with the local customs and laws. Host country licenses must be obtained when required. Training and safety should be prime considerations if a weapon is to be maintained in the home.

Illegal importation of a firearm is a serious criminal offense in many countries.

Section XIX. Children's School

When children are to be picked up at school by other than immediate family members, there should be an established procedure coordinated with school officials to assure that they are picked up only by authorized persons.

Children should be instructed in observing good security procedures such as traveling in groups, refusing rides with strangers, avoiding isolated play areas, keeping parents informed as to time and destination, reporting all strange events and attempted molestations and how to get help or call the police.

In many overseas locations it is economical to contract with a taxi company or driver to pickup and drop off students at school and home. Insist on the same driver every day and instruct children not to ride with a strange driver. In other locations car pooling may be practical.

Section XX. Coups d'etat and Emergency Evacuations

Establish contact, if not done so earlier, and maintain continuing contact with the Regional Security Officer (RSO) or Post Security Officer (PSO) at the nearest U.S. diplomatic post, i.e. Embassy or Consulate, and a designated member(s) of the Emergency Action Committee. Each post abroad formulates an Emergency Action Plan unique to its location, to deal with a coup d'etat and an attempted coup.

50

• DO NOT automatically pack and leave the country on your own initiative. Most coups only last a few days and are usually preceded by some type of advance warning, such as demonstrations, and therefore, often times can be anticipated. Contact the RSO/PSO for guidance BEFORE taking drastic action.

• Monitor local news media, TV, radio and newspapers for any evidence of anti-American activity, since such activity will have an impact on the Embassy's Emergency Action Plan.

• In certain locations, for example in some third world countries, where the political climate is right for coups and coup attempts, it is ecommended that adequate supplies of non-perishable foods and drinking water be stockpiled in your home to sustain your family for an arbitrary period of time (days or weeks) consistent with the existing threat. Maintain regular (at least daily) contact with the Embassy during such periods of high stress.

• Develop alternate routes of evacuation from your residence to be used in the event of fire or other emergency where rapid evacuation would be necessary.

• Be prepared. Have bag packed for each family member in the event you have to leave on short notice.

• Appropriate amount of currency and traveler's checks should be isolated and kept on hand.

• Keep airline tickets (without reservations) on hand for each family member.

• Maintain current passports and, where applicable, visas for a "safe haven" country.

• Prepare a list of telephone numbers for transportation companies, should emergency evacuation be necessary, i.e., taxi, airlines, private limousine service, etc. Place near the office and home telephones.

• Consolidate important personal records/files for easy access and transportation.

• Have more than one (1) evacuation plan.

• Americans should have in place a pre-planned telephonic pyramid contact system, to insure the American population in the host country is aware of what is happening. A pyramid contact system is one in which each person called with information is required to call two or three others to relay the same information.

Section XXI. Social Activities

• During social gatherings, conversations with citizens of host country, especially with reference to political, racial, economic, religious and controversial local issues, should be closely guarded and as non-committal as possible.

• Where possible, employees in high threat areas should avoid social activities which have a set place and schedule, such as the same church service every Sunday morning, shopping at the same store every Saturday, and attending well publicized American citizen functions.

Section XXII. Spouse and Dependent Activity

Each family member should be familiar with basic security procedures and techniques.

• All family members should know how to use the local telephones, both public and private.

• Family members should not reveal information concerning travel or other family plans; they should be cautious in answering such questions over the phone, even if the caller is known, to guard against the possibility of taps or other leaks.

• Family members should avoid local civil disturbances, demonstrations, crowds, or other high risk areas.

• Children, in particular, should be on guard against being approached or questioned by strangers. It is safer to drive them to school than to let them walk. If they must walk, they should not go alone. Adult escorts are preferable, but even groups of children offer some deterrence. Although children must attend school on a particular schedule, parents are encouraged to vary departures, arrivals, and routes to the extent possible. Use of carpools, especially if scheduling is on a random basis, also breaks down patterns of movement and enhances security.

51

• The location of family members should be known at all times. Causes of delays or unforeseen absences should be determined immediately. Family members should be encouraged to develop the habit of checking in before departure, after arrival, or when changing plans.

•Shopping or family outings should not conform to a set pattern or routine.

Section XXIII. Watchdogs

• A dog's extremely sensitive and discriminating senses of smell and hearing enable it to detect quickly a stranger who is not normally present in the residential area. The well-trained dog will normally bark ferociously when approached by an intruder.

• Dogs should be well trained to react only to the introduction of strangers into the residence area, to stop barking on command from the owner, and to accept food only from its master.

• Sophisticated burglars can neutralize the most ferocious of watchdogs by tossing it a meat patty laced with Demoral, which will put the dog to sleep for several hours.

• There are some liabilities attached to the presence of an animal whose role is to deter, discourage, and rout criminal intruders, particularly if the animal does not discriminate well between friend and foe.

Section XXIV. Recreation and Exercise

In order to establish a potential target's routine and evaluate the level of security awareness, terrorists usually watch their intended victims for some time before they attack. Therefore, persons in high threat areas should consider whether or not to participate in recreational or exercise activities which have a set place and schedule such as: bowling, little league sports, golf, tennis, jogging, walking, etc.

If you decide to participate in these sports, you should select jogging paths, tennis courts, golf clubs and all out-of-door activity locations with great care. For example, do not indiscriminately jog through a park with which you are not totally familiar. Use densely populated areas, if possible.

Section XXV. A Word About Illegal Drugs

Despite repeated warnings, drug arrests and convictions of American citizens are still on the increase. If you are caught with either soft or hard drugs overseas, you are subject to local and not U.S. laws. Penalties for possession or trafficking are often the same.

The laws governing the use, possession, and trafficking in illegal drugs vary widely throughout the world, as do penalties for violations of those laws. One may be legal in one country and may constitute a serious criminal offense in another. It behooves all U.S. Citizens living abroad to familiarize themselves with selected laws of the host country, especially those relating to illegal drugs.

A statement by Mr. John C. Lawn, while he was Administrator of the Drug Enforcement Administration, U.S. Department of Justice, emphasized the seriousness of violations of illegal drug laws abroad and resultant penalties:

"Possession and use of illegal drugs overseas is no casual matter. Unlike the United States, in many countries trafficking and even possessing drugs for personal use are extremely serious offenses. You may have no rights at all - no bail, no speedy trial, no jury trial - the penalties can be severe and the prisons can be frightening. You are subject to the criminal sanctions of another country. In at least two countries I know of, the penalty includes death and the U.S. State Department will not be able to help you."

It is important that the foregoing be emphasized to all family members living abroad, especially to teenage children and young adults.

Prescription Medications

It is advisable to leave all medicines in their original labeled containers if you require medication containing habit-forming drugs or narcotics. You should also carry a copy of the doctor's prescription. These precautions will make customs processing easier and also will ensure you do not violate the laws of the country where you plan to live or are currently residing.

Section XXVI. A Word About Bomb Threats, Bombings, Extortion and Kidnapping

Bomb threats, bombings, extortion, kidnapping, and hostage taking are criminal acts frequently engaged in by international terrorists. We have alluded to these techniques in this chapter in only a general way. It was not the intention of the authors to expound on these highly volatile subjects in detail, since so much has already been written about them.

Section XXVII. Conclusion

Many of us have been victimized by crime and most of us are acquainted with victims of crime. The news media daily swamps us with a barrage of stories about a wide range of criminal activities, including burglary, robbery, rape, kidnapping and murder, to name but a few. To this list have been added, in recent years, the often bizarre activities of the international political terrorist, which are nonetheless criminal acts. Yet, it is perhaps the most difficult job in the world to convince people to practice security and safety in their lives.

Crime is escalating throughout the world. It is a most serious problem which will not be solved in our lifetime, if ever. Unfortunately, we cannot delegate our personal security to the police or to anyone else. Law enforcement, as we all know, is largely reactive.

Each of us must assume responsibility for our personal security and insure that our loved ones do the same. We must adopt an attitude of continuous awareness to our vulnerabilities and always resist the temptation to yield to the complacent philosophy of "it will not happen to me."

If we do not involve ourselves, personally, in protecting ourselves, our loved ones, and our property, our vulnerability to criminal acts will increase dramatically.

Security, like safety, will never be a positive science because there are no foolproof techniques or hardware which guarantee freedom from vulnerability. Effective security must be dynamic and never static simply because the diverse risks which confront us are always changing.

Remember always to remain vigilant, especially in the unfamiliar environment of far away places

53

Part I

Employee and Family Profile

EMPLOYEE AND FAMILY PROFILE   CONFIDENTIAL

	Employee	Spouse	Children
Name			
Date of Birth			
Height			
Weight			
Color of Eyes			
Color of Hair			
Special Medication Required (yes/no)			
Photo Attached (yes/no)			
Passport: Country			
Number			
Expiration Date			
Drivers License State/Country			
Number			
Expiration Date			

Name and Address of Family Physician

Name and Address of Family Dentist

PERSONALLY OWNED VEHICLES

Make/Type	Year	Color	License

Name, Address and Telephone Number of Local Person to Contact in Event of Emergency

RESIDENTIAL SECURITY SURVEY

SECURITY FEATURE	YES	NO	REMARKS

NEIGHBORHOOD

1. Is unit in good residential area with a low crime rate?

2. Do other employees live nearby?

3. Is the police and fire protection adequate and within 10 minute response time?

4. Are there a number of alternate routes to and from the dwelling?

EXTERIOR OF SINGLE-FAMILY OR DUPLEX DWELLING

1. Is the property well-defined with a hedge, fence or wall in good condition?

2. Are the gates solid and in good condition?

RESIDENTIAL SECURITY SURVEY

SECURITY FEATURE	YES	NO	REMARKS

EXTERIOR OF SINGLE-FAMILY OR DUPLEX DWELLING, continued

3. Are gates kept locked?

4. Are there handy access routes (poles, trees, etc.) which may be used to get over the barrier?

5. Is public or residence lighting sufficient to illuminate all sides of the dwelling?

6. Are all lights working at sufficient height to prevent tampering?

7. Have hiding places near doors,

55

windows & garage or parking
area been illuminated or eliminated?

8. If garage is available,
    is it used and kept locked?

EXTERIOR OF APARTMENT

1. Are the public areas of the building
    controlled and well lighted?

2. Can lobby and elevator be
    viewed from the street?

3. Are secondary entrances to the
    building and parking controlled?

RESIDENTIAL SECURITY SURVEY

SECURITY FEATURE	YES	NO	REMARKS

EXTERIOR OF APARTMENT, continued

4. Is apartment height within the
    rescue capabilities (ladder height)
    of the fire department?

5. Is the balcony (or other apartment
    windows) accessible from another
    balcony, ledge, roof or window?

DOORS

1. Can each exterior (regular,
    sliding, French, etc.) door be
    adequately secured?

2. Does the primary lock on each
    door work?

3. Are all doors kept locked?

4. Can any door be opened from the
    outside by breaking a door glass
    or sidelight?

5. Have all unused exterior doors
    been permanently secured?

6. Are all keys accounted for?

7. Have all "hidden" keys (under
    door mat, etc.) been removed?

56

RESIDENTIAL SECURITY SURVEY

SECURITY FEATURE	YES	NO	REMARKS

DOORS, continued

8.   Are exterior hinges protected?

9.   Does each major entrance have a door viewer or interview grille?

WINDOWS

1.   Are all non-ventilating windows permanently secured?

2.   Are all windows accessible from the ground, balconies, trees, ledges, roofs and the like protected by grilles?

3.   Are all windows kept closed and locked when not in use?

4.   Have emergency escape provisions been incorporated into one or more window grilles?

5.   Are all sliding and hinged glass doors secured with a metal grille gate?

6.   Are all sliding glass doors and windows secured by a rod (charlie bar) in the slide track?

RESIDENTIAL SECURITY SURVEY

SECURITY FEATURE	YES	NO	REMARKS

WINDOWS, continued

7.   Are windows and wall air conditioners anchored and protected by steel grille-work to prevent removal from the outside?

ALARMS

1.   Are all entrance doors alarmed?

57

2. Are all non-grilled windows
   within access of the ground,
   balconies, trees, etc. alarmed?

3. Does the alarm have an external
   alerting device, such as a bell
   or siren?

4. Is the alarm linked by transmitter
   to a central monitor station?

5. Does the system have panic
   buttons placed at strategic
   locations around the residence?

6. Do the occupants test the alarm
   periodically?

RESIDENTIAL SECURITY SURVEY

SECURITY FEATURE	YES	NO	REMARKS

SAFEHAVEN

1. If a safehaven is recommended,
   can one be accommodated?

2. Does the safehaven have a solid
   core, metal, or metal-clad door?

3. Is the emergency radio kept charged
   and available in the safehaven?

4. Are toilet facilities available in
   the safehaven?

5. Is there an emergency egress from
   the safehaven?

MISCELLANEOUS CONCERNS

1. Does the dwelling have at least
   one 5 lb. or 10 lb. ABC general
   purpose fire extinguisher located
   in the kitchen?

2. Does the dwelling have at least
   one 2 1/2 gallon water type fire
   extinguisher located in the
   safehaven?

3. Are fire extinguishers checked
   periodically?

RESIDENTIAL SECURITY SURVEY

SECURITY FEATURE	YES	NO	REMARKS

MISCELLANEOUS CONCERNS,
continued

4.   Do the occupants, including older children & domestic employees, know how to use extinguishers?

5.   Is there a smoke detector in the dwelling?

6.   Are smoke detectors properly installed?

7.   Are smoke detector batteries replaced at least once a year?

8.   Are smoke detectors tested periodically?

9.   Does the dwelling have an operational emergency radio, with an outside antenna?

10.   Do the occupants, including older children and domestic employees, know how to use the radio?

11.   Are emergency phone numbers (post, fire, police, ambulance) kept near the phone?

12.   Has a background check been conducted on domestic employees?

RESIDENTIAL SECURITY SURVEY

SECURITY FEATURE	YES	NO	REMARKS

MISCELLANEOUS CONCERNS,
continued

13.   Have children and employees been briefed on security requirements (locked windows & doors, no admittance of strangers, no acceptance of packages, etc.)?

14.   Do occupants have a firearm in

59

the home?

15. Is it protected (trigger lock, disassembled, etc.) from children?

16. Have occupants been trained in its use?

RESIDENCE SECURITY SELF-EVALUATION WORKSHEET

SECURITY FEATURE/ISSUE	YES	NO

EXTERIOR

Do garden gates lock?

Are gates kept locked and the keys under your control?

Is the gate bell in working order? Are stairways lighted?

Are walls of sufficient height to deter thieves?

Are exterior lights adequate to illuminate the residence grounds, particularly around gates and doors?

If butane gas is used, are the bottles secured in a safe place?

Are there any poles, boxes, trees, or out-buildings that would help an intruder scale your wall or fence?

BUILDING DOORS

Are the exterior doors of solid wood or metal construction?

Are locks on your exterior doors of the cylinder type?

Are they the dead locking (jimmyproof) type?

Can any of your door locks be opened by breaking a glass or light wood panel next to the lock?

RESIDENCE SECURITY SELF-EVALUATION WORKSHEET

SECURITY FEATURE/ISSUE	YES	NO

BUILDING DOORS, continued

60

Do you use heavy-duty sliding deadbolts on your most used doors as auxiliary locks?

Can all your doors including porch, balcony, basement, terrace and roof be locked securely?

Are all your locks in good working order?

Does anyone other than your immediate family have a key to your residence (i.e. previous tenants, owners, servants, friends)?

Are all unused doors permanently secured?

Are all locks securely mounted?

Do you hide a spare key to your main entrance under a door mat, in a flower pot, or some other nearby, but obvious, spot?

Do you answer the door partially dressed?

Do you have a peephole or interview grille in your main door?

Do you answer the door without first checking to see who has rung the bell or knocked?

Do you lock your padlocks in place when the doors are unlocked (garage, storage room, unused servants' quarters, etc.)?

RESIDENCE SECURITY SELF-EVALUATION WORKSHEET

SECURITY FEATURE/ISSUE	YES	NO

BUILDING DOORS, continued

Are padlock hasps installed so that screws cannot be removed?

Are hasps and staple plates mounted so that they cannot be pried or twisted off?

WINDOWS

Are all your first floor windows protected?

Are unused windows permanently closed and sealed?

Are your windows properly and securely mounted?

Can window locks be opened by breading the glass?

Do you keep your windows locked when they are shut?

61

Are you as careful with securing windows on the second
floor or basement windows as you are with those on
the ground floor?

Have you locked up your ladder or relocated trellises
that might be used as a ladder to gain entry through a
second-story window?

Do you have a sliding glass doors and if so, do you have
a rod or "charlie bar" to place in the track?

RESIDENCE SECURITY SELF-EVALUATION WORKSHEET

SECURITY FEATURE/ISSUE	YES	NO

GARAGE

Do you lock your garage at night and when you are away
from home?

Are all garage doors and windows equipped with adequate
locks and are they in good working order?

Are tools and equipment left in the garage where a
burglar might be able to use them in gaining entry to
your residence?

MISCELLANEOUS

Do you have any type of fire extinguishers?

Do you know the type of fire on which to use your
extinguishers?

Has your fire fighting equipment been inspected or
recharged within the past year?

Does every member of your family and domestic staff
know how to use your fire fighting equipment?

Do you keep your cash and small valuables in a safe
storage place?

Do you have a list of serial numbers of your watches,
cameras, typewriters, computers, radios, stereo, VTRs,
etc.?

RESIDENCE SECURITY SELF-EVALUATION WORKSHEET

SECURITY FEATURE/ISSUE	YES	NO

MISCELLANEOUS, continued

Do you keep an inventory of all valuable property?

Do you have an accurate description (with photographs) of all valuable property which does not have serial numbers?

Do you avoid unnecessary display or publicity of your valuable items?

Have you given your family and servants instructions on what they should do if they discover an intruder attempting to break in or already in the house?

Have you told your family and servants to leave the house undisturbed and call the police if they find a burglary has been committed?

Do you know and have you posted near the telephone the number of the nearest police station?

Do you know how to report a fire and your dwelling location in the local language?

Do you and your family have an emergency escape plan with alternate emergency escape routes? Have you practiced this emergency plan?

Have you instructed your family and servants regarding the admission of strangers, no matter how authentic their credentials may appear?

RESIDENCE SECURITY SELF-EVALUATION WORKSHEET

SECURITY FEATURE/ISSUE	YES	NO

MISCELLANEOUS, continued

Are you, your family, and servants alert in the observations of strange vehicles or persons who may have you under surveillance or may be "casing" your residence for a burglary?

Have you verified the references and good health of your servants?

Do you know the location and telephone number of the nearest police, fire department, and hospital?

Chapter 5

Security Guidelines for Children Living Abroad

Living abroad provides both parents and children with special opportunities and experiences to share the history and culture of a foreign land. As we know, child rearing practices and standards vary widely around the world. What may be acceptable in one society may be taboo in another. You need to understand local customs—but remember, you set the standards for your child's safety and security.

Much of the information in this pamphlet you may already know, but it can serve as a useful reminder and an opportunity to review these issues with your child. You may also want to discuss it with any daycare providers you employ, as well as your child's teachers and school administrators.

Precautions in the Neighborhood

Children should:

- Be alert, cautious, and prepared.

- Know the safest route to school, stores, and friends' houses, avoid isolated areas, and be able to identify safe places to go in an emergency.

- Report any crimes, suspicious activities, or anything that does not seem quite right to the police, school authorities, and parents and guardians.

- Try to walk and play with a friend or in a group rather than alone, and always let a parent or guardian know where they are going to be.

- Stay away from known trouble spots, poorly lit or isolated areas, and strangers who hang around playgrounds, public restrooms, and schools.

- Avoid being around others who tend to engage in forms of violence or use alcohol or other drugs.

- Know to settle arguments with words rather than fists or weapons, and to walk away when others are arguing.

School and Daycare

Parents and guardians need to:

- Determine the reputation of a prospective school, daycare center, or babysitter, and find out if they are licensed, certified, or regulated in any way.

- Find out as much information as possible about individual care providers. Ask for and check references.

- Visit schools and daycare centers unannounced to assess the quality of care that is provided and to observe how the care provider relates to children.

- Consult with other parents and guardians who have used the school, daycare center, or babysitter.

- Be aware of the school or daycare center's hiring policies and practices to ensure that reference, background, and previous employment history checks have been conducted on its employees.

- Make sure a system of positive identification is in place to ensure that only authorized persons have permission to take children from the school or daycare center.

- Prohibit the care provider from taking their children on an outing without their authorization to do so.

- Inform the care provider as to who is allowed to pick up their children each day.

65

- Determine whether the facility meets relevant building codes and fire safety regulations and whether emergency plans are in place to deal with evacuation, power outages, and inclement weather.

- Be careful about individuals who have custody of their children. Such individuals should be selected for maturity, experience, and trustworthiness rather than convenience, proximity, and low cost.

Child Abuse

What is Child Abuse?

Child abuse refers to the physical or mental injury, sexual misuse or exploitation, negligent treatment, or other maltreatment of a minor.

Child abuse is usually not an isolated event but a pattern of behavior that someone in power uses in interacting with a child. Such behavior generally increases in severity and frequency and may be exhibited on either a regular or sporadic basis.

Child abuse occurs in all classes and cultures where isolation, the inability to cope with daily pressures, parental self-hate, unprepared parents, social stress, economic instability, or a misdirected sex drive exists.

Child abusers do not all fit a specific profile, but many tend to have been victims of child abuse, family violence, or substance abuse themselves.

Types of Child Abuse

Physical abuse is when someone inflicts bodily harm that leaves a physical injury on a child.

Sexual abuse is when someone in a position of power (usually an adult or older child) sexually mistreats a child either directly or indirectly.

Emotional abuse is when a child is made to feel worthless, unwanted, and unloved. It is any chronic or persistent act by an adult that endangers the mental health or emotional development of a child.

Neglect is when parents or guardians fail to provide for a child either because of ignorance of proper child care, failure to nurture, or deliberate maltreatment.

Preventing Child Abuse by Parents and Guardians

Prevention is often difficult because the line between discipline and abuse is not always clearly drawn, and the child involved is usually financially, physically, and emotionally dependent on the abuser.

Those who abuse children in their care often do so in response to emotional stress or feelings of powerlessness.

Prevention efforts need to be directed toward lessening or eliminating the factors that may cause abusive behavior. Factors can include low self-esteem, lack of education, poor child care skills, separation or divorce, social isolation, depression, illness, and financial problems. Education and counseling should be stressed.

Preventing Child Abuse by Others

Parents and guardians need to:

- Know where their children are at all times, be familiar with their children's friends, and show their children safe places in the neighborhood where they can go if they ever feel scared.

- Be alert to a teenager or adult who is paying an unusual amount of attention to their children or giving them inappropriate or expensive gifts.

- Teach their children that no one should approach them or touch them in a way that makes them feel uncomfortable. If someone does, they should tell parents or guardians immediately.

- Be careful about babysitters and any other individuals who have custody of their children. Babysitters should be selected for maturity, experience, and trustworthiness rather than convenience, proximity, and low cost.

- Keep a complete written description of their children (including hair, eye color, height, weight, date of birth, and specific physical attributes), take color photographs of their children every 6 months, ensure physician and dental records on their children are current, and arrange to have their children fingerprinted.

- Teach their children to be on the lookout for certain kinds of situations or actions rather than just certain kinds of individuals because abusers can be relatives, neighbors, friends, teachers, ministers, or strangers.

Children should:

- Know how to properly use pushbutton and dial telephones to make emergency, local, and long distance calls. They should memorize their name, address, telephone number, and parents' or guardians' work numbers.

- Be familiar with key phrases of their host country's language to enable them to communicate clearly in a time of crisis.

- Know how to answer the door and telephone when home alone. They should not let a caller at the door or on the telephone know they are home alone nor allow anyone into the home without asking permission to do so.

- Always ask their parents' or guardians' permission to leave the house, play area, or yard or to go into someone else's home.

- Understand how to operate door and window locks. However, they should not go into their home if the door is ajar or a window is broken.

- Play with a friend or in a group, try to use the buddy system, and never go places alone.

- Avoid isolated areas during the day and at night; stay in well-lit places when it is dark; and be cautious of elevators, parking lots, public restrooms, brokendown buildings, woods, and isolated fields.

- Be alert, walk confidently, pay attention to surroundings, and walk against the flow of traffic to prevent someone from following in a vehicle.

- Stay at least 15-20 feet from the door of a vehicle if someone stops to talk to them. They should never get into a car or go anywhere with any person unless they have the permission of a parent or guardian.

- Understand that no one should be asking them for directions or to help look for something, and no one should be telling them that a relative is in trouble and he or she will take them to the relative. If someone tries to take them somewhere, they should quickly get away from him or her and yell or scream "This person is trying to take me away" or "This person is not my father or mother."

- Know not to wander around if they get separated from their parent or guardian in a public place. They should go to a security office, checkout counter, or lost and found and quickly tell the person in charge they need help.

- Tell their parents or guardians if something happens that makes them feel uncomfortable or frightened in any way or if someone asks them to keep a secret, accept a gift, or pose for a picture.

- Be aware that no one should touch them on parts of the body that would be covered by a bathing suit.

If You Suspect Sexual Abuse

Young children usually do not lie about or make up the fact that have been abused. On the other hand, parents do not always believe a child who tries with a limited vocabulary to tell an experience he or she doesn't fully understand.

If you discover your child has been sexually abused, you will experience shock, outrage, and disbelief that such an experience has happened to your child. However, it is important that you try not to react too strongly, because your child's ability to cope with the abuse depends largely on how you react to the knowledge.

Knowledge of the possible changes a child might experience as a result of molestation gives parents an edge and ensures that these symptoms don't go unnoticed. No single sign is proof that there has

67

been abuse, but given groups of signals, you should be alerted that something may be wrong.

Possible physical signs include: vaginal discharge, bloody underpants, pain and itching in the genital area or genital injuries, difficulty walking or sitting.

Possible changes in behavior could include: sleep disturbances—nightmares, bedwetting, fear of sleeping, tiredness from lack of restful sleep; eating problems—loss of appetite, obesity, swallowing problems; fear of certain people or places; excessive masturbation; re-enactment of abuse using dolls, drawings, or friends; withdrawal, clinging, fear of separation.

Most children don't tell about sexual abuse because they are afraid they will be blamed, disbelieved, or even rejected by you. To protect themselves, and you, preschoolers often minimize the experience, repress the incident, and deny the pain. Your care in underreacting and assuring your child you believe and still love and trust him or her is essential to your child's healing.

What your child needs most at this critical time is your comfort, love, and support, and your reassurance that he or she is still okay—and that you're not angry with him or her. Underplay your own valid emotions of rage and injury.

If you suspect your child has been sexually abused, contact your doctor immediately. He or she will be able to recommend you to counseling professionals. Appropriate help can minimize the long-term effects of any unfortunate incidents in your child's life.

Child Abduction

Precautionary steps for parents and guardians:

- Maintain a complete identification packet on each child—including recent photographs, description, birthmarks, fingerprints, handwriting samples, voice and video recordings, and passport information.

- Teach each child a code word to indicate that the child is safe and being treated well in the event of kidnapping.

- Have on hand a complete checklist of what to do and who to contact during the initial stages of an abduction (for example, contact the Regional Security Officer, Corporation Security Director, or local police authority).

Steps parents and guardians should take if they receive a call that their child has been abducted:

- Remain calm, and maintain a cooperative but professional attitude.

- Request details of demands by caller, and identify to whom the demands are directed.

- Make a note of the caller's voice, background noise, and any other identifiable information.

- Tape record the conversation if possible.

- State that it will take time to meet the demands and to make appropriate private arrangements.

- Ask to speak with your child to know that he or she is alive. If this cannot be done, then ask a question that only your child would know the answer.

- Try to end the call on a positive note, no matter what the actual substance of the conversation. Assure the caller that his or her demands will be met.

- Dedicate the telephone number on which the call is received to receive any subsequent calls.

These are just some of the important safety and security issues facing those raising children abroad. Also, there will be other important issues unique to your location that you must consider. Ensuring that your children and those responsible for their care understand and follow safety and security practices is a never-ending job.

Notes

Chapter 6

Tips For Students Traveling or Studying Abroad

Introduction

So you are a student and you are preparing to travel abroad. You are not alone. Every year tens of thousands of American students travel overseas either unaccompanied by or in the company of their parents, friends or guardians. The purpose of these travels vary. Whereas some of the students go abroad to continue their education, in which case they take up semi-permanent residence; others go in search of summer jobs or as volunteers.

Whatever the reasons or motives for your trip, you will inevitably be exposed to the same type of problems often experienced by the majority of non-student Americans who travel abroad. This means that you should engage yourself in the same type of preparation and take the same general precautions suggested throughout this book. Like the rest of the population of Americans traveling abroad, you are concerned with security issues, health issues, time, as well as money saving opportunities. Ultimately, you want to have an exciting, safe and incident-free trip.

This book addresses precisely those issues aimed at enabling you to make a successful trip and, enabling to learn in particular, the things you need to know before you go. This theme has been echoed in several chapters throughout this book. I suggest, therefore, that you refer to the relevant chapters for those aspects of international travel that you may be interested in, that have not been addressed in this chapter.

In the course of my research and travels, I have come to appreciate the importance of a number of subjects of real interest to international student travelers. Few, if any, have matched the wishes of these students to learn about cost-saving opportunities to finance their trip. Of course, students are not alone in this category; except to say that a number of such opportunities, specifically limited to students, do exist, and

student travelers should know about them and take advantage of them.

First and foremost, you should avail yourself of the services of the Council on International Education Exchange (CIEE).

Founded in 1947, CIEE is a world-renowned organization known for its active promotion and sponsorship of International Education Exchange.

Today, CIEE services the interest of students, youths and teachers, assisting them in a variety of ways with study, hospitality and travel programs. In cooperation with member institutions world-wide, CIEE administers several study programs, including language programs, voluntary service opportunities for American students in Europe, and a variety of work camps for American and non-American youths, as well as exchange programs between secondary schools in the U.S. and in several countries of the world.

The budget-conscious student traveler may want to explore CIEE's international travel programs. CIEE distinguishes itself as a clearing house for information and services relating to all aspects of student travel. They arrange low cost transportation for individuals and groups, including students flights to Europe, Asia and various destinations in Latin America. Furthermore, CIEE provides information on low-cost hotel accommodations available to students overseas.

International Identification Cards

Further, CIEE issues a number of identification cards, including the International Student Identity Cards (ISIC), the International Teachers Identification (ITIC), and the Federation of International Youth Organization Cards (FIYTO). These cards are available from CIEE and other centers listed in the section of this chapter entitled

71

"Helping Hands". They usually have a one year expiration date, the cost is less than $20.00 each and they often require a passport photo 1 1/2 x 2 inches and some form of identification, such as a letter from your school, your grade report or transcript.

ADVANTAGES OF THE ISIC:

Although you may be able to receive just about the same services with your standard university or college I.D. card as those available to ISIC holders, the ISIC has the unique feature of being the most widely recognized proof of student status all over the world. As a holder of the ISIC, you will have access to a variety of money-saving discount opportunities and services, from airfare, bus, ferry and train rides to accommodations to museums and theaters. These money saving opportunities may not be advertised and may not be available in every country. Therefore, always initiate the request. Ask your travel or ticket agent if there are discounts available to students. If one exists, request to receive such discounts or considerations. Remember, "If You Don't Ask, You Don't Receive!" Do not forget to be polite and courteous; it could make the difference.

The other advantage of the ISIC is that, if bought in the United States, it also provides you with some amount of accident and health insurance, an important asset for every traveler going abroad.

Not the least of the ISIC advantages is its unique 'classy look'. Besides, the card serves as an important piece of identification, one that could become very useful in the event of an incident. That is the primary reason you should carry it with you at all times.

LODGING:

Finding suitable lodging overseas has not always been a problem, particularly if you have lots of money to spend. However for those on a limited budget this may not be so. Some avenues, nevertheless, exist for the budget-conscious student traveler. Some of these avenues may require some flexibility and tolerance on your part, while others may require long-term planning.

An alternative to hotels and pensions are the youth hostels. These hostels offer travelers of all ages clean, inexpensive, overnight accommodations in more than 6000 locations in over 70 countries world wide. Hostels provide dormitory-style accommodations with separate facilities for males and females. Some hostels have family rooms that can be reserved in advance. Curfews are often imposed, and membership is often required. For more information contact the American Youth Hostels, P.O. Box 37613, Washington, D.C. 20013-7613 or call (202) 783-4943. Some of the other agencies listed below in the section "Helping Hands" would be willing to assist you in finding inexpensive lodging. Should you, on the other hand, wish to use instead, a hotel or pension for lodging, present your ISIC or school I.D. card and request a discount. Who knows, they might be able to give you one.

The other alternative available to student budget travelers is to identify in the countries they plan to visit, a university or college with boarding facilities for its students, preferably, one located closest to your intended destination. Write to the "President of the Student Union/Organization/Council" of that institution requesting accommodations on campus, if possible. Your letter should explain briefly who you are, your school affiliation, your intended travel plans to that country (not your detailed day-to-day itinerary), the length of time for which you seek accommodation, and more important, that you are writing because you are traveling on a budget and do not have enough funds to cover your lodgings. Of course, you must have some funds, sufficient to subsist on for a few days in a hotel, but you do not want to include that in your request. If you succeed, that might provide you with a token gift to leave with your host or hostess. When carefully done, success with this plan has quite a number of advantages. Besides saving you money on lodging, you may be lucky enough to get free or discounted meals. As a special guest, you may have the opportunity to visit and explore many more exciting places than you probably would see in the absence of this type of accommodation.

The camaraderie created between you and your host/hostess, and their friends and relatives may provide just another opportunity for future trips at even cheaper costs.

Alternatively, you may consider renting a room in a nearby college or university (University Hostels). Several institutions abroad do have room and board facilities that are rented out to students and non-student travelers, during vacation time. The rates charged to students are usually lower than rates charged non-students. Inquiries should be directed to the Director of Housing at the respective institutions

There are, of course, several, other less conventional and cheap lodging facilities available to the international traveler. They include, farms, camps, road-side shelters and parks

Not withstanding which plans you chose, or which countries you visit, remember you are in a foreign country and that all of the precautions emphasized elsewhere in this book should be followed to safeguard your valuables, health and safety.

It is important, as with every American traveling abroad, to register immediately your presence with the Consular Section of the American Embassy immediately upon arrival. The usefulness of such registration has been stated and emphasized in elsewhere in this book.

For a country-by-country listing of foreign universities and other institutions of higher learning, including their addresses, consult your college or local public library.

USEFUL PUBLICATIONS
You will find the following publications helpful *Work, Study, Travel Abroad: The Whole World Handbook; The Teenager's Guide to Study, Travel and Adventure Abroad; The Student Travel Catalog* and *Volunteer*. These publications are produced by CIEE. The first two publications are available from CIEE and at many bookstores. The student travel catalog which is updated annually is offered free of charge. CIEE also distributes directories and brochures on foreign travel and study programs.

-LET'S GO SERIES of travel books published by Harvard Student Agencies, Inc. Cambridge, MA. (671) 495 9695. These travel books are widely available in bookstores across the country. Also check your local libraries.

Study Abroad, Published by UNESCO and *The World of Learning*, published by Europe Publications Ltd: These and other sources should be available in your local public or school library. You may, also, contact the respective education departments of the Embassies for a complete listing and location of institutions of higher learning with boarding facilities in their country.

HELPING HANDS (National and International Student Organizations)
The following organizations have a reputation for catering to the needs of students, youths and teachers traveling abroad.

They provide a wide range of services and products including bargain fares, discount travel guides, insurance, accommodation, international rail passes, and identification cards (ISIC, ITIC & FIYTO Cards). Write and request for information on their services.

Council on International Education Exchange (CIEE) 205 E. 42nd St., New York NY. 10017 (212) 661-1414. OTHER CIEE OFFICES are located in the following cities: Boston: 729 Boylston St., Boston, MA 02116. (617) 266-1926; Los Angeles: 1093 Broxton Ave., Los Angeles, CA 90024, (213) 208-3551; Chigago: 1153 N. Dearborn St., Chicago, IL 60610 (312) 951-0585; San Francisco: 919 Irvin St., San Francisco, CA 94122, (415) 566-9222, Austin : 2000 Guadelupe St. Austin TX 78705, (512) 472-4931.:The ISIC, ITIC and the YIYTO cards are administered by CIEE and are available from any of their offices.

Education Travel Center (ETC) 438 North Frances St. Madison, Wisconsin (608) 256-5551.

International Student Exchange Flights (ISE), 5010 East Shea Blvd. Suite A 104, Scottsdale, Arizona 85254. (602) 951-1177.

Let's Go Travel Services, Harvard Student Agencies Inc. Thayer Hall, B. Harvard University, Cambridge MA. 02138 (617) 495-9649.

Council Travel (is a subsidiary of CIEE. See CIEE

STA Travel, 17 East 45th St. New York, NY 10017 (800) 777-0112 or (212) 986-9470.

American Youth Hostels, P.O.Box 37613 Washington, D.C. 20013 (202) 783-4943.

Institute For Foreign Study (AIFS), 102 Greenwich Ave., Greenwich, CT 06830. (800) 727 AIFS or (203) 869-9090 or (203) 863-6087

Experiment in International Living, Kipling Rd., Brattleboro, VT. 05302, (800) 345-2929, or (802) 257-7751.

Institute of International Education, 809 United Nations Plaza, New York NY 10017, (800) 883-8200

* Your Student Office: Check with the student office of your institution. They may have valuable information, references and contacts that may save you both time and money. Some student offices do issue the ISIC card.

More Travel Tips For Students Traveling or Studying Abroad [from the U.S. Department of State]

Foreword

● *This section was to provide students, who are planning to travel or study abroad, with a few reminders about safety.*

● *Although most trips abroad are trouble free, being prepared will go a long way to avoiding the possibility of serious trouble.*

● *Become familiar with the basic laws and customs of the country you plan to visit before you travel.*

● *Remember: Reckless behavior while in another country can do more than ruin your vacation; it can land you in a foreign jail or worse! To have a safe trip, avoid risky behavior and plan ahead.*

Preparing for Your Trip Abroad

Apply early for your passport and, if necessary, any visas: Passports are required to enter and/or depart most countries around the world. Apply for a passport as soon as possible. Some countries also require U.S. citizens to obtain visas before entering. Most countries require visitors who are planning to study or work abroad to obtain visas

before entering. Check with the embassy of the foreign country that you are planning to visit for up-to-date visa and other entry requirements. (Passport and visa information is available on the Internet at http://travel.state.gov.)

Learn about the countries that you plan to visit. Before departing, take the time to do some research about the people and their culture, and any problems that the country is experiencing that may affect your travel plans. The Department of State publishes Background Notes on about 170 countries. These brief, factual pamphlets contain information on each country's culture, history, geography, economy, government, and current political situation. Background Notes are available at www.state.gov.

Read the Consular Information Sheet. Consular Information Sheets provide up-to-date travel information on any country in the world that you plan to visit. They cover topics such as entry regulations, the crime and security situation, drug penalties, road conditions, and the location of the U.S. embassy, consulates, and consular agencies.

Check for Travel Warnings and Public Announcements. Travel Warnings recommend U.S. citizens defer travel to a country because of dangerous conditions. Public Announcements provide fast-breaking information about relatively short-term conditions that may pose risks to the security of travelers.

Find out the location of the nearest U.S. embassy or consulate. If you are traveling to a remote area or one that is experiencing civil unrest, find out the location of the nearest U.S. embassy or consulate and register with the Consular Section when you arrive. (U.S. embassy and consulate locations can be found in the country's Consular Information Sheet.) If your family needs to reach you because of an emergency, they can pass a message to you through the Office of Overseas Citizens Services at 202-647-5225. This office will contact the embassy or consulate in the country where you are traveling and pass a message from your family to you. Remember consular officers cannot cash checks, lend money or serve as your attorney. They can, however, if the need arises, assist you in obtaining emergency funds from your family, help you find an attorney, help you find medical assistance, and replace your lost or stolen passport.

Find out what information your school offers. Find out whether your school offers additional information for students who are planning to study, travel, or work abroad. Many student advisors can provide you with information about studying or working abroad. They may also be able to provide you with information on any travel benefits for students (e.g. how to save money on transportation and accommodations, and other resources.)

Before committing yourself or your finances, find out about the organization and what it offers. The majority of private programs for vacation, study or work abroad are reputable and financially sound. However, some charge exorbitant fees, use deliberately false "educational" claims, and provide working conditions far different from those advertised. Even programs of legitimate organizations can be poorly administered.

How to Access Consular Information Sheets, Travel Warnings, and Public Announcements

There are four ways to obtain *Consular Information Sheets, Travel Warnings,* and *Public Announcements*:

- *Internet:* http://travel.state.gov
- *Telephone:* Dial the Office of Overseas Citizens Services at 202-647-5225.
- *Mail:* Send a self-addressed, stamped business-size envelope to: Overseas Citizens Services, Room 4811, Department of State, Washington, DC 20520-4818. On the outside envelope, write the name of the country or countries needed in the lower left corner.
- Also available at http://travel.state.gov: passport applications and procedures, foreign and U.S. visa information, travel publications (including the pamphlet *Travel Warning on Drugs Abroad)*, links to several U.S. embassy and consulate web sites worldwide, and other sources of information for students.

Top Ten Travel Tips for Students

1. Make sure you have a signed, valid passport and visas, if required. Also, before you go, fill in the emergency information page of your passport!
2. Read the Consular Information Sheets (and Public Announcements or Travel Warnings, if applicable) for the countries you plan to visit.
3. Leave copies of your itinerary, passport data page and visas with family or friends at home, so that you can be contacted in case of an emergency. Keep your host program informed of your whereabouts.
4. Make sure you have insurance that will cover your emergency medical needs (including medical evacuation) while you are overseas.
5. Familiarize yourself with local laws and customs of the countries to which you are traveling. Remember, while in a foreign country, you are subject to its laws!
6. Do not leave your luggage unattended in public areas and never accept packages from strangers.
7. While abroad, avoid using illicit drugs or drinking excessive amounts of alcoholic beverages, and associating with people who do.
8. Do not become a target for thieves by wearing conspicuous clothing and expensive jewelry and do not carry excessive amounts of cash or unnecessary credit cards.
9. Deal only with authorized agents when you exchange money to avoid violating local laws.
10. When overseas, avoid demonstrations and other situations that may become unruly or where anti-American sentiments may be expressed.

STUDENTS SHOULD LEARN AS MUCH AS POSSIBLE ABOUT THE COUNTRIES IN WHICH THEY PLAN TO TRAVEL OR STUDY

- Students should read the State Department's Consular Information Sheet for the country in which they plan

75

to study or visit, and check any Public Announcements or Travel Warnings that may pertain to that particular country. A Consular Information Sheet is available for every country in the world and provides an overview of conditions pertaining to travel in each country.

- Students to learn about the history, culture, politics and customs of the country/countries in which they travel and study, and to respect the country's customs, manners, rules and laws. For instance, various countries and cultures respect certain manners and dress codes. American students should also abide by these manners and dress codes as much as possible.

- It is a good idea for students to learn as much as they can of the language of the country in which they plan to travel or study. Learning basic phrases of the language can be helpful, and it indicates a willingness on the part of students to make an effort to communicate in the language of the country.

- The Department of State publishes *Background Notes* on countries worldwide. These are brief, factual pamphlets with information on each country's culture, history, geography, economy, government and current political situation. *Background Notes* are available for approximately 170 countries. They often include a reading list, travel notes and maps.

- It is important that students learn about the local laws abroad and obey them. **Remember, while in a foreign country, you are subject to its laws!** This year, the State Department has issued a spring break fact sheet for the Bahamas and two press releases: a press release for college newspapers on travel safety abroad for students and a press release on spring break in Cancun, reminding students about drug laws and drunk and disorderly conduct during spring and summer breaks.

WHAT STUDENTS NEED TO KNOW ABOUT OBTAINING PASSPORTS AND VISAS TO TRAVEL, STUDY AND OR WORK ABROAD

- Students must have a signed, valid passport and visas, if required. Students studying abroad must be sure that they have the proper visa to study there. A visitors visa or entry without a visa may not allow one to study. Refer to our *Foreign Entry Requirements* brochure for information on foreign visas and to *Your Trip Abroad* for U.S. passport information.

- Students should remember to fill in the emergency information page of their passport.

- It is a good idea for relatives of students abroad to obtain and maintain a valid passport as well, in case of an emergency requiring them to travel.

- Students who wish to work part-time in conjunction with their studies or when their studies are finished, should make sure that they understand the laws that apply and comply with them.

- The United States requires student visas for study in the United States.

- Students should make copies of their passport's data page and any visas. They should keep a copy separately from the originals while traveling and leave one at home with their family and with their student advisor. This will help to obtain a replacement passport in the event that a passport is lost or stolen. Refer to our brochure *Your Trip Abroad* for more information on U.S. passports.

- Students are encouraged to travel with extra photos, in case they need to get a new passport quickly. Refer to our brochures *Passports-Applying for Them the Easy Way* and *Your Trip Abroad* for more information.

STUDENTS SHOULD LEARN ABOUT MEDICAL INSURANCE AND EVACUATION INSURANCE IN CASE OF A MEDICAL EMERGENCY ABROAD

Every year, hundreds of students become ill or suffer injuries overseas. It is essential that students have medical insurance and medical evacuation insurance that would cover a medical emergency abroad. For further information, see our flyer on *Medical Information for Americans Traveling Abroad*, *Your Trip Abroad* and visit the Centers for Disease Control and Prevention's web site at http://www.cdc.gov.

STUDENTS ARE ENCOURAGED TO KNOW THE LOCATION OF THE NEAREST U.S. EMBASSY OR CONSULATE AND TO REGISTER

If students are going to be in a country for more than a couple of weeks, they should to register at the American Embassy or Consulate. This is helpful to students and their families, if there is need to locate family members in the event of an emergency. See our links to U.S. embassies and consulates worldwide.

WHAT U.S. CONSULAR OFFICERS *CAN* AND *CAN NOT* DO TO HELP U.S. CITIZENS ABROAD

- If students find themselves in trouble overseas, the Consular Officer at the nearest U.S. embassy or consulate can provide certain assistance and advice. Consular Officers can also help in the event of illness, injury, natural catastrophe, evacuations, destitution, or death. See our brochures *Crisis Abroad*, *U.S. Consuls Help Americans Abroad* and *Overseas Citizens Services* for more information.

- In the United States, the Office of Overseas Citizens Services can also assist American students abroad and their families in the USA in emergency cases. There is a 24 hour number to call (202) 647-5225.

- There are certain things that consular officers at American embassies **CAN NOT** for American citizens abroad. For example, they can not cash checks, lend money or serve as your attorney. See our brochure *U.S. Consuls Help Americans Abroad*

GENERAL PRECAUTIONS THAT STUDENTS SHOULD TAKE WHILE TRAVELING OR STUDYING ABROAD

- Remember not to leave luggage unattended and not to carry packages for anyone. The packages could contain drugs or other illegal items. Refer to

our brochure *Travel Warning on Drugs Abroad.*

- Do not become a target for thieves by wearing conspicuous clothing and expensive looking jewelry.—

There are restrictions on photography in certain countries. Students should check the Consular Information Sheet for the countries where they plan to visit or travel. -- Students should avoid demonstrations or civil disturbances, which could turn violent. Demonstrations could also turn anti-American.

- The Department of State is engaged in outreach efforts to education-related organizations to publicize road safety risks in other countries. Students, who may chose less expensive, often less reliable methods of local travel while in foreign countries, should be aware of the potential danger.

OTHER SOURCES OF INFORMATION FOR STUDENTS. [For links on the web, Go to http://travel.state.gov/studentinfo.html]

U.S. Department of State
Important Telephone Numbers
Services and Information for American Citizens Abroad
How Consular Officers Can Help In An Emergency
Centers for Disease Control and Prevention
NAFSA Home Page
Center for Global Education
students.gov
Department of Education's USNEI-U.S. Study Abroad Programs
USNEI-Foreign Students Visiting the United States
Council on International Educational Exchange for information on international study programs, international student ID cards, etc.
International Youth Hostel
International Student ID Card
Peace Corps
The University of Southern California (USC) has information on Personal Safety and Adjustment Abroad, Crisis and Risk Management and Crime and Violence Abroad.

77

Foreign Embassies in the United States

[For a complete listing of foreign embassies in the United States see **Appendix B**].

United States Embassies and Consulates Abroad

[For a complete listing of United States embassies and consulates abroad, including their addresses, telephone, fax, and telex numbers see **Appendix A**].

Planning Another Trip?

See Chapter 25 for a listing of resources available to the general traveler from the U.S. Departments of State, Customs, Transportation, Health and various government and non-government organizations. Almost all of the available International travel-related pamphlets, brochures and publications issued by the U.S. Department of State and by the U.S. Customs have been reproduced in full in this book. See Table of Contents for location.

Chapter 7

Nationality & Citizenship Issues

[The information in this chapter is reprinted verbatim from a number of bulletins issued by the U.S. State Department, Bureau of Consular Affairs. It is intended to serve as advice to Americans traveling abroad.]

Dual Nationality

The concept of dual nationality means that a person is a citizen of two countries at the same time. Each country has its own citizenship laws based on its own policy. Persons may have dual nationality by automatic operation of different laws rather than by choice. For example, a child born in a foreign country to U.S. citizen parents may be both a U.S. citizen and a citizen of the country of birth.

A U.S. citizen may acquire foreign citizenship by marriage, or a person naturalized as a U.S. citizen may not lose the citizenship of the country of birth. U.S. law does not mention dual nationality or require a person to choose one citizenship or another. Also, a person who is automatically granted another citizenship does not risk losing U.S. citizenship. However, a person who acquires a foreign citizenship by applying for it may lose U.S. citizenship. In order to lose U.S. citizenship, the law requires that the person must apply for the foreign citizenship voluntarily, by free choice, and with the intention to give up U.S. citizenship.

Intent can be shown by the person's statements or conduct. The U.S. Government recognizes that dual nationality exists but does not encourage it as a matter of policy because of the problems it may cause. Claims of other countries on dual national U.S. citizens may conflict with U.S. law, and dual nationality may limit U.S. Government efforts to assist citizens abroad. The country where a dual national is located generally has a stronger claim to that person's allegiance.

However, dual nationals owe allegiance to both the United States and the foreign country. They are required to obey the laws of both countries. Either country has the right to enforce its laws, particularly if the person later travels there. Most U.S. citizens, including dual nationals, must use a U.S. passport to enter and leave the United States. Dual nationals may also be required by the foreign country to use its passport to enter and leave that country. Use of the foreign passport does not endanger U.S. citizenship. Most countries permit a person to renounce or otherwise lose citizenship.

Information on losing foreign citizenship can be obtained from the foreign country's embassy and consulates in the United States. Americans can renounce U.S. citizenship in the proper form at U.S. embassies and consulates abroad.

ADVICE ABOUT POSSIBLE LOSS OF U.S. CITIZENSHIP AND DUAL NATIONALITY

The Department of State is responsible for determining the citizenship status of a person located outside the United States or in connection with the application for a U.S. passport while in the United States.

POTENTIALLY EXPATRIATING STATUTES

Section 349 of the Immigration and Nationality Act, as amended, states that U.S. citizens are subject to loss of citizenship if they perform certain acts voluntarily and with the intention to relinquish U.S. citizenship. Briefly stated, these acts include:

(1) obtaining naturalization in a foreign state (Sec. 349 (a) (1) INA);

(2) taking an oath, affirmation or other formal declaration to a foreign state or its political subdivisions (Sec. 349 (a) (2) INA);

(3) entering or serving in the armed forces of a foreign state engaged in hostilities against the U.S. or serving as a commissioned or non-commissioned officer in the armed forces of a foreign state (Sec. 349 (a) (3) INA);

(4) accepting employment with a foreign government if (a) one has the nationality of that foreign state or (b) a declaration of allegiance is required in accepting the position (Sec. 349 (a) (4) INA);

(5) formally renouncing U.S. citizenship before a U.S. consular officer outside the United States (sec. 349 (a) (5) INA);

(6) formally renouncing U.S. citizenship within the U.S. (but only "in time of war") (Sec. 349 (a) (6) INA);

(7) conviction for an act of treason (Sec. 349 (a) (7) INA).

ADMINISTRATIVE STANDARD OF EVIDENCE

As already noted, the actions listed above can cause loss of U.S. citizenship only if performed voluntarily and with the intention of relinquishing U.S. citizenship. *The Department has a uniform administrative standard of evidence based on the premise that U.S. citizens intend to retain United States citizenship when they obtain naturalization in a foreign state, subscribe to routine declarations of allegiance to a foreign state, or accept non-policy level employment with a foreign government.*

DISPOSITION OF CASES WHEN ADMINISTRATIVE PREMISE IS APPLICABLE

In light of the administrative premise discussed above, a person who:

(1) is naturalized in a foreign country;

(2) takes a routine oath of allegiance or

(3) accepts non-policy level employment with a foreign government

and in so doing wishes to retain U.S. citizenship need not submit prior to the commission of a potentially expatriating act a statement or evidence of his or her intent to retain U.S. citizenship since such an intent will be presumed.

When, as the result of an individual's inquiry or an individual's application for registration or a passport it comes to the attention of a U.S. consular officer that a U.S. citizen has performed an act made potentially expatriating by Sections 349(a)(1), 349(a)(2), 349(a)(3) or 349(a)(4), the consular officer will simply ask the applicant if there was intent to relinquish U.S. citizenship when performing the act. If the answer is no, the consular officer will certify that it was **not** the person's intent to relinquish U.S. citizenship and, consequently, find that the person has retained U.S. citizenship.

PERSONS WHO WISH TO RELINQUISH U.S. CITIZENSHIP

If the answer to the question regarding intent to relinquish citizenship is **yes**, the person concerned will be asked to complete a questionnaire to ascertain his or her intent toward U.S. citizenship. When the questionnaire is completed and the voluntary relinquishment statement is signed by the expatriate, the consular officer will proceed to prepare a certificate of loss of nationality. The certificate will be forwarded to the Department of State for consideration and, if appropriate, approval.

An individual who has performed **any** of the acts made potentially expatriating by statute who wishes to lose U.S. citizenship may do so by affirming in writing to a U.S. consular officer that the act was performed with an intent to relinquish U.S. citizenship. Of course, a person always has the option of seeking to formally renounce U.S. citizenship in accordance with Section 349 (a) (5) INA.

DISPOSITION OF CASES WHEN ADMINISTRATIVE PREMISE IS INAPPLICABLE

The premise that a person intends to retain U.S. citizenship is **not** applicable when the individual:

(1) formally renounces U.S. citizenship before a consular officer;

(2) takes a policy level position in a foreign state;

(3) is convicted of treason; or

(4) performs an act made potentially expatriating by statute accompanied by conduct which is so inconsistent with retention of U.S. citizenship that it compels a conclusion that the individual intended to relinquish U.S. citizenship. (Such cases are very rare.)

Cases in categories 2, 3, and 4 will be developed carefully by U.S. consular officers to ascertain the individual's intent toward U.S. citizenship.

APPLICABILITY OF ADMINISTRATIVE PREMISE TO PAST CASES

The premise established by the administrative standard of evidence is applicable to cases adjudicated previously. Persons who previously lost U.S. citizenship may wish to have their cases reconsidered in light of this policy.

A person may initiate such a reconsideration by submitting a request to the nearest U.S. consular office or by writing directly to:

Director
Office of American Citizens Services
(CA/OCS/ACS)
Room 4817 NS
Department of State
2201 C Street N.W.
Washington, D.C. 20520
Each case will be reviewed on its own merits taking into consideration, for example, statements made by the person at the time of the potentially expatriating act.

LOSS OF NATIONALITY AND TAXATION

P.L. 104-191 contains changes in the taxation of U.S. citizens who renounce or otherwise lose U.S. citizenship. In general, any person who lost U.S. citizenship within 10 years immediately preceding the close of the taxable year, whose principle purpose in losing citizenship was to avoid taxation, will be subject to continued taxation. For the purposes of this statute, persons are presumed to have a principle purpose of avoiding taxation if 1) their average annual net income tax for a five year period before the date of loss of citizenship is

greater than $100,000, or 2) their net worth on the date of the loss of U.S. nationality is $500,000 or more (subject to cost of living adjustments). The effective date of the law is retroactive to February 6, 1995. Copies of approved Certificates of Loss of Nationality are provided by the Department of State to the Internal Revenue Service pursuant to P.L. 104-191. Questions regarding United States taxation consequences upon loss of U.S. nationality, should be addressed to the U.S. Internal Revenue Service.

DUAL NATIONALITY

Dual nationality can occur as the result of a variety of circumstances. The automatic acquisition or retention of a foreign nationality, acquired, for example, by birth in a foreign country or through an alien parent, does not affect U.S. citizenship. It is prudent, however, to check with authorities of the other country to see if dual nationality is permissible under local law. Dual nationality can also occur when a person is naturalized in a foreign state without intending to relinquish U.S. nationality and is thereafter found not to have lost U.S. citizenship the individual consequently may possess dual nationality. While recognizing the existence of dual nationality and permitting Americans to have other nationalities, the U.S. Government does not endorse dual nationality as a matter of policy because of the problems which it may cause. Claims of other countries upon dual-national U.S. citizens often place them in situations where their obligation to one country are in conflict with the laws of the other. In addition, their dual nationality may hamper efforts to provide U.S. diplomatic and consular protection to them when they are abroad.

ADDITIONAL INFORMATION

See also information flyers on related subject available via the Department of State, Bureau of Consular Affairs home page on the internet at http://travel.state.gov or via our automated fax service at 202-647-3000. These flyers include:

- Dual Nationality
- Advice About Possible Loss of U.S. Citizenship and Seeking Public Office in a Foreign State
- Advice About Possible Loss of U.S. Citizenship and Foreign Military Service
- Renunciation of United States Citizenship

81

- Renunciation of U.S. Citizenship by Persons Claiming a Right of Residence in the United States

QUESTIONS

For further information, please contact the appropriate geographic division of the Office of American Citizens Services:

Africa Division at (202) 647-6060;
East Asia and Pacific Division at (202) 647-6769;
Europe Division at (202) 647-6178;
Latin America and the Caribbean Division at (202) 647-5118;
Near East and South Asia Division at (202) 647-7899.

Counsel representing persons in matters related to loss of U.S. nationality may also address inquiries to Director, Office of Policy Review and Inter-Agency Liaison, Overseas Citizens Services, Room 4817 N.S., Department of State, 2201 C Street N.W., Washington, D.C. 20520, 202-647-3666.

ADVICE ABOUT POSSIBLE LOSS OF U.S. CITIZENSHIP AND SEEKING PUBLIC OFFICE IN A FOREIGN STATE

DISCLAIMER: THE INFORMATION IN THIS CIRCULAR IS PROVIDED FOR GENERAL INFORMATION ONLY. QUESTIONS INVOLVING INTERPRETATION OF SECTION 349(A)(4) INA WITH RESPECT TO A PARTICULAR CASE SHOULD BE ADDRESSED TO THE BUREAU OF CONSULAR AFFAIRS' OFFICE OF POLICY REVIEW AND INTERAGENCY LIAISON.

The Department of State is the U.S. government agency responsible for determining whether a person located outside the United States is a U.S. citizen or national. A U.S. citizen who assumes foreign public office may come within the loss of nationality statute, which is Section 349 of the Immigration and Nationality Act of 1952 (INA), as amended, or other legal provisions as discussed below.

Currently, there is no general prohibition on U.S. citizens' running for an elected office in a foreign government. Under Article 1, section 9, clause 8 of the U.S. Constitution, however, U.S. federal government officers may not accept foreign government employment without the consent of Congress. In addition, certain retired and reserve U.S. uniformed personnel may not accept foreign government positions without the express permission of the Secretary of State and the Secretary of their department. These restrictions are reflected in the Department's regulations at 22 CFR Part 3a., and are based on 37 U.S.C. 801 Note; 22 U.S.C.2658.

With respect to loss of nationality, 349(a)(4) of the Immigration and Nationality Act (INA), as amended, is the applicable section of law. Pursuant to 349(a)(4), accepting, serving in, or performing duties of in a foreign government is a potentially expatriating act. In order to come within the Act, the person must either be a national of that country or take an oath of allegiance in connection with the position. Thus, the threshold question is whether the person's actions fall within the scope of this provision. Information used to make this determination may include official confirmation from the foreign government about the person's nationality, and whether an oath of allegiance is required.

In addition, the prefatory language of section 349 requires that expatriating act be performed voluntarily and "with the intention of relinquishing U.S. nationality." Thus, if it is determined that the person's action falls within the purview of 349(a)(4) INA, an adjudication of the person's intent must be made.

The Department has a uniform administrative standard of evidence based on the premise that U.S. citizens intend to retain U.S. citizenship when they obtain naturalization in a foreign state, subscribe to routine declarations of allegiance to a foreign state, or accept non-policy level employment with a foreign government. This administrative premise is not applicable when an individual seeks public office in a foreign state, instead, the Department of State will carefully ascertain the individual's intent toward U.S. citizenship.

Because the Department's administrative practice presumes that U.S. citizens employed in non-policy level positions in a foreign government do not have the requisite intent to relinquish U.S. citizenship, there are no efforts to seek out or adjudicate the citizenship of citizens who fall into this category of employment. On the other hand, because there is no administrative presumption that U.S. citizens who hold policy-level positions in foreign governments necessarily intend to retain their U.S. citizenship, efforts are made to fully adjudicate such cases to determine the individual's intent. (Service in a country's legislative body is considered by the Department to be a policy level position.)

An Attorney General's opinion of 1969 states that service in an important foreign political position constitutes highly persuasive evidence of intent to relinquish U.S. citizenship. In some cases, it would appear that holding a foreign office may be incompatible with maintaining U.S. citizenship (e.g. if the position necessarily entails immunity from U.S. law). The Department does not normally consider such service alone, as sufficient to sustain the burden of showing loss of U.S. citizenship by a preponderance of the evidence when the individual has explicitly expressed a contrary intent. This is particularly true when the individual continues to file U.S. tax returns, enters and leaves the U.S. on a U.S. passport, maintains close ties in the U.S. (such as maintaining a residence in the U.S.), and takes other actions consistent with an intent to retain U.S. citizenship notwithstanding the assumption of a foreign government position. Conversely, a person who publicly denied an intent to retain citizenship or who stopped paying his/her taxes, traveled to the United States on a foreign passport, and abandoned any residence in the United States might be found to have intended to relinquish U.S. citizenship notwithstanding self-serving statements to the contrary. Therefore, the Department will consider statements, as well as inferences drawn from the person's conduct, in determining one's intent to remain a U.S. citizen. Intent is determined on a case-by-case basis in light of the facts and circumstances of each individual's case. If expressed intent and conduct are consistent with a lack of intent to relinquish U.S. citizenship, the Department would generally conclude that no loss has occurred.

For further information about possible loss of U.S. citizenship and seeking public office in a foreign state, please contact:

Director
Office of Policy Review and Interagency Liaison

CA/OCS/PRI Room 4817 MS
U.S. Department of State
2201 C Street, NW
Washington, D.C. 20520-4818
(202) 647-3666

ADVICE ABOUT POSSIBLE LOSS OF U.S. CITIZENSHIP AND FOREIGN MILITARY SERVICE

A U.S. citizen who is a resident or citizen of a foreign country may be subject to compulsory military service in that country. Although the United States opposes service by U.S. citizens in foreign armed forces, there is little that we can do to prevent it since each sovereign country has the right to make its own laws on military service and apply them as it sees fit to its citizens and residents.

Such participation by citizens of our country in the internal affairs of foreign countries can cause problems in the conduct of our foreign relations and may involve U.S. citizens in hostilities against countries with which we are at peace. For this reason, U.S. citizens facing the possibility of foreign military service should do what is legally possible to avoid such service.

Federal statutes long in force prohibit certain aspects of foreign military service originating within the United States. The current laws are set forth in Section 958-960 of Title 18 of the United States Code. In *Wiborg v. U.S.*, 163 U.S. 632 (1985), the Supreme Court endorsed a lower court ruling that it was not a crime under U.S. law for an individual to go abroad for the purpose of enlisting in a foreign army; however, when someone has been recruited or hired in he United States, a violation may have occurred. The prosecution of persons who have violated 18 U.S.C. 958-960 is the responsibility of the Department of Justice.

Although a person's enlistment in the armed forces of a foreign country may not constitute a violation of U.S. law, it could subject him or her to Section 349(a)(3) of the Immigration and Nationality Act [8 U.S.C. 1481(a)(3)] which provides for loss of U.S. nationality if an American voluntarily and with the intention of relinquishing U.S. citizenship enters or serves in foreign armed forces engaged in hostilities against the United States or serves in the armed forces of any foreign country as a commissioned or non-commissioned officer.

Loss of U.S. nationality was almost immediate consequences of foreign military service and the other acts listed in Section 349(a) until 1967 when the Supreme Court handed down its decision in *Afroyim v. Rusk*, 387 U.S. 253. In that decision, the court declared unconstitutional the provisions of Section 349(a) which provided for loss of nationality by voting in a foreign election. In so doing, the Supreme Court indicated foreign election. In so doing, the Supreme Court indicated that a U.S. citizen "has a constitutional right to remain a citizen... unless he voluntarily relinquishes that citizenship."

Further confirmation of the necessity to establish the citizen's intent to relinquish nationality before expatriation will result came in the opinion in *Vance v. Terrazas*, 444 U.S. 252 (1980). The Court stated that "expatriation depends on the will of the citizen rather than on the will of Congress and its assessment of his conduct." The Court also indicated that a person's intention to relinquish U.S. citizenship may be shown by statements or actions.

Military service in foreign countries usually does not cause loss of citizenship since an intention to relinquish citizenship normally is lacking. Service as a high-ranking officer, particularly in a policy-making position, could be viewed as indicative of an intention to relinquish U.S. citizenship.

Pursuant to Section 351(b) of the Immigration and Nationality Act, a person who served in foreign armed forces while under the age of eighteen is not considered subject to the provisions of Section 349(a)(3) if, within six months of attaining the age of eighteen, he or she asserts a claim to United States citizenship in the manner prescribed by the Secretary of State.

LOSS OF NATIONALITY AND TAXATION

P.L. 104-191 contains changes in the taxation of U.S. citizens who renounce or otherwise lose U.S. citizenship. In general, any person who lost U.S. citizenship within 10 years immediately preceding the close of the taxable year, whose principle purpose in losing citizenship was to avoid taxation, will be subject to continued taxation. For the

purposes of this statute, persons are presumed to have a principle purpose of avoiding taxation if 1) their average annual net income tax for a five year period before the date of loss of citizenship is greater than $100,000, or 2) their net worth on the date of the loss of U.S. nationality is $500,000 or more (subject to cost of living adjustments). The effective date of the law is retroactive to February 6, 1995. Copies of approved Certificates of Loss of Nationality are provided by the Department of State to the Internal Revenue Service pursuant to P.L. 104-191. Questions regarding United States taxation consequences upon loss of U.S. nationality, should be addressed to the U.S. Internal Revenue Service.

ADDITIONAL INFORMATION

See also information flyers on related subject available via the Department of State, Bureau of Consular Affairs home page on the internet at http://travel.state.gov or via our automated fax service at 202-647-3000. These flyers include:

- Dual Nationality
- Advice About Possible Loss of U.S. Citizenship and Seeking Public Office in a Foreign State
- Advice About Possible Loss of U.S. Citizenship and Foreign Military Service
- Renunciation of United States Citizenship
- Renunciation of U.S. Citizenship by Persons Claiming a Right of Residence in the United States

QUESTIONS

For further information, please contact the appropriate geographic division of the Office of American Citizens Services:

Africa Division at (202) 647-6060;
East Asia and Pacific Division at (202) 647-6769;
Europe Division at (202) 647-6178;
Latin America and the Caribbean Division at (202) 647-5118;
Near East and South Asia Division at (202) 647-7899.

Counsel representing persons in matters related to loss of U.S. nationality may also address inquiries to Director, Office of Policy Review and Inter-Agency Liaison, Overseas Citizens Services,

Room 4817 N.S., Department of State, 2201 C Street N.W., Washington, D.C. 20520, 202-647-3666.

Acquisition of U.S. Citizenship By a Child Born Abroad

Birth Abroad to Two U.S. Citizen Parents in Wedlock: A child born abroad to two U.S. citizen parents acquires U.S. citizenship at birth under section 301(c) of the Immigration and Nationality Act (INA). One of the parents MUST have resided in the U.S. prior to the child's birth. No specific period of time for such prior residence is required.

Birth Abroad to One Citizen and One Alien Parent in Wedlock: A child born abroad to one U.S. citizen parent and one alien parent acquires U.S. citizenship at birth under Section 301(g) INA provided the citizen parent was physically present in the U.S. for the time period required by the law applicable at the time of the child's birth. (For birth on or after November 14, 1986, a period of five years physical presence, two after the age of fourteen is required. For birth between December 24, 1952 and November 13, 1986, a period of ten years, five after the age of fourteen are required for physical presence in the U.S. to transmit U.S. citizenship to the child.

Birth Abroad Out-of-Wedlock to a U.S. Citizen Father: A child born abroad out-of-wedlock to a U.S. citizen father may acquire U.S. citizenship under Section 301(g) INA, as made applicable by Section 309(a) INA provided:

1) a blood relationship between the applicant and the father is established by clear and convincing evidence;
2) the father had the nationality of the United States at the time of the applicant's birth;
3) the father (unless deceased) had agreed in writing to provide financial support for the person until the applicant reaches the age of 18 years, and
4) while the person is under the age of 18 years --
A) applicant is legitimated under the law of their residence or domicile,
B) father acknowledges paternity of the person in writing under oath, or
C) the paternity of the applicant is established by adjudication court.

Birth Abroad Out-of-Wedlock to a U.S. Citizen

Mother: A child born abroad out-of-wedlock to a U.S. citizen mother may acquire U.S. citizenship under Section 301(g) INA, as made applicable by Section 309(c) INA if the mother was a U.S. citizen at the time of the child's birth, and if the mother had previously been physically present in the United States or one of its outlying possessions for a continuous period of one year. 1997

Renunciation of U.S. Citizenship

A. THE IMMIGRATION & NATIONALITY ACT

Section 349(a)(5) of the Immigration and Nationality Act (INA) is the section of law that governs the ability of a United States citizen to renounce his or her U.S. citizenship. That section of law provides for the loss of nationality by voluntarily performing the following act with the intent to relinquish his or her U.S. nationality:

> "(5) making a formal renunciation of nationality before a diplomatic or consular officer of the United States *in a foreign state*, in such form as may be prescribed by the Secretary of State" (emphasis added).

B. ELEMENTS OF RENUNCIATION

A person wishing to renounce his or her U.S. citizenship must voluntarily and with intent to relinquish U.S. citizenship:

11. appear in person before a U.S. consular or diplomatic officer,
12. in a foreign country (normally at a U.S. Embassy or Consulate); and
13. sign an oath of renunciation
14.

Renunciations that do not meet the conditions described above have no legal effect. Because of the provisions of section 349(a)(5), Americans cannot effectively renounce their citizenship by mail, through an agent, or while in the United States. In fact, U.S. courts have held certain attempts to renounce U.S. citizenship to be ineffective on a variety of grounds, as discussed below.

C. REQUIREMENT - RENOUNCE ALL RIGHTS AND PRIVILEGES

In the recent case of Colon v. U.S. Department of State, 2 F.Supp.2d 43 (1998), plaintiff was a United States citizen and resident of Puerto Rico, who executed an oath of renunciation before a

85

consular officer at the U.S. Embassy in Santo Domingo. The U.S. District Court for the District of Columbia rejected Colon's petition for a writ of mandamus directing the Secretary of State to approve a Certificate of Loss of Nationality in the case because the plaintiff wanted to retain one of the primary benefits of U.S. citizenship while claiming he was not a U.S. citizen. The Court described the plaintiff as a person, "claiming to renounce all rights and privileges of United States citizenship, [while] Plaintiff wants to continue to exercise one of the fundamental rights of citizenship, namely to travel freely throughout the world and when he wants to, return and reside in the United States." See also Jose Fufi Santori v. United States of America, 1994 U.S. App. LEXIS 16299 (1994) for a similar case.

A person who wants to renounce U.S. citizenship cannot decide to retain some of the privileges of citizenship, as this would be logically inconsistent with the concept of citizenship. Thus, such a person can be said to lack a full understanding of renouncing citizenship and/or lack the necessary intent to renounce citizenship, and the Department of State will not approve a loss of citizenship in such instances.

D. DUAL NATIONALITY / STATELESSNESS

Persons intending to renounce U.S. citizenship should be aware that, unless they already possess a foreign nationality, they may be rendered stateless and, thus, lack the protection of any government. They may also have difficulty traveling as they may not be entitled to a passport from any country. Even if they were not stateless, they would still be required to obtain a visa to travel to the United States, or show that they are eligible for admission pursuant to the terms of the Visa Waiver Pilot Program (VWPP). If found ineligible for a visa or the VWPP to come to the U.S., a renunciant, under certain circumstances, could be permanently barred from entering the United States. Nonetheless, renunciation of U.S. citizenship may not prevent a foreign country from deporting that individual back to the United States in some non-citizen status.

E. TAX & MILITARY OBLIGATIONS /NO ESCAPE FROM PROSECUTION

Also, persons who wish to renounce U.S. citizenship should also be aware that the fact that a person has renounced U.S. citizenship may have no effect whatsoever on his or her U.S. tax or military service obligations (contact the Internal Revenue Service or U.S. Selective Service for more information). In addition, the act of renouncing U.S. citizenship will not allow persons to avoid possible prosecution for crimes which they may have committed in the United States, or escape the repayment of financial obligations previously incurred in the United States.

F. RENUNCIATION FOR MINOR CHILDREN

Parents cannot renounce U.S. citizenship on behalf of their minor children. Before an oath of renunciation will be administered under Section 349(a)(5) of the INA, a person under the age of eighteen must convince a U.S. diplomatic or consular officer that he/she fully understands the nature and consequences of the oath of renunciation and is voluntarily seeking to renounce his/her U.S. citizenship. United States common law establishes an arbitrary limit of age fourteen under which a child's understanding must be established by substantial evidence.

G. IRREVOCABILITY OF RENUNCIATION

Finally, those contemplating a renunciation of U.S. citizenship should understand that the act is irrevocable, except as provided in section 351 of the INA, and cannot be canceled or set aside absent successful administrative or judicial appeal. (Section 351(b) of the INA provides that an applicant who renounced his or her U.S. citizenship before the age of eighteen can have that citizenship reinstated if he or she makes that desire known to the Department of State within six months after attaining the age of eighteen. See also Title 22, Code of Federal Regulations, section 50.20).

Renunciation is the most unequivocal way in which a person can manifest an intention to relinquish U.S. citizenship. Please consider the effects of renouncing U.S. citizenship, described above, before taking this serious and irrevocable action. If you have any further questions regarding this matter, please contact the Director, Office of Policy Review & Interagency Liaison, Bureau of Consular Affairs, U.S. Department of State, Washington, DC 20520.

ADVICE ABOUT POSSIBLE LOSS OF U.S. CITIZENSHIP AND DUAL NATIONALITY

The Department of State is responsible for

determining the citizenship status of a person located outside the United States or in connection with the application for a U.S. passport while in the United States.

POTENTIALLY EXPATRIATING STATUTES

Section 349 of the Immigration and Nationality Act, as amended, states that U.S. citizens are subject to loss of citizenship if they perform certain acts voluntarily and with the intention to relinquish U.S. citizenship. Briefly stated, these acts include:

(1) obtaining naturalization in a foreign state (Sec. 349 (a) (1) INA);

(2) taking an oath, affirmation or other formal declaration to a foreign state or its political subdivisions (Sec. 349 (a) (2) INA);

(3) entering or serving in the armed forces of a foreign state engaged in hostilities against the U.S. or serving as a commissioned or non-commissioned officer in the armed forces of a foreign state (Sec. 349 (a) (3) INA);

(4) accepting employment with a foreign government if (a) one has the nationality of that foreign state or (b) a declaration of allegiance is required in accepting the position (Sec. 349 (a) (4) INA);

(5) formally renouncing U.S. citizenship before a U.S. consular officer outside the United States (sec. 349 (a) (5) INA);

(6) formally renouncing U.S. citizenship within the U.S. (but only "in time of war") (Sec. 349 (a) (6) INA);

(7) conviction for an act of treason (Sec. 349 (a) (7) INA).

ADMINISTRATIVE STANDARD OF EVIDENCE

As already noted, the actions listed above can cause loss of U.S. citizenship only if performed voluntarily and with the intention of relinquishing U.S. citizenship. *The Department has a uniform administrative standard of evidence based on the premise that U.S. citizens intend to retain United States citizenship when they obtain naturalization in a foreign state, subscribe to routine declarations of allegiance to a foreign state, or accept non-policy level employment with a foreign government.*

DISPOSITION OF CASES WHEN ADMINISTRATIVE PREMISE IS APPLICABLE

In light of the administrative premise discussed above, a person who:

(1) is naturalized in a foreign country;

(2) takes a routine oath of allegiance or

(3) accepts non-policy level employment with a foreign government

and in so doing wishes to retain U.S. citizenship need not submit prior to the commission of a potentially expatriating act a statement or evidence of his or her intent to retain U.S. citizenship since such an intent will be presumed.

When, as the result of an individual's inquiry or an individual's application for registration or a passport it comes to the attention of a U.S. consular officer that a U.S. citizen has performed an act made potentially expatriating by Sections 349(a)(1), 349(a)(2), 349(a)(3) or 349(a)(4), the consular officer will simply ask the applicant if there was intent to relinquish U.S. citizenship when performing the act. If the answer is no, the consular officer will certify that it was **not** the person's intent to relinquish U.S. citizenship and, consequently, find that the person has retained U.S. citizenship.

PERSONS WHO WISH TO RELINQUISH U.S. CITIZENSHIP

If the answer to the question regarding intent to relinquish citizenship is **yes**, the person concerned will be asked to complete a questionnaire to ascertain his or her intent toward U.S. citizenship. When the questionnaire is completed and the voluntary relinquishment statement is signed by the expatriate, the consular officer will proceed to prepare a certificate of loss of nationality. The certificate will be forwarded to the Department of State for consideration and, if appropriate, approval.

An individual who has performed **any** of the acts made potentially expatriating by statute who wishes to lose U.S. citizenship may do so by affirming in writing to a U.S. consular officer that the act was performed with an intent to relinquish U.S. citizenship. Of course, a person always has the option of seeking to formally renounce U.S. citizenship in accordance with Section 349 (a) (5) INA.

DISPOSITION OF CASES WHEN ADMINISTRATIVE PREMISE IS INAPPLICABLE

The premise that a person intends to retain U.S. citizenship is **not** applicable when the individual:

> (1) formally renounces U.S. citizenship before a consular officer;

> (2) takes a policy level position in a foreign state;

> (3) is convicted of treason; or

> (4) performs an act made potentially expatriating by statute accompanied by conduct which is so inconsistent with retention of U.S. citizenship that it compels a conclusion that the individual intended to relinquish U.S. citizenship. (Such cases are very rare.)

Cases in categories 2, 3, and 4 will be developed carefully by U.S. consular officers to ascertain the individual's intent toward U.S. citizenship.

APPLICABILITY OF ADMINISTRATIVE PREMISE TO PAST CASES

The premise established by the administrative standard of evidence is applicable to cases adjudicated previously. Persons who previously lost U.S. citizenship may wish to have their cases reconsidered in light of this policy.

A person may initiate such a reconsideration by submitting a request to the nearest U.S. consular office or by writing directly to:

Director
Office of American Citizens Services
(CA/OCS/ACS)
Room 4817 NS

Department of State
2201 C Street N.W.
Washington, D.C. 20520
Each case will be reviewed on its own merits taking into consideration, for example, statements made by the person at the time of the potentially expatriating act.

LOSS OF NATIONALITY AND TAXATION

P.L. 104-191 contains changes in the taxation of U.S. citizens who renounce or otherwise lose U.S. citizenship. In general, any person who lost U.S. citizenship within 10 years immediately preceding the close of the taxable year, whose principle purpose in losing citizenship was to avoid taxation, will be subject to continued taxation. For the purposes of this statute, persons are presumed to have a principle purpose of avoiding taxation if 1) their average annual net income tax for a five year period before the date of loss of citizenship is greater than $100,000, or 2) their net worth on the date of the loss of U.S. nationality is $500,000 or more (subject to cost of living adjustments). The effective date of the law is retroactive to February 6, 1995. Copies of approved Certificates of Loss of Nationality are provided by the Department of State to the Internal Revenue Service pursuant to P.L. 104-191. Questions regarding United States taxation consequences upon loss of U.S. nationality, should be addressed to the U.S. Internal Revenue Service.

DUAL NATIONALITY

Dual nationality can occur as the result of a variety of circumstances. The automatic acquisition or retention of a foreign nationality, acquired, for example, by birth in a foreign country or through an alien parent, does not affect U.S. citizenship. It is prudent, however, to check with authorities of the other country to see if dual nationality is permissible under local law. Dual nationality can also occur when a person is naturalized in a foreign state without intending to relinquish U.S. nationality and is thereafter found not to have lost U.S. citizenship the individual consequently may possess dual nationality. While recognizing the existence of dual nationality and permitting Americans to have other nationalities, the U.S. Government does not endorse dual nationality as a matter of policy because of the problems which it may cause. Claims of other countries upon dual-national U.S. citizens often place them in situations where their obligation to one country are

88

in conflict with the laws of the other. In addition, their dual nationality may hamper efforts to provide U.S. diplomatic and consular protection to them when they are abroad.

ADDITIONAL INFORMATION
See also information flyers on related subject available via the Department of State, Bureau of Consular Affairs home page on the internet at http://travel.state.gov or via our automated fax service at 202-647-3000. These flyers include:

- Dual Nationality
- Advice About Possible Loss of U.S. Citizenship and Seeking Public Office in a Foreign State
- Advice About Possible Loss of U.S. Citizenship and Foreign Military Service
- Renunciation of United States Citizenship
- Renunciation of U.S. Citizenship by Persons Claiming a Right of Residence in the United States

QUESTIONS
For further information, please contact the appropriate geographic division of the Office of American Citizens Services:

Africa Division at (202) 647-6060;
East Asia and Pacific Division at (202) 647-6769;
Europe Division at (202) 647-6178;
Latin America and the Caribbean Division at (202) 647-5118;
Near East and South Asia Division at (202) 647-7899.

Counsel representing persons in matters related to loss of U.S. nationality may also address inquiries to Director, Office of Policy Review and Inter-Agency Liaison, Overseas Citizens Services, Room 4817 N.S., Department of State, 2201 C Street N.W., Washington, D.C. 20520, 202-647-3666.

MARRIAGE OF UNITED STATES CITIZENS ABROAD

Who May Perform Marriages Abroad
American diplomatic and consular officers are NOT permitted to perform marriages (Title 22, Code of Federal Regulations 52.1). Marriages abroad are almost always performed by local (foreign) civil or religious officials.

As a rule, marriages are not performed on the premises of an American embassy or consulate. The validity of marriages abroad is not dependent upon the presence of an American diplomatic or consular officer, but upon adherence to the laws of the country where the marriage is performed. Consular officers may authenticate foreign marriage documents. The fee for authentication of a document is $32.00.

Validity of Marriages Abroad
In general, marriages which are legally performed and valid abroad are also legally valid in the United States. Inquiries regarding the validity of a marriage abroad should be directed to the attorney general of the state in the United States where the parties to the marriage live.

Foreign Laws and Procedures
The embassy or tourist information bureau of the country in which the marriage is to be performed is the best source of information about marriage in that country. Some general information on marriage in a limited number of countries can be obtained from Overseas Citizens Services, Room 4811, Department of State, Washington, DC 20520. In addition, American embassies and consulates abroad frequently have information about marriage in the country in which they are located.

Residence Requirements
Marriages abroad are subject to the residency requirements of the country in which the marriage is to be performed. There is almost always a lengthy waiting period.

Documentation and Authentication
Most countries require that a valid U.S. passport be presented. In addition, birth certificates, divorce decrees, and death certificates are frequently required. Some countries require that the documents presented to the marriage registrar first be authenticated in the United States by a consular official of that country. This process can be time consuming and expensive.

Parental Consent
The age of majority for marriage varies from one country to another. Persons under the age of 18 must, as a general rule, present a written statement

of consent executed by their parents before a notary public. Some countries require the parental consent statement to be authenticated by a consular official of that foreign country in the United States.

Affidavit of Eligibility to Marry

All civil law countries require proof of legal capacity to enter into a marriage contract in the form of certification by competent authority that no impediment exists to the marriage. No such document exists in the United States. Unless the foreign authorities will allow such a statement to be executed before one of their consular officials in the United States, it will be necessary for the parties to a prospective marriage abroad to execute an affidavit at the American embassy or consulate in the country in which the marriage will occur stating that they are free to marry. This is called an affidavit of eligibility to marry and the fee for the American consular officer's certification of the affidavit is $55.00, subject to change. Some countries also require witnesses who will execute affidavits to the effect that the parties are free to marry.

Additional Requirements

Many countries, like the United States, require blood tests.

Some countries require that documents presented to the marriage registrar be translated into the native language of that country.

Loss of U.S. Nationality

In some countries, marriage to a national of that country will automatically make the spouse either a citizen of that country or eligible to become naturalized in that country expeditiously. The automatic acquisition of a second nationality will not affect U.S. citizenship. However, naturalization in a foreign country on one's own application or the application of a duly authorized agent may cause the loss of American citizenship. Persons planning to apply for a foreign nationality should contact an American embassy or consulate for further information.

Marriage to an Alien

Information on obtaining a visa for a foreign spouse may be obtained from any office of the Immigration and Naturalization Service, U.S. embassies and consulates abroad, or the Department of State Visa Office, Washington, DC 20520-0113. General information regarding visas may be obtained by calling the Visa Office on 202-663-1225.

DIVORCE OVERSEAS

DISCLAIMER: THE INFORMATION IN THIS CIRCULAR IS PROVIDED FOR GENERAL INFORMATION ONLY AND MAY NOT BE TOTALLY ACCURATE IN A PARTICULAR CASE. QUESTIONS INVOLVING INTERPRETATION OF SPECIFIC U.S. STATE OR FOREIGN LAWS SHOULD BE ADDRESSED TO LEGAL COUNSEL IN THAT JURISDICTION.

STATE v. FEDERAL JURISDICTION: Marriage and divorce generally are considered matters reserved to the states rather than to the federal government. See, *Sosna v. Iowa, 419 U.S. 393, 404 (1975) and Armstrong v. Armstrong, 508 F. 2d 348 (1st Cir. 1974).* There is no treaty in force between the United States and any country on enforcement of judgments, including recognition of foreign divorces.

RECOGNITION BASED ON COMITY: A divorce decree issued in a foreign country generally is recognized in a state in the United States on the basis of comity *(Hilton v. Guyot, 159 U.S. 113, 163-64 (1895),* provided both parties to the divorce received adequate notice, i.e., service of process and, generally, provided one of the parties was a domiciliary in the foreign nation at the time of the divorce. Under the principle of comity, a divorce obtained in another country under the circumstances described above receives "full faith and credit" in all other states and countries that recognize divorce. Although full faith and credit may be given to an *ex parte* divorce decree, states usually consider the jurisdictional basis upon which the foreign decree is founded and may withhold full faith and credit if not satisfied regarding domicile in the foreign country. Many state courts which have addressed the question of a foreign divorce where both parties participate in the divorce proceedings but neither obtains domicile there have followed the view that such a divorce invalid *(Weber v. Weber, 200 Neb. 659, 265 N.W.2d 436 (1978); Everett v. Everett, 345 So. 2d 586 (La. Ct. App. 1977); Kugler v. Haitian Tours, Inc., 120 N.J. Super. 260, 293 A.2d 706 (1972); Estate of Steffke v. Wisconsin Department of Revenue, 65 Wis.2d 199, 222 N.W.2d 628 (1974); Commonwealth v.*

Doughty, 187 Pa. Super. 499, 144 A.2d 521 (1958); Bobala v. Bobala, 68 Ohio App. 63, 33 N.E.2d 845 (1940); Golden v. Golden, 41 N.M. 356, 68 P.2d 928 (1937).

AUTHORITY COMPETENT TO DETERMINE VALIDITY OF FOREIGN DIVORCE IN A U.S. STATE

Questions regarding the validity of foreign divorces in particular states in the United States should be referred to the office of the Attorney General of the state in question. It may be necessary to retain the services of a private attorney if the office of the state Attorney General does not provide such assistance to private citizens. Provide counsel with copies of foreign marriage certificates, divorce decrees and copies of foreign laws concerning divorce which may be available from the foreign attorney who handled the divorce.

MIGRATORY DIVORCES: "Foreign "migratory" divorces fall into four basic categories: (Nichols, Recognition and Enforcement: American Courts, Look at Foreign Divorces, 9 Family Advocate 9-10, 37 (1987).

-- "Ex Parte" divorces, based on the petitioner's physical presence in the foreign nation, with notice or constructive service given to the absent defendant;

-- "Bilateral" divorces, based on the physical presence of both parties in the divorcing nation, or the physical presence of the petitioner and the voluntary "appearance" by the defendant through an attorney;

-- "Void" divorces, where an *ex parte* divorce is obtained without notice, actual or constructive, to the absent defendant. Courts do not recognize or enforce this type of divorce;

-- "Practical recognition" divorces, wherein practical recognition may be afforded such decrees because of estoppel, laches, unclean hands, or similar equitable doctrines under which the party attacking the decree may be effectively barred from securing a judgment of invalidity. 13 A.L.R. 3d 1419, 1452. Many jurisdictions will prohibit the spouse who consented to the divorce from attacking it later under a principle of fairness called "estoppel". Thus, a party may be precluded from attacking a foreign divorce decree if such an attack would be inequitable under the circumstances. *Scherer v. Scherer, 405 N.E. 2d 40, 44 (Ind. App. 1980), Rosenstiel v. Rosenstiel,*

16 N.Y.2d 64, 209 N.E.2d 709, 262 N.Y.S.2d 86 (1965), and *Yoder v. Yoder, 31 Conn.Supp. 345, 330 A.2d 825 (1974).*

REGISTERING FOREIGN DIVORCES AND THE ROLE OF U.S. EMBASSIES AND CONSULATES ABROAD

There are no provisions under U.S. law or regulation for registration of foreign divorce decrees at U.S. embassies or consulates abroad. 22 C.F.R. 52 does provide for authentication of foreign marriage and divorce records. This is not a form a registration, but simply the placing of the seal of the U.S. embassy or consulate, or other competent authority in countries party to the Hague Legalization Convention, over the seal of the foreign court. See below for a detailed discussion of the authentication process.

UNIFORM STATE LAWS AND REGISTRATION OF DIVORCES: The Uniform Act on Marriage and Divorce (1970, 1973), 9A Unif. Laws. Ann. 461 (Supp. 1965), is in force in Arizona, Colorado, Georgia, Illinois, Kentucky, Minnesota, Montana, and Washington state. Section 314(c) of the Uniform Act on Marriage and Divorce establishes a procedure for the clerk of court where the divorce decree is issued to register the decree in the place where the marriage itself was originally registered. The Uniform Divorce Recognition Act, 9 Unif. Laws Ann. 644 (1979), specifically denies recognition to a divorce decree obtaining in another jurisdiction when both spouses were domiciled in the home state. The Uniform Divorce Recognition Act is in force in California, Nebraska, New Hampshire, North Dakota, Rhode Island, South Carolina and Wisconsin. Information about uniform state laws is available from the national Conference of Comissioners on Uniform State Laws, 676 North St. Clair Street, Suite 1700, Chicago, Illinois 60611, tel: 312-915-0195 or via the Internet at http://www.law.upenn.edu/library/ulc/ulc.htm.

U.S. CONSULAR CERTIFICATES OF WITNESS TO MARRIAGE: With the repeal of the old 1860 statute on "solemnization of marriages", 22 U.S.C. 4192 on November 9, 1989, U.S. consular officers ceased issuing "Certificates of Witness to Marriage". Copies of witness to marriage issued between 1860 -1989 are available from the Office of passport Services,Vital Records Section, CA/PPT/PS/PC, Suite 510. 1111

19th Street, N.W., Washington, D.C. 20522, 202-955-0307. See also the passport Services Section of the Consular Affairs home page at http://travel.state.gov.

FOREIGN MARRIAGE CERTIFICATES: In the absence of the issuance of a "Certificate of Witness to Marriage," copies of foreign marriage certificates may be obtained directly from the civil registrar in the foreign country where the marriage occurred. Contact the embassy or consulate of the foreign country in the United States for guidance on how to obtain copies of foreign public documents. The documents may then be authenticated for use in the United States as explained below. English translations may be certified by translators in the United States before a notary public. When requesting copies of foreign public documents such as marriage or divorce records, it may be advisable to write to the foreign authorities in the language of the foreign country. Enclose copies of pertinent documents and any required fees in the form of an international money order.

PROOF OF FOREIGN DIVORCE: Obtain a certified copy of the foreign divorce decree from the court in the foreign country where the divorce decree was issued. Then have the document authenticated for use in the United States as explained below. Finally, obtain a certified English translation of the divorce decree (the translator executes a certificate before a notary public in the United States). When requesting copies of foreign public documents such as marriage or divorce records, it may be advisable to write to the foreign authorities in the language of the foreign country. Enclose copies of pertinent documents and any required fees in the form of an international money order.

AUTHENTICATION OF DIVORCE AND MARRIAGE RECORDS: It may be necessary for you to provide foreign authorities or your attorney with authenticated, translated copies of your foreign divorce decree and any other pertinent documents. Consult your foreign attorney before going to this expense

U.S. SSA, VA and IRS DETERMINATIONS REGARDING FOREIGN DIVORCES: There have been a number of determinations by the U.S. Social Security Administration, Veterans Administration and Internal Revenue Service regarding the validity of foreign divorces based on the laws of the state of residence applicable with respect to claims for benefits. For SSA, see http://www.ssa.gov/. See also, 20 C.F.R. 404.314, SSR 66-1; 20 CFR 404.328(a), 404.1101, and 404.1104, SSR 72-61; 20 CFR 404.335(a), SSR 73-10a; 20 CFR 404.336, SSR 75-16; SSR 61-65; 20 CFR 404.340(c), SSR 88-15c, Section 202(g)(1)(A) of the Social Security Act (42 U.S.C. 402(g)(1)(A) *(Slessinger v. Secretary of Health and Human Services, 1A Unempl. Ins. Rep. (CCH),* 17,843 (1st Cir. 1987). *(Cunningham v. Harris, 658 F.2d 239, 243 (4th Cir. 1981).; Thompson v. Harris, 504 F. Supp. 653, 654 (D. Mass. 1980); Lugot v. Harris, 499 F. Supp. 1118 (D. Nev. 1980).* For Veterans Administration, see 27 FR 6281, July 3, 1962, as amended by 35 FR 16831, October 31, 1970; 40 FR 53581, November 19, 1975; 52 FR 19349, May 22, 1987. For the IRS, see *Estate of Felt v. Comm'r, 54 T.C.M. (CCH) 528 (1987).* It is our understanding that when obtained in good faith and not a sham for tax-avoidance purpose, the Internal Revenue Service recognizes foreign divorces.

OTHER CONTACTS: It may be helpful for American attorneys not familiar with enforcement and recognition of foreign divorces to consult the following resources:

ABA - the Family Law Section of the American Bar Association, 750 N. Lake Shore Drive, Chicago, IL 60611, 312-988-5000;
ABA Center on Children and the Law, 740 15th St., N.W., Washington, D.C. 20005, tel: 202-662-1740, http://www.abanet.org:80/child/home.html;
State or local bar association;
American Academy of matrimonial Lawyers, 150 N. Michigan Avenue, Ste. 2040, Chicago, IL 50501, 312-263-6477, http://www.aaml.org/;
International Academy of matrimonial Lawyers, Secretariat, 13 Claybury, Bushey, Herts WD2 3ES, United Kingdom, tel: (011)(44) 0181-950-6452; fax: (011)(44) 0181.950-8895; http://www.iaml-usa.com/;
International Society of Family Law, Brigham Young University School of Law, 518 JRCB, Provo, UT 84602;
International Bar Association (IBA), 2 Harewood Place, Hanover Square, London, WIR9HB, England, Tel: (011) (44) (171) 629-1206; Fax: (011) (44) (171) 409-0-456.

Library of Congress Law Library, Room 240, James Madison Bldg., 101 Independence Avenue, S.E., Washington, D.C. 20540, tel: 202-707-5079.

TREATIES: The United States is not a party to the Hague Convention on the Recognition of Divorces and Legal Separations of June 1, 1970 (978 U.N.T.S. 399 (975). See also, 5 Int'l Legal Materials 389, 393 (1966); 14 Am. J. Comp. L. 697, 700 (1966); 8 Int'l Legal Materials 31, 34 (1969); 8 Int'l Legal Materials 787, 800 (1969); 18 Int'l and Comp. L.Q. 488 (1969); 5 Family L.Q. 321 (1971); Reese, The Hague Draft Convention on Recognition of Foreign Divorces: A Comments, 14 Am. J. Comp. L. 692 (1966); Von Mehren, Draft Convention on the Recognition of Divorces and Legal Separations: Introductory Note, 16 Am. J. Comp. L. 580 (1968); Hampton, Hunning, & Wadsley, Current Legal Developments, Hague Convention on Recognition of Divorce and Legal Separation, 18 Int'l and Comp. L.Q. 483, 488 (1969). The Convention relates to such recognition but not to any ancillary matters such as findings of fault, orders for maintenance or custody of children. The Convention is in force in Australia, Cyprus, Czech Republic, Denmark, Egypt, Finland, Italy, Luxembourg, the Netherlands, Norway, Poland, Portugal, Romania, Slovenia, Sweden, Switzerland and the United Kingdom.

ENFORCEMENT OF JUDGMENTS: The Department of State, Office of Overseas Citizens Services has available a general information flyer on the subject of enforcement of judgments which is accessible via our automated fax service or our home page on the Internet as explained below.

SELECTED REFERENCES:
24 Am. Jur. 2d, Divorce and Separation, Sec. 971, 972. 27B C.J.S. Divorce Sec. 364-366.
Berke, Mexican Divorces, 7 Prac. Law. 84 (1961).
Bronstein, The Question of Haitian and Dominican Divorces, 166 N.Y.L.J., Sept. 21, 1971.
Ceschini, Divorce Proceedings in Italy: Domestic and International Procedures, 28 Family Law Quarterly, American Bar Association, 143, 150 (1994).
Comment, Mexican Bilateral Divorce -- A Catalyst in Divorce Jurisdiction Theory?, 61 Nw. U.L. Rev. 584 (1966).

Domestic Relations - Jurisdiction, Extension of Comity to Foreign Nation Divorce, 46 Tenn. L. Rev. 238, 241 (1978).
Dyer, Recognition and Enforcement Abroad, 9 Family Advocate No. 4, ABA Family Law Section, 5, 11-14 (1987).
Forscher, Haitian, Dominican Laws of Divorce Evaluated, 166 N.Y.L.J., (October 19-20, 1971).
Foreign Divorces, A Question of Jurisdiction, 5 Southern University L. Rev. 139 (1984).
Fulton, Caribbean Divorce for Americans: Useful Alternative or Obsolescent Institution?, 10 Cornell Int'l L. J. 116, 133 (1976).
Glassman, Recognition and Enforcement at Home, 9 Family Advocate No. 4, ABA Family Law Section, 4, 6-8, (1987).
Hackworth, Digest of International Law, Office of the Legal Adviser, U.S. Department of State, Vol. II, Chapter VI, Section 168, 382-391 (1941).
Holden, Divorce in the Commonwealth, 20 Int'l and Comp. L.Q. 58, 74 (1971).
Howe, The Recognition of Foreign Divorce Decrees in New York State, 40 Colum. L. Rev. 373, 376 (1940); 23 Colum. L. Rev. 782 (1923).
Juenger, Recognition of Foreign Divorces: British and American Perspectives, 20 Am. J. Comp. L. 1 (1972).
Mendes da Costa, The Canadian Divorce Law of 1968 and its Provisions on Conflicts, 17 Am. J. Comp. L. 214 (1969).
Nichols, American Courts Look at Foreign Decrees, 9 Family Advocate No. 4, ABA Family Law Section, 9-10, 37 (1987).
Pedersen, Recent Trends in Danish Family Law and Their Historical Background, 20 Int'l and Comp. L.Q. 332, 341 (1971).
Swisher, Foreign Migratory Divorces: A Reappraisal, 21 J. Fam. L. 9, 25n, 71-72 (1982).
Stone, The New Fundamental Principles of Soviet Family Law and Their Social Background, 18 Int'l and Comp. L.Q. 392, 406 (1969).
Turner, Divorce: Australian and German "Breakdown" Provisions Compared, 18 Int'l and Comp. L.Q. 896, 937 (1969).
Whiteside, Domestic Relations - The Validity of Foreign Divorce Decrees in North Carolina (Mayer v. Mayer) 20 Wake Forest L. Rev. 765 (1984).

ADDITIONAL INFORMATION The Office of American Citizens Services has available general information flyers on international judicial assistance , many of which are available through

93

our automated fax system or via our home page.

Using the Autofax System:
Dial (202) 647-3000 using the phone on your fax machine. Follow the prompts to obtain the information that you need.

Using the Internet: Many of our judicial assistance flyers are also available on the Internet via the Department of State, Bureau of Consular Affairs home page under Judicial Assistance

QUESTIONS: Additional questions may be addressed to the U.S. Department of State, Bureau of Consular Affairs, Office of American Citizens Services, Room 4817 N.S., 2201 C Street, N.W., Washington, D.C. 20520, tel: (202) 647-5225 or 202-647-5226.

Chapter 8

Getting Help Abroad from U.S. Consuls

[The information in this chapter is reprinted verbatim from a bulletin issued by the U.S. State Department, Bureau of Consular Affairs. It is intended to serve as advice to Americans traveling abroad.]

U.S. Consuls Help Americans Abroad

There are U.S. embassies in 160 capital cities of the world. Each embassy has a consular section. Consular officers in consular sections of embassies do two things:

> they issue visas to foreigners;

> they help U.S. citizens abroad.

There are also consular officers at about 60 U.S. consulates general and 20 U.S. consulates around the world. (Consulates general and consulates are regional offices of embassies.)

U.S. consuls usually are assisted by local employees who are citizens of the host country. Because of the growing number of Americans traveling abroad, and the relatively small number of consuls, the expertise of local employees is invaluable.

In this chapter, we highlight ways in which consular officers can assist you while you are traveling or residing abroad.

To help us help you while you are abroad, register with the nearest U.S. embassy or consulate. This makes it easier for consular officers to reach you in an emergency or to replace a lost passport.

Consular officers provide a range of services - some emergency, some nonemergency.

EMERGENCY SERVICES

Replace A Passport - If you lose your passport, a consul can issue you a replacement, often within 24 hours. If you believe your passport has been stolen, first report the theft to the local police and get a police declaration.

Help Find Medical Assistance - If you get sick, you can contact a consular officer for a list of local doctors, dentists, and medical specialists, along with other medical information.

If you are injured or become seriously ill, a consul will help you find medical assistance and, at your request, inform your family or friends. (Consider getting private medical insurance before you travel, to cover the high cost of getting you back to the U.S. for hospital care in the event of a medical emergency.)

Help Get Funds - Should you lose all your money and other financial resources, consular officers can help you contact your family, bank, or employer to arrange for them to send you funds. In some cases, these funds can be wired to you through the Department of State.

Help In An Emergency - Your family may need to reach you because of an emergency at home or because they are worried about your welfare. They should call the State Department's Citizens Emergency Center (202) 647-5225. The State Department will relay the message to consular officers in the country in which you are traveling. Consular officers will attempt to locate you, pass on urgent messages, and, consistent with the Privacy Act, report back to your family.

Visit In Jail - If you are arrested, you should ask the authorities to notify a U.S. consul. Consuls cannot get you out of jail (when you are in a foreign country you are subject to its laws). However, they can work to protect your legitimate interests and ensure you are not discriminated against. They can provide a list of local attorneys, visit you, inform you generally about local laws, and contact your family and friends. Consular officers can transfer money, food, and clothing to the prison authorities from your family or friends. They can try to get relief if you are held under

95

inhumane or unhealthful conditions.

Make Arrangements After The Death Of An American - When an American dies abroad, a consular officer notifies the American's family and informs them about options and costs for disposition of remains. Costs for preparing and returning a body to the U.S. may be high and must be paid by the family. Often, local laws and procedures make returning a body to the U.S. for burial a lengthy process. A consul prepares a Report of Death based on the local death certificate; this is forwarded to the next of kin for use in estate and insurance matters.

Help in a Disaster/Evacuation - If you are caught up in a natural disaster or civil disturbance, you should let your relatives know as soon as possible that you are safe, or contact a U.S. consul who will pass that message to your family through the State Department. Be resourceful. U.S. officials will do everything they can to contact you and advise you. However, they must give priority to helping Americans who have been hurt or are in immediate danger. In a disaster, consuls face the same constraints you do - lack of electricity or fuel, interrupted phone lines, closed airports.

NONEMERGENCY SERVICES

Issue a Consular Report of Birth - A child born abroad to U.S. citizen parents usually acquires U.S. citizenship at birth. The parents should contact the nearest U.S. embassy or consulate to have a "Report of Birth Abroad of a U.S. Citizen" prepared. This is proof of citizenship for all purposes.

Issue a Passport - Consuls issue approximately 200,000 passports abroad each year. Many of these are issued to persons whose current passports have expired.

Distribute Federal Benefits Payments - Over a half-million people living overseas receive monthly federal benefit payments. In many countries, the checks are mailed to the U.S. embassy or consulate and distributed through the local postal service.

Assist in Child Custody Disputes - In an international custody dispute, a consul can try to locate a child abroad, monitor the child's welfare,

and provide general information to the American parent about laws and procedures which may be used to effect the child's return to the United States. Consuls may not take custody of a child, or help a parent regain custody of a child illegally or by force or deception.

Help In Other Ways - Consuls handle personal estates of deceased U.S. citizens, assist with absentee voting and Selective Service registration, notarize documents, advise on property claims, and provide U.S. tax forms. They also perform such functions as adjudicating U.S. citizenship claims and assisting U.S. courts in legal matters.

WHAT CONSULAR OFFICERS CANNOT DO
In addition to the qualifications noted above, consular officers cannot act as travel agents, banks, lawyers, investigators, or law enforcement officers. Please do not expect them to find you employment, get you residence or driving permits, act as interpreters, search for missing luggage, or settle disputes with hotel managers. They can, however, tell you how to get help on these and other matters.

If you need to pick up mail or messages while traveling, some banks and international credit card companies handle mail for customers at their overseas branches. General Delivery (Poste Restante) services at post offices in most countries will hold mail for you.

PRIVACY ACT
The provisions of the Privacy Act are designed to protect the privacy rights of Americans. Occasionally they complicate a consul's efforts to assist Americans. As a general rule, consular officers may not reveal information regarding an individual American's location, welfare, intentions, or problems to anyone, including family members and Congressional representatives, without the expressed consent of that individual. Although sympathetic to the distress this can cause concerned families, consular officers must comply with the provisions of the Privacy Act.

For more information, contact Overseas Citizens Services, Department of State, Room 4800, Washington, D.C. 20520.

Chapter 9

Crises Abroad-What the State Department Does

*[The Information in this chapter is reprinted verbatim from a bulletin issued by the
U.S. State Department, Bureau of Consular Affairs. It is intended to serve as advice
to Americans traveling abroad.]*

Crisis Abroad - What the State Department Does

**What can the State Department's Bureau of Consular Affairs do for Americans caught in a disaster or
a crisis abroad?**

Earthquakes, hurricanes, political upheavals, acts of terrorism, and hijackings are only some of the events
threatening the safety of Americans abroad. Each event is unique and poses its own special difficulties.
However, for the State Department there are certain responsibilities and actions that apply in every disaster
or crisis.

When a crisis occurs, the State Department sets up a task force or working group to bring together in one set
of rooms all the people necessary to work on that event. Usually this Washington task force will be in touch
by telephone 24 hours a day with our Ambassador and Foreign Service Officers at the embassy in the
country affected.

In a task force, the immediate job of the State Department's Bureau of Consular Affairs is to respond to the
thousands of concerned relatives and friends who begin to telephone the State Department immediately after
the news of a disaster is broadcast.

Relatives want information on the welfare of their family members and on the disaster. The State
Department relies for hard information on its embassies and consulates abroad. Often these installations are
also affected by the disaster and lack electricity, phone lines, gasoline, etc. Nevertheless, foreign service
officers work hard to get information back to Washington as quickly as possible. This is rarely as quickly as
the press is able to relay information. Foreign Service Officers cannot speculate; their information must be
accurate. Often this means getting important information from the local government, which may or may not
be immediately responsive.

Welfare & Whereabouts
As concerned relatives call in, officers of the Bureau of Consular Affairs collect the names of the Americans
possibly involved in the disaster and pass them to the embassy and consulates. Officers at post attempt to
locate these Americans in order to report on their welfare. The officers work with local authorities and,
depending on the circumstances, may personally search hotels, airports, hospitals, or even prisons. As they
try to get the information, their first priority is Americans dead or injured.

Death
When an American dies abroad, the Bureau of Consular Affairs must locate and inform the next-of-kin.
Sometimes discovering the next-of-kin is difficult. If the American's name is known, the Bureau's Office of
Passport Services will search for his or her passport application. However, the information there may not be
current.

The Bureau of Consular Affairs provides guidance to grieving family members on how to make
arrangements for local burial or return of the remains to the U.S. The disposition of remains is affected by

97

local laws, customs, and facilities which are often vastly different from those in the U.S. The Bureau of Consular Affairs relays the family's instructions and necessary private funds to cover the costs involved to the embassy or consulate. The Department of State has no funds to assist in the return of remains or ashes of American citizens who die abroad. Upon completion of all formalities, the consular officer abroad prepares an official Foreign Service Report of Death, based upon the local death certificate, and sends it to the next-of-kin or legal representative for use in U.S. courts to settle estate matters.

A U.S. consular officer overseas has statutory responsibility for the personal estate of an American who dies abroad if the deceased has no legal representative in the country where the death occurred. The consular officer takes possession of personal effects, such as convertible assets, apparel, jewelry, personal documents and papers. The officer prepares an inventory and then carries out instructions from members of the deceased's family concerning the effects. A final statement of the account is then sent to the next-of-kin. The Diplomatic Pouch cannot be used to ship personal items, including valuables, but legal documents and correspondence relating to the estate can be transmitted by pouch. In Washington, the Bureau of Consular Affairs gives next-of-kin guidance on procedures to follow in preparing Letters Testamentary, Letters of Administration, and Affidavits of Next-of-Kin as acceptable evidence of legal claim of an estate.

Injury
In the case of an injured American, the embassy or consulate abroad notifies the task force which notifies family members in the U.S. The Bureau of Consular Affairs can assist in sending private funds to the injured American; frequently it collects information on the individual's prior medical history and forwards it to the embassy or consulate. When necessary, the State Department assists in arranging the return of the injured American to the U.S. commercially, with appropriate medical escort, via commercial air ambulance or, occasionally, by U.S. Air Force medical evacuation aircraft. The use of Air Force facilities for a medical evacuation is authorized only under certain stringent conditions, and when commercial evacuation is not possible. The full expense must be borne by the injured American or his family.

Evacuation
Sometimes commercial transportation entering and leaving a country is disrupted during a political upheaval or natural disaster. If this happens, and if it appears unsafe for Americans to remain, the embassy and consulates will work with the task force in Washington to charter special air flights and ground transportation to help Americans to depart. The U.S. Government cannot order Americans to leave a foreign country. It can only advise and try to assist those who wish to leave.

Privacy Act
The provisions of the Privacy Act are designed to protect the privacy and rights of Americans, but occasionally they complicate our efforts to assist citizens abroad. As a rule, consular officers may not reveal information regarding an individual Americans location, welfare, intentions, or problems to anyone, including family members and Congressional representatives, without the expressed consent of that individual. Although sympathetic to the distress this can cause concerned families, consular officers must comply with the provisions of the Privacy Act.

Chapter 10

Overseas Citizens Services/The Citizens Emergency Center

*[The information in this chapter is reprinted verbatim from a bulletin issued by the
U.S. State Department, Bureau of Consular Affairs. It is intended to serve as advice
to Americans both at home and abroad.]*

The Office of Overseas Citizens Services

When You Need Help...

Overseas Citizens Services
Overseas Citizens Services (OCS) in the State
Department's Bureau of Consular Affairs is
responsible for the welfare and whereabouts of
U.S. citizens traveling and residing abroad. OCS
has three offices: American Citizens Services and
Crisis Management, the Office of Children's Issues
and the Office of Policy Review and Interagency
Liaison.

AMERICAN CITIZENS SERVICES AND CRISIS MANAGEMENT (ACS)
American Citizens Services and Crisis
Management corresponds organizationally to
American Citizens Services offices set up at U.S.
embassies and consulates throughout the world.
ACS has five geographical divisions with case
officers who assist in all matters involving
protective services for Americans abroad,
including arrests, death cases, financial or medical
emergencies, and welfare and whereabouts
inquiries. The office also issues Travel Warnings,
Public Announcements and Consular Information
Sheets and provides guidance on nationality and
citizenship determination, document issuance,
judicial and notarial services, estates and property
claims, third-country representation, and disaster
assistance.

Arrests
Over 2,500 Americans are arrested abroad
annually. More than 30% of these arrests are drug
related. Over 70% of drug related arrests involve
marijuana or cocaine.

The rights an American enjoys in this country do
not travel abroad. Each country is sovereign and
its laws apply to everyone who enters regardless of
nationality. The U.S. government cannot get
Americans released from foreign jails. However, a
U.S. consul will insist on prompt access to an
arrested American, provide a list of attorneys, and
provide information on the host countrys legal
system, offer to contact the arrested Americans
family or friends, visit on a regular basis, protest
mistreatment, monitor jail conditions, provide
dietary supplements, if needed, and keep the State
Department informed.

ACS is the point of contact in the U.S. for family
members and others who are concerned about a
U.S. citizen arrested abroad.

Deaths
Approximately 6,000 Americans die outside of the
U.S. each year. The majority of these are long-
term residents of a foreign country. ACS assists
with the return of remains for approximately 2,000
Americans annually. When an American dies
abroad, a consular officer notifies the next of kin
about options and costs for disposition of remains.
Costs for preparing and returning a body to the
U.S. are high and are the responsibility of the
family. Often local laws and procedures make
returning a body to the U.S. for burial a lengthy
process.

Financial Assistance
If destitute, Americans can turn to a U.S. consular
officer abroad for help. ACS will help by
contacting the destitute person's family, friends, or
business associates to raise private funds. It will
help transmit these funds to destitute Americans.

ACS transfers approximately 3 million dollars a
year in private emergency funds. It can approve
small government loans to destitute Americans
abroad until private funds arrive. ACS also

99

approves repatriation loans to pay for destitute Americans' direct return to the U.S. Each year over $500,000 are loaned to destitute Americans.

Medical Assistance

ACS works with U.S. consuls abroad to assist Americans who become physically or mentally ill while traveling. ACS locates family members, guardians, and friends in the U.S., assists in transmitting private funds, and, when necessary, assists in arranging the return of ill or injured Americans to the U.S. by commercial carrier.

Welfare and Whereabouts of U.S. Citizens

ACS receives approximately 12,000 inquiries a year concerning the welfare or whereabouts of an American abroad. Many inquiries are from worried relatives who have not heard from the traveler. Others are attempts to notify the traveler about a family crisis at home. Most welfare/whereabouts inquiries are successfully resolved. However, occasionally, a person is truly missing. It is the responsibility of local authorities to investigate and U.S. consuls abroad will work to ensure their continued interest in cases involving Americans. Unfortunately, as in the U.S., sometimes missing persons are never found.

Consular Information Program

ACS issues fact sheets on every country in the world called *Consular Information Sheets* (CIS). The CIS contains information on entry requirements, crime and security conditions, areas of instability and other details relevant to travel in a particular country.

The Office also issues *Travel Warnings*. Travel Warnings are issued when the State Department recommends deferral of travel by Americans to a country because of civil unrest, dangerous conditions, terrorist activity and/or because the U.S. has no diplomatic relations with the country and cannot assist an American in distress.

Consular Information Sheets and *Travel Warnings* may be heard anytime, by dialing the Office of Overseas Citizens Services travelers' hotline at (202) 647-5225 from a touchtone phone. They are also available via Consular Affairs' automated fax system at (202) 647-3000, or at any of the 13 regional passport agencies, at U.S. embassies and consulates abroad, and through the airline computer reservation systems, or, by sending a

self-addressed, stamped business size envelope to the Office of Overseas Citizens Services, Bureau of Consular Affairs, Room 4811, U.S. Department of State, Washington, D.C. 20520-4818. If you have a personal computer and Internet access, you obtain them and other consular handouts and publications through the Consular Affairs web site at http://travel.state.gov

Disaster Assistance

ACS coordinates the Bureau's activities and efforts relating to international crises or emergency situations involving the welfare and safety of large numbers of Americans residing or traveling in a crisis area. Such crises can include plane crashes, hijackings, natural disasters, civil disorders, and political unrest.

CHILDREN'S ISSUES (CI)

The Office of Children's Issues (CI) formulates, develops and coordinates policies and programs, and provides direction to foreign service posts on international parental child abduction and international adoptions. It also fulfills U.S. treaty obligations relating to the abduction of children.

International Adoptions

CI coordinates policy and provides information on international adoption to the potential parents. In 1994, over 8,000 foreign born children where adopted by U.S. citizens. The Department of State cannot intervene on behalf of an individual in foreign courts because adoption is a private legal matter within the judicial sovereignty of the country where the child resides. This office can, however, offer general information and assistance regarding the adoption process in over 60 countries.

International Parental Child Abductions

In recent years, the Bureau of Consular Affairs has taken action in thousands of cases of international parental child abduction. The Bureau also provides information in response to thousands of additional inquiries pertaining to international child abduction, enforcement of visitation rights and abduction prevention techniques. CI works closely with parents, attorneys, other government agencies, and private organizations in the U.S. to prevent international abductions. The Hague Convention provides for the return of a child to his or her habitual place of residence if the child has been wrongfully removed or retained. CI has been

100

designated by Congress as the Central Authority to administer the Hague Convention in the United States.

POLICY REVIEW AND INTERAGENCY LIAISON (PRI)

The Office of Policy Review and Interagency Liaison (PRI) provides guidance concerning the administration and enforcement of laws on U.S. citizenship, and on the documentation of Americans traveling and residing abroad. The Office also provides advice on matters involving treaties and agreements, legislative matters, including implementation of new laws, conducts reconsiderations of acquisition and loss of U.S. citizenship in complex cases abroad, and administers the overseas federal benefits program.

Consular Conventions and Treaties

PRI works closely with other offices in the State Department in the negotiation of consular conventions and treaties, including prisoner transfer treaties. As a result of these prisoner transfer treaties, many U.S. citizens convicted of crimes and incarcerated abroad have returned to the U.S. to complete their sentences.

Federal Benefits

Over a half-million people receive monthly federal benefits payments outside the U.S. In many countries, the monthly benefits checks are mailed or pouched to the consular post and then distributed through the local postal service. In other countries, the checks are mailed directly into the beneficiaries foreign bank accounts. Consular officers assist in the processing of individual benefits claims and problems; investigate claims on behalf of the agency concerned; and perform other tasks requested by the agencies or needed by the beneficiaries or survivors.

Legislation

PRI is involved with legislation affecting U.S. citizens abroad. The Office participates in hearings and provides testimony to Congress on proposed legislation, particularly legislation relating to the citizenship and welfare of U.S. citizens. They also interpret laws and regulations pertaining to citizens consular services, including the administration of the Immigration and Nationality Act.

Privacy Act

PRI responds to inquires under the Privacy Act. The provisions of the Privacy Act are designed to protect the privacy and rights of Americans but occasionally complicate efforts to assist U.S. citizens abroad. As a general rule, consular officers may not reveal information regarding an individual Americans location, welfare, intentions, or problems to anyone, including family members and Congressional representatives, without the expressed consent of that individual. In all potential cases, consular officers explain Privacy Act restrictions and requirements so that all individuals involved in a case understand the Privacy Act's constraints.

Hours of Operation:

OCS is open Monday-Friday, 8:15 a.m. to 5:00 p.m. Eastern time. The OCS toll-free hotline at 1-888-407-4747 is available from 8:00 a.m. to 8:00 p.m. Eastern time, Monday-Friday, except U.S. federal holidays. Callers who are unable to use toll-free numbers, such as those calling from overseas, may obtain information and assistance during these hours by calling 317-472-2328. **For after-hours emergencies, Sundays and holidays, please call 202-647-4000 and request the OCS duty officer.**

101

Chapter 11

The State Department Travel Advisories

[The information in this chapter is reprinted verbatim from a number of bulletins issued by the U.S. State Department, Bureau of Consular Affairs. It is intended to serve as advice to Americans traveling abroad.]

TRAVEL WARNINGS AND CONSULAR INFORMATION SHEETS

What Are Travel Warnings, Consular Information Sheets & Public Announcements?

Travel Warnings are issued when the State Department decides, based on all relevant information, to recommend that Americans avoid travel to a certain country. Countries where avoidance of travel is recommended will have Travel Warnings as well as Consular Information Sheets.

Public Announcements are a means to disseminate information about terrorist threats and other relatively short-term and/or trans-national conditions posing significant risks to the security of American travelers. They are made any time there is a perceived threat and usually have Americans as a particular target group. In the past, Public Announcements have been issued to deal with short-term coups, bomb threats to airlines, violence by terrorists and anniversary dates of specific terrorist events.

Consular Information Sheets are available for every country of the world. They include such information as location of the U.S. Embassy or Consulate in the subject country, unusual immigration practices, health conditions, minor political disturbances, unusual currency and entry regulations, crime and security information, and drug penalties. If an unstable condition exists in a country that is not severe enough to warrant a Travel Warning, a description of the condition(s) may be included under an optional section entitled "Safety/Security." On limited occasions, we also restate in this section any U.S. Embassy advice given to official employees. Consular Information Sheets generally do not include advice, but present information in a factual manner so the traveler can make his or her own decisions concerning travel to a particular country.

You can access Consular Information Sheets, Travel

Warnings and Public Announcements 24-hours a day in several ways.

Internet
The most convenient source of information about travel and consular services is the Consular Affairs home page. The web site address is http://travel.state.gov. If you do not have access to the Internet at home, work or school, your local library may provide access to the Internet.

Fax
From your fax machine, dial **(202) 647-3000**, using the handset as you would a regular telephone. The system will instruct you on how to proceed.

Telephone
Consular Information Sheets and Travel Warnings may be heard any time by dialing the office of American Citizens Services at **(202) 647-5225** from a touchtone phone.

In Person/By Mail
Consular Information Sheets, Travel Warnings and Public Announcements are available at any of the regional passport agencies and U.S. embassies and consulates abroad, or, by writing and sending a self-addressed, stamped envelope to the Office of American Citizens Services, Bureau of Consular Affairs, Room 4811, U.S. Department of State, Washington, D.C. 20520-4818.

103

Travel Warnings as of July 9, 2003

Nigeria - 6/26/2003
Colombia - 6/16/2003
Indonesia - 6/12/2003
Liberia - 6/6/2003
Yemen - 5/23/2003
Kenya - 5/16/2003
Saudi Arabia - 5/13/2003
Iran - 5/12/2003
Taiwan - 5/9/2003
Lebanon - 5/6/2003
Iraq - 4/25/2003
Burundi - 4/23/2003
Israel, the West Bank and Gaza - 4/17/2003
Pakistan - 4/17/2003
Algeria - 4/9/2003
Central African Republic - 4/7/2003
Democratic Republic of the Congo - 4/7/2003
Afghanistan - 4/2/2003
Sudan - 3/26/2003
Angola - 3/24/2003
Somalia - 3/4/2003
Venezuela - 2/19/2003
Zimbabwe - 1/27/2003
Tajikistan - 12/20/2002
Cote d'Ivoire - 12/9/2002
Libya - 10/7/2002
Bosnia - 6/4/2002
Macedonia - 5/21/2002

Public Announcements as of July 9, 2003

East Timor - 6/24/2003, expires on 12/23/2003
Mauritania - 6/9/2003, expires on 9/9/2003
East Africa - 5/14/2003, expires on 9/12/2003
Malaysia - 5/14/2003, expires on 11/14/2003
SARS - 5/12/2003, expires on 9/7/2003
Kyrgyz Republic - 5/6/2003, expires on 10/31/2003
Middle East Update - 5/5/2003, expires on 10/1/2003
Peru - 5/2/2003, expires on 7/24/2003
Worldwide Caution - 4/21/2003, expires on 9/20/2003
Uzbekistan - 4/5/2003, expires on 10/1/2003
Guatemala - 4/2/2003, expires on 12/1/2003
Djibouti - 3/18/2003, expires on 7/17/2003
SOLOMON ISLANDS - 3/17/2003, expires on 9/14/2003

Philippines - 3/7/2003, expires on 9/4/2003
Republic of Congo - 2/28/2003, expires on 8/20/2003
Laos - 2/26/2003, expires on 8/13/2003
Return to Consular Information Sheets and Travel Warnings Page

State Department Electronic Subscriptions

You can automatically receive via email full texts of selected U.S. Department of State documents and publications that provide key official information on U.S. foreign policy; you also can receive notifications of travel warnings and Foreign Travel Per Diem updates.

To subscribe to any one of the email lists for the following information, **complete the online subscription form** or send an email to **LISTSERV@LISTS.STATE.GOV** and type in the message body "SUBSCRIBE LISTNAME YOURNAME". (Omit the quotation marks, and be sure to replace the YOURNAME portion above with your own name -- or, if preferred, ANONYMOUS -- and the LISTNAME with the name of the list below that you wish to subscribe to.)

The DOSIRAQ list. This list will distribute speeches, interviews, press briefings and other documents and releases that are pertinent to Iraq. You can expect the DOSIRAQ list to generate a substantial number of email messages per month.

The DOSINTLWMN list. This list will distribute an electronic newsletter, fact sheets, speeches, reports and other releases that are pertinent to International Women's Issues. You can expect the DOSINTLWMN list to generate 2 - 3 messages per month.

The DOSCOALITION list. This list provides official statements on the State Department's efforts to Build a Global Coalition Against Terrorism following the Attack on America September 11,

104

2001. You can expect the DOSCOALITION list to generate a substantial number of email messages per month.

The DOSTRAVEL list. This list provides notification of updates to the Travel Warnings issued when the State Department decides, based on all relevant information, to recommend that Americans avoid travel to a certain country. Countries where avoidance of travel is recommended will have Travel Warnings as well as Consular Information Sheets. You can expect the DOSTRAVEL list to generate an average of 10-15 email messages per month.

The DOSSCHEDULE list. The Daily Appointments Schedule of Secrtary of State Colin L. Powell and Deputy Secretary of State Richard Armitage. DOSSCHEDULE will generate a daily email.

The DOSSEC list. The Secretary of State regularly addresses various groups and testifies before Congress. Full texts of Secretarial addresses and remarks are disseminated by the Office of Electronic Information, Bureau of Public Affairs, for posting to the DOSSEC list as soon as they are released. You can expect the DOSSEC list to generate an average of 10-15 email messages per month.

The DOSSDO list. Senior State Department officials regularly address various groups and testify before Congress. These postings to the DOSSDO list are disseminated by the Office of Electronic Information, Bureau of Public Affairs, as soon as they are provided by the senior official's office. You can expect the DOSSDO list to generate about 8-12 email messages per month.

The DOSBRIEF list. The State Department conducts press briefings, usually Monday through Friday. The Office of the Spokesman, Bureau of Public Affairs, releases the press briefings the same day unless otherwise indicated in the Department of State State Department's daily press briefing calendar; full texts of these briefings are distributed via DOSBRIEF. You can expect the DOSBRIEF list to generate about 4-5 email messages per week.

The DOSFACTS list. Fact Sheets are concise (1 or 2-page) summaries of U.S. policy on current foreign affairs issues. They are updated irregularly. You can expect this listserv to generate 2-3 emails a week.

The DOSPRESS list. The Office of the Spokesman, Bureau of Public Affairs, releases about 2-5 press statements or notices to the press each day. You can expect the DOSPRESS list to generate about 20 email messages per month; each day's releases will be compiled into one message. Press statements are posted to our web site as they are released throughout the day.

The DOSBACK list. Background Notes are updated periodically and include information on U.S. bilateral relations with foreign countries and on their governments, political conditions, and foreign relations. Via DOSBACK you will receive the full-text version of newly released Background Notes. You can expect the DOSBACK list to generate about 3-4 email messages per month.

The DOSPDIEM list. This list provides notification of updates to the Maximum Travel Per Diem Allowance for Foreign Areas, Section 925, a supplement to the Standardized Regulations (Government Civilians, Foreign Areas). Foreign Travel Per Diem Rates are released monthly by the State Department's Office of Allowances. Via DOSPDIEM you will receive monthly notification of the availability of Travel Per Diem Rate updates.

The DOSPPT list. This list provides

105

subscribers with updated passport information, including new requirements, fee changes, etc. In an effort to keep U.S. citizens informed, Passport Services will send out updated information as soon as it is made available to the public. You can expect the DOSPPT list to generate 2-3 emails a year.

The DOSPPTTRV list. This list provides travel agent subscribers with updated passport information, including new requirements, fee changes, etc. In an effort to keep travel agents (and their clients) informed, Passport Services will send out updated information as soon as it is made available to the public. You can expect the DOSPPTTRV list to general 3-6 emails a year.

106

Chapter 12

Travel Warnings on Drugs Abroad

[The Information in this chapter is reprinted verbatim from a bulletin issued by the U.S. State Department, Bureau of Consular Affairs. It is intended to serve as advice to Americans traveling abroad.]

Things You Should Know Before You Go Abroad

HARD FACTS

Each year, 2,500 Americans are arrested overseas. One third of the arrests are on drug-related charges. Many of those arrested assumed as U.S. citizens that they could not be arrested. From Asia to Africa, Europe to South America, U.S. citizens are finding out the hard way that drug possession or trafficking equals jail in foreign countries.

There is very little that anyone can do to help you if you are caught with drugs. It is your responsibility to know what the drug laws are in a foreign country before you go, because "I didn't know it was illegal" will not get you out of jail.

In recent years, there has been an increase in the number of women arrested abroad. The rise is a result of women who serve as drug couriers or "mules" in the belief they can make quick money and have a vacation without getting caught. Instead of a short vacation, they get a lengthy stay or life sentence in a foreign jail.

A number of the Americans arrested abroad on drug charges in 1994 possessed marijuana. Many of these possessed one ounce or less of the substance. The risk of being put in jail for just one marijuana cigarette is not worth it. If you are purchasing prescription medications in quantities larger than that considered necessary for personal use, you could be arrested on suspicion of drug trafficking.

Once you're arrested, the American consular officer **CANNOT** get you out! You may say "it couldn't happen to me" but the fact is that it could happen to you if you find yourself saying one of the following:
... *"I'm an American citizen and no foreign government can put me in their jail."*
... *"If I only buy or carry a small amount, it won't be a problem."*

If you are arrested on a drug charge it is important that you know what your government **CAN** and **CANNOT** do for you.

The U.S. Consular Officer *CAN*
- visit you in jail after being notified of your arrest
- give you a list of local attorneys (The U.S. Government cannot assume responsibility for the professional ability or integrity of these individuals or recommend a particular attorney.)
- notify your family and/or friends and relay requests for money or other aid -- but only with your authorization
- intercede with local authorities to make sure that your rights *under local law* are fully observed and that you are treated humanely, according to internationally accepted standards
- protest mistreatment or abuse to the appropriate authorities

The U.S. Consular Officer *CANNOT*

- demand your immediate release or get you out of jail or the country!
- represent you at trial or give legal counsel
- pay legal fees and/or fines with U.S. Government funds

If you are caught buying, selling, carrying or using drugs -- from hashish to heroin, marijuana to mescaline, cocaine to quaaludes, to designer drugs like ecstacy....

IT COULD MEAN:

Interrogation and Delays Before Trial - including mistreatment and solitary confinement for up to one year under very primitive conditions
Lengthy Trials - conducted in a foreign language, with delays and postponements
Weeks, Months or Life in Prison - some places include hard labor, heavy fines, and/or lashings, if found guilty
The Death Penalty - in a growing number of countries (e.g., Malaysia, Pakistan and Turkey)
Although drug laws vary from country to country, it is important to realize before you make the mistake of getting involved with drugs that foreign countries do not react lightly to drug offenders. In some countries, anyone who is caught with even a very small quantity for personal use may be tried and receive the same sentence as the large-scale trafficker.

DON'T LET YOUR TRIP ABROAD
BECOME A NIGHTMARE!

This information has been provided to inform you before it is too late.

SO THINK FIRST!

- A number of countries, including the Bahamas, the Dominican Republic, Jamaica, Mexico and the Philippines, have enacted more stringent drug laws which impose mandatory jail sentences for individuals convicted of possessing even small amounts of marijuana or cocaine for personal use.
- Once you leave the United States, you are not covered by U.S. laws and constitutional rights.
- Bail is not granted in many countries when drugs are involved.
- The burden of proof in many countries is on the accused to prove his/her innocence.
- In some countries, evidence obtained illegally by local authorities may be admissible in court.
- Few countries offer drug offenders jury trials or even require the prisoner's presence at his/her trial.
- Many countries have mandatory prison sentences of seven years or life, without the possibility of parole for drug violations.

REMEMBER!

- If someone offers you a free trip and some quick and easy money just for bringing back a suitcase.... *SAY NO!*
- Don't carry a package for anyone, no matter how small it might seem.
- The police and customs officials have a right to search your luggage for drugs. If they find drugs in **your** suitcase, **you** will suffer the consequences.
- You could go to jail for years and years with no possibility of parole, early release or transfer back to the U.S.
- Don't make a jail sentence part of your trip abroad.

The Department of State's Bureau of Consular Affairs' Office of Overseas Citizens Services provides emergency services pertaining to the protection of Americans arrested or detained abroad, the search for U.S. citizens overseas, the transmission of emergency messages to those citizens or their next of kin in the United States and other emergency and non-emergency services. Contact the Office of Overseas Citizens Services from Monday through Friday, 8:15 a.m. to 10:00 p.m. at (202) 647-5225. For an emergency after hours or on weekends and holidays, ask for the Overseas Citizens Services' duty officer at (202) 647-4000. Internet home page: http://travel.state.gov

108

Chapter 13

Parental Child Abduction

*[The information in this chapter is reprinted verbatim from a bulletin issued by the
U.S. State Department, Bureau of Consular Affairs. It is intended to serve as advice
to Americans at home and abroad.]*

INTRODUCTION

Parental child abduction is a tragedy. When a child is abducted across international borders, the difficulties are compounded for everyone involved. This pamphlet is designed to assist the adult most directly affected by international child abduction, the left-behind parent.

The Department of State considers international parental child abduction, as well as the welfare and protection of U.S. citizen children taken overseas, to be important, serious matters. We place the highest priority on the welfare of children who have been victimized by international abductions.

The Department of State's Office of Children's Issues (CA/OCS/CI) is designated to provide assistance to the left-behind parents of international parental child abduction. Since the late 1970's, we have been contacted in the cases of approximately 16,000 children who were either abducted from the United States or prevented from returning to the United States by one of their parents. This booklet discusses what the Department of State can and cannot do to help you. In addition, because we are only part of the network of resources available to you, we mention other avenues to pursue when your child has been abducted across international borders.

The Office of Children's Issues is prepared to assist you as you pursue recovery of your abducted child. Because it can be a bewildering experience, we have prepared both a questionnaire for the left-behind parents of children taken to countries not party to the Hague Abduction Convention (See Table 1) and an application for left-behind parents of children taken to Hague Convention member countries (See Table 2)). To report an abduction case to CA/OCS/CI, call our office and follow-up with a copy of either the completed questionnaire or the completed application. Likewise, in order for us to provide the best service, we need to be informed of any developments in your case. Every child and every

case is unique, and we will work with you to apply this information to your particular situation.

If you have any further questions, please call us at 202-736-7000. You may also fax us at 202-312-9743, or write to us at:

U.S. Department of State
The Office of Children's Issues

2401 E Street, N.W., Room L127
Washington, D.C. 20522

You can receive additional information by dialing the State Department's Bureau of Consular Affairs' automated fax system at 202-647-3000 (from your fax) or visit
http://travel.state.gov/children's_issues.html.

PART I: PREVENTION

HOW TO GUARD AGAINST

INTERNATIONAL CHILD ABDUCTION

How Vulnerable is Your Child?
You and your child are most vulnerable when your relationship with the other parent is troubled or broken, the other parent has close ties to another country, and/or the other country has traditions or laws that may be prejudicial against a parent of your gender or to non-citizens in general. However, anyone can be vulnerable.

Cross-cultural Marriages: Should You or Your Child Visit the Country of the Other Parent?
Many cases of international parental child abduction are actually cases in which the child traveled to a foreign country with the approval of both parents, but was later prevented from returning to the United States. Sometimes the marriage is neither broken nor troubled, but the foreign parent, upon returning to his or her country of origin, decides not to return to the U.S. or to allow the child to do so. A person who has assimilated a second culture may find a return to

his or her roots disturbing and may feel pulled to shift loyalties back to the original culture. Furthermore, a person's behavior may change when he or she returns to the culture where he or she grew up.

In some societies, children must have their father's permission and a woman must have her husband's permission to travel. If you are a woman, to prevent your own or your child's detention abroad, find out about the laws and traditions of the country you plan to visit or plan to allow your child to visit, and consider carefully the effect that a return to his traditional culture might have on your child's father; in other societies, children need the permission of both parents to travel and the refusal of one parent to give that permission may prevent the departure of a child from that country. For detailed advice in your specific case, you may wish to contact an attorney in your spouse's country of origin. Many US Embassies/Consulates list attorneys on their websites which is, accessible via http://travel.state.gov.

Precautions That Any Parent Should Take

In international parental child abduction, an ounce of prevention is worth a pound of cure. Be alert to the possibility and be prepared:

- Keep a list of the addresses and telephone numbers of the other parent's relatives, friends, and business associates both here and abroad;

- Keep a record of important information about the other parent, including: physical description, passport, social security, bank account, and driver's license numbers, and vehicle description and plate number;

- Keep a written description of your child, including hair and eye color, height, weight, fingerprints, and any special physical characteristics; and

- Take full-face color photographs and/or videos of your child every six months - a recent photo of the other parent may also be useful.

If your child should be abducted, this information could be vital in locating your child. In addition, the National Center for Missing and Exploited Children (NCMEC), www.missingkids.org, at telephone 1-800-843-5678, suggests that you teach your child to use the telephone, memorize your home phone number, practice making collect calls, and instruct him or her to call home immediately if anything unusual happens. Discuss possible plans of action with your child in the case of abduction. Most important, however, if you feel your child is vulnerable to abduction, seek legal advice. Do not merely tell a friend or relative about your fears.

The Importance of a Custody Decree

Under the laws of the United States and many foreign countries, **if there is no decree of custody prior to an abduction, both parents may be considered to have equal legal custody of their child.** (IMPORTANT: Even though both parents may have custody of a child, it still may be a crime for one parent to remove the child from the United States against the other parent's wishes.) If you are contemplating divorce or separation, or are divorced or separated, or even if you were never legally married to the other parent, ask your attorney, as soon as possible, if you should obtain a decree of sole custody or a decree that prohibits the travel of your child without your permission or that of the court. If you have or would prefer to have a joint custody decree, you may want to make certain that it prohibits your child from traveling abroad without your permission or that of the court.

How to Draft or Modify a Custody Decree

A well-written custody decree is an important line of defense against international parental child abduction. NCMEC, in its publication *Family Abduction: How to Prevent an Abduction and What to Do If Your Child is Abducted*, makes several recommendations to help prevent the abduction of your child if your spouse is a legal permanent resident alien or a U.S. citizen with ties to a foreign country. For instance, it may be advisable to include court-ordered supervised visitation and a statement prohibiting your child from traveling without your permission or that of the court. If the country to which your child might be taken is a member of the Hague Convention on the Civil Aspects of International Child Abduction (Hague Convention), your custody decree should state that the terms of the Hague Convention apply if there is an abduction or wrongful retention. The American Bar Association (ABA) also suggests having the court require the non-citizen parent or the parent with ties to a foreign country to post a bond. This may be useful both as a deterrent to abduction and, if forfeited because of an abduction, as a source of revenue for you in your efforts to locate and recover your child. For further prevention information, you should contact the NCMEC.

> Reminder: *Obtain several* **certified** *copies of your custody decree from the court that issued it. Give a copy to your child's school and advise school personnel to whom your child may be released.*

U.S. Passports

The Department of State's Passport Lookout Program can help you determine if your child has been issued a U.S. passport. You may also ask that your child's name be entered into the State Department's Children's Passport Issuance Alert Program. This will enable the Department to notify you or your attorney if an application for a U.S. passport for the child is received anywhere in the United States or at any U.S. embassy or consulate abroad. If you have a court order that either grants you sole custody, joint legal custody, or prohibits your child from traveling without your permission or the permission of the court, the Department may also refuse to issue a U.S. passport for your child. **The Department may not, however, revoke a passport that has already been issued to the child.** There is also no way to track the use of a passport once it has been issued, since there are no exit controls of people leaving the U.S.

To inquire about a U.S. passport or to have your child's name entered into the passport alert program complete the request form in Appendix 3 and mail or fax it to:

Office of Children's Issues
Children's Passport Issuance Alert Program
(CPIAP)
2401 E Street, N.W., Room L127
Washington, D.C. 20522
Tel. (202) 736-7000
Fax (202) 312-9743

Change in Passport Regulations

A new law, which took effect in July 2001, requires the signature of both parents prior to issuance of a U.S. passport to children under the age of 14.

Requirements:

Both parents, or the child's legal guardians, must execute the child's passport application and provide documentary evidence demonstrating that they are the parents or guardians; or the person executing the application must provide documentary evidence that such person has sole custody of the child; has the consent of the other parent to the issuance of the passport; or is acting in place of the parents and has the consent of both parents, of a parent with sole custody over the child, or of the child's legal guardian, to the issuance of the passport.

Exceptions:

The law does provide two exceptions to this requirement: (1) for exigent circumstances, such as those involving the health or welfare of he child, or (2) when the Secretary of State determines that issuance of a passport is warranted by special family circumstances. For additional information, see the Bureau of Consular Affairs home page on the Internet at http://travel.state.gov.

Foreign Passports - the Problem of Dual Nationality

Many United States citizen children who fall victim to international parental abduction possess, or may have a claim to dual nationality. While the Department of State will make every effort to avoid issuing a United States passport if the custodial parent has provided a custody decree, the Department cannot prevent embassies and consulates of other countries in the United States from issuing their passports to children who are also their nationals. You can, however, ask a foreign embassy or consulate not to issue a passport to your child. Send the embassy or consulate a written request, along with certified complete copies of any court orders you have which address custody or the overseas travel of your child. In your letter, inform them that you are sending a copy of this request to the United States Department of State. If your child is *only* a United States citizen, you can request that no visa for that country be issued in his or her United States passport. No international law requires compliance with such requests, but some countries may comply voluntarily.

The United States government does not have exit controls at the border. There is no way to stop someone with valid travel documents at the United States border. The U.S. government does not check the names or the documents of travelers leaving the United States. Many foreign countries do not require a passport for entry. A birth certificate is sufficient to enter some foreign countries. If your child has a valid passport from

111

any country, he or she may be able to travel outside the United States without your consent.

PART II

WHAT THE STATE DEPARTMENT CAN AND CANNOT DO

WHEN A CHILD IS ABDUCTED ABROAD

When a United States citizen child is abducted abroad, the State Department's Office of Children's Issues (CA/OCS/CI) works with United States embassies and consulates abroad to assist the child and left-behind parent in a number of ways. *Despite the fact that children are taken across international borders, child custody disputes remain fundamentally civil legal matters between the parents involved, over which the Department of State has no jurisdiction.* If a child custody dispute cannot be settled amicably between the parties, it often must be resolved by judicial proceedings in the country where the child is located.

WHAT THE STATE DEPARTMENT CAN DO:

- Act as the primary point of contact for left-behind parents;
- Act as a liaison with federal and state agencies, including law enforcement officials;
- In cases where the Hague Convention on the Civil Aspects of International Child Abduction applies (see Part IV), assist parents in filing an application with foreign authorities for return of or access to the child;
- Attempt to locate, visit and report on the child's general welfare;
- Provide the left-behind parent with information on the country to which the child was abducted, including its legal system, custody laws, and a list of local attorneys willing to accept American clients;
- Inquire as to the status of judicial or administrative proceedings overseas;
- Assist parents in contacting local officials in foreign countries or contact them on the parent's behalf;
- Provide information concerning how federal warrants against an abducting parent, passport revocation, and extradition from a foreign country may

affect return of a child to the United States;
- Alert foreign authorities to any evidence of child abuse or neglect; and
- If the child is in the Children's Passport Issuance Alert Program, contact the left-behind parent when application is made for a new U.S. passport for the child.

WHAT THE STATE DEPARTMENT CANNOT DO:

- Intervene in civil legal matters between the parents;
- Enforce an American custody agreement overseas (United States custody decrees are not automatically enforceable outside of United States boundaries);
- Force another country to decide a custody case or enforce its laws in a particular way;
- Assist the left-behind parent in violating foreign laws or reabducting the child to the United States;
- Pay legal or other expenses;
- Act as a lawyer, give legal advice or represent parents in court;
- Take custody of the child; and
- Revoke the child's passport.

PART III

HOW TO SEARCH FOR A CHILD ABDUCTED ABROAD

Where to Report Your Missing Child

1. If your child is missing or has been abducted, file a missing person report with your local police department and request that your child's name and description be entered into the "missing person" section of the National Crime Information Center (NCIC) computer. This is provided for under the National Child Search Act of 1990. The abductor does not have to be charged with a crime when you file a missing person report. It is not always a good idea to file criminal charges against the abducting parent at the same time you file a missing person report, although local law enforcement authorities may urge you to do so *(see cautionary note on page 17)*. In addition, through INTERPOL, the international police organization, your local police can request that a search for your child be conducted by the police in the country

where you believe your child may have been taken. If your local law enforcement is unaware of the legal requirements for immediate entry into NCIC please contact the Office of Children's Issues at (202) 736-7000.

2. Contact the National Center for Missing and Exploited Children (NCMEC) at 1-800-THE LOST/1-800-843-5678. With the searching parent's permission, the child's photograph and description may be circulated to the media in the country to which you believe the child may have been taken.

3. Request information about a possible United States passport and have your child's name entered into the United States Children's Passport Issuance Alert Program. A United States passport for a child under 16 years expires after 5 years. If you do not know where your child is, but information about the child is in the name check system, it may be possible to locate him or her through the passport application process. All United States passport agencies and United States embassies and consulates are on-line with the name check system (See the information in Part I on U.S. Passports)

After Your Child Is Located

A consular officer overseas, working with this information, will try to confirm the location of your child. If the consular officer is unable to find the child based on the information provided, he or she may also request information from local officials on your child's entry or residence in the country. Please note, however, that most countries do not maintain such records in a retrievable form, and some countries will not release such information.

We may also ask you for photographs of both your child and the abducting parent because these are often helpful to foreign authorities trying to find a missing child.

The Department of State, when requested to do so, may conduct visits to determine the welfare and whereabouts of American citizens abroad. The Office of Children's Issues communicates such requests to the United States embassy or consulate responsible for the area to which you believe your child has been abducted. A welfare and whereabouts visit cannot be conducted if the abducting parent refuses access. Your signed letter requesting such a visit and containing the following information can be faxed to us at 202-312-9743:

- Child's full name (and any aliases);
- Child's date and place of birth;
- Full name (and any aliases) of the abductor; and
- Information which may assist the embassy or consulate in locating the abductor, such as the names, addresses, and telephone numbers of friends, relatives, place of employment, or business connections there.

Further Steps to Take in Your Search

It is possible that none of the institutions mentioned (the police, the NCMEC, or the Department of State) will succeed in locating your child right away and you will need to carry on the search on your own. As you search, you should, however, keep these institutions informed of your actions and progress.

- One of the best ways to find your child overseas is through establishing friendly contact with relatives and friends of the other parent, either here or abroad. You may have more influence with such persons than you suspect, and their interest in your child's welfare may lead them to cooperate with you.

- The United States Department of Health and Human Services, Office of Child Support Enforcement maintains the Federal Parent Locator Service (FPLS). The primary purpose of this service is to locate parents who are delinquent in child support payments, but the service will also search for parental abductors when requested to do so by an authorized person. Generally speaking, an authorized person is a state court judge, police officer, prosecutor, or other state official seeking to enforce a child custody order. Please ask your local law enforcement to request a search.

To learn how to access the services of the FPLS, contact your local or state Child Support Enforcement office. These offices are listed under government listings in your telephone directory.

- You can contact the principal of the school to obtain information on requests that may have been made by the

113

abductor to your child's school for the transfer of your child's records.

- You can find out from the National Center for Missing and Exploited Children how to prepare a poster on your child. A poster may assist foreign authorities in attempting to locate your child.

- You can ask your district attorney to contact the United States Postal Inspection Service to see if a "mail cover" can be put on any address that you know of in the United States to which the abductor might write.

- It may be possible for local law enforcement authorities to obtain, by subpoena or search warrant, credit card records that may show where the abductor is making purchases. Check with state and local authorities if anything can be done. In the same manner, you can try to obtain copies of telephone bills of the abductor's friends or relatives who may have received collect calls from the abductor. Law enforcement may also be able to track usage of a cell phone or emails the abductor may be sending.

PART IV

THE BEST SOLUTION: SETTLING OUT OF COURT

Promoting Communication Between Parents and Children

Legal procedures can be long and expensive. You may have greater success negotiating with the abducting parent. In some cases, friends or relatives of the abductor may be able to help you reach a compromise with the abductor. A decrease in tension might bring about the return of your child, but, even if it does not, it can increase your chances of being able to visit the child and participate in some way in the child's upbringing. In some cases compromise and some kind of reconciliation are the only realistic option.

Obtaining Information on Your Child's Welfare

If you know your child's location and your child is a United States citizen you can request that a United States consular officer attempt to visit your child. If the consul obtains the other parent's permission to visit the child, he or she will do so and report back to you about your child. Sometimes consular officers are also able to send

you letters or photos from your child. Contact the Office of Children's Issues (CA/OCS/CI) at (202) 736-7000 to request such a visit.

Working With Foreign Authorities

In child abduction cases, consular officers routinely maintain contact with local child welfare and law enforcement officers. If there is evidence of abuse or neglect of the child, the United States embassy or consulate may request that local authorities become involved.

The Question of Desperate Measures/Reabduction

Consular officers cannot take possession of a child abducted by a parent or aid parents attempting to act in violation of the laws of a foreign country. Consular officers must act in accordance with the laws of the country to which they are accredited. The Department of State strongly discourages taking desperate and possibly illegal measures to return your child to the United States. Attempts to use self-help measures to bring an abducted child to the United States from a foreign country may endanger your child and others, prejudice any future judicial efforts you might wish to make in that country to stabilize the situation, and could result in your arrest and imprisonment in that country. In imposing a sentence, the foreign court will not necessarily give weight to the fact that the would-be abductor was the custodial parent in the United States or otherwise had a valid claim under a United States court order (e.g., failure of the foreign parent to honor the terms of a joint custody order). *Should you be arrested, the United States Embassy will not be able to secure your release.*

If you do succeed in leaving the foreign country with your child, you and anyone who assisted you may be the target of arrest warrants and extradition requests in the United States or any other country where you are found. Even if you are not ultimately extradited and prosecuted, an arrest followed by extradition proceedings can be very disruptive and disturbing for both you and your child.

Finally, there is no guarantee that the chain of abductions would end with the one committed by you. A parent who has reabducted a child may have to go to extraordinary lengths to conceal his or her whereabouts, living in permanent fear that the child may be reabducted again. Please consider how this might affect the child.

114

If you are contemplating such desperate measures, you should read the information available from the National Center for Missing and Exploited Children (NCMEC) about the emotional trauma inflicted on a child who is a victim of abduction and reabduction. The NCMEC advises against reabduction not only because it is illegal, but also because of possible psychological harm to the child.

PART V

ONE POSSIBLE SOLUTION: THE HAGUE CONVENTION

One of the most difficult and frustrating elements for a parent of a child abducted abroad is that United States laws and court orders are not automatically recognized abroad and therefore are not directly enforceable abroad. Each country has jurisdiction within its own territory and over people present within its borders. No country can tell another country how to decide cases or enforce laws. Just as foreign court orders are not automatically enforceable in the United States, United States court orders are not automatically enforceable abroad.

At the Hague Conference on Private International Law in 1976, 23 nations agreed to draft a treaty to deter international child abduction. Between 1976 and 1980, the United States was a major force in preparing and negotiating the Hague Convention on the Civil Aspects of International Child Abduction (Hague Convention or the Convention). The Convention was incorporated into U.S. law and came into force for the United States on July 1, 1988. As of July 2001, the Convention is in force between the United States and 50 other countries. The Convention applies to wrongful removals or retentions that occurred on or after the date the treaty came into force between those two countries. The dates vary for each country and more countries are considering signing on to the Convention all the time. Check the most recent list prepared by the Office of Children's Issues to learn whether the Convention was in force in a particular county at the time of the wrongful removal or retention.

What Is Covered by the Convention

The Hague Convention is a civil legal mechanism available to parents seeking the return of, or access to, their child. As a civil law mechanism, the parents, not the governments, are parties to the legal action.

The countries that are party to the Convention have agreed that a child who is habitually resident in one party country, and who has been removed to or retained in another party country in violation of the left-behind parent's custodial rights, shall be promptly returned to the country of habitual residence. The Convention can also help parents exercise visitation rights abroad.

There is a treaty obligation to return an abducted child below the age of 16 if application is made **within one year** from the date of the wrongful removal or retention, unless one of the exceptions to return apply. If the application for return is made after one year, the court may use its discretion to decide that the child has become resettled in his or her new country and refuse return of the child. In any case, a court may refuse to order a child returned if there is:

15. A grave risk that the child would be exposed to physical or psychological harm or otherwise placed in an intolerable situation in his or her country of habitual residence;

16. If the child objects to being returned and has reached an age and degree of maturity at which the court can take account of the child's views (the treaty does not establish at what age children reach this level of maturity: that age and the degree of weight given to children's views varies from country to country); or If the return would violate the fundamental principles of human rights and freedoms of the country where the child is being held.

Note: Interpretation of these exceptions varies from country to country.

How to Use the Hague Convention

The Convention provides a legal mechanism for you to seek return of your child or exercise your visitation rights. **You do *not* need to have a custody decree to use the Convention**. However, to apply for the return of your child, you must have had and been actually exercising a "right of custody" at the time of the abduction, and you must not have given permission for the child to be removed or, in the case of a retention, to be retained beyond a specified, agreed-upon period of time. The Convention defines "rights of custody" as including "rights relating to the care of the person of the child and, in particular, the right to

115

determine the child's place of residence." This right need not be sole custody. If there was no court order in effect at the date of the abduction, these "rights of custody" may be established by the law in the state in which your child was living before his or her removal. In some cases it may be advisable to get a determination (as per Article 15 of the Convention) in your local court that 1) you have a right of custody to your child, and 2) the removal or retention was wrongful. Use of the Convention is not restricted to U.S. citizens.

An application should be submitted as soon as possible after an abduction or wrongful retention has taken place. As stated above, there is a time factor of one year involved. Do not wait until you get a custody order. That order would be irrelevant anyway. Copies of the application form can be found in Table 2.

Each country that is party to the Convention has designated a Central Authority to carry out specialized duties under the Convention. The Central Authority for the United States is the Department of State's Office of Children's Issues (CA/OCS/CI). You may submit your application directly to the Central Authority or foreign court of the country where the child is believed to be held, but, in order to ensure that you receive all available assistance it is best to submit your application to the U.S. Central Authority.

The Role of the United States Central Authority
The responsibilities of the Central Authority for the Hague Abduction Convention are set forth in Articles 7-12 and 21 of the Convention[1]. The United States Central Authority is prohibited from acting as an agent or attorney in legal proceedings arising under the Convention[2]. The United States Central Authority was not intended to be and has never been a party to such proceedings.

> 1 Although article 7(f) of the Convention and 22 C.F.R. 94.6(d) and (h) refer to legal proceedings under the Convention, they do not assign the U.S. Central Authority a direct role in such proceedings.
> [2] 22 C.F.R. 94.4

The United States Central Authority's role in proceedings in the United States under the Convention is that of an active facilitator. We seek to promote cooperation among the relevant parties and institutions and act as a source of information about proper procedures under the Convention and the contents and status of applications for assistance. The Central Authority in the country where your child is located, however, has the primary responsibility for processing your application.

The Office of Children's Issues will review your application to ensure that it is complete and that your request complies with the requirements of the Convention. If it does, we will forward it to the foreign Central Authority and work with that authority until your case is resolved. If the abducting parent does not voluntarily agree to the return of your child, you may be required to retain an attorney abroad to present your case under the Hague Convention to the foreign court. If you need to retain an attorney abroad, see Using the Civil Justice System - How to Proceed .

The Office of Children's Issues works with the applicant and the other Central Authority to facilitate communication between the parties involved and work toward resolving the case as quickly as possible. While specific operations and procedures under the Convention differ in each country party to the treaty, we stand ready to help applicants understand the process and monitor all cases in which assistance is sought.

Immigration and the Hague Convention
The Hague Convention on the Civil Aspects of International Child Abduction focuses on issues of residency, not citizenship. It is important to note that the Convention does not confer any immigration benefit. Anyone seeking to enter the United States who is not a United States citizen must fulfill the appropriate entry requirements, even if that person was ordered by a court to return to the United States. This applies to children and parents involved in any child abduction case including a Hague Convention case.

When a taking parent in a Hague Abduction Convention case is ineligible to enter the United States under United States immigration laws, the parent may be paroled for a limited time into the United States through the use of a Significant Public Benefit Parole in order to participate in custody or other related proceedings in a United States court.

Good News for Applicants Under the Hague Convention

The Hague Convention on International Child Abduction has improved the likelihood and speed of return of abducted or wrongfully retained children from countries that are party to the Convention. The Convention's success is encouraging more countries to become party to the Convention. As of July 2001, fifty-five countries have joined since the United States became the 10th country in July 1988. In addition, the reputation of the Hague Convention is such that, when an abducting or retaining parent learns that a Hague application has been or will be filed, he or she may return the child voluntarily and no further civil action will be taken. The majority of Hague cases still, however, require the left behind parent to retain an attorney in the country where the child is located and petition the court for return.

A note of caution: Criminal charges may have an unintended negative effect on the operation of the Hague Convention. With the Hague Convention, the emphasis is on the swift return of a child to his or her place of habitual residence where the custody dispute can then be resolved, if necessary, in the courts of that jurisdiction. Courts in some countries, including the United States, have denied return of children solely because the taking parent would be arrested if they accompanied the child home. Many of these courts, United States and foreign, have held that the arrest of the parent would expose the child to psychological harm under Article 13(b) of the Convention. This varies by country and the type of criminal charge. Please contact CI to discuss this matter further.

Children Abducted to the United States

The Hague Convention applies to children abducted to and from countries party to the Convention. If a child is abducted to the United States from one of our Hague treaty partners the parent left behind in the country may apply for return under the Convention. Even if the child was born in the United States, if the child is now found to be "habitually resident" in another country the child may be ordered to return to that country under the Convention. the U.S., provided the case meets the requirements of the Hague and the child's country of habitual residence is a signatory to the Hague Convention.

As of September 5, 1995, by agreement between the National Center for Missing and Exploited Children (NCMEC), the Department of State, and the Department of Justice, applications seeking return of or access to children in the United States are processed on behalf of the Office of Children's Issues by the NCMEC (See References)

PART VI

LEGAL SOLUTIONS WHEN THE HAGUE CONVENTION DOES NOT APPLY

If your child has been abducted to a country that is *not* a party to the Hague Convention, or if the Convention does not apply in your case, you can seek other legal remedies against the abductor, in the United States and abroad, from both the civil and criminal justice systems. The family court system from which you get a custody decree is part of the civil justice system. At the same time you are using that system, you can also use the criminal justice system consisting of the police, prosecutors, and the FBI.

Using the Civil Justice System: How To Proceed

In addition to obtaining a custody decree in the United States, you may have to use the civil justice system in the country to which your child has been abducted. The Office of Children's Issues (CA/OCS/CI) can provide general information on the customs and legal practices for many countries around the world. We can also give you general information on legal service of process abroad or obtaining evidence, and on how to have documents authenticated for use in a foreign country. You may write or telephone CA/OCS/CI for information sheets, such as Retaining a Foreign Attorney, and Authentication (or Legalization) of Documents in the United States for Use Abroad.

To obtain authoritative advice on the laws of a foreign country or to take legal action in that country, you should retain an attorney there. United States consular and diplomatic officers are prohibited by law from performing legal services. (22 C.F.R. 92.81) We can, however, provide you with a list of attorneys in a foreign country. United States embassies and consulates abroad prepare these lists. The United States Department of State can neither guarantee attorney services nor pay attorney fees.

Cautionary note: *Attorney fees can vary widely from country to country. The fee agreement that you make with your local attorney should be put into writing as soon as possible to avoid a potentially serious misunderstanding later.*

Although officers at United States embassies and consulates cannot take legal action on behalf of United States citizens, consular officers may be able to assist in communication problems with a foreign attorney. Consular officers can sometimes inquire about the status of proceedings in the foreign court, and they may be able to coordinate with your attorney to ensure that your rights as provided for by the laws of that foreign country are respected.

Your foreign attorney may ask for a certified copy of your custody decree and/or state and federal warrants regarding the abducting parent which have been authenticated for use abroad. It is also advisable to send copies of your state's laws on custody and parental kidnapping or custodial interference, the Federal Parental Kidnapping Prevention Act, and copies of reported cases of your state's enforcement of foreign custody decrees under Section 23 of the Uniform Child Custody Jurisdiction Act. Your U.S. attorney can help you gather this information.

What Are Your Chances of Enforcing Your United States Custody Order Abroad?

Just as a foreign court order has no direct effect in the United States, a custody decree issued by a court in the United States has no binding legal force abroad, although it may have persuasive force in some countries. Courts decide child custody cases on the basis of their own domestic relations law and the decision whether to recognize a foreign order is at the court's discretion. This may give a "home court" advantage to a person who has abducted a child to the country of his or her origin. You could also be disadvantaged if the country has a cultural bias in favor of a mother or a father. A United States custody decree may, however, be considered by foreign courts and authorities as evidence and, in some cases, it may be recognized and enforced by them on the basis of comity (the voluntary recognition by courts of one jurisdiction of the laws and judicial decisions of another). Your chances of having your United States court order enforced depend, to a large degree, upon the tradition of comity that the legal system of the country in question has with the United States legal system. While CA/OCS/CI can give you some information on these traditions, you should consult with your attorney in that country on how to proceed.

PART VII

USING THE CRIMINAL JUSTICE SYSTEM

There are many factors to consider in determining whether or not to file criminal charges against the abductor. The child's safe return is the primary objective in any missing child case, and criminal charges may actually complicate child recovery

efforts. While the threat of outstanding criminal charges may intimidate some abductors into returning the child, others may react by increasing their efforts to remain undetected.

The Pros of Using the Criminal Justice System

In the event that a left-behind parent is both unaware of the whereabouts of the child and does not have access to the child, using the criminal justice system may be helpful as a tracking tool. There are a multitude of federal and state agencies that work in conjunction with local law enforcement to help locate a missing child and abductor in foreign countries. The FBI is the primary source of law enforcement assistance and can provide investigative support and coordinate the issuance of federal warrants. The United States Customs Service and the Immigration and Naturalization Service utilize the Interagency Border Inspection System (IBIS) to simultaneously access and query several federal databases for warrants, and entry or exit restrictions. INTERPOL coordinates activities with foreign law enforcement to trace and locate fugitives and abductors.

What Are the Risks?

Formal resort to the criminal justice system (filing of charges, issuance of an arrest warrant, transmission of an extradition request to a foreign government under an applicable treaty, and criminal prosecution) should be considered carefully. This is especially true if the other country concerned is a party to the Hague Convention. You should be aware that, while you may have a degree of control over the ongoing civil procedures, you may not be able to affect the course of criminal actions once charges are filed. Check with the police and prosecutor to determine if your wishes would be considered in a criminal action.

Furthermore, law enforcement authorities in the United States and some countries abroad may be valuable sources of information and assistance. However, they may be unfamiliar with international parental child abduction. If this is the case, please call the Office of Children's Issues (CA/OCS/CI) as soon as possible.

Your decision on whether or not to try to utilize the criminal justice system depends upon the circumstances of your case. You should also realize that **neither extradition nor prosecution of the abductor guarantees the return of your child**

118

and may in some cases complicate, delay, or ultimately jeopardize return of your child.

Presumably, your primary interest is to obtain the return of your child. That is not the primary responsibility of the prosecutors. When the criminal justice system becomes involved in a case, there are several interests at stake, some of which may be in conflict:

- The interests of the child;
- The interests of each parent/guardian and other immediate family members;
- The interests of the civil justice system in a stable and workable custody arrangement; and
- The interests of the criminal justice system in apprehending, prosecuting, and punishing those who have violated the criminal laws of their jurisdiction in connection with a parental child abduction.

Another factor to consider is the possible reaction of the abductor to the filing of criminal charges and the threat of prosecution and punishment. Although some individuals may be intimidated enough to return the child (with or without an agreement by a prosecutor to the condition that the charges be dropped), others might go deeper into hiding, particularly if they are in a country where they have family or community support. If an abductor is ultimately brought to trial, how far are you willing to go in pursuing criminal prosecution? Unless you are prepared to testify in court against the abductor, you should not pursue criminal prosecution. A final factor to consider is the effect on the child of seeing the abducting parent prosecuted and perhaps incarcerated, with you playing an active role in that process.

Steps to Take in Case You Decide to Use the Criminal Justice System
Once you have decided to pursue criminal remedies, you or your attorney may contact your local prosecutor or law enforcement authorities to request, if provided for by your state law, that the abducting parent be criminally prosecuted and an arrest warrant be issued. In some states, parental child abduction or custodial interference is a misdemeanor; however, under many state laws it may be a crime depending on the circumstances of the removal. If you are able to obtain a state warrant, the local prosecutor can contact the F.B.I. or the United States Attorney to request the issuance of a federal *Unlawful Flight to Avoid Prosecution* (UFAP) warrant for the arrest of the

abductor. The federal Parental Kidnapping Prevention Act of 1980 provides for the issuance of this warrant.

Furthermore, the International Parental Kidnapping Crime Act (IPKCA) of 1993 (H.R. 3378) makes it a federal offense to remove a child from the United States or retain a child (who has been in the United States) outside the United States with intent to obstruct the exercise of parental rights (custody or visitation). An unlawful retention begun after 1993 could violate the statute, even though the actual removal of the child may have occurred before the date of enactment. The F.B.I. is responsible for investigating the abduction.

Prosecution of Agents or Accomplices of the Abductor
Find out if your state, through consultation with a lawyer, has laws that allow legal action to be taken against agents or accomplices to an abduction. Consider whether such actions would be useful in learning your child's whereabouts or compelling the return of your child.

Implications of an Arrest Warrant for a United States Citizen

If the abducting parent is a United States citizen and the subject of a federal arrest warrant, the F.B.I. or United States Attorney's office can ask the Department of State's Passport Office to revoke the person's United States passport. This may or may not be a burden to an abducting parent who is entitled to hold a foreign passport as well as a United States passport. However, an abducting parent who is only a United States citizen becomes an undocumented alien in a foreign country if his or her United States passport is revoked. Some countries may deport undocumented aliens or at least make it difficult for them to remain in the country.

For a United States passport to be revoked, the F.B.I. or United States Attorney must send a request for such action and a copy of the federal warrant to the Department of State's Office of Passport Policy and Advisory Services (telephone 202-663-2662). The regulatory basis for revocation of passports is found in the Code of Federal Regulations (22 C.F.R. 51.70, et seq.)

In certain circumstances, you may decide that revoking the abducting parent's passport will not achieve the desired result. For example, if you know the location of the other parent, there may be a possibility of negotiation and a settlement or, at least, the possibility of communication with your child. If the abducting parent is threatened with passport revocation, he or she might choose to flee with your child again.

Implications of a Warrant for a Non-United States Citizen

Even if the abductor is not a United States citizen, the existence of a federal warrant is important. Such a warrant may encourage the abducting parent to return the child voluntarily, especially if he or she has business or other reasons to travel to the United States. The warrant also serves to inform the foreign government that the abduction of the child is a violation of United States law and that the abductor is a federal fugitive. An arrest warrant is also necessary if you wish to have authorities seek extradition of the abductor. Note that the United States does not have an extradition treaty with every country, and even if a treaty exists extradition may not always be possible.

The Possibility of Extradition

The United States Department of Justice, not the United States Department of State, is responsible for pursuing extradition of wanted persons. Through INTERPOL and other international links, national law enforcement authorities in many countries regularly cooperate in the location and apprehension of international fugitives. Extradition, the surrender of a fugitive or prisoner by one jurisdiction for criminal prosecution or service of a sentence in another jurisdiction, is rarely a viable approach in international child abduction cases. Extradition is utilized only for criminal justice purposes in cases that prosecutors believe can be successfully prosecuted due to the sufficiency of the evidence. Prosecutors may decide not to proceed with a request for extradition for a number of different reasons. Moreover, it must be remembered that extradition **does not** apply to the abducted or wrongfully retained child, but only to the abductor. There is no guarantee that the child will be returned by foreign authorities in connection with extradition of the alleged wrongdoer. Threatened with impending extradition, abducting parents may hide the child or children with a friend or relative in the foreign country.

Another reason that extradition may not be useful is that the offenses of parental child abduction or custodial interference are covered by only a few of the extradition treaties now in force between the

United States and more than 100 foreign countries. Most of these treaties contain a list of covered offenses and were negotiated before international parental child abduction became a widely recognized phenomenon. With respect to these older treaties, there was no intent on the part of the negotiators to cover such conduct, and it cannot therefore be validly argued that parental child abduction is a covered extraditable offense, even if the language used in the list of offenses covered by a given treaty appears somewhat broad (e.g., "abduction" or "kidnapping" or "abduction/kidnapping of minors").

In negotiating more modern extradition treaties, the United States has tried to substitute a "dual criminality" approach for a rigid list of extraditable offenses, or at least has tried to combine the two. Under an extradition treaty with a dual criminality provision, an offense is covered if it is a felony in both countries. Accordingly, if the *underlying conduct* involved in parental child abduction or custodial interference is a felony in both the United States and the foreign jurisdiction involved, then that conduct is an extraditable offense under an extradition treaty based on dual criminality.

Despite the fact that parental child abduction may be covered by certain extradition treaties, you should be aware of potential difficulties in utilizing them. Apart from the possible counterproductive effects already discussed, specifically, most all civil law countries (in contrast with common law countries like the United States, United Kingdom, Canada, and Australia) refuse to extradite their own nationals. Nearly all the nations of Latin America and Europe are civil law countries. Whatever the terms of any applicable extradition treaty, experience has also shown that foreign governments are generally reluctant (and often simply unwilling) to extradite anyone (their own citizens, United States citizens, or third country nationals) for parental child abduction. For extradition to be possible, therefore:

- The local and/or federal prosecutor must decide to file charges and pursue the case, and you should be prepared to testify in any criminal trial;
- There must be an extradition treaty in force between the United States and the country in question;
- The treaty must cover parental child abduction or custodial interference;
- If the person sought is a national of the

country in question, that country must be willing to extradite its own nationals; and,

- The country in question must be willing to extradite persons for parental child abduction/custodial interference (i.e., not refuse to do so for "humanitarian" or other policy reasons).

The Possibility of Prosecution of an Abductor in a Foreign Country

A final possibility in the area of criminal justice is prosecution of the abductor by the authorities of the foreign country where he or she is found. In many countries (but not the United States), nationals of the country can be prosecuted for acts committed abroad if the same conduct would constitute a criminal offense under local law. United States law enforcement authorities can request such prosecution by forwarding to the foreign country the evidence that would have been used in a United States prosecution. United States witnesses may, of course, have to appear and testify in the foreign proceeding. Like the courses of action discussed above, this approach also risks being counterproductive and will not necessarily result in the return of the child.

PART VIII

REFERENCES

Directory - Where to Go for Assistance

Consular Assistance
United States Department of State
The Office of Children's Issues
2401 E Street, N.W., Room L127
Washington, D.C. 20522
Phone: 202 736-7000
Fax: 202 312-9743
Fax-on-Demand: 202 647-3000
After hours: 202 647-5225
Web Site:
http://travel.state.gov/children's_issues.html

Children's Passport Issuance Alert Program
United States Department of State
The Office of Children's Issues
2401 E Street, N.W., Room L127
Washington, D.C. 20037
Phone: 202 736-7000
Fax: 202 312-9743
Fax-on-Demand: 202 647-3000
Web Site:

http://travel.state.gov/children's_issues.html

National Center for Missing and Exploited Children (NCMEC)

699 Prince Street , Alexandria, VA 22314-3175;
Phone: 703 522-9320; Fax: 703 235-4067; Web Site: http://www.missingkids.org

24-hour hot line for emergencies: 1-800-THE-LOST
TTD: 1-800-826-7653

For American Bar Association Publications
American Bar Association (ABA)
750 North Lake Shore Drive
Chicago, IL 60611
Phone: 312 988-5555
Web Site:
http://www.abanet.org/store/catalog.html

Federal Parent Locator Service (FPLS)
Note: The FPLS can be accessed through local and state Child Support Enforcement offices. The names of those offices are available in telephone books and from the address below.
Department of Health and Human Services
Office of Child Support Enforcement
Federal Parent Locator Service (FPLS)
370 L'Enfant Promenade, S.W.
Washington, D.C. 20447
Phone: 202 401-9267
Web Site: http://www.acf.dhhs.gov/programs/cse/

Office of Victims of Crime (OVC)
United States Department of Justice
633 Indiana Ave., N.W.
Washington, D.C. 20531
Phone: 1-800-627-6872
Web Site: http://www.ojp.usdoj.gov/ovc/

International Social Services/American Branch
700 Light Street
Baltimore, MD 21230
Phone: 410 230-2734
Web Site: http://www.iss-usa.org

UNIFORM STATE AND FEDERAL LAWS ON CUSTODY, PARENTAL CHILD ABDUCTION, AND MISSING CHILDREN

Uniform Child Custody Jurisdiction Act (UCCJA) (9 ULA at 123): Determines when a state has jurisdiction to make a custody order and provides procedures for interstate enforcement of

121

orders in custody conflicts.

Uniform Child Custody Jurisdiction and Enforcement Act (UCCJEA)

(9 ULA at 115 (Part 1): Enhances the UCCJA by awarding priority to the child's home state, clarifies the limits of emergency jurisdiction, and grants exclusive jurisdiction to the state making the original custody determination.

MISSING CHILDREN ACT (28 USC 534):

Requires law enforcement to enter complete descriptions of missing children into the National Crime Information Center's (NCIC) Missing Person File, even if the abductor has not been charged with a crime.

NATIONAL CHILD SEARCH ASSISTANCE ACT (42 USC 5779 & 5780):

Mandates elimination of waiting periods before law enforcement takes a missing child report, including family abduction cases; Requires immediate entry of information into the NCIC Missing Person file; Requires close liaison with the National Center for Missing and Exploited Children (NCMEC).

INTERNATIONAL CHILD ABDUCTION REMEDIES ACT (42 USC 11601 et seq.):

Establishes procedures to implement the Hague Convention. Empowers state and federal courts to hear cases under the Convention and allows the Central Authority access to information in certain American records regarding the location of a child and abducting parent.

PARENTAL KIDNAPPING PREVENTION ACT (PKPA)(28 USC 1738A):

Requires authorities of every state to enforce and not modify orders made by the state court exercising proper jurisdiction. Authorizes the use of the Unlawful Flight to Avoid Prosecution (UFAP) warrant and the Federal Parent Locator Service (FPLS) in family abductions.

INTERNATIONAL PARENTAL KIDNAPPING CRIME ACT (IPKCA)(18 USC 1204):

Makes it a federal felony to remove a child under 16 from the United States, or to retain a child outside the United States with the intent to obstruct the lawful exercise of parental rights.

FUGITIVE FELON ACT (18 USC 1073):

Enhances the ability of states to pursue abductors beyond state and national borders; Permits the FBI to investigate cases that would otherwise be under state jurisdiction and authorizes use of UFAP warrants in parental kidnapping cases.

EXTRADITION TREATIES INTERPRETATION ACT of 1998 (Note 18 USC 3181):

Authorizes the United States to interpret extradition treaties listing "kidnapping" as encompassing the offense of parental kidnapping.

READING LIST

This list is intended to give some idea of the relevant literature, but should not be regarded as complete or authoritative.

Atwood, "Child Custody Jurisdiction and Territoriality," 52 *Ohio St. L.J.* 369 (1991)

Charlow, "Jurisdictional Gerrymandering and the Parental Kidnapping Prevention Act," 25 *Fam. L.Q.* 299 (1991)

Coburn, *Runaway Father: One Man's Odyssey from Revenge to Love*. Red Fox Publishing. Bellevue, WA. (1998)

Copertino, "Hague Convention on the Civil Aspects of International Child Abduction: An Analysis of its Efficacy," 6 *Conn. J. Int'l L.* 715 (1991)

Crawford, "Habitual Residence of the Child as the Connecting Factor in Child Abduction Cases: A Consideration of Recent Cases," *Jurid. Rev.* 177 (1992)

Crouch, "Use, Abuse, and Misuse of the UCCJA and PKPA," 6 *Am. J. Fam. L.* 147 (1992)

Davis, "The New Rules on International Child Abduction: Looking Forward to the Past," 3 *Aust'l J. Fam. L.* 31 (1990)

De Hart, *International Child Abduction: A Guide to Applying the 1988 Hague Convention, with Forms* (A publication of the Section of Family Law, American Bar Association) (1993)

Edwards, "The Child Abduction Agony," 140 *New L.J.* 59 (1990)

Evans, "International Child Abduction," 142 *New L.J.* 232 (1992)

Frank, "American and International Responses to International Child Abductions," 16 *N.Y.U. J. Int'l L. & Pol.* 415 (1984)

Girdner, "Obstacles to the Recovery and Return of Parentally Abducted Children," 13 *Children's Legal Rts J.* 2 (1992)

Hilton, "Handling a Hague Trial," 6 *Am. J. Fam. L.* 211 (1992)

Hoff, *Parental Kidnapping: How to Prevent an Abduction and What to Do If your Child Is Abducted* (A publication of the National Center for Missing and Exploited Children. No charge.)

Kindall, "Treaties - Hague Convention on Child Abduction - Wrongful Removal - Grave Risk or Harm to Child" 83 *Am. J. Int'l L.* 586 (1989)

Marks, "Fighting Back: The Attorney's Role in a Parental Kidnapping Case," 64 *Fla. B.J.* 23 (1990)

Murray, "One Child's Odyssey Through the Uniform Child Custody Jurisdiction and Parental Kidnapping Prevention Acts," 1993 *Wis. L. Rev.* 589

Oberdorfer, "Toward a Reasoned Response to Parental Kidnapping," 75 *Minn. L. Rev.* 1701 (1991)

Pfund, "The Hague Convention on International Child Abduction, the International Child Abduction Remedies Act, and the Need for Availability of Counsel for All Petitioners," 24 *Fam. L.Q.* 35 (1990)

Rutherford, "Removing the Tactical Advantages of International Parental Child Abductions under the 1980 Hague Convention on the Civil Aspects of International Child Abductions," 8 *Ariz. J. Int'l & Comp. L.* 149 (1991)

Sagatun, "Parental Child Abduction: The Law, Family Dynamics, and Legal System Responses,"18 *Journal of Crim. Just.* (1990)

Sharpless, "The Parental Kidnapping Prevention Act: Jurisdictional Considerations Where There are Competing Child Custody Orders," 13 *J. Juv. L.* 54 (1992)

Shirman, "International Treatment of Child Abduction and the 1980 Hague Convention," 15 *Suffolk Transnat'l L.J.* 222 (1991)

Stotter, "The Light at the End of the Tunnel: The Hague Convention on International Child Abduction Has Reached Capitol Hill," 9 *Hastings Int'l and Comp. L. Rev.* 285 (1986)

Stranko, "International Child Abduction Remedies," *The Army Lawyer* 28 (Department of the Army pamphlet 27-50-248, July 1993)

Family Advocate, A Practical Journal of the American Bar Association Family Law Section, Spring 1987. (Special issue on divorce law around the world and international parental child abduction.)

Family Advocate, A Practical Journal of the American Bar Association Family Law Section, Spring 1993. (Special issue on international family law.)

Family Law Quarterly, Spring 1994. (Special issue on international family law.)

"The Hague International Child Abduction Convention and the International Child Abduction Remedies Act: Closing Doors to the Parent Abductor," 2 *Transnat'l Law* 589 (1989)

"The Hague Convention on International Child

Abduction: A Practical Application," 10 *Loy. L.A. Int'l & Comp. L.J.* 163 (1988)

"International Child Abduction and the Hague Convention: Emerging Practice and Interpretation of the Discretionary Exception," 25 *Tex. Int'l L.J.* 287 (1990)

"International Parental Child Abduction: The Need for Recognition and Enforcement of Foreign Custody Decrees," 3 *Emory J. Int'l Dispute Resolution* 205 (1989)

"More Than Mere Child's Play: International Parental Abduction of Children," 6 *Dick. L. Rev.* 283 (1988)

"You Must Go Home Again: Friedrich v. Friedrich, The Hague Convention and the International Child Abduction Remedies Act," 18 *N.C. J. Int'l L. & Com. Reg.* 743 (1993)

United States Government Documents on the Hague Convention

Department of State notice in the *Federal Register* of March 26, 1986, pp. 10494-10516.

Senate Treaty Doc. 99-11, 99th Congress, 1st Session.

For the legislative history of the International Child Abduction Remedies Act, Public Law 100-300, see S.1347 and H.R. 2673, and H.R. 3971-3972, 100th Congress, and related hearing reports.

Table 1

Questionnaire for Non-Hague Convention Parents

Your situation is difficult, but there are things that you can do. This list assumes that you know, or strongly suspect, that your child has been abducted abroad to a country that is *not* a party to the Hague Convention on International Child Abduction. If the country *is* a party to the Hague Convention, read this chapter to determine if your situation meets the requirements of the Convention. If you have a Hague case, please submit the Application for Assistance Under The Hague Convention on International Child Abduction.

If you do not have a Hague case, then please complete this checklist/report in detail and forward a **copy** to the Office of Children's Issues when you report the abduction of your child. It is critically important that you also continue to update our office on the status of any developments in your case. You should send us **updated** copies of this checklist when developments occur.

Please fill out a separate checklist for each child.

Name of child (last, first, middle):
Child is currently located (name of country):
Dates of child's birth (month/day/year):
Place of birth:
Is the child a United States citizen? YES NO
Child's United States passport number:
Your name (last, first, middle):
Your nationality:
Address:
Home Phone Number:
Work Phone Number:
Cell Phone Number:
Pager Number:
Home Fax Number:
Work Fax Number:
E-mail Addresse(s):
Your relationship to child:
Abductor's Name (last, first, middle):
Last known United States address:
Telephone numbers (United States and foreign):
Fax number (United States and foreign):
Abductor's relationship to child:
Legal relationship between parents:
> Married
> Divorced
> Never Married
> Separated with custody order
> Separated with no custody order
> Paternity established
> Paternity not established

1. **Emergency Action - What to do Right Away**
- Has your child been taken abroad?
> If yes, please contact the Office of Children's Issues at 202 736-7000.
> If no, please contact the National Center for Missing and Exploited Children at 1-800-THE-LOST.
- If known, please give exact location of child.
> Country:
> Address:
> Telephone, fax numbers and e-mail:
- What is the license plate number of a vehicle the abductor may use to transport the child?
- Have local law enforcement authorities entered that number into the National

Crime Information Center (NCIC) computer? YES NO
- What are the probable airlines and flight numbers the abductor may use to depart the United States?
- Have you filed a missing person report with your local police department?
- YES NO
> Date police report filed:
> Name of police officer:
> Address, e-mail, phone and fax numbers of police officer:

- Have you reported the abduction to the F.B.I.? YES NO
> Date of report to F.B.I.:
> Name of F.B.I. agent:
> Address, e-mail, phone and fax numbers of agent:

- Have you obtained a decree of sole custody or one that prohibits your child from traveling without your permission? In most states, you may be able to obtain such a decree even after a child is abducted. Please submit copies of all court orders.

Dates of all custody orders:
Names of courts in which orders were issued:

Address, e-mail, phone and fax numbers for court (if known)

- Has your child ever been issued a United States passport? YES NO
- Has your child's name been entered in the United States Children's Passport Issuance Alert Program? YES NO
Date United States passport lookout entered:

Passport case number:
- Does the taking parent have ties to another country? YES NO
- May your child have a claim to citizenship of another country? YES NO
- If yes, have you informed the embassy and consulates of the foreign country of

124

your custody decree and asked them not to issue a foreign passport to your child? YES NO
Country contacted:
Date foreign embassy contacted:
Name of official contacted:

- Has your child ever been issued a passport for another country? YES NO

- Might the taking parent transit any other country en route to the country to which he or she has ties? YES NO

- If yes, have you informed the embassy and consulates of that country of your custody decree and asked them not to issue a visa to your child? YES NO
Country contacted:
Date foreign embassy contacted:
Name of official contacted:

- Do you have a valid passport in case you need to travel overseas? YES NO

Your passport number:

- Is this a United States passport? YES NO

If not United States, what country?

Date passport issued:

Date passport expires:

Place passport issued:

(Make a copy of your passport information page, in case you need to submit it.)

1. **The Search**
- Have you tried to establish contact with relatives or friends of the abducting parent? If so, please list their names, addresses, telephone and fax numbers and the dates contacted (Continue on a separate sheet if necessary.)

- Have you contacted the principal of your child's school and asked to be informed of requests for transfer of your child's school records? YES NO

- Have you contacted the registrar of

official records to see if they can block the issuance of a duplicate birth certificate for your child? YES NO

- Have you asked local law enforcement authorities to ask the United States Postal Inspection Service to put a "mail cover" on addresses in the United States to which the abductor might write? YES NO

Date of "mail cover":

Name, address, telephone and fax numbers of investigator doing cover:

- Have you asked local law enforcement authorities to help you obtain information from telephone and credit card companies on the whereabouts of the abductor? YES NO

If yes, please give the date this was done, the contact information for the person who did it, and the results of the search:

- Have you contacted the Office of Victims Assistance in the U.S. Department of Justice (See References)? YES NO

If yes, please provide CA/OCS/CI with details of whom you contacted, and the assistance they were or were not able to provide

Have you contacted the NCMEC to have search posters created (See References)? YES NO

3. After Your Child Has Been Located Abroad
- Have you retained the services of a foreign attorney?

Date attorney retained:

Name of attorney:

Address, e-mail, telephone and fax numbers for attorney:

Date of court hearing abroad:

- Have you sent certified authorized

125

copies of the custody decree, court orders, state and federal warrants, as well as copies of state custody and parental child abduction laws and the Federal Parental Kidnapping Prevention Act to the foreign attorney?

Date sent:

Please list the specific Documents sent:

Table 2

Instructions for Completing the Hague Convention Application

To invoke the Hague Convention, submit **two** completed applications for each child. The application form may be photocopied. Type or print all information in black or blue ink. Furnish as much of the information called for as possible, using an additional sheet of paper if you need more space. If you have further questions about the form, you may wish to refer to the text of the Convention. You may also call CA/OCS/CI at 202-736-7000.

Translation of the supporting documents into the official language of the requested country may be necessary. Translations can speed up the overall process. Foreign attorneys and judges tend to respond more favorably with such documents. Ask CA/OCS/CI for more information about supporting documents.

You may fax your Hague application to CA/OCS/CI, fax number 202-312-9743. Send originals and supporting documents by mail, express mail, or courier service to:

Department of State
CA/OCS/CI, Room L127
2401 E Street, N.W.
Washington, D.C. 20522

Be sure to sign and date the application.

Checklist and Instructions for Completing the Hague Application

Information Block and Details Needed
Identity of Child and Parents
Child's Name - The child's full name: last name, first, middle
Date of Birth - Month/Day/Year

Place of Birth - City/State/Country
Address - Child's address in the country of habitual residence **at the time of** the abduction or removal.
United States Social Security Number - A nine-digit number: 000-00-0000 (if known)
Passport/Identity Card - Issuing country and passport or I.D. number (if known)

Nationality - Include all nationalities of the child, (eg. U.S., Canadian)
Height - Feet and inches
Weight - Pounds
Sex - Male or female
Color of Hair - Child's hair color
Color of Eyes - Child's eye color (Include color photo, if available.)

Father

Name - Full name of father: last name, first, middle
Date of Birth - Month/Day/Year
Place of Birth - City/State/Country
Nationalities - Include all nationalities
Occupation - Usual or last known
Passport/Identity Card - Issuing country and number (if known)
Current Address and Tel. - Include zip code as well as telephone and fax numbers for work and home.
United States Social Security Number - A nine-digit number: 000-00-0000 (if known)
Country of Habitual Residence - Of the father **before** the abduction or retention, particularly if different from that of the child.
Date & Place of Marriage and Divorce, if applicable - Indicate dates and location of marriage and divorce or the parent of the child. It is important to clearly state the marital status at the time of the abduction or retention.

Mother

Name - Full name of mother of child: last name, first, middle (Include maiden name.)
Date of Birth - Month/Day/Year
Place of Birth - City/State/Country
Nationality - Include all nationalities
Passport/Identity Card - Issuing country and number (if known)
Current Address and Tel. - Include zip code as well as telephone and fax numbers for work and home.
Occupation - Usual or last known
United States Social Security Number - A nine-digit number: 000-00-0000 (if known)
Country of Habitual Residence - Of the mother **before** the abduction or retention, particularly if different from that of the child.
Date & Place of Marriage And Divorce, if applicable - Indicate date and location of marriage and divorce, as applicable, of the parents of the child. It is important to clearly indicate the parents'

marital status at the time of the abduction or retention.

II. Person Seeking Return of/Access to Child

This section is for information concerning the person or institution applying for the return of the child to the United States.

Name - Provide the full name of the person or institution asking for the child to be returned.
Nationalities - Of the requester
Relationship to Child - Relationship of the requester to the child (eg, mother, father)
Current Address and Telephone Number - Include home, work and fax number.
Occupation - Of the requester (if a person).
Name, Address and Telephone Number of Legal Adviser, if any - Include zip code as well as telephone and fax numbers. *Some of this information may be the same as that already given.*

III. Information Concerning the Person Alleged to Have Wrongfully Removed or Retained Child
The information about the abducting parent is needed to assist in locating the child. Please provide all requested information and any additional facts that may help authorities locate the child.

Name - Full name of parent who has abducted or wrongfully retained the child.
Relationship to Child - Relationship of the abductor to the child (eg, mother, father)
Known Aliases - Any other names the abductor may use.
Date of Birth - Month/Day/Year
Place of Birth - City/State/Country
Nationalities - Include all nationalities.
Occupation, Name and Address of Employer - Provide any employment information that may be helpful in locating the abductor, such as usual type of work, potential employers or employment agencies.
Passport/Identity Card - Country and number.
United States Social Security Number - A nine-digit number: 000-00-0000 (if known)
Current Location - Of the abductor in the country where the child was taken.
Height - Feet and inches
Weight - Pounds
Color of Hair - Abductor's hair color
Color of Eyes - Abductor's eye color
Other Persons with Possible Additional Information - Provide names, addresses and

telephone numbers of anyone in the Information Relating to the Whereabouts of country to which the child was taken who could give the Central the Child Authority in that country information on the child's location.

IV. Time, Place, Date, and Circumstances of the Wrongful Removal or Retention

Provide the date, to the best of your knowledge, that the child left the United States or when the wrongful retention began. Include the place from which the child was taken. Describe the legal relationship existing between you and the abducting parent when the child was removed. What were the circumstances leading up to the removal or retention? How did you learn of the removal/retention? Did the other parent take the child during a scheduled visitation? Did the other parent take the child for what you believed would be a short visit and then inform you that they were staying? Did they purchase round-trip air tickets to show that they intended to return? Had you and your family moved to the other country, and then you decided to return to the United States?

Take this opportunity to tell your story. Try to anticipate what claims the other parent may make and provide your explanation.
Do not limit yourself to the space provided on the form. Additional pages may be attached to fully narrate the circumstances. However, please be concise.

V. Factual or Legal Grounds Justifying Request

Provide information and documentation establishing that you had, and were exercising, a right of custody at the time of the child's removal. Generally, a right of custody is created by a custody order when parents are divorced, or by operation of state law when parents are still married or were never married when the child was taken. As stated, the Convention defines "rights of custody" as including "rights relating to the care of the child and, in particular, the right to determine the child's place of residence." Thus, you may have a "right of custody" as defined by the Convention even if you do not have court-ordered joint or sole custody of the child.

IMPORTANT

If there is no applicable court order, please provide a copy of the state statute, case law or an affidavit of law prepared by an attorney that establishes your right of custody at the time of the

child's removal. This provision of the law may sometimes be found in the estate and wills section of the state code. Remember, you are not attempting to show that you would have an equal right to obtain custody in a subsequent custody proceeding, but that you **had** and were exercising a right of custody when the child was taken.

SEND IN YOUR HAGUE APPLICTION IMMEDIATELY
Do NOT wait to get an order of custody. Orders issued after removal/retention are irrelevant in a Hague hearing.

VI. Civil Proceeding in Progress, If Any

Indicate any civil action (in the United States or abroad) that may be pending (e.g.. custody, divorce). Name court and hearing dates.

VII. Child Is to Be Returned To:

Name - of person to whom child will be returned.
Date of Birth - of person to whom child will be returned.
Place of Birth - of person to whom child will be returned.
Address - of person to whom child will be returned.
Telephone Number - of person to whom child will be returned.

Proposed Arrangements for Return - Provide means by which you propose the child Return Travel of Child will return to the United States if this is ordered. For example, would you travel to pick up the child, or would someone go in your place? Is the child old enough to travel by him or herself? Is there someone in the foreign country who could return with the child? Would the child travel by car, train, airplane? Be specific.

VIII. Other Remarks

State here whether you are applying for return or access under the Convention. You should include here any additional information that you believe may be pertinent to the Hague application.

Sign and date the application in black or blue ink.

HAGUE APPLICATION CHECKLIST

(Check with country officer for specific requirements.)

_____ **Application form** - signed original, one

for each child. Note: Country may require use of special application form.

_____ **Marriage Certificate** (if applicable) May need to be certified copy.

_____ **Birth Certificate of child** May need to be certified copy.

_____ **Divorce Decree** (if applicable) May need to be certified copy.

_____ Evidence of custodial right

- Custody order, or
- Copy of state statute, or
- Affidavit of law regarding presumption of custody under state law, or
- Article 15 determination by state court.

_____ Other pertinent court documents

_____ Photographs of taking parent and child

_____ Statement regarding circumstances of removal or retention

_____ Other documents specifically required by receiving country. (e.g. - Article 28 Statement - power of attorney to foreign Central Authority

_____ Translations (if applicable)

_____ Application for legal assistance (if applicable)

Table 3

Children's Passport Issuance Alert Program

The Children's Passport Issuance Alert Program is a service for the parents and legal guardians of minor children. It enables the Department of State's Office of Children's Issues to notify a parent or court ordered legal guardian, when requested, before issuing a United States passport for his or her child. The parent, legal guardian, legal representatives, or the court of competent jurisdiction must submit a written request for entry of a child's name into the program to the Office of Children's Issues.

Passport Issuance to Children under Age 18

On July 2, 2001, the Department of State began implementation of a new law regarding the passport applications of minor U.S. citizens under the age of 14. A person now applying for a passport for a child under 14 must show that both parents consent to the issuance or that the applying

parent has sole authority to obtain the passport. Passport applications made in the U.S. and at consular offices abroad will both be covered by the new law. Exceptions to this requirement may be made in special family circumstances or exigent circumstances necessitating the immediate travel of the child.

Once a passport is issued, its use is not tracked or controlled by the Department of State. There are no exit controls for American citizens leaving the United States. If you believe that your child may be abducted internationally, immediately contact the Office of Children's Issues *and* inform appropriate law enforcement officials.

Information regarding the issuance of a passport to a minor is available to either parent, regardless of custody rights, as long as the requesting parents' rights have not been terminated. The Department of State's Children's Passport Issuance Alert Program is a program to alert us when an application for a United States passport is made. This is not a program for tracking the use of a passport. This program can be used to inform a parent or a court when an application for a United States passport is executed on behalf of a child. The alert program generally remains in effect until each child turns 18. It is very important that parents keep us informed in writing of any changes to contact information and legal representation. Failure to notify CA/OCS/CI of a current address may result in a passport issuance for your child without your consent.

Passports - General Information

A passport is a travel document issued by competent authority showing the bearer's origin, identity, and nationality, which is valid for the entry of the bearer into a foreign country (8 United States C 1101(3)). Under United States law, United States citizens must enter and depart the United States with valid United States passports (8 United States C 1185(b)). This requirement is waived, however, for travel from countries within the Western Hemisphere, with the exception of Cuba (22 CFR 53.2). However, each foreign country has its own entry requirements concerning citizenship, passports and visas. Information regarding those requirements may be obtained from the appropriate foreign embassy or consulate. The addresses and telephone numbers for the foreign embassy or consulate near you are found in our Foreign Entry Requirements booklet.

The Privacy Act and Passports

Passport information is protected by the provisions of the Privacy Act (PL 93-579) passed by Congress in 1974. Information regarding a minor's passport is available to either parent. Information regarding adults may be available to law enforcement officials or pursuant to a court order issued by the court of competent jurisdiction in accordance with (22 CFR 51.27). If you want us to forward to the Foreign Embassy the information contained in your request to the Office of Children's Issues, please complete and sign the Foreign Embassy Contact Form. That form contains a waiver of your Privacy Act Rights and the rights of your minor children. For further information regarding the issuance or denial of United States passports to minors involved in custody disputes, or about international child abduction, please contact us at 202-736-7000 (this is a recorded message which provides access to country officers). See the Chapter on Passports. While we make every effort to be of assistance, the Office of Children's Issues can assume no legal responsibility for the services provided.

Dual Nationality for Children

Many children, whether born in the United States or born abroad to a United States citizen parent, are citizens of both the United States and another country. This may occur through the child's birth abroad, through a parent who was born outside the United States, or a parent who has acquired a second nationality

through naturalization in another country. There is no requirement that a United States citizen parent consent to the acquisition of another nationality.

The inability to obtain a United States passport through the Children's Passport Issuance Alert Program does not automatically prevent a dual national child from obtaining and traveling on a foreign passport. There is no requirement that foreign embassies adhere to United States regulations regarding issuance and denial of their passports to United States citizen minors who have dual nationality. If there is a possibility that the child has another nationality, you may contact the country's embassy or consulate directly to inquire about denial of that country's passport. The addresses and telephone numbers for the foreign embassy or consulate near you are found in our Foreign Entry Requirements booklet.

More information about the child-related services available to parents through the Bureau of Consular Affairs is available by calling the Office of Children's Issues at 202-736-7000 and speaking to an officer who deals with a specific country. You may prefer using the Fax-on Demand System by calling 202-647-3000 from the fax machine telephone. There is additional information about the prevention of International Parental Child Abduction in the department of State's web page.

ENTRY INTO THE CHILDREN'S PASSPORT ISSUANCE ALERT PROGRAM

REQUEST FORM. Complete one form for EACH child, and submit the completed and SIGNED request to the Office of Children's Issues by mail or fax.

1. **Please provide information about each child in order to make the alert system effective. Please PRINT CLEARLY OR TYPE the information.**
   Child's Full Name:
   Date of Birth:
   Place of Birth:
   Sex:
   Social Security Number:
   US Passport Number(s):
   Foreign Passport Number(s), List any other country involved:

2. **Please provide the following information about yourself so that we can acknowledge your request, and alert you in the future.**
   Your Name:
   Relationship to the child shown above:
   Mailing Address:

   Telephone Numbers/Fax Numbers

   I request that my child's name, as shown above, be entered into the Children's Passport Issuance Alert Program. Please notify me of any pending United States passport applications, and any United States passports still valid for travel.

Signed:_____
Dated:_____
(Customary legal signature of parent or guardian) Please *mail or fax the completed, signed form(s) to the Office of Children's Issues, 2401 E Street, NW, SA-1, Room L-127,*

Washington, DC 20037; FAX: 202-312-9743. You will receive written acknowledgement and information.

INTERNATIONAL PARENTAL CHILD ABDUCTION

ISLAMIC FAMILY LAW

DISCLAIMER: THE INFORMATION IN THIS CIRCULAR RELATING TO THE LEGAL REQUIREMENTS OF SPECIFIC FOREIGN COUNTRIES IS PROVIDED FOR GENERAL INFORMATION ONLY. QUESTIONS INVOLVING INTERPRETATION OF SPECIFIC FOREIGN LAWS SHOULD BE ADDRESSED TO FOREIGN COUNSEL.
NOTE:

The information contained in this flyer is intended as an introduction to the basic elements of Islamic family law. It is not intended as a legal reference.

It is designed to make clear the basic rights and restrictions resulting from marriages sanctioned by Islamic law between Muslim and non-Muslim partners. For Americans, the most troubling of these restrictions have been:

-- the inability of wives to leave an Islamic country without permission of their husbands;-- the wives' inability to take their children from these countries without such permission; and-- the fact that fathers have ultimate custody of children.

MARRIAGE
In Islam, the act of marriage occurs with the conclusion of the marriage contract. The marriage contract itself is completed by an offer and acceptance, both of which must be made on the same occasion by two qualified parties. If a marriage has been contracted by competent persons in the presence of two witnesses and has been adequately publicized, it is complete and binding. **It requires no religious or other rites and ceremonies because in Islamic law formalities have no value insofar as contracts are concerned. Such marriages are conducted only if both parties are willing.**

MIXED MARRIAGES
With few exceptions, a Christian or Jew who marries a Muslim and resides in an Islamic country will be subject to provisions of Islamic family law in that country. In these circumstances:
-- Any children born to the wife will be considered Muslim. They will usually also be considered citizens of the father's country.

-- **The husband's permission is always needed for the children to leave an Islamic country despite the fact that the children will also have, for example, American citizenship.** Foreign immigration authorities can be expected to enforce these regulations. The ability of U.S. consular officers to aid an American woman who wishes to leave the country with her children is very limited.

-- The wife may be divorced by her husband at any time with little difficulty and without a court hearing.
-- At a certain point in age, the children will come under the custody of the father or his family.
-- In Islamic countries, the wife will need the permission of her husband to leave the country.

CHILDREN'S RIGHTS
There are three types of guardianship which are fixed for a child from the time of its birth:
-- The first is guardianship of upbringing, which is overseen by women during the age of dependence. The age at which this period of dependence terminates varies: anywhere from 7 years for a son and 9 for a daughter to 9 and 11, respectively. In the case of divorced parents, it is permissible for a daughter to remain with her mother **if the parents agree.** But such an agreement cannot be made for a son.

-- The second is the child's spiritual guardianship. The spiritual guardian may be the father or a full blooded male relative of the father.

-- The third is guardianship over the child's property which usually is carried out by the father.

Chapter 14

International Adoptions

[The information in this chapter is reprinted verbatim from a bulletin issued by the U.S. State Department, Office of Citizens Consular Services. It is intended to serve as advice to Americans at home and abroad.]

INTRODUCTION

American citizens are seeking to adopt children in ever increasing numbers. With the reduction in children available for adoption in the United States, more and more U.S. citizens have adopted children from other countries. This year, thousands of children came to the United States from foreign countries, either adopted abroad by U.S. citizens or as potential adoptees. This chapter provides both information and guidance to U.S. citizens seeking information about international adoptions.

International adoption is essentially a private legal matter between a private individual (or couple) who wishes to adopt, and a foreign court, which operates under that country's laws and regulations. U.S. authorities cannot intervene on behalf of prospective parents with the courts in the country where the adoption takes place. However, the Department of State does provide extensive information about the adoption processes in various countries and the U.S. legal requirements to bring a child adopted abroad to the United States. The Office of Children's Issues in the Bureau of Consular Affairs provides brochures describing the adoption process in numerous countries. Adoption information is also available on our automated facsimile system and Internet (see Section C). In addition, we provide recorded information on international adoption for several countries on a twenty-four hour basis through our recorded telephone messages at (202) 736-7000 and at our Internet site at http://travel.state.gov. If you have questions, please call us at 202-312-9700. You may also fax us at 202-312-9743, or write us at:

Office of Children's Issues
U.S. Department of State

CA/OCS/CI
1800 G Street, NW
Suite 2100
Washington, D.C. 20006

I. General Information

The Role of the State Department:
The State Department **CAN**:
- Provide information about international adoption in foreign countries
- Provide general information about U.S. visa requirements for international adoption
- Make inquiries of the U.S. consular section abroad regarding the status of a specific adoption case and clarify documentation or other requirements
- Ensure that U.S. citizens are not discriminated against by foreign authorities or courts

The State Department **CANNOT**:
- Locate a child or children available for adoption
- Become directly involved in the adoption process in another country
- Act as an attorney or represent adoptive parents in court
- Order that an adoption take place or that a visa be issued

Other Sources of Information:
The Office of Children's Issues frequently receives requests for general information about international adoption. Questions range from how to begin the adoption process to how to find an agency, or what countries to consider. The public library and local telephone yellow pages (see "Adoption Services") are good sources of general information, including adoption agencies and attorneys who specialize in adoption, support

133

groups and books and magazines related to adoption (See Appendices A and B). Additionally, a number of umbrella organizations provide extensive general information that can be very helpful both before and after the adoption. Several of these organizations publish articles and lists of adoption agencies. For specific information about agencies operating in your area, call your state social services agency or the U.S. Department of Health and Human Services (HHS) office.

Adoption opportunities, regulations, and even the social climate may change at any time, making it impossible to categorically state in which country adoptions will proceed smoothly. For example, social and religious restrictions in Africa and the Middle East make adoption difficult in those regions. However, the Department of State does maintain statistics indicating the number of visas (IR-3 and IR-4) for adoption issued yearly by country. Section C C, Part III (page 19) directs you the Consular Affairs' Internet site so that you can view the most recent list of the top 20 countries. Since countries do change their adoption regulations, it is necessary for you to thoroughly investigate a country before initiating an adoption.

II. Guidelines on International Adoption

To complete an international adoption and bring a child to the United States, prospective adoptive parent(s) must fulfill the requirements set by the United States Bureau of Citizenship and Naturalization Services in the Department of Homeland Security (BCIS), the foreign country in which the child resides and sometimes the state of residence of the adoptive parent(s). Although procedures and documentary requirements may seem repetitive, you should procure several copies of each document in the event they are needed to meet the requirements of BCIS, the foreign country and your home state. The process is designed to protect the child, the adoptive parent(s) and the birth parent(s).

The U.S. Immigration and Nationality Act (INA) is the U.S. immigration law regarding the issuance of visas to nationals of other countries, including children adopted abroad or coming to the United States for adoption. The basic statutory provision concerning adopted children is in INA Section 101(b)(1)(E). Which provides immigrant classification for "a child adopted while under the age of sixteen years if the child has been in the legal custody of, and has resided with, the adopting parent or parents for at least two years." This so-called "two-year provision" is for individuals who are temporarily residing abroad and wish to adopt a child in accordance with the laws of the foreign state where they reside. Most adoptive parents, however, are not able to spend two years abroad living with the child. Therefore, they seek benefits under another provision of the INA, Section 101(b)(1)(F), which grants immigrant classification to orphans who have been adopted or will be adopted by U.S. citizens. Under this section of the law, both the child and the adoptive parents must satisfy a number of requirements established by the INA and the related regulations, but the two-year residency requirement is eliminated. Only after it is demonstrated that both the parents and the child qualify, can the child be issued a visa to travel to the United States.

For specific information about BCIS requirements, see the U.S. Department of Justice, Bureau of Citizenship and Naturalization Services in the Department of Homeland Security, brochure M-249Y, The Immigration of Adopted and Prospective Adoptive Children. The BCIS also has a toll-free information number, from which you can obtain form M-249 booklets and the telephone numbers of local BCIS offices in the United States. The toll-free number is 1-800-375-5283 or ins.usdoj.gov.

Your adoption agency or attorney will require specific documents, as will your state of residence. These requirements may appear daunting. The chart, in Section C, Part IV, serves as a checklist for many of the documents that you will be expected to provide. In general, all agencies, whether state or private, require proof of citizenship, marriage (if a married couple), health, financial stability and information about arrests or certification of a clean criminal record. In addition, the home study (a report on the family prepared by a licensed social worker or other person licensed to perform home studies) normally is required by both the foreign government and the BCIS. The local government of the country from which you wish to adopt, your chosen adoption agency, or attorney may request additional documents.

Bureau of Citizenship and Naturalization Services in the Department of Homeland Security Approval

Adoptive and prospective adoptive parent(s) must comply with U.S. immigration procedures, initiated through the BCIS in the United States in order to bring an adoptive child to the U.S. Simply locating a child in a foreign country and going to the U.S. Embassy to obtain a visa for the child will not meet these requirements. An orphan cannot be brought to the United States without a visa, which is based upon an BCIS approved petition (form I-600). To facilitate the process, we suggest that you contact the BCIS office that has jurisdiction over your place of residence in the United States for information, early in the pre-adoption process.

The Orphan Petition form has two parts: I-600 and I-600A. The I-600 is used when the adoptive parents have identified a specific child. The I-600 is filed with the appropriate office of the BCIS in the United States. The BCIS adjudicates all aspects of the I-600 petition - including the suitability of the adoptive parent(s), compliance with any state pre-adoption requirements (if the child is to be adopted after entry into the United States), and the qualifications of the child as an orphan within the meaning of section 101(b)(1)(F) of the Immigration and Nationality Act (See BCIS brochure M-249Y). When the petition has been approved, the BCIS notifies the U.S. embassy or consulate that processes visas for residents of the child's country. At the same time, the approved I-600 petition and supporting documents are sent to the National Visa Center in New Hampshire, where the petition is assigned a computer tracking code and then mailed to the appropriate U.S. consular office abroad.

The I-600A form should be filed if the prospective adoptive parent(s) have not yet identified a child or intend to go abroad to locate a child for adoption. Like the I-600, this application is filed at the local BCIS office in the United States with jurisdiction over the place of residence of the adoptive parent(s). BCIS evaluates the suitability of the prospective adoptive parent(s). When the application is approved, notification is sent to the adoptive parents and to the appropriate U.S. mission in the country where the parents have indicated they would like to adopt. Once the parents have located a specific child, they must file an I-600 Petition. The parents may file the I-600 petition either with their local BCIS office in the United States or with the BCIS or U.S. consular office overseas. Although only one parent must be physically present to file the I-600 petition overseas, that parent must be a U.S. citizen. A third party may not file the petition on the parents' behalf, even with a valid Power of Attorney. In addition, if only one of the two parents travels, the petition must nevertheless be properly executed (signed) by both parents after it has been completely filled out. This means one parent cannot sign for the other parent and neither parent may sign the petition until all the details about the child have been entered on the form. The traveling parent can, however, use express mail service to obtain the other parent's signature.

The Foreign Adoption Process
Although adoption procedures vary from country to country, most countries require that prior to any court action, a child placed for adoption be legally recognized as an orphan or, in the case where a parent is living, be legally and irrevocably released for adoption in a manner provided for under local foreign law. In addition, the adoption laws in most countries require the full adoption of the child in the foreign court after the child has been declared an orphan or released by the living parent to an appropriate foreign authority. Some countries do allow simple adoption, which means that the adopting parent(s) can be granted guardianship of the child by the foreign court. This will permit child to leave the foreign country to be adopted in the country of the adopting parent(s). A few countries do allow adoptive parents to adopt through a third party without actually traveling to that country. It is important to note that a foreign country's determination that the child is an orphan does not guarantee that the child will be considered an orphan under the U.S. Immigration and Nationality Act, since the foreign country may use different standards. Questions, which involve interpretation of specific foreign laws, should be addressed to a foreign attorney operating in the country where the adoption will take place.

Some countries accept the properly authenticated home study of the prospective adoptive parent(s) at face value, while other countries also require a personal appearance by the adoptive parent(s) before the foreign court. Sometimes, countries require a period of residence by one or both adoptive parents. In these cases, prospective adoptive parents may find it necessary to spend an extended period in the foreign country awaiting the completion of the foreign adoption documents. Additionally, several countries require a post-adoption follow-up conducted by the adoption agency or the foreign country's consul in the United States.

III. Immigrant Visas
When the foreign adoption (or guardianship

process in those countries that allow guardianship) is completed, the adoptive parent(s) can apply for an immigrant visa (IR-3 for a child adopted abroad or IR-4 for a child to be adopted in the United States) at the appropriate U.S. consular office abroad. In addition to the notification of the approved I-600 or I-600A petition from the BCIS, the consular officer also requires specific documentation to conduct a visa interview and to approve visa issuance. Some of these requirements are discussed below. However, we strongly suggest that adoptive parents contact the consular section conducting the visa interview prior to the actual scheduling of the interview. Remember, a visa is not permission to enter the United States. Final authority to enter the U.S. rests with the BCIS at the port of entry.

Meeting with the consular officer prior to the interview allows parents to obtain a list of the visa requirements and necessary forms and provides an opportunity to discuss any questions or concerns. In addition, if time permits, an early meeting may allow the consular officer to see the child for whom the visa is necessary. "Visual inspection" of the child is a requirement. It may be more convenient for all parties involved for the prospective adoptive parents not to be distracted with the child(ren) during the final visa interview. Some consular sections schedule special times to handle orphan petitions, facilitating the workflow and ensuring availability of consular staff and facilities for the adoptive parents and children.

Another visa requirement is the medical examination of the child by a designated physician. The U.S. embassy or consulate must approve the physician conducting the examination. The medical examination focuses primarily on detecting certain serious contagious diseases or disabilities that may be a basis for visa ineligibility. If the child is found to have any of these illnesses or disabilities, the child may still be issued a visa after the illness has been treated and is no longer contagious, or after a waiver of the visa eligibility is approved by the BCIS. If the physician or the consular official notes that the child has a serious disease or disability, the parents will be notified and asked if they wish to proceed with the child's immigration. Prospective adoptive parents should not rely on this medical examination to detect all possible disabilities or illnesses. You may wish to arrange an additional private medical examination if there are concerns about the child's health.

The fee for an immigrant visa is $260 for the application and $65 for the visa, which must be paid either in local currency or U.S. dollars in cash, money order, cashier's check or certified check. Neither personal checks nor credit cards are accepted.

The Visa Interview
The consular section will schedule the final visa interview once all the required documents have been provided and the file is complete.
This documentation includes:

- notification by the BCIS of the I-600 or I-600A approval
- final adoption decree or proof of custody from the foreign government
- the child's birth certificate
- the child's passport (from the country of the child's nationality)
- the completed and signed medical examination report
- necessary photographs of the child
- the visa application (Form OF 230)
- completed I-600 petition (if it was not previously approved by BCIS)

Although the final visa interview appears to involve a single action which may be completed quickly, the consular officer must perform several different steps required by law and regulation. The officer must review the I-600 petition, verify the child's status as an orphan, establish that the prospective parent(s) have legal custody, survey the child's medical condition and confirm that the child has the required travel documentation.

Questions concerning legal custody or proper documentation for the child must be resolved in accordance with the law of the country of the child's nationality or residence. Since requirements vary from country to country, the consular section can be helpful in explaining requirements in their local area. Nevertheless, the adoptive parent(s) or the adoption agent is responsible for meeting these requirements. As explained earlier, the child's ability to qualify for an immigrant visa as an orphan is determined by U.S. law. An adoption by a court decree or comparable order by a competent authority does not automatically qualify a child for an immigrant visa for entry into the United States.

The Orphan Definition
The consular officer must verify 1) the identity of the child and 2) the child's status as an "orphan"

as defined by the INA. Webster's Dictionary defines an orphan as "a child whose parents are dead" and a child who meets that definition will indeed be considered an orphan according to U.S. immigration law. The INA, however, also defines an orphan as a child who has no parents due to several other circumstances. Prospective adoptive parents should be aware that U.S. law, and not a foreign court, determines if a particular child qualifies for an orphan visa. As a rule, most children who are in orphanages will qualify as "orphans" whereas children whose parents legally relinquished them to an adoption agency or adoptive parent will not. If there are doubts about a particular child's eligibility as an orphan, the consular officer cannot approve the petition and must forward the case to BCIS.

Filing a Petition

The adoptive parents should file the I-600 Petition to Classify an Orphan as an Immediate Relative with the BCIS office having jurisdiction over their place of residence. If the adopting parent(s) have submitted an I-600A Application for Advance Processing to the BCIS and the approval notice has been forwarded to the U.S. Embassy or Consulate in the child's home country, the parent(s) may file the I-600 in person at that Embassy or Consulate. If there is no BCIS office in that country, a consular officer has the authority to approve the I-600, relying upon the approved I-600A as demonstration of the suitability of the prospective adoptive parent(s) and their compliance with any applicable state pre-adoption requirements.

Adopted or To-Be-Adopted

U.S. law distinguishes between orphans adopted overseas and orphans coming to the United States for adoption. An orphan fully adopted overseas may receive an IR-3 visa. To qualify for an IR-3, the child must also have been seen by both parents prior to or during the adoption proceedings. An orphan who has not been fully adopted, or whose adoptive parents did not see him/her prior to the adoption's finalization, may receive an IR-4 visa. Any child who enters the U.S. on an IR-4 immigrant visa must be re-adopted after he/she enters the United States, in accordance with applicable laws of the state in which the family resides. Thus, before an IR-4 visa can be issued, the consular officer must be sure that pre-adoption requirements by the child's future state of residence have been met. Adoptive parent(s) should determine in advance the requirements of their own particular state of residence. This information is available through the state social services agency or many adoption practitioners.

The Medical Examination

Every immigrant visa applicant must undergo a physical examination by a physician who has been certified by the U.S. Government (the Centers for Disease Control) for that purpose. The U.S. Embassy or Consulate can provide a list of such physicians within the foreign country. The medical examination focuses primarily on detecting certain serious infectious or contagious diseases or medical disabilities that may be a basis for visa ineligibility. If the child is found to have any of these illnesses or disabilities, the child may still be issued a visa after the illness has been successfully treated, or after a waiver of the visa eligibility is approved by the BCIS. If the physician or the consular official notes that the child has a serious disease or disability, the parents will be notified and asked if they wish to proceed with the child's immigration. Prospective adoptive parents should not rely on this medical examination to detect all possible medical conditions and may wish to arrange an additional private medical examination if they have concerns about the child's health.

While the physician conducts the medical examination, the consular officer must complete the I-604 Report on Overseas Orphan Investigation. This report consists of a review of the facts and documents to verify that the child qualifies as an orphan. In addition, the consular officer ensures that the adoptive parents are aware of any medical problems that the medical examination may have uncovered. Only when this report is completed can the consular officer finally approve the I-600 petition and/or immigrant visa.

Cases Referred to BCIS

The authority to approve petitions rests with BCIS. This authority has been delegated to consular officers only in limited circumstances and then only when the case is "clearly approvable." Occasionally, the I-604 Report does not confirm that the child is an orphan as defined by the INA. In such a case, the consular officer will provide the adoptive parents or their agent with an opportunity to submit additional information. If the outstanding questions can be answered, the case can be completed. If an issue cannot be resolved, however, the consular officer cannot approve the petition and must refer the petition to the appropriate BCIS office for adjudication.

137

When a petition has been referred to BCIS, questions about the status of the case must be addressed to the appropriate office of that agency. Since different BCIS offices can have jurisdiction, it is important to understand to which BCIS office the petition has been referred. Several scenarios may occur:

1) BCIS reviews the documentation and approves (or re-affirms) the petition. The BCIS will then notify the Embassy or Consulate and the consular officer will continue processing of the visa application.

2) BCIS reviews the documents and requests that the consular officer conduct a field investigation to ensure that no fraud or illegal activity was involved. The embassy or consulate conducts the investigation and reports its findings to the BCIS for a final decision.

3) BCIS can deny the petition. If BCIS denies the petition, the adoptive parents can appeal the denial to the BCIS Associate Commissioner for Examinations, Administrative Appeals Office for a legal ruling. Alternatively, adoptive parents can discuss other options with the BCIS office having jurisdiction over their case.*

*In rare and exceptional circumstances, children deemed ineligible for admission to the United States may qualify for "humanitarian parole" and gain entry. Only BCIS has the authority to grant humanitarian parole.

IV. Prevention of Adoption Fraud

International adoptions have become a lucrative business because of the huge demand for adoptable children. The combination of people motivated by personal gain and parents desperate to adopt a child under any circumstances, creates the potential for fraudulent adoptions. Take care to avoid these adoption scams.

You can avoid the heartache of losing a potentially adoptable child by using only reputable agencies, attorneys, and facilitators. If the answers to your questions appear to be contradictory, vague, or unrealistic, be wary. The consular section in the U.S. Embassy or Consulate in the country of planned adoption can provide accurate information concerning local legal practices. If you have problems with agencies or intermediaries in the United States, you should report these concerns immediately to the appropriate state authorities, i.e., your state social services office, District Attorney, Better Business Bureau, or state Attorney General's office. The BCIS should be notified of these concerns as well.

The lack of state regulatory requirements for international adoption agencies in some states has permitted some individuals, inexperienced in the area of foreign adoptions, to set up businesses. Some prospective adoptive parents are charged exorbitant fees. Two common abuses are 1) knowingly offering a supposedly healthy child for adoption who is later found to be seriously ill, and 2) obtaining prepayment for adoption of a nonexistent or ineligible child. In some countries, it is advisable to have the child examined by a physician before completing adoption procedures. This examination is separate from the routine medical examination required after completion of the adoption for visa purposes. Some states have moved to revoke licenses or prosecute the individuals connected with these fraudulent activities after receiving complaints. However, it should be noted that most adoption practitioners in the United States are legitimate professionals with experience in domestic and international adoptions.

In the international area, the Department of State consistently takes a strong stand against fraudulent adoption procedures. This policy flows from our general obligation to respect host country laws, to discourage any illegal activities and to avoid the possibility that a country may prohibit international adoptions entirely. The Department of State has unfailingly expressed its support for measures taken by foreign states to reduce adoption abuses.

V. Validity of Foreign Adoptions in the United States

In most cases, the formal adoption of a child in a foreign court is legally acceptable in the United States. A U.S. state court, however, is not required to automatically recognize a foreign adoption decree. This does not suggest that the United States does not respect foreign procedures or recognize the authority of the foreign country in relation to the child. Nonetheless, the status of the involved child may be subject to challenge in state court unless an adoption decree is entered in a state in the United States. Many adoption practitioners recommend that the child adopted abroad be re-adopted in a court of his/her state of residence in the United States as a precautionary measure.

Following a re-adoption in the state court, parents can request that a state birth certificate be issued. This should be recognized in all other U.S. states. In some instances, re-adoption of the child in the United States is required. This often occurs if the adoptive parent (or only one of a married couple) did not see the child prior to or during the adoption proceedings abroad. The child must be re-adopted in the U.S. in such circumstances, even if a full final adoption decree has been issued in the foreign country.

VI. Automatic Acquisition of U.S. Citizenship for an Adopted Child

How is this possible?
On February 27, 2001, the Child Citizenship Act of 2000 became effective. The aim of this law, which, among other things, amends Section 320 of the Immigration and Nationality Act (INA), is to facilitate the automatic acquisition of U.S. citizenship for both biological and adopted children of U.S. citizens who are born abroad and who do not acquire U.S. citizenship at birth.

What are the requirements?
The following are the Act's requirements:
1. At least one parent of the child must be a U.S. citizen, either by birth or naturalization.
2. The child must be under the age of 18.
3. In the case of an adopted child, the adoption must be final.

VII. Frequently Asked Questions

Q: Will a child who has met the requirements of the Child Citizenship Act of 2000 need to apply for a passport from the State Department or a Certificate of Citizenship from the Bureau of Citizenship and Naturalization Services in the Department of Homeland Security (BCIS) in order to become a citizen?
A: No. As soon as the law's requirements have been met, the child acquires U.S. citizenship automatically without the need to apply for either a passport or a Certificate of Citizenship.

Q: What documents are required to obtain a passport for a child who became a U.S. citizen under the Child Citizenship Act of 2000?
A: (1) Evidence of the child's relationship to a U.S. citizen parent (a certified copy of the final adoption decree); (2) the child's foreign passport with BCIS's I-551 stamp or the child's resident alien card; and (3) the parent's valid identification.

Q: How does a child demonstrate adoption in order to obtain a passport and/or Certificate of Citizenship?
A: By presenting a certified copy of a final adoption decree.

Q: What if I live abroad and have no address in the United States? Can my adopted child become a U.S. citizen?
A: Yes. Adoptive parents who wish to naturalize their children but who will continue to reside abroad may enter their adoptive children with a B-2 visa and complete the expeditious naturalization process. This requires that they coordinate with the BCIS office which has jurisdiction over their case and which will set an appointment for the procedure. To obtain a B-2 visa, adoptive parents must demonstrate that the child qualifies either under the two-year physical/legal custody rule or present an approved I-600. When applying for a nonimmigrant visa, the adoptive parents must also prove that they have made all the necessary arrangements with the BCIS office and that they intend to depart the U.S. to continue their residence abroad. Adoptive parents can show proof of arrangements made with the BCIS by presenting an BCIS General Call-in Letter (Form G-56). Note that parents who qualify under the two-year legal/physical custody rule and who will continue to reside abroad can avoid the cost and paperwork of both the I-130 and the I-600 by using this procedure. Expeditious naturalization in all cases must be complete before the child turns 18.

Q: Where do I obtain information on adopting abroad?
A: The Office of Children's Issues maintains a file of country-specific adoption information sheets. In addition, adoption agencies, parent support groups, adoption magazines and newsletters can provide a wealth of information. Talking with families who have adopted children and specialists in adoption issues can be a helpful measure to prepare for the issues involved with an international adoption.

Q: How can I check the credentials of an adoption provider?
A: There are several ways to investigate the credentials of an adoption provider before engaging its services. It is helpful to talk with other families or individuals in your adoptive support group who have had prior experience with the agency, attorney or individual you are planning

139

to select. The Better Business Bureau may be able to advise you if there has been a negative report about a business but would not necessarily have information concerning individuals claiming to be adoption experts. The adoption section of the state social services office and the state Attorney General's office can usually be of assistance. Finally, ask for references and check them thoroughly.

Q: How should I prepare to travel abroad?
A: What you should take when traveling abroad will depend on the country (climate and season), the length of your stay, and the particulars of the child you will adopt (age, health, etc.). In countries with limited resources, it is advisable to bring supplies from the United States. In most countries, disposable diapers and disposable bottles are unavailable or very expensive. A good travel agent should be able to provide information about the availability of products and services in a country. Alternatively, you might request information from the foreign embassy or consulate of the country to which you plan to travel. The foreign country's holidays can also affect court dates, office workdays, and the country's embassy or consulate can also provide you with this information.

Q: Is it safe to travel to . . . ?
A: The U.S. Department of State, Office of American Citizens Services and Crisis Management (ACS) issues Public Announcements and Travel Warnings for particular countries and Consular Information Sheets for all countries. (See Section C, Part I) For assistance from ACS, call 202-647-5225. You may also wish to register with the U.S. embassy or consulate in the foreign country where you plan to adopt.

Q: How should I approach the adoption process abroad?
A: Adoption can be an emotionally stressful process, particularly while facing the additional challenges of adjusting to another culture. Gathering information on the culture of the country prior to travel and even setting aside time for sightseeing can reduce stress and make the experience more positive. It will also provide invaluable information and experiences to relate to your child in later years. If you become ill, the U.S. embassy or consulate can provide you with a list of local attorneys and hospitals to assist if necessary.

Q: How should I obtain multiple copies of foreign documents?
A: Before you depart the country with your child, you should be sure to obtain several duplicate certified/authenticated copies of your child's foreign birth certificate, adoption decree and any other relevant documents. Often these documents are necessary at home, and it can be difficult to obtain copies from the foreign government later.

Q: How can I obtain information concerning attorneys, interpreters or translators in a foreign country?
A: U.S. embassies and consulates maintain lists of English-speaking foreign attorneys and have information about interpreters and translators and can refer you to other sources. Copies of lists of attorneys are also available from the U.S. Department of State's Office of American Citizens Services and Crisis Management or on the web at: http://travel.state.gov/adopt.html.

SECTION A

General Adoption Information

The information provided below is designed to provide a sampling of the many organizations involved in adoption. The agencies listed are not placement agencies. The Department of State does not endorse or recommend any particular organization.

National Adoption Organizations and Parent Support Groups
*National Adoption Information Clearinghouse (NAIC)
P.O. Box 1182
Washington, DC 20013-1182
Tel: 703-352-3488 / 888-251-0075
Fax: 703-385-3206
Internet address: http://www.calib.com/naic
Internet e-mail:
naic@calib.commailto:naic@calib.commailto:naic
@calib.com
*This organization was established by Congress to provide the general public with easily accessible information on all aspects of adoption. NAIC publishes a variety of fact sheets on adoption issues, directories of adoption-related services, and a catalog of audiovisual materials on adoptions. NAIC does not place children for adoption or provide counseling. It does, however, make referrals for such services.
Adoptive Families Magazine

P.O. Box 5159
Brentwood, TN 37024
Tel: 212-877-1839
1-800-372-3300
Internet address:
http://www.adoptivefamiliesmagazine.com
Committee for Single Adoptive Parents, Inc.
P.O. Box 15084
Chevy Chase, MD 20825
Tel: 202-966-6367

FACE (Families Adopting Children Everywhere)
Face Inc.
P.O. Box 28058
Baltimore, MD 21239
Tel: 410-488-2656 (Help-line)
Internet address: http://www.face2000.org

International Concerns Committee for Children
911 Cypress Drive
Boulder, CO 80303
Tel: 303-494-8333
Internet address: http://www.iccadopt.org

Joint Council on International Children's Services
1320 19th St., NW, Suite 200
Washington, DC 20036
Tel: 202-429-0400
Internet address: http://www.jcics.org

*North American Council on Adoptable Children
(NACAC)
970 Raymond Avenue, Suite 106
St. Paul, MN 55114
Tel: 651-644-3036
Fax: 651-644-9848
Internet address: http://www.nacac.org

*This organization can provide a list of parent
support groups in a specific region of the United
States.

National Council for Adoption
1930 17th Street NW
Washington DC 20009
Tel: 202-328-1200
Internet address: http://www.ncfa-usa.org

SECTION B

Magazines and Books

Magazines
Adoptive Families (formerly OURS magazine)
1-800-372-3300

Complimentary copy available by calling the
above number

ODS News
Open Door Society of Massachusetts
1-800-93A-DOPT
Single Parents With Adopted Kids
4108 Washington Rd. #101
Kenosha, WI 53144

Books

General Information
Adamec, Christine and Pierce, William L. The
Encyclopedia of Adoption. Facts on File, Inc.:
June 1991.
Adamec, Christine. There Are Babies To Adopt.
Windsor Publishing Corporation: 1991.
Alexander-Roberts, Colleen. The Essential
Adoption Handbook. Taylor Publishing Co.:1993.
Erichsen, Heino and Nelson-Erichsen, Jean. How
To Adopt Internationally: A Guide for Agency-
Directed & Independent Adoption. Los Ninos
International Adoption & Information Center:
1993.
Gilman, Lois. The Adoption Resource Book: All
the Things You Need to Know & Ought to Know
about Creating an Adoptive Family. Harper
Collins Publishers, Inc.: 1987.
Independent Adoption Manual. Advocate Press:
June 1993.
Knoll, Jean and Murphy, Mary-Kate. International
Adoption: Sensitive Advice for Prospective
Parents. Chicago Review Press: 1994.
Hicks, Randall B. ADOPTING IN AMERICA:
How to Adopt Within One Year (revised 1996-97
edition). WordSlinger Press: 1995.
Hicks, Randall B. Adoption Stories for Young
Children. WordSlinger Press: 1995.
Wirth, Eileen and Worden, Joan. How to Adopt a
Child from Another Country. Abingdon Press:
1993.

Adoption of Older Children
Jewett, Claudia. *Adopting the Older Child.*
Harvard Common Press: 1978.
Kadushin, Alfred. *Adopting Older Children.*
Columbia University Press: 1970.
Mansfield, Gianforte and Waldmann. *Don't Touch
My Heart - Healing the Pain of an Unattached
Child.* Pinon Press: 1994.

Children's Literature
Bloom, Suzanne. *A Family for Jamie: An Adoption
Story.* Crown Books for Young Readers: 1991.

141

Krementz, Jill. *How It Feels to Be Adopted*. Alfred A. Knopf, Inc.: 1988.

Cultural and Racial Differences
Erichsen, Heino R. and Nelson, Erichsen, Jean. *Butterflies in the Wind: Spanish-Indian Children with White Parents*. Los Ninos International Adoption & Information Center: 1992.

Single Parent Adoption
Marindin, Hope, ed. *Handbook for Single Adoptive Parents*. Committee for Single Adoptive Parents: 1992.

Parenting and Adjustment
Bartels-Rabb, Lisa and Van Gulden, Holly. *Real Parents, Real Children: Parenting The Adopted Child*. Crossroad Publishing Co.: 1993.
Brodzinsky, David; Schechter, Marshall; and Henig, Robin. *Being Adopted: The Lifelong Search for Self*. Doubleday & Company, Inc.: 1993.
Register, Cheri. *Are Those Kids Yours?: American Families with Children Adopted from Other Countries*. Free Press: 1990.

SECTION C

Additional Information on Adoptions and Foreign Travel

Part 1: Government Information

Automated Fax Service
A number of Office of Children's Issues adoption flyers are available by automated fax for anyone with a fax machine equipped with a telephone handset. The telephone number for all information through the autofax is 202-647-3000. Callers should follow the prompts to select the information that they wish to receive. All Travel Warnings, Public Announcements and Consular Information Sheets are also available through this service.

Internet
General information on international adoption and specific information on adoption in a number of foreign countries and on foreign travel is also available via Internet at http://travel.state.gov/adopt.html.

Mail In Requests
All of the flyers available on the automated fax service are also available in printed form. The order form, section two of Section C, can be used to obtain these flyers. Simply circle the flyer(s) that you wish and send the order form to:

Office of Children's Issues
1800 G Street, NW
Suite 2100
Washington, D.C. 20006
Phone: (202) 736-7000
Fax: (202) 312-9743

Please enclose a large stamped, self-addressed envelope.
For printed copies of Travel Warnings, Public Announcements, Consular Information Sheets and other general travel-related information, send a 8 1/2 X 11 inch self-addressed envelope with $3 in stamps attached to the Office of American Citizens Services and Crisis Management, Room 4811A, U.S. Department of State, Washington, D.C. 20520-4818.

Part II: Country-Specific Adoption Information Flyers

- To order by mail, simply circle the flyer(s) that you wish and send the order form with your name and address to the Office of Children's Issues, 1800 G Street, NW, Suite 2100, Washington, D.C. 20006. Please enclose an 8 1/2 X 11 inch stamped, self-addressed envelope. For Country-specific Adoption Information Flyers visit the State Department Website at http://travel.state.gov/

Part III: TWENTY-FIVE SOURCE COUNTRIES

Countries of Nationality Ranked by Number of U. S. Adoption Visas Issued*

Russia	3,816
China	3,597
S. Korea	1,654
Guatemala	788
Romania	621
Vietnam	425
India	352
Colombia	233
Philippines	163
Mexico	152
Bulgaria	148
Haiti	142
Latvia	108
Brazil	91
Ethiopia	82

Lithuania	78
Poland	78
Bolivia	77
Hungary	72
Cambodia	66

*Statistics compiled from U.S. Department of State Report of Immediate Relative Visas Issued. For up-to-date information on the number of visas issued by country please visit our web site at http://travel.state.gov/orphans_numbers.html

Section IV: Document Checklist

The adoption agency, attorney, U.S. embassy, BCIS or the state may require some or all of the following items.

- Birth Certificate
- Child Abuse Clearance
- Divorce/Death Certificate
- Financial Statement
- Foreign Adoption/Custody Decree
- Foreign Birth Certificate for the Child
- Foreign Passport for the Child
- Home Study
- Letters of Recommendation
- "Orphan" Status Document
- Photographs of the Family
- Photographs of the Child
- Physician's Report
- Physician's Report of the Child
- Police Certificate
- Power of Attorney
- Verification of Employment
- 1040- Front Two Pages

Authentication:

Some countries require legalization of documents. This process is called authentication. Generally, U.S. civil records, such as birth, death, and marriage certificates must bear the seal of the issuing office, state capitol, then by the U.S. Department of State Authentication's Office. The U.S. Department of State Authentication's Office is located at 518 23rd Street, NW, State Annex 1, Washington, DC 20520, Tel: 202-647-5002. Walk-in service is available 7:30 a.m. to 11 a.m., Monday-Friday, except holidays. The Department charges $5.00 per document for this service, payable in the form of a check drawn on a U.S. bank or money order made payable to the U.S. Department of State.

HAGUE CONVENTION ON INTERCOUNTRY

ADOPTION

(*This document is provided for information purposes only.*)

The final text of the Convention on Protection of Children and Co-operation in Respect of Intercountry Adoption (Hague Adoption Convention), a multilateral treaty, was approved by 66 nations on May 29, 1993 at The Hague. The Convention covers adoptions between countries that become parties to it and sets out for such adoptions certain internationally agreed-upon minimum norms and procedures. The goal of the Convention is to protect the children, birth parents and adoptive parents involved in intercountry adoptions and to prevent child-trafficking and other abuses. On May 1, 1995, the Convention entered into force between the first three countries that ratified it: Mexico, Romania, and Sri Lanka. As of mid-May 2002, 46 countries had become parties to the Convention and 13 had signed but not yet ratified.

The United States signed the Convention on March 31, 1994, signaling its intent to proceed with efforts to ratify the Convention. In summer 1998, President Clinton transmitted the Convention, with an article-by-article legal analysis of its provisions, to the U.S. Senate for advice and consent to ratification. Concurrently, the Administration-proposed draft implementing legislation, prepared by an interagency committee with significant input from the adoption community, was transmitted to both Houses of Congress.

In summer 2000, both Houses of Congress passed bills for implementation of the Convention with relatively minor differences that were resolved in final legislation – "The Intercountry Adoption Act of 2000" (IAA) – that was passed by both Houses in late September 2000. At approximately the same time, the U.S. Senate gave its advice and consent authorizing U.S. ratification of the Hague Convention once U.S. preparations for its implementation are in place. The IAA was signed by the President on October 6, 2000. Since that time, efforts have been under way to prepare and issue federal regulations to: (1) set out the requirements entities must meet to qualify for designation to accredit or approve adoption service providers as required by the Convention and the IAA; (2) specify the standards to be met by agencies and individuals seeking to become Hague Convention accredited or approved to be able to provide adoption services for adoptions covered by the Convention; and (3) set out the procedures to be followed for incoming and outgoing adoptions involving the United States that are safeguarded by the Hague Convention and the IAA.

It is hoped that preparations for U.S. implementation of the Convention and the IAA by the federal government, State courts and authorities, accrediting entities and those seeking to become accredited or approved to provide Convention adoption services will permit the United States to ratify the Convention and bring it into force between the United States and other party countries by some time in 2004.

MAJOR ADVANTAGES OF THE CONVENTION AND ITS IMPLEMENTATION

- Provides, for the first time, formal international and intergovernmental recognition of intercountry adoption.
- Recognizes intercountry adoption, as regulated by the Convention, as a means of offering the advantage of a permanent family to a child for whom a suitable family has not been found in the child's country of origin.
- Establishes a set of internationally agreed minimum requirements and procedures uniformly to govern intercountry adoptions in which a child moves from one Convention party country to another.
- Requires that a Central Authority be established in each party country to be the authoritative source of information and point of contact in that country; to carry out certain functions; to cooperate with other Central Authorities; and to ensure effective implementation of the Convention in the United States.
- Provides a means for ensuring that adoptions made pursuant to the Convention will generally be recognized and given effect in other party countries.
- Will facilitate the adoption by U.S. adoptive parents of children from other party countries through a new category of children, safeguarded by the Convention, who will qualify for immigration and automatic naturalization in the United States.

SUMMARY OF THE CONVENTION'S PROVISIONS

- The Convention will apply to adoptions in which children move from one Convention party country to another.
- Such an adoption may take place only if: the country of origin has established that the child is adoptable, that due consideration has been given to the child's adoption in its country of origin and an intercountry adoption is in the child's best interests, and that after counseling, the necessary consents to the adoption have been given freely. AND, the receiving country has determined that the prospective adoptive parents are eligible and suited to adopt, and that the child they wish to adopt will be authorized to enter and reside permanently in that country.
- Every country must establish a Central Authority to carry out certain functions which include cooperating with other Central Authorities, overseeing the implementation of the Convention in its country, and providing information on the laws of its country.
- Adoption agencies and individual providers of international adoption services may be authorized to perform designated functions with regard to individual adoption cases provided they have become Hague Convention accredited or approved.
- Persons wishing to adopt a child resident in another party country must initially apply to a designated authority in their own country.
- The Convention provides that, with limited exceptions, there can be no contact between the prospective adoptive parents and any parent or other person/institution which cares for the child until certain requirements have been met.
- The Convention requires the recognition of Convention adoptions certified as such, unless recognition would be manifestly contrary to the country's public policy, taking into account the best interests of the child.

SUMMARY OF THE PROVISIONS OF THE INTERCOUNTRY ADOPTION ACT OF 2000 (IAA)

- The State Department will serve as the U.S. Central Authority (USCA).

- The State Department is to establish and oversee the process of accreditation/approval of U.S. adoption service providers, and will designate at least one non-federal qualified accrediting entity to perform the actual Convention accreditation/approval function pursuant to published standards and procedures.
- The State and Justice Departments (BCIS) will establish a case registry for all incoming and outgoing adoptions covered by the Hague Convention and non-Convention intercountry adoptions.
- All home studies on U.S. prospective adoptive parents must be approved by a Convention-accredited adoption agency.
- The State Department must report annually to Congress on the activities of the U.S. Central Authority, including specified data and information.
- With specified exceptions, adoption services for Convention adoptions may be offered and provided only by (1) accredited agencies (non-profit) or (2) approved persons (other agencies and individuals), by (3) smaller agencies qualifying for registration for temporary accreditation and (4) adoption service providers acting under the supervision and responsibility of an accredited agency or approved person.
- The Act lists specific requirements/standards for Convention accreditation and imposes essentially the same requirements/standards for Convention approval.
- Convention accreditation or approval is subject to possible suspension, cancellation, or non-renewal if identified deficiencies are not timely corrected.
- Permanent and temporary debarment of a provider is possible, and an agency or person charged with certain egregious and specified violations may be subject to civil or criminal penalties.
- The Act provides for certain certifications to be made in support of the requirement that Convention adoptions be accorded recognition.
- Convention adoptions will be recognized and given effect in the United States, subject to the exception provided in the Hague Convention that has been summarized above.
- The Immigration and Nationality Act (INA) is amended by providing for a new category of children who are qualified to receive immigrant visas either because of their Convention adoption abroad or their placement abroad with U.S. prospective adoptive parents for Convention adoption in the United States.
- Children residing in the United States and being adopted by persons residing in another party country may be adopted in the United States or placed in the United States for adoption in the receiving country only if the requirements of the Convention to safeguard the child and the parents involved are determined by the appropriate local court in the United States to have been met.
- The Act provides for the preservation of records about Convention adoptions held by the State and Justice Departments (BCIS) under regulations to be issued by the State Department.
- Convention adoptions made among party countries before the Convention enters into force for the United States are to be accorded recognition in the United States.

Note: The requirements of the Hague Convention and the IAA will be fleshed out in federal regulations that are being prepared with the benefit of input from the public during their preparation and eventual written public comments on the proposed draft regulations that will be published in the Federal Register.

PREPARATIONS FOR IMPLEMENTATION OF THE HAGUE CONVENTION

The preparations for U.S. implementation of the Convention and IAA are expected to take until some time in 2004. Their completion will permit the United States to ratify the Convention and bring it into force between the United States and other countries that have become parties to it. These preparations include the following:

- establishment and staffing within the Office of Children's Issues in the Consular Affairs bureau of the State Department to meet its U.S. Central Authority functions

145

- establishment of a computerized case-tracking system for intercountry adoptions involving the United States (incoming and outgoing)
- designation of one or more entities to accredit non-profit U.S. adoption agencies to offer/provide adoption services for Convention adoptions; to approve other bodies and individuals wishing to offer/provide adoption services for such adoptions; and to register qualified smaller agencies for temporary accreditation
- State Department promulgation of regulations (1) establishing requirements/procedures for the designation and monitoring of accrediting entities; (2) setting the standards that must be met for non-profit adoption agencies to qualify for Convention accreditation and for other agencies and individuals to qualify for Convention approval; (3) governing the registration of smaller community-based agencies for temporary accreditation; and (4) providing the procedures and requirements for incoming and outgoing Convention adoptions.
- preparations by designated accrediting entities to process applications for Convention accreditation and approval and registration for temporary accreditation, to deal with complaints, and continuously to monitor the compliance by accredited agencies and approved persons with the requirements of the Convention, the IAA and the regulations
- preparation by the accrediting entities and the USCA of the first list of providers authorized under the Convention to offer and provide adoption services for Convention adoptions
- establishment of educational materials and programs for the U.S. adoption community – national adoption organizations, adoption service providers, State courts and other authorities and future prospective adoptive parents -- concerning their future roles in U.S. compliance with and implementation of the Convention, the IAA and the related federal regulations

- Deposit of the U.S. instrument of ratification and entry into force of the Convention between the United States and other party countries about three months later.

HOW WILL THE UNITED STATES IMPLEMENT THE HAGUE CONVENTION?

While the Convention and the IAA provide many details about U.S. implementation, the regulations that are still in preparation will provide many further details. The following general information can be provided subject, however, to some possible changes as the details to be set out in the regulations are worked out.

The U.S. Central Authority (USCA) will be established in the U.S. Department of State, and the Bureau of Consular Affairs, Office of Children' Issues, will have primary responsibility. That Office will receive additional staff to handle its new tasks, services and responsibilities. The USCA will have programmatic and oversight responsibility for U.S. implementation of the Convention and will be the point of contact from within the United States and from abroad for all matters related to the Convention and to adoptions to and from the United States. The USCA will not itself be an adoption service provider – a function that will continue to be left to adoption agencies and individual adoption service providers. However, for Convention adoptions such providers must qualify to provide these services through Convention accreditation, Convention approval, or through registration for temporary accreditation, or by providing such services under the supervision and responsibility of an accredited agency or approved person. The USCA will manage a computer-based case-tracking system with BCIS that is to maintain a continuous, step-by-step record of all incoming and outgoing Hague Convention and non-Hague intercountry adoptions.

The USCA will be able to refer inquiries about U.S. State and other adoption laws to a reliable source for such information. It will be the point of contact for the Central Authorities of other countries about the status of any particular case and for the discussion and resolution of intergovernmental problems that may arise – systemic problems as well as problems involving particular cases. The USCA will be responsible for representation of the United States at intergovernmental special commission sessions of the Hague Conference on Private International Law dealing with implementation of the Hague Intercountry Adoption Convention and related matters.

The case-specific adoption services and functions set out in Convention Articles 14-21 are to be performed in the United States by Convention-accredited agencies. The case-specific functions set out in Articles 15-21 may, so far as the United States is concerned, also be performed by individual U.S. providers of adoption services, such as lawyers and social workers, and by for-profit agencies, provided they have qualified as Convention-approved persons in the United States. Others may provide adoption services provided they do so under the responsibility and supervision of an accredited agency or approve person. Smaller community-based agencies may qualify for registration for temporary accreditation for one or two years.

The Department of State will eventually designate one or more entities to accredit agencies, approve persons and register smaller agencies for temporary accreditation. These entities will require a number of months after their designation to prepare to perform their functions. All Convention-accredited agencies and Convention-approved persons will need to meet essentially the same standards to qualify to offer and provide adoption services for adoptions covered by the Convention and to maintain their accreditation or approval. Convention accreditation or approval will be for a set number of years and will be subject to renewal. Accreditation and approval will be subject to suspension, loss or non-renewal if an agency or person fails to maintain required standards. Serious or willful non-compliance may result not only in loss of accreditation or approval and thereby loss of the right to provide adoption services for Convention adoptions, but also referral of the matter for possible civil and criminal prosecution.

The activities of accrediting entities will be monitored by the State Department to ensure that they are effectively and uniformly screening agencies and persons and maintaining the accreditation or approval of only those agencies and persons that are complying with the requirements of the Convention, the IAA and applicable federal regulations.

The IAA requires annual reports to Congress with

regard to certain aspects of Convention and IAA implementation. These reports will become available to the general public and to the Central Authorities of other countries beginning about one year after the Convention enters into force for the United States.

The IAA amends the Immigration and Nationality Act (INA). In view of the safeguards for the children, the birth parents and the adoptive parent(s) involved in Convention adoptions, incoming children whose adoption or placement for adoption abroad is covered by the Convention will qualify for immigrant visas even if they have two surviving parents, provided they have consented to termination of their legal relationship with the child, and provided they also meet other requirements.

Adoptions and placements for adoption made in the United States are currently subject only to State law and procedures and not to any federal law. Upon the Convention's entry into force for the United States the U.S. State, territory or commonwealth of residence of the child that is to emigrate to another Convention party country will be required to make the determinations set out for sending states in Articles 4 and 17 of the Hague Convention and to meet other requirements before an adoption or placement for adoption may proceed. Compliance with the requirements of the Convention and the IAA will be a new task for State authorities and will require close cooperation between the State Department and U.S. State courts and other authorities to ensure that the United States meets its treaty obligations to other countries party to the Convention.

SOURCES FOR LIST OF COUNTRIES PARTIES TO THE HAGUE INTERCOUNTRY ADOPTION CONVENTION, THE TEXTS OF THE HAGUE CONVENTION, AND THE INTERCONTRY ADOPTION ACT OF 2000

For up-to-date list of countries party to the Hague Convention go to http://www.hcch.net/e/status/stat33e.html. For the text of the 1993 Hague Convention, go to http://www.hcch.net/e/conventions/text33e.html, or see Senate Treaty Doc. 105-51; 32 *International Legal Materials 1139 (1993)* . For the text of the Intercountry Adoption Act of 2000, see 42 U.S.C. 14901 et seq.; 114 Stat. 825; P.L. 106-279; 41 *International Legal Materials* 222 (2002); http://thomas.loc.gov.

147

INTERNATIONAL ADOPTION

SAFEGUARDS

Legal protections for internationally adopted children in the United States

To complete an international adoption and bring a child to the United States, U.S. citizen prospective adoptive parent(s) must fulfill the requirements set by the United States Bureau of Citizenship and Naturalization Services in the Department of Homeland Security (BCIS), the U.S. Department of State, the foreign country in which the child resides and any additional requirements of the U.S. state in which the prospective adoptive child will live. This two-step process, first petitioning to classify an orphan as an Immediate relative (I-600), and then applying for that child's immigration to the United States, is designed to protect the child, the birth parent(s) and the adoptive parent(s). Simply locating a child in a foreign country and going to the U.S. embassy to apply for a visa for the child will not meet these requirements.

United States law establishes that in order to obtain an Immigrant visa for the child to live in the U.S., the U.S. Bureau of Citizenship and Naturalization Services in the Department of Homeland Securitys (BCIS, within the U.S. Department of Justice) must determine that the prospective adoptive parents are suitable to adopt. A lengthy screening process is required before such a determination can be made. Parents must submit to the BCIS a home study, or report based on interviews and meetings with a social worker licensed in their state, which assesses the family's ability to parent an adoptive child. All prospective adoptive parents must submit copies of birth, divorce and marriage certificates and proof of citizenship. Each prospective adoptive parent, and all other adult members within the household, must be fingerprinted, and those fingerprints must be checked for any criminal record by state and United States Federal police authorities (i.e. the Federal Bureau of Investigation - FBI). Police authorities must confirm that the prospective adoptive parents have no record of child abuse. Prospective adoptive parents must submit a physician's report concerning each parent's medical condition and letters verifying their employment and moral character. Furthermore,

additional documentation bearing on the parent's fitness to adopt may be required by the state governments and the adoption agency as well. Only after it is demonstrated that both the parents are qualified to adopt may they submit a petition (I-600) to have an Immigrant visa issued to an adoptive child. Much of this screening can be done prior to identifying a specific child for adoption by filing an advance processing petition (I-600A) with the BCIS. Additionally, as a part of the Immigrant visa application process, a legally binding affidavit of support (I-864), complete with specific, mandatory supporting documents is required.

Furthermore, the Government of the United States has specific requirements regarding the status of the adoptive child which ensure that the child is an orphan under U.S. law, or that the child has been legally and irrevocably released for emigration and adoption in a manner provided for under local foreign law. The U.S. government is particularly concerned with the identity of the child; the child's orphan status and that any release by a sole surviving parent is unconditional and voluntary. Questions concerning legal custody or proper documentation for the child must be resolved in accordance with the law of the country of the child's nationality or residence.

The U.S. government abhors fraudulent adoption procedures and the harm they cause children and families. In the international area, the Department of State consistently takes a strong stand against fraudulent adoption procedures. This policy flows from our general obligation to respect host country laws, to discourage any illegal activities and to facilitate the appropriate international movement of adoptive children. The Department of State has unfailingly expressed its support for measures taken by foreign states to reduce adoption abuses.

Moreover, the child protection laws in the us. at both Federal and State levels, apply to all children whether they are U.S. citizens or not, and whether they are in the U.S. for the purpose of being adopted or they have already been adopted. Although child protection laws vary from State to State, they all provide certain basic protections which are embedded in the U.S. Child Abuse Prevention and Treatment Act and in the child welfare sections of the Social Security Act.
These protections include:
-- Persons in specified occupations are identified as "mandated reporters," meaning that they must report to the local authorities any evidence or

reasonable suspicion of either child neglect or child abuse. Typically, mandated reporters include: nurses, physicians and other medical personnel; school teachers and guidance counselors; law enforcement personnel; and others who regularly come in contact with children and may be expected to observe abuse if it occurs, or to learn of neglect or abuse. The reports are made to the local public child welfare agency or, in some instances, to the police. Reporters' names are kept confidential.

-- Local public child welfare agencies maintain a 24 hour-a-day, 365 day-a-year capacity to receive allegations of child abuse or neglect. They publish the agency's phone number or special "hotline" numbers and ensure that the phones are staffed around the clock or that calls are forwarded to a designated person after hours. Child abuse investigators are designated to be on call after hours and on weekends. In some jurisdictions the police receive calls of child abuse, or abuse or neglect.

-- Allegations of abuse are acted on promptly; if there is danger of harm to a child agencies will respond to a report immediately. It is not uncommon for police and social services officials to go together to visit the family. As appropriate, children are taken to medical facilities for examination and necessary treatment. All jurisdictions in the U.S. have a minimum period of time -- usually 48 to 72 hours -- in which non-emergency investigations are to begin. Not all reports of abuse or neglect actually require a field visit, of course, but agencies take every report seriously and analyze each for its urgency.

-- When social workers/child abuse investigators get involved in a case, they first determine whether the allegation is "founded" or "unfounded." Where it is determined that there is no basis for the allegation of neglect or abuse, the case will be closed without action. If the allegation is determined to be founded, the local public child welfare agency may decide on one of a number of options. These include: 1) counseling the family and closing the case; 2) providing in-home services to assure the child's safety while working with the family to resolve the underlying problem(s); 3) removing the perpetrator from the family; or 4) removing the child from the family and placing the child in foster care.

-- When a child is removed from her family, efforts are made to work with the family to resolve

problems and correct dangerous behaviors or situations, in order to reunite the child with her family. In cases in which the child cannot be reunited with her family, the agency may then seek to terminate the parents' legal rights, in order to free the child for adoption.

In the U.S. every placement in foster care must be approved by a court, and the public agencies must return to court periodically so the child's case may be reviewed and a judge may determine whether the child is being well cared-for, and whether there are other actions the agency should take to hasten the time a child will be returned home or another permanent placement found.

Child welfare funds provided by the federal government to the States include (for fiscal year 1998):

for Child Welfare Programs $333,240,000
for Family Preservation & Support $255,000,000
for Child Abuse and Neglect $68,015,000

The States and localities, in the aggregate, spend much more than these amounts on child protection and child welfare services. In addition, the Federal government in FY 1998 will provide $4,311,000,000 in financing for foster care, adoption assistance, and independent living services for adolescents in foster care. Again, the States and localities expend considerably more than this in support of child welfare.

Post-adoption services, which States are encouraged to provide, are among the child welfare services for which Federal funds may be expended.

If a child is seen to be at risk of harm or neglect, public child welfare agencies will respond without regard to whether the child is a U.S. citizen, and without regard to whether an adoption has been completed. If it is necessary to remove a child from the custody of his family or other legal custodians, and the child is not a U.S. citizen, the child welfare agency will seek the best placement for the child, usually in the U.S. (In some cases, the child's relatives are in another country and the best placement for that child is with his relatives in that other country.)

Similarly, in the event an adoptive placement disrupts, the local public child welfare agency will take responsibility for the child, and provide a safe

149

environment, whether the child is a U.S. citizen or not. And if the child cannot be reunited with her adoptive parents, the agency will take responsibility for finding another permanent home for that child.

International Adoptions: Guidelines on Immediate Relative Petitions
Bureau of Consular Affairs

Only US citizens may petition for the immediate immigration of foreign adopted children. There is no provision in US immigration law for the entry of newly adopted children of legal permanent residents (green card holders) and long term nonimmigrant visa holders. Legal permanent residents who do adopt abroad can only expect frustration in trying to bring their adopted children to the US.

The United States Department of State reports cases each year of non-citizen parents who have legally adopted a child internationally and then find that the child cannot join them in the United States. The parents and child face only anguish and heartbreak. The best solution is for legal permanent residents to first naturalize as US citizens and for long term nonimmigrant visa holders to return to their home countries before adopting.

The problem lies in the definition of "child" in the Immigration and Nationality Act (INA). Long term nonimmigrant visa holders and legal permanent residents can bring their spouses and children with them when they enter the United States or have them enter later. The INA divides the definition of "child" into several sub-groups: natural born children, step-children, and adopted children. The INA recognizes as a "child" one who has been adopted before the age of sixteen and who has resided with, and been in the legal custody of, the parent for two years. What this means is that a child born overseas to the principal applicant after his or her entry to the US may receive the appropriate dependent visa immediately. A child adopted overseas by a non-citizen must first meet the two year co-residence requirement. The INA does not provide any way for the child to enter the US to satisfy this requirement.

The following example illustrates the problem: An Australian researcher in the US on a J-1 Exchange Visitor visa adopts a baby girl from the People's Republic of China. The child has not lived with the researcher for two years. She does not meet the definition of "child." The US consulate cannot issue her a J-2 visa (dependent of exchange visitor) to join her parent. If the researcher leaves the US and lives with his adopted daughter for two years, she can then receive a J-2 visa for future exchange visits to the US.

Long term nonimmigrant visa classes include: E1/E2 Treaty Traders or Investors, F-1 Students, I Journalists, J-1 Exchange Visitors, H, O, or P Visa Temporary Workers, L-1 Intra-company Transfers, and R-1 Religious Workers. Different rules cover diplomats and officials in the US on A or G visas. The employing embassy or international organization should contact the Department of State for information.

The situation is even more difficult for legal permanent residents. The adopting resident parent must first satisfy the two year co-residence requirement, before he or she can begin the immigration process. At the same time, a resident cannot reside outside the US making the two year requirement a near impossibility. At the end of two years' co-residence, if the parent could have complied, he or she would file a second family category (child of a legal permanent resident) petition. The family must then wait for the petition to become current: the backlog in this category is now four years. Therefore, a resident faces a wait of six years or more before his or her adopted child may immigrate.

Once a legal permanent resident naturalizes as a United States citizen, he or she may petition for the immediate immigration of an adopted (or to be adopted) orphan. There are strict limits on who may qualify as an orphan but there is no two year co-residence requirement . Other adopted children would still have to meet the two year requirement. A single US citizen over twenty-five years of age or a married US citizen of any age may petition. The spouse of a married citizen need not be a US citizen but he or she must agree to the orphan adoption.

For Further Information Please Call the Public Affairs Staff at: (202) 647-1488

Chapter 15

Know Before You Go: U.S. Customs Hints for Returning Residents

[The information in this chapter is reprinted verbatim from a bulletin issued by the Department of the Treasury, U.S. Customs Service. It is intended to serve as advice to Americans traveling abroad.]

KNOW BEFORE YOU GO: US CUSTOMS HINTS (including customs duties)

Introduction: The U.S. Customs Service is America's frontline against the smuggling of drugs and other prohibited goods. Customs has discovered large amounts of drugs in baggage, vehicles, and on passengers themselves.

When you return to the United States, we will treat you in a courteous, professional manner. We realize that very few travelers actually violate the law, but we may still need to examine your baggage or your vehicle, which, by law, we are allowed to do. We may ask you about your citizenship, your trip, and about anything you are bringing back to the United States that you did not have with you when you left.

If you need help clearing Customs, please do not hesitate to ask the Customs inspector for assistance.

"Duty" and "dutiable" are words you will find frequently throughout this chapter Duty is the amount of money you pay on items coming from another country. It is similar to a tax, except that duty is collected only on imported goods. Dutiable describes items on which duty may have to be paid. Most items have specific duty rates, which are determined by a number of factors, including where you got the item, where it was made, and what it is made of.

To "declare" means to tell the Customs officer about anything you're bringing back that you did not have when you left the United States. For example, you would declare alterations made in a foreign country to a suit you already owned, and you would declare any gifts you acquired overseas.

U.S. Customs Mission We are the guardians of our Nation's borders - America's frontline. We serve and protect the American public with integrity, innovation, and pride. We enforce the laws of the United States, safeguard the revenue, and foster lawful international trade and travel.

When You Return to the United States

When you come back, you'll need to declare everything you brought back that you did not take with you when you left the United States. If you are traveling by air or sea, you may be asked to fill out a Customs declaration form. This form is almost always provided by the airline or cruise ship. You will probably find it easier and faster to fill out your declaration form and clear Customs if you do the following:

Keep your sales slips! As you read this chapter, you'll understand why this is especially important for international travelers. Try to pack the things you'll need to declare separately. Read the signs in the Customs area. They contain helpful information about how to clear Customs.

Be aware that under U.S. law, Customs inspectors are authorized to examine luggage, cargo, and travelers. Under the search authority granted to Customs by the U.S. Congress, every passenger who crosses a U.S. border may be searched. To stop the flow of illegal drugs and other contraband into our country, we need your cooperation. If you are one of the very few travelers selected for a search, you will be treated in a courteous, professional, and dignified manner. If you are searched and you believe that you were not treated in such a manner, or if you have any concerns about the search for any reason whatsoever, we want to hear from you. Please contact the Executive Director, Passenger Programs.

What You Must Declare

You Must Declare

Items you purchased and are carrying with you upon return to the United States.

Items you received as gifts, such as wedding or birthday presents.

Items you inherited.

Items you bought in duty-free shops or on the ship or plane.

Repairs or alterations to any items you took abroad and then brought back, even if the

repairs/alterations were performed free of charge.

Items you brought home for someone else.

Items you intend to sell or use in your business.

Items you acquired (whether purchased or received as gifts) in the U.S. Virgin Islands, American Samoa, Guam, or in a Caribbean Basin Economic Recovery Act country (please see section on $600 exemption for a list of these countries) that are not in your possession when you return. In other words, if you acquired things in any of these island nations and asked the merchant to send them to you, you must still declare them when you go through Customs. (This differs from the usual procedure for mailed items, which is discussed in the section on Sending Goods to the United States.

You must state on the Customs declaration, in United States currency, what you actually paid for each item. The price must include all taxes. If you did not buy the item yourself - for example, if it is a gift - get an estimate of its fair retail value in the country where you received it. If you bought something on your trip and wore or used it on the trip, it's still dutiable. You must declare the item at the price you paid or, if it was a gift, at its fair market value.

Joint Declaration Family members who live in the same home and return together to the United States may combine their personal exemptions. This is called a joint declaration. For example, if Mr. And Mrs. Smith travel overseas and Mrs. Smith brings home a $600 piece of glassware, and Mr. Smith buys $200 worth of clothing, they can combine their $400 exemptions on a joint declaration and

not have to pay duty.

Children and infants are allowed the same exemption as adults, except for alcoholic beverages.

Register Items Before You Leave the United States If your laptop computer was made in Japan - for instance - you might have to pay duty on it each time you bring it back into the United States, unless you could prove that you owned it before you left on your trip. Documents that fully describe the item - for example, sales receipts, insurance policies, or jeweler's appraisals - are acceptable forms of proof. To make things easier, you can register certain items with Customs before you depart - including watches, cameras, laptop computers, firearms, and tape recorders - as long as they have serial numbers or other unique, permanent markings. Take the items to the nearest Customs Office and request a Certificate of Registration (Customs Form 4457). It shows Customs that you had the items with you before leaving the U.S. and all items listed on it will be allowed duty-free entry. Customs inspectors must see the item you are registering in order to certify the certificate of registration. You can register items with Customs at the international airport from which you're departing. Keep the certificate for future trips.

Duty-free Exemption

The duty-free exemption, also called the personal exemption , is the total value of merchandise you may bring back to the United States without having to pay duty. You may bring back more than your exemption, but you will have to pay duty on it. In most cases, the personal exemption is $800, but there are some exceptions to this rule, which are explained below.

Exemptions Depending on the countries you have visited, your personal exemption will be $600, $800, or $1,200. (The differences are explained in the following section.) There are also limits on the amount of alcoholic beverages, cigarettes, cigars, and other tobacco products you may include in your duty-free personal exemption.

The duty-free exemptions ($600, $800, or $1,200) apply if:

● The items are for your personal or household use.

● They are in your possession (that is, they

152

accompany you) when you return to the United States. Items to be sent later may not be included in your $800 duty-free exemption.

● They are declared to Customs. If you do not declare something that should have been declared, you risk forfeiting it. If in doubt, declare it.

● You are returning from an overseas stay of at least 48 hours. For example, if you leave the United States at 1:30 p.m. on June 1, you would complete the 48-hour period at 1:30 p.m. on June 3. This time limit does not apply if you are returning from Mexico or from the U.S. Virgin Islands. (See the section on the $200 exemption.)

● You have not used your exemption, or any part of it, in the past 30 days. If you use part of your exemption - for example, if you go to England and bring back $150 worth of items - you must wait another 30 days before you are allowed another $800 exemption. (However, see the section on the $200 exemption.) The items are not prohibited or restricted as discussed in the section on Prohibited and Restricted Items. Note the embargo prohibitions on products of Cuba.

$200 Exemption If you can't claim other exemptions because you've been out of the country more than once in a 30-day period or because you haven't been out of the country for at least 48 hours, you may still bring back $200 worth of items free of duty and tax. As with the exemptions discussed earlier, these items must be for your personal or household use.

Each traveler is allowed this $200 exemption, but, unlike the other exemptions, family members may not group their exemptions. Thus, if Mr. and Mrs. Smith spend a night in Canada, each may bring back up to $200 worth of goods, but they would not be allowed a collective family exemption of $400.

Also, if you bring back more than $200 worth of dutiable items, or if any item is subject to duty or tax, the entire amount will be dutiable. Let's say you were out of the country for 36 hours and came back with a $300 piece of pottery. You could not deduct $200 from its value and pay duty on $100. The pottery would be dutiable for the full value of $300.

You may include with the $200 exemption your choice of the following: 50 cigarettes and 10 cigars and 150 milliliters (5 fl. oz.) of alcoholic beverages or 150 milliliters (5 fl. oz.) of perfume containing alcohol.

$800 Exemption If you are returning from anywhere other than a Caribbean Basin country or a U.S. insular possession (U.S. Virgin Islands, American Samoa, or Guam), you may bring back $800 worth of items duty-free, as long as you bring them with you (this is called accompanied baggage).

Duty on items you mail home to yourself will be waived if the value is $200 or less. (See sections on "Gifts" and "Sending Goods to the United States.") Antiques that are at least 100 years old and fine art may enter duty-free, but folk art and handicrafts are generally dutiable.

This means that, depending on what items you're bringing back from your trip, you could come home with more than $800 worth of gifts or purchases and still not be charged duty. For instance, say you received a $700 bracelet as a gift, and you bought a $40 hat and a $60 color print. Because these items total $800, you would not be charged duty, because you have not exceeded your duty-free exemption. If you had also bought a $500 painting on that trip, you could bring all $1300 worth of merchandise home without having to pay duty, because fine art is duty-free.

Tobacco Products: Passengers/travelers may import previously exported tobacco products only in quantities not exceeding the amounts specified in exemptions for which the traveler qualifies. Any quantities of previously exported tobacco products not permitted by an exemption will be seized and destroyed. These items are typically purchased in duty-free stores, on carriers operating internationally, or in foreign stores. These items are usually marked "Tax Exempt. For Use Outside the U.S.," or "U.S. Tax Exempt For Use Outside the U.S." For example, a returning resident is eligible for the $800 exemption, which includes not more than 200 cigarettes and 100 cigars. If the resident declares 400 previously exported cigarettes, the resident would be permitted 200 cigarettes, tax-free under the exemption and the remaining 200 previously exported cigarettes would be confiscated. If the resident declares 400 cigarettes, of which 200 are previously exported and 200 not previously exported, the resident would be permitted to import the 200 previously exported cigarettes tax free under the exemption and the resident would be charged duty and tax on the remaining 200 not previously exported cigarettes.

The tobacco exemption is available to each person. Tobacco products of Cuban origin, however, are prohibited unless you actually acquired them in Cuba and are returning directly or indirectly from that country on licensed travel. You may not, for example, bring in Cuban cigars purchased in Canada. Persons returning from Cuba may bring into the U.S. no more than $100 worth of goods.

Alcoholic Beverages: One liter (33.8 fl. oz.) of alcoholic beverages may be included in your exemption
if:
You are 21 years old.
It is for your own use or as a gift.
It does not violate the laws of the state in which you arrive.

Federal regulations allow you to bring back more than one liter of alcoholic beverage for personal use, but, as with extra tobacco, you will have to pay duty and Internal Revenue Service tax.

While federal regulations do not specify a limit on the amount of alcohol you may bring back for personal use, unusual quantities are liable to raise suspicions that you are importing the alcohol for other purposes, such as for resale. Customs officers are authorized by Alcohol Tobacco and Firearms (ATF) make on-the-spot determinations

that an importation is for commercial purposes, and may require you to obtain a permit to import the alcohol before leasing to you. If you intend to bring back a substantial quantity of alcohol for your personal use you should contact the Customs port you will be re-entering the country through, and make prior arrangements for entering the alcohol into the U.S.

Having said that, you should be aware that State laws may limit the amount of alcohol you can bring in without a license. If you arrive in a state that has limitations on the amount of alcohol you may bring in without a license, that state law will be enforced by Customs, even though it may be more restrictive then Federal regulations. We recommend that you check with the state government before you go abroad about their limitations on quantities allowed for personal importation and additional state taxes that might apply.

In brief, for both alcohol and tobacco, the quantities discussed in this booklet as being eligible for duty-free treatment may be included in your $800 (or $600 or $1,200) exemption, just as any other purchase would be. But unlike other kinds of merchandise, amounts beyond those discussed here as being duty-free are taxed, even if you have not exceeded, or even met, your personal exemption. For example, if your exemption is $800 and you bring back three liters of wine and nothing else, two of those liters will be dutiable. Federal law prohibits shipping alcoholic beverages by mail within the United States.

$600 Exemption If you are returning directly from any one of the following 24 Caribbean Basin countries, your customs exemption is $600:

Antigua and Barbuda, Aruba, Bahamas, Barbados, Belize, British Virgin, Islands, Costa Rica, Dominica, Dominican Republic, El Salvador, Grenada, Guatemala, Guyana, Honduras, Jamaica, Montserrat, Netherlands, Antilles, Nicaragua, Panama, Saint Kitts, and Nevis, Saint Lucia, Saint Vincent and the Grenadines, Trinidad
and Tobago

You may include two liters of alcoholic beverages with this $600 exemption, as long as one of the liters was produced in one of the countries listed above (see section on Unaccompanied Purchases from Insular Possessions and Caribbean Basin Countries).

Travel to More Than One Country If you travel to a U.S. possession and to one or more of the Caribbean countries listed above (for example, on a Caribbean cruise), you may bring back $1,200 worth of items without paying duty. But only $600 worth of these items may come from the Caribbean country(ies); any amount beyond $600 will be dutiable unless you acquired it in one of the insular possessions. For example, if you were to travel to the U.S. Virgin Islands and Jamaica, you would be allowed to bring back $1,200 worth of merchandise duty-free, as long as only $600 worth was acquired in Jamaica. (Keeping track of where your purchases occurred and having the receipts ready to show the Customs inspectors will help speed your clearing Customs.)

If you travel to any of the Caribbean countries listed above and to countries where the standard personal exemption of $800 applies - for example, a South American or European country - up to $800 worth of merchandise may come from the non-Caribbean country. For instance, if you travel to Venezuela and Trinidad and Tobago, your exemption is $600, only $200 of which may have been acquired in Venezuela.

$1,200 Exemption If you return directly or indirectly from a U.S. Insular possession (U.S. Virgin Islands, American Samoa, or Guam), you are allowed a $1,200 duty-free exemption. You may include 1,000 cigarettes as part of this exemption, but at least 800 of them must have been acquired in an insular possession. Only 200 cigarettes may have been acquired elsewhere. For example, if you were touring the South Pacific and you stopped in Tahiti, American Samoa, and other ports of call, you could bring back five cartons of cigarettes, but four of them would have to have been bought in American Samoa.

Similarly, you may include five liters of alcoholic beverages in your duty-free exemption, but one of them must be a product of an insular possession. Four may be products of other countries (see section on Unaccompanied Purchases from Insular Possessions and Caribbean Basin Countries).

Gifts Gifts you bring back from a trip abroad are considered to be for your personal use. They must be declared, but you may include them in your personal exemption. This includes gifts people gave you while you were out of the country, such as wedding or birthday presents, and gifts you've brought back for others. Gifts intended for business, promotional, or other commercial purposes may not be included in your duty-free exemption.

Gifts worth up to $100 may be received, free of duty and tax, by friends and relatives in the United States, as long as the same person does not receive more than $100 worth of gifts in a single day. If the gifts are mailed or shipped from an insular possession, this amount is increased to $200. When you return to the United States, you don't have to declare gifts you sent while you were on your trip, since they won't be accompanying you.

By federal law, alcoholic beverages, tobacco products, and perfume containing alcohol and worth more than $5 retail may not be included in the gift exemption.

Gifts for more than one person may be shipped in the same package, called a consolidated gift package, if they are individually wrapped and labeled with each recipient's name. Here's how to wrap and label a consolidated gift package:

Be sure to mark the outermost wrapper with:

- the words "UNSOLICITED GIFT" and the words "CONSOLIDATED GIFT PACKAGE" :
  - the total value of the consolidated package;
  - the recipients' names; and
- the nature and value of the gifts inside (for example, tennis shoes, $50; shirt, $45; toy car, $15).

Packages marked in this way will clear Customs much more easily. Here's an example of how to mark a consolidated gift package:

Unsolicited gift-consolidated gift package- total value $135 To John Jones-one belt, $20; one box of candy, $5; one tie, $20 To Mary Smith-one skirt, $45; one belt, $15; one pair slacks, $30.

If any item in the consolidated gift parcel is subject to duty and tax or worth more than the $100 gift allowance, the entire package will be dutiable.

You, as a traveler, cannot send a "gift" package to yourself, and people traveling together cannot send "gifts" to each other. But there would be no reason to do that anyway, because the personal exemption for packages mailed from abroad is $200, which is twice as much as the gift exemption. If a package is subject to duty, the United States Postal Service will collect it from the addressee along with any postage and handling charges. The sender cannot prepay duty; it must be paid by the recipient when the package is received in the United States. (Packages sent by courier services are not eligible for this duty waiver.)

Duty-free or Reduced Rates
Items from Certain Countries The United States gives duty preferences - that is, free or reduced rates - to certain developing countries under a trade program called the Generalized System of Preferences (GSP). Some products that would otherwise be dutiable are not when they come from a GSP country. For details on this program, as well as the complete list of GSP countries, please ask your nearest Customs office for a copy of our pamphlet *GSP & The Traveler.*

Similarly, many products of Caribbean and Andean countries are exempt from duty under the Caribbean Basin Initiative, Caribbean Basin Trade Partnership Act, and Andean Trade Preference Act. Most products of certain sub-Saharan African countries are exempt from duty under the African Growth and Opportunity Act. Most products of Israel may also enter the United States either free of duty or at a reduced rate. Check with Customs for details on these programs.

The North American Free Trade Agreement (NAFTA) went into effect in 1994. If you are returning from Canada or Mexico , your goods are eligible for free or reduced duty rates if they were grown, manufactured, or produced in Canada or Mexico, as defined by the Act. Again, check with Customs for details.

Personal Belongings and Household Effects

What Items are Duty-free?
Personal Belongings Your personal belongings can be sent back to the United States duty-free if they are of U.S. origin and if they have not been altered or repaired while abroad. Personal belongings like worn clothing can be mailed home and will receive duty-free entry if you write the words "American Goods Returned" on the outside of the package.

Household Effects Household effects include furniture, carpets, paintings, tableware, stereos, linens, and similar household furnishings. Tools of trade, professional books, implements, and instruments that you've taken out of the United States will be duty-free when you return.

You may import household effects you acquired abroad duty-free if:

You used them for at least one year while you were abroad.
They are not intended for anyone else or for sale.

Clothing, jewelry, photography equipment, portable radios, and vehicles are considered personal effects and cannot be brought in duty-free as household effects. However, the amount of duty collected on them will be reduced according to the age of the item.

Paying Duty
If you're bringing it back with you, you didn't have it when you left, and its total value is more than your Customs exemption, it is subject to duty.

The Customs inspector will place the items that have the highest rate of duty under your exemption. Then, after subtracting your exemptions and the value of any duty-free items, a flat rate of duty will be charged on the next $1,000 worth of merchandise. Any dollar amount beyond this $1,000 will be dutiable at whatever duty rates apply. The flat rate of duty may only be used for items for your own use or for gifts. As with your exemption, you may use the flat-rate provision only once every 30 days. Special flat rates of duty apply to items made and acquired in Canada or Mexico. The flat rate of duty applies to purchases whether the items accompany you or are shipped.

The flat duty rate will be charged on items that are dutiable but that cannot be included in your personal exemption, even if you have not exceeded the exemption. The best example of this is liquor: Say you return from Europe with $200 worth of items, including two liters of liquor. One liter will be duty-free under your exemption; the other will be dutiable at 4 percent, plus any Internal Revenue Service tax.

Family members who live in the same household and return to the United States together can combine their items to take advantage of a combined flat duty rate, no matter which family member owns a given item. The combined flat duty rate for a family of four traveling together would be $4,000.

If you owe duty, you must pay it when you arrive in the United States. You can pay it in any of the following ways:

U.S. currency (foreign currency is not acceptable).
Personal check in the exact amount, drawn on a U.S. bank, made payable to the U.S. Customs Service. You must present identification, such as a passport or driver's license. (The Customs Service does not accept checks bearing second-party endorsements.)
Government check, money order, or traveler's check if it does not exceed the duty owed by more than $50.
In some locations, you may pay duty with credit cards, either MasterCard or VISA.

Sending Goods to the United States

Items mailed to the United States are subject to duty when they arrive. They cannot be included in your Customs exemption, and duty on them cannot be prepaid.

If you are mailing merchandise from the U.S. insular possessions or from Caribbean Basin countries, you should follow different procedures than if you were mailing packages from any other country. These special procedures are described, in the section on " Unaccompanied Purchases ".

In addition to duty and, at times, taxes, Customs collects a user fee on dutiable packages. Those three fees are the only fees Customs collects; any additional charges on shipments are for handling by freight forwarders, Customs brokers, and couriers or for other delivery services. Some carriers may add other clearance charges that have nothing to do with Customs duties.

Note: Customs brokers are not U.S. Customs employees. Brokers' fees are based on the amount of work they do, not on the value of the items you ship, so travelers sometimes find the fee high in relation to the value of the shipment. The most cost-effective thing to do is to take your purchases with you if at all possible.

Unaccompanied Luggage Unaccompanied baggage is anything you do not bring back with you, as opposed to goods in your possession - that accompany you - when you return. These may be items that were with you when you left the United States or items that you acquired (received by any means) while outside the United States. In general, unaccompanied baggage falls into the following three categories.

U.S. Mail Shipments Shipping through the U.S. mail, including parcel post, is a cost-efficient way to send things to the United States. The Postal Service sends all foreign mail shipments to Customs for examination. Customs then returns packages that don't require duty to the Postal Service, which sends them to a local post office for delivery. The local post office delivers them without charging any additional postage, handling costs, or other fees.

If the package does require payment of duty, Customs attaches a form called a mail entry (form CF-3419A), which shows how much duty is owed, and charges a $5 processing fee as well. When the post office delivers the package, it will also charge a handling fee.

Commercial goods - goods intended for resale - may have special entry requirements. Such goods may require a formal entry in order to be admitted into the United States. Formal entries are more complicated and require more paperwork than informal entries. (Informal entries are, generally speaking, personal packages worth less than $2,000.) Customs employees may not prepare formal entries for you; only you or a licensed customs broker may prepare one. For more information on this subject, please request the Customs pamphlet U.S. Import Requirements or contact your local Customs office.

If you believe you have been charged an incorrect amount of duty on a package mailed from abroad, you may file a protest with Customs. You can do this in one of two ways. You can accept the package, pay the duty, and write a letter explaining why you think the amount was incorrect. You should include with your letter the yellow copy of the mail entry (CF-3419A). Send the letter and the form to the Customs office that issued the mail entry, which you'll find on the lower left-hand corner of the form.

The other way to protest duty is to refuse delivery of the package and, within five days, send your protest letter to the post office where the package is being held. The post office will forward your letter to Customs and will hold your package until the protest is resolved.

For additional information on international mailing, please ask Customs for the pamphlet International Mail Imports .

Express Shipments Packages may be sent to the United States by private-sector courier or delivery service from anywhere in the world. The express company usually takes care of clearing your merchandise through Customs and charges a fee for its service. Some travelers have found this fee to be higher than they expected.

Freight Shipments Cargo, whether duty is owed on it or not, must clear Customs at the first port of arrival in the United States. If you choose, you may have your freight sent, while it is still in Customs custody, to another port for Customs clearance. This is called forwarding freight in bond. You (or someone you appoint to act for you) are responsible for arranging to clear your merchandise through Customs or for having it forwarded to another port.

Frequently, a freight forwarder in a foreign country will take care of these arrangements, including hiring a customs broker in the United States to clear the merchandise through Customs. Whenever a third party handles the clearing and forwarding of your merchandise, that party charges a fee for its services. This fee is not a Customs charge. When a foreign seller entrusts a shipment to a broker or agent in the United States, that seller usually pays only enough freight to have the shipment delivered to the first port of arrival in the United States. This means that you, the buyer, will have to pay additional inland transportation, or freight forwarding charges, plus brokers' fees, insurance, and possibly other charges.

If it is not possible for you to secure release of your goods yourself, another person may act on your behalf to clear them through Customs. You may do this as long as your merchandise consists of a single, noncommercial shipment (not intended for resale) that does not require a formal entry-in other words, if the merchandise is worth less than $2,000. You must give the person a letter that authorizes him or her to act as your unpaid agent. Once you have done this, that person may fill out the Customs declaration and complete the entry process for you. Your letter authorizing the person to act in your behalf should be addressed to the "Officer in Charge of Customs" at the port of entry, and the person should bring it along when he or she comes to clear your package. Customs will not notify you when your shipment arrives, as this is the responsibility of your carrier, If your goods are not cleared within 15 days of arrival you could incur storage fees.

Unaccompanied Purchases from Insular Possessions and Caribbean Countries

Unaccompanied purchases are goods you bought on a trip that are being mailed or shipped to you in the United States. In other words, you're not carrying them with you when you return. If your unaccompanied purchases are from an insular possession or a Caribbean Basin country and are being sent directly from those locations to the United States, you may enter them as follows:

Up to $1,200 worth will be duty-free under your personal exemption if the merchandise is from an insular possession.

Up to $600 worth will be duty-free if it is from a Caribbean Basin country.

Of these amounts ($1,200 or $600), up to $400 worth will be duty-free if the merchandise was acquired elsewhere than the insular possessions or the Caribbean Basin. However, merchandise that qualifies for the $400 exemption must be in your possession when you return (must accompany you) in order for you to claim the duty-free exemption. The duty-free exemptions for unaccompanied baggage apply only to goods from the insular possessions and the Caribbean Basin countries listed earlier.

An additional $1,000 worth of goods will be dutiable at a flat rate if they are from an insular possession, or from a Caribbean Basin country.(See chart under Paying Duty.)

If you are sending back more than $2,200 from an insular possession or more than $1,600 from a Caribbean Basin country, the duty rates in the Harmonized Tariff Schedules of the United States will apply. The Harmonized Tariff Schedule describes different rates of duty for different commodities; linen tablecloths, for example, will not have the same duty rates as handicrafts or plastic toy trucks.

Here's how you can take advantage of the duty-free exemption for unaccompanied tourist purchases from an insular possession or a Caribbean country:

Step 1. At place and time of purchase, ask your merchant to hold your item until you send him or her a copy of Customs Form CF-255 (Declaration of Unaccompanied Articles), which must be affixed to the package when it is sent.

Step 2. (a) On your Customs declaration (form CF-6059B), list everything you acquired on your trip, except the things you already sent home as gifts. (b) Check off on the declaration those items you are not bringing with you--that is, the unaccompanied items. (c) Fill out a separate Declaration of Unaccompanied Articles (form CF-255) for each package or container that will be sent to you after you arrive in the United States . You can often get this form where you make your purchase, but if not, ask a Customs officer for one when you clear Customs.

Step 3. When you return to the United States, the Customs officer will: (a) collect duty and tax, if

158

any is owed, on the goods you've brought with you; (b) check to see that your list of unaccompanied articles, which you indicated on the Customs declaration, agrees with your sales slips, invoices, and so on; and (c) validate the CF-255 as to whether your purchases are duty-free under your personal exemption ($1,200 or $600) or whether they are subject to a flat rate of duty. Two copies of this three-part form will be returned to you.

Step 4. Send the yellow copy of the CF-255 to the foreign shopkeeper or vendor holding your purchase, and keep the other copy for your records. (When you make your purchase, it is very important to tell the merchant not to send your package to the United States until he or she gets the copy of form CF-255.)

Step 5. When the merchant gets your CF-255, he or she will put it in an envelope and attach the envelope securely to the outside wrapping of the package or container. The merchant must also mark each package "Unaccompanied Purchase." Please remember that each package or container must have its own CF-255 attached. This is the most important step to follow in order to gain the benefits allowed under this procedure.

Step 6. If your package has been mailed, the Postal Service will deliver it after it has cleared Customs. If you owe duty, the Postal Service will collect the duty along with a postal handling fee. If your package is delivered by a commercial courier, the delivery service will notify you of its arrival so you can go to the Customs office holding the shipment and complete the entry procedure. If you owe duty or tax, you can pay it at that time. Alternatively, you may hire a customs broker to do this for you, but be aware that brokers are not U.S. Customs employees, and they charge fees for their services.

Storage Charges: If freight or express packages from your trip are delivered before you return and you have not made arrangements to pick them up, Customs will place them in storage after 15 days. This storage will be at your risk and expense. If they are not claimed within six months, the items will be sold at auction.

Packages sent by mail and not claimed within 30 days will be returned to the sender unless the amount of duty is being protested.

Duty-Free Shops

Many travelers are confused by the term "duty-free" shops. Travelers often think that what they buy in duty-free shops won't be dutiable when they return home and clear Customs. But this is not true: Articles sold in a duty-free shop are free of duty and taxes only for the country in which that shop is located. So if your purchases exceed your personal exemption, items you bought in a duty-free shop, whether in the United States or abroad, will almost certainly be subject to duty.

Articles sold in foreign duty-free shops are subject to U.S. Customs duty and other restrictions (for example, only one liter of liquor is duty-free), but you may include these items in your personal exemption. Articles sold in duty-free shops are meant to be taken out of the country; they are not meant to be used, worn, eaten, drunk, etc., in the country where you purchased them. Articles purchased in American duty-free shops are also subject to U.S. Customs duty if you bring them into the United States. For example, if you buy liquor in a duty-free shop in New York before entering Canada and then bring it back into the United States, it may be subject to duty and Internal Revenue Service tax.

Prohibited and Restricted Items

The Customs Service has been entrusted with enforcing some 400 laws for 40 other government agencies, such as the Fish and Wildlife Service and the Department of Agriculture. These other agencies have great interest in what people bring into the country, but they are not always at ports of entry, guarding our borders. Customs is always at ports of entry - guarding the nation's borders is what we do.

The products we want to keep out of the United States are those that would injure community health, public safety, American workers, children, or domestic plant and animal life, or those that would defeat our national political interests. Sometimes the products that cause injury, or have the potential to do so, may seem fairly innocent. But, as you will see from the material that follows, appearances can be deceiving.

Before you leave for your trip abroad, you might want to talk to Customs about the items you plan to bring back to be sure they're not prohibited or restricted. Prohibited means the item is forbidden by law to enter the United States, period. Examples are dangerous toys, cars that don't protect their occupants in a crash, or illegal substances like absinthe and Rohypnol. Restricted means that special licenses or permits are required from a federal agency before the item is allowed to enter the United States. Examples are firearms and certain fruits, vegetables, pets, and textiles.

Cultural Artifacts and Cultural Property (Art/Artifacts) Most countries have laws that protect their cultural property (art/artifacts/antiquities; archaeological and ethnological material are also terms that are used).Such laws include export controls and/or national ownership of cultural property. Even if purchased from a business in the country of origin or in another country, legal ownership of such artifacts may be in question if brought into the U.S. Make certain you have documents such as export permits and receipts, although these do not necessarily confer ownership. While foreign laws may not be enforceable in the U.S., they can cause certain U.S. law to be invoked. For example, as a general rule, under the U.S. National Stolen Property Act, one cannot have legal title to art/artifacts/antiquities that were stolen, no matter how many times such items may have changed hands. Articles of stolen cultural property (from museums or from religious or secular public monuments) originating in any of the countries party to the 1970 UNESCO Convention specifically may not be imported into the U.S.

In addition, U.S. law may restrict importation into the U.S. of specific categories of art/artifacts/antiquities:

1. U.S. law restricts the import of any Pre-Colombian monumental and architectural sculpture and murals from Central and South American countries.

2. U.S. law specifically restricts the importation of Native American artifacts from Canada; Maya Pre-Colombian archaeological objects from Guatemala; Pre-Colombian archaeological objects from El Salvador and Peru; archaeological objects (such as terracotta statues) from Mali; Colonial period objects such as paintings and ritual objects from Peru; Byzantine period ritual and ecclesiastic objects (such as icons) from Cyprus; Khmer stone archaeological sculpture from Cambodia.

Importation of items such as those above is permitted only when the items are accompanied by an export permit issued by the country of origin (where such items were first found). Purveyors of such items have been known to offer phony export certificates. As additional U.S. import restrictions may be imposed in response to requests from other countries, it is wise for the prospective purchaser to visit the State department's cultural property Web site. This Web site also has images representative of the categories of cultural property for which there are specific U.S. import restrictions.

Absinthe The importation of Absinthe and any other liquors or liqueurs that contain an excess of Artemisia absinthium is prohibited.

Automobiles Automobiles imported into the United States must meet the fuel-emission requirements of the Environmental Protection Agency (EPA) and the safety, bumper, and theft-prevention standards of the Department of Transportation (DOT). (Please see Customs pamphlets Importing a Car and Pleasure Boats.) Trying to import a car that doesn't meet all the requirements can be a vexing experience. Here's why:

Almost all cars, vans, sport utility vehicles, and so on that are bought in foreign countries must be modified to meet American standards. Passenger vehicles that are imported on the condition that they be modified must be exported or destroyed if they are not modified acceptably.

And even if the car does meet all federal standards, it might be subject to additional EPA requirements, depending on what countries you drove it in. Or it could require a bond upon entry until the conditions for admission have been met. So before you even think about importing a car, you should call EPA and DOT for more information.

Information on importing vehicles can be obtained from the Environmental Protection Agency, Attn.: 6405J, Washington, DC 20460, telephone (202) 564-9660 , and the Department of Transportation, Office of Vehicle Safety Compliance (NEF 32) NHTSA, Washington, DC 20590.

Copies of the Customs Service's pamphlet Importing or Exporting a Car, can be obtained by writing to the U.S. Customs Service, P.O. Box 7407, Washington, DC 20044. EPA's Automotive

Imports Fact Manual can be obtained by writing to the Environmental Protection Agency, Washington, DC 20460. Cars being brought into the United States temporarily (for less than one year) are exempt from these restrictions.

Trademarked and Copyrighted Articles U.S. Customs enforces laws relating to the protection of trademarks and copyrights. Articles that infringe a federally registered trademark or copyright, i.e., that use the protected right without the authorization of the trademark or copyright owner, are subject to detention and seizure.

Articles bearing marks that are counterfeit of a federally registered trademark are subject to seizure and forfeiture. Additionally, the importation of articles bearing counterfeit marks may subject an individual to a civil monetary penalty if the registered trademark has also been recorded with Customs. Articles bearing marks that are confusingly similar to a registered trademark, and gray market articles (goods bearing genuine marks not intended for importation into the United States) may be subject to detention and seizure.

However, passengers arriving into the United States are permitted to import one article, which must accompany the person, bearing a counterfeit, confusingly similar or restricted gray market trademark, provided that the article is for personal use and is not for sale. This exemption may be granted not more than once every thirty days. The arriving passenger may retain one article of each type accompanying the person. For example, an arriving person who has three purses, whether each bears a different infringing trademark, or whether all three bear the same infringing trademark, is permitted one purse. If the article imported under the personal exemption provision is sold within one year after the date of importation, the article or its value is subject to forfeiture.

In regard to copyright infringement, articles that are determined to be clearly piratical of a federally registered copyright, i.e., unauthorized articles that are substantially similar to a material protected part of a copyright, are subject to seizure. Articles that are determined to be possibly piratical may be subject to detention and possible seizure. A personal use exemption similar to that described above also applies in respect of copyrighted articles.

You may bring back genuine trademarked and copyrighted articles (subject to duties). The copyrighted products most commonly imported include CD-ROMs, tape cassettes, toys, stuffed animals, clothing with cartoon characters, videotapes, videocassettes, music CDs, and books.

Ceramic Tableware Although ceramic tableware is not prohibited or restricted, you should know that such tableware made in foreign countries may contain dangerous levels of lead in the glaze; this lead can seep into foods and beverages. The Food and Drug Administration Recommends that if you buy ceramic tableware abroad - especially in Mexico, China, Hong Kong, or India - you have it tested for lead release when you return, or use it for decorative purposes only.

Dog and Cat Fur It is illegal in the United States to import, export, distribute, transport, manufacture, or sell products containing dog or cat fur in the United States. As of November 9, 2000, the Dog and Cat Protection Act of 2000 calls for the seizure and forfeiture of each item containing dog or cat fur.

The Act provides that any person who violates any provision may be assessed a civil penalty of not more that $10,000 for each separate knowing and intentional violation, $5,000 for each separate gross negligent violation, or $3,000 for each separate negligent violation.

Drug Paraphernalia It is illegal to bring drug paraphernalia into the United States unless they have been prescribed for authentic medical conditions - diabetes, for example. Customs will seize any illegal paraphernalia. The importation, exportation, manufacture, sale, or transportation of drug paraphernalia is prohibited by law. If you're convicted of any of these offenses, you will be subject to fines and imprisonment.

Firearms The Bureau of Alcohol, Tobacco and Firearms (ATF) regulates and restricts firearms and ammunition; it also approves all import transactions involving weapons and ammunition. If you want to import (or export) either of them, you must do so through a licensed importer, dealer, or manufacturer. Also, if the National Firearms Act prohibits certain weapons, ammunition, or similar devices from coming into the country, you won't be able to import them unless the ATF specifically authorizes you, in writing, to do so.

161

You don't need an ATF permit if you can demonstrate that you are returning with the same firearms or ammunition that you took out of the United States. The best way is to register your firearms and related equipment by taking them to any Customs office before you leave the United States. The Customs officer will register them on the same form CF-4457 used to register cameras or computers (see "Register Items Before You Leave the United States").

For further information about importing weapons, contact the Bureau of Alcohol, Tobacco and Firearms, U.S. Department of the Treasury, Washington, DC 20226; or call (202) 927-8320 .

Many countries will not allow you to enter with a firearm even if you are only traveling through the country on the way to your final destination. If you plan to take your firearms or ammunition to another country, you should contact officials at that country's embassy to learn about its regulations. And please visit your nearest Customs office before your departure to learn the latest requirements for weapons and ammunition registration.

Fish and Wildlife Fish, wildlife, and products made from them are subject to import and export restrictions, prohibitions, permits or certificates, and quarantine requirements. We recommend that you contact the U.S. Fish and Wildlife Service before you depart if you plan to import or export any of the following:

Wild birds, land or marine mammals, reptiles, fish, shellfish, mollusks, or invertebrates. Any part or product of the above, such as skins, tusks, bone, feathers, or eggs. Products or articles manufactured from wildlife or fish.

Endangered species of wildlife, and products made from them, generally may not be imported or exported. You'll need a permit from the Fish and Wildlife Service to import virtually all types of ivory, unless it's from a warthog. The Fish and Wildlife Service has so many restrictions and prohibitions on various kinds of ivory - Asian elephant, African elephant, whale, rhinoceros, seal, pre-Endangered Species Act, post-CITES (Convention on International Trade in Endangered Species), and many others - that they urge you to contact them before you even think of acquiring ivory in a foreign country. They can be reached at (800) 358-2104 .

But you may import an object made of ivory if it's an antique; that is, if it's at least 100 years old. You will need documentation that authenticates the age of the ivory. You may import other antiques containing wildlife parts with the same condition: they must be accompanied by documentation proving they are at least 100 years old. (Certain other requirements for antiques may apply.)

For example: If you plan to buy such things as tortoiseshell jewelry, leather goods, or articles made from whalebone, ivory, skins, or fur, please, before you go, contact the U.S. Fish and Wildlife Service, Division of Law Enforcement, P.O. Box 3247, Arlington, VA 22203-3247, or call (800) 358-2104 . Hunters can get information on the limitations for importing and exporting migratory game birds from this office as well. Ask for the pamphlet Facts About Federal Wildlife Laws .

The Fish and Wildlife Service has designated specific ports of entry to handle fish and wildlife entries. If you plan to import anything discussed in this section, please also contact the Customs Service. We'll tell you about designated ports and send you the brochure Pets and Wildlife, which describes the regulations we enforce for all agencies that oversee the importation of animals.

Some states have fish and wildlife laws and regulations that are stricter than federal laws and regulations. If you're returning to such a state, be aware that the stricter state laws and regulations have priority. Similarly, the federal government does not allow you to import into the United States wild animals that were taken, killed, sold, possessed, or exported from another country if any of these acts violated foreign laws.

Game and Hunting Trophies If you plan to import game or a hunting trophy, please contact the Fish and Wildlife Service before you leave at (800) 358-2104 . Currently, 14 Customs ports of entry are designated to handle game and trophies; other Customs ports must get approval from the Fish and Wildlife Service to clear your entry.

Depending on the species you bring back, you might need a permit from the country where the animal was harvested. Regardless of the species, you'll have to fill out a Fish and Wildlife form 3-177, Declaration for Importation or Exportation.

Trophies may also be subject to inspection by the U.S. Department of Agriculture's Animal and

Plant Health Inspection Service (APHIS) for sanitary purposes. General guidelines for importing trophies can be found in APHIS's publication Traveler's Tips. Contact USDA-APHIS-PPQ, Permit Unit, 4700 River Road, Unit 133, Riverdale, MD 20737, or call (301) 734-8645.

Also, federal regulations do not allow the importation of any species into a state with fish or wildlife laws that are more restrictive than federal laws. And if foreign laws were violated in the taking, sale, possession, or export to the United States of wild animals, those animals will not be allowed entry into the United States.

Warning: There are many regulations, enforced by various agencies, governing the importation of animals and animal parts. Failure to comply with them could result in time-consuming delays in clearing your trophy through Customs. You should always call for guidance before you depart.

Food Products You may bring bakery items and certain cheeses into the United States. APHIS publishes a booklet, Traveler's Tips, that offers extensive information about bringing food products into the country. For more information, or for a copy of Traveler's Tips, contact USDA-APHIS (see the section on "Game and Hunting Trophies" section).

Some imported foods are also subject to requirements of the Food and Drug Administration.

Meats, Livestock, and Poultry The regulations governing meat and meat products are very strict: you may not bring back fresh, dried, or canned meats or meat products from most foreign countries. Also, you may not bring in food products that have been prepared with meat.

The regulations on importing meat and meat products change frequently because they are based on disease outbreaks in different areas of the world. APHIS, which regulates meats and meat products as well as fruits and vegetables, invites you to call for more information on importing meats. Contact USDA-APHIS Veterinary Services, National Center for Import/Export (NCIE), 4700 River Road, Unit 40, Riverdale, MD 20737-1231; call (301) 734-7830.

Fruits and Vegetables Bringing home fruits and vegetables can be quite troublesome. That apple you bought in the foreign airport just before boarding and then didn't eat? Whether Customs will allow it into the United States depends on where you got it and where you're going after you arrive in the United States. The same is true for those magnificent Mediterranean tomatoes. Fresh fruits and vegetables can carry plant pests or diseases into the United States.

You may remember the Med fly hysteria of the late 1980s: Stories about crop damage caused by the Mediterranean fruit fly were in the papers for months. The state of California and the federal government together spent some $100 million to get rid of this pest. And the source of the outbreak? One traveler who brought home one contaminated piece of fruit.

It's best not to bring fresh fruits or vegetables into the United States. But if you plan to, call APHIS and get a copy of Traveler's Tips, which lists what you can and can't bring, and also items for which you'll need a permit. For more information, visit http://www.aphis.usda.gov/travel/ or www.aphis.usda.gov/ppq/permits.

Plants The plants, cuttings, seeds, unprocessed plant products, and certain endangered species that are allowed into the United States require import permits; some are prohibited entirely. Threatened or endangered species that are permitted must have export permits from the country of origin. Every single plant or plant product must be declared to the Customs officer and must be presented for USDA inspection, no matter how free of pests it appears to be. Address requests for information to USDA-APHIS-PPQ, 4700 River Road, Unit 139, Riverdale, MD 20737-1236; phone (301) 734-8295 ; or visit www.aphis.usda.gov/travel/.

Gold Gold coins, medals, and bullion, formerly prohibited, may be brought into the United States. However, under regulations administered by the Office of Foreign Assets Control, such items originating in or brought from Afghanistan, Cuba, Iran, Iraq, Libya, Serbia, and Sudan are prohibited entry. Copies of gold coins are prohibited if not properly marked by country of issuance.

Medication Rule of thumb: When you go abroad, take the medicines you'll need, no more, no less.

Narcotics and certain other drugs with a high

potential for abuse - Rohypnol, GHB, and Fen-Phen, to name a few - may not be brought into the United States, and there are severe penalties for trying to bring them in. If you need medicines that contain potentially addictive drugs or narcotics (e.g., some cough medicines, tranquilizers, sleeping pills, antidepressants, or stimulants), do the following:

● Declare all drugs, medicinals, and similar products to the appropriate Customs official.
● Carry all drugs, medicinals, and similar products in their original containers.
● Carry only the quantity of such substances that a person with that condition(e.g., chronic pain)
would normally carry for his/her use.
● Carry a prescription or written statement from your physician that the substances are being
used under a doctor's supervision and that they are necessary for your physical well-being
while traveling.

U.S. residents entering the United States at international land borders, who are carrying a validly obtained controlled substance (except narcotics such as marijuana, cocaine, heroin, or LSD), are subject to certain additional requirements. If a U.S. resident wants to bring in a controlled substance other than narcotics such as marijuana, cocaine, heroine, or LSD, but does not have a prescription for the substance issued by a U.S.-licensed practitioner (e.g., physician, dentist, etc.) registered with and authorized by the Drug Enforcement Administration (DEA) to prescribe the mediation, the individual may not import more than 50 dosage units of the medication. if the U.S. Resident has a prescription for the controlled substance issued by a DEA registrant, more than 50 dosage units may be imported by that person, provided all other legal requirements are met.

Please note that only medications that can be legally prescribed in the United States may be imported for personal use. Be aware that possession of certain substances may also violate state laws.

Warning: The Food and Drug Administration (FDA) prohibits the importation, by mail or in person, of fraudulent prescription and nonprescription drugs and medical devices. These include unorthodox "cures" for such medical conditions as cancer, AIDS, arthritis, or multiple sclerosis. Although such drugs or devices may be legal elsewhere, if the FDA has not approved them for use in the United States, they may not legally enter the country and will be confiscated if found, even if they were obtained under a foreign physician's prescription.

For specifics about importing controlled substances call (202) 307-2414 . For additional information about traveling with medication, contact your nearest FDA office or write Food and Drug Administration, Division of Import Operations and Policy, Room 12-8 (HFC-170), 5600 Fishers Lane, Rockville, MD 20857, or read the FDA's Subchapter on Coverage of Personal Importations.

Merchandise from Embargoed Countries
Generally, you may not bring in any goods from the following countries: Afghanistan, Cuba, Iran*, Iraq, Libya, Serbia, and Sudan. The Office of Foreign Assets Control of the U.S. Treasury Department enforces this ban.

You may, however, bring in informational materials - pamphlets, books, tapes, films or recordings - from these countries, except for Iraq.

If you want to import merchandise from any of these countries, you will first need a specific license from the Office of Foreign Assets Control. Such licenses are rarely granted.

There are restrictions on travel to these countries. The restrictions are strictly enforced, so if you're thinking about going to any of the countries on this list, write to the Office of Foreign Assets Control, Department of the Treasury. Washington, DC 20220, before you make your plans.

*The embargo on Iranian goods is being revised to allow the importation of carpets and foods for human consumption such as caviar and pistachios. Please check with your local port to find out when the new regulations are scheduled to take effect. Until the new regulations are published, the complete embargo is still in force.

Pets

If you plan to take your pet abroad or import one on your return, please get a copy of Customs booklet, Pets & Wildlife. You should also check with state, county, and local authorities to learn if their restrictions and prohibitions on pets are more strict than federal requirements.

Importing animals is closely regulated for public health reasons and also for the well-being of the animals. There are restrictions and prohibitions on bringing many species into the United States.

Cats must be free of evidence of diseases communicable to humans when they are examined at the port of entry. If the cat does not seem to be in good health, the owner may have to pay for an additional examination by a licensed veterinarian.

Dogs , too, must be free of evidence of diseases that could be communicable to humans. Puppies must be confined at a place of the owner's choosing until they are three months old; then they must be vaccinated against rabies. The puppy will then have to stay in confinement for another 30 days.

Dogs older than three months must get a rabies vaccination at least 30 days before they come to the United States and must be accompanied by a valid rabies vaccination certificate if coming from a country that is not rabies-free. This certificate should identify the dog, show the date of vaccination and the date it expires (there are one-year and three-year vaccinations), and be signed by a licensed veterinarian. If the certificate does not have an expiration date, Customs will accept it as long as the dog was vaccinated 12 months or less before coming to the United states. Dogs coming from rabies-free countries do not have to be vaccinated.

You may import birds as pets as long as you comply with APHIS and U.S. Fish and Wildlife requirements. These requirements may include quarantining the birds at one of APHIS' three Animal Import Centers at your expense. You must make advance reservations at the quarantine facility. If you intend to import a bird, call APHIS' National Center for Import and Export at (301) 734-8364 for more information. In any case, birds may only be imported through ports of entry where a USDA port veterinarian is on duty, any you must make arrangements in advance to have the bird examined by a USDA port veterinarian at the first U.S. port of entry. There is a user fee for this service of a minimum of $23.00 based on an hourly rate of $76/hour. For more information, you may contact the USDA, APHIS, Veterinary Services, National Center for Import and Export (NCIE), 4700 River Road, Unit 40, Riverdale, MD 20737-1231; phone number (301) 734-8364 .

Textiles and Clothing In general, there is no limit to how much fabric and clothing you can bring back as long as it is for your personal use, that is, for you or as gifts. (You may have to pay duty on it if you've exceeded your personal exemption, but the amount you may bring in is not limited.)

Unaccompanied shipments (packages that are mailed or shipped), however, may be subject to limitations on amount. The quantity limitations on clothing and textiles are called "quotas." In order to enter the United States, clothing and textiles may need to be accompanied by a document - you could think of it as a passport for fabrics - called a "visa." Sometimes, instead of a visa, an export license or certificate is required from the country that produced the clothing. A formal entry must be filed for all made-to-order suits from Hong Kong, no matter what their value, unless they accompany you and an export license issued by Hong Kong is presented with this entry. If you plan to get clothing or fabric on your trip and have it sent to you by mail or courier, check with Customs about quota and visa requirements before you travel.

Money and Other Monetary Instruments
You may bring into or take out of the country, including by mail, as much money as you wish. But if it's more than $10,000, you'll need to report it to Customs. Ask the Customs officer for the Currency Reporting Form (CF 4790). The penalties for not complying can be quite severe.

"Money" means monetary instruments and includes U.S. or foreign coin currently in circulation, currency, traveler's checks in any form, money orders, and negotiable instruments or investment securities in bearer form.

Traveling Back and Forth Across the Border
If you cross the U.S. border into a foreign country and reenter the United States more than once in a short time, you might not want to use your personal exemption ($800 in this example) until you've returned to the United States for the last time. Here's why:

When you leave the United States, come back, leave again, and then come back again, all on the same trip, you can lose your Customs exemption, since you've technically violated the "once every 30 days" rule. So if you know that your trip will involve these so-called "swing-backs," you can choose to save your personal exemption until the end of your trip.

For example, say you go to Canada, buy a liter of liquor, reenter the United States, then go back to Canada and buy $500 worth of merchandise and more liquor. You would probably want to save your $800 exemption for those final purchases and not use it for that first liter of liquor. In this case, on your first swing-back, simply tell the Customs inspector that you want to pay duty on the liquor, even though you could bring it in duty-free. (If you did, you would lose the $800 exemption, since it's only available to you once every 30 days.) In other words, all you have to do is tell the inspector that you want to pay duty the first (or second or third) time you come back to the United States if you know that you'll be leaving again soon, buying goods or getting them as gifts, and then reentering before the 30 days are up. In such a case, you're better off saving your exemption until the last time you reenter theUnited States.

Photographic Film

Customs will not examine film you bought abroad and are bringing back unless the Customs officer has reason to believe it contains prohibited material, such as child pornography.

You won't be charged duty on film bought in the United States and exposed abroad, whether it's developed or not. But film you bought and developed abroad counts as a dutiable item.

Customer Service Programs and Other Travel-related Information

Customer Service Programs The Customs Service is expanding its methods of improving customer service to international travelers at major U.S. travel hubs. One method is having supervisory Customs inspectors, called passenger service representatives, available to travelers on a full-time basis at more than 20 international airports and some seaports and land border ports of entry. The representatives' major purpose is to help travelers clear Customs.

Photos of the passenger service reps are posted wherever the program is operating, so you can find them if you need assistance. If you have a concern or need help understanding Customs regulations and procedures, ask to speak with the passenger service rep on duty.

The second initiative involves kiosks, the sort of automated booths you see in malls, banks, department stores, and airports. Customs Service kiosks are located at international airports.

Think of them as automated passenger service reps: They're self-service computers with a touch-screen display. All you have to do is type in your country of destination and the computer will print the information for you. The screen displays a telephone number to call for more information. The kiosks also have pockets with Customs pamphlets on a variety of topics of interest to travelers: regulations on transporting currency, agriculture and food items, medicines, and pets, to name just a few.

Customs kiosks are located in the outbound passenger lounges at the following international airports: Atlanta; Boston; Charlotte, North Carolina; Chicago; Dallas/Ft. Worth; Detroit; Houston; JFK, New York; Los Angeles; Miami; Newark, New Jersey; Philadelphia; San Francisco; San Juan; and Washington/Dulles. More kiosks are planned.

If you have any questions about Customs procedures, requirements, or policies regarding travelers, or if you have any complaints about treatment you have received from Customs inspectors or about your Customs processing, please contact:

Executive Director, Passenger Programs U.S. Customs Service 1300 Pennsylvania Avenue, NW Room 5.4D Washington, DC 20229

Allegations of criminal or serious misconduct may be reported to the Office of Internal Affairs at 1-877-IA CALLS . You may also write them at P.O. Box 14475, Washington, D.C. 20044.

Other Travel-related Information Frequently, we are asked questions that are not customs matters. If you want to know about:

Immigration - The U.S. Immigration and Naturalization Service (INS) is responsible for the movement of people in and out of the United States. Please contact the Department of Justice, INS, for questions concerning resident alien and nonresident visa and passport information at 800-375-5283

Passports are issued by the U.S. Department of State's Passport Agency. Please contact the passport agency nearest you for more information. Postal clerks also accept passport application.

Baggage allowance - Ask the airline or steamship line you are traveling for more information.

Currency of other Nations - Your local bank can be of assistance.

Foreign countries - For information about the country you will visit or about what articles may be taken into that country, contact its embassy, consular office, or tourist information office.

Chapter 16

Moving Household Goods to the United States: A Guide to Customs Regulations

*[The information in this chapter is reprinted verbatim from bulletins issued by the
U.S. Department of Customs.
It is intended to serve as advice to Americans traveling abroad.]*

Determining Your Customs Status

Returning Resident

A returning resident is a citizen of the United States, or a person who has formerly resided in the United States, (including American citizens who are residents of Guam, American Samoa, the Commonwealth of the Northern Mariana Islands, or the U.S. Virgin Islands) who is returning from abroad. In order to be classified as a returning resident, it must be understood that your time out of the country was for a temporary period. If your intent was to move abroad permanently (you married a nonresident), and after a time, your plans unexpectedly changed (you became divorced), your return to the U.S. may be classified as a nonresident move. If you have lived abroad for more than three years you may enter as a nonresident.

Government/Military Employees

U.S. Government personnel are individuals employed by the U.S. Government. They must receive a paycheck from the U.S. Government. The person in the service of the United States must be returning under Government orders at the end of an extended duty assignment outside the Customs territory of the United States.
An extended duty assignment abroad must be longer than 140 days, except as noted for Navy personnel. Military and civilian personnel are entitled to free entry privileges if:

- They are returning, at any time, after an assignment of extended duty.

- They are returning to the United States on permanent change of station (PCS) orders regardless of the duration of assignment overseas.

- They are under permanent change of station (PCS) orders to another post or station abroad, requiring return of their personal and household effects to the United States.

Navy personnel serving aboard a United States naval vessel, or a supporting naval vessel when it leaves the United States on an intended deployment of 120 days or more outside the country, and who continue to serve on the vessel until it returns to the United States are entitled to the extended duty exemption.

Returning in Advance of Permanent Change of Station (PCS) Orders

Family members who have lived overseas with the employee, but return to the United States with their possessions before the employee receives his/her orders ending the extended duty assignment, cannot claim the duty-free exemption granted to military or Government personnel; for example, a spouse who returns to the United States to look for housing or a student who returns to the U.S. to enter college.

Emergency Evacuees

Any person living abroad who is ordered by the United States Government to leave a specific foreign country and return to the United States because of civil unrest or war is given the same exemption granted under the Harmonized Tariff Schedule to U.S. Military and Government Personnel. This may include government personnel, tourists, persons employed in private business - in short, anyone covered by an evacuation order.

169

Nonresident/First-Time Immigrants

First-time immigrants to the United States are considered to be nonresidents the first time they enter the United States. Every time thereafter they are considered to be returning residents as long as they have their Immigration and Naturalization Service form I-551, residency visa, a.k.a. "green card."

Part-Time Residents

A part-time resident may maintain two households, one in the United States and one in another country. They may be in the United States for business, for pleasure, or for educational purposes. The visit can be for a few weeks or for several years. A part-time resident may be classified, for Customs purposes, as either a returning resident or a nonresident. The status of either returning resident or nonresident is dependent upon several things and is usually decided on a case-by-case basis. Deciding factors include citizenship, where the traveler pays taxes, where they are employed, what country or state drivers license they possess, etc. A U.S. citizen is presumed to be a resident unless they can show that they are a resident of another country (e.g., possess a residency visa for another country, a round-trip ticket to return to another country, etc.) A citizen of another country residing in the U.S. must have an Immigration and Naturalization Service form I-551, residency visa, a.k.a. "green card," to be considered a returning resident.

Household Effects

Household effects are furniture, dishes, linens, libraries, artwork and similar household furnishings for your personal use. The articles must have either been available for your use or used in a household where you were a resident for one year and are not intended for any other person or for sale. The year of use does not need to be continuous, nor does it need to be the year immediately before the date of importation.

Personal Effects

Personal effects are items that belong to, and are used by, one person, such as wearing apparel, jewelry, photographic equipment and tape recorders. They cannot be entered as household effects.

Inherited Goods

Inherited goods imported into the United States cannot be brought in duty-free as household or personal effects unless they meet the following criteria:

- They are antiques (over 100 years old) and you have documentation to prove this.
- They were available for your use in a household where you resided for a year prior to your moving to the United States, for example, they were in your parents house while you were growing up.

Even if the above conditions do not apply to your inherited goods, because most inherited goods are used, the amount of duty assessed will most likely be small.

General Procedures for Importing Household and Personal Effects

When completing the Customs Form (CF) 6059B, "Customs Declaration," for accompanying goods, or the CF 3299 "Declaration For Free Entry of Unaccompanied Articles," the statement that the goods are "household effects" is not sufficient information. The complete inventory of imported goods will be treated as the packing list and must be provided to Customs upon request. The following is an example of an invoice description.

Furniture: Tables, chairs, sofas, bedroom, home/office and living room furniture, desks, lamps, mirrors, etc.

Kitchenware: Silverware, glassware, chinaware, pots, pans, utensils, electrical kitchen appliances, etc.

Household goods: Linens, towels, rugs, toiletries, cleaning products, decorative articles, art, framed pictures, toys, strollers, crafts, holiday decorations, fans, washers, dryers, VCRs, TVs, stereos, records, collectibles, etc.

Sport equipment: (NO FIREARMS). Bicycles, weights, stationary equipment, skis, skates, surfboards, etc.
Clothes: For women, men, boys, girls, and infants.

Books/Printed materials: Books, calendars,

personal records, photo albums, etc.
Home/Office equipment/Tools of Trade: Computers (CPU, monitor, printer, software, etc.), filing cabinets, shredders, fax machines, telephone equipment, calculators, books, etc.

Other personal effects: Item(s) not covered by previous categories should be individually described.

The quantity on the invoice must, at minimum, provide the count in boxes, crates, or pieces. This information is required for the efficient completion of Customs document review and examination.

NOTE: To safeguard against the importation of dangerous pests, the U.S. Department of Agriculture prohibits solid wood packing materials from China unless they have been fumigated and have appropriate documentation.

Goods That Accompany You
Household and personal effects that arrive in the U.S. on the same vessel, vehicle or aircraft, and on the same day that you do, are considered to accompany you. Articles that are shipped as freight on a bill of lading or airway bill are also considered to accompany you when the baggage arrives in the U.S. on the same conveyance that you arrive on. You must complete Customs Form 6059B, "Customs Declaration," listing all items with their value that you are bringing into the United States with you. Identify those you believe are entitled to duty-free entry, based on the information in this publication. Explain your status to the Customs Inspector and ask any questions that you may have before the inspection of your belongings begins.

Goods Shipped Separately
Household effects entitled to duty-free entry do not need to accompany you to the United States; you may have them shipped to your U.S. address at a later time if you choose. Your shipment of personal and/or household goods must be cleared through Customs at its first port of arrival unless you have made arrangements with a foreign freight forwarder to have your effects sent in Customs custody in-bond from the port of arrival to a more convenient port of entry for clearance. (*Ask your moving company if they offer this service.*) **Customs will not notify you that your goods have arrived**. It is the responsibility of the shipper to notify you of the arrival of your goods. After receiving this notification you must enter the

merchandise. Failure to enter the merchandise within 15 days after its arrival in port may result in the merchandise being moved to a general order warehouse. Failure to obtain that merchandise from the general order warehouse within six months may result in its sale. When you come to Customs to enter your goods, you must complete Customs Form 3299, "Declaration for Free Entry of Unaccompanied Articles," to give to the Customs officer. If you cannot come to the Customs office yourself, you may designate a friend or relative to represent you in Customs matters. You must give that person a letter addressed to "Officer in Charge of Customs" authorizing that individual to represent you as your agent on a one-time basis to clear your shipment through Customs.

Importing an Automobile or Other Vehicle
It is important to know that any imported vehicle, new or used, must comply with U.S. safety, fuel savings, and air pollution control standards. If an imported vehicle does not conform to these standards, it must be brought into conformity; otherwise it must be destroyed or exported. Both the Department of Transportation (DOT) and the Environmental Protection Agency (EPA) advise that although a nonconforming car may be conditionally admitted, modifications may be impractical, impossible, or require such extensive engineering that the labor and material cost may be prohibitive. Foreign automakers can also certify whether or not an automobile conforms to U.S. standards. Additional information on importing an automobile can be found on the U.S. Customs website at under Publications, Videos and Forms in the Importing and Exporting section, and on the DOT website and on the EPA website.

The U.S. Department of Agriculture also requires that the undercarriage of imported cars be free from foreign soil before they can be entered into the United States. This may be done by steam spray or by thorough cleaning before shipment.

Safety, Bumper and Theft Prevention Standards
Importers of motor vehicles must file form HS-7 at the time a vehicle is imported to declare whether the vehicle complies with Department of Transportation requirements. As a general rule, all imported motor vehicles less than 25 years old and items of motor vehicle equipment must comply with all applicable Federal Motor Vehicle Safety Standards in order to be imported permanently into the United States. Vehicles manufactured after

September 1, 1978, must also meet the bumper standard, and vehicles beginning with model-year 1987 must meet the theft-prevention standard.

Vehicles manufactured to meet these standards will have a certification label affixed by the original manufacturer near the driver's-side door. If you purchase a vehicle abroad that is certified to U.S. standards, you can expedite your importation by making sure the sales contract identifies this fact and by presenting the contract to U.S. Customs at the time of importation.

A vehicle must be imported as a nonconforming vehicle unless it bears the manufacturer's label certifying that it meets U.S. standards. If it is a nonconforming vehicle, the importer must contract with a DOT-registered importer (RI) to modify the vehicle and certify that it conforms to all applicable federal motor vehicle safety standards. The importer must also post a DOT bond for one-and-a-half times the vehicle's dutiable value. This bond is in addition to the normal Customs entry bond. Copies of the DOT bond and the contract with the RI must be attached to the HS-7 form. Before an RI can modify your vehicle, it must first be determined whether the vehicle is capable of being modified to comply with the Federal Motor Vehicle Safety Standards. The process of modifying your vehicle may become very complex and costly. A list of vehicles that have already been determined capable of being modified by an RI may be obtained from the RI or from the National Highway Traffic Safety Administration's (NHTSA) web site. Additional information may be obtained by writing to the National Highway Traffic Safety Administration (NSA-32), 400 7th Street, SW, Washington, DC 20590; or by faxing your request to (202) 366-1024.

If you do not have a copy of U.S. Customs' brochure Importing or Exporting a Car, the EPA standards are briefly described below. Customs will require a formal entry, regardless of value for all importations of nonconforming vehicles unless the nonresident exemption is claimed. Trailers, motorcycles, and mopeds are also subject to DOT standards.

Federal Tax

Certain imported automobiles may be subject to the gas-guzzler tax imposed by Section 4064 of the Internal Revenue Code. The tax is imposed on an automobile that has a fuel economy standard of less than 22.5 miles per gallon. Additional information may be obtained from any local district office of the Internal Revenue Service.

Emission Standards

Unless otherwise noted, importers of passenger cars, light trucks, motorcycles and heavy duty engines must complete and submit an EPA entry form (EPA Form 3520-1) to Customs upon entry. These forms may be obtained from Customs at the port of entry.

The following passenger cars, light-trucks, motorcycles and heavy-duty engines are subject to Federal emission requirements:

- Gasoline-fueled cars and light-trucks originally manufactured after December 31, 1967.

- Diesel-fueled cars originally manufactured after December 31, 1974.

- Diesel-fueled light-trucks originally manufactured after December 31, 1975.

- Motorcycles greater than 49 cubic centimeters displacement originally manufactured after December 31, 1977.

- Gasoline or diesel-fueled heavy-duty engines originally manufactured after January 1, 1970.

- Methanol-fueled vehicles or engines manufactured for 1990 or later model years.

- Compressed natural gas (CNG) or liquid petroleum gas (LPG) vehicles or engines (including propane) manufactured for 1997 or later model years.

Note that any nonconforming motor vehicle or engine, which is 21 years old or greater and has not been modified within that time, is considered by EPA to be exempted from Federal emission requirements.

Beginning with the 1996 model year, Federal emission requirements also apply to some non-road motorized equipment, such as lawn and garden equipment, and farm and construction equipment. For those vehicles that are subject to U.S.

emission standards, the following must be complied with upon entry into the United States:

Passenger Cars or Trucks Originally Manufactured to Meet U.S. Emission Standards
All 1971 and later model cars or trucks in this category can be identified by a label in a readily visible position in the engine compartment. This label will indicate that the vehicle was originally manufactured to comply with U.S. emission standards. For pre-1971 models, you should verify the original compliance of the vehicle with the vehicle manufacturer.

Vehicles originally equipped with a catalyst or oxygen sensor are no longer subject to EPA's requirement that the vehicle be bonded on entry. Vehicles that have had the catalyst and oxygen sensor removed, or had these components damaged through use of leaded fuel, are still required to have these components replaced after importation.

Passenger Cars or Trucks Not Originally Manufactured to Meet U.S. Emission Standards
These vehicles must be imported through an independent commercial importer (ICI). The EPA entry form (EPA Form 3520-1) must be submitted by the ICI, not the vehicle owner. A list of these ICIs may be obtained at the port of entry or from the EPA. There are no ICIs located overseas and the EPA does not accept conversions performed overseas. The ICI will be responsible for modifying and testing the vehicle in order to demonstrate that it complies with all U.S. emission requirements. Such conversions typically cost several thousand dollars and take several months to complete. The EPA assumes no responsibility for the quality of the work performed by an ICI or its contractual arrangements, including costs. Since ICIs do not necessarily accept all models, and some models may be difficult to convert, the EPA suggests that the importer complete arrangements with an ICI prior to shipping the vehicle to the United States.
Inquiries regarding emission requirements should be addressed to the attention of: The Environmental Protection Agency, Imports (6405-J), 1200 Pennsylvania Ave NW, Washington, DC 20460. You may also contact the EPA by phone at (202) 564-9240, fax (202) 564-2057, or access the Imports Faxback System to obtain documents including a current list of ICIs at (202) 564-9660.

Shipping Arrangements

For your own safety, security and convenience, DO NOT use your car as a container for personal belongings. The practice of shipping personal belongings packed in an automobile is discouraged for the following reasons:

- The goods in the car must be available for Customs inspection, which means you cannot lock your vehicle. If you do, Customs may break the lock to inspect the goods.

- Your personal belongings are susceptible to theft while waiting to be loaded on the carrier, while being transported to the U.S., or after being unloaded in the United States.

- Many shippers and carriers will not accept your vehicle if it contains personal belongings. The carrier is required to list the automobile and its contents on the ship's manifest. If the contents are not listed, the carrier is subject to fines or penalties.

- The vehicle and its contents may be subject to seizure and you may be subject to fines or penalties if you or your agent do not declare the complete contents of the vehicle at the time the automobile is examined by U.S. Customs.

General Rules for Liquor and Tobacco

Tobacco

Products of Cuban tobacco are prohibited to arriving U.S. citizens and residents, unless acquired in Cuba by persons authorized by the State Department to travel to Cuba. Cigarettes may be subject to a tax imposed by state and local authorities.

Liquor
You will be required to pay duty on liquor that is imported in quantities greater than the exemptions allowed for each category of persons moving to the United States. While there is no Federal limit to the amount of alcohol you may bring in, there will most likely be a state limit. This limit is determined by the state that your goods arrive in, not the state you are moving to.

173

Alcoholic beverages may not be imported into the U.S. by mail, nor can Customs release liquor in violation of the laws of the state where it is entered. As laws vary from state to state, this information may be obtained from state liquor authorities. The Bureau of Alcohol, Tobacco and Firearms (ATF) and the U.S. Customs Service have concurrent jurisdiction in the area of personal use importations of alcoholic beverages. As a practical matter, it is usually the U.S. Customs Service and the port director at the port of entry who decide whether or not a particular importation is, in fact, for personal use only. In certain circumstances, ATF may exercise joint jurisdiction with Customs in making this determination. In addition, other state, local or U.S. Customs requirements may apply. It should be noted that some states prohibit the direct shipment of alcoholic beverages to individuals. Anyone interested in importing alcohol for personal use should contact his or her state liquor control agency. If the alcohol is being imported for sale, you must have an ATF permit in advance of the goods arriving in port.

Households with personal wine cellars must remember that all alcohol over the amount eligible for duty-free treatment is dutiable at the applicable duty rate and that all Federal, state, and local taxes must be paid.

Finally, the determination of whether or not a shipment is for personal or commercial use cannot be decided solely on the size of the shipment, but must be determined on a case-by-case basis considering the circumstances surrounding the importation. However, the size of the shipment may give rise to questions resulting in the need for an investigation by Customs or the ATF. For further information contact:

Prohibited or Restricted Goods

The importation of certain classes of merchandise is prohibited or restricted to protect community health, to preserve domestic plant and animal life, and for other reasons. Should you attempt to bring in merchandise that is prohibited by law, it will be seized and you may be liable for a personal penalty. Prohibited articles include: liquor-filled candies, absinthe, lottery tickets, narcotics and dangerous drugs, drug paraphernalia, obscene articles and publications, seditious and treasonable materials, hazardous articles (e.g. fireworks, dangerous toys, toxic or poisonous substances),

products made by prison convicts or forced labor, and switchblade knives (the only exception is for a "one-armed traveler," in which case the blade must be no longer than three inches).

Merchandise that is *prohibited* from entry into the United States will be seized. Merchandise that is *restricted* from entry into the United States may be released after inspection by the Government agency that imposed the restrictions, or detained until the conditions attached to the restrictions are met. The importer of prohibited or restricted merchandise may be liable for a personal penalty, and the merchandise may be confiscated.

U.S. trade sanctions administered by the Office of Foreign Assets Control (OFAC) generally prohibit the importation into the United States (including U.S. territories), either directly or indirectly, of most goods, technology, or services (except information and informational materials) from, or which originated from, Burma, Cuba, Iran, Iraq, Libya, North Korea, Sudan or Yugoslavia (Serbia and Montenegro); from foreign persons designated by the Secretary of State as having promoted the proliferation of weapons of mass destruction; named Foreign Terrorist Organizations; designated terrorists and narcotics traffickers; the Taliban, and areas of Afghanistan controlled by the Taliban. Vessels and aircraft under the registry, ownership, or control of sanctions targets may not import merchandise into the United States. The importation of Cuban cigars is generally prohibited. Diamonds may not be imported from Angola without a certificate of origin or other documentation that demonstrates to Customs authorities that they were legally exported with the approval of the Angola Government of Unity and National Reconciliation.

Treasury Department's Office of Foreign Assets Control has amended the Iranian Transactions Regulations, 31 CFR part 560, to authorize the importation into the United States of, and dealings in, certain Iranian-origin foodstuffs and carpets and related transactions. Section 560.534(a) of this final rule authorizes the importation of Iranian-origin foodstuffs intended for human consumption that are classified under chapters 2-23 of the Harmonized Tariff Schedule of the United States (HTS). Items that are classified in chapters 2-23 of the HTS that are not foodstuffs intended for human consumption are not authorized for importation into the United States by this section. This final rule also authorizes the importation into the United

States of Iranian-origin carpets and other textile floor coverings and carpets used as wall hangings that are classified under chapter 57 or heading 9706.00.00.60 of the HTS. Items that are classified under heading 9706.00.00.60 ("Antiques of an age exceeding one hundred years/Other") that are not carpets and other textile floor coverings or carpets used as wall hangings are not authorized for importation into the United States by this section.

Import restrictions imposed against sanctions targets vary by program. Contact the Office of Foreign Assets Control at (202) 622-2490 with specific questions or concerns or visit OFAC's website.

Biological Materials

Biological materials of public health or veterinary importance (disease organisms and vectors for research and educational purposes) require import permits.

Write to Foreign Quarantine Program, U.S. Public Health Service, Center for Disease Control, Atlanta, Ga. 30333.

Books, Video Tapes, Computer Programs and Cassettes

Pirated copies of copyrighted articles (unlawfully made reproductions or articles produced without the copyright owner's authorization, e.g., music CDs, toys, clothing with cartoon characters, etc.,) are prohibited from importation into the United States. Pirated copies will be seized and destroyed.

Cultural Artifacts and Cultural Property

Most countries have laws that protect their cultural property (art/artifacts/antiquities; archaeological and ethnological material are also terms that are used.) Such laws include export controls and/or national ownership of cultural property. Even if purchased from a business in the country of origin, or in another country, legal ownership of such artifacts may be in question if brought into the United States. Make certain you have documents such as export permits and receipts, although these do not necessarily confer ownership. While foreign laws may not be enforceable in the U.S., they can cause certain U.S. laws to be invoked. For example, as a general rule, under the U.S. National Stolen Property Act, one cannot have legal title to art/artifacts/antiquities that were stolen, no matter how many times such items may have changed hands. Articles of stolen cultural property (from museums or from religious or secular public monuments) originating in any of the countries party to the 1970 UNESCO Convention may not be imported into the United States.

In addition, U.S. law may restrict importation into the U.S. of specific categories of art/artifacts/antiquities:

- U.S. law restricts the import of any Pre-Columbian monumental and architectural sculpture and murals from Central and South American countries.

- U.S. law specifically restricts the importation of Native American artifacts from Canada; Maya pre-Columbian archaeological objects from Guatemala; Pre-Columbian archaeological objects from El Salvador and Peru; archaeological objects (such as terracotta statues) from Mali; Colonial period objects such as paintings and ritual objects from Peru; Byzantine period ritual and ecclesiastic objects (such as icons) from Cyprus; Khmer stone archaeological sculpture from Cambodia.

Importation of items such as those above is permitted only when the items are accompanied by an export permit issued by the country of origin (where such items were first found), or if you came into possession of them before the treaties were signed. Purveyors of such items have been known to offer phony export certificates. As additional U.S. import restrictions may be imposed in response to requests from other countries, it is wise for the prospective purchaser to visit the State Department's cultural property website: http://e.usia.gov/edu/education/culprop/.

This website also has images representative of the categories of cultural property for which there are specific U.S. import restrictions.

Firearms and Ammunitions

Firearms and ammunition are subject to restrictions and import permits. The importation of fully automatic weapons and semi-automatic assault-type weapons is prohibited. Generally, firearms and ammunition acquired abroad may be imported, but only under permit. For complete information, write to the Bureau of Alcohol, Tobacco and Firearms, Department of the Treasury, Firearms and Explosives Import Branch, Washington, DC 20226. That agency will furnish permit applications and answer inquiries about the Gun Control Act of 1968.

Firearms and ammunition previously taken out of and returned to the United States by the same person may be released upon presentation to U.S. Customs of adequate proof of prior possession, i.e., bill of sale, household goods inventory showing serial number, or Customs registration forms 4455 or 4457.

Food and Dairy Products
Bakery items and all cured cheeses are admissible. The USDA Animal and Plant Health Inspection Service (APHIS) leaflet, *Travelers' Tips*, provides detailed information on bringing food, plant, and animal products into the United States. Imported foods are also subject to requirements of the Food and Drug Administration (FDA). Foods not approved by the FDA may not be entered into the United States.

Fruits, Plants, Vegetables
Fruits, plants, vegetables, cuttings, seeds, unprocessed plant products and certain endangered species of plants are either prohibited from entering the country or require an import permit. Canned or processed items are admissible.

Gold
Gold coins, medals, and bullion, formerly prohibited, may be brought into the United States. However, copies of gold coins are prohibited if not properly marked. Since the importation of counterfeit coins is prohibited.

Meats, Livestock, Poultry
Meats, livestock, poultry, and their by-products, such as pate' and sausage are either prohibited or restricted from entering the United States, depending upon the animal disease conditions in the country of origin. This includes fresh, frozen, dried, cured, cooked or canned items. Commercially labeled, cooked, canned meats, that do not require refrigeration and are hermetically sealed, may be brought into the United States.

Medicine/Narcotics
Narcotics and dangerous drugs are prohibited entry and there are severe penalties if imported. A traveler requiring medications containing habit-forming drugs or narcotics (e.g., cough medicines, tranquilizers, sleeping pills, depressants, stimulants, etc.) should:

- Have all drugs, medicinals, and similar products properly identified.

- Carry only the quantity that an individual having some sort of health problem might normally carry.

- Have either a prescription or written statement from his personal physician that the medicinals are being used under a doctor's direction and are necessary for the traveler's physical well being while traveling.

Drugs not approved by the Food and Drug Administration may not be imported into the United States.

Money
There is no limitation in terms of total amount of monetary instruments which may be brought into or taken out of the United States. Monetary instruments include U.S. or foreign coins, currency, traveler's checks, money orders, and negotiable instruments or investment securities in bearer form. If you do transport, or cause to be transported, by mail or other means, more than $10,000 in monetary instruments on any occasion into or out of the United States, or if you receive more than that amount, you must file a report (Customs Form 4790) with U.S. Customs (Currency & Foreign Transactions Reporting Act, 31 U.S.C. 1101, et seq.). Failure to do so can result in civil and criminal penalties.

Pets
There are controls, restrictions, and prohibitions on the entry of animals, birds, turtles, wildlife, and endangered species. Cats and dogs must be free of evidence of diseases communicable to man. Vaccination against rabies is not required for cats, or for dogs arriving from rabies-free countries. Personally owned pet birds may be entered (limit of two if of the Psittacine family), but Animal & Plant Health Inspection Services (APHIS) and Public Health Service requirements must be met, including quarantine at any APHIS facility at specified locations, at the owner's expense. Advance reservations are required. Primates, such as monkeys, apes, and similar animals, may not be imported. If you plan to take your pet abroad or

import one on your return, obtain a copy of our brochure, Pets and Wildlife.

Trademarked Articles

U.S. Customs enforces laws relating to the protection of trademarks and copyrights. Articles that infringe a trademark or copyright, which is use of the protected right without authorization of the trademark or copyright owner, are subject to detention and seizure. Additionally, the importation of articles bearing counterfeit marks may subject an individual to a civil monetary penalty. Articles bearing marks that are confusingly similar to a registered trademark and gray market articles (genuine articles not intended for importation into the Unites States,) may be subject to detention and seizure.

Passengers arriving into the United States are permitted to import one article, which must accompany the person, bearing a counterfeit, confusingly similar, or restricted gray market trademark, provided that the article is for personal use and not for sale. The arriving passenger may retain one article of each of the above types, accompanying the person. If the article imported under the personal exemption provision is sold within one year after the date of importation, the article or its value is subject to forfeiture.

With regard to copyright infringement, articles that are determined to be clearly piratical of a registered copyright are subject to seizure. Articles that are determined to be possibly piratical may be subject to detention and possible seizure.

The types of articles usually of interest to travelers are:

- Lenses, cameras, binoculars, optical goods.
- Tape recorders, CD players, musical instruments.
- Jewelry, precious metalware.
- Perfumes.
- Watches and clocks.
- Clothing.

Wildlife, Fish, Plants

Wildlife, fish, and plants are subject to certain import and export restrictions, prohibitions, permits or certificates, and quarantine requirements. This includes:

- Wild birds, mammals (including marine mammals,) reptiles, crustaceans,

fish, and mollusks.

- Any part or product, such as skins, feathers, eggs.

- Products and articles manufactured from wildlife and fish. You may write to the U.S. Customs Service, PO Box 7407, Washington, D.C. 20044, if you have a question that is not answered by the information in this section.

Endangered species of wildlife and plants, including products made from them, may be prohibited from being imported or exported, as appropriate. If you are considering purchasing articles made from wildlife, such as tortoise shell jewelry, leather goods, articles made from whalebone, ivory, skins, or fur, contact the U.S. Fish and Wildlife Service, Department of the Interior, Washington, D.C. 20240, for additional information.

Returning Residents

Duty Exemptions for Household and Personal Effects

You may import furniture, dishes, linens, libraries, artwork and similar household furnishings for your personal use free of duty. To be eligible for duty-free exemption, the articles must have either been available for your use, or used in a household where you were a resident for one year. The year of use does not need to be continuous, nor does it need to be the year immediately before the date of importation. Personal and household effects entitled to duty-free entry need not accompany you to the United States; you may have them shipped to your U.S. address at a later time if you choose. Your shipment of personal and/or household goods must be cleared through Customs at its first port of arrival, unless you have made arrangements with a foreign freight forwarder to have your effects sent in Customs custody in-bond from the port of arrival to a more convenient port of entry for clearance. (*Ask your moving company if they offer this service.*) Customs will not notify you that your goods have arrived. It is essential that the carrier notify you that your goods have arrived in port - otherwise after 15 days, they will be taken to a general order warehouse and may be sold at auction after six months. When you come to Customs to enter your goods, you must complete Customs Form 3299, "Declaration for Free Entry

177

of Unaccompanied Articles," to give to the Customs officer. If you cannot come to the Customs office yourself, you may designate a friend or relative to represent you in Customs matters. You must give that person a letter addressed to "Officer in Charge of Customs" authorizing that individual to represent you as your agent on a one-time basis to clear your shipment through Customs.

Professional Equipment/Tools of Trade
If your professional equipment or tools of trade were acquired abroad they are not entitled to duty-free consideration unless they were in your possession for one year prior to your return to the United States. If they were in your possession when you moved abroad, and are being brought back in connection with your return to the U.S. they are exempt from duty.

Liquor, Tobacco
You may bring in one liter of alcoholic beverages, free of duty and internal revenue tax, if you are at least 21 years of age, it is for your own use or for a gift, and it is not in violation of the laws of the state in which you arrive. Alcoholic beverages beyond the one-liter limitation are subject to duty and Internal Revenue tax.

Up to 100 cigars and 200 cigarettes (one carton) may be included in your exemption. Tobacco products of Cuban origin are prohibited unless acquired in Cuba by persons authorized by the State Department to travel to Cuba.

Firearms and ammunition
Firearms and ammunition previously taken out of, and returned to, the United States by the same person may be released upon presentation to U.S. Customs of adequate proof of prior possession, i.e., bill of sale, household goods inventory showing serial number, Customs Forms 4455 or 4457.

Gifts
Bona fide gifts may be mailed to friends and relatives in the U.S. free of duty and tax as long as the same person does not receive more than $100 (or $200 if from American Samoa, U.S. Virgin Islands, or Guam) in gift shipments per day. If you are bringing gifts with you, the exemption is $800 in merchandise acquired abroad; $600 from Caribbean Basin Economic Recovery Act countries; or $1200 from American Samoa, U.S. Virgin Islands, or Guam. The exemption includes both gifts and other items for personal use. Gifts must be included in the declaration of the donor when he returns to the United States. Gifts are not considered as part of household and personal effects. Alcoholic beverages, cigars, and cigarettes are not included in this exemption from duty.

Gifts that exceed the $100 or $200 retail value will be subject to customs duty based on the entire value of the gift or gifts. There is no exemption.

Government/Military Personnel

Difference between Government/Military Personnel and Returning Residents

A special provision allows U.S. Government personnel (military and civilian) to enter their personal and household effects without payment of duty and tax when returning from an extended duty assignment overseas, even if those effects have not been in the household for at least a year before importation into the U.S. - as is required for returning residents.

Duty Exemptions for Household and Personal Effects
The classifications, rates of duty, and exemptions from duty, are governed by the Harmonized Tariff Schedule of the United States (HTSUS). Under item 9805.00.50 of the Tariff Schedules, the personal and household effects of any person (military or civilian) employed by the U.S. Government, and returning members of his family who have resided with him at his post or station, may be entered free of duty unless items are restricted, prohibited, or limited - as in the case of liquor and tobacco.

The following groups of people are **not** entitled to this exemption:

- Employees of private business and commercial organizations working under contract for the U.S. Government.
- Persons under research fellowships granted by the United States Government.
- Peace Corps Volunteers, employees of UNICEF or the Red Cross.
- Persons going abroad under the Fulbright-Hays Act of 1961, or under the Mutual Educational and Cultural Exchange Act of 1961. You may write

to the U.S. Customs Service, PO Box 7407, Washington, D.C. 20044, if you have a question that is not answered by the information in this section.

Items sent by mail are eligible for duty-free entry if the articles were in the returnee's possession before leaving the duty station. A copy of the Government orders terminating the assignment must accompany the articles in a sealed envelope securely attached to the outer wrapper of the parcel. The parcel should also be marked clearly on the outside "Returned Personal Effects-Orders Enclosed."

Traveling by Military Transport
Articles that accompany you upon your return to the United States on PCS orders should be declared on Customs Form (CF) 6059B, "Customs Declaration," if you travel on a commercial carrier. If you travel on a carrier owned or operated by the U.S. Government, including charter aircraft, you will complete either Department of Defense Form (DD) 1854, "Customs Accompanied Baggage Declaration," or CF 6059B, "Customs Declaration." Be prepared to show Customs a copy of your travel orders.

Unaccompanied Baggage
If you are a Department of Defense (DoD) civilian or military member returning to the U.S. from extended duty overseas, you should complete DD Form 1252, "U.S. Customs Declaration for Personal Property Shipments," to facilitate the entry of your unaccompanied baggage and/or household goods into the United States. A copy of your PCS orders, terminating your assignment to extended duty abroad, should accompany DD Form 1252. This form is also used by a DoD sponsored or directed individual or employee of a nonappropriated fund agency that is an integral part of the military services. All other Government employees should complete CF 3299, "Declaration for Free Entry of Unaccompanied Articles," http://www.customs.treas.gov/travel/forms.htm and attach a copy to their orders. The documents are presented to Customs for clearance and are retained with the manifest.

By completing these declarations you certify that the shipment consists of personal and household effects that were in your personal possession while abroad, and that the articles are not imported for another person or intended for sale.

Employees completing CF 3299 must list restricted articles (e.g., trademarked items, firearms), and goods not subject to their exemption (e.g., excess liquor, articles carried for other persons) on the declaration and show the actual prices paid. All shipments of unaccompanied baggage will be cleared by Customs upon arrival in the United States.

Automobiles
A conforming foreign-made automobile may be included as part of your personal effects. However, an automobile purchased abroad and sent home before your Government orders are issued, or a car purchased and not in your possession before you leave (merely ordered but not delivered to you), will not be entitled to free entry as a personal or household effect under 9805.00.50. The vehicle would be subject to customs duty at the following rates:

- Autos......................................2.5%
- Trucks....................................25%
- Motorcycles, mopeds up to 700 cc................Free
  700 to 970 cc................2.4%
  over 970 cc..................Free
- Trailers..........................Free.

Duty rates are based on the market value of the vehicle and those rates are subject to change on an annual basis.

Liquor, Tobacco
In addition to the limitations stated on page X, active duty U.S. Government and military personnel who are returning with liquor are exempt from the age requirement. However, family members of the Government or military employee must be 21 years old or older.

Firearms and Ammunition

Military members (under certain conditions) may import up to three non-automatic long guns (rifles or shotguns) and 1,000 rounds of ammunition. However, you must first apply for a permit to import these items from the bureau of Alcohol, Tobacco and Firearms, and the permit must be presented to Customs when the items are being cleared. Surplus military firearms of any description are prohibited entry. The government will not ship, or pay for the shipping of ammunition. The employee will have to arrange and pay for shipping.

The Department of Defense and the U.S. Postal Service prohibit acceptance by military post offices of war trophy firearms, ammunition, and handguns for shipment through an APO or FPO of the military postal system.

Nonresidents/First-Time Immigrants

Difference between Nonresidents/First-Time Immigrants and Returning Residents

Requirements for the importation of alcohol, tobacco, automobiles and gifts by nonresidents/first-time immigrants are different than those for returning residents. Please see the following sections for specific details.

Duty Exemptions for Household and Personnel Effects

You may import furniture, dishes, linens, libraries, artwork and similar household furnishings for your personal use free of duty. To be eligible for duty-free exemption, the articles must have either been available for your use or used in a household where you were a resident for one year. The year of use does not need to be continuous, nor does it need to be the year immediately before the date of importation. Personal and household effects entitled to duty-free entry need not accompany you to the United States; you may have them shipped to your U.S. address at a later time if you choose. Your shipment of personal and/or household goods must be cleared through Customs at its first port of arrival, unless you have made arrangements with a foreign freight forwarder to have your effects sent in Customs custody in-bond from the port of arrival to a more convenient port of entry for clearance. (*Ask your moving company if they offer this service.*)

Household effects from the country where these effects were used, and meeting the above criteria, may be entered into the United States duty-free within 10 years after your initial arrival in the United States as a legal resident.

Personal effects may be shipped or mailed to you at a later date. The package should be marked "Used Personal Effects" and must have been in your possession prior to your entry into the United States. Anything included in the package that is new may be dutiable.

Professional Equipment

A person emigrating to the United States may enter professional books, implements, instruments and tools of trade, occupation or employment free of duty if the articles were owned and used abroad. These items do not need to have been in your possession for one year prior to importation, but they must be imported for your use and not for sale. Theatrical scenery, properties, or apparel and articles for use in any manufacturing establishment are not eligible for this exemption.

Automobiles

Nonresidents/First-time immigrants may temporarily import a vehicle duty-free for personal use if the vehicle is imported in connection with the owner's arrival. Vehicles do not need to accompany the owner, but should arrive in the U.S. at approximately the same time, at least within a few weeks. If a delay of more than a few weeks should occur the importer must prove that the delay was justified. Vehicles are defined as an automobile, trailer, airplane, motorcycle, boat or similar vehicle. Vehicles that don't conform to U.S. safety and emission standards must be exported within one year and may not be sold in the United States. *There is no exemption or extension of the export requirement.* Conforming vehicles imported under the duty-free exemption are dutiable if sold within one year of importation. Duty must be paid at the most conveniently located Customs office before the sale is completed. Conforming vehicles so imported may remain in the U.S. indefinitely once a formal entry is made for EPA purposes.

Foreign-made vehicles not in your possession before you leave your foreign residence, and imported into the U.S., whether new or used, (i.e., ordered for direct delivery to your U.S. residence, either for personal use or for sale) are generally dutiable at the following rates:

- Autos.....................................2.5 %

- Trucks....................................25%

- Motorcycles, mopeds up to 700 cc................Free
  700 to 970 cc...............2.4%
  over 970 cc..................Free

- Trailers.........................Free.

Duty rates are based on the market value of the

vehicle and those rates are subject to change on an annual basis.

Liquor, Tobacco

Nonresidents who are at least 21 years old may bring in, free of duty and internal revenue tax, up to one liter of alcoholic beverage - beer, wine, liquor - for personal use. Quantities above the one-liter limitation are subject to duty and internal revenue tax. You may also include in your personal exemption not more than 200 cigarettes (one carton) or 50 cigars or two kilograms (4.4 lbs.) of smoking tobacco, or proportional amounts of each. Cigars of Cuban origin are prohibited.

Firearms and Ammunition
Firearms and ammunition are subject to restrictions and import permits. The importation of fully automatic weapons and semi-automatic assault-type weapon is prohibited. Generally, firearms and ammunition acquired abroad may be imported, but only under permit. For complete information, write to the Bureau of Alcohol, Tobacco and Firearms, Department of the Treasury, Firearms and Explosives Import Branch, Washington, DC 20226. That agency will furnish permit applications and answer inquiries about the Gun Control Act of 1968.

Gifts:
Nonresidents are allowed up to $100 (or $200 if from American Samoa, U.S. Virgin Islands, or Guam) worth of merchandise, free of duty and internal revenue tax, as gifts for other people. These gifts must be included in your declaration and must accompany you. Gifts are not considered as part of household and personal effects. Nonresidents can include cigars in their $100 gift exemption, but may not include cigarettes or alcohol. Gifts originating from countries currently under sanctions with the U.S. (See Prohibited and Restricted Importation's section above) may not be eligible for the $100 gift exemption (Example: Iraq). To ensure that gifts are eligible for the $100 exemption, questions should be referred to the Office of Foreign Assets Control at 202/622-2480.

Part-Time Residents
Part-time residents are usually students attending school in one country and spending the rest of the year in another, "snowbirds" (seasonal residents), or residents who maintain a household in a foreign country as well as one in the United States. If you are a part-time resident, any goods you wish to import into your U.S. residence must have been in your foreign residence for at least one year prior to their importation into the U.S. to qualify for duty-free importation. Since part-time residents are either returning residents or nonresidents, please see the requirements for returning residents and nonresidents described earlier. Report Drug Smuggling to the U.S. Customs Service

1 (800) BE ALERT

Chapter 17

Bringing Pets, Wildlife into the U.S.

*[The Information in this chapter is reprinted verbatim from a bulletin issued by the
U.S. Department of the Treasury, U.S. Customs Service. It is intended to serve as advice
to Americans traveling abroad.]*

Pets and Wildlife
Licensing and Health Requirements

Pets and Wildlife
Travelers frequently inquire about taking their pets
with them to the United States. All such
importations are subject to health, quarantine,
agriculture, wildlife, and customs requirements
and prohibitions. Pets, except for pet birds, taken
out of the United States and returned are subject to
the same requirements as those entering for the
first time. Returning U.S. origin pet birds are
subject to different import restrictions than pet
birds of non-U.S. origin entering the United States
for the first time. For more information on
importing pet birds into the United States, see the
section on Birds or the Department of
Agriculture's Web site at
www.aphis.usda.gov/NCIE.

Pets excluded from entry into the United States
must either be exported or destroyed. While
awaiting disposition, pets will be detained at the
owner's expense at the port of arrival. The U.S.
Public Health Service requires that pet dogs and
cats brought into this country be examined at the
first port of entry for evidence of diseases that can
be transmitted to humans. Dogs coming from areas
not free of rabies must be accompanied by a valid
rabies vaccination certificate. Turtles are subject to
certain restrictions, and monkeys may not be
imported as pets under any circumstances.

The U.S. Fish and Wildlife Service (USFWS) is
concerned with the importation, trade, sale, and
taking of wildlife and with protecting endangered
plant and animal species. Some wildlife species of
dogs, cats, turtles, reptiles, and birds, although
imported as pets, may be listed as endangered.
Endangered and threatened animal and plant
wildlife, migratory birds, marine mammals, and
certain dangerous wildlife may not be imported
without special federal permits. Sportsmen will
find the section on wildlife of particular interest,
since game birds and animals are subject to special
entry requirements.

We suggest that you also check with state, county,
and municipal authorities for local restrictions on
importing pets. Some airlines require health
certificates for pets traveling with them. You
should check with your airline prior to your travel
date.

If you are taking a pet to another country, contact
that country's embassy in Washington, DC, or its
nearest consular office for information on any
requirements that you must meet.

General Customs Information

All birds and animals must be imported under
healthy, humane conditions. U.S. Department of
Agriculture (USDA) regulations require that
careful arrangements be made with the carrier for
suitable cages, space, ventilation, and protection
from the elements. Cleaning, feeding, watering,
and other necessary services must be provided.
Under the Animal Welfare Act, the Department of
Agriculture is responsible for setting the standards
concerning the transportation, handling, care, and
treatment of animals. The U.S. Fish and Wildlife
Service is responsible for ensuring humane
transport of all imported animals and birds (except
domesticated species) and all imported or exported
wildlife protected under the Convention on
International Trade in Endangered Species
(CITES).

Every imported container of pets, or package of
animal parts or products, must be plainly marked,
labeled, or tagged on the outside with the names
and addresses of the shipper and consignee, along
with an accurate invoice specifying the number of
each species contained in the shipment.

Since hours of service and availability of inspectors from the other agencies involved may vary from port to port, you are strongly urged to check with your anticipated port of arrival before importing a pet or other animal. This will assure expeditious processing and reduce the possibility of unnecessary delays.

Customs Duty

Dogs, cats, and turtles are free of duty. Other pets imported into the United States, if subject to a customs duty, may be included in your customs exemption if they accompany you and are imported for your personal use and not for sale.

Pets and Wildlife
Purebred Animals

Purebred animals other than domesticated livestock that are imported for breeding purposes are free of duty under certain conditions. A declaration is required to show that the importer is a citizen of the United States; that the animal is imported specifically for breeding purposes; that it is identical with the description in the certificate of pedigree presented; and that it is registered in the country of origin in a book of registry recognized by the U.S.
Department of Agriculture.

An application to the Department of Agriculture on VS Form 17-338 for a certificate of pure breeding must be furnished before the animal is examined at the designated port of entry. For complete information, write to the Animal and Plant Health Inspection Service, whose address is listed at the end of this pamphlet.

Birds

All birds,[a] those taken out of the country as well as those being returned[a] are subject to controls and restrictions. In addition, nearly all birds coming into the country require a permit from the U.S. Fish and Wildlife Service. To prevent the introduction of exotic diseases of poultry into the United States, the U.S. Department of Agriculture regulates the importation of all birds entering the country:

Most birds must be quarantined upon arrival for a minimum of 30 days in a USDA Animal Import Center. The birds must enter the United States through one of three ports of entry where the quarantine facilities are located:

New York, NY ------------ 718.553.1727

Miami, FL ---------------- 305.526.2926
Los Angeles, CA --------- 310.725.1970

Quarantine space must be reserved in advance by contacting one of the USDA Animal Import Centers listed above. All quarantine fees must also be paid in
full in advance.

A USDA import permit is required for most imported birds. Permit application forms can be obtained by contacting the USDA Animal Import Center directly or can be found on the USDA Web site at www.aphis.usda.gov/vs17-129.pdf.

All birds imported into the United States must be inspected by a USDA port veterinarian at the first U.S. port of entry. This inspection must be arranged in advance by contacting the port veterinarian at least 72 hours prior to travel. The phone number for the USDA port veterinarian will be located on the import permit or it can be found on the USDA Web site at www.aphis.usda.gov/NCIE/portlist.html.

A current veterinary health certificate must accompany the bird. The health certificate must be endorsed by a national veterinarian of the country of export and be issued within 30 days of importation.

Returning U.S. origin pet birds may be quarantined in the owner's home for a minimum of 30 days. In order to show proof of U.S. origin, the birds must be accompanied by a veterinary health certificate issued by a U.S. veterinarian prior to leaving the country. Birds imported from Canada are exempt from quarantine requirements. However, all birds must be examined by a USDA port veterinarian at the first U.S. port of entry. If the birds enter the United States via a U.S.-Canadian land border port, no import permit is required. If the birds enter via an airport, an import permit is required. The permit application can be obtained by calling 301.734.8364 or can be found on the USDA Web site at www.aphis.usda.gov/vs17-129.pdf.

More information on importing birds into the United States can be found on the USDA website at www.aphis.gov/NCIE/ind-3000.html, or by contacting the National Center for Import and Export, 4700 River Road, Unit 39, Riverdale, MD, 20737. The telephone number is

301.734.8364, and the fax number is 301.734.4704.

Importers and exporters of all wild birds, including captive-bred, are required to obtain clearance from the U.S. Fish and Wildlife Service. Birds that are protected under the Convention on International Trade in Endangered Species (CITES) require permits to travel from one country to another, and import of these birds may be subject to permit requirements or restrictions under the Wild Bird Conservation Act (WBCA). Birds imported or exported at other than a USFWS designated port may require payment of inspection fees.

To request a CITES and/or WBCA permit application or to obtain more information, contact the U.S. Fish and Wildlife Service, Office of Management Authority, 4401 North Fairfax Drive, Room 700, Arlington, VA 22203. The toll-free telephone number is 800.358.2104. Overseas calls should be placed to 703.358.2104.

Cats and Dogs

Importation of cats and dogs is regulated by the Centers for Disease Control and Prevention (CDC). **It is illegal in the United States to import, export, distribute, transport, manufacture, or sell products containing dog or cat fur in the United States.** As of November 9, 2000, the Dog and Cat Protection Act of 2000 calls for the seizure and forfeiture of each item containing dog or cat fur.

The Act provides that any person who violates any provision may be assessed a civil penalty of not more than $10,000 for each separate knowing and intentional violation, $5,000 for each separate gross negligent violation, or $3,000 for each separate negligent violation.

Cats — All domestic cats must be free of evidence of disease communicable to humans when examined at the port of entry. If the animal is not in apparent good health, further examination by a licensed veterinarian may be required at the owner's expense. Cats arriving in Hawaii or Guam, both of which are free of rabies, are subject to locally imposed quarantine requirements.

Dogs — Domestic dogs must be free of evidence of diseases communicable to humans when examined at the port of entry. If the animal is not in apparent good health, further examination by a licensed veterinarian may be required at the owner's expense.

Vaccinations

Dogs must be vaccinated against rabies at least 30 days before entering the United States. This requirement does not apply, however, to puppies less than three months of age or to dogs originating or located for at least six months in areas designated by the U.S. Public Health Service as being rabies-free.

The following procedures pertain to dogs arriving from areas that are not free of rabies:

A valid rabies vaccination certificate should accompany the animal. This certificate should be in English or be accompanied by a translation. It should identify the animal, the dates of vaccination and expiration, and be signed by a licensed veterinarian. If no expiration date is specified, the certificate is acceptable if the date of vaccination is no more than 12 months before the date of arrival.

If a vaccination has not been performed, or if the certificate is not valid, the animal may be admitted if it is confined immediately upon arrival at a place of the owner's choosing. The dog must be vaccinated within four days after arrival at the final destination, but no more than 10 days after arrival at the port of entry. The animal must remain in confinement for at least 30 days after being vaccinated.

If the vaccination was performed less than 30 days before arrival, the animal may be admitted but must be confined at a place of the owner's choosing until at least 30 days have passed since the vaccination.

Young puppies must be confined at a place of the owner's choosing until they are three months old, then they must be vaccinated. They must remain in confinement for 30 days after the vaccination.

Dogs that arrive in Hawaii or Guam, both of which are free of rabies, are subject to locally imposed quarantine requirements, in addition to other Public Health Service requirements listed above that may apply.

Monkeys

Monkeys and other primates may be brought into the United States for scientific, educational, or exhibition purposes by importers who are registered with the CDC. However, under no circumstances may they be imported as pets. Registered importers who wish to import or export primates for a permitted purpose in accordance with CDC requirements are also required to obtain clearance from the U.S. Fish and Wildlife Service. The Convention on International Trade in Endangered Species (CITES) requires that all primates have permits.

Turtles, Tortoises, and Terrapins

Live turtles with a shell length of less than four inches (linear measure) and viable turtle eggs may not be imported for commercial purposes. An individual may import live turtles with shells less than four inches long if the importation is not for commercial purposes, and the importation includes less than seven live turtles, less than seven viable turtle eggs, or any combination of turtles and eggs totaling less than seven. The CDC may issue a permit for importation of more than the permitted number if the importation is for a bona-fide noncommercial scientific or exhibition purpose.

There are no Public Health Service restrictions on the importation of live turtles with a shell longer than four inches. Importers and exporters of all tortoises and terrapins must obtain clearance from the U.S. Fish and Wildlife Service. Importers should check with USDA regarding import restrictions for some tortoises.

Rabbits, Guinea pigs, hamsters, ferrets, and other pet rodents

There are no CDC or USFWS restrictions or requirements on these animals if brought in as pets.

Wildlife

The following categories of wildlife and fish are subject to certain prohibitions, restrictions, permit and quarantine requirements:

Mammals, birds, amphibians, fish, insects, crustaceans, mollusks, reptiles, coral, and other invertebrates.

Any part or products, such as feathers, skins, eggs; and articles manufactured from wildlife.

Federal laws prohibit the importation or transportation of any wildlife or wildlife parts that violate state or foreign laws.

The following ports are designated for entry of all fish and wildlife: Atlanta, Baltimore. Boston, Chicago, Dallas/Ft. Worth, Honolulu, Los Angeles, Miami, New Orleans, New York/Newark, Portland, San Francisco, and Seattle. Most fish and wildlife imported or exported at a USFWS non-designated port require payment of inspection fees. All such packages and containers must be marked, labeled, or tagged to clearly indicate the name and address of the shipper and consignee, and the number and nature of contents. Wildlife in any form, including pets, imported into or exported from the United States must be declared and cleared on U.S. Fish and Wildlife Form 3-177 (Declaration for Importation or Exportation of Fish or Wildlife) by the U.S. Fish and Wildlife Service prior to release by U.S. Customs. Contact the U.S. Fish and Wildlife Service for further clearance requirements and for a copy of the pamphlets *Facts about Federal Wildlife Laws and Buyer Beware.*

Domesticated pets such as dogs, cats, hamsters, gerbils, guinea pigs, and rabbits do not require clearance from USFWS. Also contact the Animal and Plant Health Inspection Service, which is listed on the last page of this chapter, for information about importing animal and bird products such as hides, eggs, feathers, etc.

Game: Birds and Other Animals

Specimens of game birds and animals, other than protected species, that are legally killed by United States residents in Canada or Mexico may be imported for non-commercial purposes at any Customs port of entry and declared on a U.S. Fish and Wildlife Form 3-177. Game must be accompanied by a valid hunting license, tags, stamps, and by an export document from the country where taken, if such is required. Only United States residents may import game free of duty. Some game animals, such as black bear or elephant, require permits to be imported. Many countries also require export permits for all wildlife. Hunters should check with the U.S. Fish and Wildlife Service for permit and country requirements.

If the hunter wishes to import the meat, he/she must have a letter from a butcher indicating that the animal/bird was of Canadian origin and dressed at his/her butcher shop. All migratory birds must be imported with one wing attached for identification purposes.

United States residents may only import migratory game birds that they themselves have legally killed. The U.S. Fish and Wildlife Service has regulations regarding the number and species of migratory game birds that may be imported from Canada, Mexico, and other countries. Hunters should familiarize themselves with the restrictions on migratory game birds taken legally during open season in other countries; hunters should also be aware that some countries require wildlife export permits. Certain USDA restrictions may also apply. Contact the Veterinary Services (VS) Veterinarian in Charge in your state. For a list of offices and telephone numbers you should contact VS, Technical Trade Services, Animal Products Staff in Riverdale, MD which is listed in the last section of this chapter.

Game birds and waterfowl that are being imported as trophies must be sent to a taxidermy facility that has been approved by the USDA's Veterinary Services. A list of approved taxidermists in a particular state can be obtained from the Technical Trade Services, Animal Products Staff, National Center for Import-Export at 301.734.8364.

Many animals, game birds, products, and byproducts from such animals and game birds are prohibited, or allowed only restricted entry into the United States.

Specific requirements vary according to the country of export; for more information about importation by country, please call the U.S. Department of Agriculture (USDA), Animal and Plant Health Inspection Service (APHIS), the National Import-Export Center, at 301.734.3277, or by fax 301.734.8226.

Endangered Species
Some wildlife, including pets, are listed as threatened or endangered under the U.S. Endangered Species Act (ESA) and are prohibited from import or export unless authorized under a permit. The United States is a party in the Convention on International Trade in Endangered Species of Wild Fauna and Flora, commonly known as CITES. This treaty regulates trade in endangered species of wildlife, plants and their products. International trade in species listed by CITES is illegal unless authorized by limited to, articles made from whale teeth, ivory, tortoise shell, reptile, fur skins, coral, and birds. Permits to import into or export from the United States and

re-export certificates are issued by the Division of Management

Authority of the U.S. Fish and Wildlife Service. Information on wildlife and plants, including lists of endangered species, may be obtained from that agency.
www.aphis.usda.gov/ncie

Finding Additional Information
Although essential requirements are described in this chapter, all regulations cannot be covered in detail. If you have any questions, write or call your local Customs office or the specific agency mentioned. Their addresses and Web sites are:

U.S. Public Health Service

Centers for Disease Control and Prevention
Division of Global Migration and
Quarantine (E-03)
Atlanta, GA 30333
Tel: 404.498.1670
www.cdc.gov/ncidod/dq/animal.htm

Animal and Plant Health Inspection Service
Technical Trade Services, Animal Products Staff
U.S. Department of Agriculture
National Import/Export Center
4700 River Road, Unit 40
Riverdale, MD 20737-1231
Tel: 301.734.8364
Fax: 301.734.8226

To **obtain wildlife permits:**
U.S. Fish and Wildlife Service
Division of Management Authority
4401 N. Fairfax Drive, Room 700
Arlington, VA 22203
Tel: 703.358.2104
www.le.fws.gov
E-mail: LawEnforcement@fws.gov

U.S. Customs Service
1300 Pennsylvania Ave., NW
Washington, DC 20229
Tel: 202.354.1000
www.customs.gov
www.international.fws.gov

For clearance ports and inspection fees:
U.S. Fish and Wildlife Service
Office of Law Enforcement
4401 N. Fairfax Drive, Room 500

Arlington, VA 22203
Tel: 703.358.1949
U.S. Customs Service 10
U.S. Customs Service
Washington, D.C. 20229

Please visit the U.S. Customs Web Site at
http://www.customs.gov TO REPORT DRUG
SMUGGLING

Chapter 18

Tips on Bringing Food, Plant, and Animal Products into the U.S.

*[The information in this chapter is reprinted verbatim from a bulletin issued by the
U.S. Department of Agriculture, Animal and Plant Health Inspection Service.
It is intended to serve as advice to Americans traveling abroad.]*

TRAVELERS "TIPS (BRINGING AGRICULTURAL PRODUCTS INTO THE U.S)

Safeguarding United States Agriculture

The U.S. Department of Agriculture (USDA) plays an important role in keeping the United States free from destructive animal and plant pests and diseases that currently affect other countries. To accomplish this, certain limits are placed on items brought to the United States from foreign countries, as well as those brought to the mainland from Hawaii, Puerto Rico, and the U.S. Virgin Islands. Prohibited items could harbor animal and plant pests and diseases that could seriously damage America's crops, livestock, pets, and environment – pests and diseases that have no natural enemies or predators in this country.

All travelers entering the United States are required to **DECLARE** any meats, fruits, vegetables, plants, animals, and plant and animal products they may be carrying. The declaration must cover all items carried in baggage and hand luggage, or in a vehicle.

To speed up the inspection process:

• pack items where they will be readily accessible
• make sure to check "yes" for Question #11 on the U.S. Customs Declaration Form
• follow the instructions of the federal officers in the inspection area.

Upon examination of plants, animal products, and associated products, inspectors will determine if these items meet the entry requirements of the United States. Plant Protection and Quarantine (PPQ) officers are authorized under the Plant

Protection Act to seize, destroy, and if necessary, issue civil penalties for prohibited items discovered during an inspection.

Even though an item may be listed on the "General List of Approved Products" (see below), if you are unsure of the origin, DECLARE the item by checking "YES" on Question #11 of the U.S. Customs Declaration Form.

"But It's Only a Piece of Fruit..."

Travelers are often surprised when told that their "one little piece of fruit or meat" can cause serious damage. In fact, one prohibited item carelessly discarded has the potential to wreak havoc on American crops. For example, it's quite likely that a traveler carried in the wormy fruit that first brought the Mediterranean fruit flies to California. The fight to eradicate this pest still costs America taxpayers millions of dollars each year.

And, although there hasn't been a case of foot-and-mouth disease in the United States since 1929, the threat of this disease from countries outside the U.S. remains. A single link of sausage contaminated with the dreaded virus could devastate the U.S. livestock business. Economists agree that an outbreak today would cost farmers and consumers billions of dollars in lost production, higher food prices, and lost export markets.

Avoid Fines and Delays

Personal passenger baggage is checked for agricultural products by officers from USDA's Animal and Plant Health Inspection Service (APHIS), Plant Protection and Quarantine (PPQ) program.

At some ports, inspectors use Detector Dogs,

specially trained to sniff out agricultural items. At others, low energy x-ray machines adapted to reveal fruits and meats are used. In an average month, inspectors confiscate thousands of items. Always DECLARE to the inspectors everything you have that could be classified as an agricultural product. An inspector can then determine whether that item is prohibited or is allowed entry.

The declaration you are required to make may be oral, written or both. If you're traveling from abroad on a plane or ship, you will be given a U.S. Customs form on which to declare your agricultural products. You will also be asked to indicate whether you have visited a farm or ranch outside the United States. Why? Soil from other countries could harbor all kinds of pests, diseases, or both, and that soil could be stuck on your shoes, on garden tools, bicycle tires, or other areas!

Declarations Prevent Penalties

Prohibited items that are not declared by passengers are confiscated. But that's not all. Civil penalties may be assessed for violations, and now, with recent increases, may range up to $1,000 for a first-time offense. Depending on whether confiscated, undeclared items are intentionally concealed, or determined to be for commercial use, civil penalties may be assessed up to $50,000 for individuals. The same fine applies to illegal agricultural products sent through the mail.

General Guidelines

Fruits, Vegetables, and Plants
Depending on the country of origin, you may bring in some fruits, vegetables, and plants without advance permission, provided they are declared, inspected, and found free of pests. However, certain plants and any plant parts intended for growing (propagative material) require a permit in advance. For information on permits, contact the USDA/APHIS/PPQ Permit Unit. See the Information Resources section at the end of this notice for details.

Meat and Animal Products
Fresh, dried, or canned meats and meat products are prohibited entry into the United States from most foreign countries, because of the continuing threat of foot-and-mouth disease. If meat is used in preparing a product, it is also usually prohibited. Because regulations concerning meat and meat products change frequently, travelers should contact the consulate or local agricultural office in the country of origin (see U.S. Department of State section of the Resources section) for up-to-date information.

Animal hunting trophies, game animal carcasses, and hides are severely restricted. To find out specifics and how to arrange to bring them into the United States, contact USDA/APHIS Veterinary Services' National Center for Import and Export (NCIE). The Department of the Interior's US Fish and Wildlife Service (FWS) regulates the import and export of wild and endangered animals and plants and their products. More information is available in the FWS free publications, "Facts About Federal Wildlife Laws" and "Buyer Beware Guide."

Live Animals and Birds
Live animals and birds may enter the United States subject to certification, certain permits, inspection, and quarantine rules that vary with the type of animal and its origin.

Pet birds purchased abroad for personal use may enter, subject to restrictions by some state departments of agriculture. Quarantine arrangements must be made in advance because facilities are limited. For information and a permit application, contact APHIS' NCIE (see Resources section).

Valid veterinary health certificates are required in many instances; fees and waiting times vary. In addition, the US Centers for Disease Control and Prevention (CDC) regulate importation of certain animal species and have specific regulations regarding pets (including cats and dogs) and nonhuman primates. Importation for scientific or exhibition purposes is strictly controlled through a registration process. Contact the CDC (see Resources section) for detailed information.

Other Biological Materials
A permit is required to bring in most organisms, cells and cultures, monoclonal antibodies, vaccines, and related substances, whether of plant or animal origin. This category includes organisms and products used in the biotechnology industry. For information and a permit application, contact NCIE or PPQ's permit unit. Biological specimens of plant pests, in preservatives or dried, may be imported without restrictions but are subject to inspection upon arrival in the United States. This is done to confirm the nature of the material and make sure they are free of "hitchhiking" plant

pests or diseases. These items must all be declared and presented for inspection.

Soil, Sand, Minerals, and Shells

Soil-borne organisms threaten both plants and animals. As mentioned previously, if you visited a farm or ranch overseas, agricultural inspectors may have to disinfect your shoes or clothes. Vehicles must also be cleaned of any soil. No soil or earth of any kind is allowed into the United States without a permit, issued in advance by PPQ's permit unit. Pure sand, like a small container of decorative beach sand, is allowed. Always check with PPQ's permit unit in advance to find out if a permit is required.

Is There ANYTHING I Can Bring Back?

Of course. When planning your trip abroad, look over the general list of approved products that follows. Keep in mind that this list is not all inclusive, and that regulations change frequently, depending on outbreaks of plant and animal diseases in various parts of the world. So, whether or not the item in question appears on the "approved" list, you are still responsible for declaring to a federal inspection officer every agricultural product in your possession.

If you leave the United States with any U.S. agricultural products, note that you may not be allowed to bring them back in when you return to the country. If you're unsure of what's allowed, call for help. Check the phone book for the nearest office of USDA, APHIS, PPQ, or call PPQ's central office at 301-734-8645. If your question is specific to animals or animal products, contact NCIE. U.S. consulates abroad may also be able to answer many of your questions. APHIS' Web site http://www.aphis.usda.gov contains information on many related topics. Every effort is made to keep the information current.

Please – do your part to help protect American agriculture!

General List of Approved Products (as of January, 2003)

Aloe vera (above ground parts)
Bat nut or devil pod (Trapa bicornis)
Breads, cakes, cookies, and other bakery goods
Candies
Cannonball fruit
Chinese water chestnut
Coffee (roasted beans only)
Fish

Flower bulbs *
Fruits, canned
Garlic cloves (peeled)
Lily bulbs (Lilium spp.)
Maguey leaf
Matsutake
Mushrooms
Nuts (roasted only)
Palm hearts (peeled)
Sauces, canned or processed
Seaweed
Seeds *
Shamrocks, without roots or soil
St. John's Bread
Singhara nut (Trapa bispinosa)
Tamarind bean pod
Truffles
Vegetables, canned or processed
Water chestnut (Trapa natans)

*Check with the consulate or agricultural office in the country of origin to confirm that your item conforms to the above general list.

Predeparture Inspection is required for passengers traveling from Hawaii to the mainland; Puerto Rico to the mainland, and from the U.S. Virgin Islands to the mainland. Use these links to access detailed information on those areas.

Products from Canada and Mexico

Many products grown in Canada or Mexico are allowed to enter the United States. This includes most vegetables and fruits; however, seed potatoes from Canada currently require a permit.

Note: Fruits, vegetables, meats or birds taken from the United States to Mexico may not be allowed to re-enter. Consult in advance with APHIS inspectors.

All permissible agricultural products are still subject to inspection.

Information Resources for Travelers

USDA-APHIS-PPQ's Permit Unit can provide information about import requirements and permits for plants, plant parts, fruits, vegetables, and other agricultural items.

Contact:
USDA, APHIS
Plant Protection and Quarantine
4700 River Road, Unit 136
Riverdale, MD 20737-1236, Attention: Permit

Unit
www.aphis.usda.gov

Or

Look in your local phone book for the nearest office of USDA, APHIS, PPQ, or call the central office at 877-770-5990 or 301-734-8645.

USDA-APHIS-Veterinary Services' National Center for Import and Export (NCIE) can provide information about importing live animals and animal products.

Contact:
USDA, APHIS
Veterinary Services
4700 River Road, Unit 40
Riverdale, MD 20737-1231
Attn: National center for Import and Export

Or

301-734-7830 or on the web,
www.aphis.usda.gov/vs/ncie

The **US Customs Service** collects import duties and assists the US Public Health Service in regulating the importation of dogs, cats, monkeys, and birds.

Contact:
Customs Services
P.O. Box 7407
Washington, D.C. 20044 or visit
www.customs.ustreas.gov

The **US Department of State** issues passports for US citizens to travel abroad. Consular officers overseas issue visas for foreign citizens to enter the United States. Passport agencies are located in various cities around the country. Check listings in your local phone book or with a US embassy or consulate abroad. For recorded travel information, call 202-647-5225. Also check their web site at http://travel.state.gov

The **US Fish and Wildlife Service** regulates the import and export of wild and endangered plants and animals and their related products.

Contact:
US Fish and Wildlife Service
Office of Management Authority
4401 North Fairfax Drive

Arlington, VA 22203 or their web site,
www.fws.gov

The **Centers for Disease Control and Prevention (CDC)** regulate importation of certain animal species and have specific regulations regarding pets (including cats and dogs) and nonhuman primates.

Contact:
Centers for Disease Control and Prevention
Division of Quarantine
1600 Clifton Road, Mail Stop E-03
Atlanta, GA 30333
404-639-8107; fax 404-639-2599;
www.cdc.gov/travel.

Notice to Arriving Travelers (BRINGING AGRICULTURAL PRODUCTS INTO THE U.S.)**

We regret that it is necessary to take agricultural items from your baggage. They cannot be brought into the United States because they may carry animal and plant pests and diseases. Restricted items include meats, fruits, vegetables, plants, soil, and products made from animal or plant materials.

Agricultural pests and diseases are a threat to U.S. food crops and livestock. Some of these organisms are highly contagious animal diseases that could cause severe economic damage to the livestock industry and losses in production, which would mean increased costs for meat and dairy products. Other pests can affect property values by damaging lawns, ornamental plants, trees, and even homes.

Confiscated items are carefully destroyed in special facilities of the U.S. Department of Agriculture (USDA). For additional traveler information, please check the USDA's Animal and Plant Health Inspection Service's (APHIS) Web site at www.aphis.usda.gov or call 1-866-SAFGUARD. If you have any questions, please write to APHIS Plant Protection and Quarantine Port Operations Staff, 4700 River Road, Unit 60, Riverdale, MD, 20737.

The U.S. Department of Agriculture (USDA) prohibits discrimination in all its programs and activities on the basis of race, color, national origin, sex, religion, age, disability, political beliefs, sexual orientation, or marital or family status. (Not all prohibited bases apply to all programs.) Persons with disabilities who require alternative means for communication of program information (Braille, large print, audiotape, etc.) should contact USDA's TARGET Center at (202) 720-2600 (voice and TDD).

To file a complaint of discrimination, write USDA, Director, Office of Civil Rights, Room 326-W, Whitten Building, 1400 Independence Avenue, SW, Washington, DC 20250-9410 or call (202)720-5964 (voice and TDD). USDA is an equal opportunity provider and employer.

Civil Penalties Increased for Violations of Agricultural Regulations

Undeclared and smuggled agricultural products just got more expensive!
Many people arriving in the United States don't realize that one piece of fruit or meat packed in a suitcase has the potential to cause extensive damage to U.S. agriculture. Forbidden fruits, vegetables, meats, plants, seeds, plant cuttings, soil, straw, and other agricultural products can carry a range of plant and animal pests and diseases that could damage our agricultural and natural resources and cost American taxpayers millions of dollars in higher food prices and eradication costs.

The US Department of Agriculture's (USDA) Animal and Plant Health Inspection Service (APHIS) is responsible for keeping these pests and diseases from entering the United States.

Those who violate agricultural regulations, either by failing to declare agricultural products they are carrying with them or by smuggling these items into the United States, will be assessed a civil penalty. With the passage of the Plant Protection Act and the Animal Health Protection Act, APHIS now has the ability to charge even higher penalties for these violations.

Civil Penalties
For travelers entering the United States who do not declare agricultural products, APHIS can now charge up to $50,000 in fines. First-time offenders will be fined up to $1,000 in penalties if the products are not for resale. Agricultural smugglers face civil penalties of up to $250,000 per violation or criminal charges.

Those enrolled in a Dedicated Commuter Lane (DCL) should be aware that, in addition to being assessed a civil penalty of up to $50,000, violating USDA regulations can lead to the suspension of DCL decals and/or permanent removal from the DCL program. The Designated Commuter Lanes, which use an automated vehicle inspection system to screen pre-enrolled travelers who frequently cross the border and their vehicles, allow vehicles to move quickly through designated ports of entry. To obtain entry into the program, applicants must undergo an extensive background check, a vehicle inspection, and agree to comply with all applicable federal, state, and local laws.

The same fines apply to any illegal agricultural products sent through the mail. Senders face civil penalties of up to $50,000.

To avoid costly fines, declare all agricultural products you have when entering the United States. Mark yes to question #11 on the US Customs Declaration Form. Do not send prohibited agricultural products through the mail.

Detector Dogs
USDA's Detector Dog program plays an integral part in safeguarding America's agriculture. The Detector Dogs, which include USDA's Beagle Brigade, work at US border crossings, cargo warehouses, international post offices, and in most US international air and maritime ports. These dogs sniff passenger luggage, cargo, packages, and vehicles for prohibited agricultural products that could cause serious damage to America's agricultural and natural resources.

Anyone who intentionally harms or interferes with members of USDA's Detector Dog program faces fines of up to $10,000.

For more information, please visit the APHIS Web site at www.aphis.usda.gov or call 1-866-SAFGUARD for recorded traveler information.

The US Department of Agriculture (USDA) prohibits discrimination in all its programs and activities on the basis of race, color, national origin, gender, religion, age, disability, political beliefs, sexual orientation, or marital or family status. (Not all prohibited bases apply to all programs.) Persons with disabilities who require alternative means for communication of program information (Braille, large print, audiotape, etc.) should contact USDA's TARGET Center at (202)

Chapter 19

Buying a Car Overseas? Beware!

*[The information in this chapter is reprinted verbatim from a bulletin issued by the
U.S. Environmental Protection Agency. It is intended to serve as advice
to Americans who buy cars from overseas.]*

Importing Motor Vehicles

Are you planning to buy a car in a foreign country and bring it back to the United States? Many vehicles manufactured outside the United States do not conform with air pollution control requirements under the Clean Air Act. Avoid unnecessary risks! Know the difficulties of importing a car and the rules for meeting vehicle emission standards before you go!

EPA has established new rules, effective for all vehicles imported after June 30, 1988, covering the importation of "nonconforming vehicles." A "nonconforming vehicle," as the term is used in this text, is any motor vehicle (car, truck, van, motorcycle, etc.) or heavy-duty engine not originally manufactured to meet U.S. emission standards. In addition, special rules apply to any motor vehicle which was originally manufactured with a catalytic converter, or a catalytic converter and oxygen (O_2) sensor, to meet U.S. emission standards, but has been driven outside the United States, Canada, Mexico, or Japan.

Questions Buyers Ask

Q   I am a prospective buyer. Why should I be concerned with the new EPA importation rules?

A   Knowledge of the rules can affect your buying decisions overseas. By knowing the rules beforehand, you can avoid unnecessary costs and headaches-or even the risk of having your nonconforming vehicle banned from entry into the United States.

Q   Why has EPA changed the rules?

A   EPA has changed the regulations in order to make sure that imported vehicles meet U.S.

emission standards. The new rules require that if a nonconforming vehicle is allowed to enter the United States, it must be modified within 120 days to meet the same EPA emission standards that apply to vehicles built in the United States. This will mean cleaner air for everyone.

Q   Will I still be allowed to import a five-year-old or older car that does not meet standards under a one-time special exemption from EPA's rules?

A   No. The EPA policy permitting a first-time individual importer to import one nonconforming vehicle at least five model years old without modifying it to meet emission standards has been eliminated for all vehicles imported after June 30, 1988.

Q   Are there certain older vehicles that do not need to comply with EPA's new importation rules?

A   Yes. The following vehicles are not covered by the Clean Air Act and, therefore, are not subject to the new importation rules and may be imported by any individual:

•   Gasoline-fueled light-duty vehicles and gasoline-fueled light-duty trucks originally manufactured before January 1, 1968.

•   Diesel-fueled light-duty vehicles originally manufactured before January 1, 1975.

•   Diesel-fueled light-duty trucks originally manufactured before January

195

1, 1976.

- Motorcycles originally manufactured before January 1, 1978.

- Gasoline-fueled and diesel-fueled heavy-duty engines originally manufactured before January 1, 1970.

Five New EPA Requirements

1. Only parties holding valid "certificates of conformity" issued by EPA are permitted to import nonconforming vehicles (with a few exceptions).

A "certificate of conformity" is a document issued by EPA to certify that a particular class of vehicles (like 1985 Mercedes-Benz 500, 5.0 liter engine) has been tested and shown to meet U.S. emissions standards. The party who receives the certificate (the "certificate holder") is thereby authorized to import nonconforming vehicles and modify them so that they are identical to the tested vehicle. Such certificate holders must meet all EPA requirements that apply to them as motor vehicle manufacturers.

If you are considering importing a car, you can no longer do so on your own after June 30, 1988. Instead, you must arrange for the importation-and other activities like modification and testing-through a certificate holder.

2. Not all vehicles are eligible to be imported. Requirements vary with vehicle age and the qualifications of the certificate holder.

You need to determine whether your car is eligible to be imported by a certificate holder and make arrangements for importation before you buy! Even then, if the certificate holder is no longer in business when you are ready to import the vehicle, you may be unable to bring the car into the United States.

The following vehicles must comply with EPA standards and may be imported only by certificate holders:

- Vehicles less than six model years old. Whether a vehicle may be imported depends on several factors (including the year in which the vehicle will be imported and whether the certificate holder has a certificate for a vehicle like yours). Check with EPA before you buy!

- Vehicles six model years old or older: Any vehicle may be imported by a certificate holder if the holder is willing to be responsible for the modification and testing.

- Vehicles 21 model years old or older: Any vehicle may be imported and will be exempt from meeting U.S. emission standards. However, these vehicles must still be imported by a certificate holder unless they are not covered by the Clean Air Act. As explained above, vehicles that are not covered by the Clean Air Act may be imported by any individual.

Note: A vehicle's model year age is determined by subtracting the calendar year in which it was originally manufactured from the calendar year of importation. For example, a vehicle built by a European manufacturer in 1986 and imported into the United States in 1988 would be two model years old.

3. A certificate holder who imports your nonconforming vehicle is responsible for the following:

- Performing all modifications and emission testing within 120 days after the vehicle enters the United States.

- Ensuring that the vehicle contains an emission label and vacuum hose diagram, and providing you with prepaid emission warranties and maintenance instructions for the vehicle.

- Reporting the results of the modification and testing to EPA and holding the vehicle for 15 working days (or longer if EPA wishes to examine, the vehicle).

4. Certificate holders who violate the rules may be penalized and in some cases may be prohibited from importing nonconforming vehicles.

Even if you have arranged ahead of time for a certificate holder to import your car, if EPA later prohibits the holder from importing cars, the holder will not be eligible to import your car when

196

it arrives in the United States. You may then have trouble finding another certificate holder who is eligible to import your car.

- Vehicles which are equipped with a catalytic converter or a catalytic converter and O_2 sensor, and were originally built to meet U.S. emission standards (i.e., covered by a certificate of conformity) but have been driven outside of the United States, Canada, Mexico, or Japan, may be imported by individuals. However, these vehicles are subject to import restrictions.

The new rule requires that the catalytic converter, or catalytic converter and O_2 sensor, be replaced on vehicles which may have been contaminated with leaded gasoline overseas. This requirement is necessary because unleaded gasoline is still not widely available outside North America, and use of leaded fuel can damage these components. Therefore, these vehicles may be bonded with U.S. Customs at the time of entry to assure these components are replaced. Once the catalytic converter or the catalytic converter and O_2 sensor are replaced, EPA will recommend that Customs release the EPA portion of your bond.

The importation of vehicles equipped with a catalytic converter or a catalytic converter and O_2 sensor from countries other than Canada, Mexico, or Japan will be subject to the above requirements except in the following cases:

- Vehicles imported as part of a Department of State or Department of Defense shipment, and covered by the approved catalyst and O_2 sensor control program of either agency.

- Any vehicle which is equipped with a catalytic converter or catalytic converter and O_2 sensor and is included in a manufacturer's control program that has been approved by EPA. Such vehicles are identified by the statement "Catalyst Approved for Import," which may appear on or near the Department of

Transportation door-post label, or on the engine emission control label.

Warning: This is to remind you that the EPA policy which permits a first-time individual importer to import one nonconforming vehicle at least five model years old without a need to meet Federal emission standards is eliminated for all vehicles imported after June 30, 1988.

Because of the expense and potential difficulties involved with importing a vehicle not originally built to meet U.S. emission standards, EPA strongly recommends that you buy a vehicle that is labeled by the manufacturer as meeting U.S. emission standards. If you are interested in purchasing such a car while travelling in Europe, many manufacturers provide a delivery plan that enables you to pick up your U.S.-certified vehicle in Europe. Please contact your local dealership for more information.

Other Requirements

- The new EPA rules do not change the federal safety requirements to which the vehicles must comply. For information on safety requirements, contact:
 U.S. Department of Transportation
 400 7th Street, SW.
 Room 6115
 Washington, DC 20590

- A "Gas Guzzler Tax" may need to be paid n your vehicle. These taxes range from $500 to $3,850 per vehicle. For more information, contact:
 Internal Revenue Service
 Public Affairs Office
 111 Constitution Avenue, NW.
 Washington, DC 20224

- he State of California has its own program for regulating the importation of nonconforming vehicles that are sold, registered, or operated in California. For more information on California's requirements, contact:

 State of California
 Air Resources Board
 Mobile Source Control Division

197

9528 Telstar Avenue
El Monte, CA 91731

- Your state may have its own requirements for nonconforming vehicles. For more information, contact your state Department of Motor Vehicles *before you buy!*

EPA Can Help

- For more information on EPA's rules and requirements concerning imported vehicles, contact:
U.S. Environmental Protection Agency
Manufacturers Operations Division
(EN-340F)

Investigation/Imports Section
401 M Street, SW.
Washington, DC 20460
(202) 382-2504

Chapter 20

Importing a Car/Pleasure Boat

*[The information in this chapter is reprinted verbatim from a bulletin issued by the
U.S. Department of the Treasury, U.S. Customs Service. It is intended to serve as advice
to Americans importing cars into the U.S..]*

Importing or Exporting A Car

Guidelines for permanent and temporary purposes

WARNING

Imported motor vehicles are subject to safety standards under the Motor Vehicle Safety Act of 1966, revised under the Imported Vehicle Safety Compliance Act of 1988; to bumper standards under the Motor Vehicle Information and Cost Savings Act of 1972, which became effective in 1978; and to air pollution control standards under the Clean Air Act of 1968, as amended in 1977, and 1990.

If vehicles manufactured abroad conform to U.S. safety, bumper, and emission standards, it is because these vehicles are exported for sale in the United States. Therefore, it is unlikely that a vehicle obtained abroad meets all relevant standards. Be skeptical of claims by a foreign dealer or other seller that a vehicle meets these standards or can readily be brought into compliance. Vehicles entering the United States that do not conform with U.S. safety standards must be brought into compliance, exported, or destroyed.

This chapter provides essential information for U.S. residents, military or civilian government employees, and foreign nationals who are importing a vehicle into the U.S. It includes U.S. Customs requirements and those of other agencies whose regulations we enforce. Since Environmental Protection Agency (EPA) and Department of Transportation (DOT) requirements are subject to change, we recommend that you contact these agencies before buying a vehicle abroad. Their addresses are on pages xxx.

Our leaflets *Know Before You Go* (Customs Hints for Returning U.S. Residents) and

Customs Hints for Visitors Visiting the United States (Customs Regulations for Nonresidents) contain general information for persons entering the U.S. You may obtain copies from your nearest Customs office or by writing to U.S. Customs, P.O. Box 7407, Washington, D.C. 20044; or from American embassies and consulates abroad.

EPA has a detailed automotive fact manual describing emission requirements for imported vehicles. You may obtain a copy of this manual, called the *Automotive Imports Facts Manual*, or other information about importing motor vehicles by calling EPA's Imports Hotline at (202) 564-9240. You may also communicate by fax at (202) 564-2057; write to U.S. Environmental Protection Agency, Ariel Rios Building, Manufactures Operations Division (6405-J), Investigation/Import Section, 1200 Pennsylvania Avenue, N.W., Washington, D.C. 20460; or visit the Web site at www.epa.gov/otaq/imports.

You may reach DOT's vehicle hotline at 1-800-424-9393; communicate by fax at (202) 366-1024; write to the National Highway Traffic Safety Administration (NSA-32), 400 7th Street, S.W. Washington, D.C. 20590; or visit the Web site on page x.

NOTE: Importations from Afghanistan (Taliban), Cuba, Iran, Iraq, Libya, North Korea, Sudan, Serbia/Montenegro/Kosovo, or Yugoslavia that involve the governments of those countries, are generally prohibited pursuant to regulations issued by the Treasury Department's Office of Foreign Assets Control. Before attempting to make such an importation, information concerning the prohibitions and licensing policy should be obtained by contacting the Director, Office of

Foreign Assets Control, U.S. Department of the Treasury, 2nd Floor ANX, 1500 Pennsylvania Avenue, N.W., Washington, D.C. 20220; tel. (202) 622-2500, (202) 622-2480, or FAX (202) 622-1657; or by visiting the Web site at www.treas.gov/ofac.

PRIOR ARRANGEMENTS

The owner must make arrangements for shipping a vehicle. Have your shipper or carrier notify you of the vehicle's arrival date so that you can make arrangements to process it through Customs. Shipments are cleared at the first port of entry unless you arrange for a freight forwarder abroad to have the vehicle sent in bond to a Customs port more convenient to you.

Law prohibits Customs officers from acting as agents or making entries for an importer. However, you may employ a commercial customs broker to handle your entry.

DOCUMENTATION

For Customs clearance you will need the shipper's or carrier's original bill of lading, the bill of sale, foreign registration, and any other documents covering the vehicle. You will also be required to complete EPA form 3520-1 and DOT form HS-7, declaring the emissions and safety provisions under which the vehicle is being imported. Vehicles that meet all U.S. emission requirements will bear manufacturer's label on the engine compartment in English, attesting to that fact. For vehicles that lack such a label, the Customs inspector at the port of entry may require proof of eligibility to import under the EPA exemptions or exclusions specified on form 3520-1.

Vehicles that do not meet all U.S. emission requirements, unless eligible for exemption or exclusion must be imported through an independent commercial importer (ICI). EPA will not allow the vehicles' release to the vehicle owner until ICI work is complete. The ICI will perform any EPA-required modifications and be responsible for assuring that all EPA requirements have been met. Some vehicles cannot be successfully imported or modified by an ICI, however, and in general, ICI fees are very high. See the page for driver's license and tag requirements.

CLEANING THE UNDERCARRIAGE

To safeguard against importation of dangerous pests, the U.S. Department of Agriculture requires that the undercarriage of imported cars be free of foreign soil. Have your car steam-sprayed or cleaned thoroughly before shipment.

YOUR CAR IS NOT A SHIPPING CONTAINER

For your own safety, security, and convenience, DO NOT use your car as a container for personal belongings.

- Your possessions are susceptible to theft while the vehicle is on the loading and unloading docks and in transit.

- Many shippers and carriers will not accept your vehicle if it contains personal belongings.

- The entire contents of your car must be declared to Customs on entry. Failure to do so can result in a fine or seizure of the car and its contents.

- Your vehicle may be subject to seizure, and you may incur a personal penalty, if anyone uses it as a conveyance of illegal narcotics.

DUTIABLE ENTRY

Foreign-made vehicles imported into the U.S., whether new or used, either for personal use or for sale, are generally dutiable at the following rates:

Auto	2.5%
Trucks	25%
Motorcycles	either free or 2.4%

Duty rates are based on price paid or payable. Most Canadian-made vehicles are duty-free.

As a returning U.S. resident, you may apply your $400 Customs exemption and those of accompanying family members toward the value of the vehicle if:

-Accompanies you on your return;
-Is imported for personal use;
-Was acquired during the journey from which you are returning.

For Customs purposes, a returning U.S. resident is one who is returning from travel, work, or study abroad.

After the exemption has been applied, a flat duty rate of 10% is applied toward the next $1,000 of the vehicle's value. The remaining amount is dutiable at the regular duty rate.

FREE ENTRY

-U.S. CITIZENS employed abroad or government employees returning on TDY or voluntary leave may import a foreign-made car free of duty provided they enter the U.S. for a short visit, claim nonresident status, and export the vehicle when they leave.

-MILITARY AND CIVILIAN EMPLOYEES of the U.S. government returning at the end of an assignment to extended duty outside the Customs territory of the U.S. may include a conforming vehicle among their duty-free personal and household effects. The auto must have been purchased abroad and be in its owner's possession prior to departure. Generally, extended duty is 140 days or more. Navy personnel serving aboard a U.S. naval vessel or a supporting naval vessel from its departure from the U.S. to its return after an intended overseas deployment of 120 days or more are entitled to the extended-duty exemption. Conforming vehicles imported under the duty-free exemption are dutiable if sold within one year of importation. Duty must be paid at the most convenient Customs office before the sale is completed. Conforming vehicles so imported may remain in the U.S. indefinitely once a formal entry is made for EPA purposes.

-NONRESIDENTS may import a vehicle duty-free for personal use up to (1) one year if the vehicle is imported in conjunction with the owner's arrival. Vehicles imported under this provision that do not conform to U.S. safety and emission standards must be exported within one year and may not be sold in the U.S. There is no exemption or extension of the export requirements.

CARS IMPORTED FOR OTHER PURPOSES

Nonresidents may import an automobile or motorcycle and its usual equipment free of duty for a temporary stay to take part in races or other specific purposes. However, prior written approval from the EPA is required and such approval is granted only to those racing vehicles that EPA deems not capable of safe or practical use on streets and highways. If the contests are for other than money purposes, the vehicle may be admitted for 90 days without formal entry or bond if the Customs officer is satisfied as to the importer's identify and good faith. The vehicle becomes subject to forfeiture if it is not exported or if a bond is not given within 90 days of its importation. Prior written approval must be obtained from DOT. A vehicle may be temporarily imported for testing, demonstration, or racing purposes. A vehicle may be permanently imported for show or display. Written approval from DOT is required and should be obtained before the vehicle is exported from the foreign country to the U.S. Information on how to import a vehicle under show or display is available at DOT's NHTSA Web site at www.NHTSA.dot.gov/cars/rules/import. A vehicle permanently imported for show and display must comply with all U.S. emission requirements as well, and in general must be imported through an EPA-authorized ICI for modification and testing. EPA will not allow the vehicle to be released to its owner until ICI work is complete.

SAFETY, BUMPER, AND THEFT PREVENTION STANDARDS

Importers of motor vehicles must file form HS-7 at the time of vehicle is imported to declare whether the vehicle complies with DOT requirements. As a general rule, motor vehicles less than 25 years old must comply with all applicable Federal Motor Vehicle Safety Standards (FMVSS) in order to be imported permanently into the United States. Vehicles manufactured after September 1, 1978, must also meet the bumper standard, and vehicles beginning with model year 1987 must meet the theft-prevention standard.

Vehicles manufactured to meet these standards will have a certification label affixed by the original manufacturer near the driver's side door. If you purchase a vehicle abroad that is certified to U.S. standards, you may expedite your importation by making sure the sales contract identifies this fact and by presenting the contract to U.S. Customs at the time of importation.

A vehicle must be imported as a nonconforming vehicle unless it bears the manufacturer's label certifying that it meets U.S. standards. If it is a nonconforming vehicle, the importer must contract with a DOT-registered importer (RI) to modify the vehicle and certify that it conforms to all applicable FMVSS. The importer must also post a DOT bond for one and a half times the vehicle's dutiable value. This bond is in addition to the normal Customs entry bond. Copies of the DOT bond and the contract with the RI must be attached to the HS-7 form.

Before a RI can modify your vehicle, however, it must first be determined whether the vehicle is capable of being modified to comply with the FMVSS. If a vehicle has not previously been determined to be eligible for importation, it must go through a petition process to determine whether it's capable of being modified for such compliance. If the vehicle under petition is not similar to one sold in the United States, the process of bringing it into compliance becomes very complex and costly. A list of vehicles that have already been determined to be (capable of being modified to comply with the FMVSS) may be obtained from a RI or from NFTSA's Web site.

1

Available at all ports of entry.

2

The following are considered vehicles: cars, trucks, buses, multipurpose vehicles, trailer, motorcycles, mopeds, and motorized bicycles.

The cost of modifying a nonconforming vehicle and the time required to bring it into conformance may affect your decision to purchase a vehicle abroad. NHTSA strongly recommends discussing these aspects with a RI before buying and shipping a vehicle purchased overseas.

FEDERAL TAX

Certain imported automobiles may be subject to the gas-guzzler tax imposed by section 4064 of the Internal Revenue Code. An individual who imports an automobile for personal use, or a commercial importer, may be considered an importer for purposes of this tax and thus liable for payment of the tax.

The amount of the tax is based on a combined urban/highway fuel-economy (miles per gallon) rating assigned by the EPA for gas-guzzler tax purpose. This EPA rating may be different from fuel-economy ratings indicated by the manufacturer.

If the EPA has not assigned a gas-guzzler fuel- economy rating for the model automobile you import, a rating must be independently determined. No tax is imposed on automobiles that have a combined fuel-economy rating of at least 22.5 miles per gallon.

Information on determining fuel-economy rating and liability for the tax are contained in section 4064 of the Code, Revenue Procedure 86-9, 1986-1 Cumulative Bulletin 530, Revenue Procedure 87-10, 1987-1 Cumulative Bulletin 530, Revenue Procedure 87-10, 1987-1 Cumulative Bulletin 545, and Revenue Ruling 86-20, 1986-1 Cumulative Bulletin 319.

The gas-guzzler tax is reported on Form 720, Quarterly federal Excise Tax Return, and form 6197, Gas-Guzzler Tax. Additional information may be obtained from your local district office of the Internal Revenue Service.

EMISSION STANDARDS

The following passenger cars, light-duty trucks, heavy-duty engines and motorcycles are subject to federal emission standards:

-Gasoline-fueled cars and light-duty trucks originally manufactured after December 31, 1967.

-Diesel-fueled cars originally manufactured after December 31, 1974.

-Diesel-fueled light-duty trucks originally manufactured after December 31, 1975.

-Heavy-duty engines originally manufactured after December 31, 1969.

-Motorcycles with a displacement more than 49 cubic centimeters originally manufactured after December 31, 1977.

Vehicles must be certified to U.S. federal emission standards by their manufacturers for sale in the U.S. Vehicles that do not meet these requirements are considered nonconforming. A currently certified ICI, a list of which is available from the EPA, must import Nonconforming vehicles for you. The only EPA-authorized ICIs are located in the U.S. It is therefore recommended that you contact an ICI to discuss costs for modification and testing before you decide to import a nonconforming vehicle. The ICI will be responsible for assuring that your car complies with all U.S. emission requirements. (As of July 1, 1998, EPA no longer has the one-time exemption for vehicles five or more model-years old.) Be aware that EPA will deny entry to certain makers, models, and model year if an ICI is not certified or is unwilling to accept responsibility for the vehicle(s) in question.

You may obtain additional information on emission control requirements or on ICIs from the U.S. EPA Vehicle Programs and Compliance Division/Imports at tel. (202) 564-9660, FAX (202) 565-2057; or visit the Web site on page x.

Individual state emission requirements may differ from those of the federal government. Proper registration of a vehicle in a state may depend upon satisfaction of its requirements, so you should contact the appropriate state authorities prior to importation. Be aware, however, that EPA will not accept compliance with a state's emission requirements as satisfying EPA's requirements.

A WORD OF CAUTION
Both the DOT and the EPA advise that although a nonconforming car may be conditionally admitted, the modification required to bring it into compliance may be so extensive and costly that it may be impractical and even impossible to achieve such compliance. It is highly recommended that these prohibitions and modifications be investigated before a vehicle's purchased for importation.

Re-Importing A Previously Exported Vehicle
A vehicle taken from the United States for non-commercial, private use may be returned duty free by proving to U.S. Customs that it was previously owned and registered in the United States. This proof may be a State issued registration card for the automobile or a bill of sale for the car from a U.S. dealer. Repairs or accessories acquired abroad for your vehicle must be declared on your return and may be subject to duty.

In some countries, it will be difficult or impossible to obtain unleaded fuel for your vehicle. If the vehicle is driven using leaded gasoline, it will be necessary for you to replace the catalyst and oxygen sensor upon its return to the U.S. To avoid the expense of replacing these parts you may obtain authorization from EPA to remove the catalyst and oxygen sensor before the vehicle is shipped overseas. The EPA telephone number for these authorizations is (202) 564-2418. When the vehicle returns to the U.S., the original catalyst and oxygen sensor will need to be reinstalled. However, you may now reenter your U.S. version

vehicle into the U.S. without bond, upon your assurance that you will have the reinstallation performed.

-Using Conveyances to Transporting Goods of a Commercial/Personal Nature
Goods of a commercial nature that are being transported in a privately owned conveyance will require the purchase of a user fee decal and the payment of duty may be required.

Goods being transported for personal use within a privately owned vehicle do not require the purchase of this decal. However, the payment of duty may be required.

Rental vehicles may be used to transport personal goods without the purchase of a decal if the driver has not been paid to operate the vehicle.

EXCEPTIONS
The following vehicles need not conform to emission or safety requirements but may NOT be sold in the U.S. and may require EPA and DOT declarations:

-Those imported by nonresidents for personal use not exceeding one year. The vehicle must be exported at the end of that year – there are no exceptions or extensions.

-Those belonging to members of foreign armed forces, foreign diplomatic personnel, or other individuals who come within the class of persons for whom free entry has been authorized by the Department of State in accordance with international law.

-Those temporarily imported for testing, demonstration, or competition, provided they are not licensed for use, or driven on public roads. These vehicles may be operated on public roads or highways provided the operations are an integral part of the test. Parties responsible for such vehicles must submit proper documents- that is forms EPA 3520-1 and DOT HS-7—to Customs at the time entry is made. Also, applicable written approvals from these agencies must be obtained in advance and presented to customs along with these forms. Remember, the cost to return vehicles that have been refused prior approval can be very high and must be borne by the vehicle owner(s).

DRIVER'S PLATES AND PERMITS
Imported cars should bear the

International Registration Marker. The International Driving Permit, issued in five languages, is a valuable asset. Consult an international automobile federation or your local automobile club about these documents.

-U.S. RESIDENTS importing a new or used car should consult the Department of Motor Vehicles (DMV) in their state of residence about temporary license plates and what documentation their DMV would require from Customs.

-NATIONALS OF CENTRAL AND SOUTH AMERICAN countries that have ratified the Inter-American Convention of 1943 may drive their cars in the U.S. for touring purposes for one year or for the period of the validity of the documents, whichever is shorter, without U.S. license plates or U.S. driver's permits, provided the car carries the International Registration Marker and registration card, and the driver has the International Driving Permit.

-MOTORISTS VISITING THE UNITED STATES as tourists from countries that have ratified the Convention on International Road Traffic of 1949 may drive in the U.S. for one year with their own national license plates (registration tags) on their own national license plates (registration tags) on their cars and with their own personal drivers' licenses.

-MOTORISTS FROM CANADA AND MEXICO are permitted to tour in the U.S. without U.S. license plates or U.S. driver's permits, under agreements between the United States and these countries.

-MOTORISTS FROM A COUNTRY NOT A PARTY to any of the above agreements must secure a driving permit in the U.S. after taking an examination.

-FOREIGN NATIONALS employed in the U.S. may use their foreign license tags from the port of entry to their destination in the U.S.

EXPORTING A CAR

BASIC REQUIREMENTS AND PREOCEDURES

To export a motor vehicle from the United States, the exporter must provide documents that demonstrate proof of ownership.

In almost all cases, this will be the certificate of title. The original ownership documents, or a certified copy, and two copies must be presented to U.S. Customs.

If you are exporting through a land border port, you must submit the ownership documents to that port at least three days before exportation. On the date of exportation, you must present the vehicle to U.S. Customs to verify that the car being exported is the one described in the ownership documents.

The car will be subject to Customs inspection at the time of exportation. If the exportation is by ship or plane, both the vehicle and ownership documents must be presented to Customs at least 72 hours before lading, at which time Customs will conduct its inspection.

The vehicle will be authorized for export only after Customs has inspected it and certified that the ownership documents are in proper order. Your original title will then be stamped or perforated to show that your vehicle was exported from the United States.

OWNERSHIP DOCUMENTS

Only the original certificate of title, or a certified copy of the original, is considered valid proof of ownership. Other registration documents, by themselves, are not considered proof of ownership. If the car has a lien, encumbrance, or is leased, the exporter will have to attach to the certificate of title a letter from the lien holder or lease holder authorizing it to leave the country.

If the vehicle is a new car that has never been titled, it can be exported by submitting a document known as a manufacturer's statement of origin in lieu of the title. The manufacturer's statement of origin may be obtained from the auto dealer. The original and two copies must be presented to Customs.

Some very old used vehicles and some foreign vehicles purchased abroad may not have a certificate of title, or junk scrap certificate in force and for which a manufacture's statement of origin was not issued. In these cases, a bill of sale, sales invoice, right of possession, or other documents sufficient to prove lawful ownership may be used. In addition, the owner must certify in writing to Customs that the procurement of the vehicle was a bona fide transaction and that the vehicles presented for export is not stolen. Again, the original and two copies must be presented.

Check with your local Customs office about acceptable ownership documentation for cases in which a title cannot be produced. Most used vehicles, however -and this includes used cars legally bought and sold in the United States—must be accompanied by the original title, or a certified copy, as proof of ownership.

ADDITIONAL INFORMATION

Information in this section is specific to cars, trucks, and motorcycles. Other motorized vehicles, such as motorized farm equipment, lawnmowers, and construction equipment may be subject to similar rules and regulations.

Should you need additional information about exporting your vehicle, please contact the Customs port from which you plan to export it. You can find their address and phone number by accessing the Customs Web Site at www.customs.gov.

The source of the foregoing authority may be found in 19 CFR Part 192 that contains the Customs regulations.

IMPORTING PLEASURE BOATS

Pleasure Boats

When a yacht or any other type of pleasure boat arrives in the United States, the first place it docks must be at a Customs port or other place where Customs service is available. This pamphlet explains reporting requirements and other Customs formalities involving pleasure boats. For the location of reporting stations, contact the Customs port director in the area where you will be cruising, or any of the ports of entry.

Additional reporting and entry requirements may be obtained from the U.S. Customs Service, Office of Field Operations (Attn: Passenger Operations Team), Washington, DC 20229. For additional information on legal requirements, contact the U.S. Customs Service, Office of Regulations and Rulings (Attn: Entry Procedures and Carriers Branch), Washington, DC 20229.

Reporting & Entry

American pleasure boats. American pleasure boats that are not documented by the United States

Coast Guard, but are owned by citizens living in the United States, must comply with federal laws relating to identification numbers issued by a state, Puerto Rico, the U.S. Virgin Islands, Guam, American Samoa or the District of Columbia.

The master of any American pleasure boat must report to Customs immediately after arriving into the United States from a foreign port or place and must also report any foreign merchandise on his boat that is subject to duty. The report may be made by any means of communication and should include the name of the boat, its nationality, name of the master, place of docking and arrival time. If an inspection is required, the Customs officer will direct the vessel to an inspection area.

An American pleasure boat arriving in the United States from a foreign port or place is not required to make formal entry provided the vessel is not engaged in trade; the vessel has not visited any hovering vessel ; the master reports arrival as required by law and is in compliance with U.S. customs and navigation laws; and any article on board required by law to be entered or declared is reported to Customs immediately upon arrival. If these requirements are not met, the vessel must make formal entry with U.S. Customs within 48 hours after arrival.

An American pleasure boat must also obtain clearance from U.S. Customs before leaving a port or place in the U.S. and proceeding to a foreign port or place if the vessel is engaged in trade, has visited a hovering vessel, or is not in compliance with U.S. laws.

Foreign-flag pleasure boats. The master of a foreign-flag or undocumented foreign pleasure boat must report its arrival to U.S. Customs immediately and must make formal entry (see section that follows on cruising licenses) within 48 hours. In the absence of a cruising license, vessels in this category must obtain a permit before proceeding to each subsequent U.S. port.

Navigation fees will be charged for the formal entry, the permit to proceed, and for the clearance of foreign-flag pleasure boats. It is not necessary for foreign-flag vessels making formal entry and operating under a cruising license to acquire a $25 user fee decal.

The master of every foreign-flagged vessel arriving in the U.S. And required to make entry must have a complete legible manifest consisting of Customs Forms (CF) 1300 through 1304 and a passenger list.

Pleasure boats from foreign countries must obtain clearance before leaving a port or place in the U.S. And proceeding to a foreign port or place or for another port or place in the U.S.

Restrictions On Foreign-Built Or Foreign-Flag Vessels. Vessels that are foreign-built or of foreign registry may be used in the United States for pleasure purposes or in the foreign trade of the United States. However, federal law prohibits the use of such vessels in the coastwise trade - that is, the transport of passengers within the United States, including the carrying of chartered fishing parties. The documentation of foreign-built vessels is under the jurisdiction of the United States Coast Guard.

Cruising licenses. Cruising licenses exempt pleasure boats of certain countries from having to undergo formal entry and clearance procedures such as filing manifests and obtaining permits to proceed as well as from the payment of tonnage tax and entry and clearance fees at all but the first port of entry. These licenses can be obtained from the U.S. Customs port director at the first port of arrival in the United States. Normally valid for one year, a cruising license has no bearing on the dutiability of a pleasure boat.

NOTE: Under Customs policy, when a foreign-flag vessel's cruising license expires, that vessel may not be issued another license until the following three conditions have been met: (1) the vessel leaves the United States for a foreign port or place, and (2) it returns from that foreign port or place, and (3) at least 15 days have elapsed since the previous license expired. (Customs Directive 3100-06, November 7, 1988.)

Vessels of the following countries are eligible for cruising licenses (these countries extend the same privileges to American pleasure boats):

Argentina
Australia
Austria
Bahama Islands
Belgium
Bermuda
Canada
Denmark
Federal Republic
of Germany
Finland
France
Greece
Honduras
Ireland
Italy
Jamaica
Liberia
Netherlands
New Zealand
Norway
Sweden

Switzerland
Turkey
Great Britain (including Turks and Caicos Islands, St Vincent [including the territorial waters of the Northern Grenadine Islands], the Cayman Islands, the British Virgin Islands and the St. Christopher- Nevis-Anguilla Islands).

Charges and overtime. There are no charges for overtime inspections performed by U.S. Customs.

User fees. U.S. pleasure craft and foreign-flag vessels without a cruising license that are 30 feet or longer in length must pay an annual fee of $25 for the user fee decal. Contact your local customs office if you have any questions on this subject.

Immigration requirements. Every person entering the United States must be seen in person by an immigration officer, except those participating in the Canadian Border Small Boat Program. Information about this program may be obtained from any immigration office.

U.S. citizens should carry proof of citizenship such as a passport or birth certificate. (Voter registration cards are no longer valid for this purpose.) Canadian citizens should present proof of Canadian citizenship; Mexican citizens may present a border-crossing card. Canadian, Mexican, and U.S. Citizens must carry a passport if they are arriving in the U.S. from outside the Western Hemisphere.

Legal permanent resident aliens must present Immigration and Naturalization Service form I-551. Nonresident aliens other than Canadians and Mexicans must present a valid passport and visa.

Plant and animal restrictions. The importation of fruits, plants, meats, other plant or animal products, birds or other live organisms of any kind is regulated by the Department of Agriculture to prevent the introduction of pests and diseases into America's food chain. Such items cannot be brought into the United States unless advance permission is granted by the Department of Agriculture or U.S. Customs.

Emergencies. If it is necessary to make an emergency stop in the United States to preserve life or property, the master must report as soon as possible to the nearest customs, immigration, agriculture, or public health officer. He should not permit any merchandise or baggage to be removed

from the boat or any passengers or crew to depart the place of arrival without official permission, unless necessary for the protection of life, health, or property.

STAY ON BOARD! If your boat has anchored or tied up, you are considered to have entered the United States. No one shall board or leave the boat without first completing customs processing, unless permission to do so is granted by the Customs officer in charge. The only exception to this requirement is to report arrival.

If it is necessary for someone to leave the boat to report arrival to U.S. Customs, he or she must return to the boat after reporting and remain on board. No one who arrived on that boat may leave until the Customs officer grants permission to go ashore. Violations may result in substantial penalties and forfeiture of the boat.

Temporary and permanent importations

Personal exemptions

Returning u.s. residents. Customs determines if a person who formerly resided in the United States is a returning resident by considering whether, when the person departed, he or she intended to leave the United States permanently. In making this determination, Customs may consider the duration and purpose of the person's foreign stay and if, while abroad, the person maintained a home in the U.S.

A United States resident living or stationed abroad and entering the country for a short visit may import a foreign-built boat duty-free if, upon arrival, he or she claims and is given nonresident Customs status and exports the boat when leaving the United States. United States citizens employed abroad and government employees returning on TDY or leave may also be granted this status.

Permanent Importations
A returning U.S. resident who is importing a boat (i.e., bringing it in permanently, as opposed to temporarily) will be required to pay duty on that boat. The personal customs exemption toward duty owed on a foreign-built pleasure boat may be applied under the following conditions:
- The boat is imported for his or her personal use or for use by members of that household.
- The boat was acquired abroad as an

incident of the journey from which he or she is returning.

- The boat accompanies him or her at the time of return.

The head of a family returning together may make a joint declaration for all members residing in the same household and pool their customs exemption toward the duty on an imported boat.

Rates of duty. Pleasure boats are generally dutiable when imported into the United States. The following duty rates apply to boats imported for recreational purposes:

Sailboats and motorboats other than outboard motorboats
Outboard motorboats
Inflatable vessels
Canoes
Rowboats not designed for use with motors or sails

These rates are subject to change; call your local Customs port of entry to get the correct rates at the time of your trip. Duty rates for importations from Column 2 countries, as defined in the Harmonized Tariff Schedule, are considerably higher than those listed above.

If you are importing a yacht or other pleasure boat purchased abroad, please contact your nearest port of entry before you import the boat to learn more about entry requirements and the specific duty rate for your vessel.

Nonresidents. A nonresident for Customs purposes is a foreign visitor to the United States, a person emigrating to the United States, or a person who left the United States with no intent to reestablish residency.

Nonresidents may bring vessels into the United States for their own use without having to make formal consumption entry or pay duty on the vessel. Informal entry at the first port of arrival must still be made, however. If a pleasure boat that was admitted duty free is sold within one year of its importation without paying the applicable duty, the vessel or its value, which will be recovered from the importer, will be subject to forfeiture. 7

Temporary stays/importation under bond. Boats entered for the following purposes may be entered without payment of duty as temporary importations under bond:

- Alterations or repairs,

- As samples for taking orders,
- For experimental testing,
- For review, or study purposes,
- For use by illustrators and photographers solely as models in their own establishments,
- As professional equipment and tools of trade.

The length of stay in these circumstances is normally one year and may not exceed three years. There may be additional specific requirements for each of these exemptions from duty.

A pleasure boat and its usual equipment may be entered duty-free by a nonresident for a temporary stay to take part in races or other contests. If the contests are for other than money purses and the Customs officer is satisfied as to the importer's good faith, the boat may be admitted **without formal consumption entry or bond** for stays of up to 90 days. A certificate identifying the boat will be issued to the importer and must be delivered with the vessel to the Customs office at the point of departure from the country.

If the boat remains in the U.S. for longer than 90 days, the importer will be required to post a bond. (If the importer knows that the boat will be in the U.S. For longer than 90 days at the time of entry, the bond should be posted when the initial arrival takes place.) If the boat is in the U.S. For more than 90 days, and a bond has **not** been obtained to satisfy the conditions of a Temporary Importation Under Bond (TIB) the boat will be subject to forfeiture.

Bond is taken in an amount equal to twice the estimated duty. Cash may be deposited in lieu of surety on the bond. The bond (or cash) will be refunded if the boat is exported under Customs supervision within the time limit required by the TIB.

Pleasure boats brought into the country for sale, or for sale on approval, are not eligible for the Temporary Importation Under Bond program.

A final word... The United States Coast Guard administers a number of safety and documentation laws applicable to pleasure boats. With certain exceptions, a pleasure boat manufactured after November 1, 1972, may not be imported unless the manufacturer has affixed a certification label with the words "This Boat Complies with U.S.

Coast Guard Safety Standards in Effect on the Date of Certification." For further information on matters under U.S. Coast Guard jurisdiction, contact: Commandant, U.S. Coast Guard Headquarters, 2100 Second Street, SW, Washington, DC 20593. The Customs forms mentioned in this chapter may be obtained at our Web site at www.customs.gov.

Report your arrival in the United States to the U.S. Customs office nearest to your point of entry. (See Appendix for a listing of U.S. Customs Offices)

Chapter 21

Generalized Systems of Preferences & the Traveler

*[The information in this chapter is reprinted verbatim from a bulletin issued by the
Department of the Treasury, U.S. Customs Service. It is intended to serve as advice
to Americans traveling abroad.]*

Generalized System of Preferences (GSP) & the Traveler: Bringing in Articles from Developing Countries

What is GSP?
GSP (Generalized System of Preferences) is a system used by many developed countries to help developing nations improve their financial or economic condition through exports. In effect, it provides for the duty-free importation of a wide range of products that would otherwise be subject to customs duty if imported into the U.S. from non-GSP countries.

When did GSP go into effect for the United States?
GSP went into effect on January 1, 1976. The program has expired on several occasions since that time, most recently on June 30, 1999. On December 17, 1999, President Clinton signed legislation renewing the GSP retroactively from July 1, 1999, and extending it through September 30, 2001. However, duty-free treatment for eligible products made in designated sub-Saharan African countries continues through September 30, 2008.

How is GSP administered?
GSP is administered by the United States Trade Representative in consultation with the Secretary of State. The duty suspensions are proclaimed by the President under the Trade Act of 1974 as amended. The U.S. Customs Service is responsible for determining eligibility for duty-free entry under GSP.

What products are eligible?
Approximately 4,284 items have been designated as eligible for duty-free treatment from beneficiary developing countries (BCD's). The eligible articles are identified in the Harmonized Tariff Schedule of the United States Annotated and the designated countries are also listed there.

For the traveler's convenience, an advisory list of the most popular tourist items that, in general, have been accorded GSP status is included in this leaflet.

Are certain items excluded?
Under the Trade Act many items, such as most footwear, most textile articles (including clothing), watches, some electronic products, and certain glass and steel products are specifically excluded from GSP benefits.

What countries have been designated as Beneficiary Developing Countries?
Approximately 140 countries and territories have been designated. Those countries are listed on page X.

Are the articles and countries subject to change?
Yes. Articles may be excluded by Executive Order if it is determined that their importation is harmful to domestic industry. Beneficiary countries may also be excluded from the GSP program at any time, due to other trade considerations. For example, beneficiary countries may graduate from GSP if they become a "high income" country as defined by the International Bank for Reconstruction and Development. The President may also withdraw a beneficiary country's GSP eligibility for other reasons, such as the country begins to give preferential treatment to imports from other developed countries, but not the United States.

In addition, some articles from specified countries may be excluded from GSP treatment, if during the preceding year:

- The level of imports of those articles exceeded a specific dollar limit indexed to the nominal growth of the U.S. gross national product, since 1984.

- That country supplied 50 percent or more of the total U.S. imports of that product.

How has the Africa Growth and Opportunity Act (AGOA) affected GSP?

The AGOA amended the GSP to provide for the duty-free treatment of many products if made in designated sub-Saharan African countries. Those countries are listed on page X. The AGOA went into effect on October 1, 2000, and expires on September 30, 2008. More detailed information may be obtained from the Customs informed compliance publication *What Every Member of the Trade Community Should Know About: The African Growth and Opportunity Act*. This publication can be found on the Customs Web site at www.customs.gov in the Importing and Exporting section

Are there any specific requirements or qualifications I must be aware of to be sure an article qualifies for duty-free treatment?

In order to take advantage of GSP, you must have acquired the eligible article in the same beneficiary country where it was grown, manufactured, or produced. Articles may accompany you or may be shipped from the developing country directly to the United States.

What forms are required?

If they are shipped, the goods should be accompanied by the merchant's invoice. No other forms are necessary unless it is a commercial importation.

What about merchandise acquired in duty-free shops?

Most items purchased in duty free shops will not be eligible for GSP treatment unless the merchandise was produced in the country in which the duty free shop is located.

What about Internal Revenue tax?

Such items as gin, liqueur, perfume, if designated as eligible articles, may be subject to Internal Revenue Service tax despite their GSP status.

What happens if I thought an article was eligible for duty-free entry and it is not?

When merchandise claimed to be free of duty under GSP is found to be dutiable, you may include it in your Customs exemption. Articles imported in excess of your exemption will be subject to duty. If you feel your article should have been passed free of duty, you may write to the director of the Customs port where you entered, giving the information concerning your entry. A determination as to whether you are due a refund will be made.

Am I still entitled to my basic Customs exemption?

Yes, as a returning U.S. resident, you may still bring in free of duty $400 worth of articles (fair retail value) acquired abroad in addition to those items covered by GSP. This exemption is $1,200 if you are returning from the U.S. Virgin Islands, American Samoa, or Guam, and $600 if you are returning from certain Caribbean or Andean nations. (See pp. X-X for this list.) Remember that all articles acquired abroad, whether free of duty or not, including those entitled to GSP, must be declared to U.S. Customs on your return.

Visitors or nonresidents are entitled to bring in articles that are duty free under GSP in addition to their basic customs exemption.

Who should I contact if I have any questions about GSP?

Contact your nearest U.S. Customs office--there are 300 ports of entry throughout the United States. The address and telephone number of the nearest Customs office can be found in your local telephone directory on the U.S. Government pages under U.S. Treasury, or on the Customs website at www.customs.gov at the Office Locations button. If you are overseas, the U.S. Embassy or consulate can be of assistance.

General information on the GSP and downloadable guides are available at www.ustr.gov/gsp/general.shtml.

Please Note

Some products, although entitled to duty-free treatment under GSP, may be restricted or prohibited from entering the United States. For example, endangered species of wildlife and plants and products made from them, are protected by the Convention on International Trade in Endangered Species of Wild Fauna and Flora, and are prohibited from being exported or imported. Elephant ivory is also prohibited. Any elephant ivory brought into the United States is subject to seizure. If you are considering purchasing articles made from ivory, skin, fur, etc., please contact the U.S. Fish and Wildlife Service, or your nearest U.S. Customs port of entry, in advance of your trip.

Information contained in in this chapter has been prepared to serve only as an advisory guide for the traveling public for entry of non-commercial importations intended for personal use only. More specific and definitive advice in this regard should be obtained from one of the Customs field offices. Please also note that details or requirements for commercial importers are not covered here.

The U.S. Customs brochure *Know Before You Go* provides information on Customs clearance, exemptions, and restricted or prohibited items.

Information for commercial importers can be found on the Customs website under the Importing and Exporting section, or in our brochure *Import Requirements*. *Import Requirements* and *Know before You Go* are available by writing to: U.S. Customs Service, P.O. Box 7407, Washington, D.C. 20004, or by telephoning 202.354.1000.

POPULAR TOURIST ITEMS

This listing is solely an advisory guide to items designated as eligible for duty-free treatment under GSP that may be of interest to travelers for their personal use. **Note that certain items, if from a particular beneficiary country, may be excluded.** Do not hesitate to check with your nearest Customs office, or the American Embassy or consulate in the country you are visiting to verify the GSP status of any article you are considering bringing into the United States.

BASKETS or bags of bamboo, willow, or rattan.
CAMERAS, motion-picture and still, lenses, and other photographic equipment.
CANDY
CHINAWARE, bone: household ware, and other articles such as vases, statues, and figurines. Non-bone: articles other than household ware (except for non-bone chinaware or subporcelain).
CIGARETTE LIGHTERS, pocket and table.
CORK, manufactures of.
EARTHENWARE or stoneware except household ware available in sets.
FLOWERS, artificial of plastic or feathers.
FURNITURE of wood, rattan, or plastic.

GAMES, played on boards: chess. Backgammon. darts, Mah-Jongg.
GOLF BALLS and EQUIPMENT
JADE, cut but not set for use in jewelry and other articles of jade.
JEWELRY of precious stones, or of precious metal set with semi-precious stones, cameos, intaglios, amber, or coral: Silver, chief value, valued not over $18 per dozen. Necklaces and neck chains, almost wholly of gold: except rope from Israel and mixed link.
JEWELRY BOXES, unlined.
MUSIC BOXES and MUSICAL INSTRUMENTS
PAPER, manufactures of.
PEARLS, cultured or imitation, loose or temporarily strung and without clasp.
PERFUME
PRINTED MATTER
RADIO RECEIVERS, solid state (not for motor vehicles) .
RECORDS, phonograph and tapes.
SHAVERS, electric.
SHELL, manufactures of.
SILVER, tableware and flatware.
SKIS and SKI EQUIPMENT, ski boots not included.
STONES cut but not set, suitable for use in jewelry. Precious and semi-precious stones including marcasites, coral and cameos.
TAPE RECORDERS
TOILET PREPARATIONS
TOYS
WIGS
WOOD, carvings.

Beneficiary Countries
The countries listed below have been designated as beneficiary developing countries in the U.S. Generalized System of Preferences.

★Antigua and Barbuda***
★Bahamas***
★Barbados***
★Belize***
★Bolivia*
★Colombia*
★Costa Rica
★Dominica ***
★Dominican Republic
★El Salvador
★Grenada***
★Guatemala
★Guyana***
★Haiti

★Honduras
★Jamaica***
★Peru*
★Saint Kitts and Nevis
★Saint Lucia***
★Saint Vincent and the Grenadines***
★Trinidad and Tobago***
Albania
Angola
Argentina
Armenia
Bahrain
Bangladesh
Belarus
Benin
Bhutan
Bosnia-Hercegovina
Bostwana
Brazil
Bulgaria
Burkina Faso
Burundi
Cameroon
Cape Verde
Central African Republic
Chad
Chile
Comoros
Congo
Cote d'Ivoire
Croatia
Cyprus
Czech Republic
Djibouti
Ecuador*
Egypt
Equatorial Guinea
Estonia
Ethiopia
Fiji
Gambia
Ghana
Guinea
Guinea Bissau
Hungary
India
Indonesia**
Israel
Jordan
Kazakhstan
Kenya
Kiribati
Kyrgyzstan
Latvia
Lebanon

Lesotho
Lithuania
Macedonia (former Republic of Yugoslavia)
Madagascar
Malawi
Malaysia**
Maldives
Mali
Malta
Maritius
Moldova
Morocco
Mozambique
Namibia
Nepal
Niger
Oman
Pakistan
Papua New Guinea
Paraguay
Philippines**
Poland
Romania
Russia
Rwanda
São Tomé and Principe
Senegal
Seychelles
Sierra Leone
Slovakia
Slovenia
Solomon Islands
Somalia
South Africa
Sri Lanka
Sudan
Surinam
Swaziland
Tanzania
Thailand**
Togo
Tonga
Tunisia
Turkey
Tuvalu
Uganda
Ukraine
Uruguay
Uzbekistan
Vanuatu
Venezuela*
Western Samoa
Yemen Arab Republic Sanaa
Zaire
Zambia

214

Zimbabwe

*Member countries of the Cartagena Agreement-Andean Group (treated as one country).
**Association of South East Asian Nations (ASEAN)-except Brunei Darussalam, and Singapore
(treated as one country).
***Member countries of the Caribbean Common Market (CARICOM) (treated as one country).
★ Member countries of the United States–Caribbean Basin Trade Partnership Act eligible for $600 personal duty exemption (Panama and Nicaragua are also eligible for this exemption).

Non-Independent Countries and Territories

Anguilla
★Aruba
British Indian Ocean Territory
Cayman Islands
Christmas Island (Australia)
Cocos (Keeling) Islands
Cook Islands
Falkland Islands (Islas Malvinas)
French Polynesia
Gibraltar
Greenland
Heard Island and McDonald Islands
Macau
★Monserrat ***
★Netherlands Antilles
New Caledonia
Niue
Norfolk Island
Pitcairn Islands
Saint Helena
Tokelau
Turks and Caicos Islands
★Virgin Islands, British
Wallis and Futuna
West Bank and Gaza Strip
Western Sahara
***Member countries of the Caribbean Common Market (CARICOM)
★ Member countries of the United States–Caribbean Basin Trade Partnership Act eligible for $600 personal duty exemption (Panama and Nicaragua are also eligible for this exemption).

African Growth and Opportunity Act Beneficiary Countries

Benin*
Botswana
Cape Verde*
Cameroon*
Central African Republic*
Chad*
Congo*
Djibouti*
Eritrea*
Ethiopia*
Gabonese Republic
Ghana*
Guinea*
Guinea-Bussau*
Kenya*
Lesotho*
Madagascar*
Malawi*
Mali*
Mauritania*
Mauritius
Mozambique*
Namibia
Niger*
Nigeria*
Rwanda*
São Tomé and Principe*
Senegal*
Saychelles
Sierra Leone*
South Africa
Tanzania*
Uganda*
Zambia*

*Lesser developed beneficiary sub-Saharan African countries

Report Drug Smuggling to U.S. Customs Service.
1 (800) BE-ALERT

215

Chapter 22

Communicating To and From Overseas

CALLING OVERSEAS FROM THE U.S.:

You can call over 170 countries from the U.S., easily and economically. Here's how:

NOTE: *To use the services described in these section you may be required to first become a subscriber or customer of a Long Distance Carrier. This can be accomplished by signing up (before you go,) with the long distance carrier of your choice or by signing up for the particular service being offered by the long distance carrier.*

A) **HOW TO PLACE INTERNATIONAL CALLS DIRECTLY FROM YOUR HOME OR OFFICE**

Dial 011 + Country Code + City Code + Local Number
(A list of country codes is provided at the end of this chapter. Country and City Codes could also be found in Appendix 5E).

For example: to call Tokyo in Japan simply call:

011	+ 81	+ 3	+ XXXXXX
International Access Code	Country Code	City Code	Local Number

CALLING CANADA OR THE CARIBBEAN:

This procedure is even simpler since the dialing procedure is exactly the same as placing a long distance call from one U.S. state to another.

1 +	XXX +	XXXXXX
Long distance Access Code	Area Code Local	Number

INTERNATIONAL CALLING FROM YOUR HOTEL ROOM

Dialing procedure from a hotel room is the same as from your home or office, except that you start with a hotel access code.

Dial the hotel access code[1] and wait for a tone. Then dial the international access code + country code + city code + local number.

For example: to call Tokyo, simply dial

X +	011	+ 81	+ 3	+ XXXXXX
Hotel Access	International Access Code	Country Code	City Code	Local Number

HOW TO PLACE INTERNATIONAL CALLS WITH OPERATOR ASSISTANCE

There are a few countries that cannot be direct-dialed. Most of these countries however, could still be accessed with an operator's assistance.

If direct-dialing is not available to the country you are calling simply dial any of the following numbers for an International Operator.

10 + AT&T (If you need **AT&T** services or would like to use their calling card)

10333+0 (If you need **Sprint** services or would like to use their calling card)

10+222+0² (If you need **MCI** services or would like to use their calling card)

10211+0 (if you need **Frontier** services or would like to use their calling card)

10488+0 (If you need MCC services or would like to use their calling card)

C) HOW TO PLACE INTERNATIONAL CALLS FROM THE U.S. USING A CALLING CARD:

TO CALL CANADA OR THE CARIBBEAN

(a) AT&T Calling CARDHOLDERS:
Dial **00+ Country Code + City Code + Local Number**.
Remember to dial "01" instead of "011" (if you do not hear "AT&T", hang up and dial: **01 + 288** before placing your call.

(b) Sprint (FONCARD) HOLDERS:

Dial 10333+01+Country Code, City Code and Local Number plus the "#" button. Listen for a recorded prompt (on rotary phones, wait for Sprint Operator). Dial the 14 digit FONCARD number (shown on your FONCARD)

If you do not hear "Welcome to Sprint":

Dial 1-800-877-8000. Listen for a computer tone. Dial:**01 + Country Code, City Code and Local Number plus the "#" button + # sign.** Listen for a computer tone. Dial the 14 digit FONCARD number.

If Calling the Caribbean (area Code 809) or Canada

Dial **10333+0+Area Code and Local Number.** Listen for recorded prompt. Dial the 14 digit FONCARD number.

If you do not hear "Welcome to Sprint": Dial 1-800-877-8000.
Listen for a computer tone. Dial 0+Area Code and Local Number. Listen for computer tone. Dial the 14 digit FONCARD number.

(c) MCI CARDHOLDERS:

Dial: **9501022 + 01 + Country Code + City Code + Local Number (Wait for a dial Tone) + your 14 Digit Number.**

If dialing from an "809" Area Code, Dial 0 + **Area Code + Local Number**

(d) MCC CARDHOLDERS:

218

Dial: **1 + 800 + 275 + 1234 (Wait for a dial tone) + 01 +   Country Code + City Code + Local Number + # sign (Wait for a dial tone) + your 14 digit Code.**

CALLING THE U.S. FROM OVERSEAS:[3]

You may have up to five choices:

a) **Using Special Services** of a U.S. International Telephone Carrier. e.g.: " AT&T USADirect Service(r)", " Sprint Express", MCI " Call USA", "Frontier Passport USA Service," and "Metromedia International Origination Service". These services allow you (when you dial a special number provided by your preferred carrier) to talk to that carriers operator in the U.S. who will then place your call.

b) **Using a Calling Card[4]** with U.S. Operators. e.g.: " AT&T Calling Card", Sprint "FONCARD", "Frontier Calling Card", MCI Card", or "Metromedia Calling Card".

To place a call, using your calling card simply dial the " In Country Local International Operator" who will then place your call. (A Chart listing International Operator Codes is provided at the end of this chapter).

C) **Using International Direct Dialing[5]**

This service may not be available from all countries and/at in all phones in the foreign country. Check with your long distance carrier before leaving.

To direct dial just get an outside line and use the proper access code for the country you are calling from. (See Chart at the end of this chapter for a list of International Direct Dialing Codes).

Here is for example how you'd dial Boston directly from Italy:

00   +   1   +   617 +   _____
Direct U.S. Country   Boston   Local
Access Code Code   Area Code Number

Calling the U.S. from Canada:

You can use your Calling Card in Canada as easily as you do in the States. Simply dial from any phone:
0 + Area Code + Number
The operator will ask for your regular Calling Card number or you may enter it at the sound of the tone.

How To Use Special Services:

AT&T USADirect Dial: Just dial the AT&T USA Direct Service Number[-+] for the country you are calling from. This will put you directly in touch with an AT&T operator in the U.S. who will then place your call.

MCI Call USA Service: Dial the Special MCI Toll Free Access Number[++] for the country you are calling from. This will put you in touch with an MCI operator in the U.S. who will then place your call.

SPRINT Express: Dial Sprint Express overseas Access Number:[+-] This will put you in touch with a Sprint operator in the U.S., who will then place your call.

MCC: To use Direct Dial, Dial the MCC Access Number[-+] for the country you are in + 488 + 14 digit code + # sign + 4 Security Code + 1 + area code + number. (Note: Use "0" instead of "1" for National calls. "1" is used for International calls.)

219

++ *[A list of AT&T Direct Service Numbers and Access Numbers for the major long distance carriers is provided at the end of this chapter. Contact your long distance carrier for additional listings.]*

CALLING IN AND BETWEEN INTERNATIONAL LOCATIONS [e.g from Venice (Italy) to Genoa (Italy) or from Venice (Italy) to Paris (France)

This service is not available for all countries or from all locations. Check with your long distance carrier before leaving.

MCC: For those using MCC services, this facility is presently available in over 26 locations. To use this Direct Dial service to place a call between locations within the same country (e.g. Venice (Italy) to Genoa (Italy) dial

1. Enter Direct Dial Access Number from the country you are   in
2. Enter 488 + 14 **Digit Code** + **# sign**
3. Enter 4 Digit Security Code
4. Press "0" For National Call + City Code + Phone   number + **# sign**
OR "1" for International Call + Country + City Code   +   Phone number + **# sign**

SHIP AND SEA SERVICES

AT&T HIGH SEAS SERVICE:

a) **Calling from U.S. Shores to Ships.**

Use AT&T High Seas Service by dialing **1-800-SEA-CALL**. Give the operator the name of the ship and the person you wish to call. The operator will connect you once the contact is made.

b) **Calling from Ship to Shore.**

Before you go on your cruise, preregister your AT&T Calling Card number by calling **1-800-SEA-CALL**. Then, aboard ship, simply ask for AT&T High Seas Service, and the connection to a U.S. operator is made.

SPRINT INMARSAT/MCC MARSAT Services:

Sprint customers can enjoy direct-dial services to ships at sea using this dialing pattern: **DIAL 011 + Ocean Region Code + Ships   Telephone Number**

The Ocean Region Code will vary depending on the ship's location:

INMARSAT Regions Ocean Codes
Atlantic Ocean Region (East)   871
Atlantic Ocean Region (West)   874
Indian Ocean Region   873
Pacific Ocean Region 872

FOR ADDITIONAL INFORMATION/CUSTOMER SERVICE CALL:

Frontier: 1-800-836-8080
MCI: 1-800-444-3333
MCC: 1-800-275-2273

220

To obtain an AT&T Calling Card:

1-800-CALL-ATT
1-800-874-4000
When outside the U.S., use AT&T USADirect Service and call (816) 654-6688, collect.

For further information on the AT&T USADirect service call 1-800-874-4000

ENDNOTES

1. Check with the hotel operator for Hotel Access Code. The number is usually "8" or "9". Some hotels prefer to place International calls for their guests.

2. This is true in most places in the Northeast part of the United States except in large metropolitan areas. RCI however, will allow domestic collect calls in these areas.

3. To successfully use the services in this section, you must first become an approved customer of that carrier's calling service. In other words, you should not expect to just dial the access number and then place your calls. It is therefore, important to first inquire, and preferably, sign up with your long distance carrier before commencing on your trip.

4. Direct dialing is usually available from pay phones or specially marked phones in conjunction with your calling card.

In the absence of pay phones or specially marked phones, direct dialing will require going through a foreign operator for an outside line.

5. By using a calling card you avoid foreign surcharges. Furthermore, it allows you to have your calls billed to your card. This service however, may not be available in all foreign countries and/or at all phones in the foreign country. Check with your long distance carrier for availability before you go.

Country	-Country Local Int'l. Operator	Int'l. Direct Dialing Code	AT&T USA Direct Service Number	MCI Toll Free Access Number	SPRINT Express Overseas Codes	Int'l. Country
Algeria	16	00	na	na	na	213
Anguilla	na	1	1-800-872-2881	na	na	809
Argentina	300 or 953 8000	00	001-800-200-1111	001-800-777-1111	001-800-777-1111	54
Aruba	121	0c0	800-1011	na	na	297
Australia	0101	0011	0014-881-011	022-903-012	0014-881-877	61
Austria +	09	900	022-903-011	0114-881-100	022-903-014	43
Bahamas	0	1	1-800-872-2881	1-800-624-1000	1-800-389-2111	809
Bahrain	151	0	800-001	800-002	na	973
Belgium +	1222	00	078-11-0010	078-11-00-12	078-11-0014	32
Belize	115	00	555	na	556	501
Bermuda	na	na	1-800-872-2881	1-800-623-0484	1-800-623-0877	809
Bolivia	35-67-00	00	na	na	0800-3333	591
Brazil	000-111	00	000-8010	000-8012	000-8016	55
Bulgaria	0123	na	na	na	na	359
Canada	0	1	na	na	na	01
Cayman Islands	na		na	1872	1-624	809
Chile +	122 & 123	00	00*-0312	00*0316	00*0317	56
China	115 Beijing	00	10811	na	108-13	86
Colombia	09	90	980-11-0010	980-16-0001	980-13-0010	57

221

Country							
Costa Rica	116	00		114	162	163	506
Cyprus	na	na		080-90010	080-90-000	na	357
Czech Republic	102 & 108		00	00-420-00101		na	42
Denmark+	0016	009		8001-0010	801-0022	8001-0877	45
Ecuador	116	00		119	na	171	593
Egypt	120	00		356-0020	355-5770	na	20
El Salvador	119	00		190	na	191	503
Finland+	09	990		9800-100-10	980-102-80	9800-1-0284	358
France+	19-3311	19		19*0011	19*-00-19	19*0087	33
Gambia	na	na		00111	na	na	220
Germany (xxx)	0010	00		0130-0010	0130-0012	0130-0013	
Great Britain	155	010		0800-89-0011	0800-89-0222	0800-89-0877	
Greece	161	00		00-800-1311	00-800-1211	008-001-411	30
Grenada	na	1		872	na	na	809
Guam	013	011		018-872	950-1022	na	671
Guatemala	171	00		190	189	195	502
Haiti	09	001		001-800-872-2881	001-800-999-1234	na	509
Honduras	197	00		123	na	001-800-1212000	504
Hong Kong	011	001		008-1111	008-1121	008-1877	852
Hungary	09	00		00*-36-0111	00-800-01411	00*800-01-877	36
Iceland	na	90		999-001	na	na	354
India	186 & 187	00		na	na	000-137	91
Indonesia	101	00		00-801-10	na	00-801-15	62
Iraq	105	00		na	00-801-11	na	964
Ireland	114	16		1-800-550-000	1-800-551-001	1-800-55-2001	353
Israel	18	00		177-100-2727	177-150-2727	177-102-2727	972
Italy+	170	00		172-1011	172-1022	172-1877	39
Jamaica	na	00		0-800-872-2881	na	na	809
Japan+	0051	001		0039-111	0039-121	0039-131	81
Jordan	10217	00		na	na	na	962
Kenya	0196	na		0800-10	na	na	254
Korea, South	007	001		009-11	na	009-16	82
Kuwait	102 & 104	00		800-288	na	800-777	965
Liberia	na	00		797-797	na	na	231
Libya	16	00		na	na	na	
Liechtenstein	na	na		155-00-11	155-0222	155-9777	41
Luxembourg	0010	00		0800-0111	na	na	352
Macau	na	na		0800-111	na	0800-121	853
Malaysia	108	007		800-0011	800-0012	800-0016	60
Mexico	09	95		Designated	na	na	52
Monaco	na	19		19*0011	19*-00-19	19*0087	33
Montserrat	na	1		1-800-872-2881	na	na	809
Morocco	12	00		na	na	na	212
Netherlands, The+	0010	09		06-022-9111	06*-022-91-22	06*-022-9119	31
Netherlands Antilles		021		00	001-800-872-2881	na	599
New Zealand	0170	00		000-911	000-915	000-999	64
Nicaragua	114/116	00		64 **	na	161 (Managua)	505
Nigeria	171	009		1881	na	na	234
Norway+	0115	095		050-12-011	050-12912	050-12-877	47
Oman	15 & 195	00		na	na	na	968
Pakistan	0102	00		na	na	na	92
Panama	106	00		109	108	115	507
Paraguay	0010	00		0081-800	na	008-12-800	595
Peru	108	00		191	special phones only	196	51
Philippines+	108	00		105-11	na	105-01	63
Poland	901 & 900	00		(0)-010-480-0111	na	0010-480-0115	48
Portugal	098	097		05017-1-288	05-017-1234	05017-1-877	351
Qatar	1 & 150	0		Designated	na	na	974
Romania	071	00		na	na	na	40
St. Kits	na	na		1-800-872-288	na	na	809
San Marino	na	na		na	172-1022	172-1877	39
Saudi Arabia	900	00		1800-100	1-800-11	na	966
Singapore+	104	005		800-0011	800-0012	800-177-177	65
So. Africa	090 & 093	09 or 091		na	na	na	27
Spain	005	07		900-99-0011	900-99-0014	900-99-0013	34
Sweden+	018	009		020-795-611	020-795-922	020-799-011	46
Switzerland	114	00		155-00-11	155-0222	155-9777	41
Taiwan	100	002		0080-10288-0	Airport phones only	0080-14-0877	886

Thailand	100	001	001-999-1111	na	001-999-13-877	66
Tunisia	na	00	na	na	na	216
Turkey	528-23-03	99	919-8001-2277	99-8001-1177	99800-1-4477	90
United Arab Emirates		150 & 160	00	800-1-0010	800-1-0011	
Uruguay	007 & 02007	00	00-0410	000-412	000417	
U.S.A.	0	011	-	-	-	
Russia	339-62-66 &	810	na	na	na	7
Vahcau	271-90-20	na	na	na	na	
Vatican City	na	na	na	172-1022	172-1877	na
Venezuela	122	00	Designated	na	800-1111-0	na
Yugoslavia	981	na	99-38-0011	na	na	na
Zambia	na	na	00-899	na	na	na
Zimbabwe	na	na	110-899	na	na	na

+ Public phones require deposit
* Wait for second dial tone
** Use 02-64 for locations outside Managua.
xxxAccess only for locations in the geographic area formerly known as West Germany.

Note:
New access numbers are continually being added by the long distance carriers mentioned in this chapter.
distance carriers.

For up-to-date information on available countries access numbers and rates, call their customer service at:

AT&T: 1-800-874-4000, when overseas call: (412) 553-7458, collect.
MCI: 1-800-275-0200
Sprint: 1-800-888-0800

[See Appendix T for a complete listing of country codes, including codes of major cities.]

223

Chapter 23

Passports

*[The Information in this chapter is reprinted verbatim from a bulletin issued by the
U.S. State Department, Bureau of Consular Affairs. It is intended to serve as advice
To Americans applying for passport.]*

[Applying For Them The Easy Way] The Department of State's Bureau of Consular Affairs has
prepared this publication to assist you in applying for your U.S. passport. This guide provides information
on how, when and where to apply for your passport.

Other Than at Passport Agencies, Where Can I Apply for a Passport?
You can apply for a passport at over 5,000 passport acceptance facilities nationwide that include many
Federal, state and probate courts, many post offices, some libraries and a number of county and municipal
offices. These designated acceptance facilities are usually more convenient because they are near your home
or workplace. (Most of the 13 passport agencies are designated to serve only those departing urgently and
appointments are required.

When Do I Have to Apply in Person?
You must always apply in person if you are 13 or older and if you do not meet all of the requirements for
renewing a previous passport by mail. *(SeeShould Youl Apply for a Passport by Mail?)*
Usually, for children age 12 and under, only a parent or legal guardian need appear to apply for a passport
on behalf of a child.

What Do I Need to Do to Apply for a Passport in Person?
See How to Apply in Person for a Passport.

Where Can I Get Passport Forms?
Passport acceptance facilities stock passport forms. (See Other Than at Passport Agencies, *Where do I get a
Passport Applicationt?* Passport forms can also be downloaded from the Internet at http://travel.state.gov or
obtained by calling the National Passport Information Center at 1-900-225-5674 or from the passport
agencies.

May I Apply for a Passport by Mail?
See How to Apply for a Passport Renewal.

When Should I Apply for a Passport?
Apply several months in advance of your planned departure. If you will need visas from foreign embassies,
allow more time.

What Happens to My Passport Application After I Submit It?
If you apply at a passport acceptance facility, the same day that you apply, your application will be sent to
Passport Services for processing. Your will receive your passport within 6 weeks via first class mail. If you
apply at a passport agency, you will receive your passport within 5 weeks (25 business days) via first class
mail. Your passport will be mailed to the mailing address you provided on your application. If you need
your passport sooner, *see What If I Need a Passport in a Hurry?*

What Should I Do if My Passport Is Lost or Stolen?
If your still valid passport is lost or stolen, you can report the loss when you apply for a new passport. In addition to Form DS-11, you will need to complete a Form DS-64, "Statement Regarding a Lost or Stolen Passport." You may also call 202-955-0430, which has voice mail for nonbusiness hours, Eastern Time.

If you are abroad, immediately report the loss to local police authorities and the Consular Section of the nearest U.S. Embassy or Consulate. For more information, *see How to Replace a Lost or Stolen Passport.*

Do I Need to Obtain a Separate Passport for My Baby?
Yes. All persons, including newborn infants, are required to obtain passports in their own names.

What Do I Do if My Name Changes?
If you need to get a valid passport amended due to a name change, use Form DS-19. See May I Apply for a Passport by Mail? for the documentation needed to accompany the form and your current passport for amendment.

What If I Need a Passport in a Hurry?
If you are leaving on an emergency trip, apply in person at the nearest passport agency, presenting your tickets or airline-generated itinerary, as well as other required items listed in this publication. to ensure that customers with imminent travel receive their passports in time for their trips, many passport agencies are now operating by appointments and are generally serving only those leaving in less than 14 days.

If you do not live near a passport agency, but your overnight delivery service is reliable, departures within 7 to 10 business days may often be accommodated by appointments at a nearby passport acceptance facility. You will need to pay the additional $60 fee for expedited service and include a self-addressed, prepaid, two-way, overnight delivery envelope. (We have found that for states not densely populated and/or far from our Pittsburgh, PA cashiering facility, overnight service is not always reliable.) For all those customers leaving within 6 or fewer business days, apply at a passport agency. Whichever way you apply, be sure to include your departure date and travel plans on your application.

What Else Should I Know About Passports?
Before traveling abroad, make a copy of the identification page so it is easier to get a new passport, should it be necessary. It is also a good idea to carry two extra passport-size photos with you. If you run out of pages before your passport expires, submit Form DS-19, along with your passport to one of the passport agencies. (Please allow time for processing of the request.) If you travel abroad frequently, you may request a 48-page passport at the time of application.

Some countries require that your passport be valid at least 6 months beyond the dates of your trip. Check with the nearest embassy or consulate of the countries that you plan to visit to find out their entry requirements. In addition to foreign entry requirements, U.S. law must be considered. With certain exceptions, it is against U.S. law for U.S. citizens to enter or leave the country without a valid U.S. passport. Generally for tourists, the exceptions refer to direct travel within U.S. territories or between North, South, or Central America (except Cuba).

Passport Fees
Effective February 1, 1998

Routine Services (Form DS-11)*

Non-Refundable
Age 16 and older: The passport fee is $55. The execution fee is $30. The total is $85.
Under Age 16: The passport fee is $40. The execution fee is $30. The total is $70.
Note: When applying at other than one of the 13 Regional Passport Agencies and paying by check or money order, these fees must be paid separately because the $30.00 Execution Fee is retained locally by our 4,500

designated passport application acceptance facilities across the U.S. (Regional Passport Agencies also accept V, MC, D, and AE. Acceptance facilities may or may not accept credit cards.)

Passport Renewal (Form DS-82)
Non-Refundable

You may use this form if your previous passport:
1. Was issued when you were 16 or older.
2. Was issued in the last 15 years.
3. Is not damaged.
4. Is submitted with your application.

The total fee is $55.

Expedited Service - Add $60 for each application
For any service - e.g., first-time application, renewal, additional pages, name change

Additionally, to receive your passport as soon as possible, we strongly suggest that you arrange overnight delivery service for:
1. Sending your passport application
AND
2. Returning your passport to you.

How Long Will it Take to Process a Passport Application?

If you apply 1. At a Passport Acceptance Facility* or 2. By Mail for renewal, additional pages, amendment) and choose Routine Service, you will receive your passport within about 6 Weeks

If you apply 1. At a Passport Acceptance Facility* or 2. By Mail for renewal, additional pages, amendment) and choose Expedited Service or Expedited Service Plus Overnight delivery service for 1) Sending your application and 2) Returning your passport to you , you will receive your passport within about 2 Weeks

NOTE: • Passport Agencies assist customers with urgent travel needs - generally if you are traveling within 2 weeks.
• Most Passport Agencies are open by appointment only and require proof of your travel date or need for foreign visas. See List of Regional Passport Agencies.

How Can You Check the STATUS of the Application You ALREADY SUBMITTED?
To check status Call The National Passport Information Center

CALL
The National Passport Information Center (NPIC)
1-900-225-5674
1-888-362-8668
(for credit card users with Visa, MasterCard, American Express)
The Department of State receives NO income from the NPIC.
• 1-900: Automated information is 55 cents per minute.
• 1-900: Operator assisted calls are $1.50 per minute.
(Operators are available 8:30 a.m. to 5:30 p.m., Eastern Time, Monday - Friday, except Federal holidays; you must speak with an operator to check the status of a pending passport application.)
• 1-888: Flat rate is $5.50 per call.
• TDD - 1-900-225-7778 (for the hearing impaired)

- TDD - 1-888-498-3648 (for the hearing impaired)

Child Support Payments and Getting a U.S. Passport

Section 51.70 (a) (8) of Title 22 of the Code of Federal Regulations states, in part, that if you are certified to Passport Services by the U.S. Department of Health and Human Services (HHS) to be in arrears of child support payments in excess of $5,000, you are ineligible to receive a U.S. passport. If this applies to you, Passport Services strongly recommends that you contact the appropriate State child support enforcement agency to make payment arrangements before applying for a passport. This is because:

- The State agency must certify to the U.S. Department of Health and Human Services (HHS) that acceptable payment arrangements have been made.
- Then, HHS must notify Passport Services by the removal of your name from the electronic list HHS gives to Passport Services. (Passport Services cannot issue a passport until your name has been deleted by HHS.)
-

Please note that it can take 2-3 weeks from the time you make payment arrangements with the State agency until your name is removed from HHS' electronic list. Passport Services has no information concerning individuals' child support obligations and has no authority to take action until HHS removes your name from its list.

Please direct any questions to the appropriate State child support enforcement agency. You may go to the Department of Health and Human Services - State Child Support Enforcement Web Site for a listing of HHS state and local agencies.

Frequently Asked Questions:
Passports and Citizenship Documents
Where do I get a passport application?

- You may download forms from the State Department web site.
- Forms are also available at public offices like Post Offices, courthouses or municipal offices where passport applications are accepted.

Where are the instructions for filling out the passport forms?
Instructions are on the back of the forms.

I am traveling very soon. How do I get a passport in a hurry?
See How to Get Your Passport in a Hurry.

How do I renew my passport?
See How to Apply for a Passport Renewal.

I have never had a U.S. passport/My passport was lost or stolen. How do I get one?
See How to Apply in Person for a Passport.

My child who is under 18 needs a passport. How do I get it?

If your child is: Under 14 • then....
Your child need not appear in person.
- Both parents or legal guardians, can apply for your child.
- New legislation requires both parents' or legal guardians' consent for applications for minors under age 14. Both parents or legal guardians must show current, valid ID.
- If you do not have acceptable ID, someone with current, valid ID must vouch for you.

If your child is: 14 to 17
- Your child must appear in person.
- Your parental consent may be requested.

228

Is it true that passport applications for minors under 14 require the consent of both parents or legal guardians?
Effective July 2, 2001, Public Law 106-113, Section 236 requires that U.S. passport applications for children under the age of 14 require both parents' or legal guardians' consent.

What is the Children's Passport Issuance Alert Program (CPIAP)?
Separate from the Two-Parent Consent requirement for U.S. passport issuance for minors under the age of 14, parents may also request that their children's names be entered in the U.S. passport name-check system. The Children's Passport Issuance Alert Program provides:
- Notification to parents of passport applications made on behalf of minor children, and
- Denial of passport issuance if appropriate court orders are on file with CPIAP.

For more information, contact the Office of Children's Issues at 202-736-7000, or, by fax at 202-312-9743

I was recently married/divorced. How do I change my name on my passport?
You will need to complete Form DS-19, Passport Amendment/Validation Application and submit it along with the following:
- Certified documentation of your name change (e.g., marriage certificate, divorce decree with your new name); and
- Your current, valid passport.

My passport was lost/stolen. How do I report it?
Please apply for a new passport immediately. You may report your lost or stolen passport when you apply for the new one. Along with your application, you must submit the Statement Regarding Lost or Stolen Passport, Form DS-64.

If you decide not to apply for a new passport immediately, you may report your lost or stolen passport by completing Form DS-64 and mailing it to:

US Department of State
Passport Services
Consular Lost/Stolen Passport Section
1111 19th Street, NW, Suite 500
Washington, DC 20036
Or call us 24 hours/day at: (202) 955-0430
Voice mail - For non-business hours, Eastern Time

I was born abroad. How do I get a birth certificate proving my U.S. citizenship?
If one or both of your parents was a U.S. citizen when you were born abroad, your parent(s) should have registered your birth at a U.S. embassy or consulate, and, received a Consular Report of Birth Abroad, Form FS-240. This form is acceptable legal proof of birth and U.S. citizenship.

What should I do if my baby is born abroad?
As U.S. citizen parent(s), you should report your child's birth abroad as soon as possible to the nearest U.S. embassy or consulate to establish an official record of the child's claim to U.S. citizenship at birth. The official record will be the Consular Report of Birth of a Citizen of the United States of America, Form FS-240. This document, know as the Consular Report of Birth Abroad, is a basic United States citizenship document. An original FS-240 document will be given to you at the time registration is approved. (We have more information on these documents.)

A Consular Report of Birth can only be prepared at a U.S. embassy or consulate. It cannot be prepared if the child has been brought back into the United States, or, if the person is 18 years of age or older at the time the application is made.

What do I do if there is no birth record on file for me?
If you were born in the U.S. and there is no birth record on file, you will need several different documents

229

to substantiate your citizenship. You will need:

A letter from the Vital Statistics office of the state of your birth with your name and what years were searched for your birth record. An official of the Vital Statistics office needs to issue a letter of no record found.

In addition, you will need early public records to prove your birth in the U.S.

If you were born outside the U.S. and your U.S. parent(s) did not register your birth at the U.S. embassy or consulate, you may:
Apply for a U.S. passport.
You will need:
Your foreign birth certificate that includes your parents' names; and
Evidence of your parent(s) U.S. citizenship; and
Your parents' marriage certificate.

I'm renewing my passport. Do I get the old one back?
Yes, we return the old, cancelled passport to you. It is a good idea to keep it in a safe place as it is considered proof of your U.S. citizenship.

My child is too young to sign his/her own passport. How do I sign my child's passport?
In the space provided for the signature, the mother or father must print the child's name and sign their own name. Then, in parenthesis by the parent's name, write the word (mother) or (father) so we know who signed for the child.

How do I get a certified copy of my birth certificate?
Contact the Vital Statistics office in the state where you were born.

How long is a passport valid?
If you were 16 or Older when the passport was issued then your passport is valid for 10 Years

If you were 15 or Younger when the passport was issued then your passport is valid for 5 Years

Who should maintain a valid U.S. passport?
Passport Services recommends that the following U.S. citizens maintain valid U.S. passports.... Those
- with family living or traveling abroad
- thinking about a vacation abroad, or
- with a job that could require international travel.

In the event of an emergency involving a family member abroad, a short-notice airfare bargain, or an unexpected business trip, already having a valid U.S. passport will save time, money and stress.

What if there is an error in the passport I just received?
Passport Services apologizes for the error in your passport. (Our error rate is significantly below 1 percent, but, when it happens to you, that does not mean very much.) In order for us to correct the error as quickly as possible, please submit the following:

Your new passport;
Completed Form DS-19, Amendment/Validation Application; and
Evidence to document the correct information, such as a certified birth certificate, previous U.S. passport, certified marriage certificate, or naturalization/citizenship certificate.
Please include your departure date on Form DS-19. **Mail the above to the Rewrite Desk of the Passport Agency that issued your passport.**

How to Apply in Person for a U.S. Passport

IF . . .	Should You Apply In Person?
You are applying for a U.S. passport for the first time.	Yes
Your previous U.S. passport was lost, stolen, or damaged.	Yes
Your previous U.S. passport has expired & was issued more than 15 years ago.	Yes
Your previous passport has expired and it was issued when you were under 16.	Yes
Your name is changed since your passport was issued and you do not have a legal document formally changing your name.	Yes
You are a minor child 14 or older	Yes

NOTE:

For All Minors Under Age 14:
• The child need not routinely appear in person.
However, we reserve the right to request that your child appear.
• All applications for children under 14 require both parents' or legal guardians' consent.
(See Special Requirements for Children Under Age 14.)
•

For All Minors Age 14 to 17
• The minor MUST appear in person.
• For security reasons, parental consent may be requested.
• If your child does not have identification of his/her own, you need to accompany your child, present identification and co-sign the application.

To Apply in Person for a U.S. Passport You MUST:
1. Provide Application for Passport, Form DS-11   •   Or, forms can be obtained from any passport agency or acceptance facility. (Call to check hours of availability.)
• Many travel agents stock application forms for their clients as well.
NOTE: *Please do NOT sign the DS-11 application form until the Passport Acceptance Agent instructs you to do so.*

2. Present Proof of U.S. Citizenship   **You may prove U.S. Citizenship with any one of the following:**
• Previous U.S. Passport
• Certified birth certificate issued by the city, county or state
NOTE: A certified birth certificate has a registrar's raised, embossed, impressed or multicolored seal, registrar's signature, and the date the certificate was filed with the registrar's office, which must be within 1 year of your birth
• Consular Report of Birth Abroad or Certification of Birth
• Naturalization Certificate
• Certificate of Citizenship
A Delayed Birth Certificate filed more than one year after your birth may be acceptable if it:
• Listed the documentation used to create it and
• Signed by the attending physician or midwife, or, lists an affidavit signed by the parents, or shows early public records.
If you do NOT have a previous U.S. passport or a certified birth certificate, you will need:
1. Letter of No Record
Issued by the State with your name, date of birth, which years were searched for a birth record and that there is no birth certificate on file for you.
2. **AND as many of the following as possible:**
• baptismal certificate
• hospital birth certificate
• census record
• early school record
• family bible record
• doctor's record of post-natal care

NOTES:
- *These documents must be early public records showing the date and place of birth, preferably created within the first five years of your life.*
- *You may also submit an Affidavit of Birth, form DS-10, from an older blood relative, i.e., a parent, aunt, uncle, sibling, who has personal knowledge of your birth. It must be notarized or have the seal and signature of the acceptance agent.*

NOTE: *The following are NOT proof of citizenship*
- Voter registration cards
- Army discharge papers

We have new information on foreign-born children adopted by U.S. citizens.

NOTE: If you travel extensively, you may request a larger, 48-page passport at no additional cost. To do so, please attach a signed request for a 48-page passport to your application.

FOR MINORS UNDER THE AGE OF 14:
The citizenship evidence submitted for minors under the age of 14 must list both parents' names. Read more information on the citizenship requirements for minors under the age of 14.

3. Present Proof of Identity   You may prove your identity with any one of these, if you are recognizable:
- Previous U.S. passport
- Naturalization Certificate
- Certificate of Citizenship
- Current, valid
- Driver's license
- Government ID: city, state or federal
- Military ID: military and dependents

NOTE: *Your Social Security Card does NOT prove your identity.*

If none of these are available, you will need:

1.   **Some signature documents, not acceptable alone as ID**

(ex: a combination of documents, such as your Social Security card, credit card, bank card, library card, etc.)

AND

2.   **A person who can vouch for you. He/she must**
- Have known you for at least 2 years,
- Be a U.S. citizen or permanent resident,
- Have valid ID, and
- Fill out a Form DS-71 in the presence of a passport agent.

FOR MINORS UNDER THE AGE OF 14:
Normally, a child under the age of 14 does not need to appear in person. However, passport agents reserve the right to require the appearance of your child. Both parents or legal guardians must present evidence of identity when they apply for a minor under the age of 14. Read more information on the identity requirements for minors under the age of 14.

FOR MINORS 14 to 17:
- Your child MUST appear in person.
- For security reasons, parental consent may be requested.
- If your child does not have identification of his/her own, you need to accompany your child, present identification and co-sign the application.

4. Provide Two Passport Photos   **Your photographs must be:**
- 2x2 inches in size
- Identical
- Taken within the past 6 months, showing current appearance

232

- Color or black and white
- Full face, front view with a plain white or off-white background
- Between 1 inch and 1 3/8 inches from the bottom of the chin to the top of the head
- Taken in normal street attire
- Uniforms should not be worn in photographs except religious attire that is worn daily.
- Do not wear a hat or headgear that obscures the hair or hairline.
- If you normally wear prescription glasses, a hearing device, wig or similar articles, they should be worn for your picture.
- Dark glasses or nonprescription glasses with tinted lenses are not acceptable unless you need them for medical reasons. A medical certificate may be required.

NOTE: *Vending machine photos are not generally acceptable*

5. Pay the Applicable Fee   Passport Agencies Accept:
Credit Cards - VISA, MasterCard, American Express, Discover
Debit Cards (without pin numbers and not ATM cards)
Checks, money orders, bank drafts

Passport Acceptance Facilities:
All accept checks, money orders, bank drafts
Most accept exact cash
Some accept credit cards
Expedite Fee: (See How to Get Your Passport in a Hurry.)

Provide a Social Security Number   If you do not provide your Social Security Number, the Internal Revenue Service may impose a $500 penalty. If you have any questions please call your nearest IRS office.

Where to Apply for a Passport in the U.S.

Special Requirements for Children Under Age 14
As required by Public Law 106-113
Effective July 2, 2001
Effective July 2, 2001,Minors Under Age 14 MUST:

1. Provide Application Form DS-11
- Or, forms can be obtained from any passport agency or acceptance facility. (Call to check hours of availability.)
- Many travel agents stock application forms for their clients as well.
NOTE: *Please do NOT sign the DS-11 application form until the Passport Acceptance Agent instructs you to do so.*

2. Submit Proof of U.S. Citizenship (for minors under age 14) Note: Previous U.S. passports are not acceptable as proof of relationship to the applying parent(s)/guardian(s). Please see box #3 for documents that are acceptable as proof of relationship.
You will need to submit one of the following:
- Certified U.S. birth certificate; or
- Previous fully valid U.S. Passport; or
- Report of Birth Abroad (Form FS-240); or
- Certification of Birth Abroad (Form DS-1350); or
- Certificate of Citizenship or Naturalization from INS.
NOTE: *A certified birth certificate has a registrar's raised, embossed, Impressed or multicolored seal, registrar's signature, and the Date the certificate was filed with the registrar's office, which must be within 1 year of your birth*
A Delayed Birth Certificate filed more than one year after your birth may be acceptable if it:

233

- Listed the documentation used to create it and
- Signed by the attending physician or midwife, or, lists an affidavit signed by the parents, or shows early public records.

If you do NOT have a previous U.S. passport or a certified birth certificate, you will need:
1.   Letter of No Record
Issued by the state with your name, date of birth, which years were searched for a birth record and that there is no birth certificate on file for you.
2.   AND as many of the following as possible:
- Baptismal certificate
- Hospital birth certificate
- Census record
- Early school record
- Family bible record
- Doctor's record of post-natal care

NOTES:
- *These documents must be early public records showing the date and place of birth, preferably created within the first five years of your life.*
- *You may also submit an Affidavit of Birth, form DS-10A, from an older blood relative, i.e., a parent, aunt, uncle, sibling, who has personal knowledge of your birth. It must be notarized or have the seal and signature of the acceptance agent.*

NOTE: The following are NOT proof of citizenship
- Voter registration cards
- Army discharge papers

NOTE: If you travel extensively, you may request a larger, 48-page passport at no additional cost. To do so, please attach a signed request for a 48-page passport to your application.

3. Present Evidence of Child's Relationship to Parents/Guardians (for minors under age 14)   Note: Previous U.S. passports are not acceptable as proof of relationship to the applying parent(s)/guardian(s).

You will need to submit one of the following:
- Certified U.S. birth certificate **(with parents' names)**; or
- Certified Foreign Birth Certificate **(with parents' names and translation, if necessary)**; or
- Report of Birth Abroad **(Form FS-240) (with parents' names)**; or
- Certification of Birth Abroad **(Form DS-1350) (with parents' names)**; or
- Adoption Decree **(with adopting parents' names)**; or
- Court Order Establishing Custody; or
- Court Order Establishing Guardianship.

NOTE: If the parent(s)'/guardian's name(s) is/are other than that on these documents, evidence of legal name change is required.
4. Provide Parental Identification (for minors under age 14)   Each parent or guardian must submit one of the following:
- Valid Drivers License
- Valid Official U.S. Military ID
- Valid U.S. Gov't ID
- Valid U.S. or Foreign Passport with recognizable photo
- Naturalization/Citizenship Certificate from INS with recognizable photo
- Alien Resident Card from INS

NOTE: *Your Social Security Card does NOT prove your identity.*
If none of these are available, you will need:
1.   Some signature documents, not acceptable alone as ID

(ex: a combination of documents, such as your Social Security card, credit card, bank card, library card, etc.)

AND

2.   **A person who can vouch for you. He/she must**
- Have known you for at least 2 years,
- Be a U.S. citizen or permanent resident,
- Have valid ID, and
- Fill out a Form DS-71 in the presence of a passport agent.

5. Present Parental Application Permission Documentation (for minors under age 14)

1. Both parents must appear together and sign **or**

2. One parent appears, signs, **and** submits second parent's Statement of Consent: Issuance of a Passport to a Minor Under Age 14, Form DS-3053 authorizing passport issuance for the child **or**

3. One parents appears, signs, and submits primary evidence of sole authority to apply (such as one of the following):

- Child's certified U.S. or foreign birth certificate (with translation, if necessary) listing only applying parent; or
- *Consular Report of Birth Abroad (Form FS-240) or Certification of Birth Abroad (Form DS-1350)* listing *only* applying parent; or
- Court order granting sole custody to the applying parent (unless child's travel is restricted by that order); or
- Adoption decree (if applying parents is *sole* adopting parent); or
- Court order specifically permitting applying parent's or guardian's travel with the child; or
- Judicial declaration of incompetence of non-applying parent; or
- Death certificate of non-applying parent.

If none of the above documentation is available, the applying parent/guardian should submit Form DS-3053: Statement of Consent: Issuance of a Passport to a Minor Under Age 14.

NOTE:

A third-party in loco parentis applying on behalf of a minor under the age of 14 must submit a notarized written statement or affidavit from both parents or guardians authorizing a third-party to apply for a passport. When the statement or affidavit is from only one parent/guardian, the third-party must present evidence of sole custody of the authorizing parent/guardian.

6. Provide Two Passport Photos   **Your photographs must be:**
- 2x2 inches in size
- Identical
- Taken within the past 6 months, showing current appearance
- Color *or* black and white
- Full face, front view with a plain white or off-white background
- Between 1 inch and 1 3/8 inches from the bottom of the chin to the top of the head
- Taken in normal street attire
- Uniforms should not be worn in photographs except religious attire that is worn daily.
- Do *not* wear a hat or headgear that obscures the hair or hairline.
- If you normally wear prescription glasses, a hearing device, wig or similar articles, they should be worn for your picture.

Dark glasses or nonprescription glasses with tinted lenses are not acceptable unless you need them for medical reasons. A medical certificate may be required.

NOTE: *Vending machine photos are not generally acceptable*

7. Pay the Applicable Fee

Passport Agencies Accept: Credit Cards – VISA, MasterCard, American Express, Discover
Debit Cards (without pin numbers and not ATM cards) Checks, Money orders, Bank drafts
Passport Acceptance Facilities:
All accept Checks, Money orders, Bank drafts
Most accept Exact Cash

Some accept credit cards
Expedite Fee: (*See How to Get Your Passport in a Hurry* .)

8. Provide a Social Security Number   If you do not provide your Social Security Number, the Internal Revenue Service may impose a $500 penalty. If you have any questions please call your nearest IRS office.

How to Apply for a Passport Renewal

Should You Apply for a Passport Renewal by Mail?
YES, If You...
1.   Already have a passport that is not damaged; **and**
2.   Received it within the past 15 years; **and**
3.   Were over age 16 when it was issued; **and**
4.   Still have the same name as in passport (or you can legally document your name change).
NOTES:
•   Residents abroad should renew their passports at nearest U.S. Embassy or U.S. Consulate.
•   Passports renewed by mail in the U.S. can only be forwarded to U.S. addresses.
•   If you mutilate or alter your U.S. passport, you may invalidate it and risk possible prosecution under the law (Section 1543 of Title 22 of the U.S. Code).
•   If your passport has **been mutilated, altered or damaged**, you cannot apply by mail. You must **apply in person.** (*See How to Apply in Person.*)

If you can, then How Do You Renew Your Passport By Mail?
1. Complete Application For Passport By Mail, form DS-82
•   Be sure to sign and date your application.
2. Attach to it:
•   Your most recent passport
•   Two identical passport photographs
•   And, a $55 fee.
•   If you need your passport urgently, you may request Expedited Service.
NOTE: Your previous passport will be returned to you with your new passport.

NOTE: If you travel extensively, you may request a larger, 48-page passport at no additional cost. To do so, please attach a signed request for a 48-page passport to your application.

3. If your name has changed since your passport was issued:
•   Enclose a certified copy of the legal document specifying your name change (e.g. marriage certificate, divorce decree, adoption decree, or court order).
•   No photocopies accepted.
NOTE: If your name has changed by other means, you must apply in person. (See How to Apply in Person.)

4. Mail in a padded envelope to:
National Passport Center
P.O. Box 371971
Pittsburgh, PA 15250-9971
5. If you use an overnight delivery service that does not deliver to a post office box, then send it to:
        Passport Services - Lockbox
Attn: Passport Supervisor 371971
500 Ross Street, Rm. 154-0670
Pittsburgh, PA 15262-0001
NOTE: Include a prepaid overnight return envelope. Please note that overnight service will not speed up processing time unless the $60 fee for expedited service is also included.

How Can You Get Your Passport in a Hurry?

After you apply - You will receive your passport

Expedited Service

- Cost, **in addition** to regular application fees, is **$60** per application plus overnight delivery costs.
- Two-way overnight delivery is strongly suggested.
- If you mail in - clearly mark **Expedited** on the envelope.
- Anyone may request expedited service for any type of application (e.g., first-time applications, renewals, amendments of existing passports, etc.) See:
- How do I change my name on my passport?
- How to add extra visa pages to my passport?
- How do I apply to renew my passport?
- Passport applications sent together or at the same time do not necessarily remain together.
- Passports will be mailed separately.

Ordinarily, if you paid additionally for expedited service and two-way overnight delivery
Within about 2 weeks

Routine Service   • Include your departure date on your application. ordinarily, Within 6 weeks
Life or Death Emergencies   Call The National Passport Information Center

Payment Method

Passport Agency

- Major Credit Card - Visa, MasterCard, American Express, Discover or debit card (Not ATM and without a pin)
- Personal Check
- Bank Draft, Postal or Commercial Money Order

Mail-in

- Personal Check or Money Order (Pay to "U.S. Department of State")
- NO CASH

Post Office, Clerk of Court, Other Location

- Check with the facility for type of payment accepted.

Protect Yourself From Identity Fraud!
How to Report Your Lost or Stolen Passport

Please, provide detailed answers to all questions, sign, and submit Form DS-64, Statement Regarding a Lost or Stolen Passport, to:
US Department of State
Passport Services
Consular Lost/Stolen Passport Section
1111 19th Street, NW, Suite 500
Washington, DC 20036
Or call us 24 hours/day at: (202) 955-0430
Voice mail - For non-business hours, Eastern Time

IMPORTANT NOTICE

The information you provide on the DS-64, Statement Regarding a Lost or Stolen Passport will be entered in our Consular Lost/Stolen Passport System.

Passports reported lost or stolen are invalidated and can no longer be used for travel.

If you recover the passport after you have reported it lost or stolen, please submit it to the address listed above. When you submit it, if requested - we will cancel it and return it to you. If not requested, it will be destroyed.

Once a passport is reported lost or stolen, it cannot be re-validated.

237

How to Replace a Lost or Stolen Passport
See How to Replace a Lost or Stolen Passport.

How to Replace a Lost or Stolen Passport
To Replace Your Lost or Stolen Passport You Should:
1. Complete, Application for Passport, Form DS-11
Complete Question #18 as follows:
* Write your name as it appeared in your passport
* Write the approximate date of issue.
* Include the passport number if known
* Under "DISPOSITION", mark the appropriate box.
* If your passport was expired, write "EXPIRED" next to the "OTHER" box.
Note: If you travel extensively, you may request a larger, 48-page passport at no additional cost. To do so, please attach a signed request for a 48-page passport to your application.

2. Complete, Statement Regarding Lost Or Stolen Passport, Form DS-64
* **ONLY IF** your lost/stolen passport is **still valid.**
* Fill in as much of the passport information as you can.
* Answer all the other questions in detail.
3. Submit your form(s)
* To a passport acceptance facility.
* You will also need photos, documentation and fees.
See How to Apply in Person.

How to Add Extra Pages to Your U.S. Passport
IF:
1. Your passport pages are full **Then:** Mail completed form DS-19, Passport Amendment/Validation Application, with
your passport to the following address:
Charleston Passport Center
Attention: Amendments
1269 Holland Street
Charleston, SC 29405
* Under "Other Action Requested" write Add extra pages

2. **IF** You travel extensively and need a new passport **Then:** You may request a larger, 48-page passport at no additional cost. To do so, please attach a
signed request for a 48-page passport to your application.
NOTE: There is no fee for this service unless you require expedited service.
(See How do I get my passport in a hurry?)

See Special Requirements for Children Under Age 14.

How to Change Your Name in Your Valid U.S. Passport
IF:
Then:
1. **Your name has been legally changed since your passport was issued**
* Send a completed form DS-19, Passport Amendment/Validation Application, a certified copy of your marriage certificate or your name change court decree, and your current valid passport to the following address:
Charleston Passport Center
Attention: Amendments
1269 Holland Street
Charleston, SC 29405

238

**Photocopies and notarized copies are not acceptable
for passport purposes.**
•   If your name has changed by other means, you must apply in person. See How to **Apply in
Person**
NOTE: There is no fee for this service unless you require expedited service.
(See How do I get my passport in a hurry?)

U.S. Passports Will No Longer be Issued Abroad
**All passports, except those required for urgent travel, will be issued in the United States
using the new more secure photo-digitized imaging system.**
Effective April 8, 2002, American citizens residing or traveling abroad, who require issuance of a U.S.
passport, will be issued the latest, state-of-the-art passport. It incorporates a digitized image with other
enhanced security features. Because this technology is not available at U.S. embassies and consulates,
overseas passport issuance is being transferred to the National Passport Processing Center in Portsmouth,
New Hampshire.

Travel documents in the post-September 11 world have become even more important. The new passport has
many features that make it one of the most secure travel documents produced anywhere in the world.
Getting these more secure passports into circulation will help minimize the misuse of American passports by
criminals, terrorists, and others.

This new procedure will increase processing time at U.S. embassies and consulates, but the Department is
committed to ensuring that American citizens receive secure documents in a timely manner. American
citizens overseas are encouraged to apply early for renewal of expiring passports.

U.S. embassies and consulates will continue to issue passports that are needed for urgent travel. However,
such passports will be limited in validity, and cannot be extended. Bearers will be required to exchange, at
no additional cost, their limited-validity passports for a full-validity digitized passports upon completion of
their urgent travel. Information on applying for a U.S. passport, passport application forms and
requirements, and other travel-related information can be accessed through the Department of State's web
site at: http://travel.state.gov.

Chapter 24

More Information and Advice from the U.S. State Department, Customs, Transportation, Agriculture, Social Security...

[The information in this chapter is reprinted verbatim from the various U.S. government Departments It is intended to serve as advice to Americans traveling abroad.]

TRAVELING OUT OF/INTO THE U.S.; NEW GUIDELINES/PROCEDURES

(INFORMATION FROM THE U.S. TRANSPORTATION SECURITY ADMINISTRATION Post 9-11)

Prepared for Takeoff?

The following is the Transportation Security Administration's (TSA) comprehensive travel guide for you, the flying public. Here you will find everything you need to know about new airport security measures. You will discover a list of timesaving tips, information on assistance for special needs, the latest list of <u>prohibited and permitted items</u>, and other information that will help guide you smoothly through the security process.

Do you know what shoes you can wear that will help you move through the security line more quickly? Check "<u>Travel Preparation</u>" for suggestions on what to wear to the airport and how to pack for your trip.

Do you know that you can bring a paper cup of coffee through the passenger checkpoint but not a can of soda? See the section "<u>Security Procedures</u>" to learn about new procedures and to find timesaving tips that will help you minimize your wait time at the airport.

Do you require special assistance? Do you have religious or cultural concerns? Are you flying with family or traveling with film or sports equipment? See the " <u>Special Considerations</u>" section for answers and guidance.

The Prepare for Takeoff Campaign
The Prepare for Takeoff campaign reflects TSA's commitment to provide world-class security and world-class customer service. TSA's goal is to supply the traveling public with information that will not only help to ensure security, but will make air travel more efficient and less stressful for all.

Everyone needs to play an active role in contributing to air travel security. Together, airlines, airports, travel agents, government officials, and the public can contribute to making air travel safe, secure, and efficient.

Interested in Becoming a Partner?
The TSA is working in partnership with members of the travel and tourism community, and with disability groups and others, to get the word out to the traveling public. Using information provided by the TSA, partners are updating their own websites, providing links to the TSA website and distributing information to passengers through their own customer service departments.

Permitted & Prohibited Items
Can I Take It With Me? - Permitted and Prohibited Items
Prohibited items are weapons, explosives, incendiaries, and include items that are seemingly harmless but may be used as weapons-the so-called "dual use" items. You may not bring these items to security checkpoints without authorization.

What Happens to Prohibited Items?
If you bring a prohibited item to the checkpoint, you may be criminally and/or civilly prosecuted or, at the least, asked to rid yourself of the item. A screener and/or Law Enforcement Officer will make this determination, depending on what the item is and the circumstances. This is because bringing a prohibited item to a security checkpoint - even accidentally - is illegal.

241

Your prohibited item may be detained for use in an investigation and, if necessary, as evidence in your criminal and/or civil prosecution. If permitted by the screener or Law Enforcement Officer, you may be allowed to: consult with the airlines for possible assistance in placing the prohibited item in checked baggage; withdraw with the item from the screening checkpoint at that time; make other arrangements for the item, such as taking it to your car; or, voluntarily abandon the item. Items that are voluntarily abandoned cannot be recovered and will not be returned to you.

The prohibited and permitted items list is not intended to be all-inclusive and is updated as necessary. To ensure everyone's security, the screener may determine that an item not on this chart is prohibited.

The list of items applies to flights originating within the United States. Please check with your airline or travel agent for restrictions at destinations outside of the United States.

The following chart outlines items that are permitted and items that are prohibited in your carry-on or checked baggage. You should note that some items are allowed in your checked baggage, but not your carry-on. Also pay careful attention to the "Notes" included at the bottom of each section – they contain important information about restrictions.

The prohibited and permitted items chart is not intended to be all-inclusive and is updated as necessary. To ensure everyone's security, the screener may determine that an item not on the prohibited items chart is prohibited. In addition, the screener may also determine that an item on the permitted chart is dangerous and therefore may not be brought through the security checkpoint.

The chart applies to flights originating within the United States. Please check with your airline or travel agent for restrictions at destinations outside of the United States.

For updates and for more information, visit our website at www.TSATravelTips.us or call our Consumer Response Center toll-free at 1-866-289-9673 or email TellTSA@tsa.dot.gov.

Can I take it?	Carry-on	Checked
Personal Items		
Cigar Cutters	Yes	Yes
Corkscrews	Yes	Yes
Cuticle Cutters	Yes	Yes
Eyeglass Repair Tools (including screwdrivers)	Yes	Yes
Eyelash Curlers	Yes	Yes
Knitting and Crochet Needles	Yes	Yes
Knives, round-bladed butter or plastic	Yes	Yes
Nail Clippers	Yes	Yes
Nail Files	Yes	Yes
Personal care or toiletries with		
aerosols, in limited quantities (such as hairsprays, deodorants)	Yes	Yes
Safety Razors (including disposable razors)	Yes	Yes
Scissors-plastic or metal with blunt tips	Yes	Yes
Scissors-metal with pointed tips	No	
Toy Transformer Robots	Yes	Yes
Toy Weapons (if not realistic replicas)	Yes	Yes
Tweezers	Yes	Yes
Umbrellas (allowed in carry-on baggage once they have been inspected to ensure that prohibited items are not concealed)	Yes	Yes
Walking Canes (allowed in carry-on baggage once they have been inspected to ensure that prohibited items are not concealed)	Yes	Yes

Note Some personal care items containing aerosol are regulated as hazardous materials. The FAA regulates hazardous materials. This information is summarized at http://cas.faa.gov/these.html

Medication and Special Needs Devices
Braille Note-Taker, Slate and Stylus, Augmentation Devices Yes   Yes
Diabetes-Related Supplies/Equipment, (once inspected to ensure prohibited items are not concealed) including: insulin and insulin loaded dispensing products; vials or box of individual vials; jet injectors; pens; infusers; and preloaded syringes; and an unlimited number of unused syringes, when accompanied by insulin; lancets; blood glucose meters; blood glucose meter test strips; insulin pumps; and insulin pump supplies. Insulin in any form or dispenser must be properly marked with a professionally printed label identifying the medication or manufacturer's name or pharmaceutical label.
                    Yes   Yes
Nitroglycerine pills or spray for medical use (if properly marked with a professionally printed label identifying the medication or manufacturer's name or pharmaceutical label Yes   Yes
Prosthetic Device Tools and Appliances, including drill, allen wrenches, pullsleeves used to put on or remove prosthetic devices, if carried by the individual with the prosthetic device or his or her companion
                    Yes   Yes
Electronic Devices
Camcorders   Yes   Yes
Camera Equipment
The checked baggage screening equipment will damage undeveloped film in camera equipment. We recommend that you either put undeveloped film and cameras containing undeveloped film in your carry-on baggage or take undeveloped film with you to the checkpoint and ask the screener to conduct a hand-inspection.

	Yes	Yes
Laptop Computers	Yes	Yes
Mobile Phones	Yes	Yes
Pagers	Yes	Yes
Personal Data Assistants (PDA's)	Yes	Yes

Note Check with your airline or travel agent for restrictions on the use of these and other electronic items during your flight.

Sharp Objects

Box Cutters	No	Yes
Ice Axes/Ice Picks	No	Yes
Knives (any length and type except round-bladed, butter, and plastic cutlery) No		
Yes		
Meat Cleavers	No	Yes
Razor-Type Blades, such as box cutters, utility knives, razor		
blades not in a cartridge, but excluding safety razors	No	Yes
Sabers	No	Yes
Scissors – metal with pointed tips		
Scissors with plastic or metal blunt tips are permitted in your carry-on. No		Yes
Swords	No	Yes

Note Any sharp objects in checked baggage should be sheathed or securely wrapped to prevent injury to baggage
handlers and inspectors.

Sporting Goods

Baseball Bats	No	Yes
Bows and Arrows	No	Yes
Cricket Bats	No	Yes
Golf Clubs	No	Yes
Hockey Sticks	No	Yes
Lacrosse Sticks	No	Yes
Pool Cues	No	Yes
Ski Poles	No	Yes
Spear Guns	No	Yes

Note Any sharp objects in checked baggage should be sheathed or securely wrapped to prevent injury to baggage handlers and security screeners.

Guns and Firearms
Ammunition
Check with your airline or travel agent to see if ammunition is permitted in checked baggage on the airline you are lying. If ammunition is permitted, it must be declared to the airline at check-in. Small arms ammunitions for personal
 use must be securely packed in fiber, wood or metal boxes, or other packaging specifically designed to carry small
amounts of ammunition. Ask about imitations or fees, if any, that apply.

	No	Yes
BB guns	No	Yes
Compressed Air Guns	No	Yes
Firearms	No	Yes
Flare Guns	No	No
Gun Lighters	No	No
Gun Powder	No	No

244

Parts of Guns and Firearms	No	Yes
Pellet Guns	No	Yes
Realistic Replicas of Firearms	No	Yes
Starter Pistols	No	Yes

Note Check with your airline or travel agent to see if firearms are permitted in checked baggage on the airline you are flying. Ask about limitations or fees, if any, that apply. Firearms carried as checked baggage MUST be unloaded, packed in a locked hard-sided gun case, and declared to the airline at check-in. Only you, the passenger, may have the key or combination.

Tools

Axes and Hatchets	No	Yes
Cattle Prods	No	Yes
Crowbars	No	Yes
Hammers	No	Yes
Drills (including cordless portable power drills)	No	Yes
Saws (including cordless portable power saws)	No	Yes
Screwdrivers (except those in eyeglass repair kits)	No	Yes
Tools (including but not limited to wrenches and pliers)	No	Yes
Wrenches and Pliers	No	Yes

Note Any sharp objects in checked baggage should be sheathed or securely wrapped to prevent injury to baggage handlers and security screeners.

Martial Arts/Self Defense Items

Billy Clubs	**No**	**Yes**
Black Jacks	No	Yes
Brass Knuckles	No	Yes
Kubatonsq	No	Yes

Mace/Pepper Spray
One 118 ml or 4 Fl. oz. container of mace or pepper spray is permitted in checked baggage provided it is equipped with a safety mechanism to prevent accidental discharge. For more information on these and other hazardous materials, visit http://cas.faa.gov/these.html .

	No	Yes
Martial Arts Weapons	No	Yes
Night Sticks	No	Yes
Nunchakus	No	Yes

Martial Arts/Self Defense Items

Stun Guns/Shocking Devices	No	Yes
Throwing Stars	No	Yes

Note Any sharp objects in checked baggage should be sheathed or securely wrapped to prevent injury to baggage handlers and security screeners.

Explosive Materials

Blasting caps	No	No
Dynamite	No	No
Fireworks	No	No
Flares in any form	No	No
Hand Grenades	No	No
Plastic Explosives	No	No

Flammable Items

Aerosol (any except for personal care or toiletries in limited quantities) No		No

Fuels (including cooking fuels and any flammable liquid fuel)	No	No
Gasoline	No	No
Gas Torches	No	No
Lighter Fluid	No	No
Strike-anywhere Matches	No	No
Turpentine and paint thinner	No	No

Note There are other hazardous materials that are regulated by the FAA. This information is summarized at http://cas.faa.gov/these.html

Disabling Chemicals and Other Dangerous Items		
Chlorine for pools and spas	No	No
Compressed Gas Cylinders (including fire extinguishers)	No	No
Liquid Bleach	No	No
Spillable Batteries (except those in wheelchairs)	No	No
Spray Paint	No	No
Tear Gas	No	No

Note There are other hazardous materials that are regulated by the FAA. This information is summarized at http://cas.faa.gov/these.html

Travel Preparation

There are preparations you can make before you arrive at the airport to help you move more quickly and efficiently through the new security processes. Here you will find suggestions on what to wear to the airport and how to pack for your trip. We've also included a pre-flight checklist to help you *Prepare for Takeoff.*

Dress the Part
Security does not require any particular style or type of clothing. However, certain clothing and accessories can set off an alarm on the metal detector and slow you down. Here you will find tips to help you through the checkpoint.

Pack Smart
There are restrictions on what you can pack in your carry-on and checked baggage. All of your baggage will be screened and possibly hand-searched as part of the new security measures. This inspection may include emptying most or all of the articles in your bag. Here you will find tips to help you pack.

Final Checklist
You're dressed, packed and ready to go. Or are you? Here is a pre-flight checklist to help you Prepare for Takeoff. Contact your airline or travel agent for additional information.

By familiarizing yourself with the security process and following these tips and recommendations you will be able to play an active role in ensuring your own safety and comfort.

Be Prepared - Dress the Part

Be aware that any metal detected at the checkpoint must be identified. If you set off the alarm, you will be required to undergo a secondary screening, including a hand-wanding and a pat-down inspection.

You can remove metal items at the security checkpoint and place them in the bins provided. The bins will be sent through the X-ray machine. You can save time, however, by not wearing metal items or by placing such items in your carry-on baggage before you get in line.

TIP: Avoid wearing clothing, jewelry, or other accessories that contain metal when traveling.

- Jewelry (pins, necklaces, bracelets, rings, watches, earrings, body piercings, cuff links, lanyard or bolo tie)
- Shoes with steel tips, heels, shanks, buckles or nails
- Clothing with metal buttons, snaps or studs

246

- Metal hair barrettes or other hair decoration
- Belt buckles
- Under-wire brassieres

Hidden items such as body piercings may result in a pat-down inspection. You may ask to remove your body piercing in private as an alternative to the pat-down search.

TIP: Avoid placing metal items in your pockets.

- Keys, loose change, lighters
- Mobile phones, pagers, and personal data assistants (PDAs)

TIP: Instead, place jewelry and other metal items in your carry-on baggage until you clear security.

TIP: Pack your outer coat or jacket in your baggage when possible.

Outer coats including trench coats, ski jackets, leather jackets, overcoats and parkas must go through the X-ray machine for inspection. If you choose to wear an outer coat to the checkpoint, you will need to either place it in your carry-on or put it in the bin that is provided for you. You will not need to remove suit jackets or blazers unless requested by the screener.

Plan Ahead - Pack Smart

Carry-on Baggage is a small piece of luggage you take onboard the airplane with you. You are allowed one carry-on in addition to one personal item such as a laptop computer, purse, small backpack, briefcase, or camera case.

Checked Baggage is luggage you check in at the ticket counter or at curbside. It will not be accessible during your flight.

Packing Tips

Below are a number of tips for packing your checked baggage that will help to speed your trip and ensure that your checked bag makes the flight with you.

- Don't put film in your checked baggage, as the screening equipment will damage it.
- Pack shoes, boots, sneakers, and other footwear on top of other contents in your luggage.
- Avoid over-packing your bag so that the screener will be able to easily reseal your bag if it is opened for inspection. If possible, spread your contents over several bags. Check with your airline or travel agent for maximum weight limitations.
- Avoid packing food and drink items in checked baggage.
- Don't stack piles of books or documents on top of each other; spread them out within your baggage.

The following general packing tips apply to both carry-on and checked baggage and will help you to move through the screening process more quickly:

- Do NOT pack or bring prohibited items to the airport. See permitted and prohibited items.
- Put all undeveloped film and cameras with film in your carry-on baggage. If your bag will pass through the X-ray machine more than 5 times ask for a hand inspection to prevent damage.
- Check ahead of time with your airline or travel agent to determine the airline's baggage policy, including number of pieces you can bring and size and weight limitations.
- Carry-on baggage is limited to one carry-on bag plus one personal item. Personal items include laptops, purses, small backpacks, briefcases, or camera cases. Remember, 1 + 1.
- Don't forget to place identification tags with your name, address and phone number on all of your baggage, including your laptop computer. It is a good idea to place an identification tag inside your baggage as well.
- Avoid overpacking so that your articles don't spill out if your bag is opened for inspection.
- Think carefully about the personal items you place in your carry-on baggage. The screeners may have to open your bag and examine its contents.
- Consider putting personal belongings in clear plastic bags to reduce the chance that a TSA screener will have to handle them.
- Wait to wrap your gifts. Be aware that wrapped gifts may need to be opened for inspection. This applies to both carry-on and checked baggage.

Baggage Security Checkpoints

As of January 1, 2003, TSA began screening

247

100% of checked baggage at all 429 commercial airports across the United States. You will encounter one of the processes described below at the airport. Please be aware that you will not be able to access your bags after they are screened no matter which process you encounter. Therefore, you should remove everything that you want to take on the plane with you before you hand over your checked bag for screening.

Checked Bag Screening Processes
No change -- You check in at the ticket counter or with the skycaps as you have in the past. The new screening equipment will be out of your view and the screening of your checked baggage will occur behind the scenes.

Ticket counter first -- You will still check-in at the ticket counter or with the skycap as you have in the past, but you will next proceed to a new baggage screening area nearby. At most airports, you will next take your checked bag to the checked baggage screening area, where it will be screened there and afterwards delivered directly to your airline for loading. At some airports, someone will take your checked baggage from you at the ticket counter and deliver it to the screening area. In a growing number of airports, you will have the option to drop off your bags at the screening area and proceed directly to your gate without waiting for your bags to be screened.

Baggage screening first -- You will go first to the checked baggage screening area in the airport lobby. After baggage screening, the screener will direct you to the ticket counter and an authorized person will bring your bag from the screening area to the ticket counter for you to complete the check-in process.

Please watch for signs and other instructions that will direct you to the correct line. Unless you see signs directing you otherwise, go to the ticket counter to check-in with your airline.

Several methods are being used to screen 100% of checked baggage. The most common methods that you will encounter involve electronic screening, either by an Explosives Detection System (EDS) or Explosives Trace Detection (ETD) device.

The EDS machines are the large machines that can be over 20 feet long and weigh up three tons. Your baggage will be loaded on a conveyor belt of the EDS machine by a screener for screening. If your bag requires further inspection, it may be brought to an ETD machine.

The ETD machine are much smaller machines, and are the primary machine used in many airports. When your bag is screened with an ETD machine, the screener will take a swab of your bag and then place the swab into the ETD machine for analysis.

There are other methods that may be used at airports to ensure that 100% of all bags are screened. Regardless of which system is used, all checked bags will be screened before they are loaded onto the plane.

Unlocking Checked Bags
TSA suggests that you help prevent the need to break your locks by keeping your bags unlocked. In some cases, screeners will have to open your baggage as part of the screening process. If your bag is unlocked, then TSA will simply open the bag and screen the bag. However, if the bag is locked and TSA needs to open your bag, then locks may have to be broken. You may keep your bag locked if you choose, but TSA is not liable for damage caused to locked bags that must be opened for security purposes. If you are transporting a firearm, please refer to the on "Transporting Firearms and Ammunition" section at the bottom of this page for directions on locking your bag.

If TSA screeners open your bag during the screening procedure, they will close it with a tamper evident seal and place a notice in your bag alerting you to the fact that TSA screeners opened your bag for inspection.

In the near future, TSA will provide seals at the airport for you to use to secure your bags as an alternative to locks. Until that time, you may want to consider purchasing standard "cable ties," which can be found at your local hardware store. The 4 to 5 inch variety cable ties generally work best since they are the easiest to remove at your destination and can be used to close almost every bag with zippers. If TSA needs to inspect your bag, the screeners will cut off the seal and replace it with another seal.

Missing Contents
TSA screeners exercise great care during the screening process to ensure that your contents are returned to your bag every time a bag needs to be opened. TSA will assess, on an individual basis, any loss or damage claims made to TSA. You may

call the TSA Consumer Response Center toll-free at 1-866-289-9673 if you have questions.

See the section on "Travel Preparation" for a complete listing of other packing and timesaving tips.

Transporting Firearms and Ammunition

Subject to state, local, and airline restrictions, you may still transport a firearm and ammunition in your checked baggage provided it is declared to the aircraft operator (airline) at check in and that you comply with other applicable regulations. Please note that you should never unlock your bag if you are carrying a firearm and your bag serves as the locked, hard-sided case for transporting your firearm.

See the section "Travel Preparation, Frequently Asked Questions" for more details on transporting firearms and ammunition.

Travelers & Consumers

Can I still transport a firearm in checked baggage?

Subject to state and local restrictions on transporting firearms, you may still transport a firearm in your checked baggage. However, you should first check with your airline or travel agent to see if firearms are permitted in checked baggage on the airline you are flying. Ask about limitations or fees, if any, that apply. Firearms carried as checked baggage MUST be unloaded, packed in a locked hard-sided gun case, and declared to the airline at check-in. Only you, the passenger, may have the key or combination.

Ammunition may be packed in the same locked container as the firearm, so long as it is not loaded in the firearm. Small-arms ammunition must also be declared to the air carrier and placed in an appropriate container ? securely packed in fiber, wood or metal boxes or other packaging specifically designed to carry small amount of ammunition. In addition, small-arms ammunition must also be declared to the air carrier and placed in an appropriate container: "securely packed in fiber, wood, or metal boxes, or other packaging specifically designed to carry small amounts of ammunition." Ammunition may be packed in the same locked container as the firearm, so long as it is not loaded in the firearm.

What happens if my belongings are missing from my bag when I arrive at my destination?

TSA screeners exercise great care during the screening process to ensure that your contents are returned to your bag every time a bag needs to be opened. TSA will assess any claims made to TSA on an individual basis.

Are there any tips on packing that will help me save time at the airport?

There are some tips that will help you to speed your trip through the screening process: 1. Don't put film in your checked baggage, as the screening equipment will damage it. 2. Consider putting personal belongings in clear plastic bags to reduce the chance that a TSA screener will have to handle them. 3. Pack shoes, boots, sneakers, and other footwear on top of other contents in your luggage. 4. Avoid over-packing your bag so that the screener will be able to easily reseal your bag if it is opened for inspection. If possible, spread your contents over several bags. Check with your airline or travel agent for maximum weight limitations. 5. Avoid packing food and drink items in checked baggage. 6. Don't stack piles of books or documents on top of each other; spread them out within your baggage.

Is the check-in procedure different now that TSA is screening all checked baggage?

This depends on the airport from which you are departing. If you are at an airport where the screening equipment is "behind the scenes," you will not notice any difference. In many airports you will see screening equipment in the lobby. Unless you see signs directing you otherwise, go to the ticket counter to check-in with your airline. In a limited number of airports, you will be directed to proceed to baggage screening before you check-in with your airline. Please watch for these signs and other instructions to ensure that you go the correct line.

Will TSA relock my bag if it is opened for screening?

If TSA screeners open your bag during the screening procedure, they will close it with a security seal. In addition, TSA will place a notice in your bag alerting you to the fact that TSA screeners opened your bag for inspection. Our highly trained screeners will take great care to secure your bag for the rest of your trip.

Should I lock my luggage?

In some cases, the TSA will have to open your baggage as part of the screening process. If your bag is unlocked, then TSA will simply open the bag and screen the bag. However, if the bag is

249

locked and TSA needs to open your bag, then locks may have to be broken. Therefore, TSA suggests that you help prevent the need to break your locks by keeping your bag unlocked. In the near future, TSA will provide seals at the airport for you to use to secure your luggage as an alternative to locking your bag. Until that time, you may want to consider purchasing standard cable ties to secure your bags if it has zippers.

Will all checked baggage be screened on January 1?

The TSA will be screening all checked baggage on January 1 using several methods. Some of the screening equipment will be visible in the lobby while other equipment will be "behind the scenes." Whether you see differences or not, please be assured that all checked bags will be screened.

How early should I arrive at the airport?

Check with your airline or travel agent. Recommended check-in times differ by airline and airport.

Can I access the gate area if I am not a passenger?

1) UNACCOMPANIED CHILD, ELDERLY PERSON, OR SPECIAL NEEDS: If you are going to assist an unaccompanied child, elderly person, or person with special needs through the security checkpoint, you will need to get a gate pass/authorization at the airport ticket counter of your airline. 2) FREQUENT FLYERS CLUBS AND LOUNGES: When airline and airport clubs and lounges are located beyond the passenger security checkpoint, passengers without tickets should contact their airline representative to gain access. Access to the security checkpoints is controlled by the airlines. In regards to Frequent Fliers Clubs and Lounges, when airline and airport clubs and lounges are located beyond the passenger security checkpoint, passengers without tickets should contact their airline representative to gain access. Access to the security checkpoints is controlled by the airlines.

What are prohibited items?

Prohibited items are weapons, explosives, incendiaries, and include items that are seemingly harmless but may be used as weapons-the so-called "dual use" items. You may not bring these items to security checkpoints without authorization. A non-exclusive list of prohibited items is available at www.tsa.dot.gov.

What may happen to my prohibited item at the security checkpoint?

Your prohibited item may be detained for use in an investigation and, if necessary, as evidence in your criminal and/or civil prosecution. If permitted by the screener or law enforcement officer, you may be allowed to: consult with the airlines for possible assistance in placing the prohibited item in checked baggage, withdraw with the item from the screening checkpoint at that time, make other arrangements for the item, such as taking it to your car, or voluntarily abandon the item. Items that are voluntarily abandoned cannot be recovered and will not be returned to you.

What may happen to me if I bring a prohibited item to a security checkpoint?

You may be criminally and/or civilly prosecuted or, at the least, asked to rid yourself of the item. A screener and/or law enforcement officer will make this determination, depending on what the item is and the circumstances. This is because bringing a prohibited item to a security checkpoint-even accidentally-is illegal.

Can I transport guns or firearms?

Guns and firearms are NOT permitted in your carry-on baggage, but depending on the policy of your airline, they may be included with your checked baggage. Check with your airline or travel agent to see if firearms are permitted in checked baggage on the airline you are flying. Firearms carried as checked baggage MUST be unloaded, packed in a locked hard-sided gun case, and declared to the airline at check-in. Only you, the passenger, may have the key or combination.

What about ammunition?

Ammunition is NOT permitted in your carry-on baggage, but depending on the policy of your airline, may be included with your checked baggage. Check with your airline or travel agent to see if ammunition is permitted in checked baggage on the airline you are flying. If ammunition is permitted, it must be declared to the airline at check-in. Small arms ammunitions for personal use must be securely packed in fiber, wood or metal boxes, or other packaging specifically designed to carry small amounts of ammunition. Ask about limitations or fees, if any, that apply.

Final Checklist

Before You Arrive - Final Checklist

Check with your airline or travel agent

- To determine how early to arrive at the airport. Recommended check-in times differ by airline and airport.
- To determine whether you need a boarding pass and photo identification to enter the passenger checkpoint. You can also check the TSA website by looking under "Access Requirements" for a current list of airports with this requirement.

Check with your airport

- To confirm which parking lots are open if you will be parking at the airport. Some lots may be closed for security reasons. Be sure to allow extra time for parking and shuttle transportation.

Check to make sure you

- Bring a boarding pass, ticket, or ticket confirmation, such as a printed itinerary, as well as a government-issued photo ID. Children under the age of 18 do not require an ID. At some airports, only boarding passes will be accepted to enter the passenger checkpoint.
- Bring evidence verifying you have a medical implant or other device if it is likely to set off the alarm on the metal detector, bring evidence verifying this condition. Although this is not a requirement, it may help to expedite the screening process.
- Have removed prohibited items such as pocketknives, metal scissors with pointed tips (metal or plastic scissors with blunt tips are permitted), and tools from your carry-on baggage. Double check the list of prohibited and permitted items to determine what can be placed in carry-on or checked baggage if you have any questions.
- Have reviewed TSA's guidance on unlocking checked baggage.

Have a safe trip and enjoy your flight!

Travel Tips

TSA suggests that you help prevent the need to break your locks by keeping your bag unlocked
In some cases, screeners will have to open your baggage as part of the screening process. If your bag is unlocked, then TSA will simply open the bag and screen the bag. However, if the bag is locked and TSA needs to open your bag, then locks may have to be broken. You may keep your bag locked if you choose, but TSA is not liable for damage caused to locked bags that must be opened for security purposes.

Check with your airline or travel agent

- To determine how early to arrive at the airport. Recommended check-in times differ by airline and airport.
- To determine whether you need a boarding pass and photo identification to enter the passenger checkpoint. You can also check the TSA website by looking under "Access Requirements" for a current list of airports with this requirement.

Check with your airport

- To confirm which parking lots are open if you will be parking at the airport. Some lots may be closed for security reasons. Be sure to allow extra time for parking and shuttle transportation.

Check to make sure you

- Bring a boarding pass, ticket, or ticket confirmation, such as a printed itinerary, as well as a government-issued photo ID. Children under the age of 18 do not require an ID. At some airports, only boarding passes will be accepted to enter the passenger checkpoint.
- Bring evidence verifying you have a medical implant or other device if it is likely to set off the alarm on the metal detector, bring evidence verifying this condition. Although this is not a requirement, it may help to expedite the screening process.
- Have removed prohibited items such as pocketknives, metal scissors with pointed tips (metal or plastic scissors with blunt tips are permitted), and tools from your carry-on baggage. Double check the list of prohibited and permitted items to determine what can be placed in carry-on or checked baggage if you have any questions.
- Have reviewed TSA's guidance on unlocking checked baggage.

Security Procedures

TSA has Implemented New Security Procedures in U.S. Airports

The Transportation Security Administration has instituted standardized screening procedures at airports across the country. The information here describes the new enhanced procedures you will encounter. Familiarizing yourself with these procedures - particularly those that are new or different from what you may have experienced in the past - will assist you in moving quickly through your security screening.

Each passenger must go through two stages of screening:

- Baggage Checkpoints
- Passenger Checkpoints

Some passengers may go through an additional stage of screening:

- Gate Screening

For your security, only certain individuals are permitted to enter the screening area.

- Access Requirements

See Baggage checkpoints

Passenger Security Checkpoints

Passenger checkpoints are now the second checkpoints you will encounter.

You must pass through this checkpoint to access your departure gate. Security screeners will screen you and your carry-on baggage. You should find this screening process familiar, although enhanced security measures are in place.

The passenger checkpoint includes 3 primary steps you may want to become familiar with:

Step 1. X-ray machine

At the passenger security checkpoint, you will place all carry-on baggage and any items you are carrying with you on the belt of the X-ray machine. You will need to lay all items flat.

Laptop computers must be removed from their carrying cases and placed in one of the bins provided. You will also need to remove your outer coat or jacket and place it in one of the bins. These items go through the X-ray machine.

"IN - OUT - OFF"

- Place all metal items IN your carry-on baggage before you reach the front of the line.
- Take your computer OUT of its carrying case and place it in one of the bins provided.
- Take OFF your outer coat or jacket so that it can go through the X-ray machine (you do not need to remove your suit jacket, sport coat, or blazer unless you are asked to do so by one of the passenger screeners.)

Step 2. Walk-through metal detector

You will next walk through a metal detector, (or you may request a pat-down inspection instead). Objects on your clothing or person containing metal may set off the alarm on the metal detector.

You will undergo a secondary screening if you set off the alarm on the metal detector, or if you are chosen for additional screening. (See below)

TIP: Pack all metal items, including the contents of your pockets, in your carry-on baggage. Mobile phones, pagers, keys, lighters, and loose change are examples of items containing metal.

If you refuse to be screened at any point during the screening process, the screener must deny you entry beyond the screening area. You will not be able to fly.

Step 3. Secondary screening

Secondary screening occurs when an individual sets off the alarm on the metal detector, or if he or she is selected for additional screening. This screening includes a hand-wand inspection in conjunction with a pat-down inspection.

If you must go through a secondary screening, the screener will direct you from the metal detector to a screening station where he or she will brief you on the next steps.

- At this time, you should let the screener know of any personal needs you may have due to a religious or cultural consideration, disability, or other medical concern.
- Except in extraordinary circumstances, a screener of your gender will conduct your secondary screening. You may request that your search be conducted in private.

While you will be separated from your carry-on

baggage during this process, every effort will be made to help you maintain visual contact with your carry-ons.

Hand-Wand Inspection
The hand-wand inspection helps the screener to identify what may have set off the alarm on the metal detector. During the wanding procedure, you will be asked to stand with your feet apart and the screener will pass the wand over your entire body without actually touching you with the wand. Every effort will be taken to do this as discretely as possible. Please take note of the following:

- Areas of the body that have body piercings, thick hair, hats, and other items may require a pat-down inspection.
- You may ask to remove your body piercing in private as an alternative to the pat-down search.
- The screener may ask you to open your belt buckle as part of the process.
- The screener may ask you to remove your shoes, and your shoes may be X-rayed separately.

TIP: It is recommended (but not a requirement) that individuals with a pacemaker, or other device that is likely to alarm the metal detector, bring identification verifying the condition. This may help to expedite the screening process.

Your Carry-On Baggage
If your bag is selected for secondary screening, it may be opened and examined on a table in your presence. Please DO NOT attempt to assist the screener during the search, and do not attempt to retrieve the item before the screener has advised you that the search is complete and your baggage is cleared.

Your baggage might also be inspected with an Explosive Trace Detection machine (ETD), which is separate from the X-ray machine.

Pat-Down Inspection
A pat-down inspection complements the hand-wand inspection. In order to ensure security, this inspection may include sensitive areas of the body. Screeners are rigorously trained to maintain the highest levels of professionalism.
You may request that your pat-down inspection be conducted in private.

Gate Screening
Additional Screening May Occur at the Departure Gate
Some passengers may be selected for additional screening at the departure gate. The procedures are very similar to the secondary screening process, (See STEP 3) used at the checkpoints.

Special Considerations
Do You Require Additional Assistance during the Screening Process?
The Transportation Security Administration (TSA) has developed standardized security screening procedures for all airports. Therefore, you can expect that you will encounter essentially the same procedures at each airport you visit. You can also expect to be treated with the same courtesy and respect.

While the same screening procedures are used for virtually all passengers, we recognize that some passengers may have special needs or require additional assistance during the screening process. To maintain excellent security and customer service, TSA security screeners have been trained to be sensitive to and respectful of the needs of all passengers.

The Security Process & Preparation Tips
We have identified some helpful information that explains the security screening procedures as they may apply to groups with special needs. If you fall into any one of the categories identified below, you may want to familiarize yourself with this information before arriving at the airport.
- Persons with disabilities or medical concerns
- Religious or cultural needs
- Traveling with Children
- Pets
- Film
- Sports Equipment

Your knowledge of the procedures, and observance of the tips and recommendations, will help you move through the security checkpoint quickly and efficiently.

If you have any questions while at the airport, ask for the TSA screening supervisor. You may also contact our Consumer Response Center toll-free at 1-866-289-9673 Monday - Friday between 8am - 6pm (24 hour voicemail). You may also email us at TellTSA@tsa.dot.gov.

This information will be updated from time-to time. We recommend that you periodically check TSA's web site to obtain the latest information.

Persons with Disabilities or Medical Concerns

Do You Have a Disability?
This section provides information pertaining to specific disabilities including mobility, hearing, visual and hidden disabilities and the use of dog guides, service dogs and hearing dogs. You will also find information on medical devices for persons with diabetes, pacemakers, assistive devices and mobility aids.

Do You Have a Medical Concern?
This section provides information addressing general medical concerns, including temporary aids, injectable medication, medical implants, medical documentation, pain or sensitivity and medical, lifesaving evidentiary or scientific items and crematory containers

Before You Go
Information to be aware of and Tips for the screening process.

At the Passenger Security Checkpoint
Mobility Disability
- Don't hesitate to ask a screener for assistance with your mobility aid and carryon items as you proceed through the security checkpoint.
- Let the screener know your level of ability (e.g., whether you can walk, stand or perform an arm lift) - it will expedite the screening process.
- Inform the screener about any special equipment or devices that you are using and where this equipment is located on your body - this will help the screener be careful during a physical search if one is needed.
- Ensure that all bags and satchels hanging from, or carried on, your equipment are put on the X-ray belt for inspection.
- Ask the screener to reunite you with your carryon items and assistive device after screening is completed.

- Let the screener know if you need assistance removing your shoes when additional screening is necessary.
- Let the screener know if your shoes cannot be removed because of your disability so that alternative security procedures can be applied to your shoes.
- Ask the screener to monitor your items during the screening process and reunite you with them and assistive devices once x-ray inspection is completed.

Hearing Disability
If the screening process is unclear to you, ask the screener to write the information down or look directly at you and repeat the information slowly.

Visual Disability
You may ask the screener to:
- Explain the security process to you.
- Verbally communicate to you throughout each step of the screening process.
- Let you know where the metal detector is located.
- Let you know when you will be going though the metal detector.
- Let you know when there are obstacles you need to avoid.
- Find someone to escort you through the security process.
- Perform a hand inspection of equipment (e.g., Braille note-takers) if the X-ray inspection will damage them.
- Reunite you with all of your carryon items and assistive devices after the X-ray or physical inspection of the items is completed, including electronic equipment which has been specially adapted for your use.
- Verbally direct you toward your gate once the screening has been completed.

Hidden Disability
Persons with a hidden disability can, if they choose, advise screeners that they have a hidden disability and may need some assistance, or need to move a bit slower than others.
- Family members or traveling companions can advise screeners when they are traveling with someone who has a hidden disability, which may cause that person to move a little

254

slower, become agitated easily and/or need additional attention.

- Family members or traveling companions can offer suggestions to screeners on the best way to approach and deal with the person with a hidden disability, especially when it is necessary to touch the person during a pat-down inspection.
- Notify the screener if you need to sit down before and/or during the screening process.

Persons with Diabetes

- Notify the screener that you have diabetes and are carrying your supplies with you. The following diabetes related supplies and equipment are allowed through the checkpoint once they have been screened:
  - insulin and insulin loaded dispensing products (vials or box of individual vials, jet injectors, pens, infusers, and preloaded syringes),
  - unlimited number of unused syringes when accompanied by insulin, and
  - lancets, blood glucose meters, blood glucose meter test strips, insulin pumps, and insulin pump supplies.
- Insulin in any form or dispenser must be properly marked with a professionally printed label identifying the medication or manufacturer's name or pharmaceutical label.
- Notify screeners if you are wearing an insulin pump and, if necessary, advise the screener that it cannot be removed since it is surgically implanted.
- Insulin pumps and supplies must be accompanied by insulin with professionally printed labels identifying the medication or manufacturer's name or pharmacy label.
- Advise screeners if you are experiencing low blood sugar and are in need of medical assistance.
- It is recommended that used syringes be transported in your checked baggage; however, when used syringes need to be in carry-on, ensure they are in a hard, plastic-capped container (i.e. sharps disposable container) for safety and containment.

Persons with Pacemakers

- It is recommended (but not a requirement) that individuals with a pacemaker carry a Pacemaker Identification Card (ID) when going through airport security.
- It is recommended (but not required) that you advise the screener that you have an implanted pacemaker.
- Show the screener your pacemaker ID, if you have one, and ask the screener to conduct a pat-down inspection of you rather than having you walk through the metal detector or be hand-wanded.

Persons with Assistive Devices and Mobility Aids: Canes, Walkers, Crutches, Prosthetic Devices, Body Braces, and Other Devices

- Crutches, canes and walkers will need to go through the X-ray machine.
- Notify the screener if your device requires special handling.
- Ask for assistance with your device(s) if you need it.
- The screener will perform a hand inspection of your equipment if it cannot fit through the X-ray machine.
- Collapse canes whenever possible before they are put on the X-ray belt.
- Once devices have been screened, screeners should hand back your device to you in such a manner that helps you proceed without difficulty.
- Screeners may need to see and touch your prosthetic devices and body braces as part of the inspection process.
- You can ask for a private screening for the inspection of your prosthetic device or body brace.
- Notify screeners if you need assistance during the inspection of your prosthetic devices or body braces such as a chair or someone to lean on.
- You may bring tools and appliances (e.g. wrenches, pull sleeves, etc.) used to put on or take off prosthetic devices through the security checkpoint once they have been screened.

Service Animals

- It is recommended that persons using a dog for assistance carry appropriate identification. Identification may include: cards or documentation, presence of a harness or markings on

255

the harness, tags, or other credible assurance of the passenger using the dog for their disability.

- Advise the screener how you and your dog can go through the metal detector as a team (i.e. whether walking together or with the dog walking in front of or behind you while you continually maintain control of the dog with the leash and/or harness.
- The dog's harness will likely set off the alarm on the metal detector. In such cases, screener will perform a hand inspection of the dog and its belongings (collar, harness, leash, backpack, vest, etc.) The belongings will not be removed from your dog at any time.
- If necessary, remind the screener that you should not be separated from your dog and that removal of your dog's belongings is a sign to the dog or other service animal that it is off work.

Temporary Aids
Passengers who are temporarily using a wheelchair or assistive devices due to an injury, surgery, or medical procedure should refer to the "Mobility Disability" and/or "Persons with Assistive Devices and Mobility Aids" sections under "Persons with Disabilities." The information found there will help guide you through the screening process.

Injectable Medication
Make sure injectable medications are properly labeled (professionally printed label identifying the medication or a manufacturer's name or pharmaceutical label). Notify the screener if you are carrying a hazardous waste container, refuse container, or a sharps disposable container in your carry-on baggage used to trainsport used syringes, lancets, etc.

Medical Implants
Notify the screener if you have any implanted medical devices such as an artificial hip or knee, bone shafts, cranial plates, shrapnel, staples, pins, or metal ports that may set off the alarm on the metal detector.

Medical Documentation
If you have medical documentation regarding your medical condition, you may present this information to the screener to help inform him or her of your situation. This documentation is not required and will not exempt you from the screening process.

Pain or Sensitivity
If you are required to undergo a personal search, you can notify the screener if you are in pain due to a recent surgery or medical procedure (e.g. area where you have just undergone surgery, have staples, sutures, reconstruction areas, or newly implanted devices) that will require greater care.

Notify the screener when you have a special situation requiring sensitivity if a pat-down inspection is necessary. You may request a private area for your personal search.

Medical, Lifesaving, Evidentiary or Scientific Items and Crematory Containers
These items may be allowed through the security checkpoint and aboard an aircraft if you have made pre-arrangements with the airline. The airline and screener will confirm that you have the appropriate documents to verify the contents and establish your identity. Screeners will treat the items with the appropriate respect and dignity.

Before You Go
- Provide advance notice to your airline or travel agent if you require assistance at the airport.
- If you require a companion or assistant to accompany you through the security checkpoint to reach your gate, speak with your airline representative about obtaining a gate pass for your companion before entering the security checkpoint.
- The limit of one carry-on and one personal item (purse, briefcase or computer case) does not apply to medical supplies, equipment, mobility aids and/or assistive devices carried by a person with a disability.
- Make sure all your carry-on items. equipment, devices, etc., have an identification tag attached.
- Mobility aids and assistive devices permitted through the security checkpoint include: wheelchairs, scooters, canes, walkers, crutches, prosthetic devices, body braces, augmentation and communication devices (e.g. Braille note takers, slate and stylus), dog guides, service dogs.

256

hearing dogs, and diabetes related equipment and supplies.

- If you have a medical device (implanted on the interior or exterior of your body) check with your Doctor prior to traveling to determine if it is safe for you to go through the walk-through metal detector or be handwanded. If your Doctor indicates that you should not go through the metal detector or be handwanded or if you are concerned, ask the screener for a pat-down inspection instead.
  See the Service Animals section on the Persons with Disabilities page for information on animals assisting passengers.

Tips for the Screening Process

- If a personal search is required, you may choose to remain in the wanding area or go to a private area for your screening. If you refuse either option you will not be able to fly.
- You should be offered a private screening before the beginning of a pat-down inspection if the pat-down will require the removal or lifting of clothing and/or display of a covered medical device.
- You may request a private area for your personal search at any time during the screening process.
- You may ask for a chair if you need to sit down during the screening process.
- You may request a pat-down in lieu of going through the walk-through metal detector or being hand-wanded. You do not need to disclose why you would like this option.
- If you have a disability, condition, or implant that you would like to remain private and confidential, ask the screener to please be discreet when assisting you through the screening process.

Religious or Cultural Needs

General Screening Considerations for Religious or Cultural Needs

- If you do not want to go through the metal detector, you may request a

personal search (pat-down inspection) as an alternative.

- You may also ask the screener for a private area for this personal search. You will be provided a screener of the same gender, except in extraordinary situations. In the unlikely situation where a screener of the same gender is not available, you will be provided with alternatives, which may include waiting for a same-gender screener to arrive, or consenting to a search by a screener of the opposite gender.
- If you refuse appropriate screening you will not be allowed to pass the security checkpoint and you will be unable to board your plane.

Head Coverings

It may be necessary for you to remove your head covering during the screening process. If the screener asks you to remove a head covering, you may request a private area to provide privacy while the head cover is removed, inspected, and restored.

Religious, Cultural or Ceremonial Items

- There are items in this category that are not permitted through the security checkpoint (e.g., religious knives, swords). Therefore, it is advised that you place such items in your checked baggage. Check the permitted/prohibited list for more information.
- If the screener asks you to provide a religious, cultural or ceremonial item for screening, you may request a hand-inspection. If the item is prohibited from the cabin of the aircraft you will be asked to place the item in your checked baggage or speak to your airline about checking the item. If the item is delicate or fragile, or special handling is otherwise required, please let the screener know so that he or she can handle the item accordingly.

If the screener requests that you put a delicate or fragile item through the X-ray machine, you may want to ask the screener to ensure that there is no baggage immediately before or after the item so that it will not be damaged. Bins are available at the X-ray machine.

257

Traveling with Children

Are You Traveling with Children?

Every person, regardless of age, must undergo screening to proceed beyond the security checkpoint. Even babies must be individually screened. You will not be asked to do anything that will separate you from your child or children.

Screeners are specially trained and understand your concerns regarding children. Your children will be approached gently and treated with respect. If your child becomes uncomfortable or upset, you will be consulted about the best approach to resolving your child's concern.

The Screening Process
X-Ray

- All carry-on baggage, including children's bags and items, must go through the X-ray machine. Examples include: diaper bags, blankets, and toys.
- All child-related equipment that will fit through the X-ray machine must go through the X-ray machine. Examples include: strollers, umbrella strollers, baby carriers, car and booster seats, backpacks, and baby slings.
- When you arrive at the checkpoint, you should collapse or fold child-related equipment and secure items that are in the pockets, baskets, or attached to the equipment. You will place these items on the X-ray belt for inspection. Plastic bins are provided to deposit such items.
- When child-related equipment does not fit through the X-ray machine, the equipment must be visually and physically inspected.
- Ask screeners for assistance to help reunite you with your bags and child-related equipment, if needed.

ALERT! Babies should NEVER be left in an infant carrier while it goes through the X-ray machine.

For information regarding what is permitted or prohibited from being in carry-on luggage, please refer to our prohibited items section.

The Walk Through Metal Detector

The screener will need to resolve the alarm for both adult and child if something sets off the alarm as you are carrying a child through the metal detector.

- Babies and children must be removed from their strollers or infant carriers so they can be individually screened.
- You may not pass the child to another person behind you or in front of you during this process.
- Do not pass your child to the screener to hold.
- The screener may ask for your assistance with secondary screening of your child.
- If your child can walk unassisted, it would be best to have the child walk through the metal detector independently.

Child with a Disability

If your child has a disability, screeners may ask you what abilities your child has in order to determine the best method for screening (e.g. carry the child through the walk-through metal detector, hand-wand procedure).

If your child has a disability, screeners will never attempt to remove the child from his or her equipment. This will only be done at the discretion of the accompanying adult.

Family Travel Tips

TIPS Before you reach the airport

- Please allow yourself and your family extra time to get through security - especially when traveling with younger children.
- Call your airline or travel agent for information on recommended check-in times for your departure airport.
- Talk to your children before coming to the airport and let them know that it's against the law to make threats such as, "I have a bomb in my bag." Threats made jokingly (even by a child) can result in the entire family being delayed and could result in fines.

TIPS At the airport

- Speak to your children again about the screening process so that they will not be frightened or surprised. Remind them to not joke about threats such as bombs or explosives.

- Advise your children that their bags (backpack, dolls, etc.) will be put in the X-ray machine and will come out at the other end and be returned to them.
- Let your children know that a screener may ask to see Mom or Dad's shoes, but that these too will be returned after the inspection.
- You may want to consider asking for a private screening if you are traveling with more than one child.

Pets

Traveling with a Pet?

Security procedures do not prohibit you from bringing a pet on your flight. You should contact your airline or travel agent, however, before arriving at the airport to determine your airline's policy on traveling with pets.

Security Screening

If you are planning to bring an animal on-board the plane with you, you will need to present the animal to the security checkpoint screeners for screening. You may walk your animal through the metal detector with you. If this is not possible, your animal will have to undergo a secondary screening, including a visual and physical inspection.

Your animal will NEVER be placed through an X-ray machine. You may be asked to remove your animal from its carrier so that the carrier can be placed on the X-Ray machine.

Film

WARNING: Equipment used for screening checked baggage will damage your undeveloped film.

- Never place film in your checked baggage.
- Place film in your carry-on baggage* or request a hand inspection.

*Carry-on screening equipment might also damage film if the film passes through more than 5 times. None of the screening equipment - neither the machines used for checked baggage nor those used for carry-on baggage - will affect digital camera images or film that has already been processed, slides, videos, photo compact discs, or picture discs.

General use film*

You should remove all film from your checked baggage and place it in your carry-on baggage. The X-ray machine that screens your carry-on baggage at the passenger security checkpoint will not affect undeveloped film under ASA/ISO 800.

If the same role of film is exposed to X-ray inspections more than 5 times before it is developed, however, damage may occur. Protect your film by requesting a hand-inspection for your film if it has already passed through the carry-on baggage screening equipment (X-ray) more than 5 times.

TIP: Remember the 5x X-ray limit for your carry-on.

TIP: You may request a hand-inspection of any undeveloped film.

Specialty film*
(film with an ASA/ISO 800 or higher and typically used by professionals)

At the passenger security checkpoint, you should remove the following types of film from your carry-on baggage and ask for a hand inspection:

- Film with an ASA/ISO 800 or higher
- Highly sensitive X-ray or scientific films
- Film of any speed which is subjected to X-ray surveillance more than 5 times (the effect of X-ray screening is cumulative)
- Film that is or will be underexposed
- Film that you intend to "push process"
- Sheet film
- Large format film
- Medical film
- Scientific film
- Motion picture film
- Professional grade film

Other Tips and Precautions

- If you plan to request a hand inspection of your film, you should consider carrying your film in clear canisters, or taking the film out of solid colored canisters and putting it into clear plastic bags, to expedite the screening process.
- If you are going to be traveling through multiple X-ray examinations with the same rolls of undeveloped film, you may want to request a hand-inspection

259

of your film. However, non-U.S. airports may not honor this request.

- If you plan to hand-carry undeveloped film on an airplane at an international airport, contact the airport security office at that airport to request a manual inspection.
- Consider having your exposed film processed locally before passing through airport security on your return trip.
- We recommend that you do not place your film in lead-lined bags since the lead bag will have to be hand-inspected. If you have concerns about the impact of the X-ray machine on your undeveloped film, you can request a hand inspection.
- You may still consider bringing a lead-lined bag if you are traveling through airports in other countries as their policies may vary. Check with your airline or travel agent for more information on foreign airports.

* This guidance was developed in cooperation with the International Imaging Industry Association (I3A).

Sports Equipment

Are You Traveling with Sports Equipment?

New screening guidelines prohibit certain sporting equipment from being brought on-board an aircraft. These items include:

- baseball bats
- bows and arrows
- cricket bats
- golf clubs
- hockey sticks
- hunting knives
- martial arts devices
- pool cues
- scuba knives
- ski poles
- spear guns
- any other equipment determined by the screener to be dangerous

While these items are prohibited from your carry-on baggage, they may be transported to your destination in your checked baggage. Any sharp opbjects in checked baggage should be sheathed or securely wrapped to prevent injury to baggage

handlers and security screeners.

You may bring items such as baseballs, soccer balls, and basketballs through the passenger security checkpoint. They will need to be screened. See "Permitted and Prohibited Items" for full list.

We Welcome Your Comments and Questions

If you would like to pass on any positive feedback or concerns to TSA regarding your experience, you should contact a screener supervisor. You may also contact the TSA Consumer Response Center, toll-free, at: 1-866-289-9673 Monday - Friday between 8am - 6pm (24 hour voicemail). You may also e-mail us at TellTSA@tsa.dot.gov. The Transportation Security Administration (TSA) takes all input very seriously and will respond promptly and appropriately to all complaints or comments.

Road Safety

An estimated 1.17 million deaths occur each year worldwide due to road accidents. The majority of these deaths, about 70 percent, occur in developing countries. Sixty-five percent of deaths involve pedestrians and 35 percent of pedestrian deaths are children. Over 10 million people are crippled or injured each year. It is estimated that more than 200 U.S. citizens die each year due to road accidents abroad. The majority of road crash victims (injuries and fatalities) in developing countries are not the motor vehicle occupants, but pedestrians, motorcyclists, bicyclists and non-motor vehicles (NMV) occupants. U.S. citizens are urged to review the Road Safety segment of Department of State, Bureau of Consular Affairs Consular Information Sheets at http://travel.state.gov/travel_warnings.html and the country-specific links below for any country in which you intend to drive or travel by road as a passenger. Check with the embassy or consulate of the countries where you will visit to learn about requirements for driver's license, road permits, and auto insurance. It is important to be aware of the rules of the road in other countries, and the fact that road conditions can vary widely. It is also important to be aware of security concerns when driving abroad. Driving under the influence can have severe criminal penalties in other countries. The issue of international road safety continues to be a matter of growing concern to governments, international organizations, non-government organizations and private citizens. In 1998, the World Health Organization ranked road accidents as the 9th leading cause of mortality and disease.

Road Security

The Overseas Security Advisory Council's (OSAC) publications provide information about security and auto travel abroad. Potential victims of kidnapping and assault are probably most vulnerable when entering or leaving their homes or offices. Always carefully observe surroundings for possible surveillance upon leaving and returning. Never enter a car without checking the rear seat to ensure that it is empty. Do not develop predictable patterns. If possible, exchange company cars or swap with coworkers occasionally. Know the location of police, hospital, military, and government buildings. Avoid trips to remote areas, particularly after dark. Select well-traveled streets as much as possible. Keep vehicles well-maintained at all times. When driving, keep automobile doors and windows locked. Be constantly alert to road conditions and surroundings. Never pick up hitchhikers. Carry 3 x 5 cards printed with important assistance phrases to aid with language problems. Always carry appropriate coins for public phones. Practice using public telephones. Report all suspicious activity to the company security contact if applicable. Always lock the doors when parking a car, no matter where it is located.

Information for Students

The Department of State is engaged in outreach efforts to education-related organizations to publicize road safety risks in other countries. Students, who may chose less expensive, often less reliable methods of local travel while in foreign countries, should be aware of the potential danger. See the Center for Global Education, USC, travel and transportation web site at Travel and Transportation and the personal safety site at USC, Center for Global Education for more information. Students traveling abroad should also be aware of the dangers of potentially reckless behavior, including careless driving or driving under the influence. It should also be noted that penalties for persons judged responsible for automobile accidents resulting in injury or fatalities are treated very seriously by foreign authorities and can result in extremely stiff prison sentences. See our information for students and the Consular Information Sheet for the country you are visiting.

International Driving Permits

Although many countries do not recognize U.S. driver's licenses, most countries accept an international driving permit (IDPs). IDPs are honored in more than 150 countries outside the U.S. (See AAA's application form for the list of countries. They function as an official translation of a U.S. driver's license into 10 foreign languages. These licenses *are not intended to replace* valid U.S. state licenses and should only be used as a supplement to a valid license. *IDPs are not valid in an individual's country of residence.*

Before departure, you can obtain one from an automobile association authorized by the U.S. Department of State to issue IDPs. Article 24 of the United Nations Convention on Road Traffic (1949) authorizes the U.S. Department of State to empower certain organizations to issue IDPs to those who hold valid U.S. driver's licenses. The Department has designated the American Automobile Association (AAA) and the American Automobile Touring Alliance as the only authorized distributors of IDPs. Many foreign countries require deposit of a customs duty or an equivalent bond for each tourist automobile entering its territory, and the motoring associations are equipped with the necessary facilities for providing expeditiously a standard bond document (Article 3 of the Convention). The Convention is not applicable to United States motorists using their cars in the United States.

HOW TO APPLY FOR AN INTERNATIONAL DRIVING PERMIT: Before departure, you can obtain one at a local office of one of the two automobile associations authorized by the U.S. Department of State: the American Automobile Association (AAA) and the American Automobile Touring Alliance.

AAA (American Automobile Association), 1000 AAA Drive, Heathrow, FL 32745-5063. The application is available on-line.

American Automobile Touring Alliance (AATA), 1151 E. Hillsdale Blvd., Foster City, CA 94404, tel: 800-622-7070; fax: 650-294-7105 (www.thenac.com)

To apply for an international driving permit, you must be at least age 18, and you will need to present two passport-size photographs and your valid U.S. license. The cost of an international driving permit from these U.S. State Department authorized organizations is under $20.00.

INTERNATIONAL DRIVING PERMITS ISSUED BY UNAUTHORIZED PERSONS: The Department of State is aware that IDPs are being sold over the Internet and in person by persons not authorized by the Department of State pursuant to the requirements of the U.N. Convention of 1949. Moreover, many of these IDPs are being sold for large sums of money, far greater than the sum charged by entities authorized by the Department of State. Consumers experiencing problems should report problems to their local office of the U.S. Postal Inspector, Federal Trade Commission (FTC), the Better Business Bureau, or their state or local Attorney General's Office.

Auto Insurance
Car rental agencies overseas usually provide auto insurance, but in some countries, the required coverage is minimal. When renting a car overseas, consider purchasing insurance coverage that is at least equivalent to that which you carry at home. In general, your U.S. auto insurance does not cover you abroad. However, your policy may apply when you drive to countries neighboring the United States. Check with your insurer to see if your policy covers you in Canada, Mexico, or countries south of Mexico. Even if your policy is valid in one of these countries, it may not meet that country's minimum requirements. For instance, in most of Canada, you must carry at least $200,000 in liability insurance, and Mexico requires that, if vehicles do not carry theft, third party liability, and comprehensive insurance, the owner must post a bond that could be as high as 50% of the value of the vehicle. If you are under-insured for a country, auto insurance can usually be purchased on either side of the border.

Driving Abroad
The U.S. Department of State, Overseas Security Advisory Council (OSAC) provides brochures for American families and business travelers abroad for guidance about driving overseas.

TIPS ON DRIVING ABROAD
Obtain an International Driving Permit (IDP).
Carry both your IDP and your state driver's license with you at all times.
As many countries have different driving rules. If possible, obtain a copy of the foreign country's rules before you begin driving in that country. Information may be available from the foreign embassy in the United States

(http://www.embassy.org/embassies/index.html), foreign government tourism offices: (http://www.towd.com/), or from a car rental company in the foreign country.

Some countries have a minimum and maximum driving age.

Certain countries require road permits, instead of tolls, to use on their divided highways, and they will fine those found driving without a permit.

Always "buckle up." Some countries have penalties for people who violate this law.

Many countries require you to honk your horn before going around a sharp corner or to flash your lights before passing.

Before you start your journey, find out who has the right of way in a traffic circle.

If you rent a car, make sure you have liability insurance. If you do not, this could lead to financial disaster.

f the drivers in the country you are visiting drive on the opposite side of the road than in the U.S., it may be prudent to practice driving in a less populated area before attempting to drive during the heavy traffic part of the day.

Always know the route you will be traveling. Have a copy of a good road map, and chart your course before beginning.

Do not pick up hitchhikers or strangers.

When entering your vehicle, be aware of your surroundings.

RETAINING A FOREIGN ATTORNEY

DISCLAIMER: THE INFORMATION IN THIS CIRCULAR IS PROVIDED FOR GENERAL INFORMATION ONLY. THE DEPARTMENT OF STATE MAKES NO WARRANTY REGARDING THE ACCURACY OF THIS INFORMATION. WHILE SOME OF THE INFORMATION IS ABOUT LEGAL ISSUES, IT IS NOT LEGAL ADVICE. QUESTIONS INVOLVING

INTERPRETATION OF SPECIFIC FOREIGN LAWS SHOULD BE ADDRESSED TO FOREIGN ATTORNEYS.

PROVISO: Officers of the Department of State and U.S. Embassies and Consulates abroad are prohibited by federal regulation from acting as agents, attorneys or in a fiduciary capacity on behalf of U.S. citizens in private legal disputes abroad. (22 CFR 92.81; 10.735-206(a)(7); 72.41; 71.5.)

RECOMMENDING A FOREIGN ATTORNEY: 22 CFR 92.82 provides that Foreign Service officers shall refrain from recommending a particular foreign attorney, but may furnish names of several attorneys, or refer inquiries to foreign law directories, bar associations or other organizations.

FOREIGN ATTORNEYS REPRESENTING THE U.S. GOVERNMENT ABROAD: U.S. embassies and consulates abroad generally do not have foreign attorneys on a retainer to represent the interests of the U.S. Government. (See 22 U.S.C. 2698(a); 28 C.F.R. 0.45; Volume 2, Foreign Affairs Manual (FAM), Department of State, Sec. 283; Volume 9, Foreign Affairs Manual, Sec. 971.2.)

BACKGROUND: This information flyer was devised primarily for the lay person confronted with a private legal problem abroad. It contains general practical suggestions for dealing with a foreign attorney. General information concerning foreign legal aid is also discussed. For American lawyers facing the task of retaining foreign legal counsel, see Lewis, Selecting and Working With Foreign Counsel, The International Lawyer's Deskbook, American Bar Association, 393-410 (1996) and Epstein & Snyder, International Litigation: A Guide to Jurisdiction, Practice and Strategy, 2nd, 2.10-2.13, p. 2-17 - 2-24 (1994).

WHAT TYPE OF LAWYER WILL YOU NEED:
Barristers and Solicitors: In some foreign countries it may be necessary to retain the services of both a solicitor and a barrister. In such jurisdictions, barristers are allowed to appear in court, including trial courts and higher courts of appeal or other courts. Solicitors are allowed to advise clients and sometimes represent them in the lower courts. They may also prepare cases for barristers to try in the higher courts..**Notaries,**

"Notaires", "Notars", and "Huissiers": In some countries, notaries public, "notaires", "notars" and "huissiers" can perform many of the functions performed by attorneys in the United States. A notary in a civil law country is not comparable to a notary public in the United States. Their education and training differs from that of most notaries public in the United States. They frequently draft instruments such wills and conveyances. In some countries a notary is a public official appointed by the Ministry of Justice, whose functions include not only preparing documents, but the administration and settlement of estates. Such notaries serve as repositories for wills and are empowered to serve legal documents. In some countries "huissiers" serve documents. They are not lawyers, but are very specialized members of the foreign legal profession. They may not plead cases in court. Your foreign attorney may delegate certain functions to a notary, "notaire", "notar" or "huissier".

Foreign Legal Consultants: These are U.S. law firms with offices in foreign countries. They may or may not be licensed to practice law abroad.

Selecting an Attorney: When you receive a list of attorneys, consider contacting several attorneys, briefly describing the nature of the services you desire. Find out the attorney's qualifications and experience. Find out how the attorney plans to represent you. Ask specific questions and expect the attorney to explain legal activities in language that you can comprehend. Do not turn over documents or funds until you are satisfied that the attorney understands your problem and is willing to handle your case. Find out the rules of the foreign country concerning attorney-client confidentiality.

GUIDELINES ON HOW TO DEAL WITH YOUR FOREIGN ATTORNEY:
Understanding Your Attorney: Ask your attorney to analyze your case, giving you the positive and negative aspects and probable outcome. Do not expect your attorney to give a simple answer to a complex legal question. Be sure that you understand the technical language in any contract or other legal document prepared by your attorney **before** you sign it.

Fees: Find out what fees the attorney charges and how the attorney expects to be paid. In some countries fees are fixed by local law. Establish a billing schedule that meets your requirements and

263

is acceptable to the foreign attorney. Foreign lawyers may be unaccustomed to including a description of work performed in connection with billing. Some foreign attorneys may expect to be paid in advance; some may demand payment after each action they take on your behalf and refuse to take further action until they are paid; and some may take the case on a contingency or percentage basis, collecting a pre-arranged percentage of moneys awarded to you by the foreign court. Request an estimate of the total hours and costs of doing the work. Be clear who will be involved in the work and the fees charged by each participant. Determine costs if other attorneys or specialists need to be consulted, such as barristers. See "Payment of Attorneys and Litigation Expenses in Selected Foreign Nations", U.S. Library of Congress, Law Library, Doc. LL-95-2 (March 1995) (Includes information on Australia, Canada, China, France, Germany, Great Britain, Greece, India, Italy, Japan, Mexico, Netherlands, Poland, Sweden and Taiwan.)

Method of Payment: Find out the expected means of payment (corporate check, bank check, personal check, international money order, wire transfer), specify currency and exchange rates (when and where applicable or feasible).

Progress Reports: Ask that your attorney keep you informed of the progress of your case according to a pre-established schedule. Remember that most foreign courts work rather slowly. You may, therefore, wish the attorney to send you monthly reports, even though no real developments have ensured, simply to satisfy your doubts about the progress of the case. Ask what the fee will be for progress reports.

Language: Is the attorney fluent in English? This may or may not be important to you. If the foreign attorney does not speak or write in English, you can arrange for translation of correspondence. Attorneys on lists prepared by the U.S. embassies and consulates abroad do speak English.

Document Translations: If you need to provide complex or technical documents to your attorney, you may wish to consider having the documents translated into the attorney's native language. Remember that even a fundamental knowledge of English may not be enough to enable the attorney to understand technical documents you provide. Discuss with your attorney whether it is preferable to translate the documents in the U.S. or in the

foreign country. Compare the costs.

Communication: Remember your responsibility to keep your attorney informed of any new developments in your case. Be honest and frank with your attorney. Tell the attorney every relevant fact in order to get the best representation of your interests. Establish how you be communicate with your foreign attorney (mail, phone, fax, Internet.)

Time: Find out how much time the attorney anticipates the case may take to complete. (Note: in some countries the courts recess for a period of several months. In addition, even if the case is resolved, currency control laws may delay the transfer of funds awarded to you from the foreign country for an indefinite period of time. Discuss these issues with your attorney to ensure there is no confusion.

Authentication and Translation of Documents: It may be helpful for you to provide foreign authorities or your attorney with authenticated, translated copies of pertinent documents. Consult your foreign attorney before going to this expense. An information flyer explaining the authentication process is available from the Office of American Citizens Services, either by mail or via our Internet Consular Affairs home page described below under "Additional Information". These topics include Hague Legalization Convention and General Authentication Flyer. See also the U.S. State Department's Authentications Office home page.

Records: Consider requesting copies of all letters and documents prepared on your behalf. Inquire about the costs of mailing you such documents.

Complaints Against Foreign Attorneys: If the services of your foreign attorney prove unsatisfactory, in addition to notifying the U.S. Department of State and/or the consular section of the U.S. embassy or consulate abroad, you may address your complaints to the local foreign bar association. Information about foreign bar associations may be obtained from the U.S. embassy or consulate abroad. Foreign embassies and consulates in the U.S. may also have information on this subject.

Assistance of U.S. Embassies and Consulates: Should your communication with a foreign attorney prove unsatisfactory, a U.S. consular officer may, if appropriate, communicate with the attorney on your behalf. In addition, complaints against foreign attorneys whose names appear on the consular list of attorneys can result in the removal of their names from the list.

Coordination with Attorneys in the U.S.:
American attorneys may not be in a position to represent your interests abroad, particularly because generally they will not be permitted to participate in foreign court proceedings under the laws of the foreign country. American attorneys experienced in international law procedure may be helpful in explaining the complex legal issues involved in your case and some may have associates abroad to whom they can refer you.

Finding A Foreign Attorney:

U.S. Department of State, Bureau of Consular Affairs, Office of American Citizens Services and Crisis Management, (CA/OCS/ACS), Room 4811A, 2201 C Street N.W., Washington, D.C. 20520; tel: 202-647-5225 or 5226. Please send a stamped, self addressed envelope, 8 1/2 x 11, to accommodate postage for 20 sheets of paper or more. These lists of attorneys are also being added to the Internet home pages of our U.S. embassies and consulates. Lists of attorneys are prepared by U.S. embassies and consulates triennially (every three years). The lists include names, addresses, telephone numbers, etc., and information concerning the foreign attorney's educational background, areas of specialization, and language capability. When compiling the lists, U.S. consular officers send letters and questionnaires to the attorneys in their consular district in the foreign country. American attorneys licensed to practice in the foreign country or working as foreign legal consultants are also included. Local foreign bar associations are used as a resource in determining whether an attorney is in good standing. See Volume 7, Department of State Foreign Affairs Manual 990 (8/30/94) and 22 CFR 92.82.

Law Directories:

DISCLAIMER: The Department of State assumes no responsibility for the professional ability or integrity of the firms or persons whose names appear in the attached list. The order in which they appear has no significance.
Martindale-Hubbell Law Directory, 800-526-4902, on-line via Lexis. See also the Martindale-Hubbell home page.
Campbell's List - A Directory of Selected

Lawyers, 407-644-8298.
Russell Law List - Legal Correspondents International, 410-820-4475.
The American Lawyer - Practice Directories, 212-973-2800.
American Bar Association, 1995 Directory of Lawyer Referral Services in the U.S. and Canada.

ABA INTERNATIONAL LIAISON SECTION:
While the ABA does not provide international referrals, it can provide the names and addresses of national or local bar associations as well as the names of several reference guides. Contact the Section by e-mail at intlliaison@abanet.org or call 312-988-5107 or visit the Section's home page at American Bar Association, International Liaison Office.

LEGAL AID: There may be facilities in the foreign country for low cost or free legal services. If information is not included in the consular list of attorneys, ask the local foreign bar association or Ministry of Justice about the availability of legal aid. Contact the legal attaché or consular section of the foreign embassy in Washington for specific guidance. Legal aid information may also be available from a local branch of the International Social Service. The agencies' headquarters are in Geneva, Switzerland, but information or assistance may be available through its New York branch at 10 W. 40th Street, New York, N.Y. 10018, 212-532-6350. See also, American Bar Association, Directory of State and Local Lawyer Assistance Programs in the U.S. and Canada.

BAR ASSOCIATIONS:

DISCLAIMER: The Department of State makes no warranty or guarantee concerning the accuracy or reliability of the content of other web sites. The order in which they appear has no significance.

American Bar Association, 750 N. Lake Shore Drive, Chicago, IL 60611, 312-988-5000.
American Bar Association, Section of International Law and Practice
American Society of International Law, 2223 Massachusetts Avenue, N.W., Washington, D.C. 20008, Tel: (202) 939-6000; Fax: (202) 797-7133.
Inter-American Bar Association (IABA), 1211 Connecticut Avenue, N.W., Suite 202, Washington, D.C. 20036; tel: 202-393-1217; fax: 202-393-1241
International Bar Association (IBA), 2 Harewood

Place, Hanover Square, London, WIR9HB, England, Tel: (011) (44) (171) 629-1206; Fax: (011) (44) (171) 409-0-456.

Inter-Pacific Bar Association (IPBA), Nashiazabu Sonic Building, 3-2-12 Nichiazabu, Minato-Ku, Tokyo, 106, Japan, Tel: (011) (81) (3) 34085079; Fax: (011) (81) (3) 334085505.

Law Association for Asia and the Pacific, 33 Barrack Street, 3rd Floor, Perth, W.A., 6000, Australia, Tel: (011) (61) (9) 221-5914.

National Asian Pacific Bar Association (NAPABA) Union Internationale des Avocats (UIA), 25 Rue de Jour, Paris, France, 75001, Tel: (011) (33) (1) 4508-8231; Fax: (011) (33) (1) 4508-8231.

World Jurist Association, 1000 Connecticut Avenue, N.W., Suite 202, Washington, D.C. 20036, Tel: (202) 466-5428; Fax: (202) 452-8540.

Other Resources:

Library of Congress Law Library, Room 240, James Madison Bldg., 101 Independence Avenue, S.E., Washington, D.C. 20540, tel: 202-707-5079

SELECTED REFERENCES:

American Bar Association, Report on the Regulation of Foreign Lawyers (1977).

Aranson, The United States Percentage Contingent Fee System: Ridicule and Reform From An International Perspective, 127 Texas Int'l L.J. 755-793 (1992).

Bader-Ginsburg, Chairman, The Availability of Legal Services to Poor People and People of Limited Means in Foreign Systems, 6 Int'l Law. 128 (1971).

Barrager, The Great Lawyer Lockout, The Journal of the American Chamber of Commerce in Japan, 10-18, (November 1991).

Barsade, The Effect of EC Regulations upon the Ability of U.S. Lawyers to Establish a Pan-European Practice, 28 Int'l Law. 313 (1994).

Bisconti, Reform of the Professional Law in Italy, 14 Int'l Legal Prac. 55 (1989).

Boyd, Mutual Recognition of Lawyers' Qualifications, Bus. L. Rev. 163 (June 1986).

Brown, The Foreign Lawyer in France, 59 A.B.A.J. 365 (1973).

Busch, The Right of United States Lawyers to Practice Abroad, 3 Int'l Law. 297 (January, 1971).

Busch, The Right of United States Lawyers to Practice Abroad, 3 Int'l Law. 617 (April, 1971).

Comment, Providing Legal Services in Foreign Countries: Making Room for the American Attorney, 83 Colum. L. Rev. 1767, 1768-69 (1983).

Comment: International Legal Practice Restrictions on the Migrant Attorney, 15 Harv. Int'l L.J. 298 (1974).

Comment, The Legal Services Act of the Republic of Croatia -- A Guarantee of the Advocate's Independence and Autonomy, 29 Int'l Law. 209 (1995).

Dedingfield, The Contingency Fee System in America, 143 New Law Journal 1670 (Nov. 26, 1993).

Directory of Legal Aid and Advice Facilities Available Throughout the World, the International Legal Aid Association, International Bar Association, (1966).

Epstein & Snyder, International Litigation: A Guide to Jurisdiction, Practice and Strategy, 2nd, 2.10-2.13, p. 2-17 - 2-24 (1994).

Figa, The "American Rule" Has Outlived Its Usefulness; Adopt the "English Rule," 9 Nat'l L.J. 13 (1986).

Finding the Right Lawyer, American Bar Association, Law Practice Management Section, LC: 94-76852 (1995).

Friedman and Wilson, Representing Foreign Clients in Civil Discovery and Grand Jury Proceedings, 26 Va. J. of Int'l L. 327 (1986).

Georgakakis, Greece Allows Lawyers to Form Companies, Int'l Fin. L. Rev. 12 (July 1990).

Goebel, Lawyers in the European Community: Progress Towards Community-Wide Rights of Practice, 15 Fordham Int'l L. J. 556, 563 (1992).

Goebel, Professional Qualification and Educational Requirements for Law Practice in a Foreign Country: Bridging the Gap, 63 Tul. L. Rev. 443, 475 (1989).

Greiter, How to Get Your Money in Foreign Countries: A Survey of Court Costs and Lawyer's Fees in 151 Countries, (Boston, Kluwer Law and Taxation Publishers, 1988).

Harper, Bye Bye Barrister, 76 American Bar Association Journal 58-62 (Mar. 1990).

Hergen, How to Practice Family Law in Europe When You're Not European", 3 Family Advocate 25, Spring (1981).

Hieros Gamos, List of Bar Associations

Hufbauer, Europe 1992: Opportunities and Challenges, Brookings Rev., Summer 1990 at 15; Story, supra note 12, at 18, 27.

Kenadjian, R. Wohl, S. Chemtob, & G. Fukushima, Practice By Foreign Lawyers in Japan, Fordham International Law Journal, 1989-1990, Vol. 13, No. 3, pp. 390-404.

Knoppek-Wetzel, Employment Restrictions and the Practice of Law by Aliens in the United States and

Abroad, Duke L.J. 871 (1974).

Kritzer, The English Rule, 78 A.B.A.J. 54 (Nov. 1992).

Lewis, Selecting and Working With Foreign Counsel, The International Lawyer's Deskbook, American Bar Association, 393-410 (1996).

Lang, European Community Law, Irish Law and the Irish Legal Profession -- Protection of the Individual and Cooperation between Member States and the Community, 5 D.U.L.J. (n.s.) 1 (June 1983).

Lex Mundi Directory of Law Firm Associations, Alliances, Clubs, and Other Affiliations, Int'l Law. Newsletter, vol. xv, no. 6, 1993, at 26-37.

Lowry, Foreign Legal Consultants in Connecticut, 16 Int'l Legal Prac. 115 (1991).

MacMullin, Foreign Attorneys in Japan: Past Policies, The New Special Measures Law and Future Expectations, Florida International Law Journal, Fall 1988, Vol. 4, No. 1, pp. 51-84.

McCrory, Reform of the English Legal Profession: An American's Perspective, 134 Solicitor's Journal 819-821 (June 1, 1990).

Napier and Armstrong, Costs After the Event (United Kingdom), 143 New Law Journal 12 (Jan. 8, 1993)

Note, Foreign Branches of Law Firms: The Development of Lawyers Equipped to Handle International Practice, 80 Harv. L. Rev. 1284 (1967).

Payment of Attorneys and Litigation Expenses in Selected Foreign Nations, U.S. Library of Congress, Law Library, Doc. LL-95-2 (March 1995).

Pfennigstorf, The European Experience With Attorney Fee Shifting (Research Contributions of the American Bar Foundation, 1984, No. 2.), reprinted from 47 Law and Contemporary Problems 37 (1984).

Ramseyer, Lawyers, Foreign Lawyers, and Lawyer-Substitutes: The Market for Regulation in Japan, Harvard International Law Journal, 1986, Vol. 27, pp. 499-539.

Roorda, The Internationalization of the Practice of Law, 28 Wake Forest L. Rev. 141, 150 (1993).

Rubenstein, Foreign Firms Offer Quality Work at Bargain Rates, Crop. Legal Times Nov. 1992, at 12.

Ryan, The Development of Representative Proceedings in the Federal Court, 11 Aust. Bar Review 131, 139 (1993).

Saunders, The EEC and the USA: Will the Gates Be Oened for American Law Firms in 1992?, 3 Temple Int'l & Comp. L.J. 191, 214 (1989).

Schutzer, An Alien's Right to Practice Law, 38 Alb. L. Rev. 888 (1974).

Scott, The Green Paper on Contingency Fees (United Kingdom), 8 Civil Justice Quarterly 97-103 (April 1989).

Section Recommendation and Report, American Bar Association Section of International Law and Practice Report to the House of Delegates: Model Rule for the Licensing of Legal Consultants, 28 Int'l Law. 207 (1994).

Sheehey, Japan's New Foreign Lawyer Law, Law and Policy in International Business, Vol. 19, No. 2, 1987, pp. 361-383.

Sokol, Reforming the French Legal Profession, 26 Int'l Law. 1025 (1992).

Spedding, Transnational Legal Practice in the EEC and the United States, 185-200 (1987).

Stewart, Is the Siesta Over for Spanish Lawyers, Int'l Fin. L. Rev. 20 (Feb. 1991).

Sydney, Are Some Lawyers More Equal than Others?, Int'l Fin. L. Rev. 16 (Aug. 1989).

Tada, Role of Corporate Legal Departments in Japan, The International Lawyer, Winter 1988, Vol. 22, No. 4, pp. 1141-1144.

The American Lawyer: When and How to Use One, American Bar Association, Public Education Division, PC: 235-0021 (1993).

The Foreign Legal Operations Manual: A Survey and Analysis of U.S. Law Firms Overseas. (s.1.) Abacus Press, Division of Sachem International Corp., 1984.

Toumlin, The Right of Barristers to Practice in the EEC, New L.J. 1309 (1990).

Toumlin, A Worldwide Common Code of Professional Ethics?, 15 Fordham Int'l L.J. 673, 685 (1991-1993).

You and Your Lawyer: A Client's Guide, American Bar Association, General Practice Section, PC: 515-0100-1102 (1994)

Vargo, The American Rule On Attorney Fee Allocation: The Injured Person's Access to Justice (U.S., U.K. & Australia), 42 American University Law Review 1567-1639 (Spring-Summer 1993).

Warren, Monahan & Duhot, Role of the Lawyer in International Business Transactions, 58 A.B.A.J. 181 (1972).

Weil, The Proposal for a Directive on the Right of Establishment for Lawyers in the European Community, 15 Fordham Int'l L.J. 699 (1991-92).

Whetley, A Way to Pay the Piper (contingency fees for U.K. lawyers are to be introduced), The Times 27 (Aug. 17, 1993).

White, Comment, The Reform of the French Legal Profession: A Comment on the Changed Status of

Foreign Lawyers, 11 Colum. J. Transnat'l L. 435 (1972).

Wilson, EEC: Freedom to Provide Services for EEC Lawyers, 19 Harv. Int'l L.J. 379 (1978).

Wright, Firm Associations Provide Network of Global Counsel, Corp. Legal Times, Mar. 1993, at 36.

Zander, The Thatcher Government's Onslaught on the Lawyers: Who Won?, 24 Int'l Law. 753 (1990).

Zheng, The Evolving Role of Lawyers and Legal Practice in China, 36 American Journal of Comparative Law, 473 (1988).

ADDITIONAL INFORMATION: The Office of American Citizens Services has general information flyers on international judicial assistance.

Using the Internet: Many of these flyers are also available on the Internet via the Department of State, Bureau of Consular Affairs home page under Judicial Assistance. See also, the Department of State, Office of the Legal Adviser for Private International Law home page for information regarding private international law unification. See also the home pages for many of our embassies.

Questions: Additional questions may be addressed to the U.S. Department of State, Bureau of Consular Affairs, Office of American Citizens Services at (202) 647-5225 or 202-647-5226.

SOCIAL SECURITY--YOUR PAYMENTS WHILE YOU ARE OUTSIDE THE UNITED STATES

(Based on SSA Publication No. 05-10137, ICN 480085) October 2002

Part 1--Introduction
This document explains how being outside the U.S. may affect your Social Security payments. It also tells you what you need to report to us so we can make sure you receive all the Social Security payments you are entitled to receive. The information in Part 7 tells you how to report. Part 8 tells what you need to report. This document is also available in French, German, Greek, Italian and Spanish, but only in print format. Copies may be obtained by contacting your nearest U.S.

Embassy or consulate or Social Security office.

Part 2--When Are You "Outside Of The U.S."?
When we say you are outside the U.S., we mean that you are not in one of the 50 States, the District of Columbia, Puerto Rico, the U.S. Virgin Islands, Guam, the Northern Mariana Islands or American Samoa. Once you have been away from the U.S. for at least 30 days in a row, you are considered to be outside the country until you return and stay in the U.S. for at least 30 days in a row. If you are not a U.S. citizen, you may also have to establish that you were lawfully present in the U.S. for that 30-day period. For more information, you may contact the nearest U.S. Embassy or consulate or Social Security office.

Part 3--What Happens To Your Right To Social Security Payments When You Are Outside The U.S.?
If you are a U.S. citizen, you may receive your Social Security payments outside the U.S. as long as you are eligible for them.

Regardless of your citizenship, there are certain countries to which we are not allowed to send payments--see Part 5.

Part 3-A

If you are a citizen of one of the countries listed below, Social Security payments will keep coming no matter how long you stay outside the U.S., as long as you are eligible for the payments.
Austria
Belgium
Canada
Chile
Finland
France
Germany
Greece
Ireland
Israel
Italy
Japan
Korea (South)
Luxembourg
Netherlands
Norway
Portugal
Spain
Sweden
Switzerland
United Kingdom

(This list is subject to change from time to time.)

Part 3-B
If you are a citizen of one of the countries listed below, you also may receive your payments as long as you are outside the U.S., **unless you are receiving your payments as a dependent or survivor.** In that case, there are additional requirements you have to meet-see Part 4.

Albania
Antigua and
Barbuda
Argentina
Bahamas
Barbados
Belize
Bolivia
Bosnia-Herzegovina
Brazil
Burkina Faso
Colombia
Costa Rica
Croatia
Cyprus
Czech Republic
Denmark
Dominica
Dominican Republic
Ecuador
El Salvador
Gabon
Grenada
Guatemala
Guyana
Hungary
Iceland
Ivory Coast
Jamaica
Jordan
Latvia
Liechtenstein
Macedonia, Former
Yugoslav Rep. of
Malta
Marshall Islands
Mexico
Micronesia, Fed.
States of
Monaco
Nicaragua
Palau
Panama
Peru
Philippines
Poland

St. Kitts
and Nevis
St. Lucia
Samoa (formerly
Western Samoa)
San Marino
Slovak Republic
Slovenia
Trinidad-Tobago
Turkey
Uruguay
Venezuela
Yugoslavia, Fed. Rep. of
(formerly Serbia & Montenegro)
(This list is subject to change from time to time.)

Part 3-C
If you are **not a citizen** of the U.S. or a **citizen** of one of the other countries listed in Parts 3-A or 3-B above, your payments will stop after you have been outside the U.S. for 6 full calendar months unless you meet one of the following exceptions:

you were eligible for monthly Social Security benefits for December 1956; or

you are in the active military or naval service of the U.S.; or

the worker on whose record your benefits are based had railroad work which was treated as covered employment by the Social Security program; or

the worker on whose record your benefits are based died while in the U.S. military service or as a result of a service-connected disability and was **not** dishonorably discharged; or

you are a **resident** of a country with which the U.S. has a Social Security agreement. Currently, these countries are:

Australia
Austria
Belgium
Canada
Chile
Finland
France
Germany
Greece
Ireland
Italy
Korea (South)
Luxembourg
Netherlands
Norway
Portugal
Spain

269

Sweden
Switzerland
United Kingdom
(This list is subject to change from time to time.)

However, the agreements with Austria, Belgium, Germany, Sweden and Switzerland permit you to receive benefits as a dependent or survivor of a worker while you reside in the foreign country only if the worker is a U.S. citizen or a citizen of your country of residence; or

you are a citizen of one of the countries listed below and the worker on whose record your benefits are based lived in the U.S. for at least 10 years or earned at least 40 earnings credits under the U.S. Social Security system. If you are receiving benefits as a dependent or survivor, see Part 4 for additional requirements.

Afghanistan
Australia
Bangladesh
Bhutan
Botswana
Burundi
Cameroon
Cape Verde Islands
Central African
Rep.
Chad
China, People's
Rep. of
Congo Rep.
Ethiopia
Fiji
Gambia
Ghana
Haiti
Honduras
India
Indonesia
Kenya
Laos
Lebanon
Lesotho
Liberia
Madagascar
Malawi
Malaysia
Mali
Mauritania
Mauritius
Morocco
Myanmar
Nepal
Nigeria
Pakistan

St. Vincent &
Grenadines
Senegal
Sierra Leone
Singapore
Solomon Islands
Somali Dem. Rep.
South Africa,
Rep. of
Sri Lanka
Sudan
Swaziland
Taiwan
Tanzania
Thailand
Togo
Tonga
Tunisia
Uganda
Yemen
(This list is subject to change from time to time.)

If you are not a citizen of one of the countries listed above, you cannot use this exception.

If you are not a U.S. citizen and none of these exceptions applies to you, your payments will stop after you have been outside the U.S. for 6 full months. Once this happens, your payments cannot be started again until you come back and stay in the U.S. for a whole calendar month. This means you have to be in the U.S. on the first minute of the first day of a month and stay through the last minute of the last day of that month. In addition, you may be required to establish that you have been lawfully present in the U.S. for that full calendar month period. For more information, you may contact the nearest U.S. Embassy or consulate or Social Security office.

Part 4--Additional Residency Requirements for Dependents and Survivors
If you receive benefits as a dependent or survivor of the worker, special requirements may affect your right to receive Social Security payments while you are outside the U.S. If you are not a U.S. citizen, you must have lived in the U.S. for at least 5 years. During that 5 years, the family relationship on which benefits are based must have existed. For example, if you are receiving benefits as a spouse, you must have been married to the worker while living in the U.S. for at least 5 years.

Children who cannot meet the residency requirement on their own may be considered to meet it if it is met by the worker and other parent (if any). However, children adopted outside the

270

U.S. will not be paid outside the U.S., even if the residency requirement is met.

The residency requirement will **not** apply to you if you meet any of the following conditions:

you were initially eligible for monthly benefits before January 1, 1985; or

you are entitled on the record of a worker who died while in the U.S. military service or as a result of a service-connected disease or injury; or

you are a citizen of one of the countries listed in Part 3-A; or

you are a resident of one of the countries with which the U.S. has a Social Security agreement (see Part 3-C).

Part 5--Countries to Which We Cannot Send Payments

U.S. Treasury Department regulations prohibit sending payments to you if you are in Cuba or North Korea. In addition, Social Security restrictions prohibit sending payments to individuals in Cambodia, Vietnam or areas (other than Armenia, Estonia, Latvia, Lithuania and Russia) which were in the former Soviet Union. You cannot receive payments while you are in one of these countries, and we cannot send your payments to anyone for you.

If you are a U.S. citizen and are in Cuba or North Korea, you can receive all of your payments that were withheld once you leave that country and go to another country where we can send payments. Generally, if you are not a U.S. citizen, you cannot receive any payments for months in which you live in one of these countries, even though you leave that country and satisfy all other requirements.

Part 6--What You Need To Do To Protect Your Right To Benefits

If you are living outside the U.S., we will send you a questionnaire periodically to fill out and return. This lets us know whether you are still eligible for benefits. You must return the questionnaire to the office that sent it to you as soon as possible; if you do not, your payments will stop.

In addition to responding to the questionnaire, it is your responsibility to notify us promptly about changes that could affect your payments. If you fail to report something or deliberately make a false statement, you could be penalized by a fine or imprisonment. You may also lose some of your payments if you do not report changes promptly.

Part 7--How to Report

Parts 8-A through 8-M explain what you need to report. When you report, you can contact us in person, by mail or by telephone. If you live in Canada, you can send your report to the nearest U.S. Social Security office. If you live in Mexico, you can send your report to the nearest U.S. Social Security office, Embassy or consulate. If you live in the Philippines, your report can be sent to:

Veterans Affairs Regional Office
SSA Division
1131 Roxas Boulevard
Manila, Philippines

In all other countries, you can report to the nearest U.S. Embassy or consulate.

If you find it easiest to contact us by mail, send your report by airmail to the following address:

Social Security Administration
P.O. Box 17769
Baltimore, Maryland 21235-7769
USA

Be sure to include your Social Security claim number. When you contact us, include all of the following information:

name of person or persons about whom the report is being made;

what is being reported and the date it happened; and

the claim number that appears on the person's Social Security check or on the letters or other correspondence we send you. (This is a nine-digit number--000-00-0000--followed by a letter, or a letter and a number.)

Part 8--Things That Must Be Reported

Listed below are things that must be reported. An explanation of each is given in the part listed.

It is very important that you tell us if your address changes so your checks will not be lost or delayed. Even if your payments are being sent to a bank, you must report any change in your home address.

When you write to the U.S. Embassy or consulate or the Social Security Administration about a change of address, please type or print your new address carefully and be sure to include the country and ZIP or postal code. Also, be sure to list the names of all of your family members who will be receiving payments at the new address.

Part 8-B--Work Outside The U.S.

If you work or own a business outside the U.S. and you are younger than the full retirement age, notify the nearest U.S. Embassy or consulate or Social Security office right away. **You should notify us promptly.** If you don't, it could result in a penalty which could cause the loss of benefits. This loss of benefits would be in addition to those which might be withheld under one of the work tests explained later in this part.

For persons born in 1937 or earlier, **full retirement age** is 65. Beginning with persons born in 1938, full retirement age increases two months per year until it becomes age 66 for individuals born in 1943 through 1954. Then it will gradually increase until it becomes age 67 for those born in 1960 and later.

You must report your work even if the job is part-time or you are self-employed. Some examples of the types of work which should be reported are work as an apprentice, farmer, sales representative, tutor, writer, etc. If you own a business, you should notify us even if you do not work in the business or receive any income from it.

If a child beneficiary (regardless of age) begins an apprenticeship, notify the nearest U.S. Embassy or consulate or the Social Security Administration. An apprenticeship may be considered work under the Social Security program.

The following work tests may affect the amount of your monthly benefit payment. Work after full retirement age does not affect the payment of benefits.

The Foreign Work Test

A monthly benefit is withheld for each month in which a beneficiary younger than full retirement age works more than 45 hours outside the U.S. in employment or self-employment which is not subject to U.S. Social Security taxes. It does not matter how much was earned or how many hours were worked each day.

A person is considered to be working on any day he or she:

    actually works as an employee or self-employed person; or

has an agreement to work even if he or she does not actually work because of sickness, vacation, etc.; or

is the owner or part owner of a trade or business even if he or she does not actually work in the trade or business or receive any income from it.

Generally, if a retired worker's benefits are withheld because of his or her work, no benefits can be paid to any other people receiving benefits on his or her record for those months. However, the work of others receiving benefits on the worker's record affects only their own benefits.

The Annual Retirement Test

Under certain conditions, work performed outside the U.S. by U.S. citizens or residents is covered by the U.S. Social Security program. If your work is covered by U.S. Social Security, the same annual retirement test that applies to people in the U.S. will apply to you.

NOTE: Work by some U.S. citizens and residents outside the U.S. is exempt from U.S. Social Security as a result of international Social Security agreements the U.S. has concluded with the following countries:

Australia
Austria
Belgium
Canada
Chile
Finland
France
Germany
Greece
Ireland
Italy
Korea (South)
Luxembourg
Netherlands
Norway
Portugal
Spain
Sweden
Switzerland
United Kingdom
(This list is subject to change from time to time.)

If you are working in one of these countries and your earnings are exempt from U.S. Social Security taxes because of the agreement, your benefits will be subject to the Foreign Work Test described above. For further information on how your benefits may be affected by an agreement, contact the nearest U.S. Embassy or consulate or

Social Security office.

If your work is covered by the U.S. Social Security program, you can receive all benefits due you for the year if your earnings do not exceed the annual exempt amount. This limit changes each year. If you want to know the current limit, ask at any U.S. Embassy or consulate or Social Security office or write to us at the address shown under "How To Report" in Part 7.

If your earnings go over the limit, some or all of your benefits will be reduced by your earnings.

If you are younger than full retirement age, $1 in benefits will be withheld for each $2 in earnings above the limit.

In the year you reach full retirement age, your benefits will be reduced $1 for every $3 you earn over a different, higher limit until the month you reach full retirement age.

You must count your earnings for the whole year in figuring the benefits due you. For most people, this means earnings from January through December.

People who reach full retirement age or older can receive all of their benefits with no limit on their earnings.

THE YEAR YOUR BENEFITS START--In figuring your total earnings for the year in which you first become entitled to benefits, count earnings in that year for months both before and after you became entitled.

THE YEAR YOU REACH AGE 18--Your benefits as a child stop at age 18 unless you are a full-time student in an elementary or secondary school or you are disabled. Your earnings for the entire year in which you reach age 18 count in figuring the amount of benefits due you for the year regardless of whether your payments continue or stop at age 18.

Part 8-C--Disabled Person Returns To Work Or Disability Improves
If you receive payments because you are disabled, let us know right away if your condition improves or if you go back to work. You can keep receiving payments for up to 9 months while you are working. This 9-month period is called a "trial work period." The trial work period gives you a chance to test whether or not you are able to work without worrying about having your payments stopped. If, after 9 months, you are able to

continue working, you will get payments for 3 more months before they stop. If you are not able to keep working, you will continue to receive disability benefits.

Part 8-D--Marriage
Let us know if any person receiving benefits gets married. In some cases, Social Security payments stop after marriage. In other cases, the amount of the payments changes. This depends on the kind of benefits you receive and, sometimes, on whether the person you marry gets payments.

Part 8-E--Divorce Or Annulment
You should notify us if your marriage is annulled or you get a divorce. Divorce or annulment does not necessarily mean that your Social Security payments will stop. If you are receiving payments based on your own work record, divorce or annulment of your marriage will not affect your payments. Also, if you are a spouse age 62 or older and you were married to the worker for 10 years or more, your payments will continue even if you divorce. But you should still contact us if your name is changed as a result of the divorce so that we can show your new name on your payments.

Part 8-F--Adoption Of A Child
When a child is adopted, let us know the child's new name, the date of the adoption decree and the adopting parent's name and address.
Part 8-G--Child Leaves The Care Of A Wife, Husband, Widow Or Widower

If you are a wife, husband, widow or widower receiving benefits because you are caring for a child who is under age 16 or who was disabled before age 22, you should notify us right away if the child leaves your care. If you don't, it could result in a penalty which would cause an additional loss of benefits.

A temporary separation may not affect your benefits as long as you still have parental control over the child. You should tell us, though, if there is any change in where you or the child lives, or if you no longer have responsibility for the child. If the child returns to your care, you should tell us that also.

Part 8-H--Child Nearing Age 18 Is A Full-Time Student Or Is Disabled
Payments to a child will stop when the child reaches age 18 unless he or she is unmarried and either disabled or a full-time student at an

273

elementary or secondary school.

If a child age 18 or older is receiving payments as a student, we should be notified immediately if the student:

drops out of school;

changes schools;

changes from full-time to part-time attendance;

is expelled or suspended;

is paid by his or her employer for attending school;

marries; or

begins working.

If a child whose payments were stopped at age 18 either becomes disabled before age 22 or is unmarried and enters elementary or secondary school on a full-time basis before age 19, notify us so we can resume sending payments to the child. Also, a disabled child who recovers from a disability can have payments started again if he or she becomes disabled again within 7 years.

Part 8-I--Death

If a person who receives Social Security benefits dies, a benefit is not payable for the month of death. For example, if a beneficiary died any time in June, the payment dated July 3 (which is payment for June) should be returned to the sender.

Part 8-J--Inability To Manage Funds

Some people who receive Social Security payments cannot manage their own funds. When this happens, the person who takes care of the beneficiary should let us know. We can arrange to send the payments to a relative or other person who can act on behalf of the beneficiary. We call this person a "representative payee."

Part 8-K--Deportation Or Removal From the U.S.

If you are deported or removed from the U.S. for certain reasons, your Social Security benefits are stopped and cannot be started again unless you are lawfully admitted to the U.S. for permanent residence.

Even if you are deported or removed, your dependents can receive benefits if they are U.S. citizens.

If your dependents are not U.S. citizens, they can still receive benefits if they stay in the U.S. for the entire month. But they cannot receive benefits for any month if they spend any part of it outside the U.S.

Part 8-L--Changes In Parental Circumstances

Payments to a child who is not a U.S. citizen could stop or start when certain changes occur. Let us know when the child's natural, adoptive or stepparent dies, marries or gets a divorce (or annulment), even if that person does not receive Social Security payments.

Part 8-M--Eligibility For A Pension From Work Not Covered By Social Security

If, after 1985, you become entitled to a U.S. Social Security retirement or disability benefit and you also start to receive a monthly pension, such as a foreign social security or private pension, which is based in whole or in part on work not covered by U.S. Social Security, your U.S. Social Security benefit may be smaller. A different formula may be used to figure your U.S. Social Security benefit. For more information, ask at any U.S. Embassy or consulate or Social Security office for the factsheet, The Windfall Elimination Provision (Publication No.05- 10045).

Part 9--If Your Check Is Lost Or Stolen

It usually takes longer to deliver checks outside the U.S. because of the longer distances and extra handling needed. Delivery time varies from country to country and your check may not arrive the same day each month, so we ask you to be patient. But, if you do not receive your check after a reasonable waiting period, or if it is lost or stolen, contact the nearest U.S. Embassy or consulate or write directly to the Social Security Administration. Our address is:

Social Security Administration
P.O. Box 17769
Baltimore, Maryland 21235-7769
USA

We will replace your check as soon as possible. But please make every effort to keep your check safe, because it will take some time to replace a check while you are outside the country.

Part 10--Direct Deposit In Financial Institutions

You may want your Social Security payment to be deposited directly into your account at either a financial institution in the country where you live or a U.S. financial institution. Even if you use the direct deposit service, you must keep us informed of any change in your current residence address.

Direct deposit has several advantages. You never

have to worry about your check being delayed in the mail, lost or stolen. With direct deposit, you receive your payment much faster than if you are paid by check (usually 1 to 3 weeks faster than check deliveries). When direct deposit payments are sent to a financial institution, you also avoid check cashing and currency conversion fees. Some countries where direct deposit and other forms of electronic payments are available include

Anguilla
Antigua & Barbuda
Argentina
Australia
Austria
Bahama Islands
Barbados
Belgium
British Virgin Islands
Canada
Cayman Islands
Cyprus
Denmark
Dominican Republic
Finland
France
Germany
Grenada
Haiti
Hong Kong
Ireland
Italy
Jamaica
Malta
Netherlands
Netherlands Antilles
New Zealand
Norway
Portugal
St. Kitts & Nevis
St. Lucia
St. Vincent & the Grenadines
South Africa
Spain
Sweden
Switzerland
Trinidad & Tobago
United Kingdom

To determine if direct deposit is available in the country where you live--or to sign up for direct deposit--contact the nearest U.S. Embassy or consulate or U.S. Social Security office, or write to the Social Security Administration, P.O. Box 17769, Baltimore, Maryland 21235-7769, USA.

Part 11--Taxes

If you are a U.S. citizen or U.S. resident, up to 85 percent of the Social Security benefits you receive may be subject to the Federal income tax.

If you file a Federal income tax return as an "individual" and your combined income is $25,000 to $34,000, you may have to pay taxes on up to 50 percent of your Social Security benefits. "Combined income" means your adjusted gross income plus nontaxable interest plus one-half of your Social Security benefits. If your combined income is over $34,000, you may have to pay taxes on up to 85 percent of your Social Security benefits.

If you file a joint tax return, you may have to pay taxes on up to 50 percent of your Social Security benefits if you and your spouse have a combined income of $32,000 to $44,000. If your combined income is over $44,000, you may have to pay taxes on up to 85 percent of your Social Security benefits.

If you are a member of a couple and file a separate return, you probably will pay taxes on your benefits.

If you are not a U.S. citizen or a resident, Federal income taxes will be withheld from your benefits. The tax is 30 percent of 85 percent of your benefit amount.

It will be withheld from the benefits of all nonresident aliens, except those who reside in countries which have tax treaties with the U.S. that do not permit taxing of U.S. Social Security benefits (or provide for a lower tax rate). The U.S. has such treaties with **Canada, Egypt, Germany, Ireland, Israel, Italy, Japan, Romania, Switzerland and the United Kingdom** (defined as England, Scotland, Wales and Northern Ireland). In addition, the Social Security benefits paid to individuals who are citizens and residents of India are exempt from this tax to the extent that their benefits are based on Federal, State or local government employment. (This list of countries may change from time to time.)

After the end of the year, you will receive a statement showing the amount of benefits you were paid during the year.

Many foreign governments tax U.S. Social Security benefits. U.S. residents planning to live in another country should contact that country's embassy in Washington, D.C. for information.

Keep in mind that Social Security benefits are calculated in U.S. dollars. The benefits are not increased or decreased because of changes in international exchange rates.

Part 12--What You Need To Know About Medicare

Medicare is a health insurance program for eligible people who are age 65 or older or disabled. Medicare protection consists of two parts: hospital insurance and medical insurance. The hospital insurance part of Medicare pays hospital bills and certain follow-up care after you leave the hospital. Medical insurance helps pay doctor bills and other medical services.

Medicare generally does not cover health services you get outside the U.S. The hospital insurance part of Medicare is available to you if you return to the U.S. No monthly premium is withheld from your benefit payment for this protection.

If you want the Medical insurance part of Medicare, you must enroll and there is a monthly premium which normally will be withheld from your payment. Since Medicare benefits are available only in the U.S., it may not be to your advantage to sign up and pay the premium for medical insurance if you will be out of the U.S. for a long period of time. But you should be aware that your premium, when you do sign up, will be 10 percent higher for each 12-month period you could have been enrolled but were not.

If you are already covered by medical insurance and wish to cancel it, you should notify us. Medical insurance--and premiums-- will continue for one more month after the month you notify us that you wish to cancel it.

Part 13--Want More Information?

If you want more information than this document gives or if you have any questions about Social Security, ask at any U.S. Embassy or consulate or Social Security office, or write to us at the appropriate address shown under "How To Report" in Part 7.

This document is also published in French, German, Greek, Italian, and Spanish, but these foreign-language versions are available only in print format. Copies may be obtained by contacting your nearest U.S. Embassy or consulate or Social Security office.

Application for a Social Security Card
(SS-5-FS) - Foreign Service

The "Application For A Social Security Card" (Form SS-5-FS) is the form to be completed if you have never had a number before or need a duplicate or corrected card. Use this form if you are living outside the United States or are applying for a number or card on behalf of a child who is living outside the United States. If you (or the child on whose behalf you are applying) is living outside the United States, we can assign a number or issue a duplicate or corrected card if you (or the child) are: (1) a United States citizen or (2) a noncitizen admitted to the United States for permanent residence or with other INS authority to work. Otherwise, we can assign a number or issue a duplicate or corrected card only if a Social Security number is required by law as a condition of receiving a federally-funded benefit to which you (or the child) has established entitlement.

Complete the SS-5-FS following the instructions on the form. Also see the form for the evidence you will need.

Finally, you should take or mail the completed form with the required original documents or copies certified by the custodian of the record to the nearest U.S. Social Security office, U.S. Embassy or consulate, or if you live in the Philippines, to the Veterans Affairs Regional Office in Manila. If you are a U.S. military dependent or a U.S. citizen working on a U.S. military post, you may also go to the Post Adjutant or Personnel Office. These offices can copy and certify your records so that you do not have to send original documents through the mail. Do NOT mail original documents to the Social Security Administration in Baltimore, Maryland.

Your Social Security card will be mailed to you from the United States.

NOTE: Medicare: Medicare benefits are not available outside the United States. For information about Medicare see http://www.ssa.gov/mediinfo.htm and http://www.medicare.gov/

NOTE: Medicare: Medicare benefits are not

available outside the United States. For information about

TRAVEL SMART

Preparation for your trip

Start Early. Passports are required to enter and/or depart most countries around the world. Apply for a passport as soon as possible. Some countries also require U.S. citizens to obtain visas before entering. Check with the embassy of the foreign country that you are planning to visit to see if you need a visa. (Passport and visa information is available on the Internet at http://travel.state.gov. Passport information is also available by calling 1 - 900-225-5674 or, with a major credit card, 1-888-362-8668.)

Make a copy of your passport's data page. Make a copy of your passport's data page and any visas. Keep it with you, but separate from the originals, at all times while traveling.

Remember to leave an itinerary with family or friends. Leave a detailed itinerary and a copy of your passport or other citizenship documents with a friend or relative in the United States.

Find out the location of the nearest U.S. embassy or consulate. If you are traveling to a remote area or one that is experiencing civil unrest, end out the location of the nearest U.S. embassy or consulate and register with the Consular Section when you arrive. (Embassy and consulate locations can be found on the Internet at http://travel.state.gov/

Learn about the country you plan to visit. Before departing, take the time to do some research about the people and their culture, and any problems that the country is experiencing that may affect your travel plans.

Read the Consular Information Sheet. Consular Information Sheets provide up-to-date travel information on any country in the world that you plan to visit. They cover topics such as entry regulations, the crime and security situation, and the location of the U.S. embassy, consulates and consular agencies.

Check for Travel Warnings and Public Announcements. A Travel Warning advises travelers not to go to a country because of dangerous conditions. A Public Announcement provides fast-breaking information about relatively short-term conditions that pose risks to the security of travelers.

Top Ten Tips for Travelers

1. Make sure you have a signed, valid passport and visas, if required. Also, before you go, fill in the emergency information page of your passport!

2. Read the Consular Information Sheets (and Public Announcements or Travel Warnings, if applicable) for the countries you plan to visit. (See the section "Preparation for Your Trip")

3. Leave copies of your itinerary, passport data page and visas with family or friends at home, so that you can be contacted in case of an emergency.

4. Make sure you have insurance that will cover your emergency medical needs while you are overseas.

5. Familiarize yourself with local laws and customs of the countries to which you are traveling. Remember, while in a foreign country, you are subject to its laws!

6. Do not leave your luggage unattended in public areas and never accept packages from strangers.

7. While abroad, avoid using illicit drugs or drinking excessive amounts of alcoholic beverages, and associating with people who do.

8. Do not become a target for thieves by wearing conspicuous clothing and expensive jewelry and do not carry excessive amounts of cash or unnecessary credit cards.

9. Deal only with authorized agents when you exchange money or purchase art or antiques in order to avoid violating local laws.

10. When overseas, avoid demonstrations and other situations that may become unruly or where anti-American sentiments may be expressed.

PROPERTY DISPUTES: TOURIST, TRADE AND COMMERCIAL COMPLAINTS, FOREIGN CLAIMS

U.S. CUSTOMS AND TREASURY REQUIREMENTS

DISCLAIMER: THE INFORMATION IN THIS CIRCULAR IS PROVIDED FOR GENERAL INFORMATION ONLY AND MAY NOT BE TOTALLY APPLICABLE IN A PARTICULAR CASE. QUESTIONS INVOLVING INTERPRETATION OF SPECIFIC U.S. OR FOREIGN LAWS SHOULD BE ADDRESSED TO APPROPRIATE LEGAL COUNSEL.

This is an official U.S. Government source. Inclusion of non-U.S. Government links does not imply endorsement of contents.

The Department of State and U.S. consular officers abroad receive numerous inquiries about a variety of issues related to potential legal disputes involving property, tourism, trade and investment abroad. These issues are handled by a variety of offices in the Department of State and in other U.S. Government agencies. This information is designed to assist you in locating the best source of help.

FREQUENTLY ASKED QUESTIONS

What can the State Department do for me if I am involved in a legal dispute abroad?
The Department of State and officers of the Foreign Service are prohibited by Federal regulations from acting as agents, attorneys or in a fiduciary capacity on behalf of U.S. citizens in private legal disputes abroad (22 CFR 92.81). U.S. embassies and consulates can assist in facilitating communication with foreign authorities or businesses and making inquiries on behalf of U.S. citizens in tourist, trade and other commercial disputes. They may also be able to provide general information, but not legal advice, about how the legal systems work in the foreign country, and furnish you with a list of foreign attorneys. In addition, our Office of American Citizens Services and Crisis Management in the Bureau of Consular Affairs has information available about service of process and obtaining evidence abroad.

Can U.S. consular officers assist in taking possession of my belongings abroad if I am unable to do so?
Consular officers are not authorized to accept for safekeeping private property except under very limited circumstances related to the death of a U.S. citizen abroad. See our information regarding estates of U.S. citizens who die abroad. Under current U.S. law and regulations (22 U.S.C. 4195; 22 CFR Part 72), the only time a consular officer may take possession of the property of a U.S. citizen is (a) when acting as provisional conservator of the estate of a deceased American abroad; (b) when taking custody of the effects of a deceased American seaman; or (c) when taking jurisdiction over a U.S. registered vessel, its cargo or effects on board following a disaster at sea. Consular officers can assist in referring you to local shipping and storage companies that may be able to assist you. If a U.S. citizen's wallet or purse is located by local police and returned to the U.S. embassy or consulate, the consular officer will attempt to locate you and return your belongings to you. Shipping expenses must be paid by the U.S. citizen.

How do I find a foreign attorney?
Lists of foreign attorneys are available by contacting the Department of State, Bureau of Consular Affairs, Overseas Citizens Services, Office of American Citizen Services and Crisis Management at (202) 647-5225 or from U.S. embassies and consulates abroad. In addition, many U.S. embassies are now placing their lists of attorneys on their home pages. See links to home pages of U.S. embassy and consulates. Links to many U.S. embassy lists of attorneys are also available on the Bureau of Consular Affairs home page. See also our general information flyer, *Retaining A Foreign Attorney*.

Will the U.S. Government pay for my legal expenses?
The U.S. Government is not authorized to pay for the legal expenses of U.S. citizens abroad. Some foreign countries have legal aid available, available primarily in criminal matters. This topic may be discussed in the U.S. embassy list of attorneys. For additional information, contact the local foreign bar association, Ministry of Justice, or legal attache or consular section at the foreign embassy in Washington, D.C. about the availability of legal aid. Information about how to contact foreign embassies and consulates in the United States.

278

Where can a U.S. company get help with a complaint involving a foreign company?
Consumer or other contractual complaints (not collection cases) in excess of $500, in which the complainant has made an effort to settle the dispute but had not filed a legal action, may be referred to the U.S. Department of Commerce, International Trade Administration or contact the Department of Commerce's regional foreign business center. The U.S. Department of Commerce, Trade Information Center is the first stop for information about all U.S. Federal Government export assistance programs, general export counseling, and country and regional market information. Please call ITA at 1-800-USA-TRADE to receive personal export assistance from a trade specialist Monday through Friday 8:30 a.m. until 5:30 p.m. (EST) or consult the TIC home page. Other possible sources of help include chambers of commerce. See the home pages for the International Chamber of Commerce; the U.S. Chamber of Commerce, International and U.S. Chambers of Commerce Abroad.

Where can a U.S. traveler get help with a tourist complaint involving a foreign country or business?
For assistance with tourism complaints, contact the foreign embassy or consulate in the United States. It may also be useful to contact the foreign country's tourism office in the United States. In case of serious problems, contact the Department of State, Bureau of Consular Affairs, Office of American Citizen Services and Crisis Management at (202) 647-5225 or the local U.S. embassy or consulate abroad.

Where can a U.S. investor find assistance in connection with an investment dispute abroad?
Contact the Department of State, Bureau of Economic Affairs, International Finance and Development, Office of Investment Affairs (EB/IFD/OIA), at 202-647-4907; fax: 202-647-0320; email: eboia@state.gov.

U.S. Business Investment Treaty Program (BIT). BITs give U.S. investors the right to submit an investment dispute with the treaty partner's government to international arbitration. There is no requirement to use that country's domestic courts. See also information about the work of the Department of State, Coordinator for Business Affairs; See the U.S. Department of State's Bill of Right for American business.

Where can I find information about export licensing requirements?
For assistance in determining your export licensing requirements, contact the U.S. Department of Commerce, Bureau of Export Administration, Export Counseling Division or for help from the Department of Commerce or write to the U.S. Department of Commerce, Export Counseling Division, Room 2705, 14th and Pennsylvania Ave., N.W., U.S. Department of Commerce, Export Counseling Division, Washington, D.C. 20230.

Where can I find information about U.S. Treasury Restrictions and Foreign Asset Controls?
For information about licensing criteria, contact the U.S. Department of Treasury, Licensing Division, Office of Foreign Assets Control (OFAC), Info-by-Fax 202-622-0077, or write to the U.S. Department of the Treasury, OFAC, 1500 Pennsylvania Avenue, N.W., Treasury Annex, Washington, D.C. 20220.

What are U.S. Customs, Agriculture Department and Fish and Wildlife Service requirements about bringing articles, food, and animals back to the United States from overseas?
See the U.S. Customs Service *Know Before You Go* and *Pets, Wildlife, U.S. Customs*, other useful information about restricted and prohibited merchandise, medications/drugs, etc. See the U.S. Department of Agriculture's *Travelers' Tips On Bringing Food, Plant, and Animal Products Into the United States*. See also the U.S. Fish and Wildlife Service publications, *Facts About Federal Wildlife Laws* and *Buyer Beware Guide*.

What can the Department of State do to assist U.S. citizens pursuing claims against foreign governments?
The Department of State seeks to provide appropriate assistance whenever possible in claims involving United States citizens against foreign states. However, the ability of the United States to pursue individual claims formally must be determined on a case-by-case basis in accordance with generally recognized principles of international law. In order for the United States to be able to present a formal claim against a foreign government, the claimant must have been a U.S. citizen at the time the claim arose. Furthermore, the claimant must have exhausted local judicial and/or administrative remedies, or have demonstrated that to do so would be futile. Unless

these conditions are met, the United States Government can not consider formal presentation of a claim. Inquiries about such claims may be addressed to the Office of the Legal Adviser, International Claims and Investment Disputes (L/CID), Department of State, (202) 776-8430. For information about the service provisions of the Foreign Sovereign Immunities Act and guidance on how to effect service under the Act, see our Bureau of Consular Affairs information at http://travel.state.gov/fsia.html.

How do I file a claim against a foreign government under a foreign claims settlement agreement?

See the Foreign Claims Settlement Commission home page for answers to questions about pursuing claims under existing agreements. The Foreign Claims Settlement Commission of the United States is a quasi-judicial, independent agency within the Department of Justice which adjudicates claims of U.S. nationals against foreign governments, either under specific jurisdiction conferred by Congress or pursuant to international claims settlement agreements.

Office of Authentication

The Department of State is responsible for providing authentication service to U.S. citizens and foreign nationals on all documents that will be used overseas. Types of documents include corporate documents such as company bylaws and articles of incorporation, power of attorney, patent applications and trademarks, diplomas, transcripts, letters relating to degrees, non-marital status, references and job certifications, home studies, deeds of assignments, distributorship agreements, papers for adoption purposes, etc.

The Authentications Office receives a variety of documents from commercial organizations, private citizens, and officials of the Federal and State Governments. The Office is responsible for issuing certificates under the Seal of the Department of State. It also ensures that the requested information will serve in the interest of justice and is not contrary to U.S. policy.

Please note the following information must be obtained before the authentication process can begin.
1. Signed before a notary public.

2. Certified by the clerk of Court of the County in which the document is commissioned.*
3. Certified by the Secretary of State of the State in which the document is executed.
4. All seals and signatures must be originals.
5. All dates must follow in chronological order on all certifications.
6. All documents in foreign text must be accompanied with a certified (notarized) English translation.
7. Whenever a copy (if acceptable) is used, it must include a statement that it is a true and accurate copy.
8. Foreign governments require the U.S. Department of State to authenticate documents in order for the document to be considered legal. Therefore, it is suggested that you contact the embassy of the particular country to determine what documents are needed for transactions.
*Item 2 may be omitted if the authority in item 3 will certify directly to the notary.

A request for authentication services under 22 CFR, Part 131, should include the reason for authentication and the name of the country where the document will be used. Contact information is below.

Authentications Office (A/OPR/GSM/AUTH)
518 23rd Street, N.W.
State Annex 1
Washington, DC 20037
Tel: 202 647-5002
TDD: 202 663-3468
1 800 688-9889
Fax: 202 663-3636 or you can email us at AOPRGSMAUTHSTATE.GOV.
For information about American citizens who were born, married, or deceased abroad, contact the Passport Office, U.S. Department of State, 1111 19th Street, N.W., Washington, DC 20520, Tel. 202-955-0307. Copies of consular reports of birth, marriage, and deaths may be obtained from this office.

Traveling with Samples

As a business traveler, you have several options available for facilitating the movement of commercial samples into and out of the United States:

Payment of Duty
You may elect to pay any applicable duty and/or taxes upon arrival. This releases the samples to the

authorized importer, enabling them to move freely within the United States to be either sold or exported at the importers convenience.

If the imported merchandise is exported in the same condition as declared upon the original payment of duty, it may be eligible for drawback.

Temporary Importation Under Bond (TIB)
Samples used solely for taking orders for merchandise may be eligible for admittance into the United States without the payment of duty under a Temporary Importation Under Bond (TIB). The condition is that the samples not be sold and that they are exported within one year from their date of importation. An extension of the bond period can be granted for a total of three years, after which time the importer becomes liable for liquidated damages in the amount of the bond.

ATA Carnet

The "Admission Temporaire - Temporary Admission", or the ATA Carnet, is an international customs document which may be used for the temporary duty free importation of merchandise. This is in-lieu-of the usual customs documents required for entry. The carnet serves as a guarantee against the payment of duties which may become due if the merchandise is not re-exported.

A carnet is valid for one year, however, you may make as many trips as desired during the period the carnet is valid. It can also be used for moving goods within the United States as prescribed in the regulations under 19 C.F.R. Part 114.

Local associations issue carnets to their residents. In the United States, the U.S. Council for International Business, located at 1212 Avenue of the Americas, New York, NY, has been designated by the U.S. Customs Service as the issuing and guaranteeing organization for the United States. A fee is charged for this service.

What is an ATA carnet?
The ATA Carnet is an international Customs document that a traveler may use temporarily to import certain goods into a country without having to engage in the Customs formalities usually required for the importation of goods, and without

having to pay duty or value-added taxes on the goods.

The United States allows for the temporary importation of commercial samples, professional equipment and certain advertising materials by a nonresident individual.

Carnets are a security that participating countries accept as a guarantee against the payment of Customs duties that may become due on goods temporarily imported under a carnet and not exported as required. "ATA" stands for the combined French and English words "Admission Temporaire-Temporary Admission."

Why use an ATA carnet?
The ATA carnet simplifies the Customs formalities involved in temporarily importing goods into the U.S. and other countries. Without a carnet it would be necessary to go through the Customs procedures established in each country for the temporary admission of goods. The carnet allows the business traveler to use a single document for clearing certain categories of goods through Customs in several different countries. It may be used for unlimited exits from and entries into the U.S. and participating foreign countries during the one-year period of validity. They are accepted as the entry document and satisfy the importer's obligation to post a security in more than 87 countries.

Why not use Temporary Importation under Bond?
Foreign importers who choose to use a TIB to temporarily enter goods into the United States must file either Customs Form (CF) 3461, "Entry/Immediate Delivery," or 7501, "Entry Summary" to clear their shipment. This usually necessitates leaving the passenger terminal and going to the Cargo Entry Branch office, or having a Customs broker do your legwork for you. The importer will also need to secure a bond from a licensed surety. No forms, other than the carnet, need to be filed for goods entered under an ATA carnet.

What are the Importer's Obligations?
A carnet holder is obligated to present the goods and carnet to Customs to prove exportation. Failure to prove exportation on either a TIB or a carnet subjects the importer to liquidated damages equal to 110 percent of the duty and import tax. Goods imported under either a TIB or a carnet

281

may not be offered for sale.

Who issues ATA carnets?
Domestic associations in participating countries that are members of the International Bureau of Chambers of Commerce issue carnets to residents to be used abroad. The United States Council for International Business http://www.uscib.org (USCIB) has been designated by the U.S. Customs Service as the United States issuing and guaranteeing organization. A fee is charged by the Council for its service. The guaranteeing organization is held liable for the payment of liquidated damages if the carnet holder, such as the importer, fails to comply with Customs regulations.

How long is an ATA carnet valid for?
An ATA carnet is valid for one year from the date of its issuance. Merchandise listed on an ATA carnet can be imported to and exported from any of the member countries as many times as needed during the one-year life of the carnet.

What goods may be entered under an ATA carnet?
Commercial samples, professional equipment and advertising material can be imported into the United States by a nonresident.

Other countries permit the use of a carnet to import the above materials and other categories of goods such as:

- Ordinary goods such as computers, tools, cameras and video equipment, industrial machinery, automobiles, gems and jewelry, and wearing apparel.

- Extraordinary items, for example, Van Gogh's self-portrait, circus animals, jets, band instruments, satellites, human skulls, and the New York Philharmonic's equipment.

What does a ATA carnet not cover?
Merchandise not covered by the three above listed categories of goods are not eligible for importation into the U.S. by carnet. In addition, merchandise within those three categories intended for sale or sale on approval cannot be entered on a carnet – it must be entered as a regular Customs entry.

What happens if the goods are not exported?
If the holder of an ATA carnet sells, donates or otherwise disposes of any of the goods listed on the carnet, the issuing organization will be required to pay liquidated damages equal to 100 percent of the import duties and taxes. That organization in turn will attempt to collect these moneys from the holder of the carnet who violated the terms. In some cases, the country where the violation occurred will hold both the organization that issued the carnet and the importer equally responsible. The importer is liable to his/her issuing association (and, in some cases, to the Customs authorities of the country where this transpired) for all duties and/or taxes and other sums which would normally be charged on the importation of such goods, as well as the amount charged as liquidated damages. If the U.S. Customs Service finds that there was fraud involved in the importation, additional penalties may be assessed.

What happens when goods covered by a U.S.-issued ATA carnet are reimported into the U.S.?
If goods covered by a U.S.-issued carnet are brought back into the United States within the validity period of the carnet, the carnet serves as the Customs control registration document and must be presented on re-importation. Whether the re-imported goods are subject to duty depends on exemption in the Harmonized Tariff Schedule http://www.usitc.gov/taffairs.htm and not on their status as carnet goods. See 19 CFR 141.4 for goods that are exempted from entry documentation requirements and 19 CFR 141.2 for goods exempted from duty on re-importation.

What if the ATA carnet has expired?
If the expiring ATA carnet is a U.S.-issued carnet there will be no penalties or duties assessed by the United States, however, there may be penalties assessed by a foreign government if the carnet expired before the U.S. merchandise was exported from that country.

If the carnet is foreign-issued then liquidated damages will be assessed by the U.S. Customs Service due to the carnet expiring before the merchandise could be exported out of the United States.

What is contained in an ATA carnet document?
The carnet document has a green cover page which provides the names of the carnet holder and issuing association, the carnet issue date, the carnet number, the countries in which the carnet may be used and a complete description of the goods covered. Two yellow sheets in the package

are to be used upon exportation from and reimportation back into the issuing country. White sheets are used for the temporary importation into and reexportation from the second or additional countries. Blue sheets are used when transiting though   countries.

Each sheet contains two parts – a counterfoil, which remains in the carnet and describes the actions taken by Customs officers each time goods enter or leave a country, and a detachable voucher, which contains a list of the goods covered by the carnet and serves as the required Customs document.

How is a U.S.-issued ATA carnet processed by Customs?

When leaving the United States, the holder of a U.S.-issued ATA carnet presents the carnet and the covered goods to a Customs officer. The carnet is reviewed for completeness and accuracy and the goods are examined to ensure that they match the carnet list. The officer then validates the carnet document and certifies the appropriate exportation counterfoil and voucher. The carnet and the U.S. Customs-certified export voucher are returned to the carnet holder who retains the voucher as the permanent record of the Customs transaction. (Note: The carnet does not affect export control requirements such as the filing of a shipper's export declaration or the requirement to obtain export licenses.) Upon return to the United States, the holder of a U.S.-issued carnet presents the carnet and covered goods to a Customs officer for examination. The officer certifies the appropriate reimportation counterfoil and voucher and returns the carnet to the holder for further use or surrender to the issuing association. (Note: On U.S.-issued carnets only, the vouchers of the yellow exportation/reimportation sheets will not be detached, but will remain with the document when departing or returning to the United States.)

It is the responsibility of the carnet holder to present the carnet to the Customs authorities when entering or leaving a country in order that the necessary verification and certification of the appropriate vouchers and counterfoils can take place. Failure to do so may result in a claim being made. A claim is a notice from a Customs authority of the country of import that a violation of the carnet system has occurred and payment of duties, taxes, and penalty are required.

How is a non-U.S.-issued ATA carnet processed?

When processing a foreign-issued carnet, Customs must create a record of the transaction in order to protect the revenue and domestic commerce. Therefore, the U.S. Customs officer responsible for clearing the temporary importation must ensure that the port of importation, dates of Customs activities, and any departure from the original list of articles, are clearly shown in the appropriate fields.

When the merchandise leaves the U.S. the Customs officer must ensure that the required exportation dates are complied with, that the original list of articles agrees with what is being exported, and that the appropriate voucher is detached and forwarded to the port of importation.

283

What countries use the ATA carnet?

ATA carnets can be used in the following
countries:

Algeria
Andorra
Australia
Austria
Balearic Isles
Belgium
Botswana
Bulgaria
Canada
Canary Islands
Ceuta
China
Corsica
Croatia
Cyprus
Czechoslovakia
Denmark
Estonia
European Union
Finland
France
French Guiana
French polynesia- including Tahiti
Germany
Gibraltar
Greece
Guadeloupe
Bailiwick of Guernsey
Hong Kong
Hungary
Iceland
India
Ireland Isle of Man
Israel
Italy
Ivory Coast
Japan
Jersey
Korea (Rep. Of)
Lebanon
Lesotho
Liechtenstein
Luxembourg
Macedonia
Macao
Malaysia
Malta
Martinique
Mauritius

Mayotte
Melilla
Miguelon
Monaco
Morocco
Namibia
Netherlands
New Caledonia
New Zealand
Norway
Poland
Portugal
Puerto Rico
Reunion Island
Romania
St. Barthelemy
St. Martin,
French part
St. Pierre
Senegal
Singapore
Slovakia
Slovenia
South Africa
Spain
Sri Lanka
Swaziland
Sweden
Switzerland
Tahiti
Tasmania
Taiwan
Thailand
Tunisia
Turkey
United Kingdom
United States
Wallis & Futuna Islands

The listed countries are Contracting Parties to the ATA convention that established the ATA carnet system. Countries are added to the ATA system periodically. Call the Council for International Business at (212) 354-4480 to determine if the country to which you are traveling accepts carnets. The United States acceded to the ATA Convention on December 3, 1968 and began issuing ATA carnets in late 1969.

Where may I obtain additional information on the ATA carnet?

The United States Council for International Business is located at 1212 Avenue of the Americas, New York, New York 10036-1689, telephone (212) 354-4480, fax (212) 944-0012, and should be contacted for further details concerning the issuance of ATA carnets. The Internet address is http://www.uscib.org The application form for the ATA carnet can also be downloaded from that website. Other questions may be referred to the U.S. Customs Service, 1300 Pennsylvania Avenue, NW, Washington, DC 20229. Attn: Office of Trade Programs, (202) 927-0300.

Report Drug Smuggling to U.S. Customs Service

1 (800) BE ALERT

Currency Reporting

It is legal to transport any amount of currency or other monetary instruments into or out of the United States. However, if you transport, attempt to transport, or cause to be transported (including by mail or other means) currency or other monetary instruments in an aggregate amount exceeding $10,000 (or its foreign equivalent) at one time from the United States to any foreign place, or into the United States from any foreign place, you must file a report with U.S. Customs. This report is called the Report of International Transportation of Currency or Monetary Instruments, Customs Form 4790 (http://www.customs.gov/travel/forms.htm). Furthermore, if you receive in the United States, currency or other monetary instruments in an aggregate amount exceeding $10,000 (or its foreign equivalent) at one time which has been transported, mailed, or shipped to you from any foreign place, you must file a CF-4790. These forms can be obtained at all U.S. ports of entry and departure.

Monetary instruments include: 1) U.S. or foreign coins and currency; 2) traveler checks in any form; 3) negotiable instruments (including checks, promissory notes, and money orders) that are either in bearer form, endorsed without restriction, made out to a fictitious payee, or otherwise in such form that title thereto passes upon delivery; 4) incomplete instruments (including checks, promissory notes, and money orders) signed, but with they payee's name omitted; and 5) securities or stock in bearer form or otherwise in such form that title thereto passes upon delivery. However, the term "monetary instruments" does not include: 1) checks or money orders made payable to the order of a named person which have not been endorsed or which bear restrictive endorsements; 2) warehouse receipts; or 3) bills of lading.

Reporting is required under the Currency and Foreign Transaction Reporting Act (PL 97-258, 31 U.S.C. 5311, et seq.), as amended. Failure to comply can result in civil and criminal penalties and may lead to forfeiture of your monetary instrument(s).

U.S. Customs Service
1300 Pennsylvania Avenue, N.W.
Washington, D.C. 20229
Telephone (202) 927-1520

Why Are You Taking My . . .?

Plant Protection & Quarantine

If you've had food or souvenirs taken away by an inspector of the U.S. Department of Agriculture (USDA) while entering the United States at an airport, border station, or seaport, we want to be sure you understand why.

USDA restricts certain items brought into the United States from foreign countries. Prohibited items can harbor foreign animal and plant pests and diseases that could seriously damage America's crops, livestock, pets, and the environment.

Because of this threat, you are required to declare on a U.S. Customs form any meats, fruits, vegetables, plants, animals, and plant and animal products in your possession. This declaration must cover all items carried in your baggage and hand luggage. You will also be asked to indicate whether you have visited a farm or ranch outside the United States. Officers of USDA's Animal and Plant Health Inspection Service (APHIS) inspect passenger baggage for undeclared agricultural products. At some ports, APHIS personnel use beagle dogs to sniff out hidden items.

APHIS inspectors also use low-energy xray machines adapted to reveal concealed fruits and meats.
Travelers who fail to declare a prohibited item can be fined up to $1,000 or more and have their items confiscated.

Travelers are often surprised to hear that a single piece of fruit or meat can cause serious damage. In fact, one pest-infested or disease-infected item carelessly discarded can wreak havoc on American crops and livestock. The extra cost for controlling agricultural pests and diseases ripples down from farmers to consumers in the form of higher food prices. Taking prohibited agricultural items from travelers helps prevent outbreaks that could affect everyone.

Fresh Fruit
It may look luscious and wholesome, but fruit you bring into the United States from abroad could carry agricultural pests and diseases. Oranges, for example, could harbor the Mediterranean fruit fly (Medfly)—a devastating pest of more than 200 fruits, nuts, and vegetables. In fact, it's possible that individual travelers carried in the infested fruit that brought the Medfly to California in 1979 and to Florida in 1997. Medfly infestations can cause billion-dollar losses to the citrus industry.

USDA regulations regarding the importation of fresh fruit can be found in Title 7 of the Code of Federal Regulations, Part 319.56.

Meat and Meat Products
Regulations prohibit you from bringing in fresh, dried, and canned meats and meat products from most foreign countries. If any meat is used in preparing a product, that product is prohibited. Commercially canned meat is allowed if the inspector can determine from the label that the meat was cooked in the can after it was sealed to make it shelf-stable without refrigeration.

Animal disease organisms can live for months in

sausage and other meat, including many types of canned hams sold abroad. Foot-and-mouth disease and African swine fever are just two of several dreaded foreign livestock diseases that could cost the U.S. livestock industry billions to eradicate, cause higher food prices, and eliminate export markets.

USDA regulations regarding the importation of meat and meat products can be found in Title 9 of the Code of Federal Regulations, Part 94.

Plants in Soil
Some of the most notorious and varied pest hitchhikers are microscopic insects, disease agents, and weed seeds that lurk in soil and plant parts. These organisms could cause extensive harm to our crops and forests. You can import many plants legally and safely, provided you follow USDA guidelines and buy plants from reputable dealers. For information and permit applications, write USDA, APHIS, Plant Protection and Quarantine, 4700 River Road, Unit 136, Riverdale, MD, 20737-1236, Attn: Permit Unit. You can visit the PPQ permit Web site at http://www.aphis.usda.gov/ppq/permits.

In addition, APHIS' Import Authorization System currently allows customers to submit applications to import fruits and vegetables and animal products, organisms, and vectors online, as well as check the status of an existing application and submit revisions to an existing application. To apply for a permit online, visit our Web site at https://web01.aphis.usda.gov/IAS.nsf/Mainform? OpenForm. USDA regulations regarding the importation of plants in soil can be found in Title 7 of the Code of Federal Regulations, Part 319.37.

Exotic Birds
Sometimes without even showing signs of illness, parrots, parakeets, and other birds brought to the United States from other countries can carry and spread serious diseases, such as exotic Newcastle disease. Therefore, birds are subject to specific rules. Restrictions include a minimum 30-day quarantine stay in a USDA-operated import facility, which requires advance reservations and related fees. Birds must also be tested for exotic diseases while in quarantine.

To avoid confiscation of pet birds, know current restrictions and guidelines. For information, contact USDA, APHIS, Veterinary Services, 4700 River Road, Unit 39, Riverdale, MD, 20737-

1231, Attn: National Center for Import/Export. Also, visit our traveler's Web site for travel tips including importing exotic birds at http://www.aphis.usda.gov/oa/pubs/usdatips.pdf. USDA regulations regarding the importation of pet birds can be found in Title 9 of the Code of Federal Regulations, Part 92.

Hunting Trophies

The entry of hunting trophies into the United States—as well as game animal carcasses, hides, dairy products, and other animal products and byproducts—is severely restricted and in many instances prohibited. These articles can also harbor livestock disease organisms. When the product involves endangered species, restrictions of the U.S. Department of the Interior's Fish and Wildlife Service apply. For information, contact U.S. Fish and Wildlife Service, Office of Management Authority, 4401 North Fairfax Dr., Arlington, VA 22203 or visit their Web site at http://www.fws.gov. USDA regulations regarding the importation of hunting trophies can be found in Title 9 of the Code of Federal Regulations, Part 95.

Packing Material

Insects and even diseases can hide in packing material made from agricultural products like straw and burlap. Straw from wheat, if infected with an exotic wheat smut, for example, could do billions of dollars of damage to American wheat fields. Straw hats or other decorative items made from straw may be forbidden entry into the United States if derived from prohibited material. You may be surprised to hear that some agricultural pests can live on packing material for long stretches of time without any source of food. One such pest is the khapra beetle, a tiny, brownish-black pest of grain. It can hide in the folds of burlap and can survive there, without feeding, for up to 3 years. But when the beetle reaches a supply of grain, it goes on a rampage. A colony reproduces so fast and eats so much that an infested grain bin literally comes alive with wriggling larvae. A khapra beetle infestation in the United States and Mexico in the 1950s cost about $11 million to eradicate. USDA regulations regarding the importation of packing materials can be found in Title 7 of the Code of Federal Regulations, Part 319.69.

Live Snails

No live snails may be brought into the mainland United States without a permit obtained from USDA. In 1966, a small boy brought two giant African snails into Florida from Hawaii. He eventually discarded them, and shortly thereafter these voracious consumers of foliage and fruit were infesting a 16-block area near his home. It took years and half a million dollars to eradicate them. To request an application and permit information, write USDA, APHIS, PPQ. 4700 River Road, Unit 133, Riverdale, MD 20737-2346, Attn: Permit Unit. USDA regulations regarding the importation of live snails can be found in Title 7 of the Code of Federal Regulations, Part 330.200.

Do Your Part

Please do your part to help protect American agriculture and ensure that we continue to enjoy a healthy and abundant food supply. If you have questions about APHIS' inspection procedures or whether particular agricultural products can be brought into the United States, contact APHIS' Plant Protection and Quarantine (PPQ). Look in the phone book under "U.S. Department of Agriculture" for the nearest PPQ office, or contact the central office at:

USDA-APHIS-PPQ
Permit Unit
4700 River Road, Unit 136
Riverdale, MD 20737
Telephone (301) 734-8645
Fax (301) 734-5786
In addition, you can visit our Web site at http://www.aphis.usda.gov.

The U.S. Department of Agriculture (USDA) prohibits discrimination in all its programs and activities on the basis of race, color, national origin, gender, religion, age, disability, political beliefs, sexual orientation, or marital or family status. (Not all prohibited bases apply to all programs.) Persons with disabilities who require alternative means for communication of program information (Braille, large print, audiotape, etc.) should contact USDA's TARGET Center at (202) 720-2600 (voice and TDD).

To file a complaint of discrimination, write USDA, Director, Office of Civil Rights, Room 326-W, Whitten Building, 14th and Independence Avenue, SW, Washington, DC 20250-9410 or call (202) 720-5964 (voice and TDD). USDA is an equal opportunity provider and employer.

Random Exams

One of Customs missions is to ensure that travelers entering the United States comply with U.S. laws. In support of this mission, Customs conducts random compliance examinations (COMPEX).

Essentially, COMPEX examinations involve random selection of vehicles and/or air passengers that ordinarily would not be selected for an intensive examination. By combining the results of these examinations with the results of targeted examinations, Customs is able to estimate the total number of violations being committed by the international traveling public. By comparing the results of the two types of examinations we are better able to devise enforcement techniques that prevent the entry of contraband without creating undue delay of law abiding travelers. Often trends tell us what message we need to send to ensure informed compliance by travelers who were unaware of our requirements.

It is possible that upon your entry into the United States, from a foreign country, you may be selected for a COMPEX examination and experience a slight delay in your Customs processing. The Customs Service believes that this compliance examination is a critical component of our ability to ensure that our processing procedures are effective. We apologize for any delay or inconvenience you may experience and appreciate your cooperation.

What Gives Customs the Right To Search Me?

What Gives Customs the Right? This is certainly a normal question to ask when you have been referred to our secondary inspection area for an intensive examination.

The Congress of the United States has given the U.S. Customs Service broad authority to conduct searches of persons and their baggage, cargo, and means of transportation entering the United States. This authority is contained in Title 19 of the United States Code, Sections 482, 1467, 1496, 1581, and 1582.

The courts have also held that this search, seizure, and arrest authority is not dependent upon either probable cause or a search warrant as is required by police officers. One reason for this broad authority is the vulnerability of our borders to the illegal entry of a vast amount of dangerous and prohibited items.

We endeavor to use this authority wisely and with respect for human dignity. It is, however, the responsibility of a trained, professional Customs officer to determine the actual parameters of an examination. The officer is not permitted to release a traveler for entry into the U.S. until he or she is satisfied that no Customs or related Federal or State laws have been violated.

Why Did This Happen to Me?

Q: Why Does the Customs Service Search Passengers?
A: Customs officers must stop contraband, such as narcotics (drugs) from entering the United States. The narcotics are often found in cargo, but they are also found on passengers or in their baggage. Sometimes people swallow narcotics or insert them in their bodies to hide them.

The only way to be sure of finding narcotics that are hidden in baggage is to open the bags and examine them thoroughly. The only way to find narcotics hidden on or inside a person is to do a personal search of the person's clothing and body.

Q: How do Officers decide which passengers to examine?
A: When a Customs officer stops a passenger, it doesn't mean the person is accused of committing a crime. The examination process is a way to confirm the passenger's U.S. Customs declaration and to allow innocent passengers to continue on their way as quickly as possible. Customs officers receive regular training in methods of identifying passengers who may be smugglers. In addition, through on the job experience, Customs officers have acquired knowledge and expertise in detecting smugglers in action. Officers are often looking for narcotics when they choose passengers for examination. This may result in innocent passengers having to undergo a personal search.

Q: Did I fit the profile of a smuggler?
A: If all smugglers shared the same characteristics, it would be easy to identify them.

Smugglers, however, are continually adapting their ways of bringing contraband into the U.S. Since all cases of smuggling vary, there is no "profile" of a smuggler.

The Customs Service does not tolerate discrimination. Customs officers are not permitted to use race, gender, religion, or ethnic background to select a passenger for examination.

Q: How much authority do officers have to carry out examinations?
A: Customs officers have been given special authority by federal statutes and court decisions. The United States Congress and the courts recognize the extreme importance of protecting the United States from narcotics. Officers may examine all conveyances (car, boat, airplane), all persons and their baggage, and all cargo entering the United States. They may also conduct personal searches of passengers.

Q: Why aren't all passengers examined?
A: Our aim is to make our Customs officers highly professional at finding smugglers. Although officers have the authority to examine everyone and everything entering the U.S., there are two reasons why they don't. First, most passengers entering the U.S. are law-abiding travelers. Second, Customs resources are limited. Therefore, Customs officers concentrate on finding the few passengers who are breaking the law. So, for most people entering the U.S. there is little or no examination.

What Good Does It Do? Examinations help protect:

You and your family from narcotics and dangerous drugs,

Your job and employer from unfair foreign competition,

Our agriculture industry from devastation by harmful insects and diseases,

The health of you, your family, and community from contaminated foods and medicines,

You from very serious criminal elements bent on entering this country,

Random examinations allow us to validate compliance rates by the traveling public.

Of course, these are only a few of the many examples of what Customs accomplishes through our examination process.

The Examination: If you are ever selected for an examination upon your entry into the U.S., ask yourself, apart from the inevitable inconvenience to you, was your examination conducted politely, professionally and with tact. If not, we wish to know about it. Please discuss any problem with a Supervisor or Passenger Service Representative prior to leaving the Customs area. If that is not possible or you do not want to discuss the situation at that time, please write to us via the port where the incident took place. We will investigate your concern and respond to you as quickly as possible.

When you write, please include the date, approximate time of day, flight number (if applicable), and the badge numbers of the officers involved. If you feel that an examination deserves positive recognition, we would certainly enjoy hearing that also.

Why U.S. Customs Conducts Examinations

When a Customs officer stops a traveler for a Customs examination, it does not necessarily mean that the traveler is suspected of unlawful activity. In addition to enforcing narcotics related laws, Customs enforces hundreds of laws for other federal agencies. The purpose of the Customs examination is to verify the information on the Customs Declaration, which has been completed by the arriving international traveler, and to deal with issues arising from it. Frequently, Customs officers are looking for narcotics when they choose passengers for examination. This may result in having to undergo a personal search. However, there are many other reasons for a traveler to be referred for a Customs examination. For example, Customs may need to determine if:

You owe Customs duty or other taxes
You have merchandise that you did not declare on your Customs Declaration
You have commercial merchandise

289

You have merchandise that may be considered prohibited or restricted

In addition, the United States Customs Service has established a program to randomly select a small percentage of international passengers for examination. The program, called Compliance Examination (COMPEX), is designed to validate our knowledge of smuggling trends and patterns.

Why aren't all passengers examined? Although Customs officers have the authority to examine everyone and everything entering the U.S., there are two reasons why they don't. First, most passengers entering the U.S. are law-abiding travelers. Second, Customs resources are limited; therefore, Customs officers generally concentrate on finding the few passengers who are not in compliance with the law.

What can I do if I think the examination was not conducted in a professional manner? If you feel that the examination was not conducted in a professional manner, ask to speak with a supervisor immediately. A Customs supervisor is always available at the Customs facility or by telephone. Supervisors are responsible for ensuring that Customs officers treat all persons with dignity and that they behave in a professional manner.

This Customs processing facility may also employ a Customs Passenger Service Representative (PSR). The PSR is a supervisor specifically trained to handle any concerns or questions you may have.

If you have any additional comments or questions, the Customs Service wants to hear from you. You may write directly to Customs Headquarters at:

Executive Director, Passenger Operations U.S. Customs Service1300 Pennsylvania Avenue, N.W Room 5.4DWashington, D.C. 20229 Office of Overseas Schools

The mission of the Office of Overseas Schools is to promote quality educational opportunities at the elementary and secondary level for dependents of American citizens carrying out our programs and interests of the U.S. Government abroad.

Our efforts are to increase mutual understanding between the people of the United States and the people of other countries by upgrading educational institutions which serve to demonstrate American educational principles and methods employed in the United States.

Overseas Schools Advisory Council Worldwide Fact Sheet - 2002-2003

American-Sponsored Elementary and Secondary Schools Overseas

The Worldwide Context: The school-age children among overseas Americans--estimated to number nearly a quarter million--attend a wide variety of schools. Most of the children of military personnel attend schools established and operated by the U.S. Department of Defense, and a number of civilian government agency and private-sector children also attend these schools on a space-available, tuition-paying basis. However, most civilian agency dependents abroad attend non-government, coeducational, independent schools of various kinds. Although these schools include those founded by U.S. companies, church organizations, and individual proprietors, the majority are nonprofit, nondenominational, independent schools established on a cooperative basis by American citizens residing in foreign communities. Many of the schools in this latter group have received assistance and support from the U.S. government under a program administered by the Office of Overseas Schools of the U.S. Department of State. The schools that have received such assistance constitute the "American-sponsored" schools described in this Fact Sheet.

Statistics on the American-Sponsored Schools Assisted by the Department of State at a Glance: During the 2002-2003 school year, the Office of Overseas Schools is assisting 185 schools in 132 countries. The purposes of the assistance program are to help the schools provide adequate education for U.S. government dependents and to demonstrate to foreign nationals the philosophy and methods of American education. The schools are open to nationals of all countries, and their teaching staffs are multinational. Enrollment in the schools at the beginning of the 2002-2003 school year totaled 98,098, of whom 27,632 were U.S. citizens. Out of 12,106 teachers and administrators employed in the schools, 5,463 were U.S. citizens and 6,643 were foreign nationals..

Basic Characteristics: No statement about the American-sponsored overseas schools would apply without exception or qualification to all schools. Variety is one of their basic characteristics. They range from tiny schools, such as the American Embassy School in Reykjavik, Iceland, with 13 students, to large overseas schools, such as the Singapore American School with 2,923 students. School facilities range from rented homes to multi-million dollar campuses, although in-creasing numbers of overseas schools now occupy purpose-built facilities. Very few schools have boarding facilities.

The schools are not operated or controlled by the U.S. government. Ownership and policy control are typically in the hands of associations of parents of the children enrolled, who elect a school board to supervise the superintendent or chief administrator whom the board chooses to administer the school. In some schools, the organization is highly formalized, comprising corporate status in the United States or in the host country, while other schools are loosely defined cooperative entities. All schools are subject, in varying degrees and with varying effects, to host-country laws and regulations pertaining to educational practices, importation of educational materials, personnel practices, etc.

Combined annual operating budgets of the 185 schools total over $450 million. Tuition payments are the principal source of financing for the schools. Many schools derive additional support from gifts and contributions from U.S. and local business firms, foundations, individuals and local governments, and all have received some assistance from the limited funds available under the program of the Office of Overseas Schools (a total of approximately $8 million annually).

The instructional programs provide a core curriculum that will prepare students to enter schools, colleges, and universities in the United States. The language of instruction is English, supplemented in most schools with the local language. The content of the educational programs is American but can vary depending on the proportion of U.S. students. Certain schools, especially in Latin America, must also fulfill host-country curriculum requirements. The curricula tend to be largely academic, with relatively little attention given to vocational or commercial education. An out-standing characteristic of most American-sponsored schools is the use they have made of their location abroad to provide foreign language and local culture programs. The quality and range of instructional materials are excellent in increasing numbers of the schools. The extent and quality of computer programs in many overseas schools, for example, exceed that of typical schools in the United States.

In terms of faculties, most of the administrators and half of the teachers are Americans or American trained. A portion of the American staff is hired locally, and a number of these are U.S. government dependent spouses. Most staff members are college graduates, and the majority holds teaching certificates. The local and third-country teachers are usually well qualified, although some lack experience in U.S. educational methods. Hiring of staff is the responsibility of the individual schools.

For further information contact:
Dr. Keith D. Miller, Director
Office of Overseas Schools
Department of State
Washington, DC 20522-0132
Tel: 202-261-8200
Fax: 202-261-8224
E-Mail: OverseasSchools@state.gov
Web: www.state.gov/m/a/os/

CONTACT INFORMATION

The Office of Overseas Schools is staffed with a director and six regional education officers, each assigned oversight of a geographic region, who are well-informed about schools attended by U. S. citizen school-age dependent children. For information about overseas schools, you are encouraged to contact any of the following:

Director

Keith D. Miller

millerkd2@state.gov
Tel: (202) 261-8200

Regional Education Officers

Africa
Joseph P. Carney

carneyjp2@state.gov
Tel: (202) 261-8216

East Asia and Canada
Beatrice Cameron
cameronbh2@state.gov
Tel: (202) 261-8211

Eastern Europe
Marsha A. McDonough
mcdonoughma@state.gov
Tel: (202) 261-8219

**Near East, South Asia, and
the Mediterranean**
Beatrice Cameron, Acting
cameronbh2@state.gov
Tel: (202) 261-8211

Central and South America
William H. Scotti
scottiwh2@state.gov
Tel: (202) 261-8219

Western Europe
Robert R. Spillane
spillanerr2@state.gov
Tel: (202) 261-8211

Resource Center Coordinator

Carol T. Sutherland
sutherlandct@state.gov
Tel: (202) 261-8223

Office of Overseas Schools
U.S. Department of State
Room H328, SA-1,
Washington, D. C. 20522-
0132
Phone: (202) 261-8200
Fax: (202) 261-8224
E-mail:
OverseasSchools@state.gov

You will receive a written response in a timely manner. If you provide your daytime phone number, Customs will contact you directly by telephone. You may also get information and provide feedback through the Customs Web site

Chapter 25

References and Resources for Overseas Travelers & Residents

U.S. DEPARTMENT OF STATE
http://travel.state.gov

The following fourteen publications from the Department of State,(D.O.S.) Bureau of Consular Affairs (B.C.A) may be ordered, unless, otherwise indicated from the Superintendent of Documents, U.S. Government printing Office, Washington D.C. 20402; Tel. (202) 512-1800:(http://www.access.gpo.gov)

*Your Trip Abroad provides basic travel information - tips on passports, visas, immunizations, and more. It will help you prepare for your trip and make it as trouble - free as possible. (D.O.S. Publication # 10542, B.C.A. Revised April 1998)

*A Safe Trip Abroad gives travel security advice for any traveler, but particularly for those who plan trips to areas of high crime or terrorism. (D.O.S. Publication #10942, B.C.A. Revised March 2002)

*Tips for Americans Residing Abroad is prepared for the more than 2 million Americans who live in foreign countries. (D.O.S. Publication # 10391, B.C.A. Revised September 1996)

*Travel Tips for Older Americans provides health, safety, and travel information for older Americans (D.O.S. Publication, #10337, B.C.A. Revised August 1996)

*Tips for Travelers to Sub-Saharan Africa (D.O.S. Publication #10205, B.C.A. Revised October 1994)

*Tips for Travelers to the Caribbean (D.O.S. Publication #10439, B.C.A. Revised May 1997)

*Tips for Travelers to Central and South America (D.O.S. Publication #10407, B.C.A. Released October 1996)

*Tips for Travelers to Mexico (D.O.S. Publication #10571 B.C.A Revised August 1998)

*Tips for Travelers to the Middle East and North Africa (D.O.S. Publication #10850, B.C.A. Revised August 2001)

*Tips for Travelers to the People's Republic of China (D.O.S. Publication #10271, B.C.A. Revised October 1995)

*Tips for Travelers to South Asia (D.O.S. Publication)

*Tips for Travelers to Canada (D.O.S. Publication)

* Tips for Travelers to Russia. (D.O.S. Publication #10844, B.C.A. Revised May 2001)

Tips for Business Travelers to Nigeria (D.O.S. Publication #10786, February 2001)

Advance Business Scams (D.O.S. Publication)

*Tips for Students (D.O.S. Publication)

*Tips for Women Traveling Alone (D.O.S. Publication #10867, May 2002)

Other Department of State Publications and Resources

*Americans Abroad provides basic up to date information on passport, foreign laws, customs, personal safety and helpful travel tips. You may request for a free copy by writing to: Americans Abroad, Consumer Information Center, Pueblo, CO 81009. Multiple copies of 25 may be purchased from the Superintendent of Documents, U.S. Government Printing Office, Washington D.C. 20402; Tel: (202) 512-1800.

*Foreign Entry Requirements lists visa and other

293

entry requirements of foreign countries and tells you how to apply for visas and tourists cards. Updated Yearly. Order this publication for 50 cents from the Consumer Information Center, Dept. 438T, Pueblo, CO 81009. (D.O.S. Publication, B.C.A. Revised May 2002)

Key Officers of Foreign Service Posts gives addresses and telephone, telex, and FAX numbers for all U.S. embassies and consulates abroad. **(NOTE: When writing to a U.S. embassies and consulates, address the envelope to the appropriate section, such as Consular Section, rather than to a specific individual.) This publication is updated 3 times a year and may be purchased from the Superintendent of Documents, U.S. Government Printing Office, Washington, D.C. 20402; Tel. (202) 783-3238.

Diplomatic List lists the addresses, and telephone and fax numbers of foreign embassies and consulates in the U.S. including the names of key offices. This publication is updated quarterly and may be purchased from the Superintendent of Documents. U.S. Government Printing Office. (D.O.S. Publication).

*Passports the Easy Way provides information on where to apply, how to apply and the best time to apply for a U.S. Passport, including renewals; Everything you need to know about getting a passport- cost, requirements etc. (D.O.S. Publication)

Background Notes are brief, factual pamphlets on each of 170 countries. They give current information on each country's people, culture, geography, history, government, economy, and political conditions. They also include a factual profile, brief travel notes, a country map, and a suggested reading list. To place orders or for information contact: Superintendent of Documents. U.S. Government Printing Office, Washington D.C. 20402: Tel. (202) 512-1800. Be sure to indicate the specific country or area you will be traveling to with your request.

*Consular Information Sheets is part of the U.S. State Department's travel advisory instruments. It covers such matters as location and telephone number of the nearest U.S. Embassy, health conditions, entry regulations, crime and security conditions that may affect travel, drug penalties and areas of instability. Consular Information Sheets are available for most countries. For a free copy of the Consular Information Sheet for the country you plan to visit write to the state Department, Bureau of Consular Affairs, Washington D.C. 20520.

*U.S. Consul Help Americans Abroad explains some of the functions and services of U.S. Embassies and Consulates abroad. (D.O.S. Publication #10176 B.C.A. June 1994)

*Crises Abroad-What the State Department Does available free of charge from Department of State, CA/PA Rm. 5807 Washington D.C. 20520. (D.O.S. Publication #10176, B.C.A. June 1994)

International Parental Child Abduction available free of charge. Write to Office of Citizens Consular Services, Bureau of Consular Affairs, Department of State, Rm.4817 Washington D.C. 20520. (D.O.S. Publication #10862 B.C.A. Revised July 2001)

*International Adoptions discusses the issue of International Adoptions including valuable tips, guidelines and procedures. This circular (publication) is available free of charge from the Department of State, Overseas Citizens Services or call (202) 647-2688.

*Travel Warnings on Drugs Abroad available free of charge from the Department of State, CA/PA Rm. 5807 Washington D.C. 20520. (D.O.S. Publication B.C.A. Revised February 2000)

***Travel advisories, issued by the State Department, caution U.S. citizens about travel to specific countries or areas. If you are concerned about existing conditions in a given area, contact your travel agent or airline, the nearest passport agency or the Department of State's Citizens Emergency Center at (202) 647-5225.

* Security Awareness Overseas: An Overview provides guidelines and tips on a variety of topics relating to personal safety and security while overseas.(D.O.S. Overseas Security Advisory Council, Bureau of Diplomatic Security).

U.S. DEPARTMENT OF COMMERCE

* Climates of the World provides data on climatic

conditions around the world, including temperatures and precipitations. This publication may be ordered from the Superintendent of Documents, U.S. Government Printing Office. (Department of Commerce, Environmental Science Services Administration, Environmental Data Service Publication).

DEPARTMENT OF TREASURY/CUSTOMS
http://www.customs.treas.gov or
http//www.customs.gov

*Know Before You Go, Customs Hints for Returning U.S. Residents gives detailed information on U.S. Customs regulations, including duty rates. Single copies are available free from any local customs or by writing to the Department of the Treasury, U.S. Customs Service, P.O. Box 7407, Washington D.C. 20044. (U.S. Customs Publication #0000-0512

*U.S. Customs: International Mail Imports provides information on procedures and requirements pertaining to parcels mailed from abroad to the U.S. (U.S. Customs Publication No. 0000-0514, Revised September 2002).

*U.S. Customs: Importing or Eporting a Car provides essential information for persons importing a vehicle into the U.S. It also includes U.S. Custom requirements and those of other government agencies whose regulations are enforced by the U.S. Customs. (U.S. Customs Publication)

*Pleasure Boats provides essential information for persons importing pleasure boats into the U.S. It includes requirements and charges. This publication is available free of charge from the Public Information Office, U.S. Customs Service, P.O. Box 7407, Washington D.C. 20044. (U.S. Customs Publication #: 0000-0544.)

*Pets, Wildlife: U.S. Customs (U.S. Customs Publication #509. Revised September 1992)

*G.S.P. and the Traveler provides basic information regarding the Generalized System of Preference which allows some products from certain countries to be brought into the U.S. duty-free. The leaflet only treats those non-commercial importation intended for personal use only. (U.S. Customs Publication #0000-0515. Revised July 2000)

*Personal Search: What to Expect (U.S. Customs Publication)

*Why U.S. Customs Conduct Examinations (U.S. Customs Publication #0000-0119)

*Internet Purchases (U.S. Customs Publication)

*Moving Household Goods to the U.S. (U.S. Customs Publication #0000-0518. Revised April 2000)

*Pets & Wildlife (U.S. Customs Publication #0000-0509)

*Importing or Exporting A Car (U.S. Customs Publication #0000-0520)

*ATA Carnet (U.S. Customs Publication #0000-0127)
*Currency Reporting (U.S. Customs Publication #0000-0503. October 2001)

*International Mail Imports (U.S. Customs Publication #0000-0514. Revised September 2003)

U.S. DEPARTMENT OF AGRICULTURE
http://www.usda.gov

*Travelers Tips on Bringing Food, Plant, And Animal Products Into the United States lists the regulations on bringing these items into the United States from most parts of the world. Fresh fruits and vegetables, meat, potted plants, pet birds, and other items are prohibited or restricted. Obtain the publication free from the Animal and Plant Health Inspection Service, U.S. Department of Agriculture, 732 Federal Bldg., 6505 Belcrest Road, Hyattsville, Maryland 20782. Tel. (301) 734-7885. (Program Aid No. 1083. Revised December 1993).

*Shipping Foreign plants Home. Provides tips and guidelines. Obtain the publication free from the Animal and Plant Health Inspection Service, U.S. Department of Agriculture, 732 Federal Bldg., 6505 Belcrest Road, Hyattsville, Maryland 20782. Tel. (301) 734-7885. (Program Aid No. 1162. Revised September 1988)

*Travelers Tips on Prohibited Agriculture

Products Free copies may be obtained from the address above.

*Traveling By Air with Your Pet (USDA: Animal & Plant Health Inspection Service, (Miscellaneous Publication # 1536 revised October 998)

U.S. DEPARTMENT OF HEALTH

Centers For Disease Conrols-CDC (http://www.cdc.gov/travel/index.htm)

*+Health Information for International Travel is a comprehensive listing of immunization requirements of foreign governments. In addition, it gives the U.S. Public Health Service's recommendations on immunizations and other health precautions for the international traveler. Copies are available from the Superintendent of Documents, U.S. Government Printing Office, Washington, D.C. 20402; Tel. (202) 512-1800 or go to http://www.cdc.gov/travel/index.htm

DEPARTMENT OF INTERIOR

*Buyer Beware! tells about restrictions on importing wildlife and wildlife products. For a free copy, write to the Publications Unit, US Fish and Wildlife Service, Department of the interior, Washington D.C. 20240; (202) 343-5634.

ENVIRONMENTAL PROTECTION AGENCY

*Buying a Car Overseas? Beware! Free copies may be ordered from Publication Information Center PM-211B, 401 M Street S.W. Washington DC 20460 (202) 260-7751. (U.S. Environmental Protection Agency, February 1988)

DEPARTMENT OF TRANSPORTATION

*Fly Rights explains your rights and responsibilities as an air traveler (U.S. Department of Transportation, Tenth Revised Edition, September 1994)

Although essential requirements are provided in the leaflets listed above and, all regulations cannot be covered in detail. If you have any questions, or are in doubt , write or call the specific agency or organization mentioned. Their addresses including the type of subject matter they might provide some assistance are noted below.

SOCIAL SECURITY ADMINISTRATION
*Your Payments While You are Outside the United States (SSA #: 05-10137, ICN 480085, October 2002

AMERICAN SOCIETY FOR THE PREVENTION OF CRUELTY TO ANIMALS
American Society for the Prevention of Cruelty to Animals. Write to A.S.P.C.A. Education Department, 424 E. 49th Street, NY, N.Y. 10128

*Air Travel Tips (free)

*Airline Travel with Your Bird (free)

Agency/Source and Type of Inquiry/Assistance
Center For Disease Control: Travel Information
International Travelers Hotline 404-323-4559

[Telephone or fax back information about required and recommended vaccinations for foreign destinations]

U.S. Public Health Services
Centers for Disease Control
Division of Quarantine
Atlanta, Georgia 30333
Tel. (404) 539-2574

[On bringing food, plant and animal products into the U.S.]

Animal and Plant Health Inspection Service (APHIS)
U.S. Department of Agriculture
613 Federal Building
6505 Belcrest Road
Tel. (301) 734-7885,
http//www.aphis.usda.gov/travel/travel.htm

[On Importing meat and mea products]

USDA-APHIS
Verterinary Services
National Center for Import/Export (NCIE)
4700 River Rd. Unit 401
Riverdale MD 20737-1231
301-74-7830

[On bringing food, plant, and animal products into the U.S.]

U.S. Fish and Wildlife Service
Department of the Interior
Washington, D.C. 20240
Tel. (202) 343-9242,
(202) 343-5634
http://www.fws.gov

[Fish and Wildlife]

Department of the Treasury
U.S. Customs Service
P.O. Box 7407
Washington D.C. 20044
(202) 927-2095

[Imports and Exports, duties (tariffs) restricted and prohibited products]

Food and Drug Administration
Import Operations Unit
Room 12-8(HFC-131)
5600 Fishers Lane
Rockville, MD 20857

[Import of food and drugs into the U.S]

Office of Community and   Consumer Affairs

U.S. Department of Transportation
400 7th Street, S.W., Rm. 10405
Washington, D.C. 20590
(202) 366-2220

[To complain about an airline or cruise line or to check out the records of an airline or cruise line.]

Executive Director
Passenger Programs
U.S. Customs Service
1300 Pennsylvania Ave. N.W.; Rm 5.4D
Washington , DC 20229

[For information about Customs procedures, requirements or policies regarding travelers; or if you have complaints about treatment you have received from customs inspectors or about your Customs processing]

Community and Consumer
Liaison Division
APA - 400
Federal Aviation Administration

800 Independence Avenue. S.W.
Washington, D.C. 20591
(202) 267-3481

[To complain about safety hazards.]

U.S. Environmental Protection Agency
Public Information Center
PM-211B, 401 M Street
S.W. Washington, D.C. 20460
(202) 382-2504

[Environmental issues dealing with imports of certain products or goods, including cars.]

TRAFFIC U.S.A.
World Wildlife Fund - U.S.
1250 24th Street
N.W. Washington, D.C. 20520

[On import of wildlife.]

U.S. Department of State
CA/PA Rm. 5807 Washington ,D.C. 20402

(202) 647 4000 or (202) 647 1488 *[Citizen safety, whereabouts, and welfare abroad, passports, visas, U.S. embassies and consulates abroad, foreign embassies and consulates in the U.S.*

Department of Justice
800-375-5283

[For questions concerning resident Alien & Non resident visa, passport information]

Superintendent Of Documents
U.S. Government Printing Office
Washington, D.C. 20402
(202) 512-1800

[U.S. government publications, including publications of various agencies and departments of the Federal Government.]

Office Of Foreign Assets Control
Department Of The Treasury
Washington, D.C. 20220
(202) 566-2761

[Import of merchandise from foreign countries.]

Quarantines, USDA-APHIS-PPQ 6505 Belcrest

297

Rd. (301) 436-7472

[For permits and information on import of plants, meat products, livestock and poultry.]

Office Of Munitions Control
Department Of State
Washington, D.C. 20520

[Export/ import of weapons, ammunition and firearms.]

Bureau Of Alcohol, Tobacco and Firearms
Department Of The Treasury
Washington, D.C. 20226
202-927-8320

[Import of alcohol, tobacco and firearms.]

Office Of Vehicle Safety Compliance (NEF 32)
Department Of Transportation
Washington, D.C. 20590
[Import of vehicles (standards).]

U.S. Information Agency
Washington, D.C.
(202) 619-4700

[Import/export of Cultural property.]

Consumer Information Center
Pueblo, Colorado 81009   or P.O. Box 100
Pueblo Colorado 81002
[Publications of interest to the general public.]

RECOMMENDED GOVERNMENT WEBSITES

Department of Homeland Security
[http://dhs.gov]

U.S. State Department [http://travel.state.gov]

U.S. Customs [http://www.customs.gov]

Transportation Security Administration
[http://www.tsa.gov]

Federal Aviation Administration
[http://www1.faa.gov]

Office of Aviation Enforcement & Proceedings
(Aviation Consumer Protection Division)
[http://airconsumer.ost.dot.gov]

Federal Consumer Information Center
[http://www.pueblo.gsa.gov]

Centers For Disease Control
[http://www.cdc.gov]

OTHER TRAVEL WEBSITES

SENIORS:
http://www.seniors.gov
SeniorNet [http://www.seniornet.org]
Elderhostel [http://www.elderhostel.org]
American Association of Retired Persons
[http://www.aarp.org/travel)

DISABLED TRAVELERS:
Assess-Able Travel Source [http://www.access-able.com]
GlobalAccess [http://www.geocites.com]

HEALTH ADVICE:
Your Health Abroad
[http://armchair.com/info/health.html]
Healthy Flying [http://www.flyana.com]
U.S. Centers for Disease Control
[http://www.cdc.gov/travel/travel.html]
Travel Health Online [http://www.tripprep.com]
International Society of Travel Medicine
[http://www.istm.org/clinidir.html]

GAY/LESBIAN TRAVELERS

PlanetOut Travel [http://www.planetout.com]
Travelook [http://www.tavelook.com]
Out & About [http://www.outandabout.com]
-[http://www.gaytravelig.com]

FAMILY TRAVEL:

Family Travel Forum
[http://www.familytravelforum.com]
-[http://www.familytravelguides.com

SECURITY/TRAVEL ADVISORIES

298

U.S. State Department Travel Warnings
[http://travel.state.gov/travel_warnings.htm]
Kroll Travel Watch
[http://www.krollassociates.com/kts]
CIA World Factbook
[http://www.pdci.gov/cia/pulications/factbook]

OTHER TRAVEL SERVICES:

**WEATHER [http://weather.com;
http://www.accuweather.com]**

CURRENCY CONVERTER
[http://www.xe.net/currency]
[http://www.oanda.com]

FOREIGN LANGUAGES HELP
[http://www.travlang.com/languages]

PASSPORT SERVICES
[http://travel.state.gov/passport_services.html]

CREDIT CARD ATM LOCATORS [
http://visa.com/pd/atm]
[http://wwmastercard.com/atm]

ROAD SAFETY:

Association For Safe International Road Travel [
http://www.asirt.org]

299

APPENDIX A

U.S. EMBASSIES AND CONSULATES ABROAD

Note: APO/FPO addresses may only be used for mail originating in the United States. When you use an APO/FPO address, do not include the local street address. For more information See Appendix I. (List of abbreviations and symbols are provided and explained at the end of this appendix)

Albania - Tirana (E), Tirana Rruga Elbasanit 103 -- AmEmbassy Tirana, Department of State, Washington, D.C. 20521-9510, Tel [355] (42) 47285 thru 89, Fax 32222

Algeria - Algiers (E), 4 Chemin Cheikh Bachir El-Ibrahimi -- B.P. Box 408 (Alger-Gare) 16000, Tel [213] (2) 69-12-55, 69-32-22, 69-11-86, 69-14-25, Fax 69-39-79; GSO Fax 69-17-82; COM Tel 69-23-17, Fax 69-18-63; PAO Fax 69-14-88. Internet address: - usembassy.eldjazair.net.dz

Angola - Luanda (E), Rua Houari Boumedienne No. 32, Miramar, Luanda -- International Mail: Caixa Postal 6484, Luanda, Angola, or Pouch: American Embassy Luanda, Dept. of State, Washington. D.C., 20521-2550; INMARSAT: Int'l Operator 873-151-7430, Tel [244] (2) 347-028/345-481, Fax 346-924; DAO Fax 347-217; Admin/Consular Annex: Casa Inglesa, Rua Major Kanhangula No. 132/135, Angola, or use other pouch address; ADMIN Tel 392-498; CON Tel 396-927, Fax 390-515

Argentina - Buenos Aires (E), International Mail: 4300 Colombia, 1425 Buenos Aires -- APO Address: Unit 4334, APO AA 34034, Tel [54] (1) 777-4533 and 777-4534, Fax 777-0197; COM Fax 777-0673, Telex 18156

AMEMBAR

Armenia - Yerevan (E). 18 Gen Bagramian (local address) -- American Embassy Yerevan, Dept. of State, Washington, D.C. 20521-7020 (pouch address), Tel 3742-151-551, Fax 3742-151-550, Telex 243137 AMEMY. Internet address: - www.embgso@arminco.com -

Australia - Canberra (E), Moonah Pl., Canberra, A.C.T. 2600 -- APO AP 96549, Tel [61] (2) 6214-5600, afterhours Tel 6214-5900, Fax 6214-5970. Internet website: www.usis-australia.gov

Austria - Vienna (E), Boltzmanngasse 16, A-1091, Vienna, Tel [43] (1) 313-39, Fax [43] (1) 310-0682; CON: Gartenbaupromenade 2, 4th Floor, A-1010 Vienna, Tel [43] (1) 313-39, Fax 513-4351; COM Fax [43] (1) 310-6917 or 31339-2911; EXEC Fax [43] (1) 317-7826; ADM Fax [43] (1) 31339-2510; ECON/POL Fax [43] (1) 313-2916

Azerbaijan - Baku (E), Azadliq Prospekt 83, Baku 370007, Azerbaijan -- AmEmbassy Baku, Dept. of State, Washington, D.C. 20521-7050 (pouch address), Tel [9] (9412) 98-03-35, 36, 37, Fax 90-66-71; Tie Line 841-0289; EXEC Fax 98-91-79; CON Fax 98-37-55; COM Fax 98-61-17; PAO Tel & Fax 98-93-12. Internet address: http://www.usia.gov/posts/baku.html

Bahamas, The - Nassau (E), Queen St. (local/express mail address) P.O. Box N-8197; Amembassy Nassau, P.O. Box 599009, Miami, Fl. 33159-9009 (stateside address); -- Nassau, Dept. of State, Wash., D.C. 20521-3370 (pouch address), Tel (242) 322-1181, afterhours Tel 328-2206, EXEC Fax (242) 356-0222;

ECO/COM Fax 328-3495; ADM Fax 328-7838; NAS Fax 356-0918; PAO Fax 326-5579; Visas Fax 356-7174

Bahrain - Manama (E), Building No. 979, Road 3119, Block 331, Zinj District -- AmEmbassy Manama, PSC 451, FPO AE 09834-5100; International Mail: American Embassy, Box 26431, Manama, Bahrain, Tel [973] 273-300, afterhours Tel 275-126, Fax 272-594; ADM Fax 275-418; ECON/COM Fax 256-717; PAO Tel 276-180, Fax 270-547; OMC Tel 276-962, Fax 276-046. Web site address: http://www.usembassy.com.bh

Bangladesh - Dhaka (E), Diplomatic Enclave, Madani Ave., Baridhara, Dhaka 1212 or -- G.P.O. Box 323, Dhaka 1000, Tel [880] (2) 882-4700-22, Fax 882-3744; USAID Fax 882-3648; PAO address: House No. 110, Road No. 27, Banani, Dhaka 1213, Tel [880] (2) 881-3440-44, Fax 9881677; workweek: Sunday thru Thursday. E-mail address: Dhaka@usia.gov.

Barbados - Bridgetown (E), Canadian Imperial Bank of Commerce Bldg., Broad Street -- P.O. Box 302 or FPO AA 34055, Tel (246) 436-4950, Fax 429-5246. Telex 2259 USEMB BGI WB. Marine Sec. Guard, Tel 436-8995; CON Fax 431-0179; AID Fax 429-4438; PAO Fax 429-5316; MLO Fax 427-1668; LEGATT Fax 437-7772

Belarus - Minsk (E), 46 Starovilenskaya Str., 220002 Minsk · PSC 78, Box B Minsk, APO 09723, Tel [375] (17) 210-12-83 and 234-77-61, afterhours Tel 226-1601, Fax 234-78-53, CON Fax 217-7160; Fax 577-4650; PAO Tel [375] (17) 217-04-81, Fax 217-88-28

301

Belgium - Brussels (E), 27 Boulevard du Regent, B-1000 Brussels -- PSC 82, Box 002, APO AE 09710, Tel [32] (2) 508-2111, Fax [32] (2) 511-2725; COM Fax 512-6653; direct-in-dial: Amb [32] (2) 508-2444; Amb sec 508-2444; DCM 508-2446; POL 508-2475; ECO 508-2448; COM 508-2425; CON 508-2382; ADM 508-2350; RSO 508-2370; PAO 508-2412; IRM 508-2200; DAO 508-2505; ODC 508-2664; FAS 508-2437; FAA 508-2703

Belize - Belize City (E), Gabourel Lane -- P.O. Box 286, Unit 7401, APO AA 34025, Tel [501] (2) 77161 thru 63, Fax 30802; ADM Fax 35321; DAO Fax 32795; DEA Fax 33856; PC Fax 30345; IBB Tel [501] (7) 22091/22063, Fax 22147; MLO Tel 25-2009/2019, Fax 25-2553. Internet address: embbelize@belizwpoa.us-state.gov. Web site address: http://www.usemb-belize.gov

Benin - Cotonou (E), rue Caporal Bernard Anani, B.P. 2012, Tel [229] 30-06-50, 30-05-13, 30-17-92, Fax 30-14-39 and 30-19-74, workweek: Monday through Friday. Internet address: amemb.coo@intnet.bj

Bermuda - Hamilton (CG), Crown Hill, 16 Middle Road, Devonshire - P.O. Box HM325, Hamilton HMBX, Bermuda, or AmConGen Hamilton, Department of State, Wash., D.C. 20520-5300, Tel [441] 295-1342, Fax 295-1592 or 296-9233

Bolivia - La Paz (E), Ave. Arce No. 2780 -- P.O. Box 425, La Paz, Bolivia, APO AA 34032, Tel [591] (2) 430251, Fax 433900; USAID Tel 786544, Fax 786654; Direct lines: AMB [591] (2) 432524; DCM 431340; POST 1 432540; DEA 431481; CON 433758, Fax 433854; PAO Tel 432621; USAID DIR Tel 786179, USAID EXEC OFF Tel 786399

Bosnia and Herzegovina - Sarajevo (E), Alipasina 43, 71000 Sarajevo, Tel [387] (71) 445-700,

Fax [387] (71) 659-722

Botswana - Gaborone (E), P.O. Box 90, Tel [267] 353-982, afterhours Tel 357-111 or 374-498, Fax 356-947; AID Tel 324-449, Fax 324-404; CDC Tel 301-696; VOA Tel 810-932. E-mail address: usembgab@global.co.za

Brazil - Brasilia (E), Avenida das Nacoes, Quadra 801, Lote 3, Brasilia, D.F. Cep 70403-900 Brazil -- American Embassy Brasilia, Unit 3500, APO AA 34030, Tel [55] (61) 321-7272, Fax 225-9136 (Stateside address); ADM Fax 225-5857; COM Fax 225-3981; PAO Fax 321-2833, 322-0554; AID Fax 323-6875; FCS Fax 225-3981; NAS Fax 226-0171; SCI Fax 321-3615; POL Fax 223-0497; ECO Fax 224-9477. Internet address: http://www.embaixada-americana.org.br/

Brunei - Bandar Seri Begawan (E), Third Floor - Teck Guan Plaza, Jalan Sultan, Bandar Seri Begawan, Brunei Darussalam -- PSC 470 (BSB), FPO AP 96507, Emb Tel [673] (2) 220-384, 229-670, Fax [673] (2) 225-293; Amb direct line 240-763; DCM direct line 241-645; COM Fax 226-523; STU III Fax 240-761. E-mail: amembbsb@brunet.bn. Embassy website: http://members.xoom.com/amembrunei

Bulgaria - Sofia (E), 1 Saborna St. -- AMEmbassy Sofia, Dept. of State, Washington, D.C. 20521-5740, Tel [359] (2) 980-5241 thru 48, Fax 981-8977; CON Fax 963-2859; ADM/GSO/PER Fax 963-0086; COM Fax 980-6850; AGR Fax 981-6568; AID Fax 951-5070; PAO Fax 980-3646; PC Tel 980-0217, Fax 981-7525. CON Internet address: bgcons@hotmail.com

Burkina Faso - Ouagadougou (E), 602 Avenue Raoul Follerau, 01 B.P. 35, Tel (226) 30-67-23, afterhours Tel 31-26-60 and 31-27-07, Fax (226) 30-38-90. Internet address: amembouaga@ouagadougb.us-

state.gov

Burma - Rangoon (E), 581 Merchant St. (GPO 521) -- Box B, APO AP 96546, Tel [95] (1) 282055, 282182, Fax [95] (1) 280409, Telex (083) 21230 AMBYGN BM; direct-in-dial: EXEC Tel [95] (1) 283668; DAO Tel 277507; GSO Tel 543354, 542608, Fax 543353; Health Unit Tel 511072, Fax 511069; PAO Tel 221585, 223106, 223140, Fax 221262. Internet address: Embassy.info-rangoon@dos.us-state.gov

Burundi - Bujumbura (E), B.P. 1720, Avenue Des Etas-Unis, Tel [257] 22-34-54, afterhours Tel 21-48-53, Fax 22-29-26; AID/OFDA Tel 22-59-51, Fax 22-29-86. E-mail: (user last name plus initials) @bujumburab.us-state.gov

Cambodia - Phnom Penh (E), 27 EO Street 240 -- Box P, APO AP 96546, Tel [855] 23-216-436/438, Fax 23-216-811; ADM Fax 23-216437

Cameroon - Yaounde (E), rue Nachtigal, B.P. 817, Tel (237) 23-40-14, and (237) 23-05-12 -- Pouch address: American Embassy, Dept. of State, Washington, D.C. 20521-2520, Tel [237] 23-45-52, Fax 23-07-53; ADM Tel 23-13-87; IRM Tel [237] 23-43-72; DAO Tel 22-03-17. Internet address: yaounde@youndeb.us-state.gov

Canada - Ottawa, Ontario (E), 100 Wellington St., K1P 5T1 -- P.O. Box 5000, Ogdensburg, NY 13669-0430, Tel (613) 238-5335 or 238-4470, Fax 238-5720; COM Fax 238-5999

Cape Verde - Praia (E), Rua Abilio Macedo 81, C.P. 201, Tel [238] 61-56-16, Fax 61-13-55

Central African Republic - Bangui (E), Avenue David Dacko, B.P. 924, Tel [236] 61-02-00, 61-02-10, 65-25-78, Fax 61-44-94, duty phone (236) 50-12-08

Chad - N'Djamena (E), Ave. Felix

Eboue, B.P. 413, Tel [235] (51) 70-09, 51-90-52, 51-92-33, Telex 5203 KD, Fax 51-56-54, or 56-54; Direct system dialing via system 85 in Dept: AMB 924-2002, DCM 924-2112; POL 924-2372; RSO 924-2342; IRM 924-2122, Fax 924-2302. Internet Admin address: paschallrc@ndjamenab.us-state.gov

Chile - Santiago (E), Av. Andres Bello 2800, APO AA 34033, Tel [56] (2) 232-2600, Fax 330-3710; COM Fax 330-3172; AID Fax 638-0931; AGR Fax 56-2-330-3203; FBO Fax 233-4108; CON 56-2-330-3710; GSO Fax 330-3020

China - Beijing (E), Xiu Shui Bei Jie 3, 100600 -- PSC 461, Box 50, FPO AP 96521-0002, Tel [86] (10) 6532-3831, Telex AMEMB CN 22701; EXEC/ECO Fax 6532-6422; POL/ES&T/RSO Fax 6532-6423; ESO/MSG Fax 6532-6421; GSO Travel Fax 6532-2483; Health Unit Fax 6532-6424; AGR Fax 6532-2962; CUS Fax 6500-3032; INS Fax 6561-4507; PAO Fax 6532-2039; CON Fax 6532-3178; COM Tel 6532-6924 thru 27, Fax 6532-3297; ADM/Personnel Fax 6532-5141; APHIS address: 12-21 China World Trade Ctr., No. 1 Jianguomenwai Ave., Beijing, FAX [86] (10) 6505-4574; American Center for Education Exchange (ACEE) address: Jing Guang Center, Tel 6510-5242, Fax 6501-5247; Federal Aviation Administration (FAA) address: No. 15 Guang Hua Li, Jian Guo Men Wai, Chao Yang District, Tel 6504-2571, Fax 6504-5154

Colombia - Bogota (E), Calle 22D-BIS, No. 47-51, Apartado Aereo 3831, -- APO AA 34038, Tel [57] (1) 315-0811, Fax 315-2197; CON Tel. 315-1566; COM Fax [571] (315) 2171/2190; GSO Fax [571] (315) 2207

Congo, Democratic Republic of - Bogota (E), Calle 22D-BIS, No. 47-51, Apartado Aereo 3831, -- APO AA 34038, Tel [57] (1) 315-0811, Fax 315-2197; CON Tel. 315-1566; COM Fax [571] (315) 2171/2190; GSO Fax [571] (315)

2207

Congo, Republic of - Brazzaville (E), The Brazzaville Embassy Office is co-located with Embassy Kinshasa at 310 Avenue Des Aviateurs, Kinshasa, DRC. Tel [243] (88) 43608, Fax (88) 41036. Address/phone of temporary office in Brazzaville: 70 rue Bayardelle, Tel [242] 81-14-72; additional information: [243] (88) 40520 or (88) 40252

Costa Rica - San Jose (E), Pavas, San Jose -- APO AA 34020, Tel (506) 220-3939, afterhours Tel 220-3127, Fax 220-2305; COM Fax 231-4783

Cote d'Ivoire - Abidjan (E), 5 rue Jesse Owens, 01 B.P. 1712, Tel [225] 20-21-09-79 or 20-21-46-72, Fax 20-22-32-59

Croatia - Zagreb (E), Andrije Hebranga 2, 1000 Zagreb, Croatia, Tel [385] (1) 455-5500, afterhours Tel 455-5281, Fax 455-8585; EXEC Fax 455-0394; ADM Fax 455-0892; GSO Fax 481-7711. Website address: www.usembassy.hr

Cuba - **-3975; ADM Fax 66-2095, INS switchb**Havana (USINT), Swiss Embassy, Calzada between L and M Sts., Vedado, Havana, USINT Tel [53] (7) 33-3551/9, 33-3543/5, Fax 33-3700; Refugee inquiries telephone numbers 33-3546/7, afterhours Marine Post 1 33-3026; PAO direct line 33-3967, Fax 33-3869; T+T Fax 33-3975, FBO direct line: 33-4096/97, Fax 33oard 33-4511/33-3586, Fax 33-4512

Cyprus - Nicosia (E), Metochiou and Ploutarchou Streets, Engomi, Nicosia, Cyprus -- P.O. Box 24536, PSC 815 FPO AE 09836, Tel [357] (2) 776400, afterhours Tel 776934, Fax 780944; CON Fax 781146; PAO Tel 677143, Fax 668003; Internet address: amembsys@spidernet.com.cy

Czech Republic - Prague (E), Trziste 15, 11801 Prague 1, Tel

[420] (2) 5753-0663, Fax 5753-0920; GSO Fax 5753-0584; DAO Fax 5753-2718; ODC Fax 5753-1175; CON Fax 5753-4028; POL/ECO Fax 5753-2717; COM Fax 5753-1165 or 5753-1168; AGR Fax 5753-1173; Pub. Diplomacy and IRC: Hybernska 7A 11716 Prague 1, PAO Tel Fax 2422-0983

Denmark - Copenhagen (E), Dag Hammarskjolds Alle 24, 2100 Copenhagen -- PSC 73, APO AE 09716, Tel [45] 3555-3144, afterhours Tel 3555-9270, Fax 3543-0223; POL/ECO/EST Fax 3542-8075; ADM Fax 3526-9611; CON Fax 3538-9616; PAO Fax 3542-7273; AGR Fax 3543-0278; USAF Fax 3526-5108; COM Fax 3542-0175; DAO Fax 3542-2516. Embassy home page: www.usembassy.dk

Djibouti - Djibouti (E), Plateau du Serpent, Blvd. Marechal Joffre, B.P. 185, Tel [253] 35-39-95, Fax 35-39-40, afterhours 35-13-43

Dominican Republic - Santo Domingo (E), corner of Calle Cesar Nicolas Penson and Calle Leopoldo Navarro -- Unit 5500, APO AA 34041-5500, Tel [809] 221-2171, afterhours Tel 221-8100 or 562-3560, Fax 686-7437; CON Tel 221-5511, Fax 685-6959; AID Tel 221-1100, Fax 221-0444; INS Tel 221-0113, Fax 221-0110; PC Tel 685-4102, Fax 686-3241. Fax 686-4326; ADM ext. 255, Fax 686-7166; FCS ext. 400, Fax 688-4838; PAO ext. 486, Fax 541-1828; DEA ext. 381, Fax 685-7507; DAO ext. 220, Fax 687-5222; MAAG ext. 487, Fax 682-3991; APHIS ext. 357, Fax 686-0979; AGR ext. 344. Fax 685-4743; ECO/POL x 335 Fax 686-4038; website: www.usia.gov/posts/santodomingo. E-mail: Last name first, initial, middle initial@state.gov

Copenhagen, Denmark - Dag Hammarskjölds Allé 24, 2100 København Ø. Tl: +45 35 55 31 44 Fax: +45 35 43 02 23

Ecuador - Av. Patria y Av. 12 de Octubre Tel:(593) 2 256 2890

Fax:(593) 2 250 2052 Tel: de emergencia: (593) 2 223 4126

Egypt - 5, Latin America St., Garden City, Cairo, Egypt Tel: [20] [2] 797-3300 Fax: [20] [2] 797-3200

El Salvador - Boulevard Santa Elena,Urbanización Santa Elena, Antiguo Cuscatlán La Libertad, El Salvador General info: [503] 278 4444

Equatorial Guinea - Yaounde, Cameroun - Rue Nachtigal P.O. Box 817, Yaounde Tel: (237) 223-05-12 (237) 222-25-89 (237) 222-17-94 (237) 223-40-1

Eritrea - Asmara (E), Franklin D. Roosevelt St. P.O. Box 211, Asmara, Eritrea Tel: [291] (1) 120004 Fax: 127584 USAID Tel: 121895; Fax: 123093 Peace Corps Tel: 12 63 54 Fax: 122870 DAO/SAO Tel: 126381 DOD/SAO Fax: 126339

Estonia - Kentmanni 20, 15099 Tallinn, Estonia Tel: (372) 668 8100 Fax (372) 668 8134 Public E-mail:tallinn@usemb.ee **U.S. Consular Section in Tallin, Estonia** - Kentmanni 20, 15099 Tallinn, Estonia Tel: (372)-668 8100 Consular Section Fax: (372)-668 8267 Visa information: E-mail:VisaTallinn@state.gov American Citizen Services:ACSTallinn@state.gov

Addis Ababa, Ethiopia - P.O.Box 1014, Addis Ababa , Ethiopia E-mail:usemaddis@state.gov Tel. 251-1-550666, Fax 251-1-551328

U.S. Consular Section in Addis Ababa, Ethiopia - Entoto Street, P.O.Box 1014 Addis Ababa,Ethiopia Tel: 251-1-55 06 66, Fax: 251-1-55 10 94 E-mail:consaddis@state.gov

Fiji - 31 Loftus Street P.O. Box 218 Suva, Fiji Tel: (679) 3314-466 Fax: (679) 3300-081 ; **U.S. Consular Section in Suva, Fiji** - 31 Loftus Street P.O. Box 218 Suva, Fiji Tel: (679) 3314-466 Fax: (679) 3300-081 E-mail: consularsuva@state.gov.

Finland - Itäinen Puistotie 14 B, FIN-00140 Helsinki, Finland Tel: +358-9-171 931 E-mail:webmaster@usembassy.fi ;**U.S. Consular Section in Helsinki, Finland** - Itäinen Puistotie 14 B, FIN-00140 Helsinki, Finland Tel: +358-9-171 931 E-mail:consular@usembassy.fi

France - 2 avenue Gabriel 75008 Paris, France Switchboard (33) 1 43 12 22 22 Fax: (33) 1 42 66 97 83 ; **U.S. Consular Section in Paris, France** - 2, rue St. Florentin 75382 Paris, Cedex 08; Visa Services : Tel: 08-99-70-37-00 (fee charged) Fax: 01-42-86-82-91 (From outside France 33-1-42-86-82-91) ; **U.S. General Consulate in Marseille, France** - Office address: Place Varian Fr 13006 Marseille Tel: (33) 4-91-54-92-00 Fax: (33) 4-91-55-09-47 - ; Mailing address: Consulat Général des Etats-Unis d'Amérique Place Varian Fry 13286 Marseille Cedex 6 - Mailing address within the U.S.: U.S. Consulate General PSC 116 (MAR) APO AE 09777 ; **U.S. General Consulate in Strasbourg, France** - 15, Avenue d'Alsace 67082 Strasbourg Cedex Tel: (33) 3 88 35 31 04 Fax: (33) 3 88 24 06 95

Gabon - Blvd. De la Mer B.P. 4000 Libreville Gabon Tel:(241) 76.20.03 or (2004/1241) Fax: (241) 74.55.07

Georgia - 25 Atoneli Street, Tbilisi 380005, Georgia. Tel:(995-32) 98-99-67 or 98-99-68 Fax:(995-32) 92-29-53 E-mail:consulate-tbilisi@state.gov

Germany - Neustädtische Kirchstr. 4-5 10117 Berlin Federal Republic of Germany Tel: (030) 8305-0 ; **U.S. General Consulate in Düsseldorf, Germany** - Willi- Becker- Allee 10 40227 Düsseldorf ;Tel: (0211) 788 - 8927 ;**U.S. General Consulate in Frankfurt, Germany** - Siesmayerstraße 21 60323 Frankfurt Federal Republic of Germany Tel: (49) (69) 7535-0 ;**U.S. General Consulate in Hamburg, Germany** - Alsterufer 27/28 20354 Hamburg Federal Republic of Germany Tel: (040) 411 71 100 Fax: (040) 411 71 222 ;**U.S. General Consulate in Leipzig, Germany** - Wilhelm-Seyfferth- Straße 4 04107 Leipzig Federal Republic of Germany

U.S. General Consulate in Munich, Germany - Königinstraße 5 80539 Munich, Federal Republic of Germany

Ghana - Ring Road East P.O. Box 194 Accra, Ghana Tel: (233) 21 - 775-348. After Hours Emergency Number: (233) 21-775-297 Fax: (233) 21-776-008

Greece - E-mail:usembassy@usembassy.gr ; **U.S. General Consulate in Thessaloniki, Greece** - 43 Tsimiski , 7th Floor GR-54623 Thessaloniki Tel : 003 2310 242 905,6,7 Fax : 003 2310 242 927 Public Affairs Fax : 003 2310 242 910 E-mail : amcongen@compulink.gr

Grenada - St. George's (E), P.O. Box 54, St. George's, Grenada, W.I., Tel [473] 444-1173/6, Fax 444-4820. E-mail address: usemb-gd@caribsurf.com

Guatemala - Avenida Reforma 7-01, Zona 10 Ciudad de Guatemala, Guatemala.

Guinea - Rue KA 038, Conakry, Republic of Guinea Tel: (224) 41-15-20/21/23 Fax: (224) 41-15-22

Haiti - Consular Section 104, rue Oswald Durand Port au Prince, Haiti.

Holy see (Vatican City) - Via delle Terme Deciane, 26 00162 - Rome, Italy Tel: (+39) 06-4674-3428 Fax: (+39) 06-575-8346

Hong Kong and Macau -26 Garden Road, Hong Kong Tel: (852) 2523-9011 Fax: (852) 2845-1598

Honduras - La Paz, Apartado Postal No. 3453 Tegucigalpa, Honduras.

Hungary - Szabadság tér 12., H-1054 Budapest Tel: (36-1) 475-4400 After-Hours: (36-1) 475-4703/4924.

Iceland - - Laufasvegur 21, 101 Reykjavik, Iceland Tel: +354 5629100 Fax: +354 5629123

India - Shantipath, Chanakyapuri New Delhi - 110021. Tel: 011-2419-8000 E-mail:newdelhi@pd.state.gov ; U.S. General Consulate in Calcutta, India - 5/1, Ho Chi Minh Sarani Calcutta- 700071 Tel: 033-2282-3611 E- mail:pascal@pd.state.gov ;U.S. General Consulate in Mumbai, India - Lincoln House 78, Bhulabhai Desai Road Mumbai - 400026 Tel: 022-2363-3611 E-mail:webmastermumbai@state.gov ;U.S. Information Service in

Chennai, India - No. 220, Anna Salai Chennai - 600006 Tel: 044-2811-2000 E-mail:chennaic@state.gov

Indonesia - Jl. Medan Merdeka Selatan 4-5, Jakarta 10110, Indonesia Tel: (62-21) 3435-9000 Fax: (62-21) 385-7189; U.S. Consular Agency in Bali, Indonesia - Jl. Hayam Wuruk 188, Denpasar 80235, Bali, :; Indonesia Tel: (62-361) 233-605, Fax: (62-361) 222-426 E-mail:amcobali@indosat.net.id : U.S. General Consulate in Surabaya, Indonesia - alan Raya Dr. Soetomo 33 Surabaya 60264, Indonesia Tel: 62-31-568-2287 Facsimile: 62-31-567-4492

Ireland - 42 Elgin Road, Dublin 4, Ireland Tel: +353 1 6688777 / 687122 Fax: +353 1 6689946

Israel - 1 Ben Yehuda Street Tel Aviv POB 26180 Israel Tel: 972 3822 Fax: 972-3-5103828 E-mail: webmaster@usembassy-israel.org.il

Italy - Via Vittorio Veneto 119/A

00187 Roma, Italia Telephone: (+39) 06.4674.1 (switchboard) Fax: (+39) 06.4882.672 or 06.4674.2356; **U.S. General Consulate in Florence, Italy** - Lungarno Vespucci, 38 - 50123 FIRENZE, Italy Tel: +39 055-266-951 Fax:+39 055-284-088 ; **U.S. General Consulate in Milan, Italy** - Via Principe Amedeo, 2/10 - 20121 MILANO (Italy) Tel:+39 02-290-351 Fax: +39 02-2900-1165 ; **U.S. General Consulate in Naples, Italy** - Piazza della Repubblica - 80122 NAPOLI, Italy Tel:+39 081-5838-111 Fax: +39 081-7611-869

Jamaica - 2 Oxford Road, Kingston 5, Jamaica, W.I.Tel: 1 (876) 935-6053/4. Fax: 1(876) 929-3637 E-mail:opakgn@pd.state.gov

Japan - - 1-10-5 Akasaka, Minato-ku, Tokyo Japan 107-8420 Tel: 03-3224-5000 ; **U.S. Consulate in Fukuoka, Japan** - Fukuoka American Center Solaria Parkside Building 8th floor 2-2-67 Tenjin Chuo-ku, Fukuoka 810-0001 Phone: 092-733-0246 Fax: 092-716-6152; E-Mail:facres@gol.com ; **U.S. General Consulate in Osaka, Japan** - 11-5 Nishitenma 2-chome, Kita-ku, Osaka 530-8543 Tel: 06-6315-5900 Fax:06-6315-5914

Jordan - P.O. Box 354, Amman 11118 Jordan Tel: 962-6-592-0101, Fax: 962-6-592-0121.

Kazakhstan - Seyfullin Ave., 531 Almaty, Kazakstan Tel: 7 3272 633094 Fax: 7 3272 633045 E-mail:usembassy@freenet.kz

Kenya - Consular Section APO AP 96205-5550 USA

Kuwait - Bayan, Area 14, Al-Masjed Al-Aqsa Street, P. O. Box 77, Safat 13001, Tel: (965)539-5307/8; Fax: (965) 538-0282.

Laos- 19 Rue Bartholonie Vientiane, Lao P.D.R. Tel: (856-21) 212581 Fax: (856-21) 213045

Latvia - Raina Blvd.7 Riga LV-1510 Tel: +371 7036-200 Fax:+371 7820-047 E-mail:pas@usembassy.lvConsular E-mail:AskConsular@USRiga.lv

Lebanon - Beirut (E), Antelias -- P.O. Box 70-840, or PSC 815, Box 2, FPO AE 09836-0002, Tel: [961] (4) 543-600, 542-600, 544-130/131/133, Fax 544-136: ADM Fax: 544-604

Lesotho - Tel: + 266- 312666 Fax: + 266-310116 E-mail:info@embassy.org.ls

Liberia - 111 United Nations Drive, Mamba Point P.O. Box 10-0098 1000 Monrovia, 10 Liberia Telephone: (231)226-370/-380 Fax:(231)226-148

Lithuania - -2600 Akmenu 6 Vilnius, Lithuania Tel:(370-5)2665500 Fax:(370-5)2665510 E-mail:mail@usembassy.lt

Luxembourg - 22 Boulevard Emmanuel Servais L-2535 Luxembourg Tel: +352-460123 Fax: +352-461401

Macedonia - bul. Ilinden bb 1000 Skopje, Macedonia. Tel +389 2 116 180; Fax:+ 389 2 117 103 E-mail:irc@usembassy.mpt.com.mk

Madagascar - 14 - 16, rue Rainitovo - Antsahavola-Antananarivo 101 Tel.: 261 20 22 212 57/ 212 73 / 209 56 Fax: 261 20 22 345 39

Malaysia - 376 Jalaln Tun Razak, 50400 Kuala Lumpur. Tel: 603-2168-5000 Fax: 603-2142-2207.

Malta - Development House, 3rd Floor St. Anne Street, Floriana, Malta VLT 01 - P.O. Box 535, Valletta, Malta, CMR 01 Tel: (356) 2561 4000 Fax: (356) 21 243229

Marshall Islands - P.O. Box 1379 Majuro, MH 96960 Tel: (692) 247-4011 Fax: (692) 247-4012

Mauritius - 4th floor, Rogers House, John Kennedy Avenue,

Port Louis, Mauritius.Tel : (230) 202 4400 Fax: (230) 208 9534 E-mail:usembass@intnet.mu

Mexico - Av. Lopez Mateos 924 Nte.Ciudad Juarez, Mexico ; **Mexico City, Mexico** -From Mexico: Paseo de la Reforma 305 Col. Cuauhtémoc 06500 México, D.F. Tel: (01- 55) 5080 - 2000 Fax: (01- 55) 5511- 9980 From USA: American Embassy Mexico P.O. Box 9000 Brownsville, TX 78520-9000 Tel:(011- 52 - 55) 5080 - 2000 Fax: (011- 52 - 55) 5511- 9980; **U.S. General Consulate Guadalajara, Mexico** - Progreso 175, Col. Americana Guadalajara, Jalisco ZP C. 44100 Tel: (01-33) 3825-2700 Fax: (01-33) 3826-6549 Emergency phone (01-33) 3826-5553; **U.S. General Consulate in Monterrey, Mexico** - Ave. Constitución 411 Pte. Monterrey, Nuevo León. México 64000 Phone from the U.S. 011 (52 81) 8345-2120; **U.S. General Consulate in Tijuana, Mexico** - Tapachula 96, Colonia Hipódromo, Tijuana, Baja California, México 22420 Tel.: (664) 622-7400 Fax: (664) 681-8016 From USA: P.O. Box 439039, San Diego, CA 92176-9039

Micronesia - P.O. Box 1286 Kolonia, Pohnpei FSM 96941 Phone: (691) 320-2187 Fax: (691) 320-2186 E-mail:USEmbassy@mail.fmfm

Moldova - 103 Mateevivi Street, Chisinau MD-2009, Tel:373 -2 - 23 3772 Fax:373-2-233044

Mongolia - P.O. Box 21Ulaanbaatar-13 ; MONGOLIA Tel: 976-11-329095 Fax: 976-11-320776

Morocco - The international mailing address:2 Avenue de Mohamed El Fassi Rabat, Morocco Mail from the U.S. to the Embassy can be sent via APO. The address is: Embassy PSC 74 Box 021 APO AE 09718 Tel: (212)(37)-76-22-65 Fax: (212)(37)-76-56-61 After-hours telephone: (212)(37)-76-96-

39

Mozambique - Avenida Kenneth Kaunda, 193 Maputo. Mozambique Telephone: 258-1-492797 Fax: 258-1-490448 E-mail:consularmaputo@state.gov

Namibia - Mail Address Private Bag 12029 Windhoek, Namibia Street Address 14 Lossen Street Windhoek, Namibia Local Phone 221601 International Phone 264-61-221601 E-mail:kopfgb@state.gov

Nepal - U.S. Embassy, Panipokhari, Kathmandu, Nepal Tel: +977 1 4411179 Fax: +977 1 4419963

Netherlands - - Lange Voorhout 102 2514 EJ The Hague the Netherlands Tel: +31 70 310-9209 Fax: +31 70 361-4688

New Zealand - Km 4 1/2 Carretera Sur P.O. Box #: 327 TeL: 011-(505)-268-0123 Fax: 011 - (505) - 2669943

Nigeria - 7, Mambilla Street Off Aso Drive Maitama District, Abuja, Nigeria Telephone: (234)-9-523-0916/0960/5857/2235/2205 Fax: (234)-9-523-0353 E-Mail:usabuja@pd.state.gov

Norway - Drammensveien 18 0244 Oslo, Norway Tel:(+47)22 44 85 50

Samoa - Apia (E) -- P.O. Box 3430, Apia, Tel [685] 21-631, afterhours Tel 23-617, Fax 22-030.Mobile Tel [685] 7-1776. Internet address: usembassy@samoa.net

Saudi Arabia - Riyadh (E), Collector Road M, Riyadh Diplomatic Quarter or American Embassy, Unit 61307, APO AE 09803-1307, international mail: P.O. Box 94309, Riyadh 11693, Tel 966 (1) 488-3800, Fax 488-7360; PAO address: P.O. Box 94310, Riyadh 11693, Fax 488-3989; COM Fax 488-3237; POL/ECO Fax 488-3278; RSO Fax 488-7867; FMC Fax 482-2765;

GSO Fax 488-7939; ATO Tel 488-4364, ext. 1560, Fax 482-4364; ISC Fax 488-7867; ADM Fax 488-7765; workweek: Saturday–Wednesday /// Dhahran (CG). Between Aramco Hdqtrs and Dhahran Int'l Airport. P.O. Box 81, Dhahran Airport 31932 -- Unit 66803, APO AE 09858-6803, Tel [966] (3) 891-3200; ADM Fax 891-7416; COM Fax 891-8332; CON Fax 891-6816; EXEC Fax 891-0464; GSO Fax 891-3296, afterhours 891-2203 /// Jeddah (CG), Palestine Rd., Ruwais -- P.O. Box 149, Jeddah 21411, or Unit 62112, APO AE 09811, Tel [966] (2) 667-0080, Fax 669-2991; ADM Fax 669-3074; CON Fax 669-3078; COM Tel 667-0040, Fax 665-8106; ATO Tel 661-2408, Fax 667-6196; PAO Tel 660-6355, Fax 660-6367; workweek: Saturday through Wednesday /// U.S. Representative to the Saudi Arabian U.S. Joint Commission on Economic Cooperation (USREP/-JECOR), P.O. Box 5927, Riyadh, Tel [966] (1) 248-3471, ext.] 263, Fax 248-3471, ext. 857

Senegal - Dakar (E), B.P. 49, Avenue Jean XXIII, Tel [221] 823-4296 or 823-7384, Fax 822-2991; PAO Tel 823-1185 or 823-8124; AID Tel 823-5880, 823-1602, 823-6680, Fax 823-2965, Telex 21793 AMEMB SG. Fax 822-2991; E-mail user last name and initials. i.e.: doejt@state.gov

Serbia and Montenegro - Belgrade (E), American Embassy Belgrade -- U.S. Department of State, Washington, D.C. 20521-5070, Tel [381] (11) 645-655, afterhours Tel 646-481, tie line (8) 754-0000. Fax [381] (11) 645-221; E ec Fax 645-332; POL/ECO Fax 646-054; PAO Fax 646-924; CON Fax 644-053; GSO Fax 645-221. Internet address: amembassybelgrade@dos.us-state.gov./ (Operations temporarily suspended)./ Pristina (USOP), Dragodan – Nazim Hikmet 30, 38000 Pristina, Kosovo Province -- Pouch address: Embassy Skopje, Department of State, Washington, DC 20521-7120, Satellite phone

306

873 762 029 525. Fax 873 762 029 526; USAID: Dragodan - Nazim Hikmet, 38000 Pristina, Kosovo Province Tel [381] (38) 590 174, Fax [381] (38) 590438, Saturday Tel 873 761 393 321

Seychelles - Port Louis (E), Rogers House (4th Fl.), John Kennedy St., Tel [230] 208-2347, 208-2354, 208-9763 thru 9767, Fax 208-9534;Int'l. mail: P.O. Box 544, Port Louis, Mauritius; U.S. mail: Am. Emb., Port Louis, Dept. of State, Wash., D.C. 20521-2450. Internet address: usembass@intnet.mu [*Note: Port Louis is now responsible for Comoros and assumed responsibility for Seychelles on October 1, 1996.]

Sierra Leone - Freetown (E), corner of Walpole and Siaka Stevens Sts., Tel [232] (22) 226-481 through 226-485, AMB Tel 226-155, DCM Tel 227-192, Fax 225-471

Singapore - Singapore (E), 27 Napier Rd., Singapore 258508 -- PSC Box 470, FPO AP 96534-0001, Tel [65] 476-9100, Fax 476-9340. Internet home page address: http://www.homepacificnet.sg/~am emb

Slovakia - Bratislava (E), Hviezdoslavovo Namestie 4, 81102 Bratislava (int'l address), Tel [421] (7) 5443-3338, ADM Fax 5441-5148; CON Tel 5443-0809, GSO/CON Fax 5441-8861, POL Tel 5443-5990, POL/ECO Fax 5443-0096. Internet address: www.usis.sk

Slovenia - Ljubljana (E), Presernova 31, 1000 Ljubljana or -- AmEmbassy Ljubljana, Dept. of State, Washington, D.C. 20521-7140, Tel [386] (61) 200-5000, Fax 200-5555; PAO address: Cankarjeva 11 1000 Ljubljana, Tel 200-21-80, Fax 126-4284. Internet address: us-embassy@usis.si

South Africa - Pretoria (E), 877 Pretorius St., Arcadia 0083 -- P.O. Box 9536, Pretoria 0001, Tel [27]

(12) 342-1048, Fax 342-2244; PAO Tel 342-3006, Fax 342-2090; AID Tel 323-8869, Fax 323-6443 /// Cape Town (CG), Broadway Centre Hertzog Boulevard, Heerengracht, Foreshore, Cape Town, P.O. Box 6773, Roggebaai, Cape Town 8012, Tel [27] (21) 421-4280, ADM Fax 418-1989. Internet address: socapetown@pixie.co.za /// Durban (CG), 2901 Durban Bay House, 333 Smith St., Durban 4000, Tel [27] (31); 304-4737, Fax 301-0265; PAO Tel 305-5060, Fax 304-2847; COM Tel 304-4737, Fax 3301-0577 /// Johannesburg (CG), 1 River Street -- corner of Riviera, Killarney -- P.O. Box 1762, Houghton, 2041, Tel [27] (11) 646-6900, Fax 646-6913; COM Tel 442-3571, Fax 442-3770; PAO Tel 838-2231, Fax 838-3920; SCO Tel 442-3571, Fax 442-3770. E-mail address: amcongen.jhb@pixie.co.za

Spain - Madrid (E), Serrano 75, 28006 Madrid -- PSC 61, APO AE 09642, Tel [34] (1) 91587-2200, Fax 91587-2303. Inward dial (DID) numbers: AMB [34] 91587-2201; DCM 91587-2205; POL 91587-2387; ECO 91587-2286; ADM 91587-2208; IRM 91587-2308; DAO 91587-2278; PAO 91587-2502; DEA 91587-2280; FAA 91587-2300; ODC 91549-1339; CON 91587-2236; B&F 91587-2211; PER 91587-2226; RSO 91587-2230; IRM duty phone 91587-2355; EMB duty phone 619-276-782. Internet address: http://www.embusa.es /// Barcelona (CG), Paseo Reina Elisenda De Montcada 23, 08034 Barcelona -- PSC 61, Box 0005, APO AE 09642, Tel [34] (93) 280-2227, Fax (93) 205-5206; ADM Fax (93) 205-7764; PAO Fax (93) 205-5857; COM Fax (93) 205-770 /// La Coruna (CA), Canton Grande, 16-17, 8E, 15003; Tel. [34] 981213-233; Fax [34] 981228 808 /// Las Palmas (CA), Los Martinez De Escobar, 3 Oficina 7- 35007, Tel 34-928-271 259, Fax 34-928-22-58-63 /// Fuengirola (Malaga) (CA), Centro Comercial "Las Rampas" Fase 2, Planta 1, Locales 12-G-7 y 12-G-8,

Fuengirola, 29640 Malaga, Tel. 34-952-47-48-91, Fax 34-952-46-51-89 /// Palma de Mallorca (CA), Avenida Jamime 111, No. 26, Entresuelo (97) 07012; Tel. 34-971-725051, Fax 34-971-71-87-55 /// Seville (CA), Paseo de las Delicias, 7 Seville, 41012, Tel. 34-95-42 31885, Fax 34-95-42 32040 /// Valencia (CA), CL de la Paz, 6-5 Local 5, 46003 Valencia; Tel. 34-96-351-6973, Fax 34-96-352-9565

Sri Lanka - Colombo (E), 210 Galle Road, Colombo 3, Tel [94] (1) 448007, Fax 437345, 4446013; USAID: 44 Galle Road, Colombo 3, Tel [94] (1) 472855, Fax 472850; PAO: 44 Galle Road, Colombo 3, Tel [94] (1) 421121, Fax 449070; IBB: 228/1 Galle Road, Colombo 4, Tel 589245, Fax 502675; Peace Corps: 751/1 Kynsey Road, Colombo 8, Tel 687617. Internet address: http://www.usia.gov/posts/sri lanka. COM E-mail address: com@eureka.lk. Information Resource Center E-mail address: amcenter@sri.lanka.net.USAID. E-mail address: lisachiles@usaid.gov

Sudan - Khartoum (E), Sharia Ali Abdul Latif -- P.O. Box 699, APO AE 09829, Tel [249] (11) 774611 or 77-47-00, Fax [249] (11) 774137, Telex 22619 AMEM SD, Fax (873) (151) 6770

Suriname - Paramaribo (E), Dr. Sophie Redmondstraat 129 -- P.O. Box 1821, AmEmbassy Paramaribo, Dept. of State, Washington, D.C., 20521-3390, Tel [597] 472900, 477881, 476459; AMB 78300; DCM 476507; IRM 476793; GSO Fax 479829; AMB Fax 420800; ADM Fax 410972. Internet address: embuscen@sr.net

Sweden - Stockholm (E), Dag Hammarskjślds VŠg 31, S-115 89 Stockholm, Sweden -- pouch address: AmEmb Stockholm, Dept. of State, Wash. D.C. 20521-5750, Tel [46] (8) 783-5300, Fax (46) (8) 661-1964; AMB SEC Tel 783-5314; afterhours Tel 783-5310; CON Fax 660-5879; COM: Fax

660-9181; AGR: Fax 662-8495; PAO Fax 665-3303; DAO Fax 662-8046

Switzerland - Bern (E), Jubilaumsstrasse 93, 3005 Bern, Tel [41] (31) 357-7011, Fax 357-7344; Telex (845) 912603, AMB Tel 357-7259; DCM Tel 357-7258; POL/ECO Tel 357-7424; ADM Tel 357-7295; PAO Tel 357-7238, Fax 357-7379; IRM Tel 357-7201; RSO Tel 357-7296; DEA Tel 357-7367, Fax 357-7253; DAO Tel 357-7244, Fax 357-7381; AGR Tel 357-7279, Fax 357-7363; LEGATT Tel 357-7340, Fax 357-7268; CON Fax 357-7398; FCS Fax 357-7336; COM Fax 357-7336. Embassy website: www.usembassy.ch /// US Mission to the European Office of the UN and Other International Organizations (Geneva), Mission Permanente Des Etats-Unis, Route de Pregny 11, 1292 Chambesy-Geneva, Switzerland, Tel [41] (22) 749-4111, Fax 749-4880, Amb. Tel 749-4300, Fax 749-4892; DCM Tel 749-4302; PSA (POL) Tel 749-4621; IAEA (ECON) Tel 749-4629, Fax 749-4883; RMA Tel 749-4617, Fax 4671; LEGATT: 749-4460; ADM Tel 749-4391, Fax 749-4491; PAO Tel 749-4360, Fax 749-4314; RSO Tel 749-4397; LAB Tel 749-4624; IRM Tel 749-4306 /// US Trade Representative (USTR), Botanic Bldg., 1-3 Avenue de la Paix, 1202 Geneva, Switzerland, Tel [41] (22) 749-4111, Fax 749-5308 /// US Delegation to the Conference on Disarmament (CD), U.S. Mission Bldg., Route de Pregny 11, 1292 Chambesy-Geneva, Tel [41] (22) 749-4407, Fax 749-4833 /// Geneva (CA), 11 route de Pregny, 1292 Chambesy/Geneva, Tel [41] (22) 798-1605, Fax 798-1630 /// Zurich (CA), Dufourstrasse 101, 8008 Zurich, Tel [41] (01) 422-2566, Fax 383-9814

Syria - Damascus (E), Abou Roumaneh, Al-Mansur St., No. 2 -- P.O. Box 29, Damascus, Syria, Tel [963] (11) 333-1342, Fax 224-7938; 24 hours: 333-3232; PAO Tel 333-1878, 333-8413, Fax 332-

1456; CON Fax 331-9678

Taiwan - American Institute in Taiwan, No. 7 Lane 134, Hsin Yi Road, Section 3, Taipei, Taiwan, Tel [886] (2) 2709-2000, afterhours Tel 2709-2013, Fax 2702-7675. For further information, contact the Washington, D.C., office of the American Institute in Taiwan, 1700 N. Moore St. Suite 1700, Arlington, VA 22209-1996, Tel (703) 525-8474, Fax 841-1385. /// American Trade Center, Room 3207, International Trade Building, Taipei World Trade Center, 333 Keelung Road, Section 1, Taipei 10548, Taiwan, Tel [886] (2) 2720-1550; COM Fax 2757-7162 American Institute in Taiwan, 5th Fl., #2 Chung Cheng 3rd Rd. Kaohsiung, Taiwan, Tel [886] (7) 224-0154/7, Fax 223-8237

Tajikistan - Dushanbe (E), Octyabrskaya Hotel, 105A Prospect Rudaki, Dushanbe, Tajikistan 734001, Tel [7] (3772) 21-03-56, Fax [7] (3772) 21-03-62. Internet address: amemb@usis.td.silk.org

Tanzania - Dar Es Salaam (E), 140 Msese Road, Kinondoni District -- P.O. Box 9123, Tel [255] (51) 666010-5, Fax 666701. Internet address: usembassy-dar2@cats-net.com

Thailand - Bangkok (E), 120 Wireless Rd. -- APO AP 96546, Tel [66] (2) 205-4000, Fax 205-4131;COM 3rd Fl., Diethelm Towers Bldg., Tower A, 93/1 Wireless Rd., 10330, Tel 255-4365 thru 7, Fax 255-2915 /// Chiang Mai (CG), 387 Vidhayanond Rd., Chaing Mai 50300 -- U.S. Embassy, Box C, APO AP 96546, Tel [66] (53) 252-629, Fax 252-633

Togo - Lome (E), rue Pelletier Caventou and rue Vauban, B.P. 852, Tel [228] 21-29-91 thru 94, ADM Fax 21-79-52. Internet address: ustogo1#caf.tg

Trinidad and Tobago - Port-of-Spain (E), 15 Queen's Park West -- P.O. Box 752, Tel (809) 622-6372/6, 6176, Fax 628-5462;

EXEC OFF Fax 628-8134; ECO/COM Fax 622-2444

Tunisia - Tunis (E), 144 Ave. de la Liberte, 1002 Tunis-Belvedere, Tel [216] (1) 782-566, Fax 789-719; USATO Fax 785-345; CON Fax 788-923; FSI Tel 741-672 or 746-991, Fax 741-062; GSO Tel 707-166 or 715-785, Fax 715-735; PAO Tel 799-895, 789-800, 798-833, Fax 789-313; DAO Fax 794-677; ODC Fax 788-609; AGR Fax 785-345

Turkey - Ankara (E), 110 Ataturk Blvd. -- PSC 93, Box 5000, APO AE 09823, Tel [90] (312) 468-6110, Fax 467-0019; ADM/ECO Fax 468-6138; GSO Fax 467-0057; PER Fax 467-8847; POL Fax 468-4775; CON Fax 468-6131; PAO Tel 468-6102 thru 6106; PAO EXEX OFF Fax 467-3624 and 468-6145; AGR Fax 467-0056; COM Fax 467-1366. Internet address: http://www.usis-ankara.orgt.tr. /// Istanbul (CG), 104-108 Mesrutiyet Caddesi, Tepebasi, 80050 Istanbul, Turkey -- PSC 97, Box 0002, APO AE 0927-0002, Tel [90] (212) 251-3602, Fax 251-3218; ADM Fax 251-3632; CON Fax 252-7851; DEA Fax 251-5213; FAS Fax 243-5262; FCS/COM Fax 252-2417; GSO Fax 251-2554; PAO Fax 252-7986. Web site address: http://www.usisist.org.tr /// Adana (C), Ataturk Caddesi -- PSC 94, APO AE 09824, Tel [90] (322) 459-1551, Fax 457-6591. Website address: http://www.usconadana.org.tr /// Izmir (CA), PSC 88, Box 5000, APO AE 09821, Tel [90] (232) 441-0072 and 441-2203; Fax 441-2373; COM: c/o Izmir Chamber of Commerce, Ataturk Caddesi 126, Kat 5, 35210 Pasaport, Izmir, PSC 88 Box 5000, APO AE 09821, Tel 441-2446, Fax 489-0267

Turkmenistan - Ashgabat (E), 9 Puskin Street, Tel [9] (9312) 35-00-37, 35-0 0-42, 51-13-06, tie line 962-0000, Fax 51-13-05, tie line 962-2159

Uganda - Kampala (E), Parliament

Ave. -- P.O. Box 7007, Tel [256] (41) 259792/3/5, Fax 259794; ADM Tel 234142, Fax 341863; PAO Tel 233231, Fax 250314; AID Tel 235879, Fax 233417

Ukraine - Kiev (E), 10 Yuria Kotsubynskoho, 2..54053 Kiev 53, Tel [380] (44) 246-9750, afterhours Tel 216-3805, Fax 244-7350; PAO Tel 213-2532, Fax 213-3386; USAID Tel 462-5678, Fax 462-5834; COM Tel 417-2669, Fax 417-1419; PC Tel 220-1183; AGR Tel 417-1268

United Arab Emirates - Abu Dhabi (E), [post does not have access to APO/FPO] Al-Sudan St. -- P.O. Box 4009, Pouch: AmEmbassy Abu Dhabi, Dept. of State, Washington, D.C. 20521-6010, Tel [971] (2) 436-691 or 436-692, afterhours Tel 434-457, Fax 434-771; ADM Fax 435-441; CON Fax 435-786; PAO Fax 434-802; USLO Fax 434-604; COM: Blue Tower Bldg., 8th Fl., Sheikh Khalifa Bin Zayed St., Tel 273-666, Fax (2) 271-377, workweek: Saturday-Wednesday. Internet address: usembabu@emirates.net.ae /// Dubai (CG), [post does not have access to APO/FPO] Dubai World Trade Center, 21st Fl. -- P.O. Box 9343, Pouch AMCONGEN Dubai, Dept. of State, Washington, D.C., 20521-6020, Tel [971] (4) 3313-115, Fax 3314-043; COM Tel 3313-584, Fax 3313-121; PAO Tel 3314-882, Fax 3314-254; ATO Tel 3313-612/3314-063, Fax 3314-998; NRCC Tel 3311-888, Fax 3315-764, workweek: Saturday-Wednesday. Internet E-mail address: max@emirates.net.ae

United Kingdom - London, England (E), 24/31 Grosvenor Sq., W1A 1AE -- PSC 801, Box 40; FPO AE 09498-4040, Tel [44] (0207) 499-9000; ECO Fax [44] (0207) 409-1637; COM/FCS Fax [44] (0207) 408-8020; CON Fax [44] (0207) 495-5012; ADM Fax [44] (171) 629-9124. Website: www.usembassy.org.uk /// Belfast, Northern Ireland (CG), Queen's

House, 14 Queen St., BT1 6EQ -- PSC 801, Box 40, APO AE 09498-4040, Tel [44] (028) 9032-8239, Fax [44] (028) 9024-8482 /// Edinburgh, Scotland (CG), 3 Regent Ter. EH7 5BW -- PSC 801, Box 40, FPO AE 009498-4040, Tel [44] (131) 556-8315, Fax [44] (131) 557-6023. Website: www.usembassy.org.uk/scotland/ /// European Bank for Reconstruction and Development, One Exchange Square, London EC2A 2EH, Tel [44] (171) 338-6502, Fax [44] (171) 338-6487 /// Cayman Islands (CA), Office of Adventure Travel, Seven Mile Beach, Georgetown, Grand Cayman, Tel 345-945-1511, Fax 345-945-1811

United States - US Mission to the United Nations (USUN), 799 United Nations Plaza, New York, NY 10017-3505, Tel (212) 415-4000, afterhours Tel 415-4444, Fax 415-4443 /// US Mission to the Organization of American States (USOAS), Department of State, Washington, D.C. 20520, Tel (202) 647-9376, Fax 647-0911

Uruguay - Montevideo (E), Lauro Muller 1776 • APO AA 34035, Tel [598] (2) 203-6061 or 408-7777, Fax 408-7777. Internet address: www.embeeuu.gub.uy

Uzbekistan - Tashkent (E), 82 Chilanzarskaya, Tel [998] 71 120-5450, Fax 120-6335, tie-line Tel 793-0000, tie-line Fax 793-0131; PAO Fax [998] (71) 120-6224; USAID Fax 120-6309; COM Fax 120-6692; duty officer cellular Tel [998] (71) 180-4060

Venezuela - Caracas (E), Calle F con Calle Suapure, Colinas de Valle Arriba -- P.O. Box 62291, Caracas 1080-A or APO AA 34037, Tel [58] (2) 975-6411/975-7811 or 975-9821 (afterhours); IVG 643 plus ext. or 643-0000 (operator); MILGP [58] (2) 682-7749/2877, Emb Fax 975-6710; ADM Fax 975-9429; AGR Fax 975-7615; CON Fax 753-4534; CON ACS FAX 975-8991; COM and FCS Fax 975-9643; CUS Fax 975-6556; DAO

Fax 975-6542; DEA Fax 975-8519; POL and ECO FAX 975-9778; FAS Fax 975-7615; FMC Fax 975-7903; GSO Fax 975-8406; RSO Fax 975-8972; LEGATT Fax 975-9629; MILGP Fax 682-5844; NAS Fax 975-9685; PAO Fax 975-6998; PER Fax 975-6292. Website address: www.usia.gov/posts/caracas /// Maracaibo (CA), CEVAZ – Centro Venezolano-Americano del Zulia, Calle 63 Numero 3E60, Apartado 419, Maracaibo, Estado Zulia, Venezuela, Tel 58-61-982-164 or 58-61-925-953, Fax 58-61-921-098

Vietnam - Hanoi (E), 7 Lang Ha Road, Ba Dinh District, Hanoi, Vietnam (Int'l mail), U.S. Embassy-Hanoi, PSC 461, Box 400, FPO AP 96521-0002 (U.S. mail), U.S. Embassy-Hanoi, Dept. of State, Washington, D.C. 20521-4500 (pouch address), Tel [84] (4) 843-1500, ADM Fax 843-1510; CON Fax 831-3017; USDAO Fax 831-3239; AGR Fax 843-8932; POL/ECO Fax 733-2614; PAO Tel 822-5439, Fax 822-5435; USCS Tel 824-2422, Fax 824-2421 /// Ho Chi Minh City (CG), 51 Nguyen Dinh Chieu, District 3 -- PSC 461, P.O. Box 400, FPO AP 96521-0002, Tel [84] (8) 822-9433, Fax 822-9434

Yemen - Sanaa (E), Dhahr Himyar Zone, Sheraton Hotel District -- P.O. Box 22347, Sanaa, Republic of Yemen, Tel [967] (1) 238-843/52, Fax 251-563; CON Fax 238-870; PAO Tel 238-819, Fax 226-649; post one/afterhours: 238-855; RMO Fax 238-874; workweek: Saturday-Wednesday, 8:00 a.m. to 4:30 p.m. Internet address: usembassyol@y.net.ye

Zambia - Lusaka (E), corner of Independence and United Nations Aves. -- P.O. Box 31617, Tel [260] (1) 250-955 or 252-230, front office Tel 254-301, afterhours Tel 252-234, Telex AMEMB ZA 41970, Fax 252-225; AID Tel 254-303 thru 6, ext. 212, Fax 254-532; PAO Tel 227-993 thru 4, ext. 211, Fax 226-523

Zimbabwe - Harare (E), 172 Herbert Chitepo Ave. -- P.O. Box 3340, Tel [263] (4) 250-593, 250-594, 250-595, Fax 796-488; Executive Office direct line 704679, Fax 796487; Embassy Fax 797488; IPU direct tel line 708941; DAO Fax 705752; PAO Tel 758800/1, Fax 758802; USAID Tel 720630, Fax 722418, 720722; PC Tel 752273. Internet address: amembzim@africaonline.co.zw

---

Note:

ACM	Assistant Chief of Mission
ADM	Administrative Section
ADV	Adviser
AGR	Agricultural Section (USDA/FAS)
AID	Agency for International Development
ALT	Alternate
AMB	Ambassador
AMB SEC	Ambassador's Secretary
APHIS	Animal and Plant Health Inspection Service Officer
APO	Army Post Office
ATO	Agricultural Trade Office (USDA/FAS)
BCAO	Branch Cultural Affairs Officer (USIS)
Bg	Brigadier General
BIB	Board for International Broadcasting
BO	Branch Office (of Embassy)
BOB/EUR	Board of Broadcasting, European Office
BPAO	Branch Public Affairs Officer (USIS)
B.P.	Boite Postale
C	Consulate
CA	Consular Agency/Agent
CAO	Cultural Affairs Officer (USISO
Capt	Captain (USN)
CDC	Centers for Disease Control
Cdr	Commander
CEO	Cultural Exchange Officer (USIS)
CG SEC	Consul General's Secretary
CHG	Charge d' Affaires
CINCAFSOUTH	Commander-in Chief Allied Forces Southern Europe
CINCEUR	Commander-in Chief U.S. European Command
CINCUSAFE	Commander-in Chief U.S. AirForces Europe
CINCUSAREUR	Commander-in Chief U.S. Army Europe
Col	Colonel
COM (FCS)	Commercial Section
CON	Consul, Consular Section
COUNS	Counselor
C.P.	Caixa Postal
CPO	Communications Program Officer
CUS	Customs Service (Treasury)
DAC	Development Assistance Committee
DCM	Deputy Chief of Mission
DEA	Drug Enforcement Agency
DEP	Deputy
DEP DIR	Deputy Director
DIR	Director
DOE	Department of Energy
DPAO	Deputy Public Affairs Officer (USIS)
DPO	Deputy Principal Officer
DSA	Defense Supply Adviser
E	Embassy
ECO	Economic Section
ECO/COM	Economic/Commercial Section
EDO	Export Development Officer
ERDA	Energy Research and Development Administration
EX-IM	Export-Import
FAA	Federal Aviation Administration
FIC/JSC	Finance Committee and Joint Support Committee
FIN	Financial Attache (Treasury)
FODAG	Food and Agriculture Organizations
FPO	Fleet Post Office
IAEA	International Atomic Energy Agency
IAGS	Inter-american Geodetic Survey
ICAO	International Civil Aviation Organization
IMO	Information Management Officer
IO (USIS)	Information Officer
IRM	International Resources Management
IRS	Internal Revenue Service
ISM	Information Systems Manager
JUS/CIV	Department of Justice, Civil Division
JUSMAG	Joint US Military Advisory Group
LAB	Labor Officer
LO	Liaison Officer
Ltc	Lieutenant Colonel
LEGAT	Legal Attache
M	Mission
Mg	Major General
MAAG	Military Assistance Advisory Group
MILGP	Military Group
MSG	Marine Security Guard
MIN	Minister
MLO	Military Liaison Office
MNL	Minerals Officer
NARC	Narcotics
NATO	North Atlantic Treaty Organization
NAU	Narcotics Assistance Unit
OAS	Organization of American States
ODA	Office of the Defense Attache
ODC	Office of Defense Cooperation
OIC	Office in Charge
OMC	Office of Military Cooperation
PAO (USIS)	Public Affairs Officer
PO	Principal Officer
PO SEC	Principal Officer's Secretary
POL	Political Section
POL/LAB	Political and Labor Section
POLAD	Political Adviser
POL/ECO	Political/Economic Section
Radm	Rear Admiral

REDSO   Regional Economic Development Services Office
REF   Refugee Coordinator
REP   Representative
RES   Resources
RHUDO   Regional Housing and Urban Development Office
ROCAP   Regional Officer for Central American Programs
RPSO   Regional Procurement and Support Office
RSO   Regional Security Officer
SAO   Security Assistance Office
SCI   Scientific Attache
SEC DEL   Secretary of Delegation
SHAPE   Supreme Headquarters Allied Powers Europe
SLG   State and Local Government
SR   Senior
STC   Security Trade Control
UNEP   United Nations Environment Program

311

APPENDIX B
FOREIGN EMBASSIES IN THE UNITED STATES

The Republic of Afghanistan
2341 Wyoming Ave., NW,
Washington DC 20008
Telephone: (202) 234-3770
Fax: (202) 328-3516

The Republic of Albania
2100 S Street, NW, Washington
DC 20008
Telephone: (202) 223-4942
Fax: (202) 628-7342

**The Democratic and Popular
Republic of Algeria**
2118 Kalorama Road NW,
Washington DC 20008
Telephone: (202) 265-2800
Fax: (202) 667-2174
E-mail: embalgus@cais.com
http://www.algeria-us.org/

Andorra
Two United Nations Plaza, 25th
Floor, New York NY 10017

Angola
1615 M Street, NW Suite 900,
Washington DC 20036
Telephone: (202) 785-1156
Fax: (202) 785-1258
E-mail: angola@angola.org
http://www.angola.org/

Antigua and Barbuda
3216 New Mexico Avenue, NW,
Washington DC 20016
Telephone: (202) 362-5122
Fax: (202) 362-5225

The Argentine Republic
1600 New Hampshire Avenue,
NW, Washington DC 20009
Telephone: (202) 238-6400
Fax: (202) 332-3171
E-mail: argentina@veriomail.com
http://www.embassyofargentina-usa.org/

The Republic of Armenia
2225 R Street, Washington DC
20008
Telephone: (202) 319-1976
Fax: (202) 319-2982

E-mail: amembusadm@msn.com
http://www.armeniaemb.org/

Australia
1601 Massachusetts Avenue, NW,
Washington DC 20036
Telephone: (202) 797-3000
Fax: (202) 797-3168
http://www.austemb.org/

Austria
3524 International Court, NW,
Washington DC 20008-3035
Telephone: (202) 895-6700
Fax: (202) 895-6750

The Republic of Azerbaijan
927 15th Street, NW, Suite 700,
Washington DC 20035
Telephone: (202) 842-0001
Fax: (202) 842-0004
E-mail: azerbaijan@tidalwave.net
http://www.azembassy.com/

**The Commonwealth of the
Bahamas**
2220 Massachusetts Avenue, NW,
Washington DC 20008
Telephone: (202) 319-2660
Fax: (202) 319-2668

The State of Bahrain
3502 International Drive, NW,
Washington DC 20008
Telephone: (202) 342-0741
Fax: (202) 362-2192
E-mail: info@bahrainembassy.org
http://www.bahrainembassy.org/

**The People's Republic of
Bangladesh**
3510 International Drive, NW,
Washington DC 20007
Telephone: (202) 244-2745
Fax: (202) 244-5366
E-mail: bdenq@bangladoot.org
http://www.bangladoot.org/

Barbados
2144 Wyoming Avenue, NW,
Washington DC 20008
Telephone: (202) 939-9200

Fax: (202) 332-7467

The Republic of Belarus
1619 New Hampshire Avenue,
NW, Washington DC 20009
Telephone: (202) 986-1606
Fax: (202) 986-1805
E-mail: embassy@capu.net
http://www.belarusembassy.org

Belgium
3330 Garfield Street, NW,
Washington DC 20008
Telephone: (202) 333-6900
Fax: (202) 333-3079
E-mail: washington@diplobel.org

http://www.diplobel.org/usa/default.htm

Belize
2535 Massachusetts Avenue, NW,
Washington DC 20008
Telephone: (202) 332-9636
Fax: (202) 332-6888
E-mail: belize@oas.org
http://www.embassyofbelize.org/

The Republic of Benin
2124 Kalorama Road, NW,
Washington DC 20008
Telephone: (202) 232-6656
Fax: (202) 265-1996

Bhutan
(Consulate-General) 2 UN Plaza,
27th Floor, New York NY 10017
Telephone: (212) 826-1919
Fax: (212) 826-2998

Bolivia
3014 Massachusetts Avenue, NW,
Washington DC 20008
Telephone: (202) 483-4410
Fax: (202) 328-3712
http://www.bolivia-usa.org/

Bosnia and Herzegovina
2109 E Street NW, Washington DC
20037
Telephone: (202) 337-1500
Fax: (202) 337-1502
E-mail: info@bosnianembassy.org

http://www.bosnianembassy.org/

Botswana
1531-3 New Hampshire Avenue,
NW, Washington DC 20036
Telephone: (202) 244-4990
Fax: (202) 244-4164

Brazil
3006 Massachusetts Avenue, NW,
Washington DC 20008
Telephone: (202) 238-2700
Fax: (202) 238-2827
E-mail: webmaster@brasilemb.org
http://www.brasilemb.org/

Embassy of Brunei Darussalam
3520 International Court, NW,
Washington DC 20008
Telephone: (202) 237-1838
Fax: (202) 885-0560
E-mail: info@bruneiembassy.org
http://www.bruneiembassy.org/

The Republic of Bulgaria
1621 22nd Street, NW, Washington
DC 20008
Telephone: (202) 387-0174
Fax: (202) 234-7973
E-mail: office@bulgaria-
embassy.org
http://www.bulgaria-embassy.org

Burkina Faso
2340 Massachusetts Avenue, NW,
Washington DC 20008
Telephone: (202) 332-5577
Fax: (202) 667-1882
E-mail: bf@burkinaembassy-
usa.org
http://www.burkinaembassy-
usa.org/

The Republic of Burundi
2233 Wisconsin Avenue, NW, Suite
212, Washington DC 20007
Telephone: (202) 342-2574
Fax: (202) 342-2578

The Republic of Cameroon
2349 Massachusetts Avenue, NW,
Washington DC 20008
Telephone: (202) 265-8790
Fax: (202) 387-3826

Canada
501 Pennsylvania Avenue, NW,
Washington DC 20001
Telephone: (202) 682-1740
Fax: (202) 682-7726

E-mail:
webmaster@canadianembassy.org
http://www.canadianembassy.org

The Republic of Cape Verde
3415 Massachusetts Avenue, NW,
Washington DC 20007
Telephone: (202) 965-6820
Fax: (202) 965-1207

http://www.capeverdeusaembassy.o
rg/

The Central African Republic
1618 22nd Street, NW, Washington
DC 20008
Telephone: (202) 483-7800
Fax: (202) 332-9893
The Republic of Chad
2002 R Street, NW, Washington
DC 20009
Telephone: (202) 462-4009
Fax: (202) 265-1937
E-mail: info@chadembassy.org
http://www.chadembassy.org

Chile
1732 Massachusetts Avenue, NW,
Washington DC 20036
Telephone: (202) 785-1746
Fax: (202) 887-5579
http://www.chile-usa.org/

The People's Republic of China
2300 Connecticut Ave., NW,
Washington DC 20008
Telephone: (202) 328-2500
Fax: (202) 588-0032
E-mail:
chinaembassy_us@fmprc.gov.cn
http://www.china-embassy.org/

Colombia
2118 Leroy Place, NW,
Washington DC 20008
Telephone: (202) 387-8338
Fax: (202) 232-8643
E-mail: emwas@colombiaemb.org
http://www.colombiaemb.org/

**The Federal and Islamic Republic
of the Comoros**
420 E. 50th St., New York NY
10022
Telephone: (212) 972-8010
Fax: (212) 983-4712

The Republic of Congo
4891 Colorado Avenue, NW,
Washington DC 20011

Telephone: (202) 726-5500
Fax: (202) 726-1860
E-mail: info@embassyofcongo.org
http://www.embassyofcongo.org/

**The Democratic Republic of
Congo**
1800 New Hampshire Avenue,
NW, Washington DC 20009
Telephone: (202) 234-7690
Fax: (202) 234-2609

Costa Rica
2114 S Street, NW, Washington
DC 20008
Telephone: (202) 234-2945 or 46
Fax: (202) 265-4795
E-mail: embassy@costarica-
embassy.org
http://costarica-embassy.org/

**The Republic of Cote d'Ivoire
(Ivory Coast)**
2424 Massachusetts Avenue, NW,
Washington DC 20008
Telephone: (202) 797-0300

The Republic of Croatia
2343 Massachusetts Avenue, NW,
Washington DC 20008
Telephone: (202) 588-5899
Fax: (202) 588-8936
E-mail: webmaster@croatiaemb.org
http://www.croatiaemb.org/

Cuba Interests Section
2630 and 2639 16th Street, NW,
Washington DC 20009
Telephone: (202) 797-8518
Fax: (202) 986-7283
E-mail: cubaseccion@igc.apc.org

The Republic of Cyprus
2211 R Street, NW, Washington
DC 20008
Telephone: (202) 462-5772
Fax: (202) 483-6710
E-mail: cypembwash@earthlink.net
http://www.cyprusembassy.net

The Czech Republic
3900 Spring of Freedom Street,
NW, Washington DC 20008
Telephone: (202) 274-9100
Fax: (202) 966-8540
E-mail:
washington@embassy.mzv.cz
http://www.mzv.cz/washington/

Royal Danish Embassy

3200 Whitehaven Street, NW,
Washington DC 20008
Telephone: (202) 234-4300
Fax: (202) 328-1470
E-mail: wasamb@wasamb.um.dk
http://www.denmarkemb.org/

The Republic of Djibouti
1156 15th Street, NW, Suite 515,
Washington DC 20005
Telephone: (202) 331-0270
Fax: (202) 331-0302

The Commonwealth of Dominica
3216 New Mexico Avenue, NW,
Washington DC 20016
Telephone: (202) 364-6781/2
Fax: (202) 364-6791
E-mail: Embdomdc@aol.com

The Dominican Republic
1715 22nd Street, NW, Washington
DC 20008
Telephone: (202) 332-6280
Fax: (202) 265-8057
E-mail: embdomrepusa@msn.com
http://www.domrep.org/

Ecuador
2535 15th Street, NW, Washington
DC 20009
Telephone: (202) 234-7200
Fax: (202) 667-3482
E-mail: mecuawaa@erols.com
http://www.ecuador.org/

The Arab Republic of Egypt
3521 International Court, NW,
Washington DC 20008
Telephone: (202) 895 5400
Fax: (202) 244-4319
E-mail: embassy@egyptembdc.org
h
ttp://www.embassyofegyptwashingtondc.or
g/

El Salvador
2308 California Street, NW,
Washington DC 20008
Telephone: (202) 265-9671
E-mail: cbartoli@elsalvador.org
http://www.elsalvador.org
Equatorial Guinea
2020 16th Street, NW, Washington
DC 20009
Telephone: (202) 518-5700
Fax: (202) 518-5252

Eritrea
1708 New Hampshire Ave, NW,

Washington DC 20009
Telephone: (202) 319-1991
Fax: (202) 319-1304
E-mail:
veronica@embassyeritrea.org

Estonia
1730 M Street, Suite 503, NW,
Washington DC 20036
Telephone: (202) 588-0101
Fax: (202) 588-0108
E-mail: info@estemb.org
http://www.estemb.org/

Ethiopia
3506 International Drive, NW,
Washington DC 20008
Telephone: (202) 364-1200
Fax: (202) 686-9551
E-mail: info@ethiopianembassy.org
http://www.ethiopianembassy.org/

Fiji
2233 Wisconsin Avenue, NW, Suite
240, Washington DC 20007
Telephone: (202) 337-8320
Fax: (202) 337-1996
E-mail: fijiemb@earthlink.net

Finland
3301 Massachusetts Avenue, NW,
Washington DC 20008
Telephone: (202) 298-5800
Fax: (202) 298-6030
E-mail: info@finland.org
http://www.finland.org/

France
4101 Reservoir Road, NW,
Washington DC 20007
Telephone: (202) 944-6000
Fax: (202) 944-6072
E-mail: info@amb-wash.fr
http://www.ambafrance-us.org/

The Gabonese Republic
2034 20th Street, NW, Suite 200,
Washington DC 20009
Telephone: (202) 797-1000
Fax: (202) 332-0668

The Gambia
1155 15th Street, NW, Suite 1000,
Washington DC 20005
Telephone: (202) 785-1399
Fax: (202) 785-1430
E-mail: gamembdc@gambia.com

http://www.gambia.com/index.html

The Republic of Georgia
1615 New Hampshire Ave. NW,
Suite 300, Washington DC 20009
Telephone: (202) 387-2390
Fax: (202) 393-4537
http://www.georgiaemb.org/

Germany
4645 Reservoir Road, NW,
Washington DC 20007-1998
Telephone: (202) 298-4000
Fax: (202) 298-4249 or 333-2653
http://www.germany-info.org/

Ghana
3512 International Drive NW,
Washington DC 20008
Telephone: (202) 686-4520
Fax: (202) 686-4527
E-mail: ghtrade@cais.com

Greece
2221 Massachusetts Avenue, NW,
Washington DC 20008
Telephone: (202) 939-5800
Fax: (202) 939-5824
http://www.greekembassy.org/

Grenada
1701 New Hampshire Ave., NW,
Washington DC 20009
Telephone: (202) 265-2561

Guatemala
2220 R Street, NW, Washington
DC 20008
Telephone: (202) 745-4952
Fax: (202) 745-1908
E-mail: info@guatemala-
embassy.org
http://www.guatemala-
embassy.org

The Republic of Guinea
2112 Leroy Place, NW,
Washington DC 20008
Telephone: (202) 483-9420
Fax: (202) 483-8688

The Republic of Guinea-Bissau
15929 Yukon Lane, Rockville MD
20855
Telephone: (301) 947-3958

Guyana
2490 Tracy Place, NW,
Washington DC 20008
Telephone: (202) 265-6900
Fax: (202) 232-1297
E-mail:

314

Guyanaembassy@hotmail.com

http://www.guyana.org/govt/embas
sy.html

The Republic of Haiti
2311 Massachusetts Avenue, NW,
Washington DC 20008
Telephone: (202) 332-4090
Fax: (202) 745-7215
E-mail: embassy@haiti.org
http://www.haiti.org/

**Apostolic Nunciature, the Holy
See**
3339 Massachusetts Avenue, NW,
Washington DC 20008
Telephone: (202) 333-7121

Honduras
3007 Tilden Street, NW, Suite 4M,
Washington DC 20008
Telephone: (202) 966-7702
Fax: (202) 966-9751
E-mail: embhondu@aol.com
http://www.hondurasemb.org/

The Republic of Hungary
3910 Shoemaker Street, NW,
Washington DC 20008
Telephone: (202) 362-6730
Fax: (202) 966-8135
E-mail: office@huembwas.org
http://www.huembwas.org/

Iceland
1156 15th Street, NW, Suite 1200,
Washington DC 20005-1704
Telephone: (202) 265-6653
Fax: (202) 265-6656
E-mail: icemb.wash@utn.stjr.is
http://www.iceland.org/

India
2107 Massachusetts Avenue, NW,
Washington DC 20008
Telephone: (202) 939-7000
Fax: (202) 265-4351
http://www.indianembassy.org/

The Republic of Indonesia
2020 Massachusetts Avenue, NW,
Washington DC 20036
Telephone: (202) 775-5200
Fax: (202) 775-5365

Iranian Interests Section
2209 Wisconsin Avenue NW,
Washington DC 20007
Telephone: (202) 965-4990

Fax: (202) 965-1073

http://www.daftar.org/default_eng.
htm

Iraqi Interests Section
1801 P Street, NW, Washington
DC 20036
Telephone: (202) 483-7500
Fax: (202) 462-5066

Ireland
2234 Massachusetts Avenue, NW,
Washington DC 20008
Telephone: (202) 462-3939
Fax: (202) 232 5993
E-mail: ireland@irelandemb.org
http://www.irelandemb.org/

Israel
3514 International Drive, NW,
Washington DC 20008
Telephone: (202) 364-5500
Fax: (202) 364-5423
E-mail: ask@israelemb.org
http://www.israelemb.org/

Italy
3000 Whitehaven Street, NW,
Washington DC 20008
Telephone: (202) 612-4400
Fax: (202) 518-2154
http://www.italyemb.org/

Jamaica
1520 New Hampshire Avenue,
NW, Washington DC 20036
Telephone: (202) 452-0660
Fax: (202) 452-0081
E-mail: info@emjamusa.org
http://www.emjamusa.org/

Japan
2520 Massachusetts Avenue NW,
Washington DC 20008
Telephone: (202) 238-6700
Fax: (202) 328-2187
http://www.embjapan.org/

**The Hashemite Kingdom of
Jordan**
3504 International Drive, NW,
Washington DC 20008
Telephone: (202) 966-2664
Fax: (202) 966-3110
E-mail: HKJEmbassyDC@aol.com
http://www.jordanembassyus.org/

The Republic of Kazakhstan
1401 16th Street, NW, Washington

DC 20036
Telephone: (202) 232-5488
Fax: (202) 232-5845
E-mail: kazak@intr.net
http://www.kazakhstan-embassy-
us.org

Kenya
2249 R. Street, NW, Washington
DC 20008
Telephone: (202) 387-6101
Fax: (202) 462-3829
E-mail: info@kenyaembassy.com
http://www.kenyaembassy.com/

The Kyrgyz Republic
1732 Wisconsin Avenue, NW,
Washington DC 20007
Telephone: (202) 338-5141
Fax: (202) 338-5139
E-mail: Embassy@kyrgyzstan.org
http://www.kyrgyzstan.org/

The Republic of Korea
2450 Massachusetts Avenue, NW,
Washington DC 20008
Telephone: (202) 939-5600
Fax: (202) 797-0595
http://www.koreaembassy.org/

The State of Kuwait
2940 Tilden Street, NW,
Washington DC 20008
Telephone: (202) 966-0702
Fax: (202) 364-2868

**The Lao People's Democratic
Republic**
2222 S Street, NW, Washington
DC 20008
Telephone: (202) 332-6416
Fax: (202) 332-4923
http://www.laoembassy.com/

Latvia
4325 17th Street, NW, Washington
DC 20011
Telephone: (202) 726-8213
Fax: (202) 726-6785
E-mail: Embassy@Latvia-USA.org
http://www.latvia-usa.org/

Lebanon
2560 28th Street, NW, Washington
DC 20008
Telephone: (202) 939-6300
Fax: (202) 939-6324
E-mail:
info@lebanonembassyus.org
http://www.lebanonembassyus.org/

The Kingdom of Lesotho
2511 Massachusetts Avenue, NW,
Washington DC 20008
Telephone: (202) 797-5533
Fax: (202) 234-6815

The Republic of Liberia
5201 16th Street, NW, Washington
DC 20011
Telephone: (202) 723-0437
Fax: (202) 723-0436
E-mail: info@liberiaemb.org
http://www.liberiaemb.org/

Lithuania
2622 Sixteenth Street, NW,
Washington DC 20009-4202
Telephone: (202) 234-5860
Fax: (202) 328-0466
E-mail: admin@ltembassyus.org
http://www.ltembassyus.org/

Luxembourg
2200 Massachusetts Avenue, NW,
Washington DC 20008
Telephone: (202) 265-4171
Fax: (202) 328-8270
E-mail: infos@luxembourg-usa.org
http://www.luxembourg-usa.org/

The Republic of Macedonia
3050 K Street, NW, Suite 210,
Washington DC 20007
Telephone: (202) 337-3063
Fax: (202) 337-3093
E-mail: rmacedonia@aol.com

Malawi
2408 Massachusetts Avenue, NW,
Washington DC 20008
Telephone: (202) 797-1007

Malaysia
3516 International Court, NW,
Washington DC 20008
Telephone: (202) 572-9700
Fax: (202) 483-7661

The Republic of Mali
2130 R Street, NW, Washington
DC 20008
Telephone: (202) 332-2249
Fax: (202) 332-6603
E-mail: info@maliembassy-usa.org
http://www.maliembassy-usa.org

Malta
2017 Connecticut Avenue NW,
Washington DC 20008
Telephone: (202) 462-3611

Fax: (202) 387-5470
E-mail:
Malta_Embassy@compuserve.com

http://www.foreign.gov.mt/ORG/m
inistry/missions/washington2.htm

**The Republic of the Marshall
Islands**
2433 Massachusetts Avenue, NW,
Washington DC 20008
Telephone: (202) 234-5414
Fax: (202) 232-3236
E-mail: info@rmiembassyus.org

http://www.rmiembassyus.org/use
mb.html

**The Islamic Republic of
Mauritania**
2129 Leroy Place, NW,
Washington DC 20008
Telephone: (202) 232-5700
Fax: (202) 319-2623
E-mail: info@mauritaniembassy-
usa.org
http://www.mauritaniembassy-
usa.org/

Mauritius
4301 Connecticut Avenue, NW,
Suite 441, Washington DC 20008
Telephone: (202) 244-1491
Fax: (202) 966-0983
E-mail:
MAURITIUS.EMBASSY@prodigy.
net

http://www.idsonline.com/usa/embasydc.ht
ml

Mexico
1911 Pennsylvania Avenue, NW,
Washington DC 20006
Telephone: (202) 728-1600
Fax: (202) 728-1698
E-mail: mexembusa@sre.gob.mx
http://www.embassyofmexico.org

**The Federated States of
Micronesia**
1725 N Street, NW, Washington
DC 20036
Telephone: (202) 223-4383
Fax: (202) 223-4391
E-mail: fsm@fsmembassy.org
http://www.fsmembassy.org/

The Republic of Moldova
2101 S Street, NW, Washington

DC 20008
Telephone: (202) 667-1130/31/37
Fax: (202) 667-1204
E-mail: moldova@dgs.dgsys.com
http://www.moldova.org/

Mongolia
2833 M Street NW, Washington
DC 20007
Telephone: (202) 333-7117
Fax: (202) 298 9227
E-mail: monemb@aol.com
http://members.aol.com/monemb/

The Kingdom of Morocco
1601 21st Street, NW, Washington
DC 20009
Telephone: (202) 462-7979
Fax: (202) 265-0161

The Republic of Mozambique
1990 M Street, NW, Suite 570,
Washington DC 20036
Telephone: (202) 293-7146
Fax: (202) 835-0245
E-mail: embamoc@aol.com
http://www.embamoc-usa.org/

The Union of Myanmar
2300 S Street, NW, Washington
DC 20008
Telephone: (202) 332-9044
Fax: (202) 332-9046
E-mail: MEWashDC@aol.com

http://members.aol.com/mewashdc/

The Republic of Namibia
1605 New Hampshire Avenue,
NW, Washington DC 20009
Telephone: (202) 986-0540
Fax: (202) 986-0443

Royal Nepalese Embassy
2131 Leroy Place, NW,
Washington DC 20008
Telephone: (202) 667-4550
Fax: (202) 667-5534
E-mail: nepali@erols.com

Royal Netherlands Embassy
4200 Linnean Avenue, NW,
Washington DC 20008
Telephone: (202) 244-5300
Fax: (202) 362-3430
http://www.netherlands-
embassy.org/

New Zealand
37 Observatory Circle, Washington

316

DC 20008
Telephone: (202) 328-4800
Fax: (202) 667-5227
E-mail: nz@nzemb.org
http://www.nzemb.org/

The Republic of Nicaragua
1627 New Hampshire Avenue,
NW, Washington DC 20009
Telephone: (202) 939-6570
Fax: (202) 939-6542

The Republic of Niger
2204 R Street, NW, Washington
DC 20008
Telephone: (202) 483-4224
Fax: (202) 483-3169
E-mail: embassyofniger@ioip.com
http://www.nigerembassyusa.org/

The Federal Republic of Nigeria
1333 16th Street, NW, Washington
DC 20036
Telephone: (202) 986-8400
Fax: (202) 462-7124
http://www.nigeriaembassyusa.org

Royal Norwegian Embassy
2720 34th Street, NW, Washington
DC 20008
Telephone: (202) 333-6000
Fax: (202) 337-0870
http://www.norway.org/

The Sultanate of Oman
2535 Belmont Road, NW,
Washington DC 20008
Telephone: (202) 387-1980
Fax: (202) 745-4933

The Islamic Republic of Pakistan
2315 Massachusetts Avenue, NW,
Washington DC 20008
Telephone: (202) 939-6200
Fax: (202) 387-0484
E-mail: info@pakistan-
embassy.com
http://www.pakistan-embassy.com/

The Republic of Panama
2862 McGill Terrace, NW,
Washington DC 20008
Telephone: (202) 483-1407

Papua New Guinea
1779 Massachusetts Ave. NW,
Suite 805, Washington DC 20036
Telephone: (202) 745-3680
Fax: (202) 745-3679
E-mail: Kunduwash@aol.com

http://www.pngembassy.org

Paraguay
2400 Massachusetts Avenue, NW,
Washington DC 20008
Telephone: (202) 483-6960
Fax: (202) 234-4508

Peru
1700 Massachusetts Avenue, NW,
Washington DC 20036
Telephone: (202) 833-9860
Fax: (202) 659-8124
E-mail: peru@peruemb.org
http://www.peruemb.org

The Philippines
1600 Massachusetts Avenue, NW,
Washington DC 20036
Telephone: (202) 467-9300
Fax: (202) 467-9417
http://www.philippineembassy-
usa.org/

Poland
2640 16th Street, NW, Washington
DC 20009
Telephone: (202) 234 3800
Fax: (202) 328-6271
E-mail: information@ioip.com
http://www.polandembassy.org/

Portugal
2125 Kalorama Road, NW,
Washington DC 20008
Telephone: (202) 328-8610
Fax: (202) 462-3726
E-mail: portugal@portugalemb.org
http://www.portugalemb.org/

The State of Qatar
4200 Wisconsin Ave, NW, Suite
200, Washington DC 20016
Telephone: (202) 274-1600
Fax: (202) 237-0061

Romania
1607 23rd Street, NW, Washington
DC 20008
Telephone: (202) 332-4848
Fax: (202) 232-4748
E-mail: romania1@roembus.org
http://www.roembus.org/

The Russian Federation
2650 Wisconsin Avenue, NW,
Washington DC 20007
Telephone: (202) 298-5700
Fax: (202) 298-5735
http://www.russianembassy.org

The Republic of Rwanda
1714 New Hampshire Avenue,
NW, Washington DC 20009
Telephone: (202) 232-2882
Fax: (202) 232-4544
E-mail: rwandemb@rwandemb.org
http://www.rwandemb.org/

Saint Kitts and Nevis
3216 New Mexico Avenue, NW,
Washington DC 20016
Telephone: (202) 686-2636
Fax: (202) 686-5740
E-mail: info@stkittsnevis.org
http://www.stkittsnevis.org/

Saint Lucia
3216 New Mexico Avenue, NW,
Washington DC 20016
Telephone: (202) 364-
6792/93/94/95
Fax: (202) 364-6723

Saint Vincent and the Grenadines
3216 New Mexico Avenue, NW,
Washington DC 20016
Telephone: (202) 364-6730
Fax: (202) 364-6736

Royal Embassy of Saudi Arabia
601 New Hampshire Avenue, NW,
Washington DC 20037
Telephone: (202) 337-4076
E-mail: info@saudiembassy.net
http://www.saudiembassy.net/

The Republic of Senegal
2112 Wyoming Avenue, NW,
Washington DC 20008
Telephone: (202) 234-0540

The Republic of Seychelles
800 Second Avenue, Suite 400,
New York NY 10017
Telephone: (212) 687-9766
Fax: (212) 972-1786

Sierra Leone
1701 19th Street, NW, Washington
DC 20009
Telephone: (202) 939-9261
Fax: (202) 483-1793

The Republic of Singapore
3501 International Place, NW,
Washington DC 20008
Telephone: (202) 537-3100
Fax: (202) 537-0876
E-mail: singemb@bellatlantic.net

317

http://www.gov.sg/mfa/washington
/

The Slovak Republic
3523 International Court, NW,
Washington DC 20008
Telephone: (202) 237-1054
Fax: (202) 237-6438
E-mail: info@slovakembassy-us.org
http://www.slovakembassy-us.org/

The Republic of Slovenia
1525 New Hampshire Avenue,
NW, Washington DC 20036
Telephone: (202) 667-5363
Fax: (202) 667-4563
E-mail: slovenia@embassy.org
http://www.embassy.org/slovenia/

Somalia
The Embassy of the Somali
Democratic Republic ceased
operations May 8, 1991

South Africa
3051 Massachusetts Avenue, NW,
Washington DC 20008
Telephone: (202) 232-4400
Fax: (202) 265-1607
E-mail: info@saembassy.org
http://www.saembassy.org

Spain
2375 Pennsylvania Avenue, NW,
Washington DC 20037
Telephone: (202) 452-0100
Fax: (202) 833-5670
E-mail: spain@spainemb.org

http://www.spainemb.org/ingles/indexing.h
tm

Sri Lanka
2148 Wyoming Avenue, NW,
Washington DC 20008
Telephone: (202) 483-4025 to 28
Fax: (202) 232-7181
E-mail: slembassy@starpower.net
http://www.slembassyusa.org/

The Republic of the Sudan
2210 Massachusetts Avenue, NW,
Washington DC 20008
Telephone: (202) 338-8565
Fax: (202) 667-2406
E-mail: info@sudanembassyus.org
http://www.sudanembassyus.org/

The Republic of Suriname

4301 Connecticut Avenue, NW,
Suite 460, Washington DC 20008
Telephone: (202) 244-7488
Fax: (202) 244-5878

The Kingdom of Swaziland
3400 International Drive, NW,
Washington DC 20008

Sweden
1501 M Street, NW, Washington
DC 20005
Telephone: (202) 467-2600
Fax: (202) 467-2656
E-mail:
ambassaden.washington@foreign.m
inistry.se
http://www.swedish-embassy.org/

Switzerland
2900 Cathedral Avenue, NW,
Washington DC 20008
Telephone: (202) 745-7900
Fax: 202-387-2564
E-mail:
vertretung@was.rep.admin.ch
http://www.eda.admin.ch/

The Syrian Arab Republic
2215 Wyoming Avenue, NW,
Washington DC 20008
Telephone: (202) 232-6313
Fax: (202) 234-9548

The Republic of China on Taiwan
4201 Wisconsin Avenue, NW,
Washington DC 20016
Telephone: (202) 895-1800
Fax: (202) 966-0825

The United Republic of Tanzania
2139 R Street, NW, Washington
DC 20008
Telephone: (202) 939-6125
Fax: (202) 797-7408
E-mail: balozi@tanzaniaembassy-
us.org
http://www.tanzaniaembassy-
us.org/

Royal Thai Embassy
1024 Wisconsin Avenue, NW, Suite
401, Washington DC 20007
Telephone: (202) 944-3600
Fax: (202) 944-3611
E-mail: thai.wsn@thaiembdc.org
http://www.thaiembdc.org/

The Republic of Togo
2208 Massachusetts Avenue, NW,

Washington DC 20008
Telephone: (202) 234-4212
Fax: (202) 232-3190

The Kingdom of Tonga
800 Second Avenue, Suite 400B,
New York NY 10017

The Republic of Trinidad and Tobago
1708 Massachusetts Avenue, NW,
Washington DC 20036
Telephone: (202) 467-6490
Fax: (202) 785-3130
E-mail: embttgo@erols.com
http://ttembassy.cjb.net/

Tunisia
1515 Massachusetts Avenue, NW,
Washington DC 20005
Telephone: (202) 862-1850
Fax: (202) 862-1858

The Republic of Turkey
2525 Massachusetts Avenue, NW,
Washington DC 20008
Telephone: (202) 612-6700
Fax: (202) 612-6744
E-mail: info@turkey.org
http://www.turkey.org/

Turkmenistan
2207 Massachusetts Avenue, NW,
Washington DC 20008
Telephone: (202) 588-1500
Fax: (202) 588-0697
E-mail: turkmen@earthlink.net

http://www.turkmenistanembassy.o
rg

The Republic of Uganda
5911 16th Street, NW, Washington
DC 20011
Telephone: (202) 726-7100
Fax: (202) 726-1727
E-mail: ugembassy@aol.com

http://www.ugandaweb.com/ugaem
bassy/

Ukraine
3350 M Street, NW, Washington
DC 20007
Telephone: (202) 333-0606
Fax: (202) 333-0817
E-mail: infolook@aol.com
http://www.ukremb.com/

The United Arab Emirates

318

1255 22nd Street, NW, Suite 700,
Washington DC 20037
Telephone: (202) 243-2400
Fax: (202) 243-2432

The United Kingdom of Great Britain and Northern Ireland
3100 Massachusetts Ave, NW,
Washington DC 20008
Telephone: (202) 588-6500
Fax: (202) 588-7870

http://www.britainusa.com/consular
/embassy/embassy.asp

Uruguay
2715 M Street, NW, 3rd Floor,
Washington DC 20007
Telephone: (202) 331-1313
Fax: (202) 331-8142
E-mail: uruguay@erols.com
http://www.embassy.org/uruguay/

The Republic of Uzbekistan
1746 Massachusetts Avenue, NW,
Washington DC 20036
Telephone: (202) 887-5300
Fax: (202) 293-6804
E-mail: emb@uzbekistan.org
http://www.uzbekistan.org/

The Republic of Venezuela
1099 30th Street NW, Washington
DC 20007
Telephone: (202) 342-2214
Fax: (202) 342-6820
E-mail: prensa@embavenez-us.org
http://www.embavenez-us.org/

The Socialist Republic of Vietnam
1233 20th Street NW, Suite 400,
Washington DC 20037
Telephone: (202) 861-0737
Fax: (202) 861-0917
E-mail: info@vietnamembassy-usa.org
http://www.vietnamembassy-usa.org/

Independent State of Samoa
800 Second Avenue, Suite 400D,
New York NY 10017
Telephone: (212) 599-6196
Fax: (212) 599-0797

The Republic of Yemen
2600 Virginia Avenue, NW, Suite
705, Washington DC 20037
Telephone: (202) 965-4760
Fax: (202) 337-2017

E-mail: info@yemenembassy.org
http://www.yemenembassy.org

The Former S. F. Republic of Yugoslavia
2410 California Street, NW.
Washington DC 20008
Telephone: (202) 332-0333
Fax: (202) 332-3933
E-mail: yuembusa@aol.com
http://www.yuembusa.org/

The Republic of Zambia
2419 Massachusetts Avenue, NW,
Washington DC 20008
Telephone: (202) 265-9717
Fax: (202) 332-0826

The Republic of Zimbabwe
1608 New Hampshire Avenue,
NW, Washington DC 20009
Telephone: (202) 332-7100
Fax: (202) 483-9326
E-mail: zimemb@erols.com
http://www.zimembassy-usa.org/

319

APPENDIX C

KEY OFFICERS OF U.S. FOREIGN SERVICE POSTS

Guide for Business Representatives

The Key Officers Guide lists key officers at Foreign Service posts with whom American business representatives would most likely have contact. All embassies, missions, consulates general, and consulates are listed.

At the head of each U.S. diplomatic mission are the Chief of Mission (with the title of Ambassador, Minister, or Charge d'Affairs) and the Deputy Chief of Mission. These officers are responsible for all components of the U.S. Mission within a country, including consular posts.

Commercial Officers assist U.S. business through: arranging appointments with local business and government officials, providing counsel on local trade regulations, laws, and customs; identifying importers, buyers, agents, distributors, and joint venture partners for U.S. firms; and other business assistance. At larger posts, trade specialists of the US&FCS perform this function. At smaller posts, commercial interests are represented by economic/commercial officers from the Department of State.

Commercial Officers for Tourism implement marketing programs to expand inbound tourism, to increase the export competitiveness of U.S. travel companies, and to strengthen the international trade position of the United States. These officers are employees of the U.S. Travel and Tourism Administration (USTTA), an agency of the U.S. Department of Commerce with offices in various countries. Additional important markets in Europe, Asia, the Pacific, Latin America are covered by the Foreign Commercial Services and the private sector under USTTA leadership.

Economic Officers analyze and report on macroeconomic trends and trade policies and their implications for U.S. policies and programs.

Financial Attaches analyze and report on major financial developments.

Political Officers analyze and report on political developments and their potential impact on U.S. interests.

Labor Officers follow the activities of labor organizations and can supply information on wages, non-wage costs, social security regulations, labor attitudes toward American investments, etc.

Consular Officers extend to U.S. citizens and their property abroad the protection of the U.S. Government. They maintain lists of local attorneys, act as liaison with police and other officials, and have the authority to notarize documents. The Department recommends that business representatives residing overseas register with the consular officer; in troubled areas, even travelers are advised to register.

The Administrative Officer is responsible for the normal business operations of the post, including purchasing for the post and its commissary.

Regional Security Officers are responsible for providing physical, procedural, and personnel security services to U.S. diplomatic facilities and personnel; their responsibilities extend to providing in-country security briefings and threat assessments to business executives.

Security Assistance Officers are responsible for Defense Cooperation in Armaments and foreign military sales to include functioning as primary in-country point of contact for U.S. Defense Industry.

Scientific Attaches follow scientific and technological developments in the country.

Agricultural Officers promote the export of U.S. agricultural products and report on agricultural production and market developments in their area.

The Aid Mission Director is responsible for AID programs, including dollar and local currency loans, grants, and technical assistance.

The Public Affairs Officers is the post's press and

cultural affairs specialist and maintains close contact with the local press.

The Legal Attache serves as a representative to the U.S. Department of Justice on criminal matters.

The Communications Program Officer is responsible for the telecommunications, telephone, radio, diplomatic pouches, and records management programs within the diplomatic mission. They maintain close contact with the host government's information/communications authorities on operational matters.

The Information Systems Manager is responsible for the post's unclassified information systems, database management, programming, and operational needs. They liaison with appropriate commercial contacts in the information field to enhance the post's systems integrity.

Business representatives planning a trip overseas should include in their preparations a visit or telephone call to the nearest U.S. Department of Commerce District Office. The District Office can provide extensive information and assistance as well as a current list of legal holidays in the countries to be visited. If desired, the District Officer can also provide advance notice to posts abroad of the representative's visit.

The Department of State, Bureau of Diplomatic Security, can also provide current data on the security situation to interested persons planning trips abroad. American business representatives desiring this information should contact the Diplomatic Security Service, Overseas Support Programs Division (202) 647-3122.

Some of the services jointly provided by the Departments of State and Commerce to U.S. business firms interested in establishing a market for their products or expanding sales abroad include:

-The Trade Opportunities Program (TOP) that provides specific export sales leads of U.S. products and services;

World Traders Data Report (WTDR) that provides detailed financial and commercial information on individual firms abroad upon request from U.S. companies;

-Agent Distributor Service (ADS) that helps U.S. firms find agents or distributors to represent their firms and market their products abroad; and

-Information about foreign markets for U.S. products and services and U.S.-sponsored exhibitions abroad in which American firms can participate and demonstrate their products to key foreign buyers.

-In all matters pertaining to foreign trade, the nearest U.S. Department of Commerce District Office should be your first point of contact. Foreign trade specialists at these facilities render valuable assistance to U.S. business representatives engaged in international commerce.

For additional information about Foreign Service assistance to American business overseas, or for specialized assistance with unusual commercial problems, you are invited to visit, telephone, or write the Office of Commercial, Legislative, and Public Affairs, Bureau of Economic and Business Affairs, U.S. Department of State, Washington, D.C. 20520-5816. Telephone (202) 647-1942.

APPENDIX D

COMPARATIVE CLOTHING SIZES

Suits and Overcoats (men)

American	32	34	36	38	40	42	44	46
Continental	42	44	46	48	50	52	54	56
British	32	34	36	38	40	42	44	46

Dresses and Suits (women)

American		6	8	10	12	14	16	18
Continental		36	38	40	42	44	46	48
British		8	10	12	14	16	18	20

Shirts (men)

American	14	14.5	15	15.5	16	16.5	17	17.5
Continental	36	37	38	39	41	42	43	44
British	14	14.5	15	15.5	16	16.5	17	17.5

Women's Hosiery

American	8	8.5	9	9.5	10	10.5
Continental	0	1	2	3	4	5
British	8	8.5	9	9.5	10	10.5

Socks

American	8.5	9	9.5	10	10.5	11	11.5

Continental	36/37	37/38	38/39		39/40	40/41	41/42	42/43
British	8.5	9	9.5		10	10.5	11	11.5

Shoes(Men)

American	7	8	8.5	9.5	10.5	11	11.5	12	13
Contl.	39.5	41	42	43	44	44.5	45	46	47
British	6	7	7.5	8.5	9.5	10	10.5	11	12

Shoes (women)

American	6	6.5	7	7.5	8	8.5	9
Continental	38	38	39	30	40	41	42
British	4.5	5	5.5	6	6.5	7	7.5

Children's Clothes

American	2	4	6	8	10	12	14

Continental

Height (cm)	115	125	135	150	155	160	165
Age	5	7	9	12	13	14	15

British

Height (in)	38	43	48	55	58	60	62
Age	2-3	4-5	6-7	9-10	11	12	13

Shoes (children)

American	1	2	3	4.5	5.5	6.5	8	9	10	11	12	13
Continental	32	33	34	36	37	38.5	24	25	27	28	29	30
British	13	1	2	3	4	5.5	7	8	9	10	11	12

APPENDIX E

INTERNATIONAL WEIGHTS AND MEASURES

CONVERSION TABLES

DISTANCE

1 mile (Mi) = 1.609 Kilometers (Km)
1 kilometer (Km) = .6214 miles (Mi)

VOLUME (capacity)

IMPERIAL WEIGHT MEASURE

1 Imperial gallon = 4.5 liters (L)
1 liter (L) = .222 Imperial gallon (IGal)

Imperial gallons are larger than U.S. gallons
1mperial gallon = 1.2 U.S. gallons

TEMPERATURE

Degrees Fahrenheit (F') = 9/5 x Degrees
Centigrade + 32
Degrees Centigrade/Celsuis (C') = (5/9
Degrees Fahrenheit - 32)

SPEED

1 Mile per hour (MPH) = 1.6 (KMH)
1 kilometer per hour (KMH) = .625
(MPH)
1 inch = 2.54 centimeter (cm)
1 centimeter = .3937 inches (in)   1 foot
= .3048 meters (m)
1 meter = 3.281 feet (ft)

WEIGHTS

1 ounce (oz) = 28.349 grams (gm)
1 gram (gm) = .0353 ounces (oz)
1 pound (lb) = .4536 Kilograms
1Kg Kilogram (Kg) = 2.205 pounds (lb)

In = Cm
1 = 2.54
2 = 5.08
3 = 7.63
4 = 10.16
5 = 12.70
6 = 15.24
7 = 17.78
8 = 20.32
9 = 22.86
10 = 25.40
11 = 27.94
12 = 30.48

Cm = In
1 = 0.40
2 = 0.80
3 = 1.20
4 = 1.60
5 = 2.00
6 = 2.40
7 = 2.80
8 = 3.20
9 = 3.50
10 = 3.90
11 = 4.30
12 = 4.70

Lb = Kg
1 = 0.45
2 = 0.91
3 = 1.36
4 = 1.81
5 = 2.27
6 = 2.72
7 = 3.18
8 = 3.63
9 = 4.08
10 = 4.54
50 = 22.68
100 = 45.36

Kg = Lb
1 = 2.21
2 = 4.41
3 = 6.61
4 = 8.82
5 = 11.02
6 = 13.23
7 = 15.43
8 = 17.64
9 = 19.84
10 = 22.05
50 = 110.23
100 = 220.46

Mi = Km
1 = 1.61
2 = 3.22
3 = 4.83
4 = 6.44
5 = 8.05
6 = 9.66
7 = 11.27
8 = 12.88
9 = 14.48
10 = 16.09
50 = 80.47
100 = 160.90

Km = Mi
1 = 0.62
2 = 1.24
3 = 1.86
4 = 2.49
5 = 3.11
6 = 3.73
7 = 4.35
8 = 4.97
9 = 5.59
10 = 6.21
50 = 31.07
100 = 62.14

Gal = L
1 = 3.79
2 = 7.57
3 = 11.35
4 = 15.14
5 = 18.93
6 = 22.71
7 = 26.50
8 = 30.28
9 = 34.16
10 = 37.94
50 = 189.70

100 = 379.40

L = Gal
1 = 0.26
2 = 0.53
3 = 0.79
4 = 1.06
5 = 1.32
6 = 1.58
7 = 1.85
8 = 2.11
9 = 2.38
10 = 2.64
50 = 13.20
100 = 26.40

TEMPERATURE
F = C
32 = 0
40 = 5
50 = 10
60 = 15
70 = 20
75 = 25
85 = 30
105 = 40
140 = 60
175 = 80

SPEED
MPH = KMH
20 = 32
30 = 48
40 = 64
50 = 80
60 = 96
70 = 112
80 = 128
90 = 144
100 = 160

325

APPENDIX F

INTERNATIONAL SYSTEMS OF WEIGHTS & MEASURES

Country		Country		Country	
AFGHANISTAN	M	CZECH REP.	M	LAOS	M
ALBANIA	M	DENMARK	M	LATVIA	M
ANGOLA	M	DOMINICA	I*	LEBANON	M
ANGUILLA	M,I	DOMINICAN REP.	I*	LESOTHO	M
ANTIGUA &		ECUADOR	M	LIBERIA	I
BARBUDA	I*	EGYPT	M*	LIBYA	M
ARGENTINA	M	EL SALVADOR	M*	LIECHTENSTEIN	M
ARMENIA	M	EQUAT. GUINEA	M	LITUANIA	M
AUSTRALIA	M	ESTONIA	M	LUXEMBOURG	M
AUSTRIA	M	ETHIOPIA	M*	MADAGASCAR	M
AZERBAIJAN	M	FIJI	M	MALAWI	M
BAHAMAS	I	FINLAND	M	MALAYSIA	M*
BAHRAIN	M	FRANCE	M	MALI	M
BANGLADESH	I*	FRENCH GUIANA	M	MALTA	M
BARBADOS	M	FR. ANTILLES	M	MARTINIQUE	M
BELGIUM	M	FR. POLYNESIA	M	MAURITANIA	M
BELIZE	I	GABON	M	MAURITIUS	M
BERMUDA	M,I	GEORGIA	M	MEXICO	M
BHUTAN	M	GERMANY	M	MOLDOVA	M
BOLIVIA	M	GHANA	M	MONACO	M
BOTSWANA	M	GREECE	M	MONGOLIA	M
BRAZIL	M	GRENADA	M	MONTSERRAT	I*
BRITISH V.I.	I	GUADELOUPE	M	MOROCCO	M
BRUNEI	I**	GUATEMALA	M	MOZAMBIQUE	
BULGARIA	M	GUINEA	M	NAMIBIA	M
BURKINA FASO	M	GUINEA-BISSAU	M	NAURU	M
BURUNDI	M	GUYANA	M	NETHERLANDS	M
BYELARUS	M	HAITI	M	NETH. ANTILLES	M
CAMBODIA	M	HONDURAS	M*	NEW ZEALAND	M
CAMEROON	M	HONG KONG	M	NICARAGUA	M*
CANADA	M	HUNGARY	M	NIGER	M
CAYMAN IS	I	ICELAND	M	NIGERIA	M
CENTRAL		INDIA	M,I*	NORWAY	M
AFRICAN REP.	M	INDONESIA	M	OMAN	M,I*
CHAD	M	IRAN	M*	PAKISTAN	M,I*
CHILE	M	IRAQ	M*	PANAMA	M,I
CHINA,		IRELAND	I*	PAPUA	
PEOPLES REP.	M*	ISRAEL	M	NEW GUINEA	M
CHINA, TAIWAN	M	ITALY	M	PARAGUAY	M
COLOMBIA	M	JAMAICA	M,I	PERU	M
COMOROS	M	JAPAN	M	PHILIPPINES	M
CONGO,		JORDAN	M	PORTUGAL	M
PEOPLE'S REP.	M	KAZAKHSTAN	M	QATAR	M*
COSTA RICA	M	KENYA	M	REP. OF	
COTE D'IVOIRE	M	KOREA, NORTH	M	CAPE VERDE	M
CUBA	M	KOREA, SOUTH	M*	ROMANIA	M
CYPRUS	M*,I*	KUWAIT	M	RUSSIA	M
CZECHOSLO-		KYRGYZSTAN	M	RWANDA	M
				SAN MARINO	M

SAO TOME &		-----------------	
PRINCIPE	M		
SAUDI ARABIA	M	I =	Imperial system of
SENEGAL	M		Weights and
SEYCHELLES	I*		Measures is in use.
SIERRA LEONE	M		
SINGAPORE	M*	I* =	Imperial system of
SOMALIA	M,I		Weights and
SOUTH AFRICA	M		Measures is in use.
SPAIN	M		however
SRI LANKA	M*		metrication
ST. VINCENT	I		program is being
ST. KITTS			introduced.
	I	I** =	Imperial and /or
ST. LUCIA	I		local systems of
ST.PIERRE &			Weights and
MIQUELON	M		Measures are
SUDAN	I*		being used.
SURINAME	M	M =	Metric system of
SWEDEN	M		Weights and
SWITZERLAND	M		Measures is in use.
SYRIA	M	M* =	Traditional
TAJIKISTAN	M		systems of Weights
TANZANIA	M		and Measures is
THAILAND	M*		still in use.
THE GAMBIA	I*	M,I =	Metric and
TOGO	M		Imperial systems
TONGA	M		of Weights and
TRINIDAD &			Measures are in
TOBAGO	I*		use.
TUNISIA	M		
TURKEY	M		
TURKMENISTAN	M		
TURKS & CAICOS	I		
UGANDA	M		
UKRAINE	M		
UN. ARAB			
EMIRATES	I,M		
U.K	I*		
URUGUAY	M		
UZBEKISTAN	M		
VENEZUELA	M		
VIETNAM			
	M		
YEMEN, P.D.M.	I*		
YUGOSLAVIA	M		
ZAIRE	M		
ZAMBIA	M		
ZIMBABWE	M		

327

APPENDIX G

INTERNATIONAL GUIDE TO TIPPING*

	HOTELS	TAXIS	OTHERS
ANDORRA	10-20%	10%	YES
ANGUILLA	D	D	YES
ANTIGUA & BARBUDA	10%	D	YES
ARGENTINA	10-22%	10%	YES
ARMENIA	YES	OD	OD
AUSTRALIA	10%	D	YES
AUSTRIA	10-15%	10%	YES
AZERBAIJAN	YES	OD	OD
BAHAMAS	15%	15%	YES
BANGLADESH	5-10%	5-10%	YES
BARBADOS	10%	10%	YES
BELARUS	YES	OD	OD
BELGIUM	15%	D	YES
BELIZE	D 10%	D	YES
BENIN	D	D	D
BOLIVIA	10-23%	D	YES
BRAZIL	D	YES	
BURMA	10%	10%	YES
CAMEROON	10%	D	YES
CANADA	15-20%	15-20%	YES
CAYMAN IS	NC 10-15%	NC	YES
CHILE	10%	NC	YES
CHINA, PEOPLES REP.	F	F	F
CHINA, TAIWAN	D 10%	D 10%	YES
COLUMBIA	10%	NC	YES
COSTA RICA	10%	NC	YES
COTE D'IVOIRE	5-10%	5-10%	YES
CYPRUS	10%	NT	YES
CZECHOSLOVAKIA	OD 5-10%	5-10%	YES
DENMARK	15%	upto 15%	YES
DOMINICA	10%	D	YES
DOMINICAN REP.	10%		
ECUADOR	10%	NC	YES
EGYPT	10-12%	10%	YES
ETHIOPIA	5-10%	NC	YES
FIJI	D	D	YES
FINLAND	14-15%	NT	YES
FRANCE	upto 25%	15%	YES
FRENCH GUIANA	12 1/2%	NC	YES
GERMANY	10%	5%	YES
GHANA	YES	YES	YES
GIBRALTAR	10-12%	10%	YES
GREECE	10-15%	10%	YES

GRENADA	D	D	YES
GUADELOUPE	10-15%	YES	
GUATEMALA	10%	10%	YES
GUINEA	D	D	YES
GUYANA	10%	10%	YES
HAITI	NC 10%	D	YES
HONDURAS	10%	10%	YES
HONG KONG	10-15%	10%	YES
HUNGARY	OD 10-15%	YES	YES
ICELAND	NC	NC	NC
INDIA	10%	NC	YES
INDONESIA	NC 10%	NC 10%	YES
IRELAND	10-15%	YES	YES
ISRAEL	10%	NC	YES
ITALY	12-15%	15%	YES
JAMAICA	15%	10-20%	YES
JAPAN	NC 10-20%	NC	YES
JORDAN	10%	10%	YES
KAZAKHSTAN	OD	OD	OD
KENYA	10-15%	10%	YES
KOREA, SOUTH	NC 10%	NC 10-15%	YES
KUWAIT	10%	D	YES
KYRGYZSTAN	OD	OD	OD
LATVIA	NT	10-20%	YES
LIBERIA	10-15%	NC	YES
LIECHTENSTEIN	10-15%		
LITHUANIA	NC	NC	NC
LUXEMBOURG	NC 10-20%	15-20%	YES
MALAYSIA	NC 10%	NC 10%	YES
MALTA	10%	10%	YES
MARTINIQUE	10-15%	D	YES
MEXICO	7-15%	D	YES
MOLDOVA	OD	OD	OD
MONTSERRAT	10%	10%	YES
MOROCCO	10-15%	10-15%	YES
NEPAL			YES
NETHERLANDS	15%	10-15%	YES
NEW CALEDONIA		F	F
NEW ZEALAND	NC 10%	NC	
NICARAGUA	10%	NC	YES
NIGERIA	10%	D	YES
NORWAY	15%	D	YES
PAKISTAN	5-10%	D	YES
PANAMA	10-15%	NC	YES
PAPUA NEW GUINEA	NC	NC	NC
PARAGUAY	10%	5-12%	YES
PERU	5-10%	NC	YES
PHILIPPINES	10%	D 10%	YES
POLAND	10%	10%	YES
PORTUGAL	10-15%	15%	YES
ROMANIA	NC	NC	
RUSSIA	10-15%	10-15%	YES
SAUDI ARABIA	10-15%	NC	YES
SENEGAL	10%	D	YES
SEYCHELLES	10%	D	YES
SINGAPORE	OD	10%	OD

329

SOUTH AFRICA	10%	10%	YES
SPAIN	5-10%	10-15%	YES
SRI LANKA	10%	D	YES
ST. KITTS	D	D	YES
ST. LUCIA	10%	10%	YES
ST. VINCENT	10-15%	10-15%	YES
ST. MAARTEN	10%	10%	YES
SURINAME	10%	NC	YES
SWEDEN	12-15%	10-15%	YES
SWITZERLAND	12-15%	12-15%	YES
TAJIKISTAN	OD	OD	OD
TANZANIA	5%	(OD) D	YES
THAILAND	D 10%	NC	YES
TOGO	OD	OD	
TRINIDAD & TOBAGO	10%	10-15%	YES
TUNISIA	10%	10%	YES
TURKEY	10-15%	D	YES
TURKMENISTAN	OD	OD	OD
UKRAINE	OD	OD	OD
UNITED KINGDOM	12-15%	10-15%	YES
URUGUAY	10%	10%	YES
UZBEKISTAN	OD	OD	OD
VENEZUELA	10%	NC	YES
YUGOSLAVIA	10%	10%	YES
ZAIRE	10%	D	YES
ZAMBIA	10%	OD	YES

xxx		YES, persons who perform other services such as porters, luggage handlers, door persons, etc. may be tipped or may expect to be tipped. Tipping and amount of tip is at your discretion.
D	=	Tipping is expected. Amount of tip is at your discretion.
OF	=	Tipping is Officially Discouraged although privately welcome.
NC	=	Tipping is not customary, nevertheless welcome.
NT	=	Not usually tipped
F	=	Tipping is prohibited

APPENDIX H

INTERNATIONAL TIME ZONES

(TIME DIFFERENCE, IN
HOURS, BETWEEN
U.S.EASTERN STANDARD
TIME AND FOREIGN
CAPITAL CITIES)

COUNTRIES	HOURS
AFGHANISTAN	9.5
ALBANIA	6
ALGERIA**	6
AMERICAN SAMOA	6
ANDORRA	6
ANGUILLA	1
ANTIGUA &	
BARBUDA	1
ARGENTINA	2
ARMENIA	8
AUSTRALIA*	15
AUSTRIA	6
AZERBAIJAN	8
BAHAMAS	0
BAHRAIN	8
BANGLADESH	11
BARBADOS	1
BELGIUM	6
BELIZE	-1
BENIN	6
BERMUDA	1
BHUTAN	11
BOLIVIA	1
BOTSWANA	7
BRAZIL*	2
BRITISH VIRGIN IS	1
BRUNEI	13
BULGARIA	7
BURKINA FASO	5
BURMA	11.5
BURUNDI	7
BYELARUS	8
CAMBODIA	12
CAMEROON	6
CANADA*	0
CAYMAN IS	0
CENT. AFRICAN REP.	6
CHAD	6
CHILE**	1

CHINA, PEOPLES REPUBLIC.	13
CHINA, TAIWAN	3
COLUMBIA	0
COMOROS	8
CONGO, PEOPLE'S REP	6
COSTA RICA	-1
COTE D'IVOIRE	5
CUBA**	0
CYPRUS	7
CZECH REP.	6
DENMARK	6
DOMINICA	1
DOMINICAN REP.	0
ECUADOR	0
EGYPT	7
EL SALVADOR	-1
ESTONIA	8
EQUAT. GUINEA	6
ETHIOPIA	8
FAEROW IS	5
FIJI	17
FINLAND	7
FRANCE	6
FR. POLYNESIA	-5
FR. ANTILLES	1
FRENCH GUIANA	2
GABON	6
GEORGIA	6
GHANA	5
GIBRALTAR	6
GREECE	7
GREENLAND	2
GRENADA	1
GUADELOUPE	1
GUAM	15
GUANTANAMO BAY	0
GUATEMALA	-1
GUINEA	5
GUINEA-BISSAU	5
GUYANA	2
HAITI	0
HONDURAS	-1
HONG KONG	13
HUNGARY	6
ICELAND	5

INDIA	10.5
INDONESIA*	12
IRAN	8.5
IRAQ	8
IRELAND	5
ISRAEL	7
ITALY	6
JAMAICA**	0
JAPAN	14
JORDAN	7
KAZAKHSTAN	11
KENYA	8
KIRIBATI	-5
KOREA, SOUTH	14
KOREA, NORTH	14
KUWAIT	8
KYRGYZSTAN	11
LAOS	12
LATVIA	8
LEBANON	7
LESOTHO	7
LIBERIA	5
LIBYA	6
LIECHTENSTEIN	6
LITUANIA	8
LUXEMBOURG	6
MADAGASCAR	8
MALAWI	7
MALAYSIA*	13
MALDIVES	10
MALI	5
MALTA	6
MARSHALL IS	17
MAURITANIA	5
MAURITIUS	9
MAYOTTE IS	8
MEXICO*	1
MICRONESIA*	16
MOLDOVA	8
MONACO	6
MONGOLIA	13
MONTSERRAT	1
MOROCCO	5
MOZAMBIQUE	7
MUSTIQUE	1
NAMIBIA	7
NAURU	17

NEPAL	10.5		TOGO	5
NETHERLANDS	6		TONGA	18
NETHERLANDS			TRANSKEI	7
ANTILLES	1		TRINIDAD &	
NEW CALEDONIA	16		TOBAGO	1
NEW ZEALAND**	17		TUNISIA	6
NICARAGUA	-1		TURKEY	7
NIGER	6		TURKMENISTAN	10
NIGERIA	6		TURKS &	
NORWAY	6		CAICOS	**0
OMAN	9		U.S.A.	0
PAKISTAN	10		UGANDA	8
PANAMA	0		UKRAINE	8
PAPUA N. GUINEA	15		UNION IS	1
PARAGUAY	2		U.K**	5
PERU	0		UNITED ARAB	
PHILIPPINES	13		EMIRATES	9
POLAND	6		URUGUAY	2
PORTUGAL	5		UZBEKISTAN	11
PUERTO RICO	1		VATICAN CITY	6
QATAR	8		VENEZUELA	1
REP. OF DJIBOUTI	8		WESTERN SAMOA	-6
REP. OF CAPE VERDE	4		YEMEN, .P.D.R.	8
REUNION IS	9		YEMEN,	
ROMANIA	7		ARAB REP.	8
RUSSIA	8		YUGOSLAVIA	6
RWANDA	7		ZAIRE*	6
SAIPAN	15		ZAMBIA	7
SAN MARINO	6		ZIMBABWE	7
SAO TOME &				
PRINCIPE	5			
SAUDI ARABIA	8		*	Countries with
SENEGAL	5			multiple Time
SEYCHELLES	9			Zones. Hours
SIERRA LEONE	5			indicated may be
SINGAPORE	13			different
SOLOMON IS	16			depending on your
SOMALIA	8			location in these
SOUTH AFRICA	7			countries.
SPAIN	6			
SRI LANKA	10.5			
ST. MARTIN	1		**	Countries with
ST. LUCIA	1			varying time,
ST. KITTS-NEVIS	1			depending on the
ST. PIERRE & MIQUELON	2			month.
ST. VINCENT	1			
SUDAN	7			
SURINAME	2			
SWAZILAND	7			
SWEDEN	6			
SWITZERLAND	6			
SYRIA	7			
TAJIKISTAN	11			
TANZANIA	8			
THAILAND	12			
THE GAMBIA	5			

APPENDIX I

INTERNATIONAL ELECTRICITY REQUIREMENTS

COUNTRIES	Volts/AC	COUNTRIES	Volts/AC
AFGHANISTAN	20/50 AC	DENMARK	220/50
ALGERIA	110-115/50, 220/50 AC*	DOMINICA	220-240/50 AC
ANDORRA	125/50 AC	DOMINICAN REP.	110/60 AC
ANGUILLA	220	ECUADOR	110/60 AC
ANTIGUA	110/60 AC	EGYPT	220/50, 110-120/50*
ARGENTINA	220/60 AC	EL SALVADOR	110/60
ARMENIA	220/50	ESTONIA	220/50
AUSTRALIA	240 AC	EQUAT. GUINEA	220/50
AUSTRIA	220/50	ETHIOPIA	220/60 AC
AZERBAIJAN	220/50	FIJI	240/50 AC
BAHAMAS	120/60 AC	FINLAND	220/60 AC
BAHRAIN	220/50 AC	FRANCE	220/50
BANGLADESH	220 AC	FRENCH GUIANA	220 & 110/50 AC
BARBADOS	110/50 AC	GABON	220/240/50
BELGIUM	220/50 AC	GEORGIA	220/50
BELIZE	110/220/60 AC	GERMANY	220/50 AC
BENIN	220/50	GHANA	220-240/50 AC
BERMUDA	110/60 AC	GIBRALTAR	240-250/50 AC
BHUTAN	110-220/50 AC*	GREECE+	220/50 AC
BOTSWANA	220	GRENADA	220-240/50 Ac
BRAZIL+ 110/60; 220/60, 127/60 AC*		GUADELOUPE	220/50 AC
BRITISH V.I	115-210/60 AC	GUAM	120/60 AC
BULGARIA	220/50 AC	GUATEMALA	110/60 AC
BURKINA FASO	220/50	GUINEA	220/50
BURMA	220/50 AC	GUYANA	110-120/60 AC
BURUNDI	220/50	HAITI	110/60 AC
BYELARUS	220/50	HONDURAS	110 or 220/60 AC*
CAMEROON	110-220	HONG KONG + +	200-220/60 AC
CANADA	110/60 AC	HUNGARY	220/50 AC
CAYMAN ISLANDS	110/60 AC	ICELAND	220/50 AC
CENTRAL AF. REP.	220	INDIA+	220/50 AC
CHAD	220	INDONESIA	220/50 AC
CHILE+	220/50 AC	IRAN	220/50
CHINA	110/50	IRAQ	220 DC
CHINA, TAIWAN	110/60 AC	IRELAND	220/50 AC
COLOMBIA	150/60 AC, 110/60**	ISRAEL	220/50 AC
COMOROS	220/50	ITALY	220/50, 110-127/50 AC*
CONGO, REP.	220/50	JAMAICA	110/50 AC
COSTA RICA	110/60 AC	JAPAN	110/50, 100/60 AC*
COTE D'IVOIRE	220/50 AC	JORDAN	220/50 AC
CUBA	110/60	KAZAKHSTAN	220/50
CYPRUS + +	240/50 AC	KENYA	220/50 AC
ZECH REP.	220/50 AC	KOREA, SOUTH	110/60 AC

KUWAIT	240/50 AC	SOMALIA	220/50
KYRGYZSTAN	220/50	SOUTH AFRICA	220-230/50 AC
LATVIA	220/50	SPAIN	110-220/50 AC
LEBANON	110-220/50	SRI LANKA	230-240/50 AC
LESOTHO	220 AC	ST. KITTS	230/60 AC
LIBERIA	120/60 AC	ST. LUCIA	220/50 AC
LIBYA	220/50	ST. MARTIN	220/60 AC
LIECHTENSTEIN	220/50 AC	ST. VINCENT	220-230/50 AC
LITHUANIA	220/50	SUDAN	240 AC
LUXEMBOURG	220/110	SURINAME	110-115/60 AC
MADAGASCAR	220/50	SWAZILAND	240/50
MALAWI	220	SWEDEN+	220/50 AC
MALAYSIA	220/50 AC	SWITZERLAND	220/50 AC
MALI	220	TAJIKISTAN	220/50
MALTA	240/50 AC	TANZANIA	240/50/60 AC
MARTINIQUE	220/50AC	THAILAND	220/50 AC
MAURITANIA	220/50	TOGO	220/50 AC
MAURITIUS	220/230	TONGA	220 AC
MEXICO	110/60 AC	TRINIDAD & TOB.	110/60 AC
MICRONESIA	110/60 AC	TUNISIA	110-115/50, 220/50 AC*
MOLDOVA	220/50	TURKEY	220/50
MONTSERRAT	230/60 AC	TURKMENISTAN	220/50
MOROCCO	110-120/50 AC	TURKS & CAICOS	110/60
MOZAMBIQUE	220/50	U.S.A	110-115/60 AC
NAMIBIA	220/240/60	UKRAINE	220/50
NEPAL	220/50 AC	UNITED ARAB EM.	240/415 AC
NETHERLANDS		UNITED KINGDOM	220/50 AC
ANTILLES.	110-130/50,120/60 AC*	URUGUAY	220/50 AC
NETHERLANDS	220/50 AC	UZBEKISTAN	220/50
NEW CALEDONIA	220/50 AC	VENEZUELA	110/60 AC
NICARAGUA	110/60 AC	YEMEN, ARAB REP.	220/50 AC
NIGER	220-240/50	YEMEN, P.D.R	220/240/50
NIGERIA++	220/50 AC	YUGOSLAVIA	220/50 AC
NORWAY	220/50 AC	ZAIRE	220/50
OMAN	220/240/50	ZAMBIA	220/50 AC
PAKISTAN	220/240/50 AC	ZIMBABWE++	220/240/50
PANAMA	110/60 AC		
PAPUA NEW GUINEA	240 AC		
PARAGUAY+	220/50 AC	*	Electricity requirements vary in some parts of the country.
PERU	220/60 AC		
PHILIPPINES	220/60 AC		
POLAND	220/50 AC	+	Some parts of the country still use DC.
PORTUGAL	210-220/50 AC		
PUERTO RICO	110-115/60 AC	++	In some or most parts of the country, you may need three square pin plugs.
QATAR	220/50		
REP. OF DJIBOUTI	220/50		
CAPE VERDE	220/50		
ROMANIA	220/50		
RUSSIA	220/50		
RWANDA	220/50		
SAUDI ARABIA	110 & 120/60 AC		
SENEGAL	110 & 220/50 AC		
SEYCHELLES	240/50 AC		
SIERRA LEONE	220/50		
SINGAPORE++	230-250 AC		
SAO TOME & PRIN.	220/50		

APPENDIX J

INTERNATIONAL TELEPHONE DIALING CODES

COUNTRY/COUNTRY CODE   City & Codes

Albania   355
Durres 52 plus 4 digits, Elbassan 545 plus 4 digits,
Korce 824 plus 4 digits, Shkoder 224 plus 4 digits,
Tirana 42 plus 5 digits

Algeria   213

City code not required.

American Samoa   684

City code not required.

Andorra   376

Use 628 for all cities.

Anguilla   809

Dial 1 + 809 + Local Number.

Antigua   809
Dial 1 + 809 + Local Number.

Argentina   54

Bahia Blanca 91, Buenos Aires 1, Cordoba 51,
Corrientes 783, La Plata 21, Mar Del Plata 23,
Mendoza 61, Merlo 220, Posadas 752, Resistencia
772, Rio Cuarto 586, Rosario 41, San Juan 64, San
Rafael 627, Santa Fe 42, Tandil 293

Armenia   374
City codes not required

Aruba   297
Use 8 for all cities.

Ascension Island   247
City code not required.

Australia   61
Adelaide 8, Ballarat 53, Brisbane 7, Canberra 62,
Darwin 89, Geelong 52, Gold Coast 75, Hobart 02,
Launceston 03, Melbourne 3, Newcastle 49, Perth 9,
Sydne 2, Toowoomba 76, Townsville 77, Wollongong
42

Austria   43

Bludenz 5552, Graz 316, Innsbruck 5222, Kitzbuhel
5356, Klagenfut 4222, Krems An Der Donau 2732,
Linz Donau 732, Neunkirchen Niederosterreich 2635,
Salzburg 662, St. Polten 2742, Vienna 1, Villach
4242, Wels 7242, Wiener Neustadt 2622

Bahamas   809

Dial 1 + 809 + Local Number.

Bahrain   973
City code not required.

Bangladesh   880
Barisal 431, Bogra 51, Chittagong 31, Comilla 81,
Dhaka 2, Khulna 41, Maulabi Bazar 861,
Mymensingh 91, Rajshaki 721, Sylhet 821

Barbados   809

Dial 1 + 809 + Local Number.

Blarus   375
Loev 2347, Minsk 172, Mogilev 222

Belgium   32
Antwerp 3, Bruges 50, Brussels 2, Charleroi 71,
Courtrai 56, Ghent 91, Hasselt 11, La Louviere 64,
Leuven 16, Libramont 61, Liege 41, Malines 15,
Mons 65, Namur 81, Ostend 59, Verviers 87

Belize   501
Belize City (City code not required), Belmopan 08,
Benque Viejo Del Carmen 093, Corozal Town 04,
Dangviga 05, Independence 06, Orange Walk 03,
Punta Gorda 07, San Ignacio 092

Benin   229
City code not required.

Bermuda   809
Dial 1 + 809 + Local Number.

335

Bolivia 591
Cochabamba 42, Cotoga 388, Guayafamerin 47, La Belgica 923, La Paz 2, Mineros 984, Montero 92, Oruro 52, Portachuelo 924, Saavedra 924, Santa Cruz 33, Trinidad 46, Warnes 923

Bosnia-Herzegovina 387
Mostar 88, Sarajevo 71, Zenica 72

Botswana 267
Francistown 21, Gaborone 31, Jwaneng 38, Kanye 34, Lobatse 33, Mahalapye 41, Maun 26, Mochudi 37, Molepoloe 32, Orapa 27, Palapye 42, Ramotswana 39, Selibe (Phikwe) 8, Serowe 43

Brazil 55
Belem 91, Belo Horizonte 31, Brasilia 61, Curitiba 41, Fortaleza 85, Goiania 62, Niteroi 21, Pelotas 532, Porto Alegre 512, Recife 81, Rio de Janeiro 21, Salvador 71, Santo Andre 11, Santos 132, Sao Paulo 11, Vitoria 27

British Virgin Islands 809
Dial 1 + 809 + Local Number in the following cities: Anegada, Camanoe Island, Guana Island, Josh Vah Dyke, Little Thatch, Marina Cay, Mosquito Island, North Sound, Peter Island, Salt Island, Tortola, Virgin Gorda.

Brunei 673
Bandar Seri Begawan 2, Kuala Belait 3, Mumong 3, Tutong 4

Bulgaria 359
Kardjali 361, Pazardjik 34, Plovdiv 32, Sofia 2, Varna 52

Burkina Faso 226
Bobo Dioulasso 9, Fada N'Gorma 7, Koudougou 4, Ouagadougou 3

Burma 95
Akyab 43, Bassein 42, Magwe 63, Mandalay 2, Meikila 64, Moulmein 32, Pegu 52, Prom 53, Rangoon 1

Cameroon 237
City code not required.

Canada NPA's

Dial 1 + Area Code + Local Number.
Cape Verde Islands 238

City code not required.

Caymen Islands 809
Dial 1 + 809 + Local Number.

Chile 56
Chiquayante 41, Concepcion 41, Penco 41, Recreo 31, San Bernardo 2, Santiago 2, Talcahuano 41, Valparaiso 32, Vina del Mar 32

China 86
Beijing (Peking) 1, Fuzhou 591, Ghuangzhou (Canton) 20, Shanghai 21

Colombia 57
Armenia 60, Barranquilla 5, Bogota 1, Bucaramanga 73, Cali 3, Cartagena 59, Cartago 66, Cucuta 70, Giradot 832, Ibague 82, Manizales 69, Merdellin 42, Neiva 80, Palmira 31, Pereira 61, Santa Marta 56

Costa Rica 506
City code not required.

Croatia 387
Dubrovnik 20, Rijeka 51, Split 21, Zagreb 41.

Cyprus 357
Kythrea 2313, Lapithos 8218, Lamaca 41, Lefkonico 3313, Limassol 51, Moni 5615, Morphou 71, Nicosia 2, Paphos 61, Platres 54, Polis 63, Rizokarpaso 3613, Yialousa 3513. The following cities are handled by the Turkish Telephone Network. Use country code 90 for Turkey: Famagusta 536, Kyrenia 581, and Lefka 57817.

Czech Rep. 42
Brno 5, Havirov 6994, Ostrava 69, Prague (Praha) 2,

Denmark 45
City code not required.

Djibouti 253
City code not required.

Dominica 809
Dial 1 + 809 + Local Number.

Dominican Republic 809
Dial 1 + 809 + Local Number.

Ecuador 593
Ambato 2, Cayambe 2, Cuenca 7, Esmeraldas 2, Guayaquil 4, Ibarra 2; Loja 4, Machachi 2, Machala 4, Manta 4, Portoviejo 4, Quevedo 4, Quito 2, Salinas 4, Santa Domingo 2, Tulcan 2

Egypt 20

336

Alexandria 3, Answan 97, Asyut 88, Benha 13, Cairo 2, Damanhour 45, El Mahallah (El Kubra) 43, El Mansoura 50, Luxor 95, Port Said 66, Shebin El Kom 48, Sohag 93, Tanta 40

El Salvador   503
City code not required.

Estonia   372
Tallinn 2, Tartu 7.

Ethiopia   251
Addis Ababa 1, Akaki 1, Asmara 4, Assab 3, Awassa 6, Debre Zeit 1, Dessie 3, Dire Dawa 5, Harrar 5, Jimma 7, Makale 4, Massawa 4, Nazareth 2, Shashemene 6

Faeroe Islands   298
City code not required.

Fiji Islands   679
City code not required.

Finland   358
Epoo-Ebbo 15, Helsinki 0, Joensuu 73, Jyvaskyla 41, Kuopio 71, Lahti 18, Lappeenranta 53, Oulu 81, Port 39, Tammefors-Tampere 31, Turku 21, Uleaborg 81, Vaasa 61, Vanda-Vantaa 0

France   33
Aix-en-Provence 42, Bordeaux 56, Cannes 93, Chauvigny 49, Cherbourge 33, Grenoble 76, Le Havre 35, Lourdes 62, Lyon 7, Marseille 91, Nancy 8, Nice 93, Paris 1, Rouen 35, Toulouse 61, Tours 47

French Antilles   596
City code not required.

French Guiana   594
City code not required.

French Polynesia   689
City code not required.

Gabon Republic   241
City code not required.

Gambia   220
City code not required.

Georgia   7
Sukhumi 881, Tblisi 88

Germany, Fed. Rep.   49
Bad Homburg 6172, Berlin 30, Bonn 228, Bremen 421, Cologne (Koln) 221, Cottbus 355, Dresden 351,

Dusseldorf 211, Erfurt 361, Essen 201, Frankfurt am Main (west) 69, Frankfurt an der Oder (east) 335, Gera 365, Halle 345, Hamburg 40, Heidellberg 6221, Karl-Stadt 9353, Koblenz 261, Leipzig 341, Magdeburg 391, Mannheim 621, Munich 89, Numberg 911, Postdam 331, Rostock 381, Saal 38223, Schwerin 385, Stuttgart 711, Wiesbaden 6121

Ghana   233
City code not required.

Gibraltar   350
City code not required.

Greece   30
Argos 751, Athens (Athinai) 1, Corinth 741, Iraklion (Kristis) 81, Kavala 51, Larissa 41, Patrai 61, Piraeus Pireefs 1, Rodos 241, Salonica (Thessaloniki) 31, Sparti 731, Thessaloniki 31, Tripolis 71, Volos 421, Zagora 426

Greenland 299
Goatham 2, Sondre Stromfjord 11, Thule 50

Grenada   809
Dial 1 + 809 + Local Number.

Guadeloupe   590
City code not required.
Guam   671
City code not required.

Guantanemo Bay   5399
City code not required.

Guatemala 502
Guatemala City 2. All other cities 9.

Guinea   224
City code not required.

Guyana   592
Anna Regina 71, Bartica 5, Beteryerwaging 20, Cove & John 29, Georgetown 2, Ituni 41, Linden 4, Mabaruma 77, Mahaica 28, Mahalcony 21, New Amsterdam 3, New Hope 66, Rosignol 30, Timehri 61, Vreed-En-Hoop 64, Whim 37

Haiti   509
Cap-Haitien 3, Cayes 5, Gonalve 2, Port au Prince 1

Honduras   504
City code not required.

Hong Kong   852
Castle Peak 0, Cheung Chau 5, Fan Ling 0, Hong

Kong 5, Kowloon 3, Kwai Chung 0, Lamma 5, Lantau 5, Ma Wan 5, Peng Chau 5, Sek Kong 0, Sha Tin 0, Tai Po 0, Ting Kau 0, Tsun Wan 0

Hungary   36
Abasar 37, Balatonaliga 84, Budapest 1, Dorgicse 80, Fertoboz 99, Gyongyos 37, Kaposvar 82, Kazincbarcika 48, Komlo 72, Miskolc 46, Nagykaniza 93, Szekesfehervar 22, Szolnok 56, Varpalota 80, Veszprem 80, Zalaegerzeg 92

Iceland   354

Akureyi 6, Hafnafijorour 1, Husavik 6, Keflavik Naval Base 2, Rein 6, Reykjavik 1, Reyorarjorour 7, Sandgerol 2, Selfoss 9. Siglufijorour 6, Stokkseyri 9, Suoavik 4, Talknafijorour 4, Varma 1, Vik 9

India   91

Ahmedabad 272, Amritsar 183, Bangalore 812, Baroda 265, Bhopal 755, Bombay 22 Calcutta 33, Chandigarh 172, Hyderabad 842, Jaipur 141, Jullundur 181, Kanpur 512, Madras 44, New Dehli 11, Poona 212, Surat 261

Indonesia   62
Bandung 22, Cirebon 231, Denpasar (Bali) 361, Jakarta 21, Madiun 351, Malang 341, Medan 61, Padang 751, Palembang 711, Sekurang 778, Semarang 24, Solo 271, Surabaya 31, Tanjungkarang 721, Yogykarta 274

Iran   98

Abadan 631, Ahwaz 61, Arak 2621, Esfahan 31, Ghazvin 281, Ghome 251, Hamadan 261, Karadj 2221, Kerman 341, Mashad 51, Rasht 231, Rezaiyeh 441, Shiraz 71, Tabriz 41, Tehran 21
Iraq   964
Baghdad 1, Basiah 40, Diwanyia 36, Karbala 32, Kirkuk 50, Mosul 60, Nasryia 42

Ireland   353
Arklow 402, Cork 21, Dingle 66, Donegal 73, Drogheda 41, Dublin 1, Dundalk 42, Ennis 65, Galway 91, Kildare 45, Killamey 64, Sligo 71, Tipperary 62, Tralee 66, Tullamore 506, Waterford 51, Wexford 53

Israel   972
Afula 65, Ako 4, Ashkelon 51, Bat Iam 3, Beer Sheva 57, Dimona 57, Hadera 63, Haifa 4, Holon 3, Jerusalem 2, Nazareth 65, Netania 53, Rehovot 8, Tel Aviv 3, Tiberias 67, Tsefat 67

Italy   39
Bari 80, Bologna 51, Brindisi 831, Capri 81, Como 31, Florence 55, Genoa 10, Milan 2, Naples 81, Padova 49, Palermo 91, Pisa 50, Rome 6, Torino 11, Trieste 40, Venice 41, Verona 45

Ivory Coast   225
City code not required.

Jamaica   809
Dial 1 + 809 + Local Number.

Japan   81
Chiba 472, Fuchu (Tokyo) 423, Hiroshima 82, Kawasaki (Kanagawa) 44, Kobe 78, Kyoto 75, Nagasaki 958, Nagoya 52, Nahat (Okinawa) 988, Osaka 6, Sapporo 11, Sasebo 956, Tachikawa (Tokyo) 425, Tokyo 3, Yokohama 45, Yokosuka (Kanagawa) 468

Jordan   962
Amman 6, Aqaba 3, Irbid 2, Jerash 4, Karak 3, Maam 3, Mafruq 4, Ramtha 2, Sueeleh 6, Sult 5, Zerqa 9

Kazakhstan   7
Alma-Ata 3272, Chimkent 325, Guryev 312, Petropavlovsk 315.

Kenya   254
Anmer 154, Bamburi 11, Embakasi 2, Girgiri 2, Kabete 2, Karen 2882, Kiambu 154, Kikuyu 283, Kisumu 35, Langata 2, Mombasa 11, Nairobi 2, Nakuru 37, Shanzu 11, Thika 151, Uthiru 2

Kiribati   686
City code not required.

Korea   82
Chung Ju 431, Chuncheon 361, Icheon 336, Incheon 32, Kwangju (Gwangju) 62, Masan 551, Osan 339, Osan Military (333+414), Pohang 562, Pusan (Busan) 51, Seoul 2, Suwon (Suweon) 331, Taegu (Daegu) 53, Ulsan 552, Wonju (Weonju) 371

Kuwait   965
City code not required.

Kyrgyzstan   7
Osh 33222 plus 5 digits, Pishpek 3312

Latvia   371
Riga 0132

Lebanon   961
Beirut 1, Juniyah 9, Tripoli 6, Zahlah 8

Lesotho 266
City code not required.

Liberia 231

City code not required.

Libya 218

Agelat 282, Benghazi 61, Benina 63, Derma 81, Misuratha 51, Sabratha 24, Sebha 71, Taigura 26, Tripoli 21, Tripoli International Airport 22, Zawai 23, Zuara 25

Liechtenstein 41
Use 75 for all cities.

Lithuania 370
Kaunas 7, Klaipeda 6, Panevezys 54, Siauliai 1, Vilnius 2.

Luxembourg 352
City code not required.

Macao 853
City code not required.

Macedonia 389
Asamati 96, Bitola 97, Gostivar 94, Kicevo 95, Krusevo 98, Lozovo 92, Skopje 91.

Malawi 265
Domasi 531, Likuni 766, Luchenza 477, Makwasa 474, Mulanje 465, Namadzi 534, Njuli 664, Thondwe 533, Thornwood 486, Thyolo 467, Zomba 50. City code not required for other cities.

Malaysia 60
Alor Star 4, Baranang 3, Broga 3, Cheras 3, Dengil 3, Ipoh 5, Johor Bahru 7, Kajang 3, Kepala Batas 4, Kuala Lampur 3, Machang 97, Maran 95, Port Dickson 6, Semenyih 3, Seremban 6, Sungei Besi 3, Sungei Renggam 3

Maldives 960
City code not required.

Mali 223
City code not required.

Malta 356
City code not required.

Marshall Islands 692
Ebeye 871, Majuro 9

Mauritius 230
City code not required.

Mayotte Islands 269
City code not required.

Mexico 52
Acapulco 748, Cancun 988, Celaya 461, Chihuahua 14, Ciudad Juarez 16, Conzumel 987, Culiacan 671, Ensenda 667, Guadalajara 36, Hermosillo 621, La Paz 682, Mazatlan 678, Merida 99, Mexicali 65, Mexico City 5, Monterrey 83, Puebla 22, Puerto Vallarta 322, Rasarito 661, San Luis Potosi 481, Tampico 121, Tecate 665, Tijuana 66, Torreon 17, Veracruz 29

Micronesia 691
Kosrae 851, Ponape 9, Truk 8319, Yap 841

Moldova 373
Benderi 32, Kishinev 2

Monaco 33
Use 93 for all cities.

Mongolian People's Rep. 976
Ulan Bator 1

Montserrat 809
Dial 1 + 809 + Local Number.

Morocco 212
Agadir 8, Beni-Mellal 48, Berrechid 33, Casablanca (City code not required). El Jadida 34, Fes 6, Kenitra 16, Marrakech 4, Meknes 5, Mohammedia 32, Nador 60, Oujda 68, Rabat 7, Tanger (Tangiers) 9, Tetouan 96

Mustique 809
Dial 1 + 809 + Local Number.

Namibia 264
Gobabis 681, Grootfontein 673, Industria 61, Keetmanshoop 631, Luderitz 6331, Mariental 661, Okahandja 622, Olympia 61, Otjiwarongo 651, Pioneerspark 61, Swakopmund 641, Tsumeb 671, Windhoek 61, Windhoek Airport 626

Nauru Island 674
City code not required.

Nepal 977
City code not required.

Netherlands 31
Amsterdam 20, Arnhem 85, Eindhoven 40,

339

Groningen 50, Haarlem 23, Heemstede 23, Hillegersberg 10, Hoensbraoek 45, Hoogkerk 50, Hoogvliet 10, Loosduinen 70, Nijmegen 80, Oud Zuilen 30, Rotterdam 10, The Hague 70, Utrecht 30

Netherlands Antilles 599
Bonaire 7, Curacao 9, Saba 4, Eustatius 3, St. Maarten 5

Nevis 809
Dial 1 + 809 + Local Number.

New Caledonia 687
City code not required.

New Zeland 64
Auckland 9, Christchurch 3, Dunedin 24, Hamilton 71, Hastings 70, Invercargill 21, Napier 70, Nelson 54, New Plymouth 67, Palmerston North 63, Rotorua 73, Tauranga 75, Timaru 56, Wanganui 64, Wellington 4, Whangarei 89

Nicaragua 505
Boaco 54, Chinandega 341, Diriamba 42, Esteli 71, Granada 55, Jinotepe 41, Leon 311, Managua 2, Masatepe 44, Masaya 52, Nandaime 45, Rivas 461, San Juan Del Sur 466, San Marcos 43, Tipitapa 53

Niger Republic 227
City code not required.

Nigeria 234
Lagos 1 (Only city direct dial)

Niue 683

Norfolk Island 672

Norway 47
Arendal 41, Bergen 5, Drammen 3, Fredrikstad 32, Haugesund 47, Kongsvinger 66, Kristiansund N. 73, Larvik 34, Moss 32, Narvik 82, Oslo 2, Sarpsborg 31, Skien 35, Stavanger 4, Svalbard 80, Tonsberg 33, Trondheim 7

Oman 968
City code not required.

Pakistan 92
Abbotabad 5921, Bahawalpur 621, Faisalabad 411, Gujtanwala 431, Hyderabad 221, Islamabad 51, Karachi 21, Lahore 42, Multan 61, Okara 442, Peshawar 521, Quetta 81, Sahiwal 441, Sargodha 451, Sialkot 432, Sukkur 71

Palm Island 809
Dial 1 + 809 + Local Number.

Panama 507
City code not required.

Papau New Guinea 675
City code not required.

Paragua 595
Asuncion 21, Ayolas 72, Capiata 28, Concepcion 31, Coronel Bogado 74, Coronel Oviedo 521, Encarnacion 71, Hermandarias 63, Ita 24, Pedro J. Caballero 36, Pilar 86, San Antonio 27, San Ignacio 82, Stroessner: Ciudad Pte. 61, Villarica 541, Villeta 25

Peru 51
Arequipa 54, Ayacucho 6491, Callao 14, Chiclayo 74, Chimbote 44, Cuzco 84, Huancavelica 6495, Huancayo 64, Ica 34, Iquitos 94, Lima 14, Piura 74, Tacna 54, Trujillo 44

Phillippines 63
Angeles 55, Bacolod 34, Baguio City 442, Cebu City 32, Clark Field (military) 52, Dagupan 48, Davao 35, Lloilo City 33, Lucena 42, Manila 2, San Fernando: La Union 46, San Fernando: Pampanga 45, San Pablo 43, Subic Bay Military Base 89, Subic Bay Residential Housing 89, Tarlac City 47

Poland 48
Bialystok 85, Bydgoszcz 52, Crakow (Krakow) 12, Gdansk 58, Gdynia 58, Katowice 32, Lodz 42, Lubin 81, Olsztyn 89, Poznan 48, Radom 48, Sopot 58, Torun 56, Warsaw 22

Portugal 351
Alamada 1, Angra Do Heroismo 95, Barreiro 1, Beja 84, Braga 53, Caldas Da Rainha 62, Coimbra 39, Estoril 1, Evora 66, Faro 89, Horta 92, Lajes AFB 95, Lisbon 1, Madalena 92, Madeira Islands 91, Montijo 1, Ponta Del Gada 96, Porto 2, Santa Cruz (Flores) 92, Santarem 43, Setubal 65, Velas 95, Vila Do Porto 96, Viseu 32

Qatar 974
City code not required.

Reunion Island 262
City code not required.

Romania 40
Arad 66, Bacau 31, Brasov 21, Bucharest 0, Cluj-Napoca 51, Constanta 16, Crajova 41, Galati 34, Lasi 81, Oradea 91, Pitesti 76, Ploiesti 71, Satu-Mare 97, Sibiu 24, Timisoara 61, Tirgu Mures 54

Russia   7
Magadan 413, Moscow 095, St. Petersburg 812

Rwanda   250
City code not required.

St. Kitts   809
Dial 1 + 809 + Local Number.

St. Lucia   809
Dial 1 + 809 + Local Number.

St. Pierre & Miquelon 508
City code not required.

St. Vincent   809
Dial 1 + 809 + Local Number.

Saipan   670
Capitol Hill 322, Rota Island 532, Susupe City 234, Tinian Island 433

San Marino   39
Use 541 for all cities.

Saudi Arabia   966
Abha 7, Abqaiq 3, Al Khobar 3, Al Markazi 2, Al Ulaya 1, Damman 3, Dhahran (Aramco) 3, Jeddah 2, Khamis Mushait 7, Makkah (Mecca) 2, Medina 4, Najran 7, Qatif 3, Riyadh 1, Taif 2, Yenbu 4

Senegal   221
City code not required.

Seychelles Islands   248
City code not required.

Sierra Leone   232
Freetown 22, Juba 24, Lungi 25, Wellington 23

Singapore   65
City code not required.

Solomon Island   677
City code not required.

Slovakia   42
Bratislava 7, Presov 91.

Slovenia   386
Ljubljana 61, Maribor 62

South Africa   27
Bloemfontein 51, Cape Town 21, De Aar 571, Durban 31, East London 431, Gordons Bay 24, Johannesburg 11, La Lucia 31, Pietermaritzburg 331,
Port Elizabeth 41, Pretoria 12, Sasolburg 16, Somerset West 24, Uitenhage 422, Welkom 171

Spain   34
Barcelona 3, Bibao 4, Cadiz 56, Ceuta 56, Granada 58, Igualada 3, Las Palmas de Gran Canaria 28, Leon 87, Madrid 1, Malaga 52, Melilla 52, Palma De Mallorca 71, Pamplona 48, Santa Cruz de Tenerife 22, Santander 42, Seville 54, Torremolinos 52, Valencia 6

Sri Lanka   94
Ambalangoda 97, Colombo Central 1, Galle 9, Havelock Town 1, Kandy 8, Katugastota 8, Kotte 1, Maradana 1, Matara 41, Negomgo 31, Panadura 46, Trincomalee 26

Suriname   597
City code not required.

Swaziland   268
City code not required.

Sweden   46
Alingsas 322, Boras 33, Eskilstuna 16, Gamleby 493, Goteborg 31, Helsinborg 42, Karlstad 54, Linkoping 13, Lund 46, Malmo 40, Norrkoping 11, Stockholm 8, Sundsvall 60, Trelleborg 410, Uppsala 18, Vasteras 21

Switzerland   41
Baden 56, Basel 61, Berne 31, Davos 83, Fribourg 37, Geneva 22, Interlaken 36, Lausanne 21, Lucerne 41, Lugano 91, Montreux 21, Neuchatel 38, St. Gallen 71, St. Moritz 82, Winterthur 52, Zurich 1

Taiwan   886
Changhua 47, Chunan 36, Chunghsing-Hsintsun 49, Chungli 34, Fengyuan 4, Hsiaying 6, Hualien 38, Kaohsiung 7, Keelung 2, Lotung 39, Pingtung 8, Taichung 4, Tainan 6, Taipei 2, Taitung 89, Taoyuan 33

Tajikistan   7
Dushanbe 3772

Tanzania   255
Dar Es Salaam 51, Dodoma 61, Mwanza 68, Tanga 53

Thailand   66
Bangkok 2, Burirum 44, Chanthaburi 39, Chien Mai 53, Cheingrai 54, Kamphaengphet 55, Lampang 54, Nakhon Sawan 56, Nong Khai 42, Pattani 73, Pattaya 38, Ratchaburi 32, Saraburi 36, Tak 55, Ubon Ratchathani 45

341

Togo   228
City code not required.

Tonga Islands   676
City code not required.

Trinidad & Tabago   809
Dial 1 + 809 + Local Number.

Tunisia   216
Agareb 4, Beja 8, Bizerte 2, Carthage 1, Chebba 4,
Gabes 5, Gafsa 6, Haffouz 7, Hamman-Souse 3,
Kairouan 7, Kef 8, Khenis 3, Medenine 5, Tabarka 8,
Tozeur 6, Tunis 1

Turkey   90
Adana 711, Ankara 41, Antalya 311, Bursa 241,
Eskisehir 221, Gazianter 851, Istanbul 1, Izmir 51,
Izmit 211, Kayseri 351, Konya 331, Malatya 821,
Mersin 741, Samsun 361

Turka & Caicos   809
Dial 1 + 809 + Local Number.

Turkmenistan   7
Ashkkhabad 3632, Chardzhou 378

Tuvalu   688

Ukraine   380
Kharkiv 572, Kiev 44, Lviv 322
Uganda   256
Entebbe 42, Jinja 43, Kampala 41, Kyambogo 41

Union Island   809
Dial 1 + 809 + Local Number.

United Arab Emirates971
Abu Dhabi 2, Ajman 6, Al Ain 3, Aweer 58, Dhayd
6, Dibba 70, Dubai 4, Falaj-al-Moalla 6, Fujairah 70,
Jebel Ali 84, Jebel Dhana 52, Khawanij 58,
Ras-al-Khaimah   77,   Sharjan   6,   Tarif   53,
Umm-al-Quwain 6

United Kingdom   44
Belfast 232, Birmingham 21, Bournemouth 202,
Cardiff 222, Durham 385, Edinburgh 31, Glasgow
41, Gloucester 452, Ipswich 473, Liverpool 51,
London (Inner) 71, London (Outer) 81, Manchester
61, Nottingham 602, Prestwick 292, Sheffield 742,
Southampton 703

Uruguay   598
Atlantida 372, Colonia 522, Florida 352, La Paz 322,
Las Piedras 322, Los Toscas 372, Maldonado 42,

Mercedes 532, Minas 442, Montevideo 2, Parque De
Plata 372, Paysandu 722, Punta Del Este 42, Salinas
372, San Jose 342,
San Jose De Carrasco 382

Uzbekistan7
Karish 375, Samarkand 3662, Tashkent 3712

Vanuatu, Rep. of   678

Vatican City   39
Use 6 for all cities.

Venezuela   58
Barcelona 81, Barquisimeto 51, Cabimas 64, Caracas
2, Ciudad Bolivar 85, Coro 68, Cumana 93, Los
Teques 32, Maiquetia 31, Maracaibo 61, Maracay 43,
Maturin 91, Merida 74, Puerto Cabello 42, San
Cristobal 76, Valencia 41

Vietnam   84
Hanoi 4, Ho Chi Minh City 8

Wallis & Futuna Islands 681

Western Samoa   685
City code not required.

Yeman (North)   967
Al Marawyah 3, Al Qaidah 4, Amran 2, Bayt Al
Faquih 3, Dhamar 2, Hodeidah 3, Ibb 4, Mabar 2,
Rada 2, Rawda 2, Sanaa 2, Taiz 4, Yarim 4, Zabid 3

Yugoslavia   38
Belgrade (Beograd) 11, Dubrovnik 50, Leskovac 16,
Ljubjana 61, Maribor 62, Mostar 88, Novi Sad 21,
Pirot 10, Rijeka 51, Sarajevo 71, Skopje 91, Split 58,
Titograd 81, Titovo-Uzice 31, Zagreb 41

Zaire   243
Kinshasa 12, Lubumbashi 222

Zambia   260
Chingola 2, Kitwe 2, Luanshya 2, Lusaka 1, Ndola 26

Zimbabwe 263
Bulawayo 9, Harare 0, Mutare 20

APPENDIX K

WORLD COMMERCIAL HOLIDAYS

Virtually every day this year will be a holiday somewhere in the world with business and government offices closed while employees watch parades, pray, or perhaps enjoy a quiet holiday at home with their family. Seasoned business travelers build their schedules around these holidays, because the alternative can be a frustrating day wasted in a hotel room while the local people, from the top executives on down observe their traditional holiday rituals.

The following pages list alphabetically by country, the hundreds of commercial holidays around the world each year that will close business and government offices for a day or more. Major regional holidays that are observed in many countries are included, plus any other pertinent information.

In cases where holidays fall on Saturday or Sunday commercial establishments may be closed the preceding Friday or following Monday. For many countries, such as those in the Moslem world, holiday dates can be only approximated because the holidays are based on actual lunar observation and exact dates are announced only shortly before they occur. Note that references to the Moslem holidays often vary in spelling and dates, and that businesses in many Moslem countries are closed on Fridays.

Although U.S. holidays are not listed in this schedule, they should also be considered when appointments are made with U.S. and Foreign Commercial Service officers abroad. This calendar is intended as a working guide only. For some countries that have not yet announced holidays for 2003, the schedule was projected based on 2002 holidays. Corroboration of dates is suggested in final travel planning.

Algeria
March 13 Aid El Fitr; May 1 Labor Day; May 21 Aid El Adha; June 11 Awal Mouharem; June 19 Revolutionary Recovery Day; June 20 Achoura; July 5 Independence Day; August 20 El Moulid Ennaboui; November 1 Revolution Day.

Argentina
January 1 New Year's; April 1 Good Friday; May 1 Labor Day; May 25 Revolution (1810) Day; June 10 Sovereignty Day; June 20 Flag Day; July 9 Independence (1816) Day; August 17 Death of General J. de San Martin; October 12 Discovery of America; December 25 Christmas.

Australia
January 1 New Year's; January 26 Australia Day; April 14 Good Friday; April 17 Easter Monday; April 25 ANZAC Day; June 13 Queen's Birthday; December 26 Christmas; December 27 Boxing Day. [The preceding list is based on Australia's 2002 holiday schedule.]

Austria
January 1 New Year's; January 6 Epiphany; April 17 Easter Monday; May 1 Labor Day; May 25 Ascension; June 5 Whit Monday; June 6 Corpus Christi; August 15 Assumption; October 26 National Day; November 1 All Saint's; December 8 Immaculate Conception; December 25 Christmas; December 26 St. Stephen's Day.

Bahrain
January 1 New Year's; March 2-4 Eid Al Fitr; May 9-11 Eid Al Adha; May 29 Islamic New Year; June 8-9 Ashoora; August 7 Prophet's Birthday; December 16 National Day.

Bangladesh
February 21 Martyrs' Day; March 11 Shab-i-Qadr; March 13-14 Eid-ul-Fitr; March 26 Independence Day; April 14 Bangla New Year's Day; May 1 May Day; May 21-24 Eid-ul-Azha; June 20 Muharram (Ashura); August 29 Janmaausthami; November 7 Solidarity Day. (The Bangladesh Government announces holidays for the next year in late December. Muslim religious holidays vary with appearance of the moon. Religious holidays may move one or two days in either direction.)

Barbados

343

January 1 New Year's; January 21 Errol Barrow's Birthday; April 14 Good Friday; April 17 Easter Monday; May 1 May Day; June 5 Whit Monday; First Monday in August Kadooment Day; First Monday in October United Nation's Day; Last weekday of November Independence Day; December 25 Christmas; December 26 Boxing Day.

Belgium

January 1 New Year's; April 17 Easter Monday; May 1 Belgian Labor Day; May 25 Ascension; June 5 Whit Monday; July 21 Belgian Independence Day; August 15 Assumption; November 1 All Saints' Day; November 10-11 Veterans' Day; December 25 Christmas.

Brazil

January 1 New Year's; February 14-15 Carnival; April 14 Good Friday; April 21 Tiradentes' Day; June 2 Corpus Christi; September 7 Independence Day; October 12 N. Sra. Aparecida; November 2 All Souls; November 15 Proclamation of the Republic; December 25 Christmas; (The preceding list is based on Brazil's 1994 holiday schedule.)

Bulgaria

January 1 New Year's; March 3 Liberation from the Ottoman Yoke Day; May 1 Labor Day; First Monday after the Orthodox Easter Easter Monday; May 24 Cyril and Methodius Day; December 25-26 Christmas.

Canada

January 1-2 New Year's; January 3 New Year's (Quebec only); February 20 Family Day (Alberta only); April 14 Good Friday; April 17 Easter Monday; May 22 Victoria Day; June 26 St. Jean Baptiste Day (Quebec only); July 3 Canada Day; August 7 Civic Holiday (most provinces); September 4 Labor Day; October 9 Thanksgiving; November 13 Remembrance Day; December 25 Christmas; December 26 Boxing Day.

Chile

January 1 New Year's; April 1 Good Friday; April 3 Easter Sunday; May 1 Labor Day; May 21 Commemoration of the Battle of Iquique; June 2 Corpus Christi; June 29 Saint Peter and Saint Paul; August 15 Assumption; September 11 Official Holiday; September 18 Independence Day; September 19 Day of the Army; October 12 Columbus Day; November 1 All Saints' Day; December 8 Immaculate Conception; December 25 Christmas.

China

February 10-12 Spring Festival; May 1 International

Labor Day; October 1-2 Chinese National Day.

Colombia

January 1 New Year's; January 6 Epiphany*; March 19 St. Joseph's Day*; April 13 Holy Thursday; April 14 Good Friday; May 1 Labor Day; May 29 Ascension; June 19 Feast of the Sacred Heart; June 26 Corpus Christi; June 29 Saints Peter and Paul* (When holidays marked with an asterisk do not fall on Monday, they are transferred to the following Monday.)

Costa Rica

March 31 Holy Thursday; April 1 Good Friday; April 11 Juan Santamaria; June 2 Corpus Christi; June 29 Saint Peter and Saint Paul; July 25 Annexation of Guanacaste; August 2 Our Lady of Los Angeles; August 15 Assumption; September 15 Independence Day; October 12 Columbus Day; December 8 Immaculate Conception; December 26 Christmas.

Cote d'Ivoire

January 1 New Year's; March End of Ramadan; April 17 Easter Monday; May 1 Labor Day; May 25 Ascension; May Tabaski; June 5 Pentecost Monday; August 15 Assumption; August Prophet Mohammed's Birthday; October Houphouet Boigny's Birthday; November 1 All Saint's; November 15 National Peace Day; December 7 Independence Day; December 25 Christmas.

Czech Republic

January 1 New Year's; May 8 Liberation Day; July 5 Cyril & Methodius Day; July 6 Jan Hus Day; October 28 National Day; December 25 Christmas; December 26 St. Stephen's Day.

Denmark

January 1 New Year's; April 13 Maundy Thursday; April 14 Good Friday; April 17 Easter Monday; May 12 Prayer Day; May 23 Ascension; June 5 Whit Monday and Constitution Day; December 25 Christmas; December 26 Second Christmas Day.

Dominican Republic

January 1 New Year's; January 6 Epiphany; January 21 Our Lady of Grace; January 26 Duarte's Birthday; February 27 Dominican Independence; April 1 Good Friday; May 1 Dominican Labor Day; May 16 Dominican Election Day; June 2 Corpus Christi; August 16 Dominican Restoration Day; September 25 Our Lady of the Mercedes; December 25 Christmas.

Ecuador

April 1 Good Friday; May 24 Battle of Pichincha;

July 25 Founding of Guayaquil (Guayaquil only); August 10 Independence Day; November 2 All Souls' Day; November 3 Independence of Cuenca; December 6 Founding of Quito (Quito only).

Egypt
January 1 New Year's; *March 13-15 Ramadan Bairam (End of Ramadan Fasting Month); April 25 Sinai Liberation Day; May 1 Labor Day; May 2 Sham El Nessim (Spring Day); *May 20-23 Kurban Bairam (Pilgrimage); *June 10 Islamic New Year; July 23 National Day; *August 19 Moulid El Nabi (Prophet's Birthday); [*Depends on Lunar Calendar; a difference of one day may occur.]

El Salvador
January 1 New Year's; January 16 Salvadoran Peace Day; April 14 Holy Thursday; April 15 Good Friday; May 1 Labor Day; June 30 Bank Holiday; August 3-6 San Salvador Feasts; September 15 Independence Day; October 12 Columbus Day; November 2 All Souls' Day; November 5 Day of First Cry of Independence; December 25 Christmas.

Finland
January 1 New Year's; January 6 Epiphany; April 14 Good Friday; April 16 Easter; April 17 Easter Monday; May 1 May Day; May 25 Ascension; June 25 Mid-Summer Day; December 6 Independence Day; December 25-26 Christmas.

France
January 1 New Year's; April 17 Easter Monday; May 1 Labor Day; May 8 Veterans' Day (WWII); May 25 Ascension; June 5 Whit Monday; July 14 French National Day; August 15 AssumptionGabon; January 1 New Year's; April 17 Easter Monday; May 1 Labor Day; June 5 Pentecost Monday; August 15-17 Independence Day; November 1 All Saint's; December 25 Christmas; [Two muslim holidays Id el Fitr and the Last Day of Ramadan are; celebrated in Gabon, but their dates are known only at the last moment.]

Georgia
January 1 New Year's; January 7 Christmas; January 19 Baptism Day; March 3 Mother's Day; April 9 Memorial Day; May 2 Recollection of the Deceased; May 26 Independence Day; August 28 August Day of the Virgin; October 14 Svetitskhovloba; November 23 St. George's Day.

Germany
January 1 New Year's; April 14 Good Friday; April 17 Easter Monday; May 25 Ascension; June 5 Whit Monday; October 3 Day of German Unity; November 16 Repentance Day; December 25-26 Christmas; [The preceding list is based on Germany's 1994 holiday schedule.]

Greece
January 1 New Year; January 6 Epiphany; 49 days prior to Greek Easter Sunday Kathara Deftera; March 25 Independence Day; Movable Holiday Good Friday; Movable Holiday Holy Saturday; Movable Holiday Easter Sunday; Movable Holiday Easter Monday; May 1 May Day; 50 days after Greek Easter Sunday Whit Monday; August 15 Assumption; October 20 OXI Day; December 24 Christmas Eve; (half-day holiday, only shops open all day); December 25 Christmas Day; December 26 Boxing Day; December 31 New Year's Eve; (half-day holiday, only shops open all day); [Regional holidays: Liberation of Ioannina, February 20 (observed; in Ioannina only); Dodecanese Accession Day, March 7 (observed in; Dodecanese Islands only); Liberation of Xanthi, October 4 (observed; in Xanthi only); St. Demetrios Day, October 26 (observed in; Thessaloniki only); St. Andreas Day, November 30 (observed in; Patras only).]

Guatemala
January 1 New Year's; April 12 p.m.-April 15 Holy Week; May 1 Labor Day; June 30 Army Day; August 15 Feast of the Assumption; September 15 Independence Day; October 20 Revolution Day; November 1 All Saints'; December 24 (p.m. only) Christmas Eve; December 25 Christmas; December 31 (p.m. only) New Year's Eve; [In addition, the banking sector celebrates the following holidays: July 1 Bank Workers's Day, and October 12, Columbus Day. Business; travelers should avoid arriving in Guatemala on a holiday, if possible,; because of the unpredictability of transportation and other services,; especially during the Holy Week, when almost everything is shut down.]

Guinea
January 1 New Year's; Variable Holiday end of Ramadan; (in 1994, it was celebrated March 19); April 3 Anniversary of the Second Republic; May 1 Labor Day; May 25 Anniversary of Organization of African Unity (OAU); Variable Holiday Tabaski; (in 1994, it was celebrated June 8); August 25 Assumption; Variable Holiday Prophet Mohammed's Birthday; (in 1993, it was observed September 23); October 2 Independence Day; December 25 Christmas.

Honduras
January 2 New Year's Day; April 13 Holy Thursday;

April 14 Good Friday and Americas' Day; May 1 Labor Day; September 15 Honduran Independence Day; October 3 Francisco Morazan's Birthday; October 12 Discovery of America Day; October 21 Armed Forces' Day; December 25 Christmas.

Hong Kong

January 2 First Weekday after New Year's Day; January 31 Lunar New Year's Day; February 1 Second Day of Lunar New Year; February 2 Third Day of Lunar New Year; April 5 Ching Ming Festival; April 14 Good Friday; April 15 The day following Good Friday; April 17 Easter Monday; June 2 Dragon Boat Festival; August 26 The Saturday preceding the last Monday in August; August 28 Liberation Day; November 1 Chung Yeung Festival; December 25 Christmas; December 26 First Weekday after Christmas Day.

Hungary

January 1-2 New Year's; March 15 Revolution Day; April 17 Easter Monday; May 1 Labor Day; June 5 Whit Monday; August 20 National Day; October 23 Republic Day; December 25 Christmas; December 26 Boxing Day.

India

January 26 Republic Day; March 10 Mahashhivratri; March 14 Id'ul Fitr; April 14 Good Friday; April 20 Ramnavami; May 22 Bakrid; May 25 Buddha Purnima; June 20 Muharram; August 15 Independence Day; August 29 Janmashtami; October 13 Dussehra; November 3 Diwali; November 18 Guru Nanak's Birthday; [The preceding list is based on India's 1994 holiday schedule.]

Indonesia

January 1-2 New Year's; January 10 Ascension of Mohammad; March 14-15 Idulfitri 1414H; April 14 Good Friday; May 1 Ascension of Christ; May 21 Idul Adha 1414H (Haj New Year); June 11 Moslem New Year 1415H; August 17 Independence Day; August 20 Mohammad's Birthday; December 25 Christmas; December 30 Ascension Day; [The preceding list is based on Indonesia's 1994 holiday schedule.]

Ireland

January 1 New Year's Day; March 17 Saint Patrick's Day; April 16 Easter Monday; First Monday in May May Holiday; First Monday in June June Holiday; First Monday in August August Holiday; First Monday in October October Holiday; December 25 Christmas; December 26 Saint Stephen's Day; [If New Year's Day, Saint Patrick's Day, Christmas Day, or; Saint Stephen's Day fall on a weekend, the

following Monday is; a public holiday.; Most businesses close from December 24 through January 2 during; the Christmas festive period.; Certain other days are celebrated as holidays within local; jurisdictions.]

Israel

April 15 Passover (first day); April 21 Passover (last day); May 4 Independence Day; June 4 Shavuot (Pentecost); September 25 Rosh Hashana (New Year-first day); September 26 Rosh Hashana (New Year-second day); October 4 Yom Kippur (Day of Atonement); October 9 Succot (Feast of Tabernacles); October 16 Simhat Torah (Rejoicing of the Law); [Jewish holidays are determined according to lunar calendars, so their dates change from year to year.]

Italy

January 6 Epiphany; April 17 Easter Monday; April 25 Anniversary of the Liberation; May 1 Labor Day; August 15 Assumption; Patron Saint's Days are observed by the following cities: Florence, June 24, St. John's Day; Rome, June 29, St. Peter's and St. Paul's Day; Palermo, July 15, St. Rosalia's Day; Naples, September 19, St. Gennaro's Day; July and [August are poor months for conducting business in Italy; since most business firms are closed for vacation during this period. The same is true during the Christmas and New Year period. Certain; other days are celebrated as holidays within local jurisdictions. When; an Italian holiday falls on a Saturday, offices and stores are closed.]

Jamaica

January 1 New Year's; Variable Ash Wednesday; Variable Good Friday; Variable Easter Monday; May 23 National Labor Day; August 5 Independence Day; October 21 National Heroes' Day; December 25 Christmas Day; December 26 Boxing Day.

Japan

January 1 New Year's; January 15 Adult's Day; February 11 National Foundation Day; March 21 Vernal Equinox Day; April 29 Greenery Day; May 3 Constitution Memorial Day; May 4 Declared Official Holiday; May 5 Children's Day; September 15 Respect-for-the-Aged; September 23 Autumnal Equinox Day; October 10 Health/Sports Day; November 3 Culture Day; November 23 Labor Thanksgiving Day; December 23 Emperor's Birthday; [If a national holiday falls on a Sunday, the following Monday is a compensatory day off. May 4 is also a national holiday, although; it has no specific title. In addition to the above public holidays, many Japanese companies and government offices traditionally close; for several days during the New Year's holiday season (December 28- January 3). Many also close during ``Golden Week'' (April 29-May 5); and the traditional ``O-Bon'' (Festival of Souls') period for several; days in mid-August (usually August 12-15).]

Korea

January 1-2 New Year's; January 30-; February 1 Lunar New Year Days; March 1 Independence Movement Day; April 5 Arbor Day; May 5 Children's Day; May 7 Buddha's Birthday; June 6 Memorial Day; July 17 Constitution Day; August 15 Independence Day; September 8-10 Korean Thanksgiving Days; October 3 National Foundation Day; December 25 Christmas.

Kuwait

January 1 New Year's; February 25 Kuwait National Day; February 26 Kuwait Liberation Day. [A number of variable Islamic holidays are also observed in Kuwait. Government offices operate with very limited business hours during the Holy Month of Ramadan (the dates of which vary from one year to the next). Appointments should not be scheduled on Thursdays and Fridays.]

Latvia

January 1 New Year's; April 14 Good Friday; May 1 Constitution Day; June 23-24 Midsummer Holiday; November 18 Proclamation Day; December 25-26 Christmas; December 31 New Year's Eve.

Lebanon

January 1 New Year's; February 9 St. Maron's Day; Variable Feast of Ramadan; Variable Good Friday Western Rite; May 1 Labor Day; Variable Eastern Orthodox Good Friday; May 6 Martyr's Day; Variable Feast of Al-Adha; Variable Ashura; Variable Moslem New Year; August 15 Assumption; Variable Prophet's Birthday; November 1 All Saint's Day; November 22 Independence Day; December 25 Christmas.

Lesotho

March 12 Moshoeshoe Day; March 21 National Tree Planting Day; April 14 Good Friday; April 17 Easter Monday; July 4 Ascension and Family Day; July 17 King's Birthday; October 4 Independence Day; December 26 Boxing Day.

Madagascar

January 1 New Year's; March 29 Day Commemorating Martyrs; April 14 Easter; April 17 Easter Monday; May 1 Labor Day; 6th Thursday after Easter Ascension; 7th Sunday after Easter Pentecost,; followed by Pentecost Monday;

May 25 OAU Day; June 26 Independence Day; August 15 Assumption; November 1 All Saint's Day; December 25 Christmas.

Malawi

January 3 New Year's; March 3 Martyrs' Day; April 14 Good Friday; April 17 Easter Monday; May 16 Kamuzu Day; July 6 Republic Day; October 17 Mothers' Day; December 21 National Tree Planting Day; December 26 Boxing Day; December 27 Christmas observed.

Malaysia

January 1 New Year's; January 31-; February 1 Chinese New Year; February 1 Kuala Lumpur City Day; March 4 and 5 (variable, and subject to change); Hari Raya Puasa May 1 Labor Day; May 12 (variable, and subject to change) Hari Raya Haji; May 14 Wesak Day; May 31 Awal Muharam; June 3 Agong's Birthday; August 9 Prophet Mohammed's Birthday; August 31 National Day; October or November (variable) Deepavali; December 25 Christmas.

Mali

January 1 New Year; January 20 Army Day; March 14 (approximate) Ramadan; March 26 Day of Democracy; April 17 (approximate) Easter Monday; May 1 International Labor Day; May 21 (approximate) Tabaski; May 25 Day of Africa; August 21 (approximate) Mawloud; August 28 (approximate) Prophet's Baptism; September 22 Independence Day; December 25 Christmas; [Dates listed as approximate, other than Easter, are Muslim holidays; based on the lunar calendar and therefore subject to one or two days'; variation from the date given.]

Mexico

January 1 New Year's; February 5 Anniversary of Mexican Constitution; March 21 Benito Juarez' Birthday; April 14 Good Friday; May 1 Mexican Labor Day; May 5 Anniversary of Independence; September 16 Mexican Independence Day; November 2 All Soul's Day; November 20 Anniversary of the Mexican Revolution; December 25 Christmas; [The preceding list is a projection based on Mexican holidays in 2002.]

Morocco

March 3 Throne Day; March 30* Aid El Fitr; May 1 Labor Day; May 23 National Holiday; June 5* Aid El Adha; June 25* Moslem New Year; July 9 King's Birthday; August 14 Saharan Province Day; September 5* Prophet's Birthday; November 6 Green March Day; November 18 Independence Day.

[Holidays marked with an asterisk are based on the lunar calendar; and change every year.]

Mozambique

January 1 New Year's; February 3 Mozambican Heroes' Day; April 7 Women's Day; May 1 Labor Day; June 25 Independence Day; September 7 Lusaka Agreement Day; September 25 Revolution Day; November 10 Maputo City day, a holiday only for Maputo; December 25 Christmas.

Netherlands

January 1 New Year's; April 14 Good Friday; April 17 Easter Monday; April 30 Queen's Birthday; May 5 Liberation Day; May 28 Ascension; December 25 Christmas; December 26 Second Christmas Day; [Certain other days are celebrated as holidays within; local jurisdictions.]

New Zealand

January 1-3 New Year's; January 23 Wellington Anniversary Day (Wellington only); January 30 Auckland Anniversary Day (Auckland only); February 6 Waitangi Day; April 14 Good Friday; April 17 Easter Monday; April 25 ANZAC Day; June 5 Queen's Birthday; October 23 Labor Day; November 6 Marlborough Anniversary (Blenheim only); November 10 Canterbury Anniversary (Christchurch only); December 25 Christmas; December 26 Boxing Day.

Nicaragua

January 1 New Year's Day; April 13 Holy Thursday; April 14 Good Friday; May 1 Labor Day; July 19 Sandinista Revolution Day; August 1 Festival of Santo Domingo; September 14 Battle of San Jacinto; September 15 Independence Day; December 8 Immaculate Conception; December 25 Christmas.

Nigeria

January 1 New Year's; April 1 Good Friday; April 4 Easter Monday; May 1 Labor Day; October 1 National Day; December 25 Christmas; December 26 Boxing Day.

Holidays falling on Saturdays are likely to be observed on the preceding Friday, while those falling on Sunday are likely to be observed on the following Monday.

[The Muslim holidays of Eid-El-Fitri and Eid-El-Kabir are usually celebrated for two consecutive work days. Their dates, as well as the date of Eid-El-Maulud, vary and are announced by the Ministry of Internal Affairs shortly before they occur.]

Norway

April 13 Holy Thursday; April 14 Good Friday; April 17 Easter Monday; May 1 Labor Day; May 17 Independence Day; May 25 Ascension; December 25 Christmas. [Some Norwegian manufacturing plants and major businesses are closed for three to four weeks for summer holidays from mid-July to mid-August. Easter (a 10-day holiday season for many Norwegians) also is a period of low business activity.]

Oman

March 1-2 Eid Al Fitr; May 9-10 Eid Al Adha; May 30 Islamic New Year; August 18 Birth of the Prophet; November 18-19 National Day; December 29 Ascension Day. [Most of these dates are approximations. The religious holidays are determined by locally observed phases of the moon. The actual date and duration of the National Day holiday is announced shortly before the holiday is to take place].

Pakistan

March 3-5* Eid-ul-Fitr; March 23 Pakistan Day; May 1 May Day; May 12-13 Eid-ul-Azha; June 10-11* 9th and 10th of Muharram; August 10 Milad-An-Nabi; August 14 Independence Day; September 6 Defense of Pakistan Day; September 11 Death Anniversary of Quaid-i-Azam; November 9 Iqbal Day; December 25 Birthday of Quaid-i-Azam. [*Based on the Islamic lunar calendar and may differ by one or two days from the expected dates. In addition, there is often a one or two day discrepancy in timing among different parts of the country).

Panama

January 1 New Year's; January 9 Mourning Day; February 28 Carnival; April 14 Good Friday; May 1 Labor Day; November 3 Independence Day from Colombia; November 4 Flag Day; November 10 The Uprising of Los Santos; November 28 Independence Day from Spain; December 8 Mother's Day; December 25 Christmas.

Paraguay

January 1 New Year's; February 3 San Blas; March 1 Heroes' Day; April 14 Holy Thursday; April 15 Good Friday; May 1 Labor day; May 15 Independence Day; June 12 Chaco Armistice; August 15 Founding of Asuncion; December 8 Virgin of Caacupe Day; December 25 Christmas.

Philippines

January 1 New Year's; April 9 Bataan & Corregidor Day and Heroism Day; April 13 Maundy Thursday; April 14 Good Friday; May 1 Labor Day; June 12 Independence Day; August 28 National Heroes

Day; November 1 All Saints' Day; November 30 Bonifacio Day; December 25 Christmas; December 30 Rizal Day. [June 24, Manila Day, is observed only in the City of Manila, and August 19, Quezon Day, is observed only in Quezon City. In addition, special public holidays such as Election Day and EDSA Revolution Day, may be declared by the President and are observed nationwide.]

Poland

January 1 New Year's; April 17 Easter Monday; May 1 Labor Day; May 3 Constitution DayLate; May or early; June Corpus Christi; August 15 Assumption; November 1 All Saints' Day; November 11 Independence Day; December 25-26 Christmas. [One Saturday per month is by custom considered a working Saturday, but there is no consistency among institutions or exact observance as such.]

Qatar

February 22 Anniversary of the Accession of the Amir; September 3 Independence Day [Officially, Qatar uses the Gregorian calendar year for all purposes. The Hijra (Islamic) calendar is also widely used. Religious holidays vary from year to year. Eid Al-Fitr (four days) marks the end of the fasting month of Ramadan and Eid Al-Adha marks the conclusion of the pilgrimage (Haj) to Mecca.]

Romania

January 1-2 New Year's; April 23-24 Orthodox Easter; May 1-2 Labor Day; December 1 National Day; December 25 Christmas.

Russia

January 1-2 New Year's; January 7 Orthodox Christmas; March 8 International Women's Day; May 1 International Labor Day; May 2 Spring Day; May 9 Victory Day; June 12 Independence Day; November 7 Revolution Day. [When holidays occur on weekends, Russian authorities announce during the week prior to the holiday, if the day will be celebrated on the following Monday. It is likely that January 2 and 3 will be holidays in 1995 since January 1 is a Sunday.]

Saudi Arabia

Beginning about March 1 Eid al-Fitr; Beginning about May 9 Eid al-Adha; September 22 National Day. [There are two Islamic religious holidays around which most businesses in Saudi Arabia close for at least three working days. Eid al-Fitr occurs at the end of the holy month of Ramadan. Eid al-Adha celebrates

the time of year when pilgrims arrive from around the world to perform the Haj. Their timing is governed by the Islamic lunar calendar and they fall approximately 11 days earlier in each successive year. In 1995, the Eid al-Fitr holiday will begin on or about March 1 and the Eid al-Adha holiday on or about May 9.]

Senegal

January 1 New Year's; April 4 Independence Day; 1st Monday in April Easter Monday; May 1 International Labor Day; August 15 Assumption; November 1 All Saints' Day; December 25 Christmas. [The following holidays are moveable according to the religious calendar: Korite, Tabaski, Tamxarit, Mawlud, Ascension, and Pentecost (in May).]

South Africa

January 1-2 New Year's; April 6 Founders' Day; April 14 Good Friday; April 17 Family Day; May 1 Workers' Day; May 25 Ascension; May 31 Republic Day; October 10 Kruger Day; December 16 Day of the Vow; December 25 Christmas; December 26 Day of Goodwill.

Spain

January 1 New Year's; January 6 Epiphany; April 14 Good Friday; August 15 Assumption; October 12 National Day; November 1 All Saints' Day; December 6 Constitution Day; December 8 Immaculate Conception. [Regional holidays: April 13 (Holy Thursday), Bilbao/Madrid; April 17 (Easter Monday), Barcelona/Bilbao; May 2 (Labor Day), Madrid; May 16 (St. Isidro), Madrid; June 5 (Whit Monday), Barcelona; June 24 (St. John), Barcelona; July 25 (St. James), Bilbao/Madrid; September 24 (La Merced), Barcelona; November 9 (Our Lady of Almudena), Madrid; December 26, Barcelona/Madrid. The list of Spain's commercial holidays for 1995 is not available yet. It will not differ much from the preceding list for 1994.]

Sri Lanka

January 15 Thai Pongal; January 16 Duruthu Poya; February 4 National Day; February 14 Navam Poya; February 27 Maha Sivarathri; March 3 Ramazan Festival; March 16 Medin Poya; April 13 Day Prior to Sinhala and Tamil New Year; April 14 Sinhala and Tamil New Year Good Friday; April 15 Bak Poya; May 1 May Day; May 10 Hadji Festival; May 14 Vesak Poya; May 15 Day Following Vesak Poya; May 22 National Heroes' Day; June 12 Poson Poya; June 30 Special Bank Holiday; July 12 Esala Poya; August 10 Nikini Poya and Holy Prophet's Birthday; September 8 Binara Poya; October 8 Vap Poya; October 23 Deepavali Festival; November 6 Il Poya;

349

December 6 Unduvap Poya; December 25 Christmas; December 31 Special Bank Holiday. [Sri Lankan holidays are connected with the country's four religions: Buddhism, Hinduism, Islam, and Christianity. Dates change from year to year. Holidays with fixed dates include National Day (February 4), National Heroes' Day (May 22), and Christmas (December 25). Each full moon is marked by a Poya Day holiday.]

Suriname

January 1 New Year's; About March 13 Holi Phagwa; About March 27 Ied Ul Fitr; April 14 Good Friday; April 17 Easter Monday; May 1 Labor Day; July 1 Emancipation Day; November 25 Independence Day; December 25 Christmas.

Swaziland

January 1 New Year's; April 14 Good Friday; April 17 Easter Monday; April 19 King Mswati III's Birthday; April 25 National Flag Day; May 12 Ascension; July 22 Public Holiday; August or September Umhlanga (Reed Dance); September 6 Independence Day; December 25 Christmas; December 26 Boxing Day; December or January Incwala. [The preceding list is a projection based on Swaziland holidays in 1994. Swaziland holidays falling on a Sunday are observed on the following Monday. Swaziland holidays falling on a Saturday are observed on that day unless an announcement to the contrary is made by the Government.]

Sweden

January 1 New Year's; January 6 Epiphany; April 14 Good Friday; April 17 Easter Monday; May 1 Swedish Labor Day; May 25 Ascension; June 5 Whit Monday; June 24 Midsummer Day; November 4 All Saints' Day; December 25-26 Christmas. [Offices are also closed on Mid-Summer Eve, Christmas Eve, and New Year's Eve. Government and many business offices generally close 1:00 p.m. on the day before major holidays.]

Switzerland

January 1 New Year's; January 2 Baerzelistag; April 14 Good Friday; April 17 Easter Monday; May 25 Ascension; June 5 Whit Monday; August 1 Swiss National Day; December 25 Christmas; December 26 St. Stephan's Day.

Syria

Jauary 1 New Year's; March 8 Revolution Day; March 13-15 Al-Fitr Holiday; March 21 Mothers' Day; April 3 Western Easter; April 10 Eastern

Easter; April 17 In dependence Day; May 1 Labor Day; May 6 Martyrs' Day; May 22-25 Al-Adha Holiday; June 9 Muslim New Year; August 18 Prophet's Birthday; October 6 Tishree War; December 25 Christmas. [The Muslim religious holidays listed above are based on the lunar calendar; the exact dates are to be confirmed.]

Taiwan

January 1 Founding Day; Late January Mid-February Spring Festival; (Chinese New Year) March 29 Youth Day; April 4 Women and Children's Day; April 5 Tomb Sweeping Day and President Chiang Kai-Shek Day; Late May Mid-June Dragon Boat Festival September Mid-Autumn Festival; September 28 Confucius' Birthday; October 10 Double Ten National Day; October 25 Taiwan Retrocession Day; October 31 President Chiang Kai-Shek's Birthday; November 12 Dr. Sun Yat-Sen's Birthday; December 25 Constitution Day. [There are 10 holidays and three festivals in Taiwan. Dates for the three festivals which include Chinese Lunar New Year Day, Dragon Boat Festival, and Mid-Autumn (Moon) Festival change with the lunar calendar.]

Tanzania

January 1 New Year; January 12 Zanzibar Revolutionary Day; March 3-4* Idd-El-Fitr; April 14 Good Friday; April 17 Easter Monday; April 26 Union Day; May 1 International Workers' Day; May 11* Idd-El-Hajj; August 8 Peasants' Day; August 11 Maulid Day; December 9 Independence Day; December 25 Christmas; December 26 Boxing Day. [Holidays marked with an asterisk are subject to the sighting of the moon and may vary from the dates shown.]

Thailand

January 3 New Year's; February 9-10 Chinese New Year; February 25 Magha Puja Day; April 6 King Rama I Memorial and Chakri Day; April 12-14 Songkran Days; May 2 Labor Day; May 5 Coronation Day; May 24 Visakha Puja Day; July 25 Buddhist Lent Day; August 12 Her Majesty the Queen's Birthday; October 24 Chulalongkorn Day; December 5 His Majesty the King's Birthday; December 12 Constitution Day. [The preceding list is based on the list of Thailand holidays in 1994.]

Trinidad and Tobago

January 1 New Year's; April 14 Good Friday; April 17 Easter Monday; June 2 Corpus Christi; June 5 Whit Monday; June 19 Labor Day; August 1 Emancipation Day; August 31 Independence Day; September 24 Republic DayDate to be determined Divali; December 25 Christmas;

December 26 Boxing Day. [The dates for Carnival Monday and Tuesday (the Monday and Tuesday preceding Ash Wednesday) change from year to year. Carnival Monday and Tuesday are not official public holidays but most businesses are closed.]

Turkey
January 1 New Year's; March 2-5 Sugar Holiday; April 23 National Sovereignty and Children's Day; May 9-13 Sacrifice Holiday; May 19 Ataturk Memorial, Youth, and Sports Day; August 30 Zafer Bayrami (Victory Day); October 28-29 Turkish Independence Day.

Uganda
January 1 New Year's; January 26 Liberation Day; April 14 Good Friday; April 17 Easter Monday; March 8 International Women's Day; May 1 Labor Day; Date to be determined Idd-el-Fitr; Date to be determined Iddi Aduha; June 3 Uganda Martyrs' Day; June 9 National Heroes' Day; October 9 Independence Day; December 25 Christmas; December 26 Boxing Day.

United Arab Emirates
January 1 New Year's; January 19* Ascension; March 2-4 Eid Al Fitr; May 9* Waqfa; May 10-12* Eid Al-Adha; May 31* Islamic New Year; August 6 Shaykh Zayed Accession Day; August 8* Prophet's Birthday; December 2-3 UAE National Day. [UAE religious holidays are marked with an asterisk and are dependent upon the sighting of the moon.]

United Kingdom
England and Wales: January 1 New Year's; April 14 Good Friday; April 17 Easter Monday; May 1 May Day; May 29 Spring Holiday-May; August 28 Summer Bank Holiday; December 25 Christmas; December 26 Boxing Day.

Scotland
Scotland observes the above except Easter Monday, Spring Holiday, and Summer Bank Holiday, and also observes the following: January 2 Bank Holiday; April 3 Spring Holiday; May 15 Victoria Day; August 7 Bank Holiday; September 18 Autumn Holiday.

Northern Ireland:
In addition to the U.K.-listed holidays, the following are observed: March 17 St. Patrick's Day; April 18 Easter Tuesday; July 12-13 Orangeman's Day.

Venezuela
February 27-28 Carnival; April 13 Good Thursday; April 14 Good Friday; April 19 Signing of Independence; May 1 Labor Day; July 5 Independence Day; July 24 Bolivar's Birthday.

Zambia
January 1 New Year's; March 12 Youth Day; April 14 Good Friday; April 17 Easter Monday; May 1 Labor Day; May 25 African Freedom Day; July 4 Heroes' Day; July 5 Unity Day; August 1 Farmers' Day; October 24 Independence Day; December 25 Christmas.

351

APPENDIX L

COUNTRIES: BANKING, BUSINESS AND SHOPPING HOURS

AFGHANISTAN
Business/Shopping Hours: 8:AM - 6:AM (Sun-Thur)
Businesses are closed Thursday and Friday afternoons

ALGERIA
Banking Hours: 9:AM - 4:PM (Sun-Thur) Business
Hours: 8:AM - 12:Noon, 1:PM - 5:PM (Sat-Wed)
Businesses are closed Thursday and Friday

AMERICAN SAMOA
Banking Hours: 9:AM - 2:PM (Mon-Thur) 9:AM -
5:PM (Fri)

ANDORRA
Banking Hours: 9:AM - 1:PM; 3:PM - 7:PM
Business Hours: 9:AM - 1:PM; 3:PM - 7:PM,
Shopping Hours: 10:AM - 1:PM; 3:PM - 8:PM

ANGUILLA
Banking Hours: 8:AM - 12:00 Noon (Mon-Fri); 3:PM
(Fri)Business Hours: 8:AM - 4:PM, Shopping Hours:
8:AM - 5:PM (Mon-Sat)

ANTIGUA AND BARBUDA
Banking Hours: 8:AM - 1:PM (Mon,Tue,Wed,Thur)
8:AM - 1:PM & 3:PM - 5:PM (Fri); Business Hours:
8:AM - 12:Noon & 1:PM - 4:PM (Mon-Fri) Shopping
Hours: 8:AM - 12:Noon & 1:PM - 5:PM (Mon-Sat)

ARMENIA
Banking Hours: 9:AM - 6:PM
Business Hours: 9:AM - 6:PM
Shopping Hours: 8:AM - 9:PM

ARGENTINA
Banking Hours: 10:AM - 4:PM (Mon-Fri); Business
Hours: 9:AM - 6:PM (Mon-Fri); Shopping Hours:
9:AM - 8:PM (Mon-Sat)

AUSTRALIA
Banking Hours: 10:AM - 3:PM (Mon-Thur); 10:AM
- 5:PM (Fri)Banks are closed on Saturdays;
Business/Shopping Hours: 9:AM - 5:30PM (Mon-
Thur); 8:30AM - 12:Noon (Sat)

AUSTRIA

Banking Hours: 8:AM - 12:30 PM, 1:30 - 3:30 PM
(Mon, Tue, Wed, Fri); 1:30 -5:30PM(Thur) Business
Hours: 8:30 AM - 4:30 PM Shopping Hours: 8:AM
- 6:PM (Mon - Fri); 8:AM -12:Noon (Sat)

AZERBAIJAN
Banking Hours: 9:AM - 6:PM; Business Hours:
9:AM - 6:PM; Shopping Hours: 8:AM - 9:PM

BAHAMAS
Banking Hours: 9:30AM - 3:PM (Mon-Thur);
9:30AM - 5:PM (Fri)

BAHRAIN
Banking Hours: 7:30AM - 12:Noon (Sat-Wed);
7:30AM - 11:AM Thur)

BARBADOS
Banking Hours: 8:AM - 3:PM (Mon-Thur); 8:AM -
1:PM & 3:PM - 5:PM (Fri); Business Hours:
8:30AM - 4:PM (Mon-Fri); Shopping Hours: 8:AM -
4:PM (Mon-Fri); 8:AM - 12:Noon (Sat)

BANGLADESH
Banking Hours: 9:30AM - 1:30PM (Mon-Thur);
9:AM - 11:AM (Fri- Sat); Business/Shopping Hours:
9:AM - 9:PM (Mon-Fri); 9:AM - 2:PM (Sat)

BELARUS
Banking Hours: 9:AM - 6:PM
Business Hours: 9:AM - 6:PM
Shopping Hours: 9:AM - 9:PM

BELGIUM
Banking Hours: 9:AM - 3:PM (Mon-Fri); Business
Hours: 9:AM - 12:Noon & 2:PM - 5:30PM;
Shopping Hours: 9:AM - 6:PM (Mon-Sat)

BELIZE
Banking Hours: 8:AM - 1:PM (Mon-Fri); 3:PM -
6:PM (Fri)Business Hours: 8:AM - 12:Noon; 1:PM -
5:PM (Mon-Fri)Shopping Hours: 8:AM - 4:PM
(Mon-Sat)

BENIN
Banking Hours: 8:AM - 11:AM; 3:PM - 4:PM (Mon-

Fri); Business Hours: 8:AM - 12:30PM; 3:PM - 6:30PM (Mon-Fri) Shopping Hours: 9:AM - 1:PM, 4:PM -7:PM (Mon-Sun)

BERMUDA
Business/Shopping: 9:AM - 5:PM (Mon-Sat)

BOLIVIA
Banking Hours: 9:AM - 12:Noon & 2:PM - 4:PM (Mon-Fri) Business Hours: 9:AM - 12:Noon & 2:30PM - 6:PM (Mon-Fri) Shopping Hours: 9:AM - 6:PM; 9:AM - 12:Noon (Sat)

BOSNIA HERZEGOVINA
Banking Hours: 7:AM - Noon or &:AM - 7:PM; Business Hours: 8:AM - 3:30 PM; Shopping Hours: 8:AM - 8:PM (Mon-Fri)

BOTSWANA
Banking Hours: 8:15 - 12:45PM (Mon-Fri), 8:15AM - 10:45 AM (Sat) Shopping Hours: 8:AM - 6:PM (Mon-Sat)

BRITISH VIRGIN ISLANDS
Banking Hours: 9:AM - 2:PM (Mon-Fri); Business Hours: 8:30AM - 2:00PM & 4:PM - 5:PM (Mon-Fri); Shopping Hours: 8:AM - 5:PM (Mon-Sat)

BRAZIL
Banking Hours 10:AM - 4:30PM (Mon-Fri) Shopping Hours: 9:AM - 6:30PM (Mon-Fri) & 9:AM - 1:PM (Sat)

BURKINA FASO
Business Hours: 7:AM - 12:Noon, 3:PM - 5:PM (Mon-Fri) Shopping Hours: 7:AM - 12:Noon, 2:PM - 7:PM (Mon-Sat)

BURMA
Banking Hours: 10:AM - 2:PM (Mon-Fri); 10:AM - 12:Noon (Sat) Bussiness/Shopping: 9:30Am - 4:PM (Mon-Sat)

BURUNDI
Business Hours: 8:AM - 12:Noon (Mon-Fri); Shopping Hours: 8:AM - 6:PM (Mon-Sat)

CAMEROON
Banking Hours: French Speaking Part: 8:AM - 11:AM, 2:30PM - 4:PM (Mon-Fri)English Speaking Part: 8:AM - 2:PM (Mon-Fri) Business Hours: French Speaking Part: 7:30AM - 12: Noon, 2:30PM - 6:PM (Mon-Fri) English Speaking Part: 7:30AM - 2:30PM - (Mon-Fri), 7:30AM - 1:PM Shopping Hours: 8:AM - 12:30PM, 4:PM - 7:PM (Mon-Sat)

REPUBLIC OF CAPE VERDE
Banking Hours: 8:AM - 12: Noon (Mon-Fri); Business Hours: 8:AM - 12: Noon (Mon-Fri)

CAYMAN ISLANDS
Banking Hours: 9:AM - 2:30PM (Mon-Thur) & 9:AM -PM, :30PM -4:30PM (Fri) Business Hours: 8:30AM - 5:PM Shopping Hours: 8:30AM - 5:PM

CENTRAL AFRICAN REPUBLIC
Banking Hours: 8:AM - 11:30AM (Mon-Fri); Shopping Hours: 7:30AM - 9:PM (Mon-Sun)

CHAD
Banking Hours: 7:AM - 11:AM (Mon-Thur, Sat), 7:AM -10:AM (Fri) Business Hours: 7:AM - 2:PM (Mon-Thur, Sat), 7:AM -12: Noon (Fri)Shopping Hours: 8:AM - 1:PM, 4:PM - 6:PM (Mon-Sat)

CHILE
Banking Hours: 9:AM - 1:PM & 2:30PM - 6:PM (Mon-Fri); 9:AM -2:PM (Sat) Shopping Hours: 9:AM - 1:PM & 2:30PM - 6:PM (Mon-Fri)

CHINA, PEOPLES REPUBLIC
Banking Hours: varies (Mon-Sat)

CHINA, TAIWAN
Banking Hours: 9:AM - 3:30PM (Mon-Fri); 9:AM - 12:Noon (Sat)

COLUMBIA
Banking Hours: 9:AM - 3:PM (Mon-Thur); 9:AM - 3:30 (Fri); Business Hours: 8:30AM - 5:PM (Mon-Fri); Shopping Hours: 10:AM - 7:PM (Mon-Sat)

COMOROS ISLAND
Banking Hours: 9:AM - 12:30PM, 3:PM - 5:PM (Mon-Fri), 9:AM - 12:30PM (Sat); Shopping Hours: 8:AM - 8:PM (Mon-Sat)

CONGO, PEOPLE'S REPUBLIC
Banking Hours: 7:AM - 2:PM (Mon-Fri); Shopping Hours: 7:AM - 7:PM (Mon-Sat)

COSTA RICA
Banking Hours: 9:AM - 3:PM (Mon-Fri); Shopping Hours: 8:30AM - 11:30AM & 2:PM - 6:PM (Mon-Fri) 8:30AM - 11:30AM (Sat)

COTE D'IVOIRE
Banking Hours: 8:AM - 11:30AM, 2:30PM - 4:PM (Mon-Fri) Business Hours: 8:AM - 12:Noon, 2:30PM - 5:30PM (Mon-Fri) Shopping Hours: 8:30AM - 12:Noon, 2:30PM - 7:PM (Mon-Sat)

CUBA

Banking Hours: 9:AM - 3:PM (Mon-Fri); Business Hours: 8:30AM - 12:30PM & 1:30PM - 5:30PM (Mon - Fri) Shopping Hours: 9:AM - 5:PM (Mon-Fri); 9:AM - 12:Noon (Sat)

CYPRUS

Banking Hours: 8:30AM - 12: Noon (Mon-Sat); Business Hours: 8:AM - 1:PM, 2:30PM - 6:PM (Mon-Fri)8:AM -1:PM (Sat)Shopping Hours: 8:AM - 1:PM; 4:PM - 7:PM (Mon-Fri) Closed Wednesday and Saturday afternoons.

CZECH REPUBLIC

Banking Hours: 8:AM - 4:PM (Mon-Fri); Business Hours: 8:30AM - 5:PM Shopping Hours: 9:AM - 6:PM (Mon-Fri), 9:AM - 1:PM (Sat)

DENMARK

Banking Hours: 9:30AM - 4:PM; (Mon,Tue,Wed, & Fri), 9:30AM -6:PM (Thur) Business Hours: 8:AM - 4:PM (Mon-Fri) Shopping Hours: 9/10:AM - 5:30/7:PM (Mon-Thur) 9/10:AM - 7/8:PM (Fri) 9/10:AM - 1/2:PM (Sat)

REPUBLIC OF DJIBOUTI

Banking Hours: 7:15AM - 11:45AM (Sun-Thur); Shopping Hours: 7:30AM - 12:Noon, 3:30PM - 7:30PM (Sat-Thur)

DOMINICA

Banking Hours: 8:AM - 1:PM (Mon-Fri); 3:PM - 5:PM (Fri) Business Hours: 8:AM - 1:PM & 2:PM - 4:PM (Mon-Fri); 8:AM - 1:PM (Sat) Shopping Hours: 8:AM - 1:PM & 2:PM - 4:PM (Mon-Fri); 8:AM-1:PM (Sat)

DOMINICAN REPUBLIC

Banking Hours: 8:AM - 12:Noon (Mon-Fri); Business Hours: 9:AM - 6:PM (Mon-Fri) & 9:AM -12:Noon (Sat); Shopping Hours: 8:30AM - 12:Noon & 2:30PM - 6:PM (Mon-Fri); 8:30AM - 1:PM (Sat)

ECUADOR

Banking Hours: 9:AM - 1:30PM (Mon-Fri); Shopping Hours: 8:30AM - 12:30PM (Mon-Sat) & 3:30PM - 7:PM (Mon-Sat)

EGYPT

Banking Hours: 8:30AM - 1:PM (Mon-Thur, Sat), 10:AM - 12:Noon (Sat) Shopping Hours: 10:AM - 7:PM (Tue-Sat), 10:AM - 8:PM (Mon - Thur)

EL SALVADOR

Banking Hours: 8:AM - 12:Noon & 2:PM - 4:PM (Mon-Fri); Shopping Hours: 8:AM - 12:Noon & 2:30PM - 6:PM (Mon-Sat)

EQUATORIAL GUINEA

Banking Hours: 8:AM - 3:PM (Mon-Fri), 8:AM - 1:PM(Sat) Business Hours: 8:AM - 3:PM (Mon-Fri), 8:AM - 1:PM (Sat) Shopping Hours: 8:AM -3:PM, 5:PM - 7:PM (Mon-Sat)

ESTONIA

Banking Hours: 9:AM - 3:PM
Business Hours: 9:AM - 6PM
Shopping Hours: 9:am - 9:PM (Mon-Sat)

ETHIOPIA

Banking Hours: 9:AM - 5:PM (Mon-Fri); Business Hour: 8:AM - 12:Noon, 1:PM - 4:PM (Mon-Fri);Banks close for 3 hours for lunch

FIJI

Banking Hours: 10:AM - 3:PM (Mon-Thur); 10:AM - 4:PM (Fri); Business/Shopping Hours: 8:AM - 5:PM

FINLAND

Banking Hours: 9:15AM - 4:15PM (Mon-Fri); Business Hours: 8:30AM - 4:PM (Mon-Fri);Shopping Hours: 9:AM - 5/6:PM (Mon-Fri), 9:AM - 2/3:PM (Sat)

FRANCE

Banking Hours: 9:AM - 4:30PM (Mon-Fri); Business Hours: 9:AM - 12:Noon; 2:PM - 6:PM (Mon-Fri), 9:AM - 12:Noon (Sat); Shopping Hours: 9:AM -6:30PM (Tue-Sat)

FRENCH GUIANA

Banking Hours: 7:15AM - 11:45AM (Mon,Tue,Thur, Fri); 7:AM -12:Noon (Wed)

GABON

Banking Hours: 7:AM - 12:Noon (Mon-Fri); Business Hours: 8:AM - 12:Noon, 3:PM - 6:PM (Mon-Fri); Shopping Hours: 8:AM - 12:Noon, 4:PM - 7:PM (Mon-Sat)

GEORGIA

Shopping Hours: 9:AM - 7:PM

THE GAMBIA

Banking Hours: 8:AM - 1:PM (Mon-Fri); 8:AM - 11:AM (Sat); Business/Shopping Hours: 8:AM - 5:PM (Mon-Fri); 8:AM -12:Noon (Sat)

FEDERAL REPUBLIC OF GERMANY

Banking Hours: 8:30AM - 12:30PM; 1:45PM - 3:45PM (Mon-Fri), Thur- 5:45PM Business Hours:

8:AM - 5:PM Shopping Hours: 8:AM - 6:30PM (Mon-Fri), 8:AM - 2:PM (Sat)

GHANA
Banking Hours: 8:30AM - 2:PM (Mon-Fri); Business Hours: 8:30AM - 5:PM (Mon-Fri); Shopping Hours: 8:30AM - 5:PM (Mon-Sat)

GIBRALTAR
Banking Hours: 9:AM - 3:30PM (Mon-Fri), 4:30PM - 6:PM (Fri) Business Hours: 9:AM -6:PM; Shopping Hours: 9:AM - 1:PM & 3:30PM - 7:PM (Mon-Fri), 9:-1:PM (Sat)

GREECE
Banking Hours: 8:AM - 2:PM (Mon-Fri); Business Hours: 8:30AM - 1:30PM, 4:PM - 7:30PM; Shopping Hours: 8:AM - 2:30PM (Mon, Wed, Sat), 8:AM - 1:30PM, 5:PM- 8:PM (Tue, Thur, Fri)

GRENADA
Banking Hours: 8:AM - 12:Noon (Mon-Fri) & 2:30 PM - 5:PM (Fri) Business Hours: 8:AM -4:PM (Mon-Fri) 8:AM - 11:45 AM (Sat) Shopping Hours: 8:AM - 4:PM (Mon-Fri); 8:AM - 11:45 AM (Sat)

GUADELOUPE
Banking Hours: 8:AM - 12:Noon & 2:PM - 4:PM; Shopping Hours: 9:AM - 1:PM & 3:PM - 6:PM (Mon-Fri); Sat mornings

GUATEMALA
Banking Hours: 9:AM - 3:PM (Mon-Fri); Shopping Hours: 9:AM - 7:PM (Mon-Sat)

GUINEA, REPUBLIC
Banking Hours: 7:30AM - 3:PM (Mon-Sat); Business Hours: 7:30 - 3:PM (Mon-Sat); Shopping Hours: 8:AM - 6:PM (Mon-Sun)

GUYANA
Banking Hours: 8:AM - 12:30PM (Mon-Fri); Business Hours: 8:AM - 4:PM (Mon-Fri); Shopping Hours: 8:AM - 12:Noon; 2:PM - 4:PM

HAITI
Banking Hours: 9:AM - 1:PM (Mon-Fri); Business Hours: 8:AM - 5:PM (Mon-Fri); 8:AM - 12:Noon (Sat) Shopping Hours: 8:AM - 5:PM (Mon-Fri); 8:AM - 12:Noon (Sat)

HONDURAS
Banking Hours: 9:AM - 3:30PM (Mon-Fri); Shopping Hours: 8:AM - 6:30PM (Mon-Sat)

HONG KONG
Banking Hours: 10:AM - 3:PM (Mon-Fri); 9:AM - 12:Noon (Sat) Business/Shopping Hours: 9:AM - 5:PM; 9:AM - 1:Pm (Sat)

HUNGARY
Banking Hours: 8:30AM - 3:PM (Mon-Sat); Business Hours: 8:30AM - 5:PM Shopping Hours: 10:AM - 6:PM (Mon-Fri); 10:AM - 2:PM (Sat)

ICELAND
Banking Hours: 9:15AM - 4:PM (Mon-Fri); Business Hours: 9:AM - 5:PM (Mon-Fri); Shopping Hours: 9:AM - 6:PM (Mon-Fri); 9:AM - 12:Noon (Sat)

INDIA
Banking Hours: 10:30AM - 2:30PM (Mon-Fri); 10:30AM - 12:30PM (Sat); Business/Shopping Hours:Government Offices: 10:AM - 1:PM; 2:PM - 5:PM (Mon-Sat); Non-Gov't Offices: 9:30AM - 1:PM; 2:PM - 5:PM (Mon-Sat)

INDONESIA
Banking Hours: 10:AM - 3:PM (Mon-Fri); 9:AM - 12:Noon (Sat)

IRAN
Banking Hours: 8:AM - 1:PM; 4:PM - 6:PM (Sat-Thur); Business/Shopping Hours:Gov't Office: 8:AM - 4:30PM (Sat-Wed) Non-Gov't. Offices: 8:AM - 4:30PM (Sat-Thur) Offices closed on Friday

IRELAND
Banking Hours: 10:AM - 12:30PM; 1:30PM - 3:PM (Mon-Fri); Business Hours: 9:AM - 1:PM, 2:PM - 5:PM; Shopping Hours: 9:AM - 5:30PM (Mon-Sat)

ISRAEL
Banking Hours: 8:30AM - 12:30PM; 4:PM - 5:30PM (Sun-Tue,Thur) 8:30AM -12:30PM (Wed); 8:30AM -12:Noon (Fri)Business Hours: Non-Gov't Office: 8:AM - 4:PM (Mon-Fri) Offices close early on Friday

ITALY
Banking Hours: 8:35AM - 1:35PM; 3:PM - 4:PM (Mon-Fri) Business Hours: 8:30AM - 12:30PM, 3:30PM- 7:30PM Shopping Hours: 9:AM - 1:PM, 3:30/4:PM - 7:30/8:PM

JAMAICA
Banking Hours: 9:AM - 2:PM (Mon - Thur); 9:AM - 12:Noon & 2:PM- 5:PM (Fri) Business Hours: 8:AM - 4:PM Shopping Hours: 8:30AM - 4:30PM

JAPAN

Banking Hours: 9:AM - 3:PM (Mon-Fri); 9:AM - 12:Noon (Sat) Business/Shopping: 9:AM - 5:PM (Mon-Fri); 9:AM - 12:Noon (Sat)

JORDAN
Banking Hours: 8:AM - 12:30PM (Sat-Thur) Business/Shopping Hours: 8:AM - 6:PM (Sat-Thur)

KENYA
Banking Hours: 9:AM - 2:PM (Mon - Fri); 9:AM - 11;AM (1st & last saturday of month) Business Hours: 8:30AM - 4:30PM (Mon -Fri), 8:30 - 12:Noon (Sat) Shopping Hours: 8:30AM - 12:30PM, 2:PM - 5:PM (Mon - Sat)

KOREA, SOUTH
Banking Hours: 9:30AM - 4:30PM (Mon-Fri); 9:30AM - 11:PM (Sat) Business/Shopping Hours: 9:AM - 5:PM (Mon-Fri): 9:AM - 1:PM (Sat)

KUWAIT
Banking Hours: Mostly in the morning ;Business/Shopping Hours: Gov't Offices: 7:30AM - 1:30PM Non-Gov't Offices: 7:30AM - 2:30PM (Sat-Wed);7:AM - 1:PM; 5:PM - 8:PM

KYRGYZSTAN
Banking Hours: 9:AM - 6:PM
Business Hours: 9:AM - 6:PM
Shopping Hours: 8:AM - 9:PM

LATVIA
Banking Hours: 9:AM - 12:Noon
Business Hours: 9:AM - 6:PM
Shopping Hours: 8:Am - 10:PM

LEBANON
Banking Hours: 8:30AM - 12:30PM (Mon-Fri); 8:30AM -12:Noon (Sat)

LESOTHO
Banking Hours: 8:30AM - 1:PM (Mon-Fri); 9:AM - 11:AM (Sat) Business Hours: 8:AM - 4:30PM (Mon-Fri) Shopping Hours: 8:AM - 4:30PM (Mon-Fri); 8:AM - 1:PM (Sat)

LIBERIA
Banking Hours: 9:AM - 5:PM (Mon-Sat); Business Hours: 9:AM - 6:PM (Mon-Sat)
LIBYA
Banking Hours: 8:AM - 4:PM (Sat-Thur); Business Hours: 8:AM - 4:PM (Sat-Thur)

LIECHTENSTEIN
Banking Hours: 8:30AM - 12:Noon, 1:30 - 4:30PM (Mon-Fri) Business Hours: 8:AM - 12:Noon, 2:30PM

- 6:PM; Shopping Hours: 8:AM - 12:15PM, 2:PM - 6:30PM (Mon-Fri), 8:AM - 4:PM (Sat)

LITHUANIA
Banking Hours: 9:AM - 12:Noon; Business Hours: 9:AM - 1:PM, 2:PM - 6:PM (Mon-Sat)

LUXEMBOURG
Banking Hours: 9:AM - 12:Noon; 2:PM - 5:PM (Mon-Sat); Business Hours: 9:AM - 12:Noon, 2:PM - 5:30PM; Shopping Hours: 8:AM - 12:Noon, 2:PM - 6:PM (Mon-Sat)

MADAGASCAR
Banking Hours: 8:AM - 11:AM, 2:PM -4:PM (Mon-Fri); Shopping Hours: 9:AM - 6:PM (Mon-Sat); Business Hours: 8:AM - 12:Noon, 2:PM - 6:PM (Mon-Fri)

MALAWI
Banking Hours: 8:AM - 1:PM (Mon-Fri); Business Hours: 7:30AM - 5:PM (Mon-Fri); Shopping Hours: 8:AM - 6:PM

MALAYSIA
Business/Shopping Hours: 8:30/9:AM - 1:PM, 2:30PM - 4:30PM (Mon-Fri); 9:AM - 1:PM (Sat) Gov't Offices: 9:AM - 4:30Pm (Mon-Fri); 9:AM - 1:PM (Sat)

MALI
Banking Hours: 8:AM - 12:Noon, 2:PM - 4:PM (Mon-Fri); Business Hours: 7:30AM - 2:30PM (Mon-Sat), 7:30AM -12:30PM (Fri)Shopping Hours: 9:AM - 8:PM (Mon-Sat)

MALTA
Banking Hours: 8:30AM - 12:30PM (Mon-Fri), 8:30AM - 11:30AM (Sat) Business Hours: 8:30AM - 5:30PM (Mon-Fri), 8:30AM - 1:PM (Sat) Shopping Hours: 9:AM - 1:PM, 4:PM - 7:PM (Mon-Fri), 9:AM -1:PM, 4:PM - 8:PM (Sat)

MARTINIQUE
Banking Hours: 7:30AM - 4:PM (Mon-Fri); Shopping Hours: 8:30AM - 6:PM (Mon-Fri); 8:30AM - 1:PM (Sat)
MAURITANIA
Banking Hours: 8:AM - 3:PM (Sun-Thur);Business Hours: 8:AM - 3:PM (Sun-Thur); Shopping Hours: 8:AM - 1:PM, 3:PM - 6:PM (Sun-Thur)

MAURITIUS
Banking Hours: 10:AM - 2:PM (Mon - Fri), 9:30AM - 11:30AM (Sat) Shopping Hours: (Varies) 9:AM -

5:PM (Mon-Fri), 9:AM -12:Noon (Sat, Sun)

MEXICO
Banking Hours: 9:AM - 1:30PM (Mon-Fri); Business Hours: 9:AM - 6:PM (Mon-Fri) Shopping Hours: 10:AM - 5:PM (Mon-Fri); 10:AM 8:/9:PM

MICRONESIA
Banking Hours: 9:30Am - 2:30PM (Mon-Fri)

MONACO
Banking Hours: 9:AM - 12:Noon, 2:PM - 4:PM (Mon-Fri); Business Hours: 8:30AM - 6:PM Shopping Hours: 9:AM - 12:Noon, 2:PM - 7:PM (Mon-Sat)

MONTSERRAT
Banking Hours: 8:AM - 1:PM (Mon-Thur); Business Hours: 8:AM - 4:PM; Shopping Hours: 8:AM - 4:PM

MOROCCO
Banking Hours: 8:30AM - 11:30AM, 3:PM - 5:30PM (Mon-Fri) Business Hours: 8:30AM - 12:Noon, 2:30PM - 6:30PM (Mon-Fri), 8:30AM - 12:Noon (Sat) Shopping Hours: 8:30AM - 12:Noon, 2:PM - 6:30PM (Mon-Sat)

MOZAMBIQUE
Banking Hours: 7:30 -12:Noon, 2:PM - 5:PM (Mon-Fri), 7:30AM - 12:Noon (Sat) Business Hours: 7:30AM - 12:Noon, 2:PM - 5:PM (Mon-Fri), 7:30AM - 12:Noon (Sat)

NAMIBIA
Banking Hours: 9:AM - 3:30PM (Mon-Fri), 8:30AM - 11:AM (Sat) Business Hours: 8:30AM - 5:PM (Mon-Fri) Shopping Hours: 8:30AM - 5:30PM (Mon-Fri) 9:AM - 1:PM (Sat)

NEPAL
Banking Hours: 10:AM - 3:PM (Sat-Thur);10:AM - 12:Noon (Sat)

NETHERLANDS
Banking Hours: 9:AM - 4/5:PM (Mon-Fri); Business Hours: 8:30 - 5:30PM; Shopping Hours: 8:30/9:AM - 5:30/6:PM (Mon-Fri)

NETHERLANDS ANTILLES
Banking Hours: 8:30AM - 11:AM; 2:PM - 4:PM (Mon-Fri) Business/Shopping Hours: 8:AM - 12:Noon; 2:PM - 6:PM (Mon-Sat)

NEW CALEDONIA
Banking Hours: 7:AM - 10:30AM; 1:30PM - 3:30PM (Mon-Fri); 7:30 - 11:AM (Sat)

NEW ZEALAND

Banking Hours: 10:AM - 4:PM (Mon-Fri); Business/Shopping Hours: 9:AM - 5:PM (Mon-Fri)

NIGARAGUA
Banking Hours: 8:30AM - 12:Noon; 2:PM - 4:PM (Mon-Fri); 8:30AM - 11:30AM (Sat); Business/Shopping Hours: 8:AM - 5:30PM (Mon-Sat)

NIGER
Banking Hours: 7:30AM - 12:30PM, 3:30PM - 5:PM; Business Hours: 7:30AM - 12:30:PM, 3:30PM - 6:30PM; Shopping Hours: 7:30AM - 12:30PM, 3:30PM - 6:30PM

NIGERIA
Banking Hours: 8:AM - 3:PM (Mon), 8:AM - 1:30PM (Tues-Fri);Business Hours: Gov't Offices: 7:30AM - 3:30PM (Mon-Fri) Private Firms: 8:AM - 5:PM (Mon-Fri)

NORWAY
Banking Hours: 8:15AM - 3:30PM (Mon, Tue, Wed, Fri); 8:15AM - 5:PM (Thur); Business Hours: 9:AM - 4:PM; Shopping Hours: 9:AM - 5:PM (Mon-Fri); 9:AM - 6/7:PM (Thur); 9:AM- 1/2:PM (Sat)

PAKISTAN
Banking Hours: 9:AM - 1:PM (Mon-Thur); 9:AM - 11:30AM (Sat) Business/Shopping Hours: 9:30AM - 1:PM (Mon-Thur); 9:AM -10:30AM (Sat)

PANAMA
Banking Hours: 8:30AM - 1:PM (Mon-Fri); Business Hours: 8:30AM - 12:30PM & 1:30PM - 4:PM (Mon-Fri); Shopping Hours: 8:30AM - 6:PM (Mon-Sat)

PARAGUAY
Banking Hours: 7:AM - 12:Noon (Mon-Fri); Shopping Hours: 7:AM - 12:Noon & 3:PM - 7:PM

PERU
Banking Hours: 9:AM - 1:PM (Mon-Fri); Business Hours: 9:AM - 5:PM (Mon-Fri);Shopping Hours: 9:AM - 7:PM (Mon-Sat)

PHILIPPINES
Banking Hours: 9:AM - 6:PM (Mon-Fri); 9:AM - 12:30 (Sat)

POLAND
Banking Hours: 8:AM - 1:PM; Business Hours: 8:30AM - 3:30PM; Shopping Hours: 9:AM - 8:PM

PORTUGAL

Banking Hours: 8:AM - 3:PM (Mon-Fri) Business Hours: 10:AM - 6:PM Shopping Hours: 9:AM - 1:PM, 3:PM - 7:PM (Mon-Fri), 9:AM -12:Noon (Some Shops)

PUERTO RICO
Banking Hours: 9:AM - 5:PM (Mon-Fri); Business Hours: 8:AM - 5:PM (Mon-Fri); Shopping Hours: 9:AM - 6:PM (Mon-Sat)

QATAR
Banking Hours: 7:30AM - 11:30AM (Sat-Thur)

REUNION ISLAND
Business/Shopping Hours: 8:AM - 12:Noon; 2:PM - 6:PM

ROMANIA
Banking Hours: 8:30 - 11:30AM Business Hours: 8:AM - 4:PM (Mon-Fri), 8:AM - 12:30PM (Sat); Shopping Hours: 9:AM - 1:PM, 4:PM-6/8:PM

RUSSIA
Banking Hours: 9:AM - 6:PM; Business Hours: 9:AM - 6:PM; Shopping Hours: 9:AM - 9:PM (Mon-Sat)

RWANDA
Banking Hours: 8:AM - 11:AM, 2:PM - 5:PM (Mon-Fri), 8:AM -1:PM (Sat) Business Hours: 7:AM - 12:Noon, 2:PM - 6:PM (Mon-Fri) Shopping Hours: 8:AM - 6:PM (Mon-Fri), 11:AM - 6:PM (Sat)

SRI LANKA
Banking Hours: 9:AM - 1:PM (Mon-Fri); 9:am - 11:AM (Sat)

ST. KITTS & NEVIS
Banking Hours: 8:AM - 1:PM (Mon-Fri); 8:AM - 1:PM; 3:PM -5:PM (Fri) Business Hours: 8:AM - 12:Noon, 1:PM - 4:30PM (Mon, Tues); 8:AM - 12:Noon; 1:PM - 4:PM (Wed Thur, Fri) Shopping Hours: 8:AM - 12:Noon, 1:PM -4:PM Shops closed on Thursday afterNoons

ST. LUCIA
Banking Hours: 8:AM - 12:30PM (Mon-Thur); 8:AM - 12:Noon & 3:PM - 5:PM (Fri) ; Shopping Hours: 8:AM - 4:30PM (Mon-Fri); 8:AM - 1:PM (Sat)

SAN MARINO
Banking Hours: 8:30AM - 12:Noon, 2:30PM - 3:15PM; Business Hours: 8:AM - 12:Noon, 2:PM - 6:PM; Shopping Hours: 8:AM - 12:Noon 3:PM - 7:PM

ST. MAARTEN
Banking Hours: 8:30AM - 1:PM (Mon-Thur); 8:30AM - 1:PM & 4:PM - 5:PM (Fri); Business Hours: 8:AM -12:Noon & 2:PM - 6:PM; Shopping Hours: 8:AM - 12:Noon & 2:PM - 6:PM

ST. MARTIN
Banking Hours: 9:AM - 12:Noon & 2:PM - 3:PM (Mon-Fri); Shopping Hours: 9:AM - 12/12:30 & 2:PM - 6:PM (Mon-Sat)

SAO TOME AND PRINCIPE
Banking Hours: 7:30AM - 12:30PM, 2:30PM - 4:30PM (Mon-Fri); Businss Hours: 7:30AM - 12:30PM, 2:30PM - 4:30PM (Mon-Fri); Shopping Hours: 9:AM - 12:30PM, 2:30PM - 6:PM (Mon-Sat)

ST. VINCENT & THE GRENADINES
Banking Hours: 8:AM - 12/1:PM (Mon - Thur); 8:AM - 12:/1:PM & 2:/3:PM -5:PM (Fri) Business Hours: 8:AM - 12:Noon & 1:PM - 4:PM (Mon - Fri); 8:AM- 12:Noon (Sat)

SAUDI ARABIA
Banking Hours: 7/8:AM - 2:30PM (Sat-Thur); Business Hours: Gov't Offices: In Winter 8:AM - 4:PM (Sat- Wed); In Summer 7:AM - 3:PM; During Ramadan 8:AM - 2:PM Others: 8:30AM- 1:30PM; 4:30AM -8PM (Sat-Thur) closed Friday

SENEGAL
Banking Hours: 8:AM - 11:AM, 2:30PM - 4:30PM (Mon-Fri) Business Hours: 8:AM - 12:Noon, 3:PM - 6:PM (Mon-Fri), 8:AM - 12:Noon (Sat) Shopping Hours: 8:AM - 7:PM (Mon-Sat)

SEYCHELLES
Banking Hours: 8:30AM - 1:30PM (Mon-Sat) Business Hours: 8:AM - 12:Noon, 1:PM - 4:PM (Mon-Fri) Shopping Hours: 8:AM - 5:PM (Mon-Fri), 8:AM - 1:PM (Sat)

SIERRA LEONE
Banking Hours: 9:AM - 2:PM (Mon-Fri); Business Hours: 9:AM - 2:PM (Mon-Fri); Shopping Hours: 9:AM - 6:PM (Mon-Sat)

SINGAPORE
Banking Hours: 10:AM - 3:PM (Mon-Fri); 9:30AM - 11:30AM (Sat) Business Hours: Gov't: 9:AM - 4:30PM (Mon-Fri); 9:AM - 1:PM (Sat) Shopping Hours: 9:AM - 6:PM (Mon-Sat)

SOUTH AFRICA
Banking Hours: 9:AM - 3:PM (Mon,Tue,Thur,Fri);

9:AM - 1:PM (Wed); 9:AM -11:AM (Sat) Business/Shopping Hours: 8:30AM - 5:PM (Mon-Fri); 8:30AM - 12:Noon (Sat) Some stores

SPAIN
Banking Hours: 9:AM - 2:PM (Mon-Fri), 9:AM - 1:PM (Sat)Business Hours: 9:AM - 2:PM, 4:PM - 7:PM Shopping Hours: 9:AM - 1:PM, 4:PM - 8:PM

SUDAN
Banking Hours: 8:30AM - 12:Noon (Sat-Thur); Business/Shopping Hours: 8:AM - 1:PM; 5:PM - 8:PM (Sat-Thur)

SURINAME
Banking Hours: 8:AM - 3:PM (Mon-Fri); Business Hours: 7:AM - 3:PM (Mon-Fri); Shopping Hours: 7:30AM - 4:PM (Mon-Fri)

SWEDEN
Banking Hours: 9:30AM - 3:PM (Mon,Tue,Wed,Fri), 9:30AM -3:PM, 4:PM - 5:30PM (Thur) Business Hours: 8:AM - 5:PM Shopping Hours: 9:30AM - 6:PM (Mon-Fri), 9:30AM - 1:PM (Sat), Noon - 4:PM (Sun)

SWITZERLAND
Banking Hours: 8:30AM - 4:30PM (Mon-Fri); Business Hours: 8:AM - 12:Noon; 2:PM - 6:PM; Shopping Hours: 8:AM - 12:15PM, 1:30PM - 6:30AM (Mon-Fri); 8:AM - 4:PM (Sat)

SYRIA
Banking Hours: 8:AM - 12:30PM (Sat-Thur); Business Hours: 8:AM - 1:30PM; 4:30PM - 9:PM (Sat-Thur)

TANZANIA
Business/Shopping Hours: 8:AM - 5/6:PM (Mon-Sat)

TAJIKISTAN
Bankng Hours: 9:AM - 6:PM; Business Hours: 9:AM - 6:PM; Shopping Hours: 8:AM - 9:PM

THAILAND
Business/Shopping Hours: 8:30AM - 7/8:PM

TOGO
Banking Hours: 7:30AM - 11:30AM; 1:30 - 3:30PM (Mon-Fri); Business/Shopping Hours: 8:AM - 6:PM (Mon-Fri); Sat morning

TONGA
Banking Hours: 9:30AM - 4:30PM (Mon-Fri)

TRINIDAD AND TOBAGO

Banking Hours: 9:AM - 2:PM (Mon-Thur) & 9:AM - 12:Noon; 3:PM -5:PM (Fri); Shopping Hours: 8:AM - 4:PM (Mon-Fri); 8:AM - 12:Noon (Sat)

TUNISIA
Banking Hours: 8:AM - 11:AM; 2:PM - 4:PM (Mon-Fri)

TURKEY
Banking Hours: 8:30AM - 12:Noon, 1:30 - 5:PM (Mon- Fri) Business Hours: 8:30AM - 12:30PM, 1:30PM - 5:30PM Shopping Hours: 9:AM - 1:PM, 2:PM - 7:PM (Mon-Sat)

TURKMENISTAN
Banking Hours: 9:AM - 6:PM
Business Hours: 9:AM - 6:PM
Shopping Hours: 8:AM - 9:PM

TURKS AND CAICOS
Banking Hours: 8:30AM - 3:30PM
Business Hours: 8:30AM - 5:PM
Shopping Hours: 9:AM - 7:PM

UKRAINE
Banking Hours: 9:AM - 6:PM
Business Hours: 9:AM - 6:PM
Shopping Hours: 8:AM - 9:PM

UNITED KINGDOM
Banking Hours: (Varies) England & Wales: 9:AM - 3:PM (Mon-Fri) Scotland: 9:30 - 12:30PM, 1:30 - 3:30PM (Mon - Wed), 9:30AM -12:30PM, 1:30 - 3:30PM, 3:30PM -4:30PM-6PM (Thur) 9:30AM - 3:30PM (Fri), North Ireland: 10:AM - 3:30PM (Mon - Fri) Business Hours: 9:AM - 5:PM Shopping Hours: 9:AM - 5:30PM

UZBEKISTAN
Banking Hours: 9:AM - 6:PM
Business Hours: 9:AM - 6:PM
Shopping Hours: 8:AM - 9:PM

URUGUAY
Banking Hours: 1:PM - 5:PM (Mon-Fri)
Business Hours: 7:AM - 1:30PM (Mon-Fri) Summer & 12:30 - 7:PM (Mon-Fri) Winter Shopping Hours: 10:AM - 7:PM (Mon-Sat)

VENEZUELA
Banking Hours: 9:AM - 12:Noon & 3:PM - 5:PM (Mon-Fri) Business Hours: 8:AM - 12:Noon & 2:PM - 5:PM (Mon-Fri) Shopping Hours: 9:AM - 12:Noon & 2:PM - 5:PM (Mon-Sat)

VIETNAM

Banking Hours: 8:AM - 11:30AM; 2:PM - 4:PM
(Mon-Fri); 8:AM - 11:AM (Sat)

WESTERN SAMOA
Banking Hours: 9:30AM - 3:PM (Mon-Fri); 9:30AM
- 11:30AM (Sat)

YUGOSLAVIA
Banking Hours: 7:AM - 12:Noon or 7:AM - 7:PM;
Business Hours: 8:AM - 12:30PM Shopping Hours:
8:AM - 12:Noon, 4:PM - 8:PM or 8:AM - 8:PM
(Mon-Fri) 8:AM - 3:PM (Sat)

ZAIRE
Banking Hours: 8:AM - 11:30 (Mon-Fri);
Business/Shopping Hours: 8:AM - 12:Noon; 3:PM -
6:PM (Mon- Sat)

ZAMBIA
Banking Hours: 8:AM - 1:PM (Mon-Fri); 8:AM -
11:AM (Sat) Business/Shopping Hours: 8:AM - 5:PM
(Mon-Fri); 8:AM - 3:PM (Sat)

ZIMBABWE
Banking Hours: 8:30AM - 2:PM (Mon,Tue, Thur,
Fri); 8:30AM -12:Noon (Wed); 8:30AM - 11:AM
(Sat)Business/Shopping Hours: 8:AM - 5:PM

APPENDIX M

MEDICAL ASSISTANCE ORGANIZATIONS

*Several private organizations will provide medical information and insurance for overseas travelers. Most charge a fee for this service. The following is provided **FOR INFORMATIONAL PURPOSES ONLY** and in no way constitutes an endorsement, expressed or implied, by the Department of State.*

AIR AMBULANCE / MED-EVAC

U.S.-based Companies

ABLE JET
Fort Pierce, FL
800-225-3538

ACADIAN AMBULANCE & AIR MED
SERVICE, INC.
Lafayette, LA
800-259-3333

ADVANCED AIR AMBULANCE
Miami, FL
800-633-3590 / 305-232-7700

AAA - AIR AMBULANCE AMERICA
Austin, TX
800-222-3564 / 512-479-8000

AIR AMBULANCE CARE FLIGHT
INTERNATIONAL, INC.
Clearwater, FL
800-282-6878 / 1-727-530-7972 (international)

AIR AMBULANCE NETWORK
Sarasota, FL
800-327-1966

AIR AMBULANCE PROFESSIONALS
Fort Lauderdale, FL
800-752-4195 / 954-491-0555

AirEvac
Phoenix, AZ
800-421-6111

AIR MEDIC - AIR AMBULANCE OF
AMERICA
Washington, PA
800-245-9987

AIRescue INTERNATIONAL
Van Nuys, CA
800-922-4911 / 818-994-0911

AIR RESPONSE
Orlando, FL
800-631-6565 / 303-858-9967

AIR STAR INTERNATIONAL
Thermal, CA
877-570-0911 / 800-991-2869
e-mail: AirStar1@aol.com

AMERICAN CARE, INC.
San Diego, CA
800-941-2582 / 619-486-8844

AMERICAN JET AIR MEDICAL
Houston, TX
888-I-FLY-AJI / 713-641-9700

CRITICAL AIR MEDICINE
San Diego, CA
800-247-8326 / 619-571-0482

CRITICAL CARE MEDFLIGHT
Lawrenceville. GA
800-426-6557

GLOBAL CARE / MEDPASS
Alpharetta, GA
800-860-1111

INFLIGHT MEDICAL SERVICES
INTERNATIONAL INC.
Naples, FL
800-432-4177 / 941-594-0800

INTERNATIONAL SOS ASSISTANCE
Philadelphia, PA
800-523-8930 / 215-244-1500
Also provides travel insurance services.

MedAire
Phoenix, AZ
602-452-4300

MED ESCORT INTERNATIONAL INC.
Allentown, PA
800-255-7182 / 610-791-3111

MEDEX ASSISTANCE CORPORATION
Timonium, MD
888-MEDEX-00 / 410-453-6300 (call collect)
(Also provides travel insurance services.)

MEDJET ASSISTANCE
Birmingham, AL
1-800-963-3538

MEDJET INTERNATIONAL, INC.
Birmingham, AL
800-356-2161 / 205-592-4460

MEDWAY AIR AMBULANCE
Lawrenceville, GA
800-233-0655

MERCY MEDICAL AIRLIFT
Manassas, VA
800-296-1217
(Service area: Caribbean and part of Canada only.
If necessary, will meet commercial incoming
patients at JFK, Miami and other airports.)

NATIONAL AIR AMBULANCE
Ft. Lauderdale, FL
800-327-3710 / 305-525-5538

SMARTRAVEL
Alexandria, VA
800-730-3170 / 703-379-8645
Provides a range of travel medicine services.

TRAVEL CARE INTERNATIONAL, INC.
Eagle River, WI
800-524-7633 / 715-479-8881

TRAVELERS EMERGENCY NETWORK
Tierra Verde, FL
800-ASK-4-TEN
e-mail: ten@intrex.net

Foreign-based Companies

AEA INTERNATIONAL
Singapore
U.S. Phone: 800-468-5232
Service worldwide, also provides travel insurance
services

AUSTRIAN AIR AMBULANCE
Vienna, Austria
43-1-40-144

EURO-FLITE LTD.
Helsinki International Airport
Vantaa, Finland
358-9-870-2544

EUROPASSISTANCE
Johannesburg, South Africa
27-11-315-3999

GERMAN AIR RESCUE (DRF)
Filderstadt, Germany
49-0711-7007-0
e-mail: alarmzentrale@drf.de

MEDIC'AIR
Paris, France
331-41-72-14-14

TYROL AIR AMBULANCE
Innsbruck, Austria
43-512-22422

362

APPENDIX N

MEDICAL EMERGENCY KIT

Listed below are some items you may wish to include in your medical emergency kit. These items are readily available (in various brands) in your local pharmacy. Consult your physician for advice on other useful items and health matters.

Aspirin, 5 gr., or Tylenol, 325 mg.
Aluminum Hydroxide with Magnesium Trisilicate Tablets
Milk of Magnesia Tablets
Chlorpheniramine Tablets
Antihistamine Nasal Spray
Antimicrobial Skin Ointment
Calamine Lotion
Liquid Surgical Soap
Tweezers
Antifungal Skin Ointment
Zinc Undecylenate Foot Powder
Vitamin Mineral Tablets
Oil of Clove and Benzocaine Mixture
Opthalmic Ointment
Throat Lozenges
Kaolin Pectin Mixture, Tablets or Liquid
Paregoric or Lomotil
Adhesive Bandages
3-inch Wide Elastic Bandage
2-foot-by-19-Yard Gauze Bandage
4-inch by 4-inch Gauze Pad
Adhesive Medical Tape
Medium-Size Safety Pins
Thermometer
Insect Repellent
Sleeping Pills
Small Pack of Cotton Wool
Tampons
Tissues
A Pair of Scissors

APPENDIX O

INTERNATIONAL EMERGENCY CODES

Country	Emergency #	Ambulance #	Police #
Algeria			17
Andorra		182-0020	21222
Andorra	11/15	20020	
Anguilla	999		
Antigua	999		20045/20125
Argentina			101
Austria		144	133
Bahamas		3222221	3224444
Barbados			112/60800
Belgium	900/901	906	101
Belize			2222
Bermuda			22222
Bolivia	118		110
Brazil	2321234		2436716
Columbia			12
Costa Rica	2158888		117
Cyprus	999		
Czech Republic	155		
Denmark	000		
Dominican Republic			6823000
Egypt			912644
Ethiopia			91
Fiji Islands	000		
Finland	000	002/003	
France	17	12/17	
French Guiana			18
Germany	110		
Gibraltar	199		
Great Britain	999		
Greece	100		171
Guyana	999		
Haiti	0		
Hong Kong	999		
Hungary	04		
Iceland			
(Reykavik)	11100	11166	
(elsewhere dial 02 for the operator who will then place the call)			
India		102	100
Ireland	999		
Israel			100
Italy		113	112
Jamaica		110	119
Japan		119	100
Jordan	19		
Kenya	999		

Liechtenstein		144	117
Luxembourg	012		
Malaysia	0		
Malta	99		
Maltese Island		196	191
Monaco		933-01945	17
Morocco			19
Nepal	11999		
Netherlands			
Amsterdam	559-9111	5555555	222222

(elsewhere dial 008 for the operator who will then place the call)

New Zealand	111		
Norway		003	110011
Pakistan	222222		
Papua New Guinea			255555
Paraguay			49116
Peru	05		
Phillipines			599011
Poland		999	997
Portugal	115		
San Marino	113		
Singapore	999		
Spain	091		
Sri Lanka			26941/21111
St. Vincent			71121
St. Kitts & Nevis	999		
St. Lucia	95		99
Suriname	99933		711111/77777
Sweden	90000		
Switzerland		144	117
Tanzania	999		
Thailand			2810372/2815051
Tunisia			243000
U.S. Virgin Is.		922	915
Uruguay	401111		890
Venezuela			169/160
Yugoslavia	94		92

APPENDIX P

ORGANIZATIONS THAT PROVIDE SERVICES TO INTERNATIONAL TRAVELERS

Academic Travel Abroad, 3210 Grace St., N.W. 1st flr. Washington, D.C. 20007, Tel. (202) 333-3355

Airline passenger of America, 4212 King St., Alexandria, VA 22302, Tel. (703) 824-0505

Airport Operators Council International, Inc., 1220 19th St. NW, Suite 200, Washington DC, 20036, Fax. (202) 331-1362.

American Council for International Studies, 19 Bay State, Road, Boston, MA. 02215, Tel. (617) 236-2051

American Automobile Association (AAA), AAA Drive, Heathrow, Florida 32746 (404) 444-4000

American Youth Hostels, P.O. Box 37613 Washington DC 20013, Tel. (202) 783-4943.

American Association of Retired Persons (AARP), 1909 K-Street, NW Washington DC 20049 Tel. (800) 441-7575 or (800) 927-0111.

American Society of Travel Agents (ASTA), 1101 King St., Alexandria, VA 22314, Tel. (703) 739-2782

Association of Group Travel Executives, c/o Arnold H. Light A.H. Light Co., Inc. 424 Madison Ave., Suite 705. New York, NY. 10017 Tel. (212) 486-4300

Association of Corporate Travel Executives, P.O. Box 5394, Parsippany, N.J. 07054, Tel. (201) 537-4614

Citizens Emergency Center, Bureau of Consular Affairs, Rm 4811, N.S. U.S. Department of State, Washington DC 20520, Tel. (202) 647-5225.

Council on International Education Exchange (CIEE), 205 E. 42nd St., New York, NY 10017 (212) 661-1414.

Cruise Lines International Association, 500 Fifth Ave, Suite 407, New York, NY. 10110, Tel. (212) 921-0066

Fly Without Fear (FWF), 310 Madison Ave., New York, NY 10017, Tel. (212) 697-7666

Freighter Travel Club of America (FTC), P.O. Box 12693, Salem OR, 97309, Tel. (503) 399-8567

Hideaways International, 15 Goldsmith St., P.O. Box 1270, Littleton, MA 01460, Tel. (508) 486-8955, (800) 843-4433

Institute of Certified Travel Agents (ICTA), P.O. Box, 8256, 148 Linden St., Wellesley, MA. 02181 Tel. (617) 237-0280

Interexchange, 356 W. 34th St., 2nd flr. New York, NY., 10001 Tel. (212) 947-9533

International Gay Travel Association, P.O. Box 18247, Denver, CO. 80218, Tel. (303) 467-7117

International Federations of Women's Travel Organizations, 4545 N. 36th St., Suite 126, Phoenix, AZ, 85018 Tel. (602) 956-7175

International Association for Medical Assistance to Travellers (IAMAT), 417 Center St. Lewiston, NY. 14092 Tel. (716) 754-4883

International Airline Passengers Association (IAPA), 4341 Lindburg Dr., Dallas, TX, 75244, Tel. (214) 404-9980

International Association of Tour Managers, 1646 Chapel St., New Haven, CT. 06511, Tel. (203) 777-5994

International Cruise Passengers Association (ICPA), Box 886 F.D. R. Station, New York, NY 10150, Tel. (212) 486-8482

International Visitors Information Service, 733 15th Street, NW Suite 300, Washington DC 20005, Tel. (202) 783-6540.

International Bicycle Tours, Champlin Square, Box 754 Essex, CT 06426 Tel. (203) 767-7005

National Association of Cruise Only Agents, (NACOA) P.O. Box 7209, Freeport, NY. 11520

National Campers and Hikers Association, 4804 Transit Rd., Building 2, Depend, NY 1404, Tel. (716) 668-6242.

North American Vegetarian Society, P.O. Box 72, Dolgeville, NY 1339, Tel. (518) 568-7970.

SCI International Voluntary Service, Innisfree Village, Rt.2, BOX 506 Crozet, VA 22932, Tel. (804) 823-1826.

Share-A-Ride International (SARI), 100 Park Ave. Rockville, Maryland, Tel. (301) 217-0871

Society of Incentive Travel Executives, 347 Fifth Ave., Suite 610, New York, NY. 10016, Tel. (212) 725-8253

Society for the Advancement of Travel for the Handicapped (SATH), 347 Fifth Ave., Suite 610, New York, NY 10016 Tel. (212) 447-7284. 858-5483

Travel Information Service (TIS), Moss Rehabilitation Hospital , 12th St., and Tabor Rd, Philadelphia, PA. 19141, Tel. (215) 456-9600

U.S. Department of Commerce, International Trade Information Center, Tel (800) 872-8723.

U.S. Department of Transportation, Office of General Counsel, 400 7th St. SW, Rm. 10422, Washington DC 20590, Tel. (202) 366-9306 (voice), (202) 755-7687 (TDD)

U.S. Public Health Services, Centers for Disease Control, Atlanta Georgia, Tel. (404) 539-2574.

Volunteers for Peace International Work Camps, 43 Tiffany Rd., Belmont VTY 05730, Tel. (802) 259-2759.

World Ocean and Cruise Liner Society, P.O. Box 92, Stamford, CT. 06904, Tel. (203) 329-2787

Institute of Certified Travel Agents (ICTA), 148 Linden St., P.O. Box, 812059, (800) 542, 4282.

International Air Passenger Association (IAPA), P.O. Box 870188, Dallas TX. 75287, (800) 821-4274.

International Air Transport Association (IATA), 2000 Peel St., Montreal, QC Canada, H3A 2R4. (514) 844-6311.

International Airlines Travel Agent Network (IATAN), 300 Garden City Plaza, Ste. 342, Garden City, NY. 11530, (7516) 747-4716.

International Association for Medical Assistance to Travelers (IAMAT), 417 Center St., Lewiston, NY. 14092, (716) 754-4883

International Association of Convention and Visitor Bureaus (IACVB), 2000 L. St., NW., Ste. 702, Washington, D.C. 20036, (202) 296-7888.

International Civil Aviation Organization (ICAO), 1000 Sherbrooke West, Montreal, QC Canada H3A 2R2, (514) 285-8219.

National Business travel Association (NBTA), 1650 King St., STe. 301, Alexandria, VA. 22314, (703) 684-0836.

Society of Incentive Travel Executives (SITE), 21 W. 38th St., 10th Fl., New York, 10018, (212) 575-0910.

Society of Travel Agents in Government (STAG), 6935 Wisconsin Ave, Bethesda, MD. 20815, (301) 654-8595.

Travel and Tourism Government Affairs Council, 1100 New York Ave., NW., Ste. 450, Washington, DC. 20005, (202) 408-9600.

Travel and Tourism Research Association, 10200 W. 44th Ave., Ste. 304, Wheat ridge, CO. 80033, (303) 940-6557.

Travel Industry Association of America (TIA), 1100 New York AVe. NW. Ste. 450, Washington, D.C. 20005, (202) 408-8422.

U.S. Travel Data Center, 1100 New York Ave, NW., Ste. 450, Washington, D.C. 20005, (202) 408-1832.

World Travel & Tourism Council, Chaussee de La Hulpe 181, Box 10, 1170 Brussels, Belgium, (32-2) 660 20 67.

OTHER BOOKS BY THE SAME AUTHOR

Americans Traveling Abroad: What You Should Know Before You Go (3rd Ed.) Bestseller! paperback, 720 pages, ISBN: 1-890605-10-7, $39.99

Americans Living Abroad: What You Should Know While You are There. paperback, 375 pages, ISBN: 1-890605-11-5, $34.99

Traveling Abroad Post "9-11" and in the Wake of Terrorism: A Practical Guide for Americans & Other International Travelers, paperback, 265 pages, ISBN: 1-890605-13-1, $24.99

American Businesses Abroad: How to Protect Your Assets and Personnel, paperback, 320 pages, ISBN: 1-890605-12-3, $39.99; (Hard Cover, ISBN: 1-890605-26-3, $49.99)

Weapons of Mass Destruction, What You Should Know: A Citizen's Guide To Biological, Chemical and Nuclear Agents & Weapons paperback, 300 pages, ISBN: 1-890605-14-X, $39.99 (Hard Cover, ISBN: 1-890605-25-5, $49.99)

Natural Disasters and Other Emergencies, What You Should Know: A Family Planning & Survival Guide. paperback, 250 pages, ISBN: 1-890605-15-8, $29.99 (Hard Cover, ISBN: 1-890605-27-1, $39.99)

Do's and Don'ts Around the World: A Country Guide to Cultural and Social Taboos and Etiquette. paperback, available in 9 different volumes/editions: Europe, Asia, Africa, South America, The Caribbean, The Middle East, Russia and the Independent States, Oceania, USA-Canada-Australia. These books contain hundreds of country-specific do's and don'ts and much more!.

Series Title: *DO'S AND DON'TS AROUND THE WORLD: A COUNTRY GUIDE TO CULTURAL AND SOCIAL TABOOS AND ETIQUETTE*

EUROPE 1-890605-00-X; (*1-890605-17-4) 400 pages; $39.99; **SOUTH AMERICA** 1-890605-03-4; (*1-890605-20-4) 230 pages; $24.99; **AFRICA** 1-890605- 04-2 (*1-890605-16-6); 450 pages; $39.99; **THE CARIBBEAN** 1-890605-02-6; (*1-890605-19-0) 230 pages; $24.99; **ASIA** 1-890605-01-8; (*1-890605-18-2) 260 pages; $24.99; **RUSSIA & THE INDEPENDENT STATES** 1-890605-06-9; (*1-890605-22-0) 120 pages; $15.99; **USA, CANADA & AUSTRALIA** 1-890605-08-5; (*1-890605-24-7) 75 pages; $15.99; **OCEANIA & JAPAN** 1-890605-07-7; (*1-890605-23-9) 200 pages; $19.99; **THE MIDDLE EAST** 1-890605-05-0; (*1-890605-21-2) 120 pages; $15.99

Note: Books marked with * refer to a new ISBN planned for the same book under a different title called *"Ethics and Etiquette Around the World: A Country Guide To Cultural and Social Do's, Don'ts, & Taboos"*

NOTE: INDIVIDUAL COUNTRY REPORTS of the Do's & Don'ts Books ARE AVAILABLE!!! for $7 per report per country.

Individual Country Reports are only available online and may be ordered from (www.frontlinepublishers.com)

LIBRARY RECOMMENDATION FORM

(This form should be hand delivered to your local Head Librarian or Reference Librarian)

Sir/Madam:

I regularly use the following book(s) published by **Frontline Publishers (www.frontlinepublishers.com)**:

(1)_____ISBN #:_____Price $_____
(2)_____ISBN #:_____Price $_____
(3)_____ISBN #:_____Price $_____
(4)_____ISBN #:_____Price $_____
(5)_____ISBN #:_____Price $_____
(6)_____ISBN #:_____Price $_____
(7)_____ISBN #:_____Price $_____
(8)_____ISBN #:_____Price $_____
(9)_____ISBN #:_____Price $_____
(10)_____ISBN #:_____Price $_____
(11)_____ISBN #:_____Price $_____
(12)_____ISBN #:_____Price $_____

Your records indicate that the library does not carry these valuable and comprehensive travel reference books. Could you please order them for our library?

Name of Recommender: _____
Address:_____
_____
Phone:_____

371

ORDERING INFORMATION

Mail or Fax your orders to:

Frontline Publishers
P.O. Box 32674-1A,
Baltimore, MD 21282-2674 U.S.A.
Fax: (410) 922-8009.
Make check or money order payable to **Frontline Publishers**
We also accept, International Money Orders.

Shipping/Postage Cost for books:
U.S. Residents add $4.50 U.S. dollars per book for postage.
Canadian Residents add $6 U.S. dollars per book for postage.
Mexican Residents add $7 U.S. dollars per book for postage.
Other Countries: add $15 U.S. dollars for airmail delivery; $7 for surface mail delivery.

Books may also be ordered on-line at *amazon.com* or *frontlinepublishers.com*, and other major online bookstores, or from major bookstores throughout the country.

Remember, individual **Country Reports** of the *Do's and Don'ts* books are now available on-line through several sites including:
frontlinepublishers.com

ORDER FORM

Telephone Orders: Directly from the publisher- FRONTLINE PUBLISHERS at 1-410-922-4903

Fax Orders: 1-410-922-8009 (Send this form)

Postal Orders: Frontline Publishers, P.O. Box 32674-1A, Baltimore, Maryland
21282-2674-8674 U.S.A.{Tel: (410) 922-4903}. Make Check or Money Order payable to
FRONTLINE PUBLISHERS

Online Orders: Visit *amazon.com* or *frontlinepublishers.com*. Also available through
several online bookstores

☐ Please enter my order for the following books:
- **Do's and Don'ts:**

Europe	$39.99 + $____	postage: Total $____
South America	$24.99 + $____	postage: Total $____
Africa	$39.99 + $____	postage: Total $____
The Caribbean	$24.99 + $____	postage: Total $____
Asia	$24.99 + $____	postage: Total $____
Russia/The Independent States	$15.99 +$____	postage: Total $____
USA, Canada & Australia	$15.99 + $____	postage: Total $____
The Middle East	$15.99 + $____	postage: Total $____
Oceania & Japan	$19.99 + $____	postage: Total $____

(Please refer to the section containing shipping/postage information for applicable postage rates.)

- **Americans Traveling Abroad.**	$39.99 + $____	postage Total $____
- **Americans Living Abroad**	$34.99 + $____	postage Total $____
- **American. Businesses Abroad (paper)**	$39.99 + $____	postage Total $____
- **American. Businesses Abroad (Hard)**	$49.99 + $____	postage Total $____
-**Traveling Abroad Post 9-11**	$24.99 + $____	postage Total $____
- **Weapons of Mass Destruction (paper)**	$39.99 + $____	postage Total $____
- **Weapons of Mass Destruction (Hard)**	$49.99 + $____	postage Total $____
- **Natural Disasters (paper)**	$29.99 + $____	postage Total $____
- **Natural Disasters (Hard)**	$39.99 + $____	postage Total $____

- **Do's and Don'ts - COUNTRY REPORTS:** Available online for $7 at
www.frontlinepublishers.com

Sales Tax: (Maryland Residents Only) Add 5%
$_____

Enclosed is my Total Payment of $_____by

☐ Check ☐ Money Order ☐ This is a gift from:_____

Ship To:_____**Firm Name:**_____
Your Name:_____ _____**Address:**_____
City:_____**State:**_____**Zip:**_____**Country:**_____

COMMENT FORM FOR OUR BOOKS

YOUR OPINION MEANS A LOT TO US

Please use this post card to tell us how you feel about any of our books. Remember, we may quote you and/or use your comments, testimonials or suggestions in our promotions and future editions.

Title of Book:_____

Name:_____

Organization:_____**Position:**_____

Address:_____

City, State, Zip & Country:_____

_____

_____

(   ) Check here if we may quote you.

Signature:_____**Date:**_____

[Mail your comments to Frontline Publishers, P.O. Box 32674 Baltimore, MD 21282-2674, USA.]

COUNTRY REPORTS FOR *"DO'S & DON'TS"* BOOKS

[Note: Individual Country reports are currently available for $7 per country, per report
at www. frontlinepublishers.com]

AFGHANISTAN	DOMINICA	LIBYA	SINGAPORE
ALBANIA	DOMINICAN REP.	LIECHESTEIN	SLOVAK REP.
ALGERIA	ECUADOR	LITHUANIA	SLOVENIA
AMERICAN SAMOA	EGYPT	LUXEMBOURG	SOLOMON ISLAND
ANDORRA	EL SALVADOR	MACAU	SOMALIA
ANGUILLA	EQUATORIAL GUINEA	MACEDONIA	SOUTH AFRICA
ANTIGUA & BARBUDA	ERITREA	MADAGASCAR	SPAIN
ARGENTINA	ESTONIA	MALAWI	SRI LANKA
ARMENIA	ETHIOPIA	MALAYSIA	ST. PIERRE &
ARUBA	FALKLAND ISLANDS	MALDIVES	MIQUELON
AUSTRALIA	FAROE ISLAND	MALI	ST. MARTIN
AUSTRIA	FIJI	MALTA	ST. KITTS & NEVIS
AZERBAIJAN	FINLAND	MARSHALL ISLANDS	ST. LUCIA
BAHAMAS	FRANCE	MAURITIUS	ST. VINCENT
BAHRAIN	FRENCH GUIANA	MAYOTTE	SUDAN
BANGLADESH	FRENCH POLYNESIA	MEXICO	SURINAME
BARBADOS	GABON	MOLDOVA	SWAZILAND
BELGIUM	GAMBIA, THE	MONACO	SWEDEN
BELIZE	GEORGIA	MONGOLIA	SWITZERLAND
BENIN	GERMANY	MONTESERRAT	SYRIA
BERMUDA	GHANA	MOROCCO	TAJIKISTAN
BHUTAN	GIBRALTA	MOZAMBIQUE	TANZANIA
BOLIVIA	GREECE	MUSTIQUE	THAILAND
BOTSWANA	GREENLAND	MYANMAR (BURMA)	TOGO
BRAZIL	GRENADA	NAMIBIA	TONGA
BRITISH VIRGIN	GUADELOUPE	NAURU	TRINIDAD & TOBAGO
ISLANDS	GUAM	NEPAL	TUNISIA
BRUNEI-DARUSSALEM	GUANTANAMO BAY	NETHERLANDS	TURKEY
BULGARIA	GUATEMALA	NEW ZEALAND	TURKMENISTAN
BURKINA FASO	GUINEA	NEW CALEDONIA	TURKS & CAICOS
BURMA (SEE	GUINEA BISSAU	NICARAGUA	TUVALU
MYANMAR)	GUYANA	NIEU	UGANDA
BURUNDI	HAITI	NIGER	UKRAINE
BYLERUS	HONDURAS	NIGERIA	UNION ISLAND
CAMBODIA	HONG KONG	NORWAY	UNITED KINGDOM
CAMEROON	HUNGARY	OMAN	UNITED ARAB
CANADA	ICELAND	PAKISTAN	EMIRATES
CAPE VERDE, REP. OF	INDIA	PANAMA	UNITED STATES
CAYMAN	INDONESIA	PAPUA NEW GUINEA	URUGUAY
CENTRAL AFRICAN	IRAN	PARAGUAY	UZBEKISTAN
REP.	IRAQ	PERU	VENEZUELA
CHAD	IRELAND	PHILIPPINES	VIETNAM
CHILE	ISRAEL	POLAND	WESTERN SAMOA
CHINA, PEOPLE'S REP.	ITALY	PORTUGAL	YEMEN, ARAB REP.
COLOMBIA	JAMAICA	PUERTO RICO	YEMEN, P.D.R.
COMOROS	JAPAN	QUATAR	YUGOSLAVIA
CONGO, PEOPLE'S	JORDAN	REUNION ISLAND	ZAIRE
REP.	KAZAKHSTAN	ROMANIA	ZAMBIA
COOK ISLANDS	KENYA	RUSSIA	ZIMBABWE
COSTA RICA	KIRIBATI	RWANDA	
COTE'IVOIRE	KOREA, NORTH	SAIPAN	
CROATIA	KOREA, SOUTH	SAN MARINO	
CUBA	KUWAIT	SAO TOME &	
CURACAO	LAOS	PRINCIPE	
CYPRUS	LATVIA	SAUDI ARABIA	
CZECH REP.	LEBANON	SENEGAL	
DENMARK	LESOTHO	SEYCHELLES	
DJIBOUTI, REP.	LIBERIA	SIERRA LEONE	

INDEX

378

ABOUT THE AUTHOR

Dr. Gladson I. Nwanna (Ph.D.) is a university professor, a former consultant to the World Bank, and a veteran traveler. He has over the past 20 years traveled to several countries of the world, logging thousands of miles in the process. Dr. Nwanna is the author of several books.

OTHER BOOKS BY THE SAME AUTHOR

Americans Traveling Abroad: What You Should Know Before You Go (3rd Ed.) Bestseller! paperback, 720 pages, ISBN: 1-890605-10-7, $39.99

Americans Living Abroad: What You Should Know While You are There. paperback, 375 pages, ISBN: 1-890605-11-5, $34.99

Traveling Abroad Post "9-11" and in the Wake of Terrorism: A Practical Guide for Americans & Other International Travelers, paperback, 265 pages, ISBN: 1-890605-13-1, $24.99

American Businesses Abroad: How to Protect Your Assets and Personnel, paperback, 320 pages, ISBN: 1-890605-12-3, $39.99; (Hard Cover, ISBN: 1-890605-26-3, $49.99)

Weapons of Mass Destruction, What You Should Know: A Citizen's Guide To Biological, Chemical and Nuclear Agents & Weapons paperback, 300 pages, ISBN: 1-890605-14-X, $39.99 (Hard Cover, ISBN: 1-890605-25-5, $49.99)

Natural Disasters and Other Emergencies, What You Should Know: A Family Planning & Survival Guide. paperback, 250 pages, ISBN: 1-890605-15-8, $29.99 (Hard Cover, ISBN: 1-890605-27-1, $39.99)

Do's and Don'ts Around the World: A Country Guide to Cultural and Social Taboos and Etiquette. paperback, available in 9 different volumes/editions: Europe, Asia, Africa, South America, The Caribbean, The Middle East, Russia and the Independent States, Oceania, USA-Canada-Australia. These books contain hundreds of country-specific do's and don'ts and much more!.

Series Title: *DO'S AND DON'TS AROUND THE WORLD: A COUNTRY GUIDE TO CULTURAL AND SOCIAL TABOOS AND ETIQUETTE*

EUROPE 1-890605-00-X; (*1-890605-17-4) 400 pages; $39.99; **SOUTH AMERICA** 1-890605-03-4; (*1-890605-20-4) 230 pages; $24.99; **AFRICA** 1-890605- 04-2 (*1-890605-16-6); 450 pages; $39.99; **THE CARIBBEAN** 1-890605-02-6; (*1-890605-19-0) 230 pages; $24.99; **ASIA** 1-890605-01-8; (*1-890605-18-2) 260 pages; $24.99; **RUSSIA & THE INDEPENDENT STATES** 1-890605-06-9; (*1-890605-22-0) 120 pages; $15.99; **USA, CANADA & AUSTRALIA** 1-890605-08-5; (*1-890605-24-7) 75 pages; $15.99; **OCEANIA & JAPAN** 1-890605-07-7; (*1-890605-23-9) 200 pages; $19.99; **THE MIDDLE EAST** 1-890605-05-0; (*1-890605-21-2) 120 pages; $15.99

Note: Books marked with * refer to a new ISBN planned for the same book under a different title called *"Ethics and Etiquette Around the World: A Country Guide To Cultural and Social Do's, Don'ts, & Taboos"*

Individual Country Reports are *of the Do's & Don'ts Books currently* online and may be ordered for $7 per country per report (www.frontlinepublishers.com)

[See inside pages 372-372 for ordering information & ORDER FORM]

Printed in the United States
16155LVS00003B/42